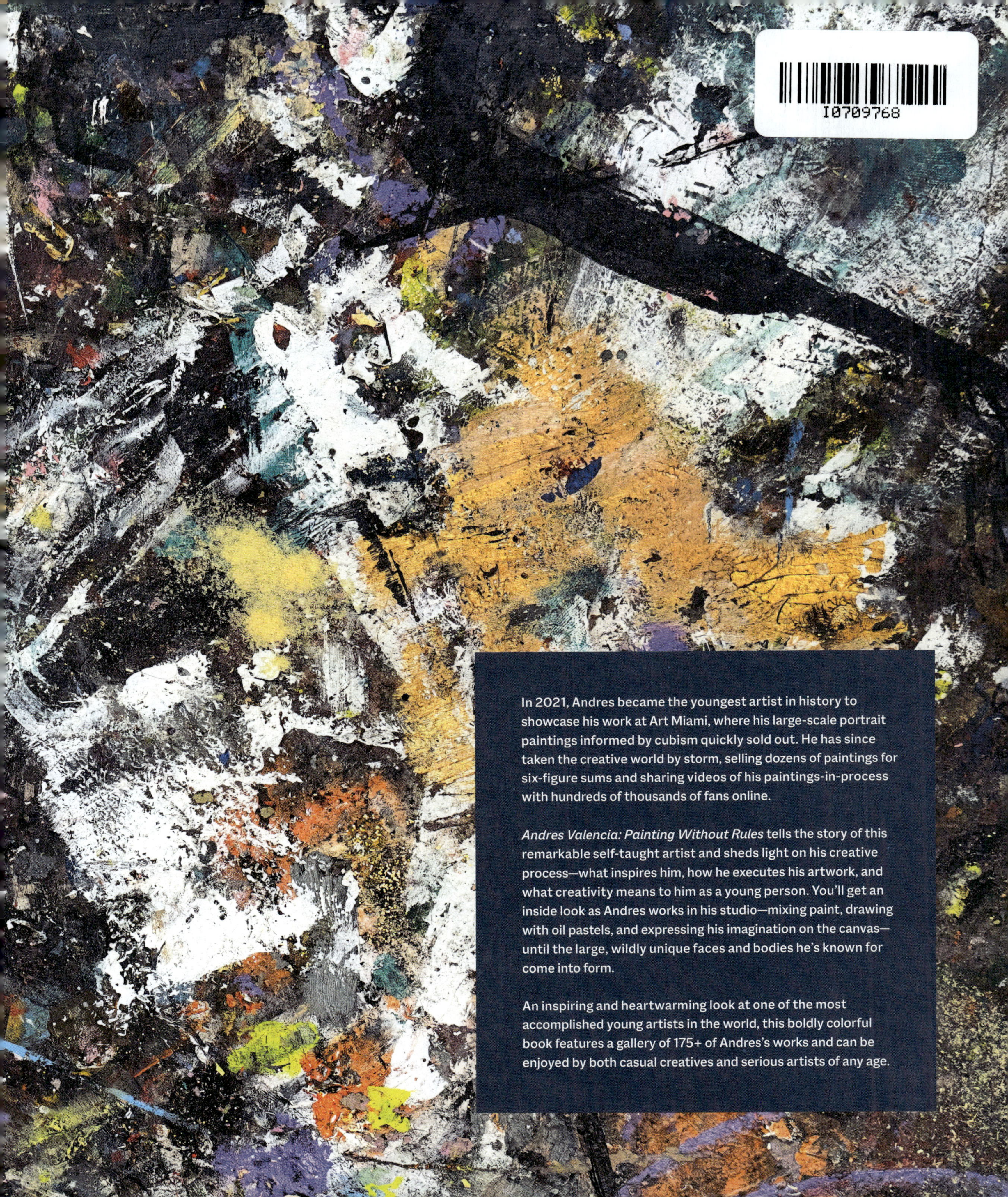

In 2021, Andres became the youngest artist in history to showcase his work at Art Miami, where his large-scale portrait paintings informed by cubism quickly sold out. He has since taken the creative world by storm, selling dozens of paintings for six-figure sums and sharing videos of his paintings-in-process with hundreds of thousands of fans online.

Andres Valencia: Painting Without Rules tells the story of this remarkable self-taught artist and sheds light on his creative process—what inspires him, how he executes his artwork, and what creativity means to him as a young person. You'll get an inside look as Andres works in his studio—mixing paint, drawing with oil pastels, and expressing his imagination on the canvas—until the large, wildly unique faces and bodies he's known for come into form.

An inspiring and heartwarming look at one of the most accomplished young artists in the world, this boldly colorful book features a gallery of 175+ of Andres's works and can be enjoyed by both casual creatives and serious artists of any age.

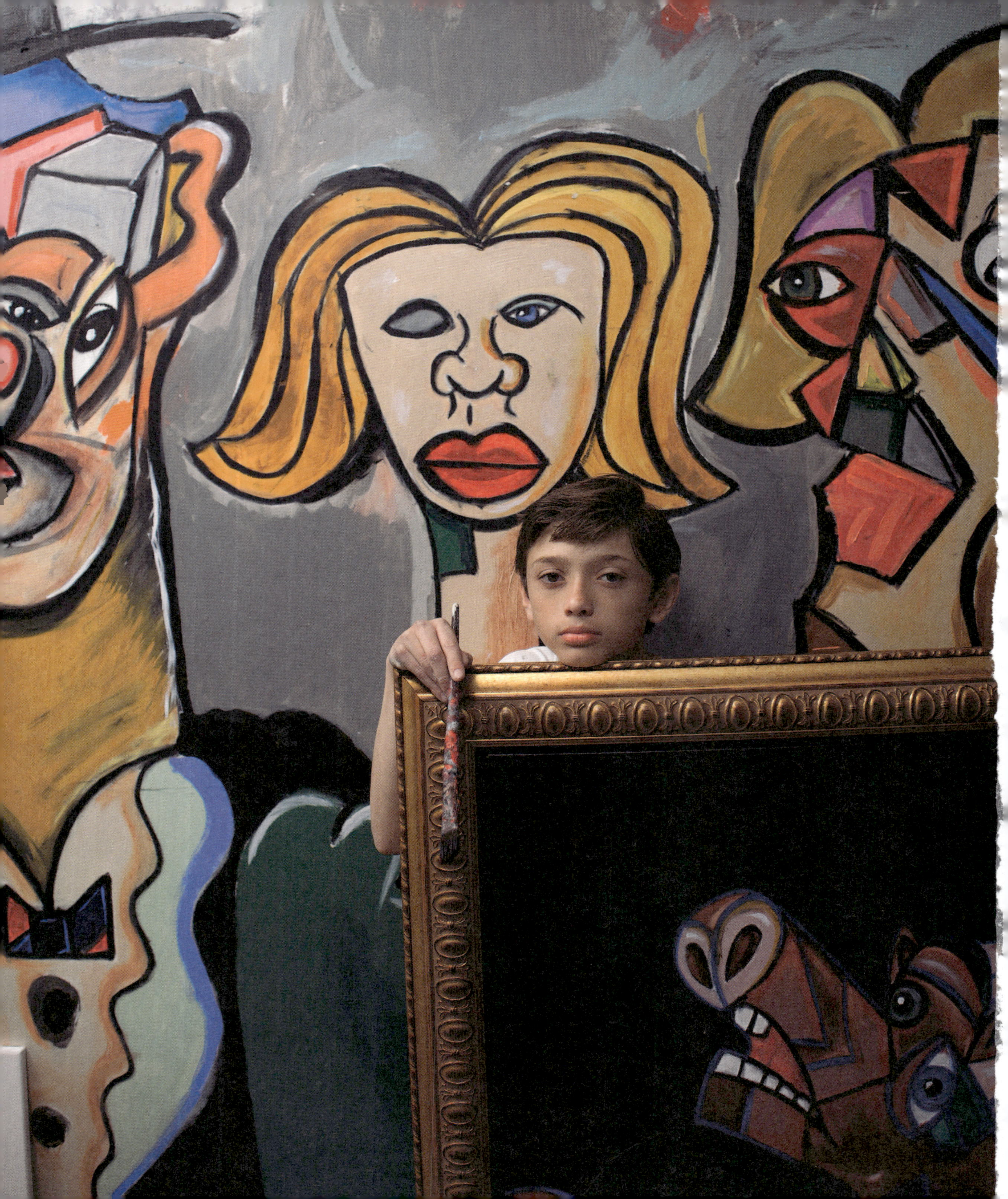

ANDRES VALENCIA

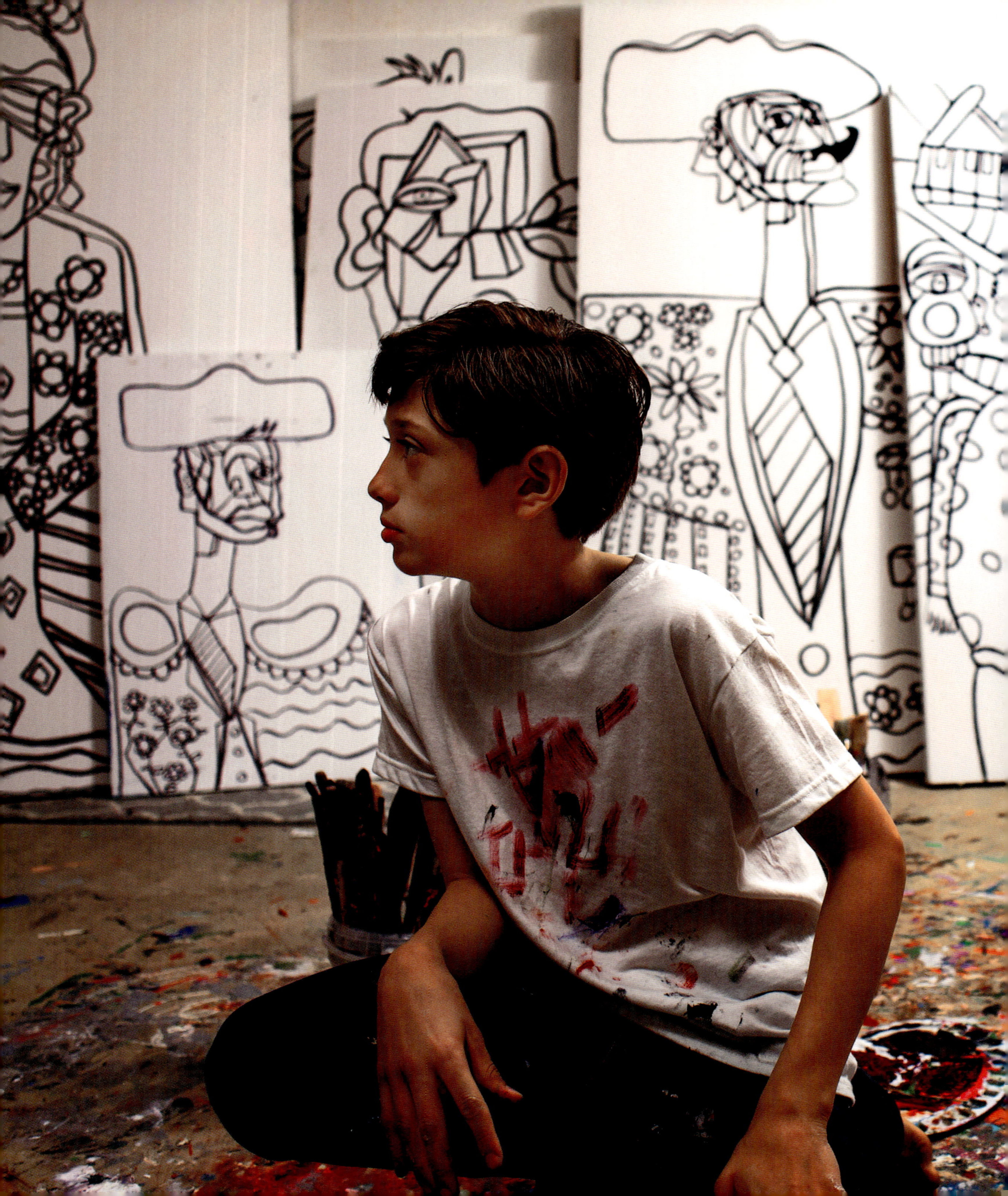

ANDRES VALENCIA

PAINTING WITHOUT RULES

with ALEXANDER M. RIGBY

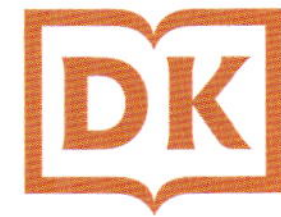

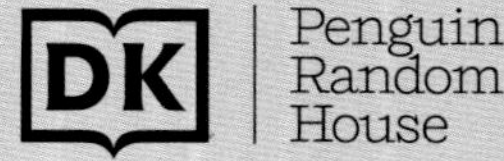

Publisher Mike Sanders
Executive Editor Alexander Rigby
Editorial Director Ann Barton
Art & Design Director William Thomas
Designer Joanna Price
Photographer Raphael Mazzucco
Developmental Editor Devon Fredericksen
Copy Editor Tiffany Taing
Proofreaders Mira S. Park, Tamanna Bhasin
Indexer Celia McCoy

First American Edition, 2025
Published in the United States by DK Publishing
1745 Broadway, 20th Floor, New York, NY 10019

The authorized representative in the EEA is Dorling
Kindersley Verlag GmbH. Arnulfstr. 124, 80636 Munich,
Germany

Library of Congress Number: 2024944879
ISBN 978-0-5938-4405-2

DK books are available at special discounts when purchased
in bulk for sales promotions, premiums, fundraising, or
educational use. For details, contact SpecialSales@dk.com

Printed and bound in China

www.dk.com

This book was made with Forest
Stewardship Council™ certified
paper – one small step in DK's
commitment to a sustainable future.
Learn more at
www.dk.com/uk/information/sustainability

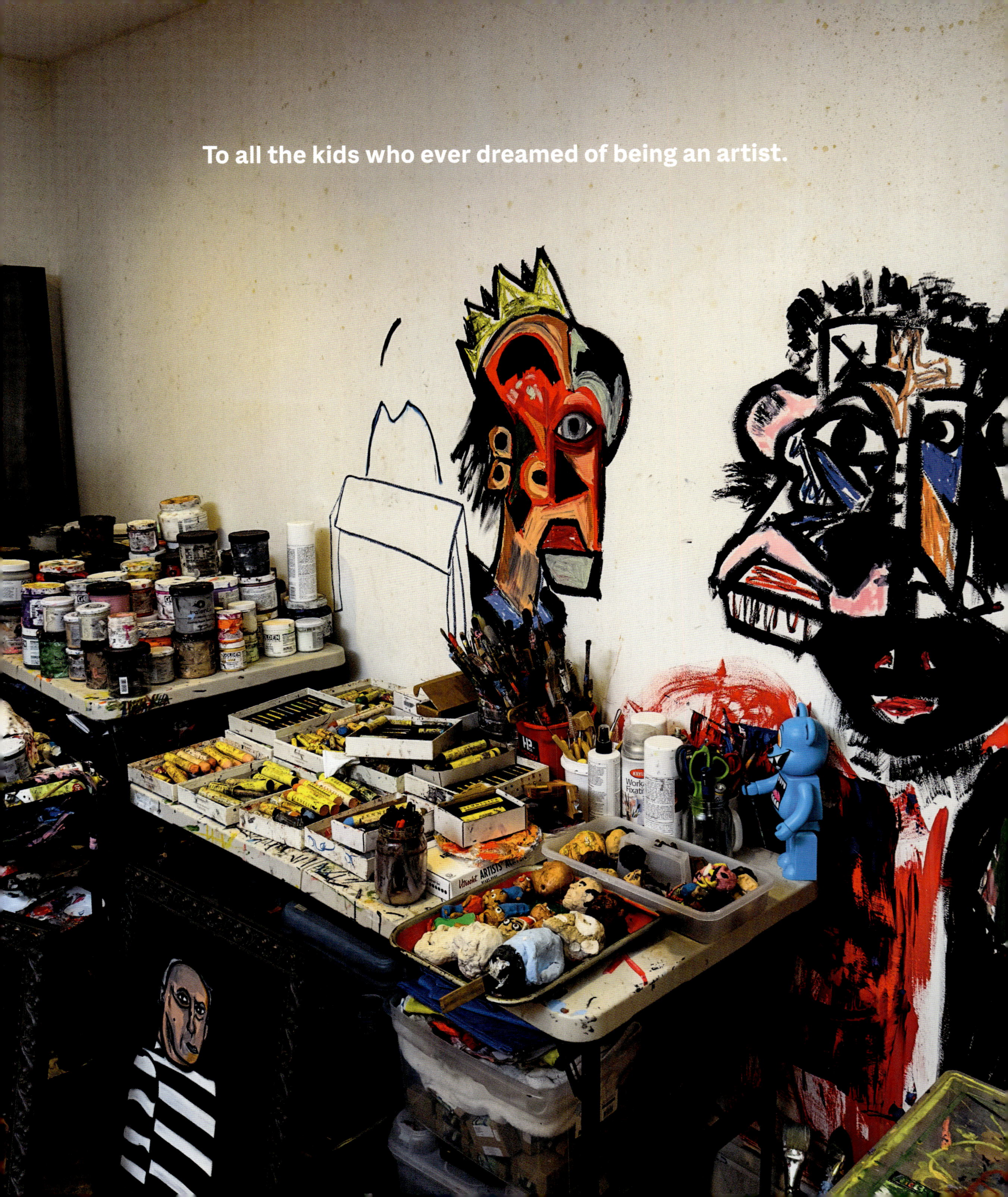
To all the kids who ever dreamed of being an artist.

Contents

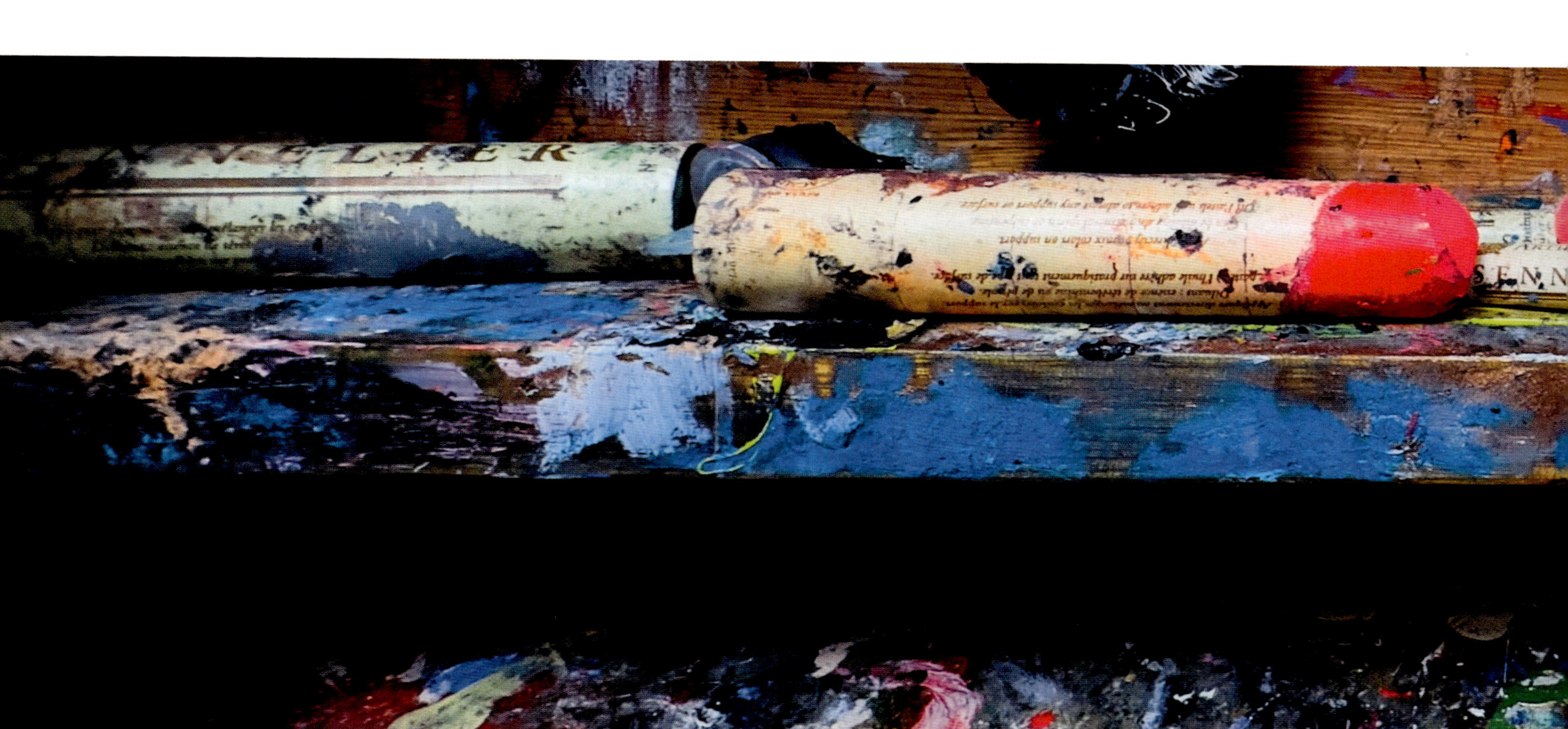

Foreword

Historically, art has been the medium through which humanity has captured its essence, history, and deepest desires. From time to time, prodigies emerge who, with freshness and originality, transform our perceptions and invite us to see the world with new eyes. Andres Valencia is one of those prodigies.

When I first contemplated Andres's art, I found myself before the work of a talented artist and the manifestation of a unique and precocious vision. His paintings, full of color, emotion, and depth, remind us that talent has no age and that young souls can capture the complexity of the world around us with surprising precision.

In Andres, the passion for art meets an unexpected maturity, resulting in works that move, challenge, and invite us to see the world in a new way. Andres has emerged as a leading figure in contemporary art, not only for his prodigious talent at an early age, but for the way his work challenges and enriches the global art scene.

This book is not only a compilation of his work; it is a window into the soul of a young man who, through art, is discovering himself and simultaneously revealing a new world to us all. Each page and image is an invitation into the mind of a child whose creativity knows no boundaries.

I am deeply excited to witness this chapter in Andres's career and to share with you the magic he creates. I am sure that, like me, you will be inspired, amazed, and moved by this young artist's talent.

Andres and I share a deep love for art, and it is an honor for me to write the foreword for this book, which I am sure will be only the first of many more to come.

Eugenio López Alonso
President of Fundación Jumex Arte Contemporáneo

Translated from Spanish by Lorena Baca.

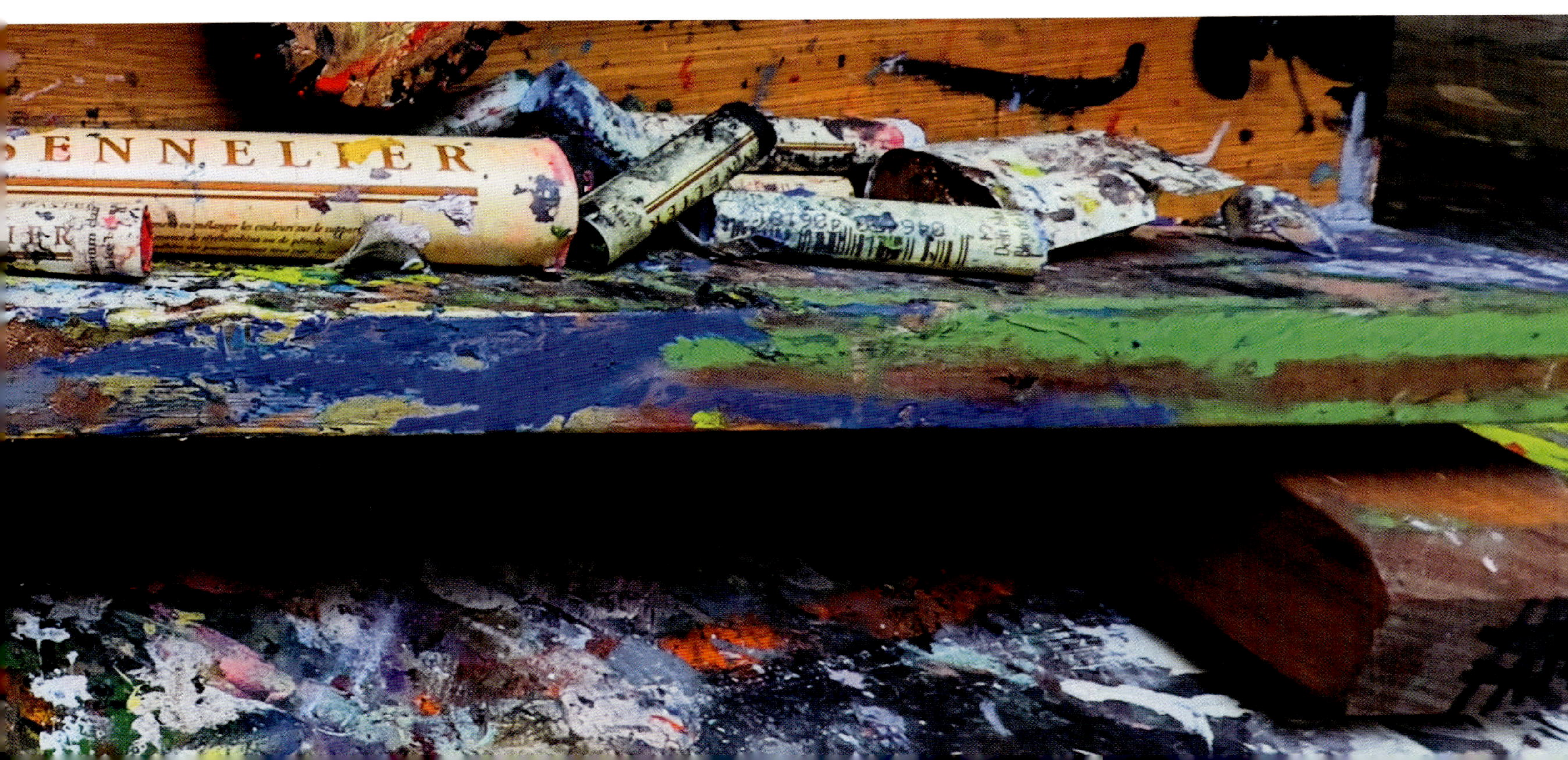

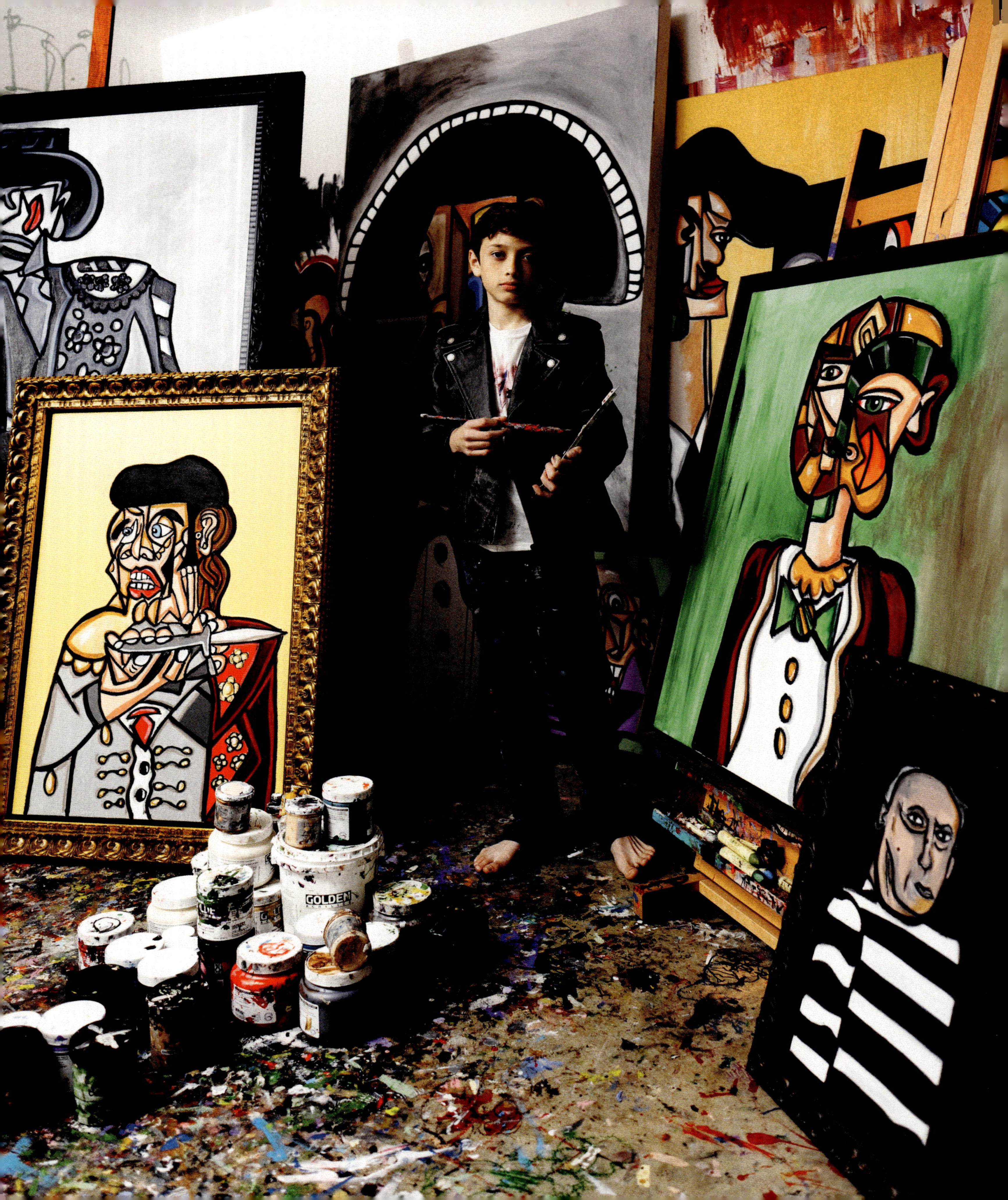

Introduction

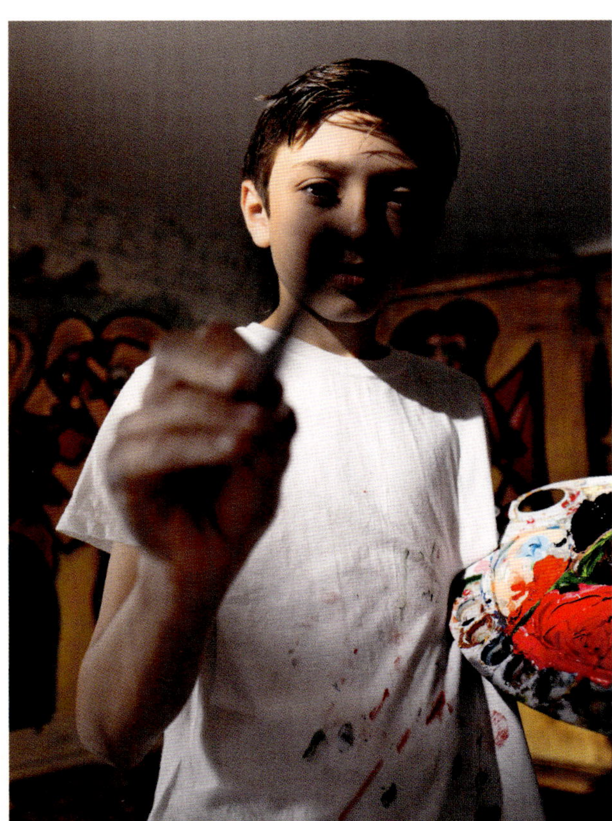

Andres Valencia has always been an artist. Since his birth in 2011, he has lived to create. Painting is as intrinsic to his identity as playing outside is to other kids. The thing is, Andres plays outside too. He is a painter, but he is also a young person living an incredibly rich childhood. His parents have expertly guided him to explore his creativity so he can reach his full artistic potential, while also encouraging him to explore the many facets of his boyhood.

Speaking with Andres is like talking to someone with an old soul. He has a calm, pleasant demeanor, and his voice is never loud. He is thoughtful with his answers, and withholds more than he shares. Instead, where he allows himself to go wild is on the canvas, creating large, abstract portraits heavily influenced by cubism. He has been painting regularly at his home in San Diego since the age of five, but it was only in 2021 that he fully burst onto the professional art scene. At ten, he showed his work at his very own booth at Art Miami, a respected art fair, making him the youngest person ever to do so. It was at this event that celebrity fans began buying his paintings. Since then, his work has sold for six-figure sums at various auctions, and he has garnered international media attention and received praise and recognition from other famous artists. Even though Andres has been painting for years, he is also just getting started.

His art is spontaneous. He usually doesn't have a plan when he starts working on a new piece, and his parents, Elsa and Guadalupe "Lupe" Valencia, encourage this freedom of expression. Andres has not taken any art classes outside the ones offered at his public school, so his artistry has been self-taught. When people question him on why he paints the way he does, he doesn't have a specific answer. As Elsa explains, "After he gets questions like these, he says to me, 'Why do they ask?' I tried to explain that people want to be guided through his creative process. And he's like, 'But there shouldn't be rules. We should just paint and draw.'"

People who see Andres's work in person or who watch the Instagram videos Elsa records of him want to hear Andres tell stories about his art. But sometimes Andres doesn't have a story to tell, and he can only explain his process by saying, "I'm just doing my art. Why do I have to explain it? I'm just doing it. I don't have to sketch or paint a certain way." Other times, there is a backstory or a specific inspiration that led him to create a certain piece. Andres is more than happy to tell you about the artists, paintings, museums, and films that have inspired

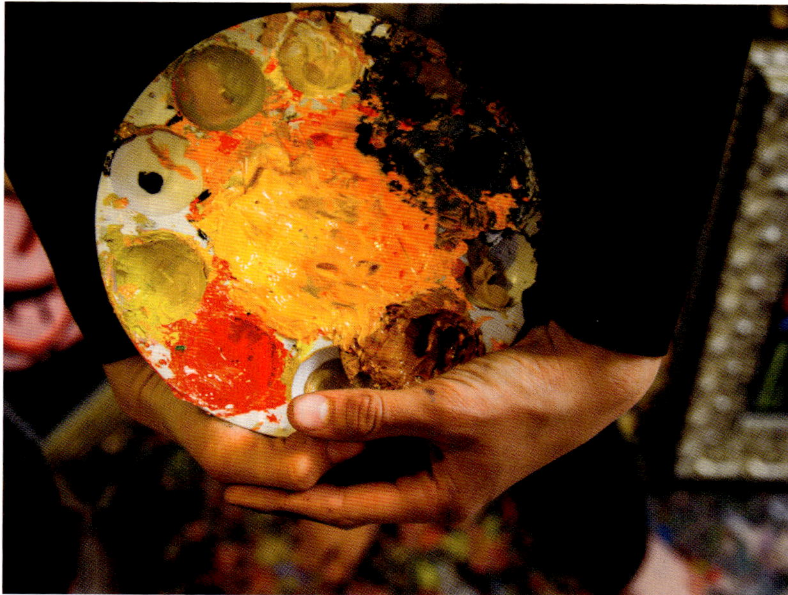

him. With Andres's art, you never know what you are going to get, and that is part of the excitement. He paints for the joy of it. He does what he wants. And there is a special kind of magic that comes with this kind of freeing, fluid process.

This book will give you an inside look into Andres's studio, share details on his creative process, and teach you about his many artistic inspirations. You will come to understand Andres and his artistic vision in a comprehensive way. If you've only watched his videos online, prepare to be more fully immersed inside the world of a one-of-a-kind child prodigy artist. Through interviews with Andres, his parents, and others, you'll hear directly from the important people who helped him find his footing in the art world at such a young age. Or if you'd rather just look at Andres's fascinating artwork, flip to the second half of the book, which contains nearly two hundred of Andres's paintings, arranged in chronological order so you can see how his work has evolved over the years.

First and foremost, Andres and his family hope this book inspires young people to believe they can do anything. "Andres is a young boy who loves art," Lupe says, "who believes in it, and is successful—he's just doing it. He's working hard, and he enjoys it. It's his passion, and he doesn't give up. I hope that young artists and artists in general see this book and get inspired by what he's doing. We also really want the world to see Andres and his art. He has been lucky to have been able to share his creative process with people on social media, and we hope this book will be another way for people to delve in deeper to how Andres paints and creates."

This book is a reflection on everything that has made Andres the artist he is and how these foundations will shape his artistic life in the future. It is about the joy of creating and pulling inspiration from a variety of influences, and also not being afraid to follow your instincts. This is a story about a young man who has been painting all his life, creating hundreds of incredible, museum-worthy pieces, while still finding happiness and spontaneity in the simple act of making something all his own—painting without rules.

Above: Andres holds his palette. **Opposite:** Sitting beside his paintings *Sofía Vergara* (pg. 245) and *Roberto* (pg. 263), March 2024.

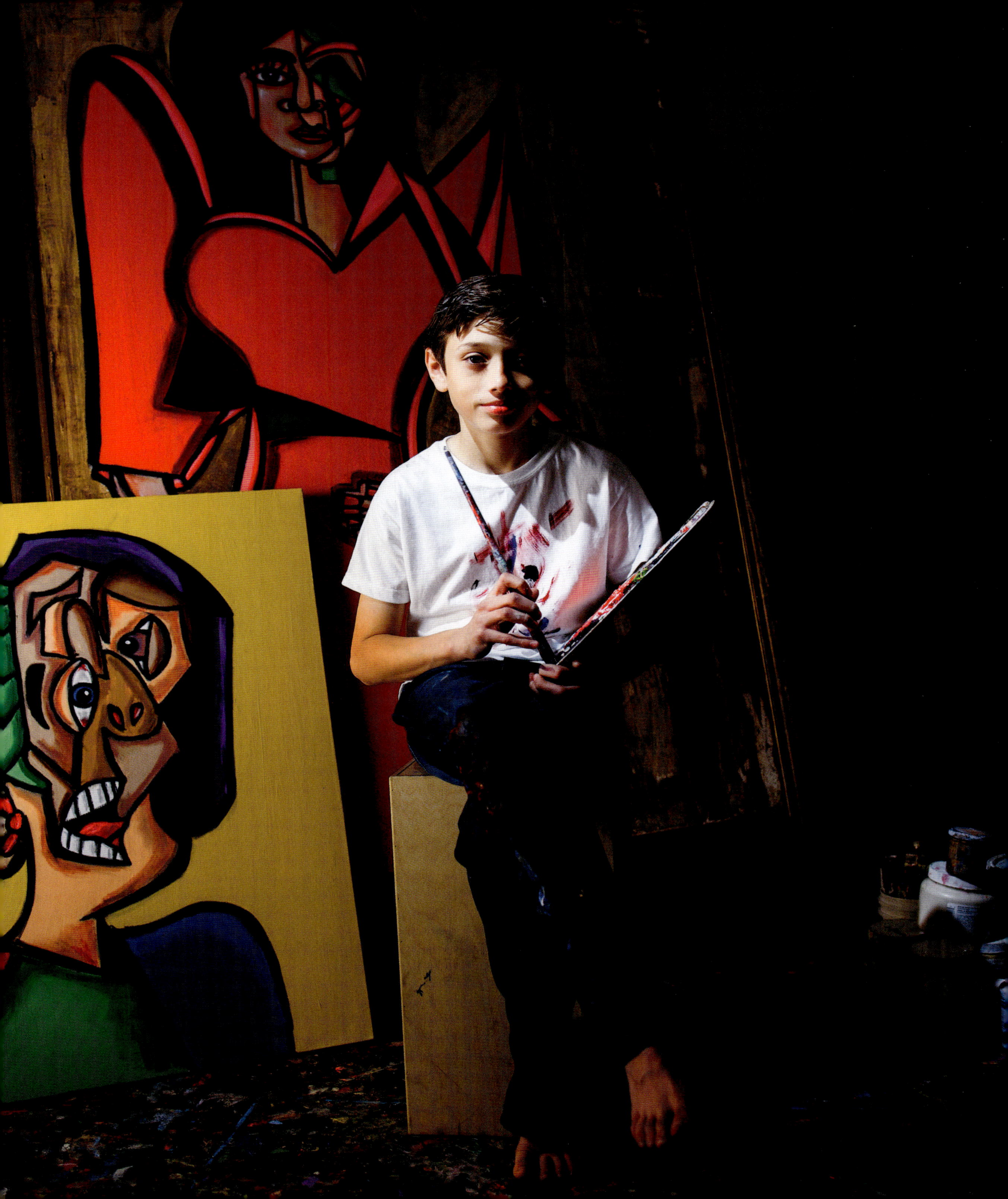

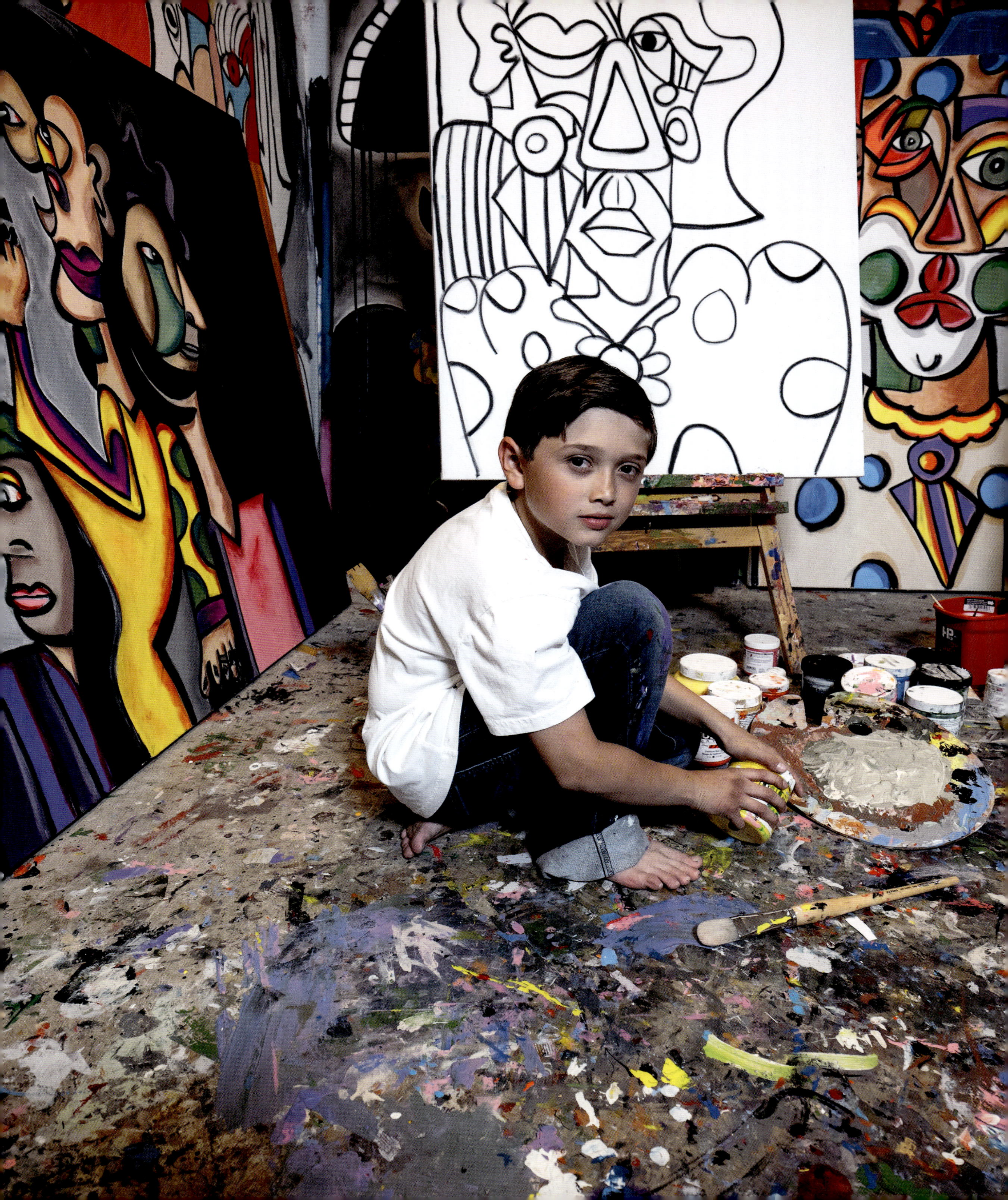

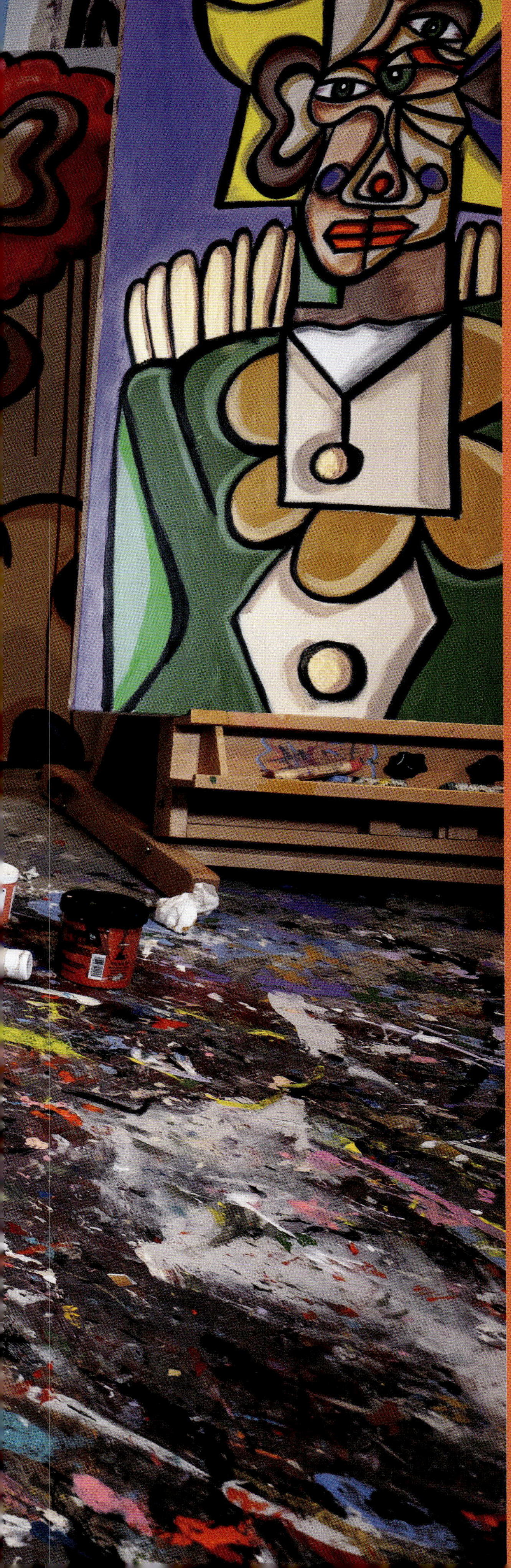

PART 1

EARLY LIFE

Since the age of five, Andres has been painting regularly. From the start, he has never followed rules or conventions. Andres paints faces the way he wants to, putting the eyes, ears, nose, and other elements wherever he feels inclined. His parents have encouraged this creativity and given him tools and supplies over the years to make hundreds of paintings. Some are on small, napkin-size pieces of paper, while others are on huge canvases over six feet tall. By pulling inspiration from other artists and the paintings that hang on the walls of his home, Andres has been able to teach himself how to paint in his own unique way. Andres is still a child, though, and regardless of how much his parents encourage his creativity and continue to help him succeed in the art space, they always stress that he is a young boy. He certainly is an artist, but he is a kid first.

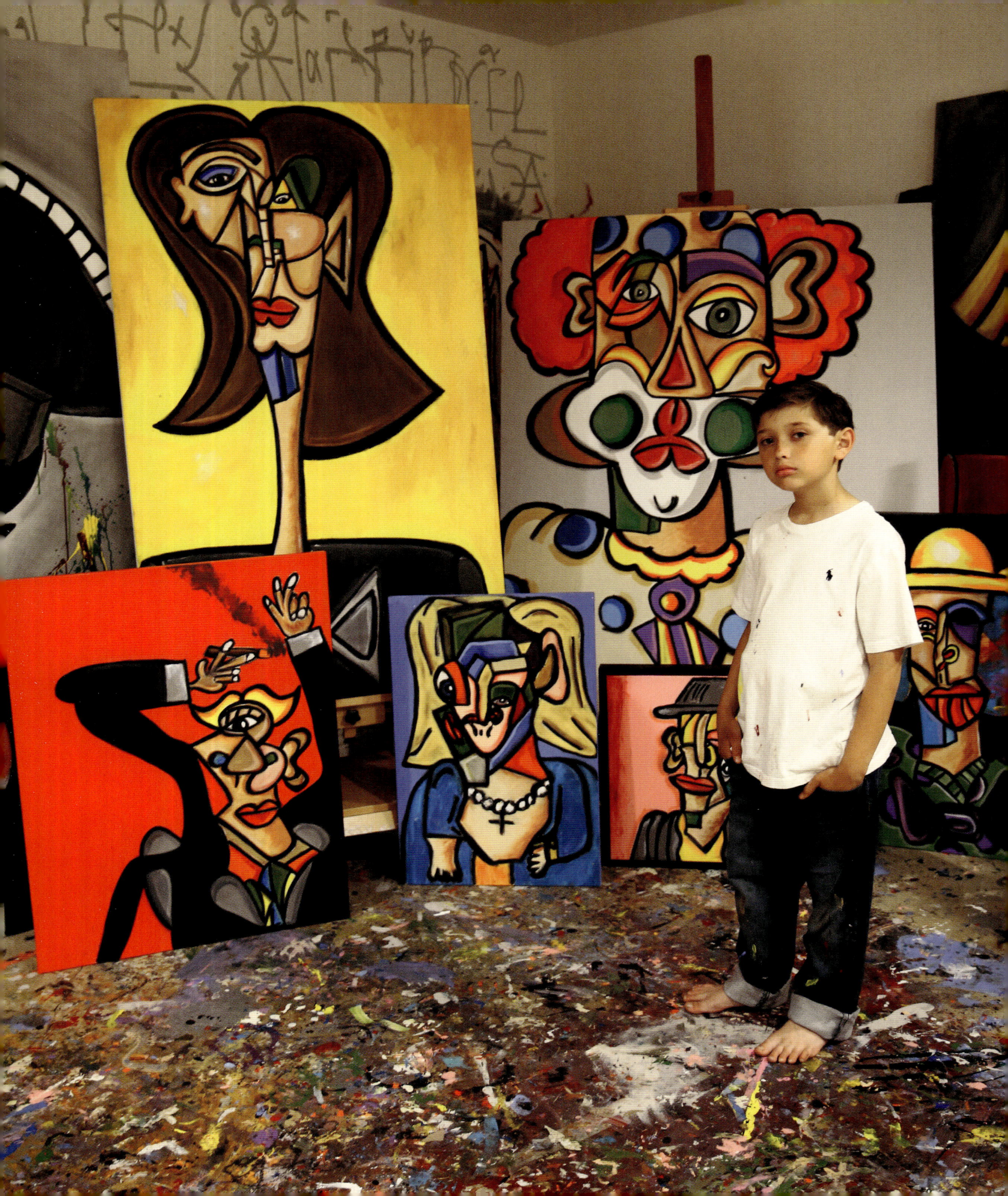

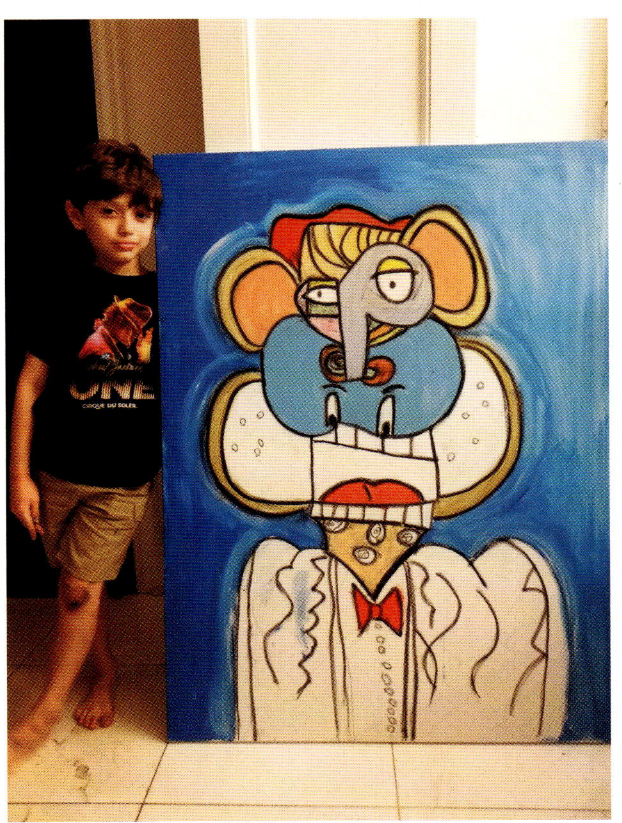

Above: Andres poses with his painting *Elephant Man* (pg. 142) as a work in progress at eight years old. **Opposite:** Surrounded by his paintings in his studio at the age of ten, April 2022.

Family Foundations

Elsa, Andres's mother, grew up in Los Angeles in a creative household, where making things was a part of regular daily life. She has been making her own clothes since she was thirteen years old. Her father was a tailor, and her mother was a seamstress. "We always had a sewing machine," she explains. "There was always some kind of designing or creativity going on at home. I was encouraged to learn. I designed a lot. I created a lot." Elsa's dad also worked as a welder, so she learned how to design with metal too. This led Elsa into designing jewelry. In middle school, she made clothes for herself and for friends. However, her parents discouraged her from pursuing these hobbies professionally—they thought the work was too hard and wouldn't lead to enough money. "But no matter what, I always loved creating," she says. When she graduated high school, she went to college to become a therapist. Still, she continued to explore her other passions, and on weekends, she would take classes on tailoring and jewelry design.

Elsa met Lupe Valencia, Andres's father, during college in Los Angeles. In 2007, after Lupe graduated from law school and Elsa became a licensed clinical therapist, they got married. The newlyweds then moved to San Diego, where they have lived ever since.

After moving to San Diego, Elsa began to focus more on jewelry design. The couple's first child, a girl named Atiana, was born that same year, and when their daughter was very young, Elsa decided to continue making jewelry on the side while working a full-time job. "To be honest," she says, "I regret not fully pursuing what I loved. If I could go back, I would completely change my career and focus on something in design instead." Even now, Elsa still designs jewelry and makes clothes from her own patterns. "Everything I create is under the umbrella of fashion," Elsa says. "I love creating."

The Valencia's second child, Andres, was born in 2011. As a very young boy, Andres was first exposed to creativity in Elsa's studio. It was there that he was able to watch her make jewelry and witness what an artist could create when they have a designated space of their own.

Exposure to Studio Creation

Since they were little, the Valencia children have always gone in and out of Elsa's studio, a room on the first floor of their home located right next to the garage. "Once Andres started walking and talking, he would just sit there in my studio and watch me work," Elsa says. She gave him little tasks to do, like filing down some of the wax off the jewelry pieces. He was always coming in and saying, "Please teach me how to do this. Please teach me." Elsa was surprised he was so interested, but she encouraged his curiosity.

Eventually, Andres asked his mother, "Why do you get to have a studio?" By this point, Andres had started to paint regularly, so when Elsa asked him what he meant, he said, "I think I deserve a studio at home too." Andres noticed how his mom was often creating, so he would go into her studio because he also wanted to participate. Elsa made jewelry pieces with wax and wouldn't let Andres touch some of the things, since she worried he could get hurt. "So then I got upset," Andres says. "I wanted my own studio. I thought it was only fair since she got hers. I turned my bedroom into a studio." After that, Andres started painting a lot more in his room. He was just five years old.

Andres's creative pursuits were not limited to painting. At the age of four, he asked Elsa if she could make sleeping bags and clothes for his vintage GI Joe action figures from the 1960s. But then he started making them himself with Elsa's help.

She would make patterns out of paper, and he would cut them out on the fabric. Since Andres didn't know how to sew, he would glue the outfits together. Andres created pairs of pants by gluing the sides together, then made miniature sleeping bags in the same way. Elsa taught him how to cut the patterns out, and he would make little shirts for his GI Joes. Mother and son started to go to the fabric store together to pick out patterns for the outfits.

The family still has some of the little pieces of clothing that Andres made then, as they were some of his first artistic creations. All this happened right before Andres really started to focus on painting.

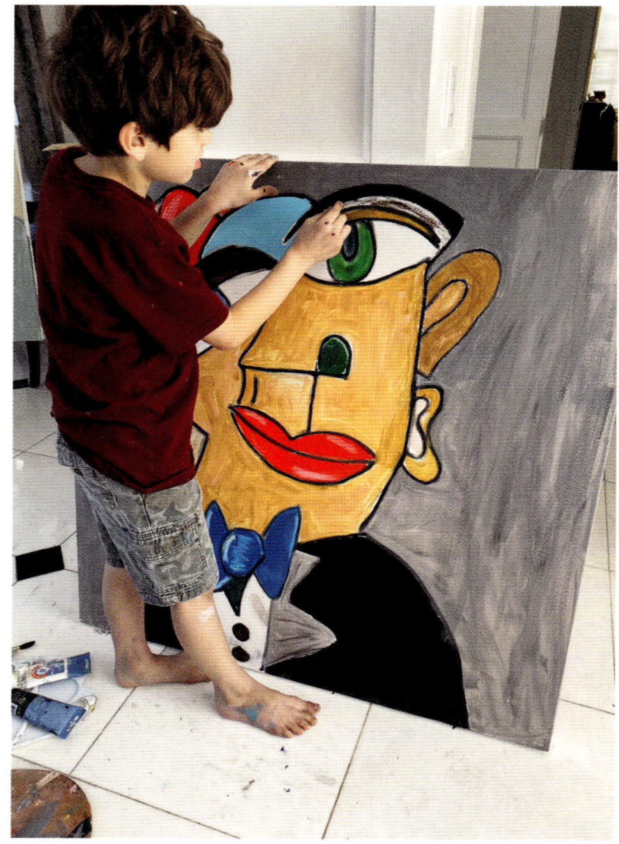

Above: Andres puts the final touches on his painting *The Judge* (pg. 148) in the family's dining room. **Opposite:** Proudly showing off his painting, *The Farmer* (pg. 149), March 2020.

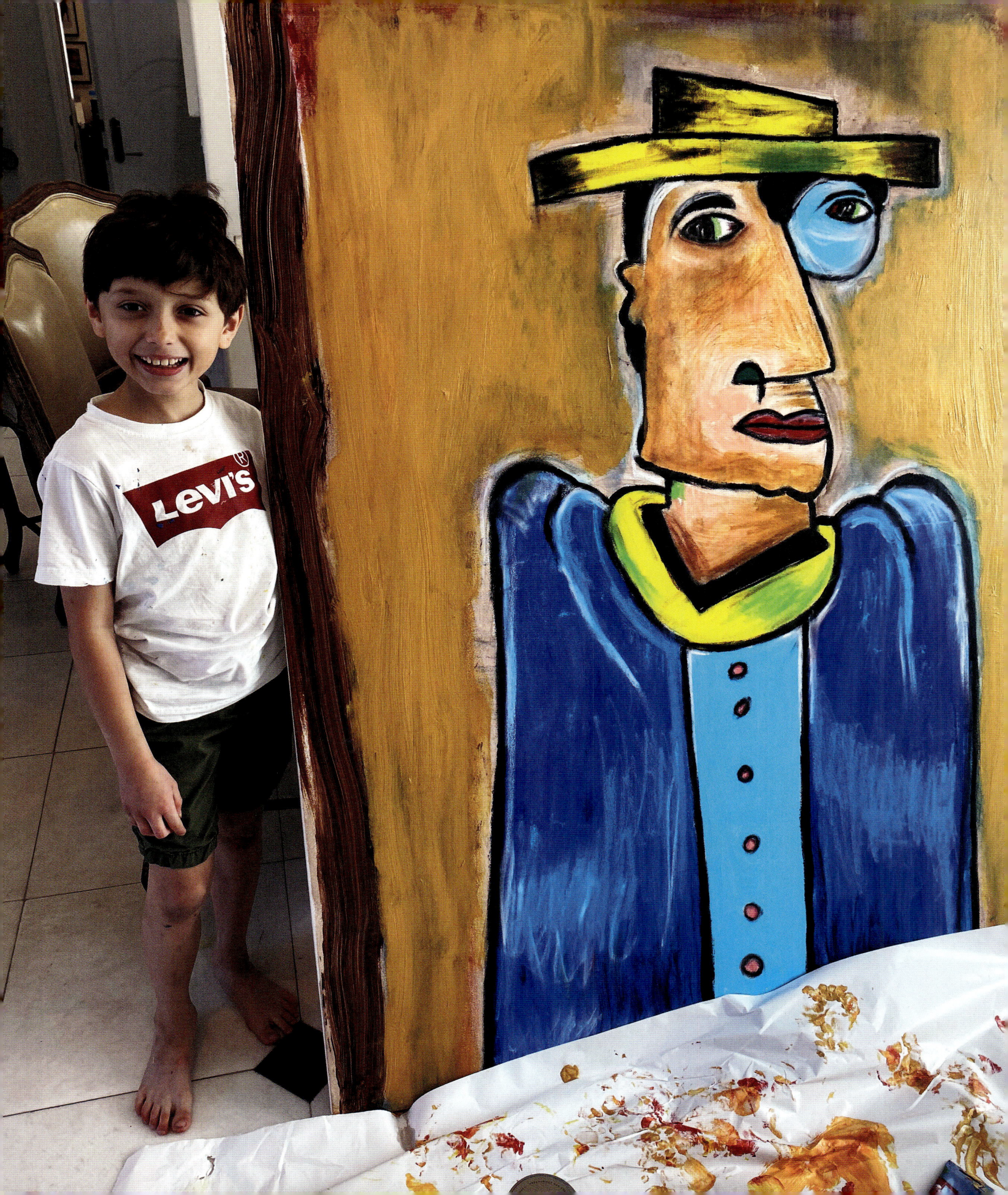

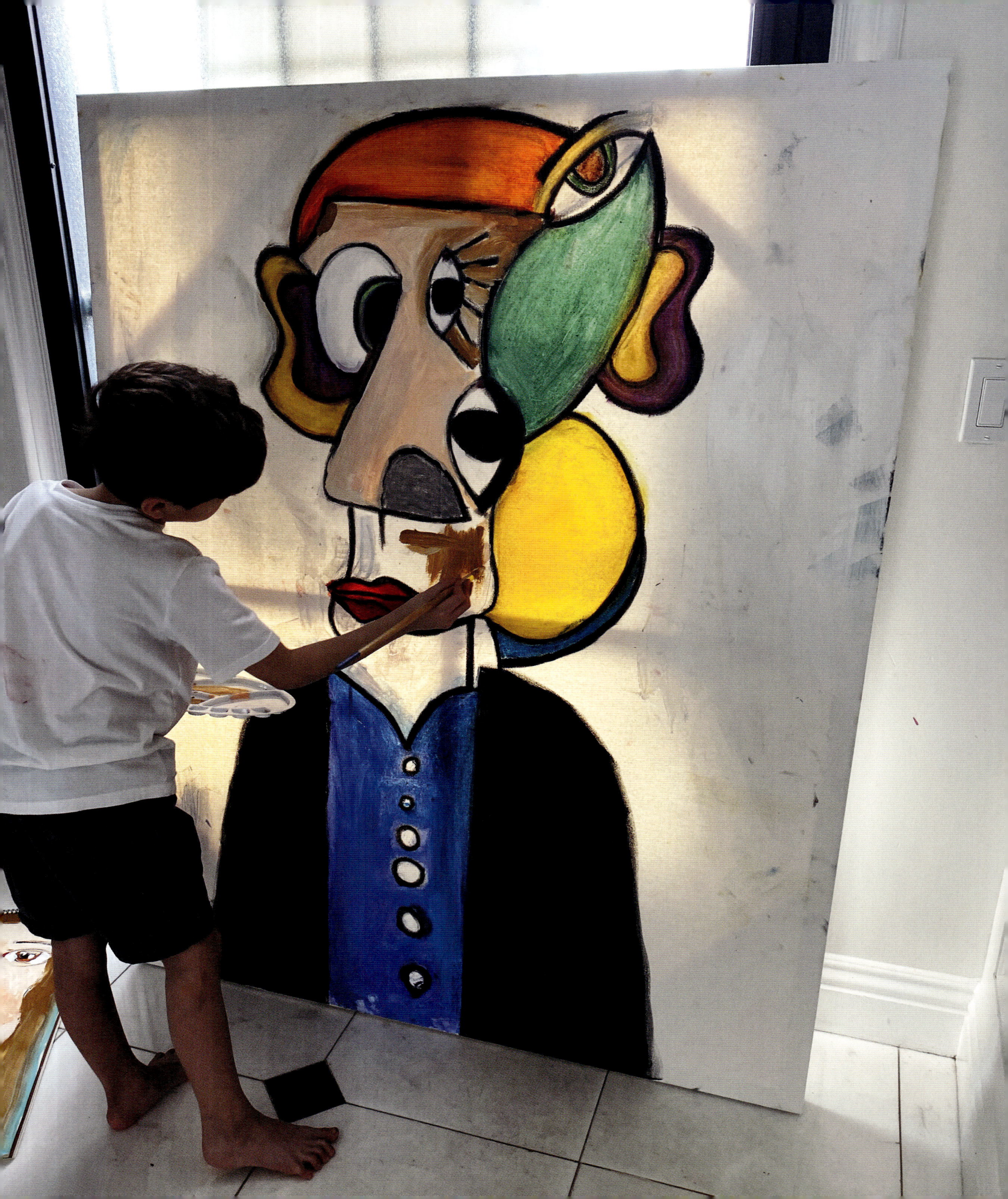

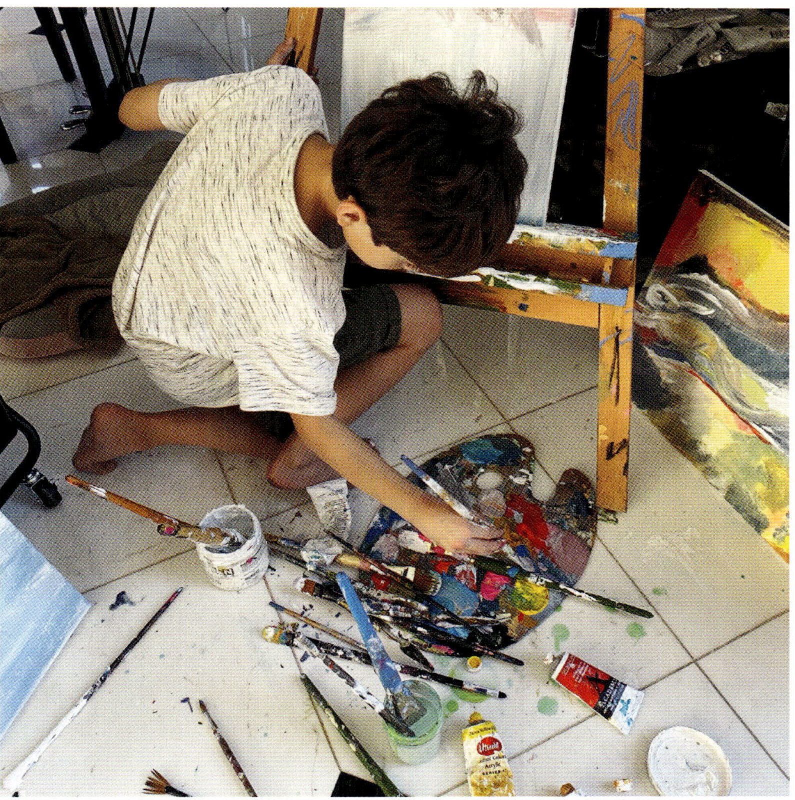

The Freedom of Expression

From birth, Andres was encouraged to create. He was influenced by Elsa's creativity and her artistic expression, especially when it came to her jewelry making and fashion design. Andres was also exposed to artwork in the home, since Lupe has always collected art and filled the walls of the house with paintings.

When Andres was a toddler, before he was regularly painting, Elsa would give him different tools and toys to express himself creatively. "I have always believed in art and the power of art therapy," Elsa says. "These kinds of practices are meant for kids to be able to express themselves and have fun." She never had rules about where the kids could paint or be creative in their house. She used to buy big rolls of white paper, put them on the floor, and give Andres and Atiana paint, brushes, and stencils, then set them loose. "My kids would get right into it and become totally covered in paint," Elsa says. "Creative expression was very therapeutic and very freeing for both of my children."

Elsa always encouraged her kids to be barefoot too. It was important to her that her children could feel free, both in their creative expression as well as their way of being and existing in the world. "I wanted them to feel the dirt and grass underneath their feet," Elsa says. "I wanted my kids to just be free. And so with the painting, I did the same thing. I didn't care if my house was a mess. It was all very freeing for them." This early encouragement to lean into freedom and spontaneity laid the foundation for Andres's free-flowing creativity, which was already beginning to take shape.

Above: Andres works on a painting on the family's living room floor, October 2020. **Opposite:** Painting the face of *The Observer* (pg. 150), April 2020.

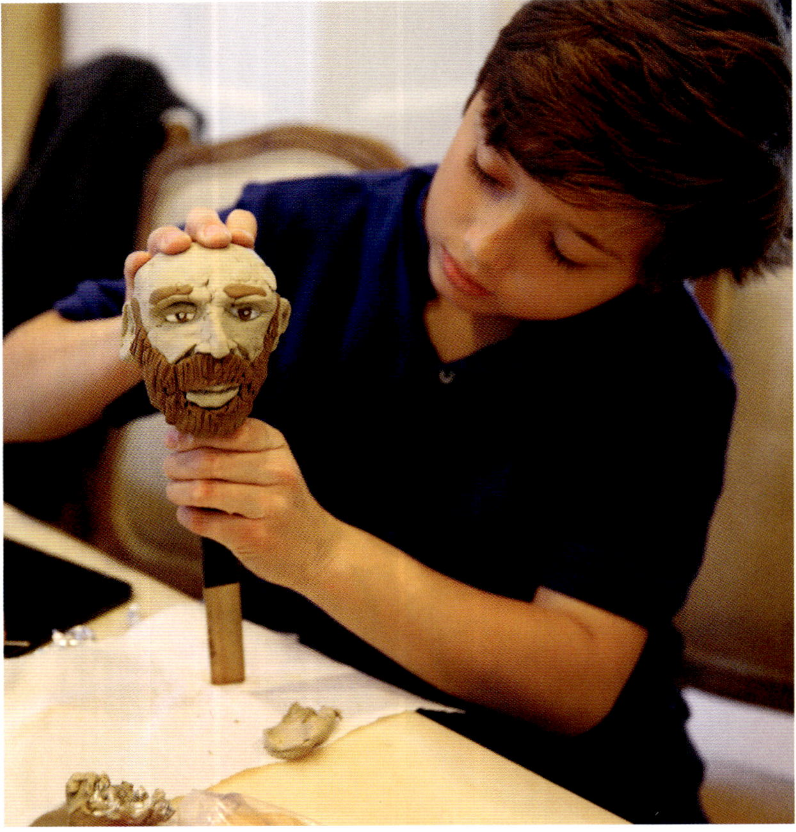

Noticing Andres Is Different

Elsa describes a young Andres as a "very funny little boy." She says, "He was always making me laugh and doing things his own way." On one occasion, Elsa hired her neighbor's sister, who was an art-school graduate, to come over and give her kids a class. She remembers both of the kids sitting at the kitchen island working on small canvases. The teacher said, "Okay, we're going to paint a vase with flowers." Andres was five at the time, and when he finished his painting, Elsa saw it had nothing to do with a vase or flowers. She thought to herself, *Oh my God, he is not following instructions.* Initially, she'd even considered, *This is not okay.*

Atiana's painting featured a beautiful vase of flowers. In contrast, Andres had used grays, blacks, and whites to paint two dripping eyes. The teacher said, "It's okay if he wants to do his own thing." But Elsa was still concerned at first, especially since he wasn't following instructions. "I didn't think he could just do whatever he wanted to do in a class," she says.

After this experience, Elsa decided further classes like this one were probably not going to work out for Andres. Elsa recalls talking to her son, "Andres, you were supposed to paint the vase with the flowers." And he responded by saying, "I didn't want to do that." She tried to explain that following instructions was how classes worked, but Andres remained unconvinced. Because he was so young, Elsa assumed he would grow out of this. Little did she know, this was just the beginning of Andres forging his own creative path.

Above: Andres sculpts the head of Vincent van Gogh using clay, November 2022. **Opposite:** Taking a break from painting as he poses on the floor of his studio at the age of ten, May 2022.

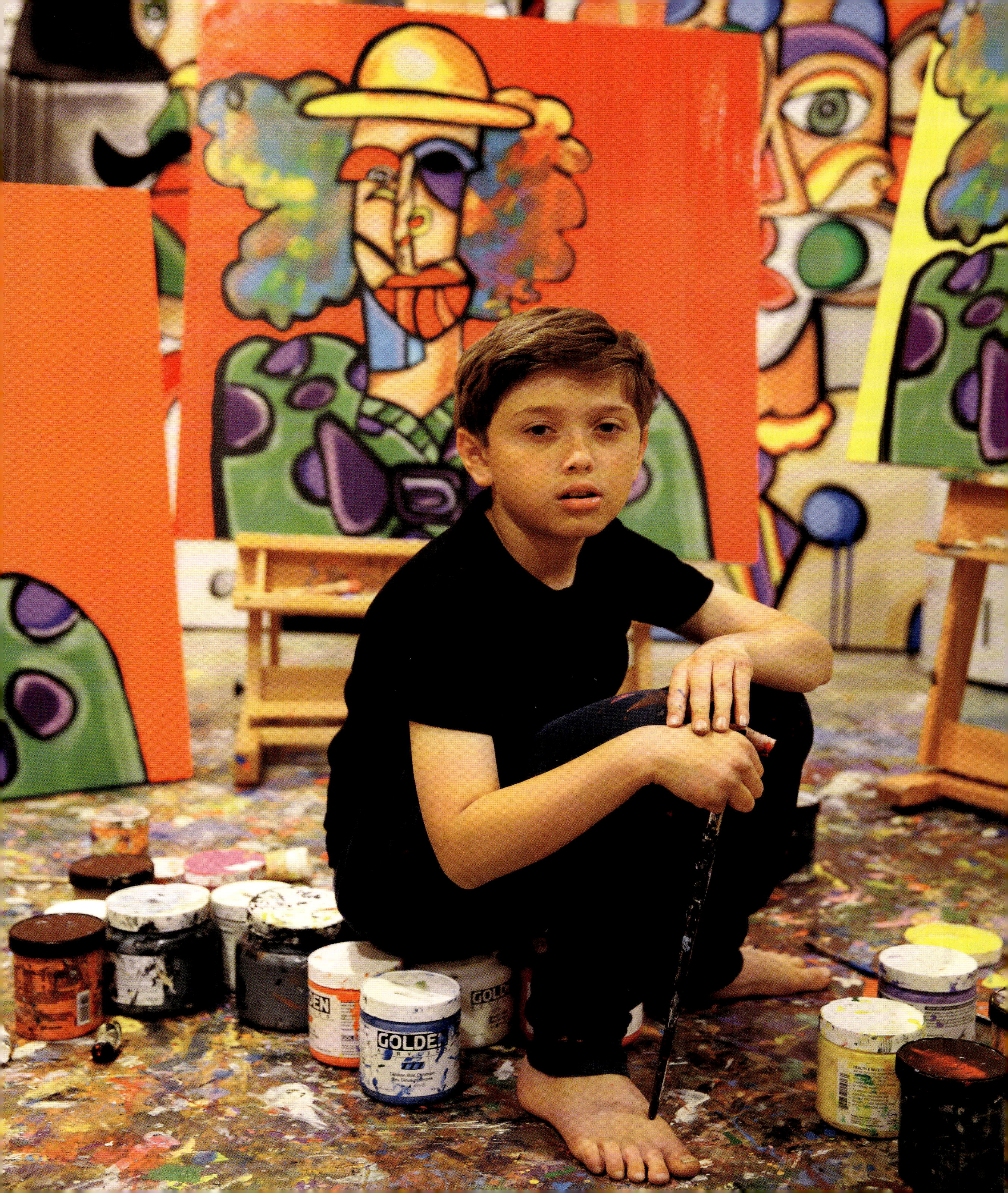

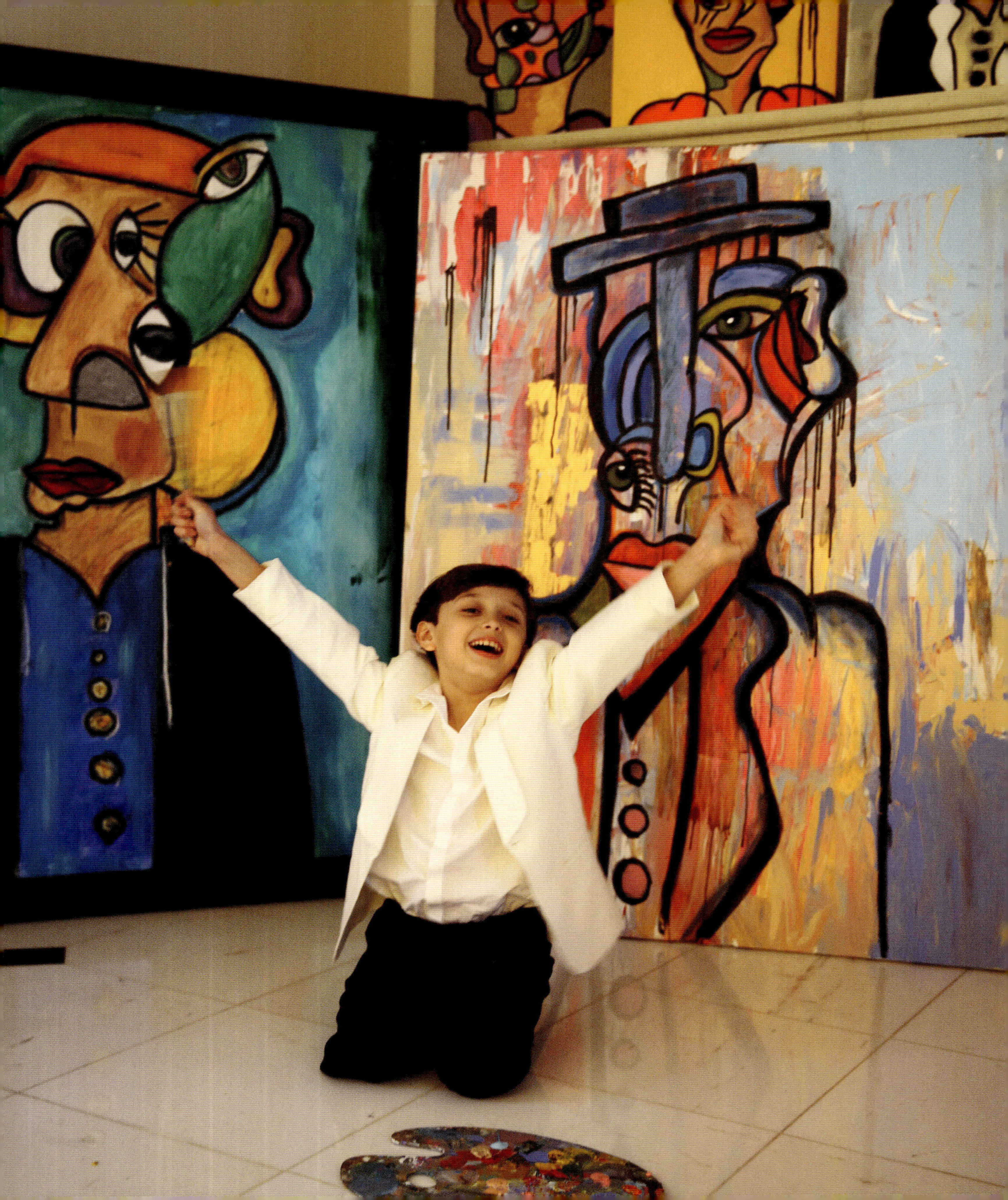

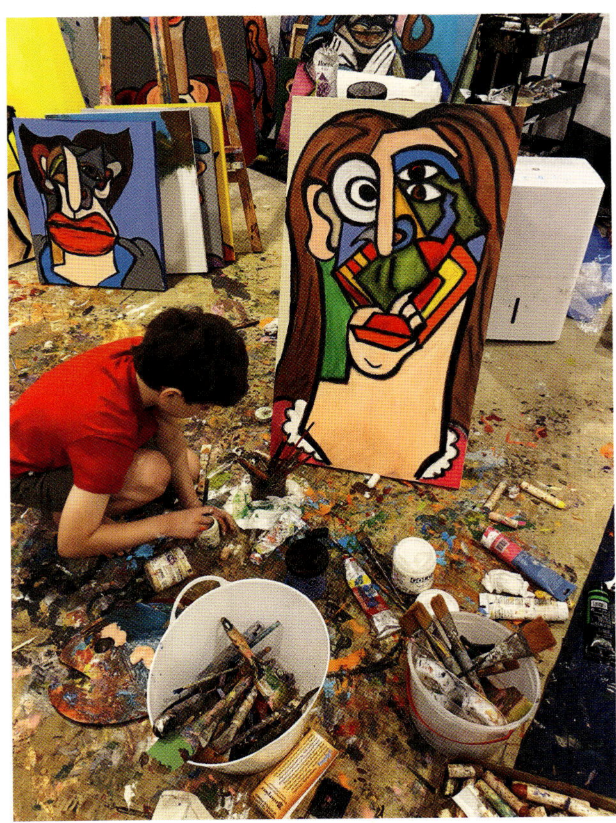

Painting His Own Way

When Andres first began drawing faces, he almost always put eyes, ears, and noses in the wrong places. Noticing this, Elsa encouraged him to look at real human faces to see how they're put together. But Andres continued to paint faces more abstractly, and his mother realized he was doing things in his own creative way. Instead of trying to correct him again, she decided to let him follow his instincts and encouraged him to express himself creatively in whatever way he wanted to.

From the beginning, Andres felt compelled to depict the abstract, cubist-like faces for which he has become famous. Making these faces is exciting to him, as he explains, "I want to do something different from a lot of other artists. As we know, there's a lot of realism out there. Making these faces my way was just something I felt passionate about."

During Andres's time in preschool, he brought some of his paintings and drawings home to show Elsa. When she saw this early work, she often thought, *What is he doing? This is different.* "I'm going to be honest, I didn't see it as free and creative at first," Elsa says. "It kind of worried me. I questioned him about it a lot. Maybe this was the therapist in me coming out. I asked him things like, 'Can you tell me why you put the nose on the forehead?' But he never had an answer. Or if he did say something, it was along the lines of 'I don't know, that's where I want it.'" Elsa tried to explain to him that "we have two eyes, one nose, and one mouth, and they're always meant to go in the same place." But she doesn't think he really listened.

Andres's art is often compared to Pablo Picasso's, but Andres wasn't exposed to Picasso's work until after he had begun developing his own style. When Andres started painting, he was still too young to pay much attention to other works of art or to be familiar with any of the artists he loves now.

When asked why he likes to make faces less realistic and more fantastical, Andres explains, "I like to be different, because it makes you stand out. To be honest, though, I didn't even know I was doing it differently at first. It just poured out of me. I had to do it."

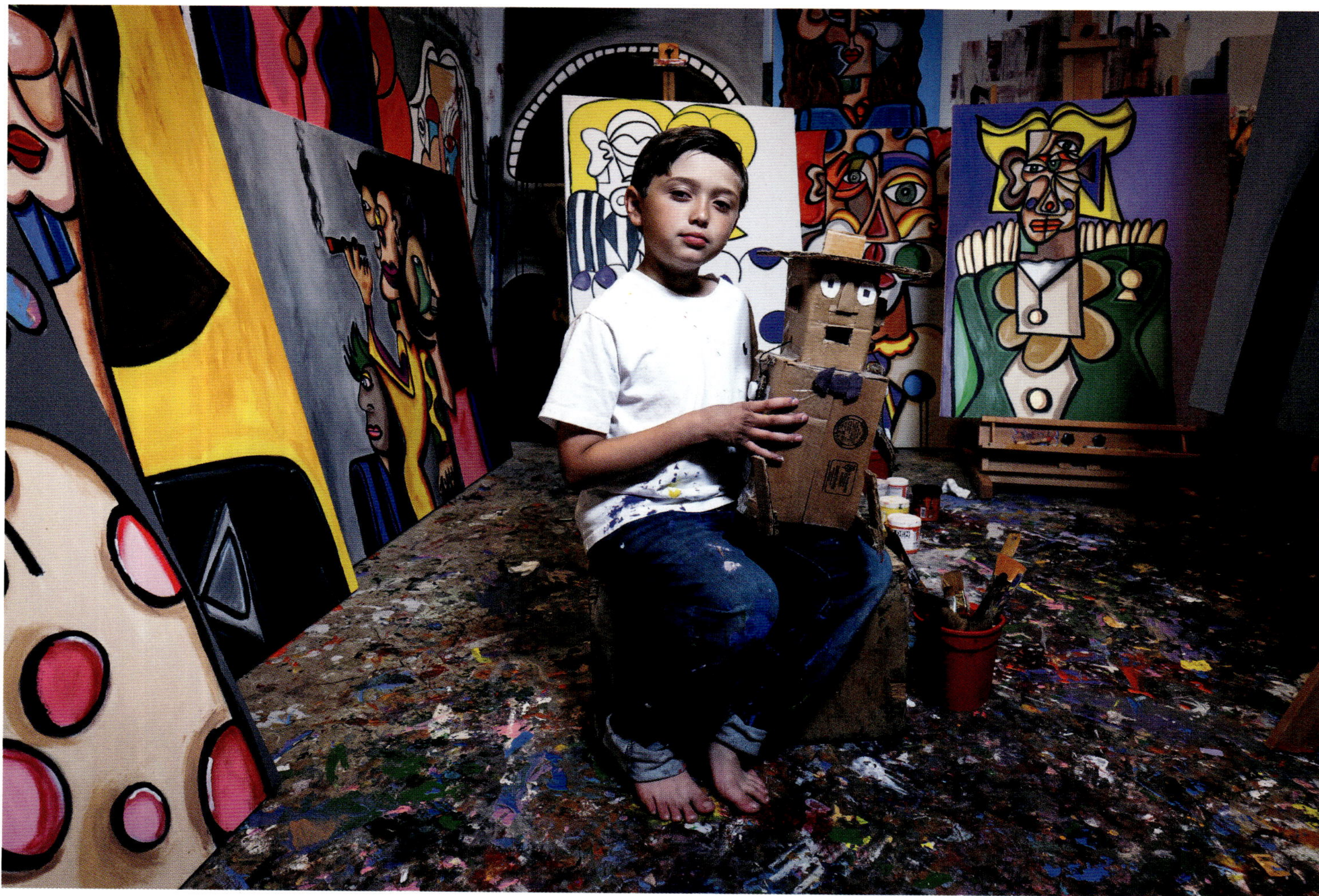

Elsa stopped asking Andres about his art after she went to his classroom when he was in the first grade to help with a holiday party. All the corners of the room were set up with different activities, and one was a corner where you could draw or paint whatever you wanted. "Of course," she says, "Andres went over there and got to work." When he finished, the whole class ran over to him. They were all excited. They wanted to see what he'd made. They knew he was an artist. "That's when this little light bulb inside me turned on, and I thought, *Oh my God, the kids are loving it*," Elsa says. "So I said to myself, 'Okay, you know what, I am going to just allow him to be.'"

From this point forward, Elsa began to appreciate how differently Andres sketched and created faces. She started to encourage Andres and told him about some of the artists who also painted in a similar way. Elsa showed him books about Picasso and other artists and talked to him about the art hanging in the Valencia home. Pretty soon, mother and son were regularly talking about the paintings in these books and the pieces they owned. They had conversations about what they liked and didn't like, as well as the artist's color choices and methods. These early discussions helped lay the foundation for Andres's impressive knowledge in the field of art history.

Above: Andres holding a cardboard sculpture he made in his studio, age ten. **Opposite:** Working on the painting *Valentina* (pg. 216), 2022. *Photos by Sye Williams.*

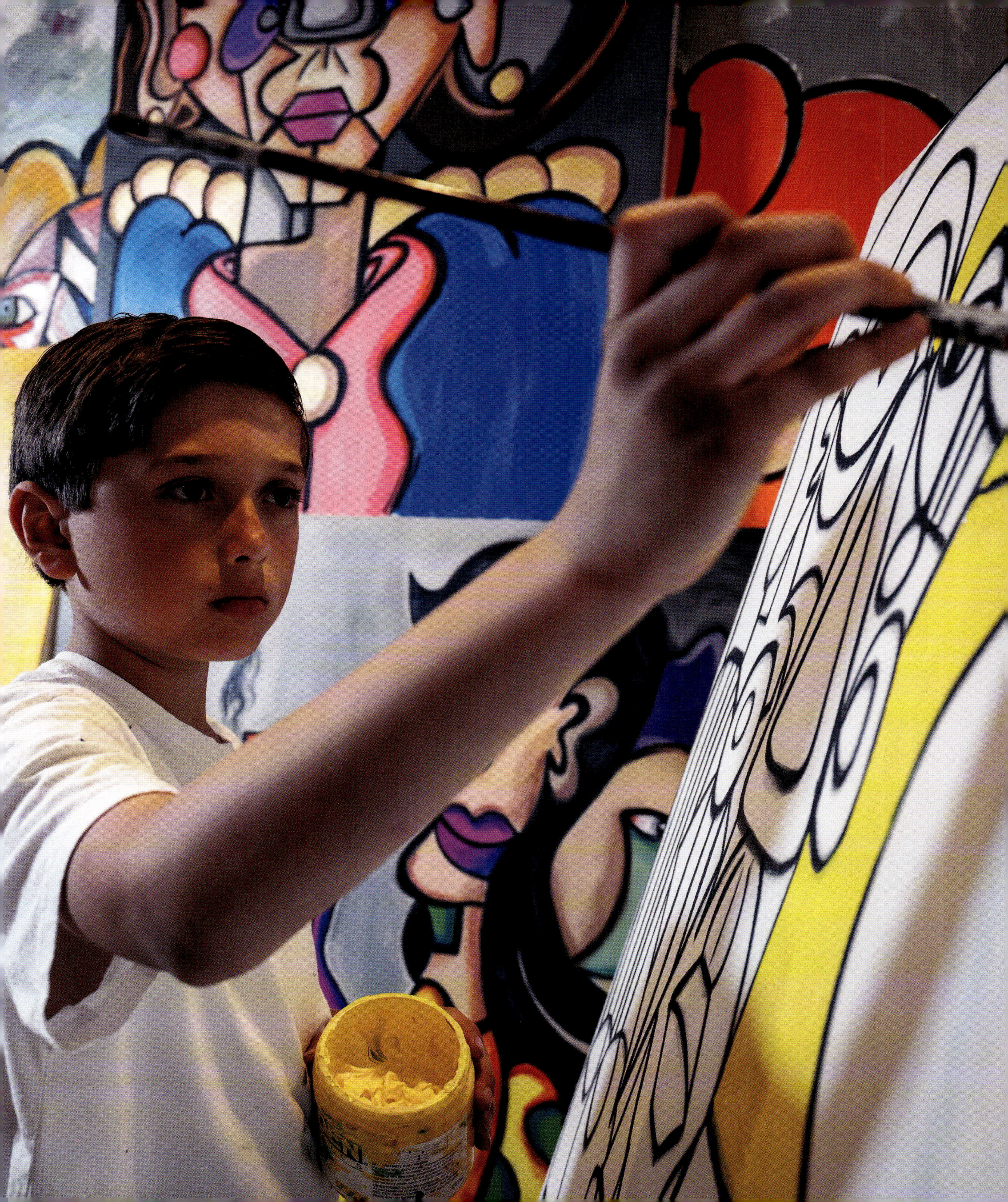

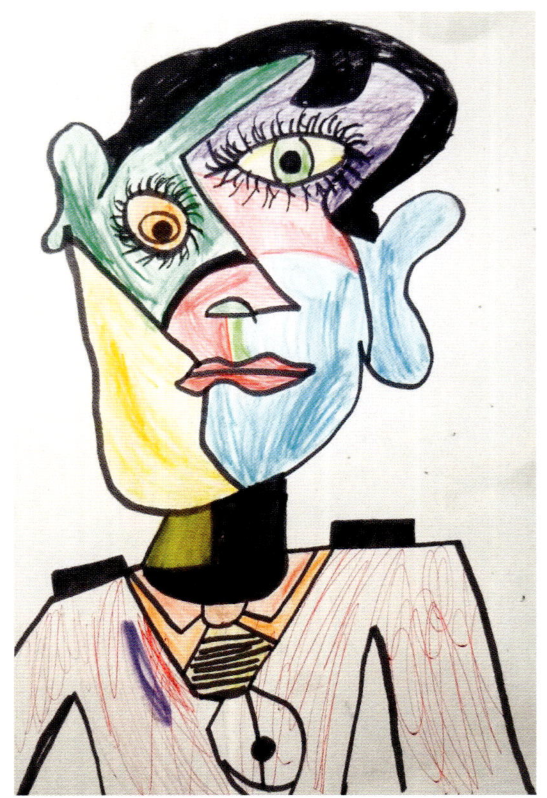
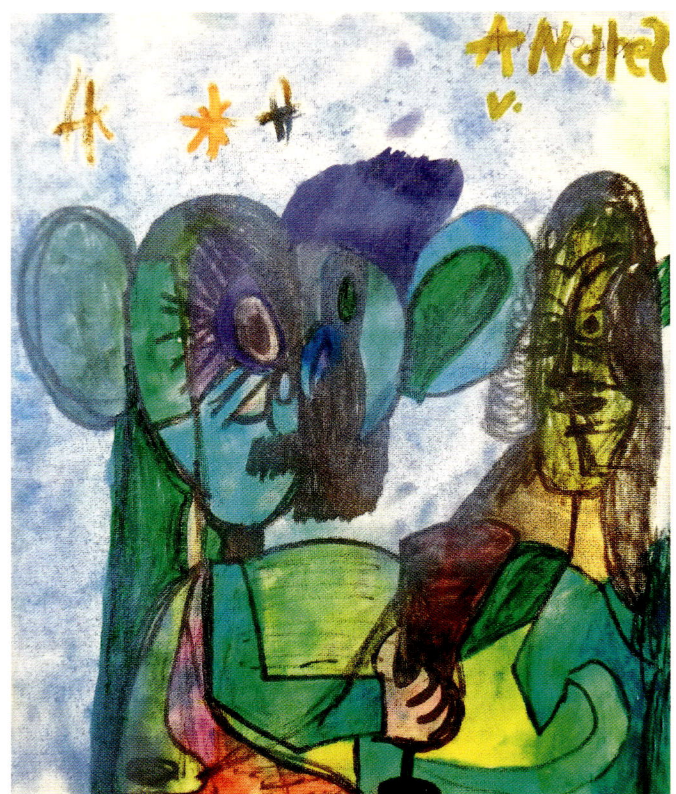
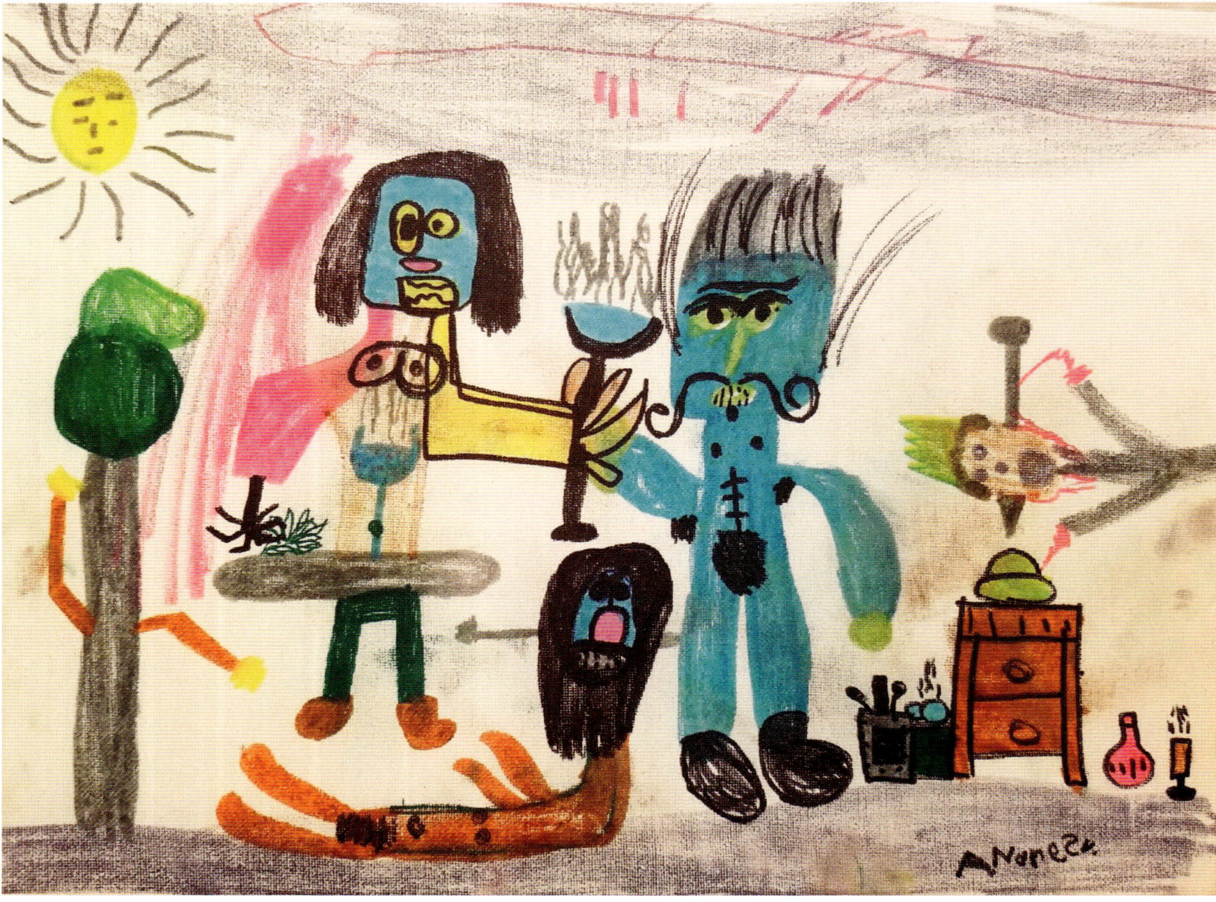

Above: Early sketches on paper from 2018. **Opposite:** Three sketches from 2019; one sketch from 2020 (bottom right).

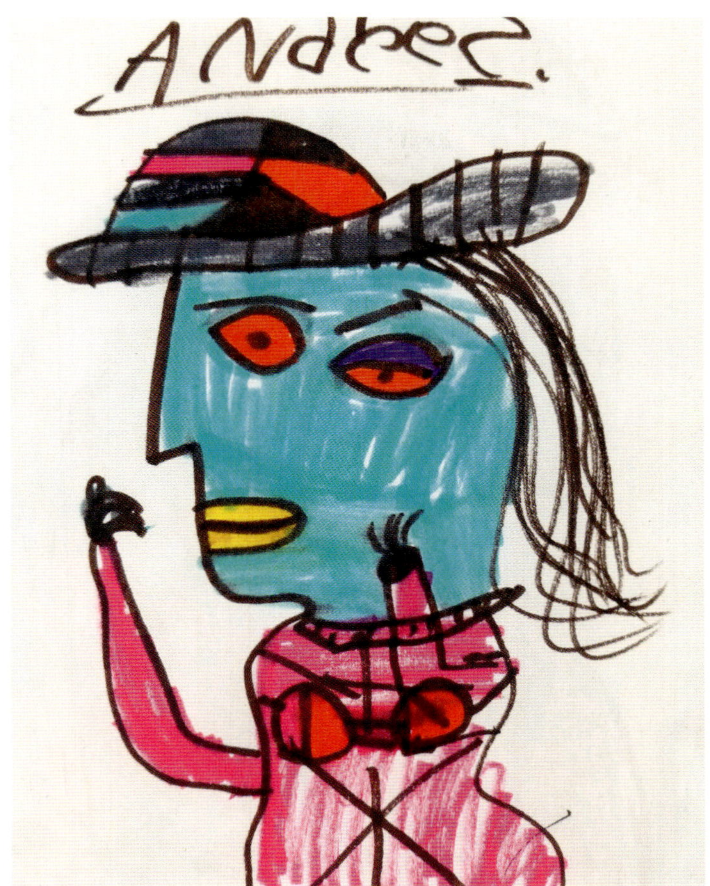

A Ndrez.

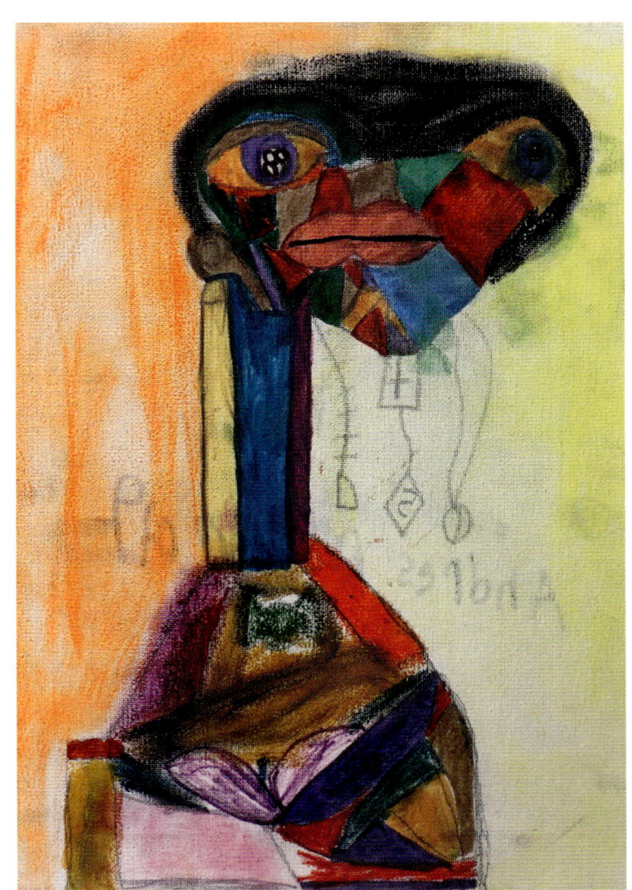

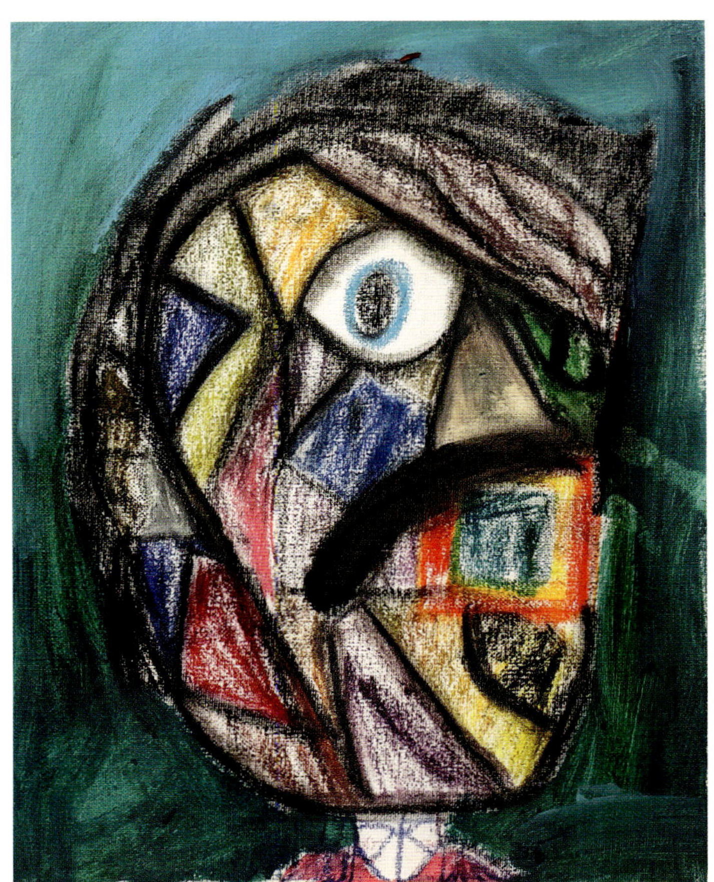

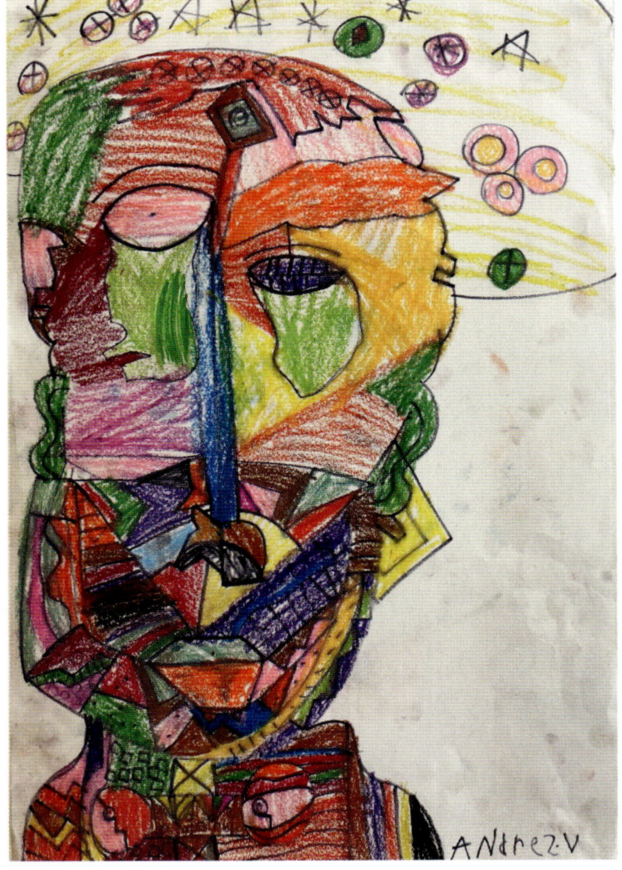

ANdrezV

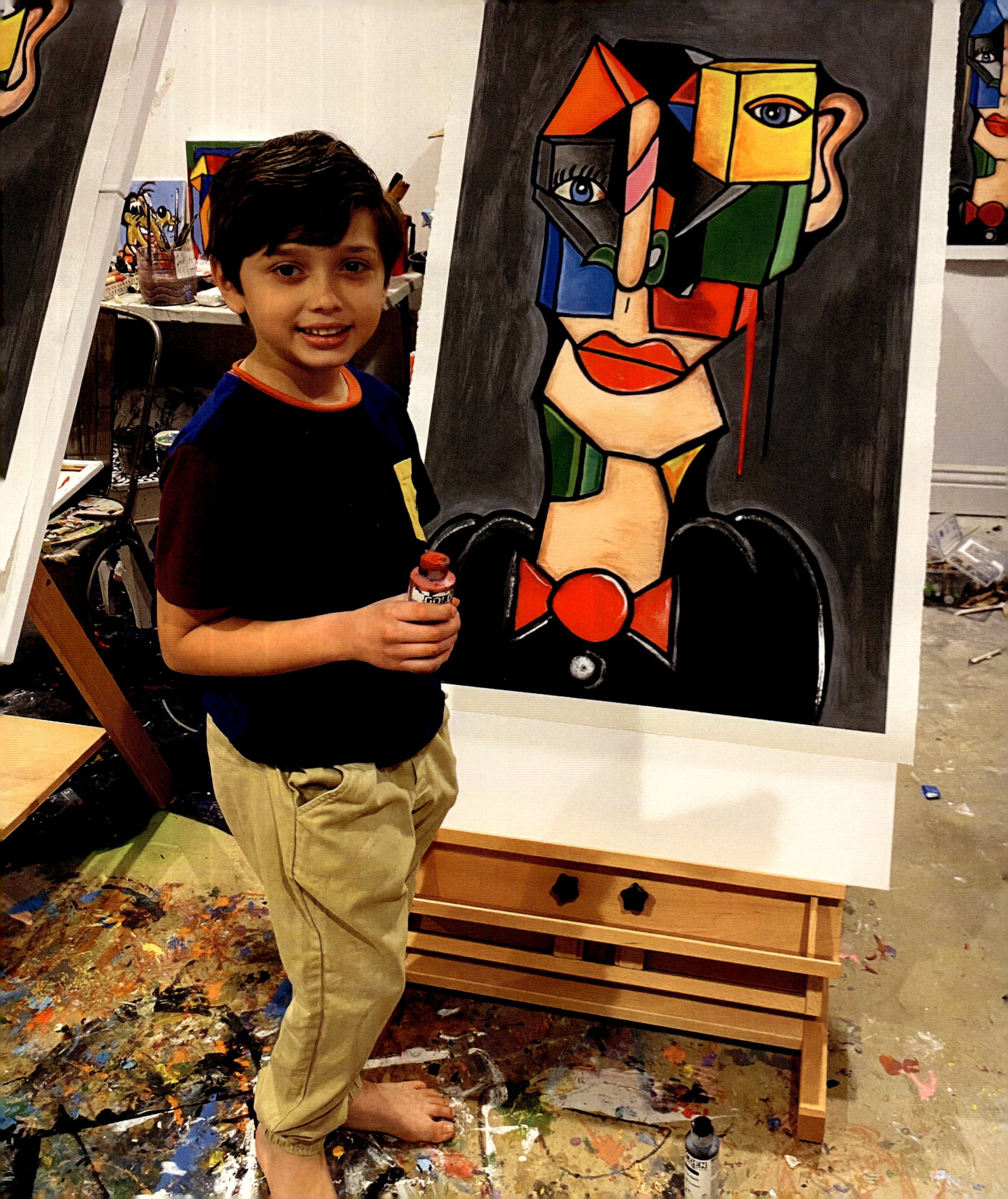

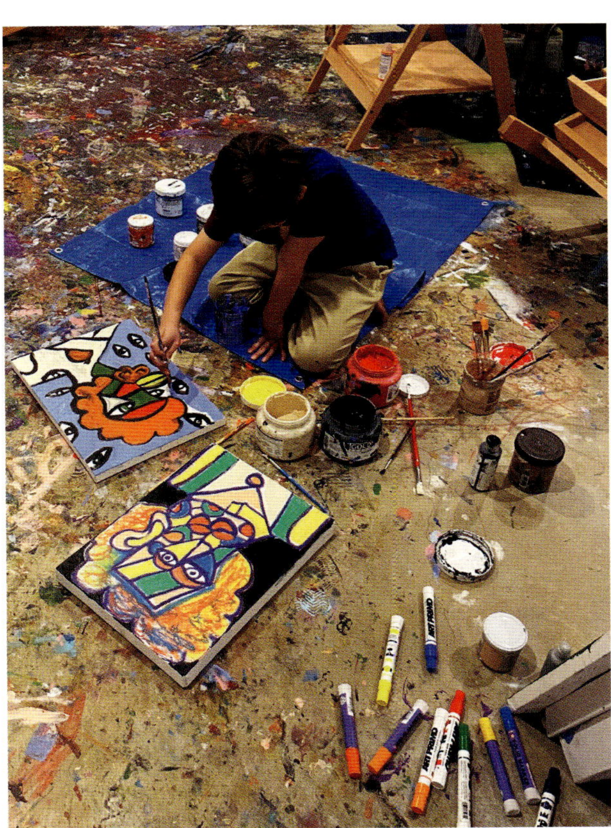

A Child Artist

When Andres was first exploring his creativity, one painting on the walls of the Valencia's home was an abstract piece by the artist RETNA, a contemporary artist best known for his graffiti-like art. Andres was drawn to the painting and tried to copy it, sketching as fast as he could. He tried to use the same colors, not with paint, but with colored pencils. As they watched him work, his parents realized Andres was exhibiting an unusual skill, and they fully leaned in to encouraging his creative endeavors. He was only five years old.

By the age of six, Andres had requested his own studio space and often sketched and painted in his bedroom. "He always had access to paint," Elsa says. "We didn't have canvases for him at this point, but we gave him a lot of paper to use." Andres would make something in his room and leave it in there. Whenever he finished, Elsa would go in to check it out. "I was regularly surprised by the originality of what he created," Elsa says. "I'd grab the piece and take it to my husband. Lupe would see it and say something like, 'Oh my God, that's amazing. That's very cool.'"

Recognizing Andres's talent, his parents started buying him canvases to paint on. Elsa took him to art stores so Andres could pick out his own supplies and paint colors. Having both his parents support as well as access to art supplies and tools are advantages that have helped Andres fully explore his creativity.

From the start, he was very interested in color. He studied books about art and guides on how to mix and match colors to achieve specific shades. At this point, Elsa recalls thinking, *Maybe this is just a little artistic stage he will go through.* But it was never just a stage. Instead, it was the beginning.

Andres brought art into nearly everything he did. While other kids in the neighborhood set up lemonade stands to sell cold, refreshing drinks, Andres set up an art stand to try and sell his art. "Art for sale! Art for sale!" he would holler, while his sister and her friends sold lemonade on the other corner. At that point, an original Andres Valencia painting could be had for just one dollar, a very small fraction of the price his work would later command.

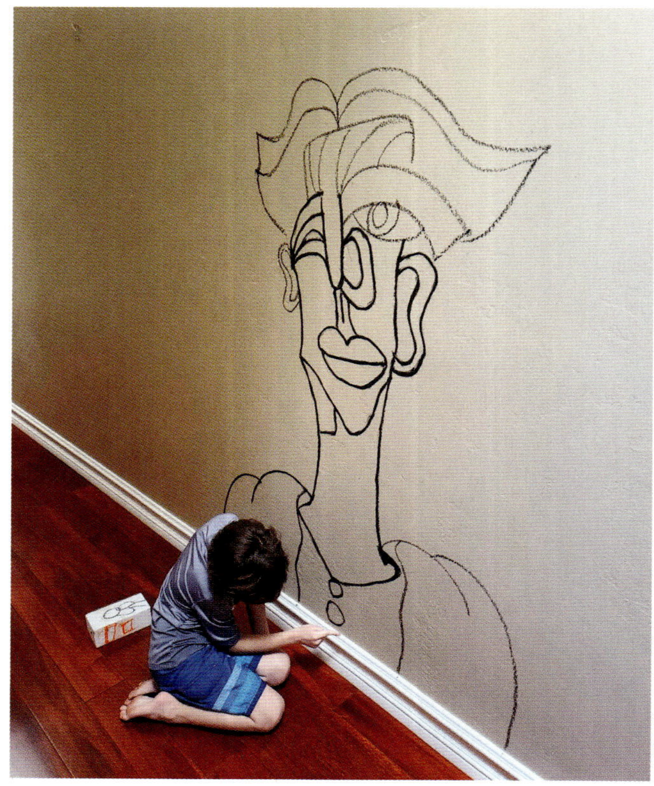

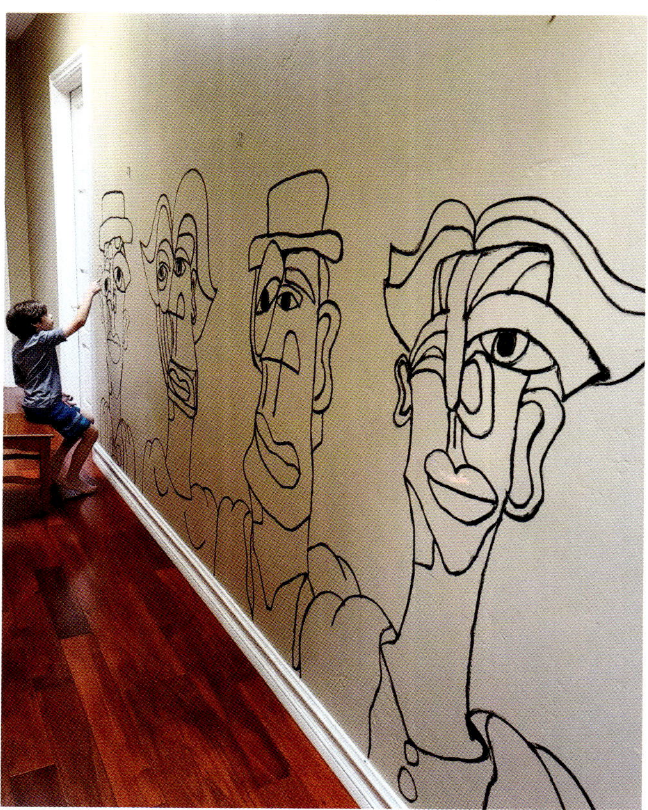

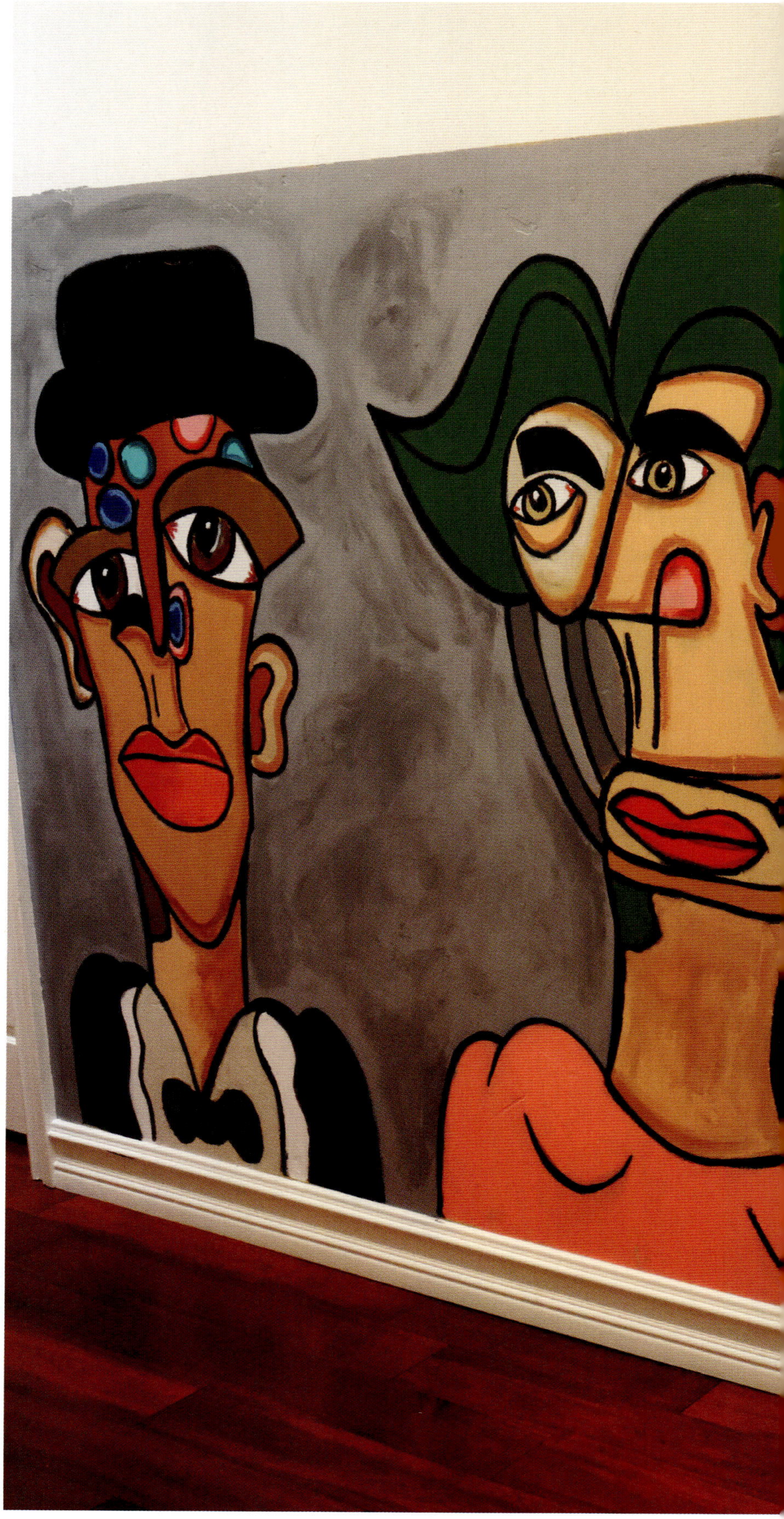

Above: In September 2020, Andres was asked to create a mural at the home of art collector, Marc Chase. These photos show the work in progress. **Opposite:** The completed mural features four distinct characters.

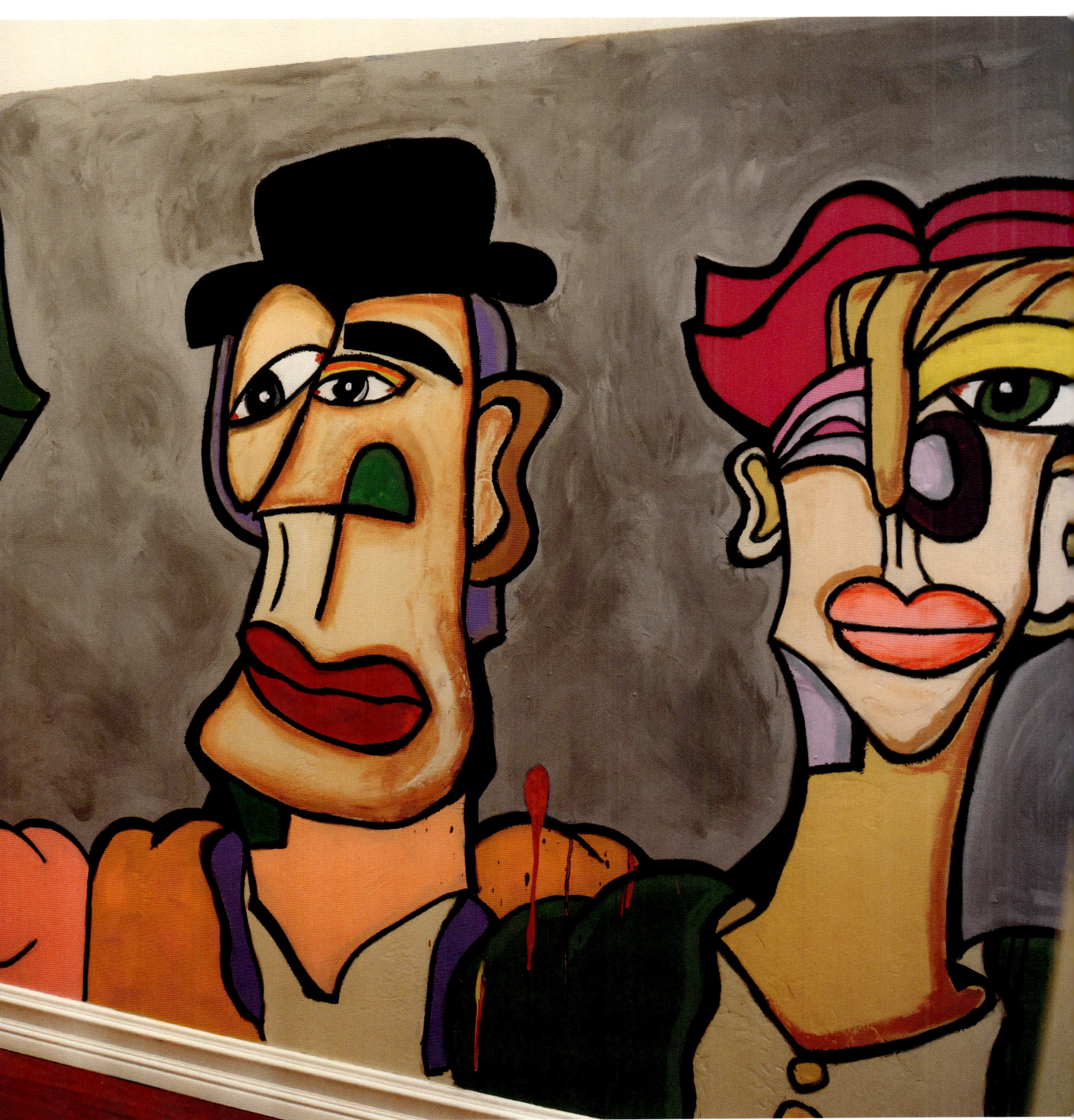

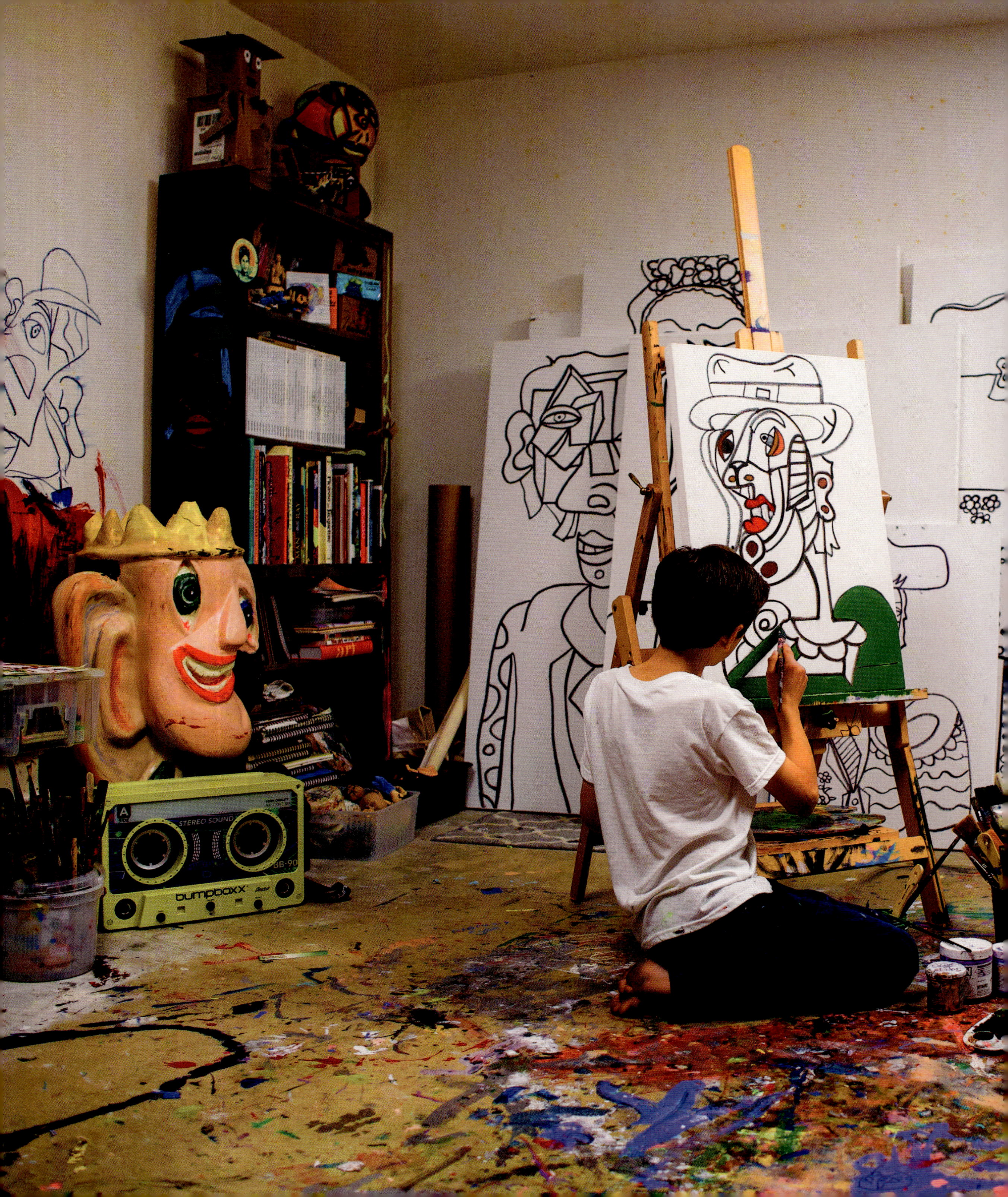

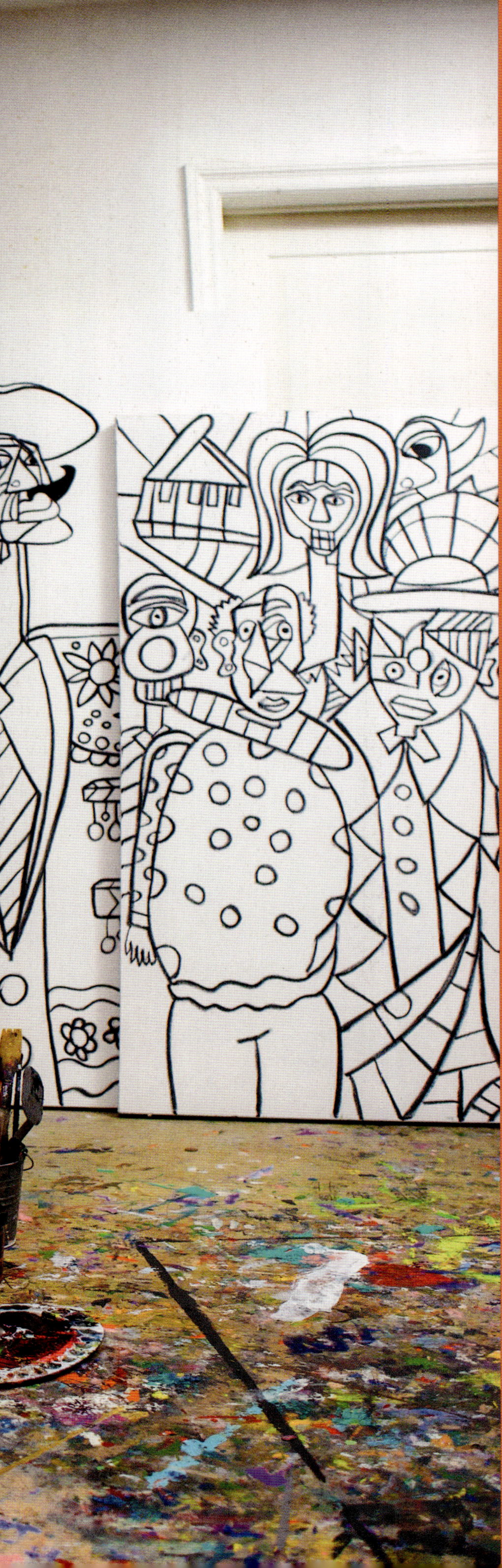

INSPIRATION

Andres has been compared to Pablo Picasso since he first started painting. He was even referred to as "little Picasso" when he first made a big splash in the art scene at the age of ten. His cubist portraits are reminiscent of the Spanish painter's work in terms of form, color, and emotion. While Andres does consider Picasso one of his favorite artists and a big inspiration, he cites Amedeo Modigliani and George Condo as two other major influences. The elongated style of Modigliani's figures are apparent in Valencia's work, as he often plays around with typical human proportions, and Condo's geometric shapes and intentionally haphazard placement of facial features are seen on Andres's characters as well.

Although he's entirely self-taught, Andres consistently seeks inspiration from other artists, studying art books and watching documentaries about other well-known creatives. He picks and chooses elements of each artist he is drawn to most, mixing in his own painting aesthetic as he works to define his unique style. No specific teacher has guided his creative process. Instead, Andres has informed his own painting style by pulling inspiration from a number of sources, both in the art world and from popular culture at large.

Andres painting in his studio, March 2024.

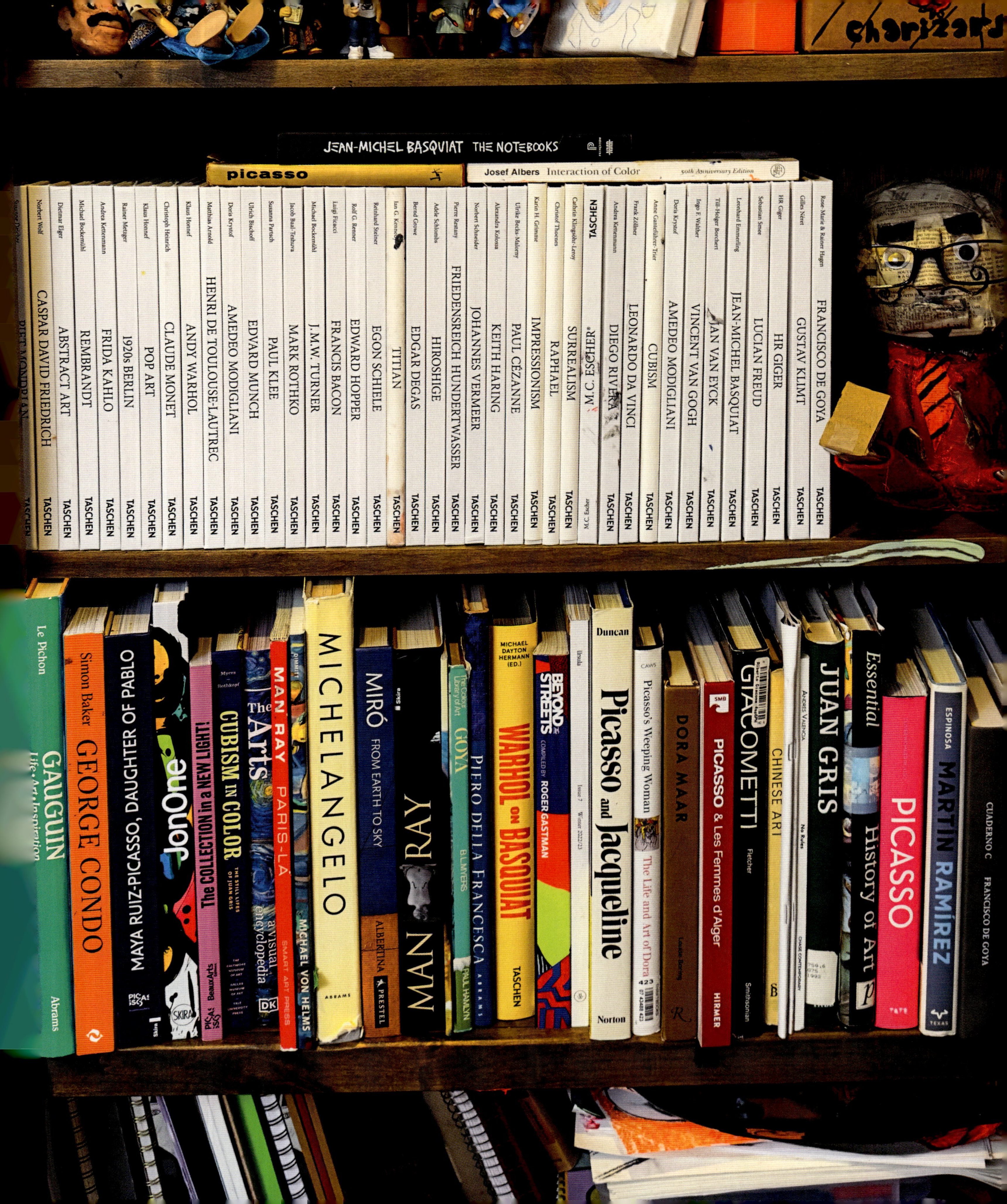
JEAN-MICHEL BASQUIAT THE NOTEBOOKS
picasso
Josef Albers Interaction of Color
50th Anniversary Edition
PIET MONDRIAN
CASPAR DAVID FRIEDRICH
ABSTRACT ART
REMBRANDT
FRIDA KAHLO
1920s BERLIN
POP ART
CLAUDE MONET
ANDY WARHOL
HENRI DE TOULOUSE-LAUTREC
AMEDEO MODIGLIANI
EDVARD MUNCH
PAUL KLEE
MARK ROTHKO
J.M.W. TURNER
FRANCIS BACON
EDWARD HOPPER
EGON SCHIELE
TITIAN
EDGAR DEGAS
HIROSHIGE
FRIEDENSREICH HUNDERTWASSER
JOHANNES VERMEER
KEITH HARING
PAUL CÉZANNE
IMPRESSIONISM
RAPHAEL
SURREALISM
M.C. ESCHER
DIEGO RIVERA
LEONARDO DA VINCI
CUBISM
AMEDEO MODIGLIANI
VINCENT VAN GOGH
JAN VAN EYCK
JEAN-MICHEL BASQUIAT
LUCIAN FREUD
HR GIGER
GUSTAV KLIMT
FRANCISCO DE GOYA
TASCHEN
Le Pichon
GAUGUIN
Abrams
Simon Baker
GEORGE CONDO
MAYA RUIZ-PICASSO, DAUGHTER OF PABLO
JonOne
SKIRA
The COLLECTION in a NEW LIGHT!
CUBISM IN COLOR
The Arts
a visual encyclopedia
DK
MAN RAY
PARIS-LA
SMART ART PRESS
MICHAEL VON HELMS
MICHELANGELO
ABRAMS
MIRÓ FROM EARTH TO SKY
ALBERTINA
PRESTEL
MAN RAY
GOYA
PIERO DELLA FRANCESCA
PAUL HAMLYN
MICHAEL DAYTON HERMANN (ED.)
WARHOL ON BASQUIAT
TASCHEN
BEYOND STREETS
COMPILED BY ROGER GASTMAN
Duncan
Picasso and Jacqueline
Norton
Picasso's Weeping Woman
The Life and Art of Dora
DORA MAAR
PICASSO & Les Femmes d'Alger
HIRMER
GIACOMETTI
Fletcher
Smithsonian
CHINESE ART
JUAN GRIS
Essential
History of Art
PICASSO
TATE
ESPINOSA
MARTIN RAMÍREZ
CUADERNO C
FRANCISCO DE GOYA
charizard

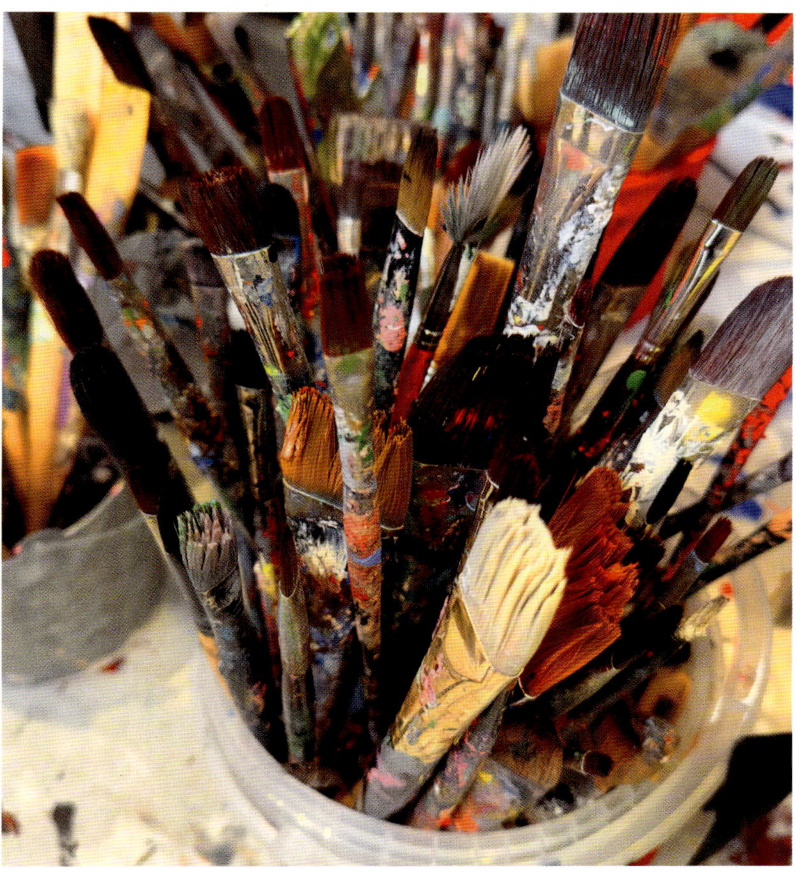

An Appreciation for Art History

When asked about why he is drawn to certain artists over others, Andres often cites details from the artists' personal lives. He displays a comprehensive knowledge of not only their artworks, but their personal histories too. "Andres could tell you Picasso's entire life story," Elsa says. "He could tell you every woman Picasso was married to and all his kids' names. I think it's not just the art that he is drawn to, but it's also the whole package, the entirety of an artistic life."

Once, when Andres and Elsa were at a museum in Los Angeles, Andres quickly walked up to a painting and said, without hesitation, "This is a Pollock."

"Wait, how do you know that?" Elsa responded. "I don't think we've read about him."

"Oh, yes, he was an alcoholic," Andres replied, without answering the question. He instead offered more insight he'd learned from watching videos about Pollock on YouTube, getting into further details about his life, and even sharing facts about Pollock's wife, fellow artist and abstract expressionist painter Lee Krasner.

Instances like this occur often, as Andres holds an encyclopedic amount of knowledge about the famous artists who inspire him. If you ask him a question about Picasso, Condo, or Modigliani, you will get not only the answer to your question but also other details about their lives and their works.

Above: Paintbrushes in Andres's studio. **Opposite:** The shelves in Andres's studio are full of books about famous artists.

Andres's Favorite Artists

Pablo Picasso

While the inspiration Andres has pulled from Picasso is undeniable, one painting in particular has influenced him the most: *Guernica*, Picasso's huge 1937 oil painting that depicts violence and suffering among people and animals in the namesake Spanish town after it was bombed by Nazi Germany. Even though this 11.5 ft (3.5 m) tall and 25.5 ft (7.8 m) wide painting is entirely in black and white, the emotions Picasso is able to bring forth from each character is visceral.

Andres was lucky enough to see *Guernica* in 2023 when he visited the Museo del Prado in Madrid, Spain, with his family. "I had always looked at books that have that painting in it," Andres says. "It was something I always wanted to see because I knew so much about it. Seeing it in person was a dream come true." Andres spent thirty minutes staring at it, trying to figure out how Picasso made it.

In response to the Russian invasion of Ukraine, Andres was inspired to create a painting in the vein of *Guernica*: a large canvas in color called *Invasion of Ukraine* (pg. 199). Just like Picasso's painting, the brutality of war and the fraught emotions of the victims caught in the chaos are apparent in the scene. "The painting shows a Russian soldier invading a Ukrainian village, and the Ukrainians are fighting back," Andres says. "I wanted to show how Ukraine is not going to give up. With *Guernica*, Picasso kind of kept that awfulness alive. He didn't want anyone to forget what happened to these people and the struggles they went through. It was just a little village that got bombed. So then I kind of felt I had to do the same for Ukraine." With his painting, Andres wanted to make a difference and help those in need. The family decided to create a limited print run of Andres's original painting with five hundred copies. All the earnings have been donated directly to charities that are working to support the people of Ukraine.

"My favorite thing about Picasso's paintings is how different they are from other artists," Andres says. "Around his time, you see all these artists doing realism and making the face look like it's supposed to look, but he wanted to do something else. He was the only artist at the time who was doing things like this and using cubism, not being realistic, but still being really, really creative." In addition to *Guernica*, Andres likes Picasso's dove sketches and the blue paintings.

When Andres is asked what he thinks of some people referring to him as "little Picasso," he replies by saying, "I like it, but I also want to be my own artist." An astute point from a young boy who is still defining his own identity.

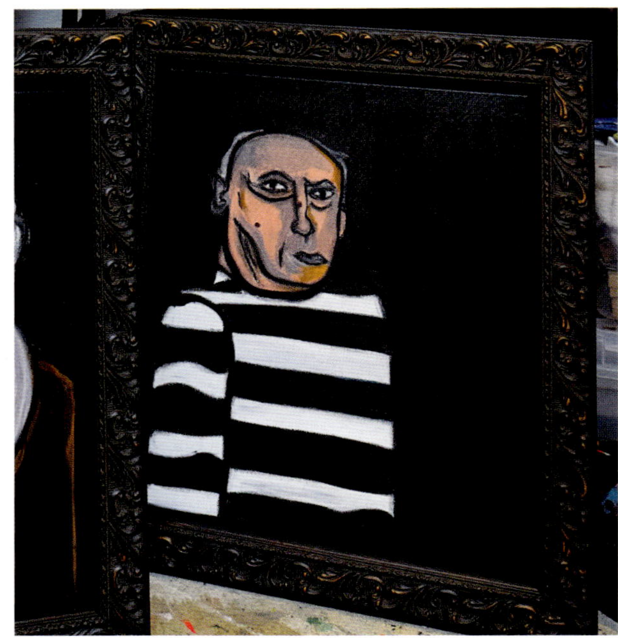

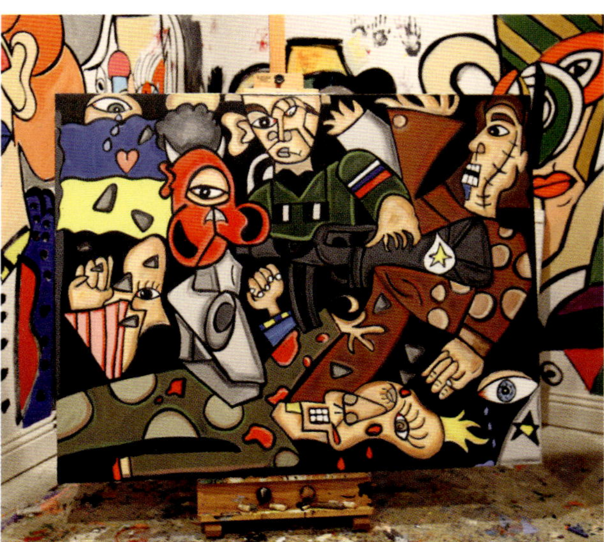

Top: Andres's painting of *Pablo Picasso* (pg. 235) resting on the floor of his studio. **Above:** The completed painting, *Invasion of Ukraine* (pg. 199). **Opposite:** Andres working on the Ukraine painting in his studio, March 2022.

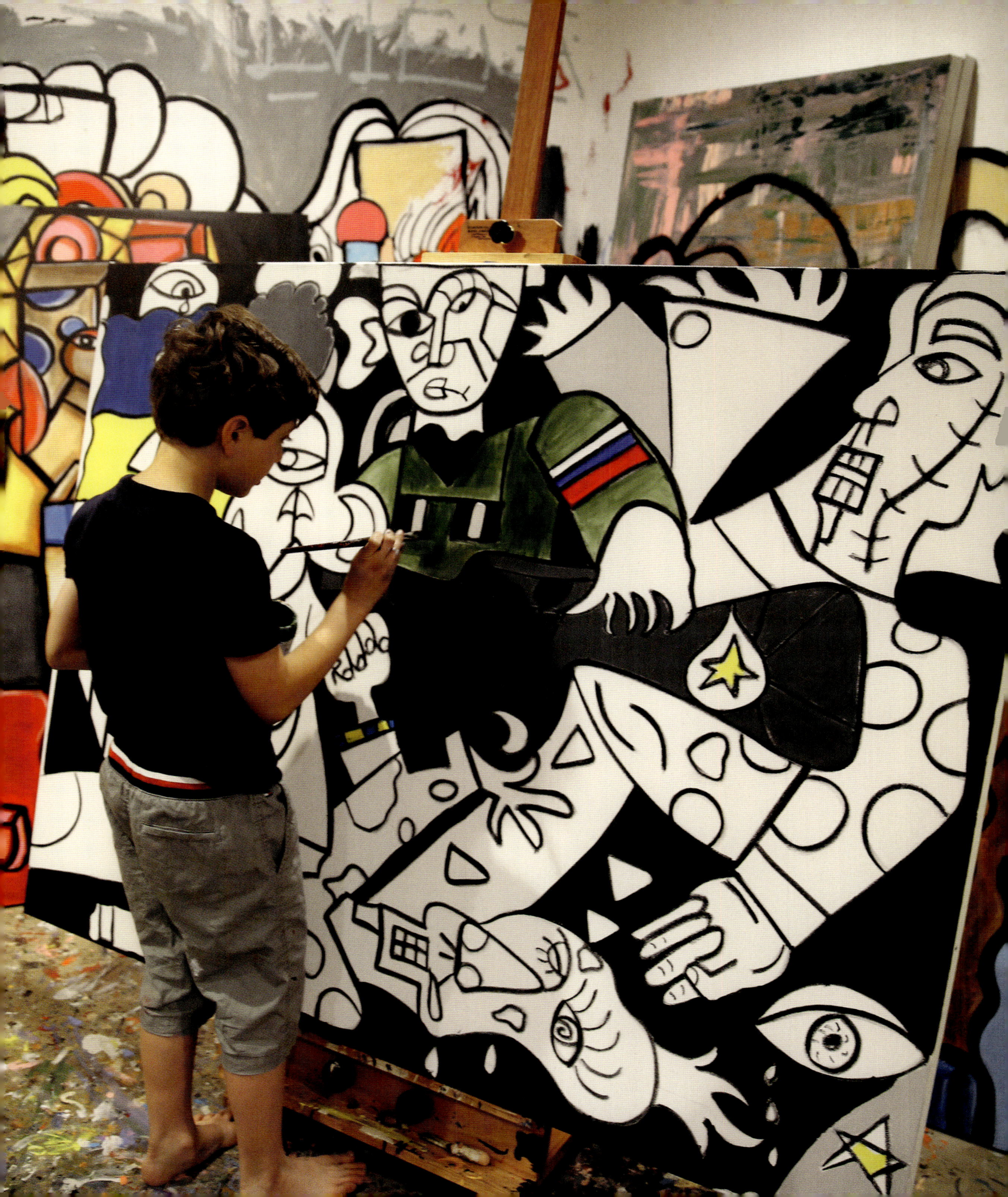

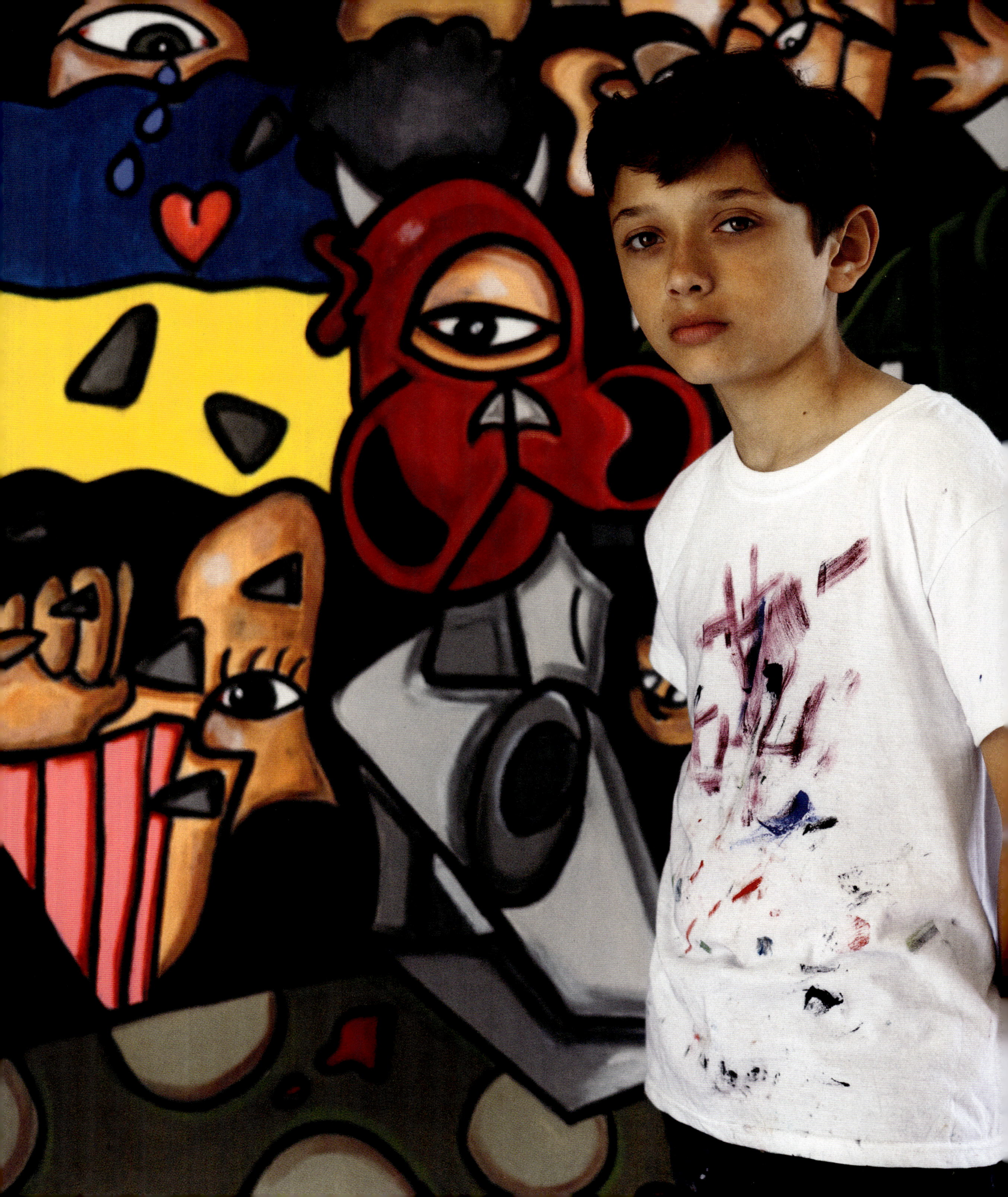

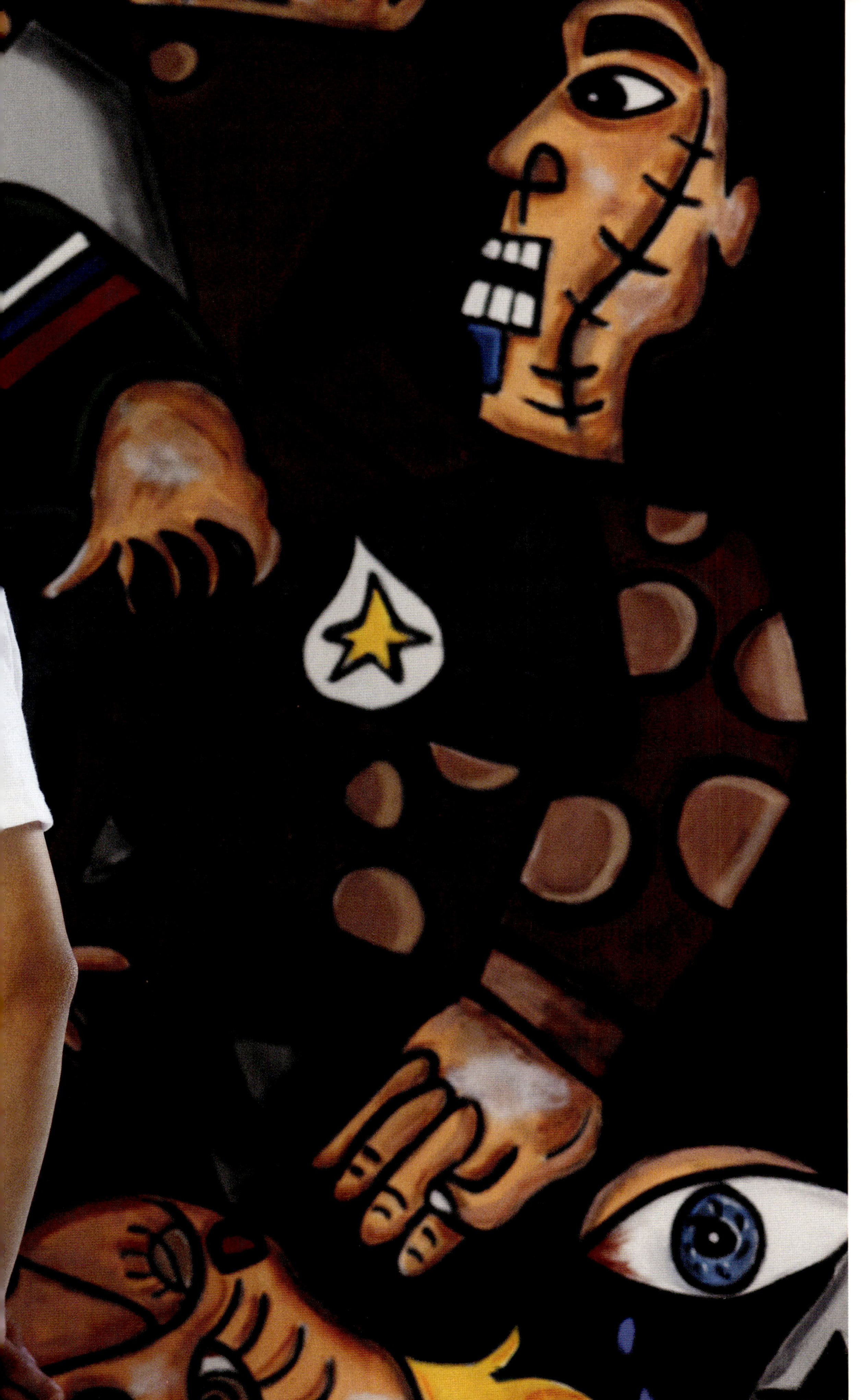

Andres poses in front of his large painting, *Invasion of Ukraine* (pg. 199), at the family home, March 2024.

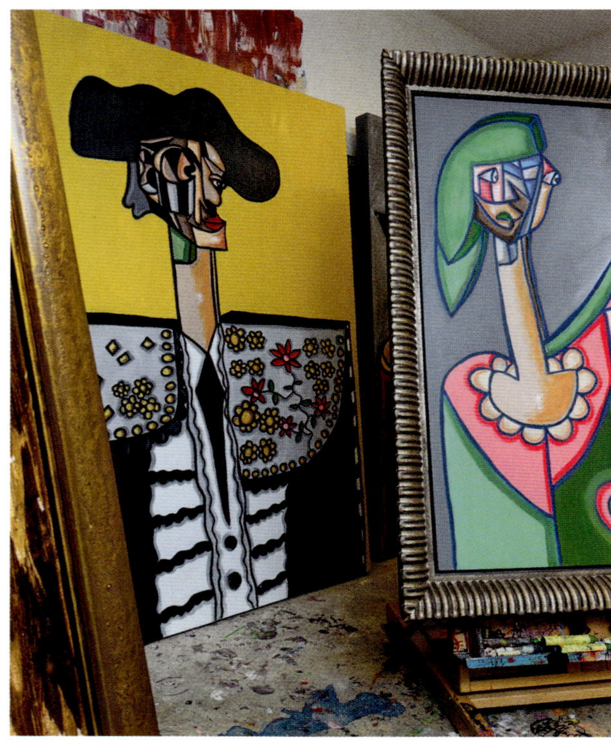

George Condo

When asked which famous artist he'd like to meet and have a conversation with, Andres's answer is always George Condo, the New York–based contemporary artist who is known for his "artificial realism" paintings. Andres's interest in Condo began in second grade, when he started regularly watching YouTube videos that featured Condo and his paintings. This was a time when he really wanted to learn more about art and how other artists created their works.

"Those videos of George Condo are what helped Andres figure out what oil pastel was," Elsa says. "He didn't even know what oil pastel was before this. He would watch these videos of Condo and figure out what he was using to create his art. So really, he got empowered by watching George Condo work. Condo was definitely one of his first loves. He would constantly tell me how he thought his art was cool. Learning about art through YouTube in this way was really, really big for him."

Andres explains further: "I first learned about George Condo because I was looking at Picasso paintings, and there were recommendations about other artists I might like, and one of them was George. I started looking at his work, and it was just so cool to me what he did." So for hours, Andres would watch his videos on YouTube, drawing like him. "If I could meet any artist who is still alive today, it would be him," Andres says.

Amedeo Modigliani

Modigliani is known for painting a lot of interesting faces and portraits that aren't super realistic. His willingness to shy away from realism when creating human characters is something from which Andres has been able to pull inspiration. "My favorite thing about his work is the long necks he does," Andres says. "He uses a lot of exaggeration where he changes the size and shape of people's proportions. I like doing this too." Modigliani also painted self-portraits, along with a portrait drawing of Picasso, which is one of Andres's favorites. Modigliani and Picasso knew each other and had a bit of a rivalry, a fact that Andres finds fascinating.

Andres enjoys how Modigliani painted his portraits in his own unique fashion, in the way he saw the subject. Often, the models who sat for Modigliani or the clients who hired him to paint their portraits didn't like the finished work because they felt the portraits were not accurate representations. Andres relates to Modigliani because of this, as he also leans into painting portraits his own way—not focusing on realism but instead allowing abstract emotions to come alive on the canvas.

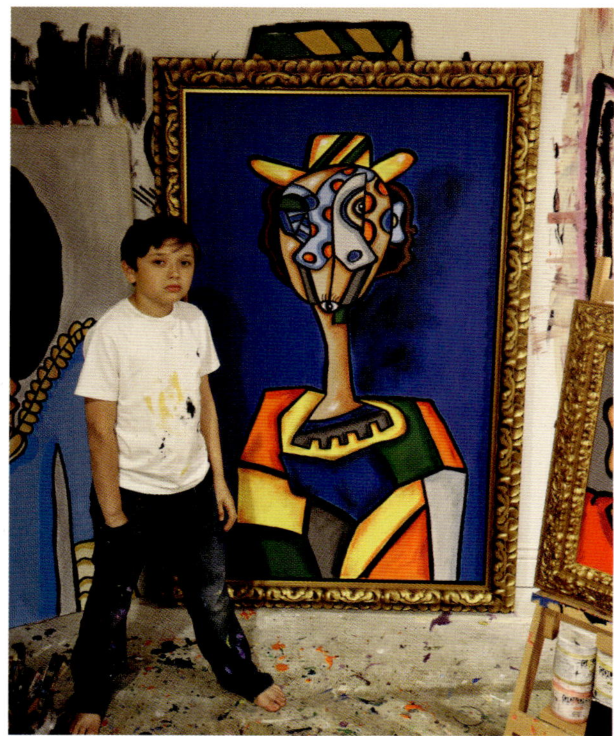

Top: *Romero* (pg. 256) and *Lourdes* (pg. 227) are two of Andres's paintings that feature long necks, a characteristic Modigliani often used in his work. **Above:** Andres with his painting *The Cowboy* (pg. 237), April 2023. **Opposite:** Standing before a Condo piece at an art exhibit, December 2022.

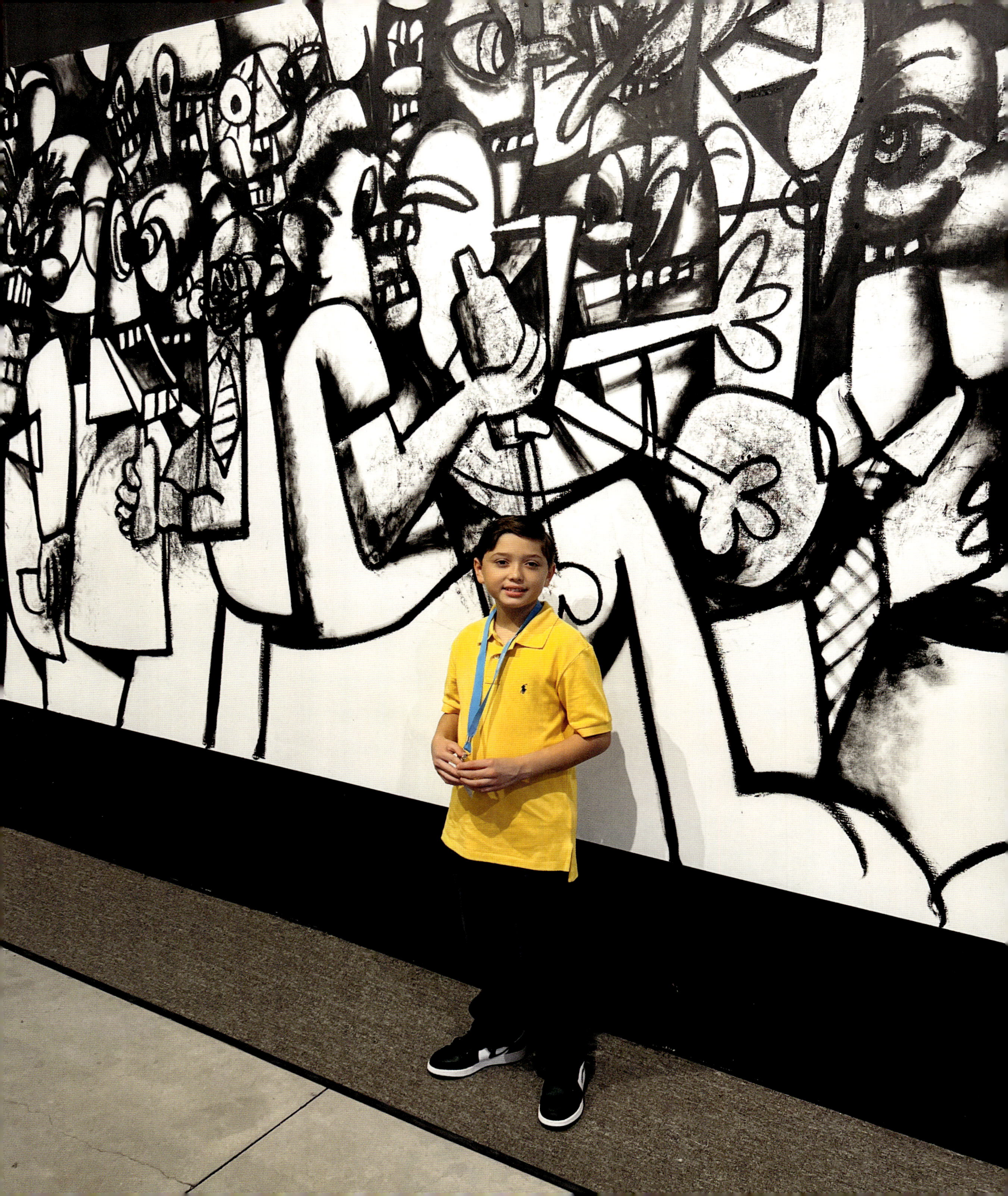

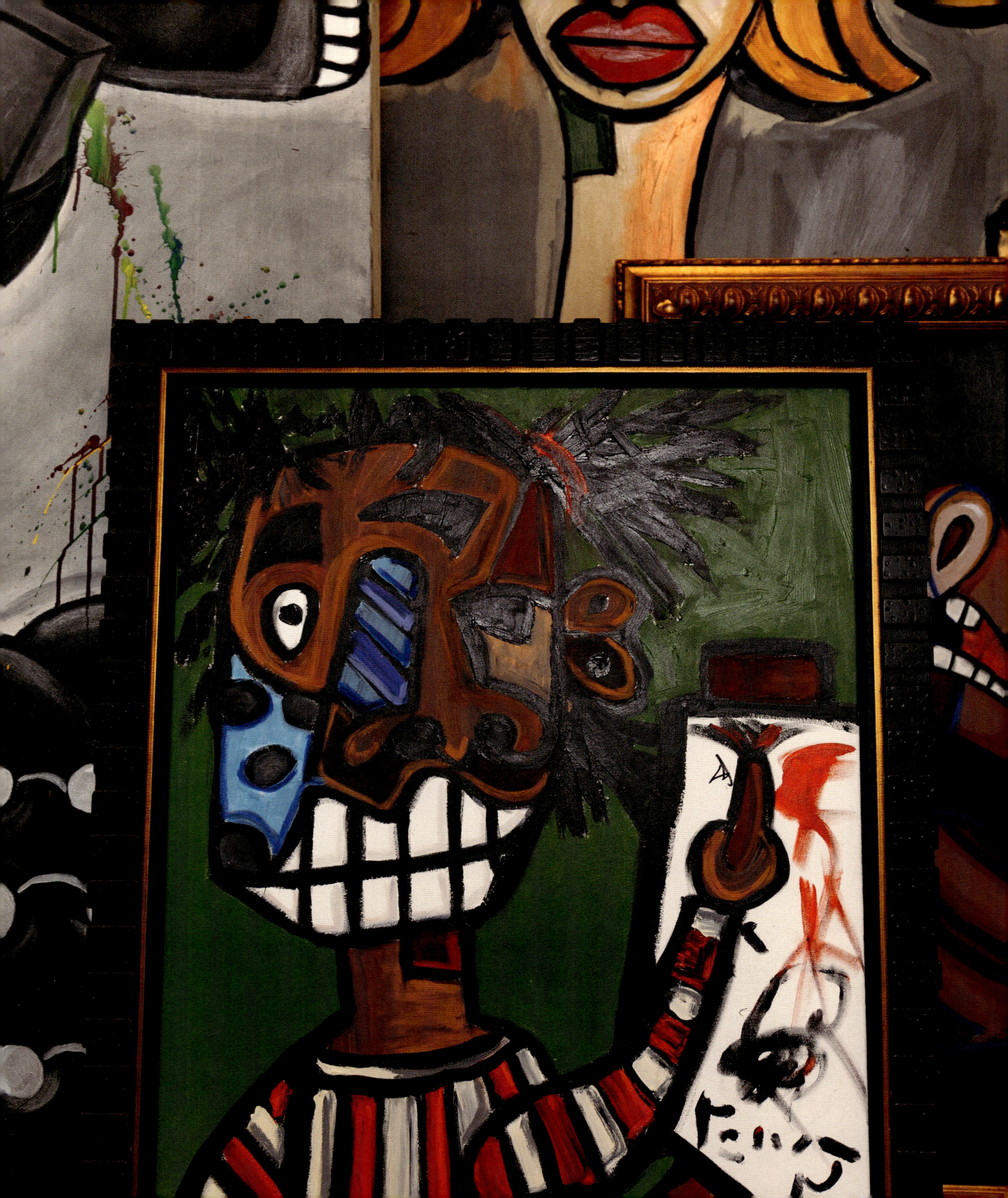

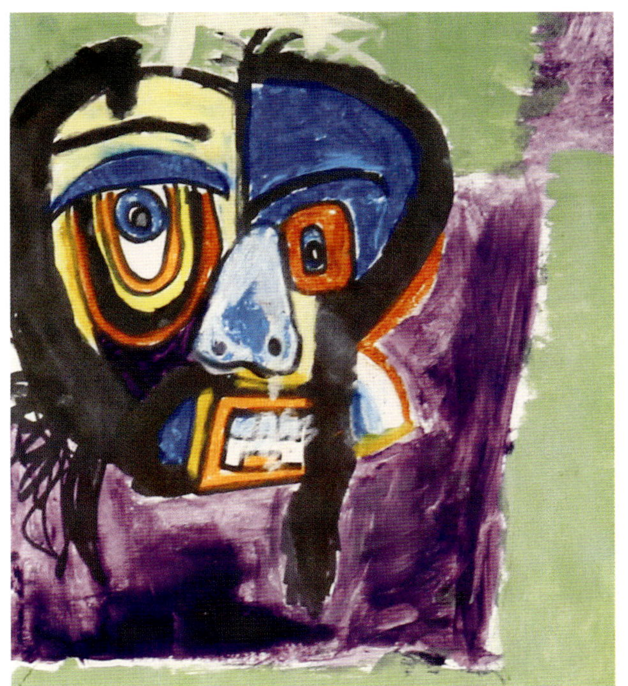

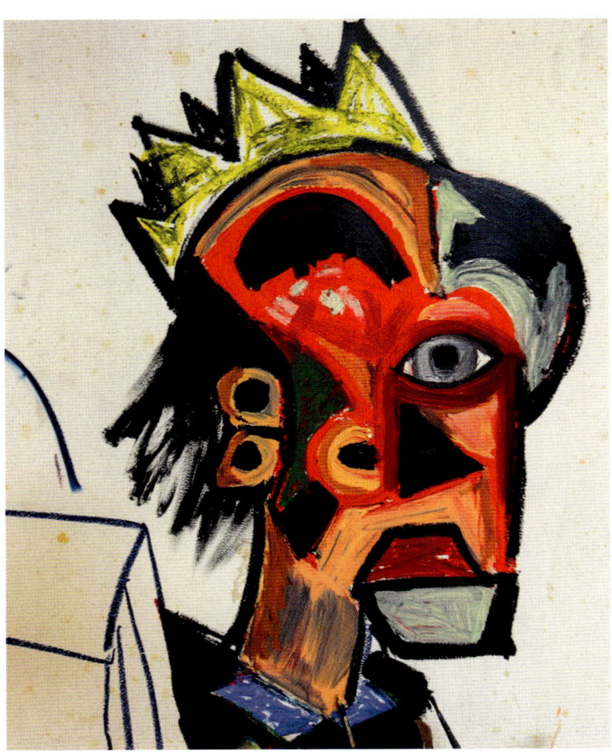

Jean-Michel Basquiat

When he was nine years old, Andres watched a documentary about Jean-Michel Basquiat and told his father, quite simply, "I can do that." So Lupe bought him several large-scale canvases. This was in 2020, during the pandemic, when the family spent a lot of time at home together. It wasn't long before Andres was painting works that were reminiscent of Basquiat's striking, abstract portraits, which were completed with meandering lines and bleeding colors. Andres continued to work in this portraiture style, finding a happy medium somewhere between surrealism and cubism, two styles that Basquiat also experimented with.

Andres watches *The Radiant Child* documentary about Basquiat all the time. "My favorite thing about Basquiat is how unique he was, and not only just his artwork, but even his hair," Andres says. "His artwork looks simple, but it has such a big story behind it. I like the way he uses a bunch of different colors and layers, and it looks like he's not even trying to do it. It just happens. His work reminds me that it's okay to say, 'I'm going to go for this and see what happens.' It's almost like an accident. He just throws paint on there."

Andres is clearly drawn to other artists who create in a way that feels liberating. His artistic expression is an act of freedom and pure creation. For a while, Andres was putting drips and splatters on his paintings in a similar way to Basquiat. He was drawn to this randomness and fluidity because it didn't feel planned out or organized.

Vincent van Gogh

When Andres was in first grade, a visiting art program came to his school. Each time they visited, they would pick a different artist to discuss with the class. The guest instructors taught the students about the artist, showed them examples of the artist's work, and then had the students create something in a similar style. One instructor came in to talk about Vincent van Gogh, and after she went through her session, Andres raised his hand and said, "You forgot something." When the instructor asked him what she forgot, he said, "Van Gogh was schizophrenic, and you forgot to tell everybody."

The instructor was surprised that a first grader knew the word and that he felt the urge to make sure the rest of the class knew this truth about Van Gogh too. Afterward, the instructor recounted the story to Elsa and asked her how Andres knew about this. Elsa explained to the instructor that she and Andres had read a lot about Van Gogh together. When the diagnosis came up in a book, Elsa discussed it with him; since she works as a clinical therapist, she was able to explain schizophrenia in simpler terms so Andres was able to understand.

Since Andres loved Van Gogh's art so much, he asked his mom to buy books about him. On top of that, Andres learned more about Van Gogh from videos he watched on his iPad. He studied the artist for so long that he learned all about Van Gogh's life and work. "In school, they don't really tell you that much [about him]," Andres says. "They just tell you he painted this, he painted that. But I like getting more into details." Andres's favorite Van Gogh paintings are *The Starry Night* and the Sunflowers series, along with a couple of his self-portraits.

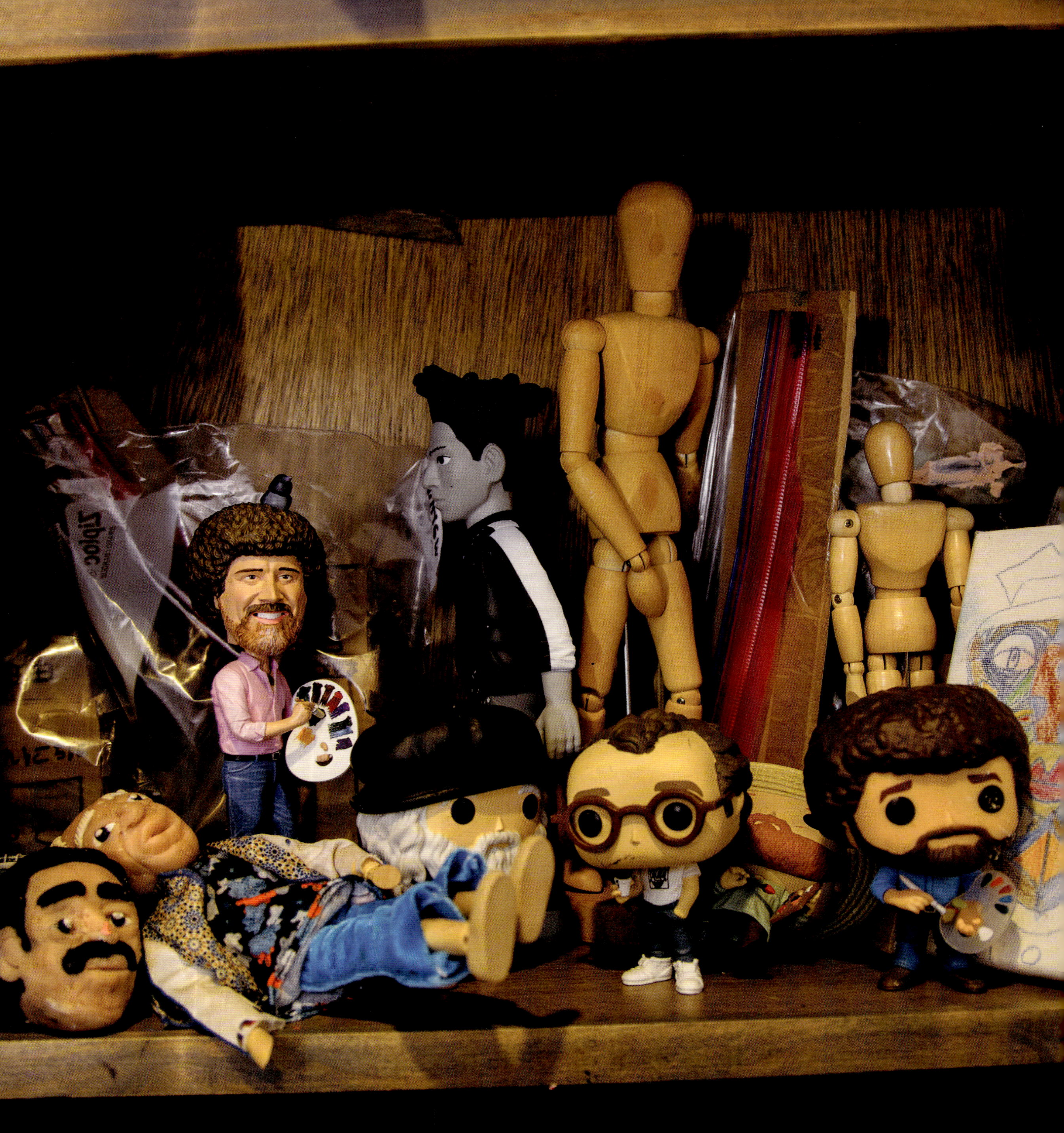
JEAN-MICHEL BASQUIAT THE NOTEBOOKS
Josef Albers Interac

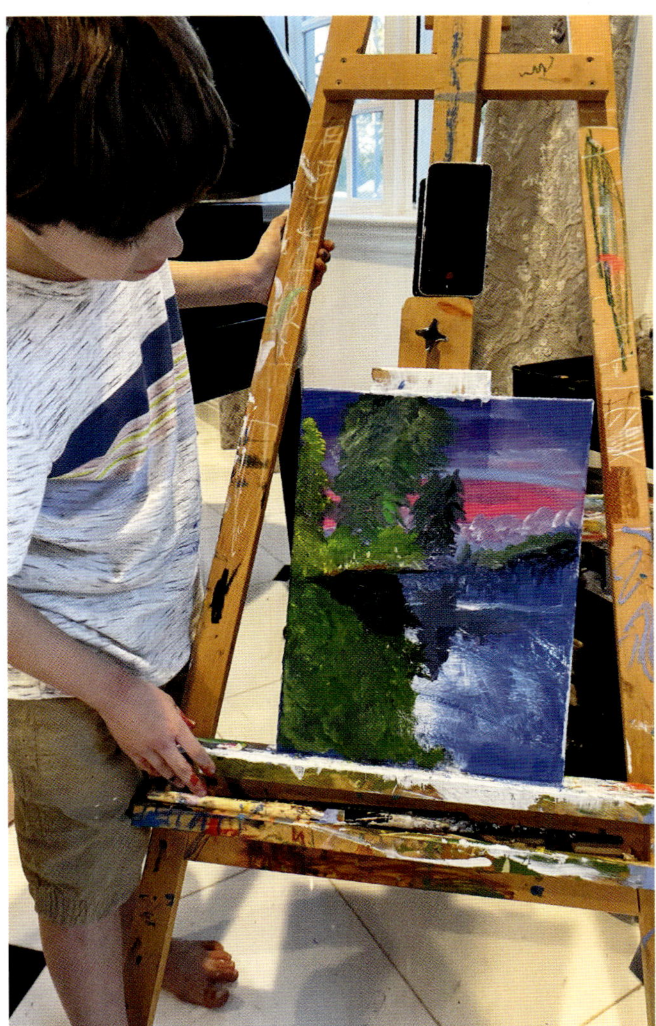

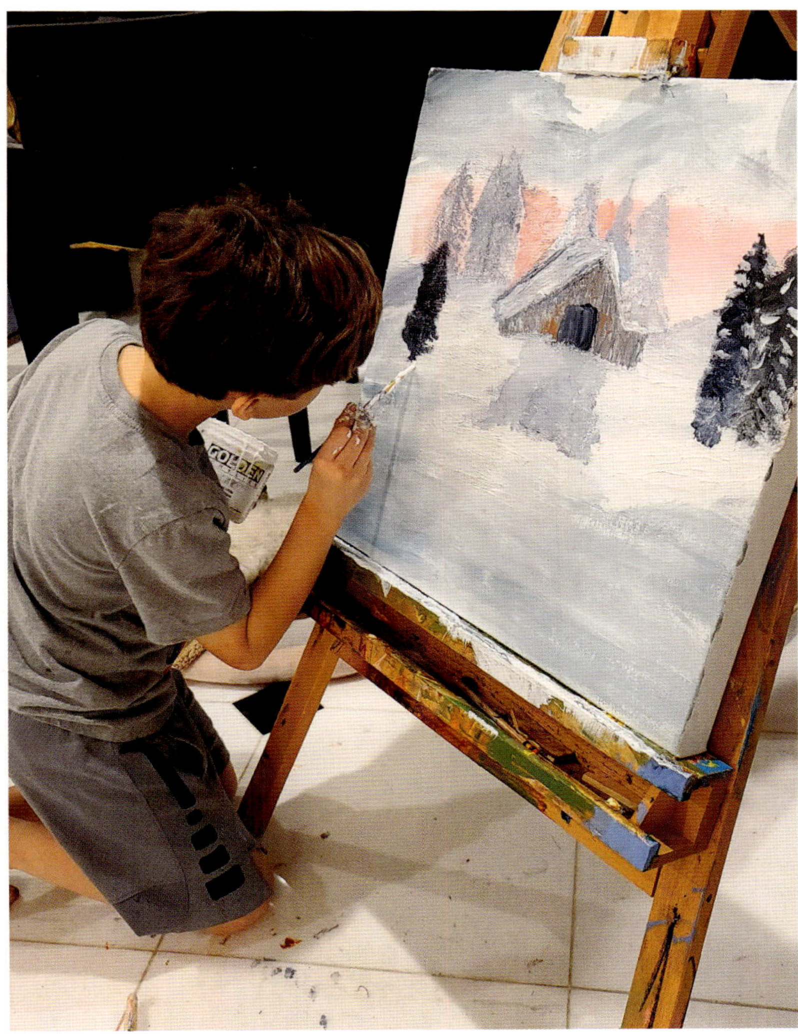

Bob Ross

One painter Andres enjoys a great deal was less of a fine artist and more of a cultural icon in the art world. When Andres found out about Bob Ross he told Elsa, "I want to do some landscapes like Bob Ross." So he got on YouTube, and he watched Bob Ross paint, and then he painted about three or four canvases of landscapes reminiscent of Ross's work. "He did them so quick," says Lupe. "He was watching the Bob Ross video, and then the next thing you know, he's painted these really cool landscapes. I looked at Andres, and I was like, 'Oh my God, this child just did these landscapes.' They were incredible."

"He's a fan favorite," Andres says of Bob Ross. "I wanted to learn about Bob Ross because I'd always see his paintings in videos, and what he was doing looked so fun." Andres started drawing landscapes along with Ross while watching his videos just for fun. "And while I was doing this, I thought maybe I could put a Bob Ross–style landscape in the background of my work," Andres says. "Then I could draw a portrait on top of it, like the *Mona Lisa*. For landscapes, there are more rules if you really want to make it look real. There's a lot to learn, and watching Bob Ross helped me get some techniques down to make these things look good."

RETNA

The Valencia family has a professional connection to the contemporary Los Angeles-based artist RETNA, and one of his pieces hangs in their living room. From a young age, Andres was captivated by this painting and could often be found sitting in front of it, trying to replicate it on his sketch pad. Andres especially loves RETNA's "Brimstone" character series.

Andres says that it's because of the RETNA painting hanging in their house that he got into art. "I sat in front of it almost every day for hours, just trying to copy it exactly, but I never got it right because it has so many lines," Andres says. "But eventually this led to me making my own. I have known RETNA my whole life, even before I was really getting attention for my art."

A few years after Andres's family bought the RETNA painting, the two artists created two different pieces together. One was on Andres's birthday, when the family was in Los Angeles and RETNA joined them for dinner. He and Andres sketched something small during the meal. "I started drawing on this little napkin," Andres says. "And then he started drawing on it too. So that was our first sketch together. I still have this little sketch framed." Later on, Andres wanted to create something bigger with RETNA. "So he came to my studio, and we just put on the music and then started painting this piece together, and it just kind of worked out."

"This was a pretty amazing moment because Andres always looked up to RETNA as an artist," Lupe says. "He knew of him since he was young, and then all of a sudden, this little boy is doing a collaboration with him." The large piece RETNA and Andres made together now hangs in the dining room of the Valencia family home in San Diego.

Opposite: The collaboration painting Andres created with RETNA hangs on the wall in the Valencia family's dining room.

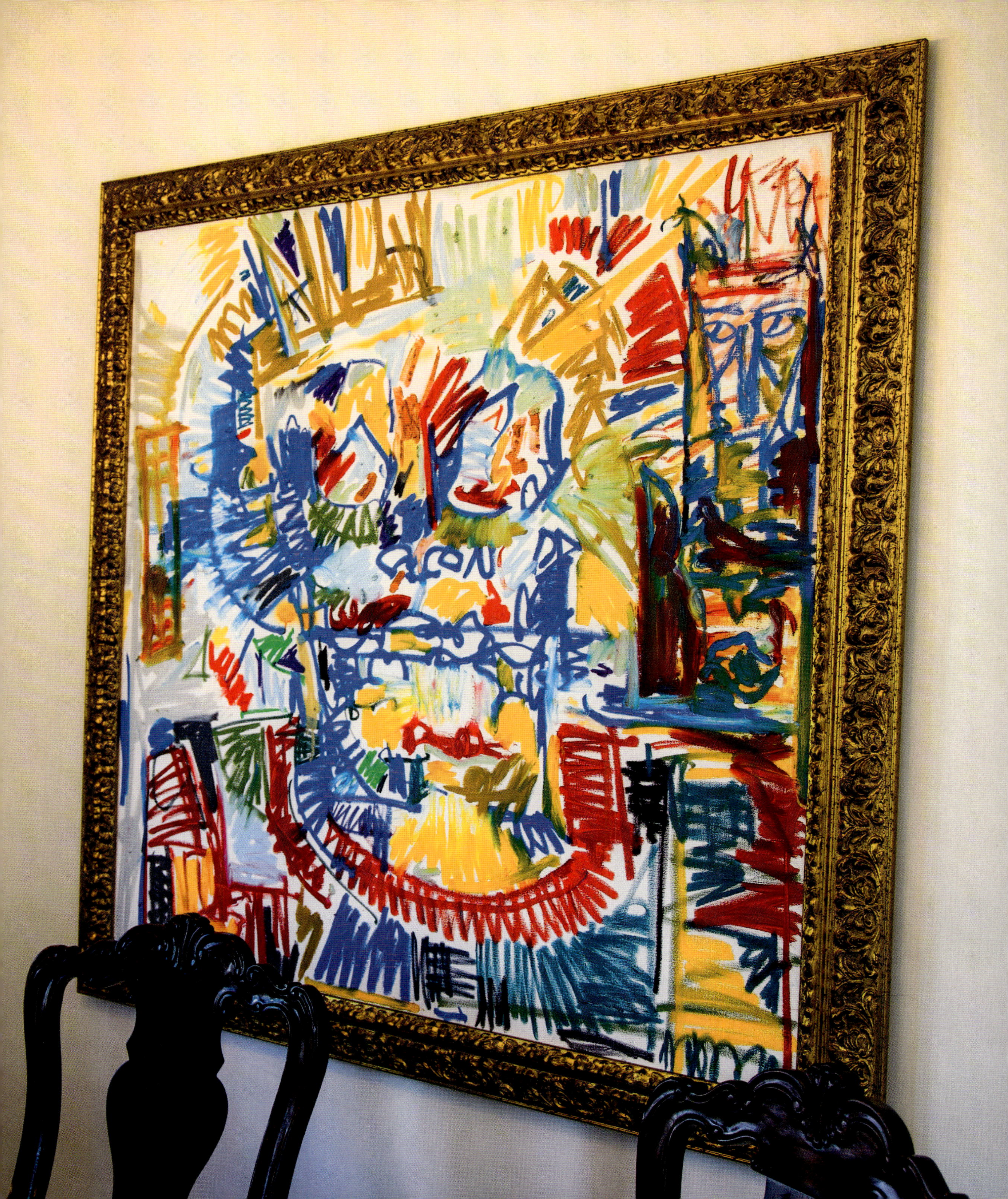

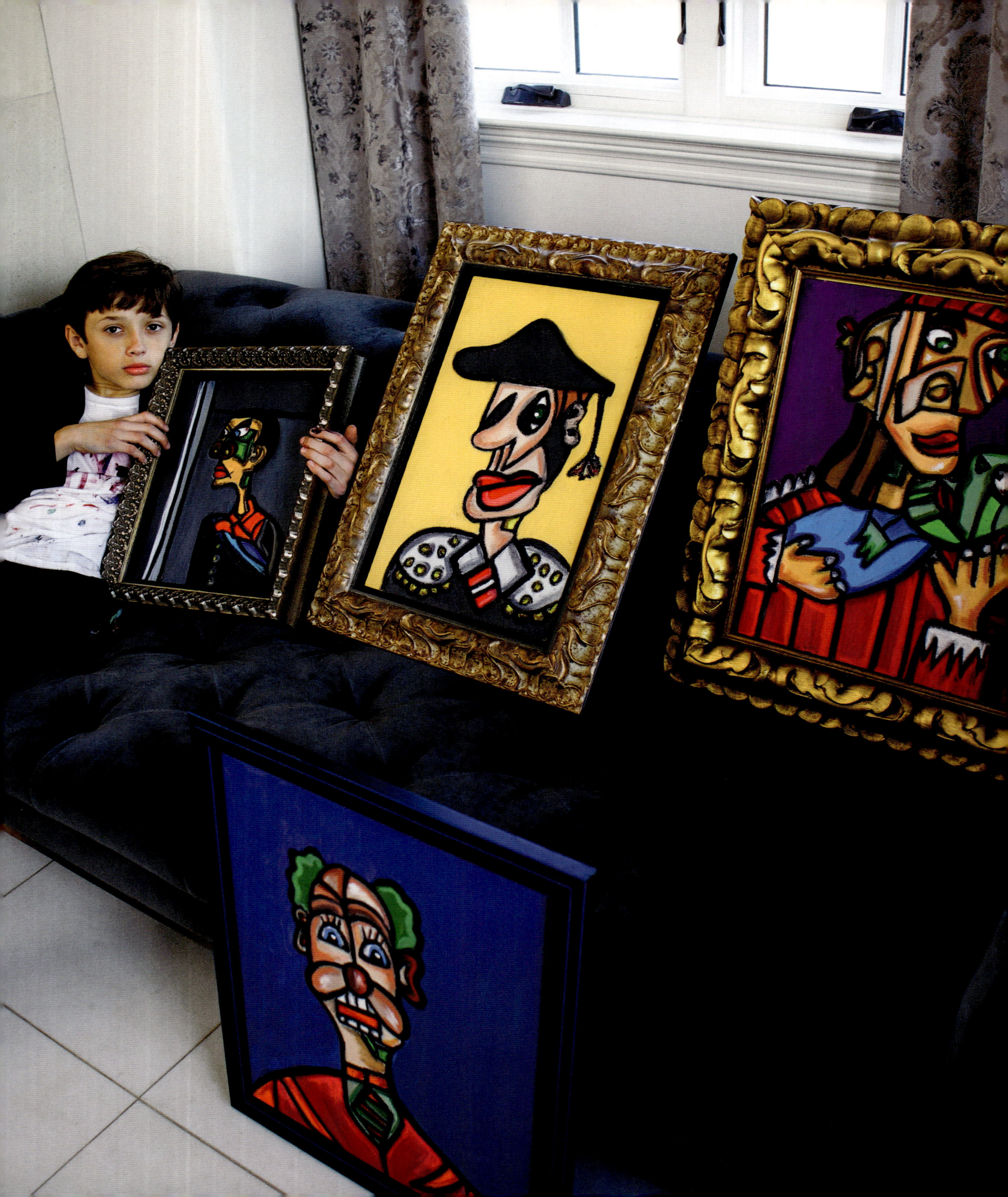

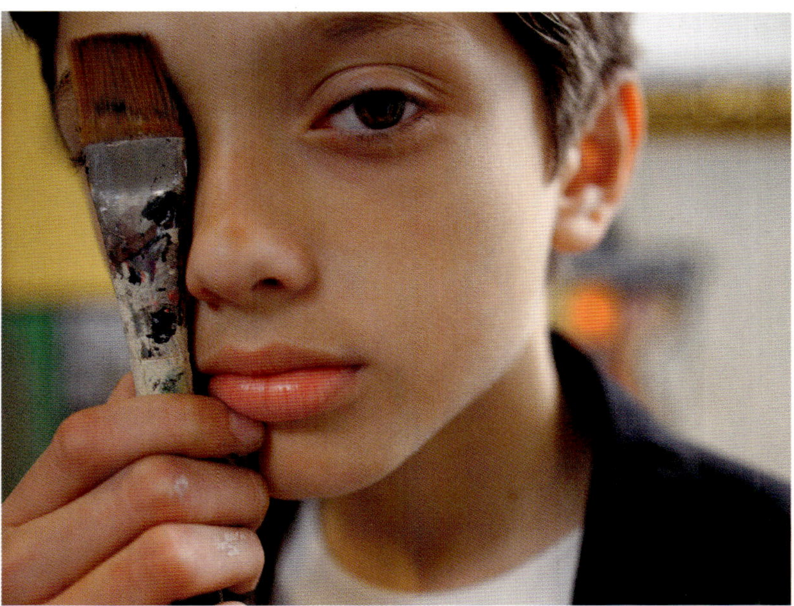

Portraits

Andres has become well-known for his cubist portraits, which feature surreal faces that are endlessly interesting to look at. There is a certain sense of playfulness in each portrait he creates. He never shies away from new compositions, placing the eyes, nose, and ears wherever he wishes, with little regard to actual human anatomy. Yet each of his portraits is still recognizably his, as he has created a distinct style that can be molded and adapted to depict all sorts of characters.

"A lot of famous artists started by doing portraits—like our old masters," Andres says. He's practiced his portraiture further by watching YouTube videos of other artists creating portraits, taking note of how each painter tries to capture the enigmatic human face in their own special way.

Andres enjoys creating portraits because he feels they capture the magical quality of someone's essence, almost like a photograph but in a more shifting, artistic form. "When some of our old masters were doing portraits, it was because there were no cameras," Andres says. "This is how important people like kings would get their portraits out there—with paintings." Since cameras do exist in today's world, Andres isn't interested in creating a lifelike, realistic portrait of someone. "If we wanted a realistic portrait of someone, we could just take a nice photo," he explains. Instead, Andres wants to take it further and make something different. By leaning into the inventive and imaginative, Andres unlocks hidden magic in each unique face he paints. Andres has even created portrait paintings of some of his favorite artists: two small pieces depicting Pablo Picasso and Francisco Goya, a medium-size painting of Jean-Michel Basquiat, and a large-scale painting of Frida Kahlo that is nearly six-feet tall.

Andres has also done a few self-portraits. "I have some old ones, and I have newer ones," he says. "They're all sketches on my sketch pad. Once, I drew myself because I wanted to practice some realism, and I wondered, *Who should I draw?* I didn't have my phone with me, and I just wanted

Above: Andres with one of his many paintbrushes.
Opposite: Andres sits on the couch in his family's living room holding the painting *Lady Gloria* while the paintings *Salvador, Mama and Baby* (pg. 231), and *Tommy* (pg. 236) rest beside him.

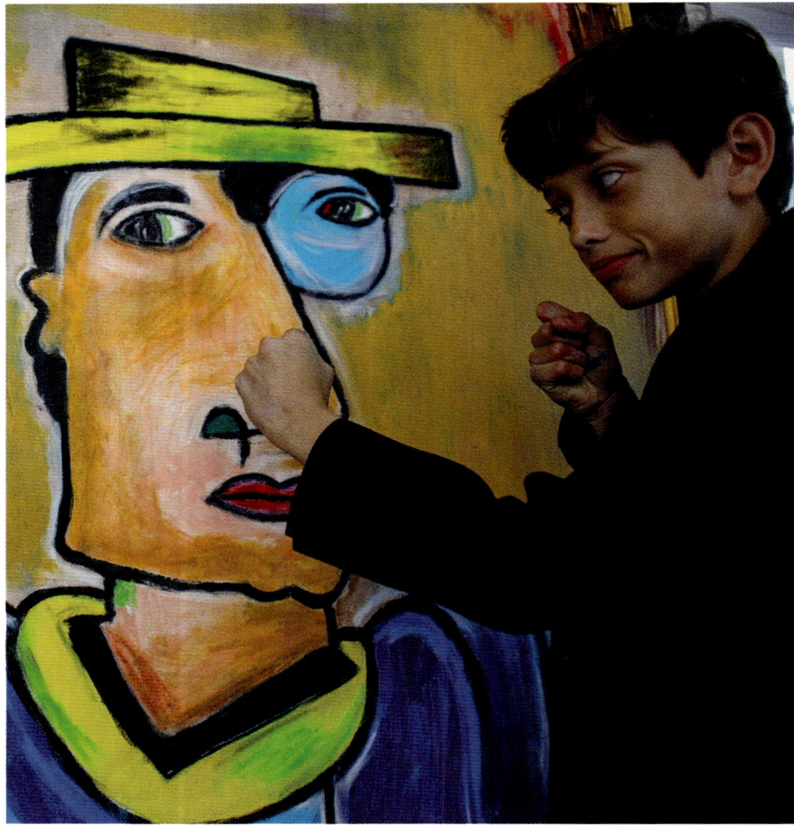

to draw. There was a mirror beside me, so I looked at it and said, 'Okay, I'll just draw myself.'"

The human face contains multitudes, and even if Andres continues to focus on painting his own distinct version of portraiture, there's never going to be two of his paintings that turn out exactly the same. "I think that's what he enjoys," Elsa says. "The endless options and opportunities to play and explore."

Still, Andres is aware of some of the more negative comments people have whispered about his portraits. "Why do people say I have to learn how to do realistic, lifelike portraits before I'm an artist?" Andres asks. "I think I'm an artist now." When her son asks these kinds of questions, Elsa responds in a positive, encouraging way, urging Andres to continue to follow his artistic instincts. She tells him, "You *are* an artist, and you don't have to worry about what other people think the rules should be."

You can make your own rules. That's the beauty of art. Even at a young age, Andres understands this well, perhaps better than most. He isn't afraid to lean into creating his cubist portraits again and again, because that's what he loves best.

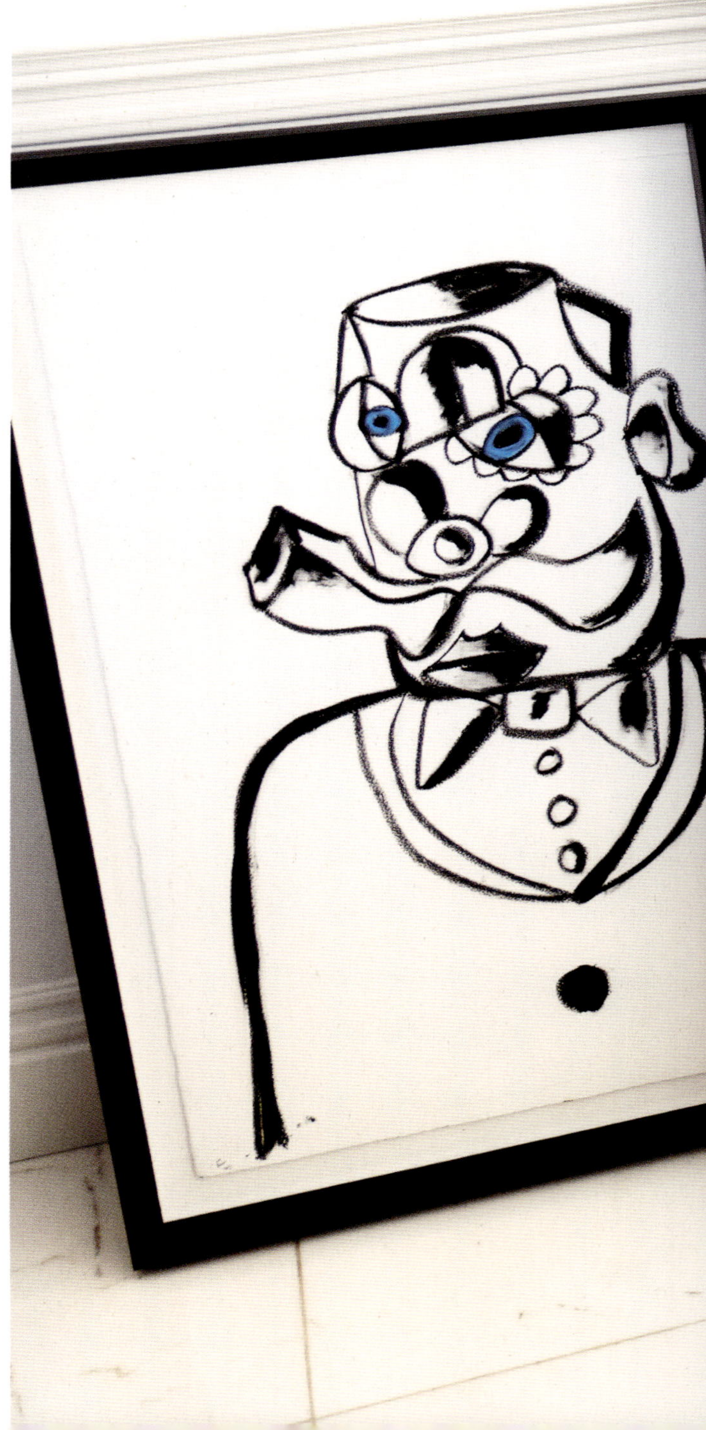

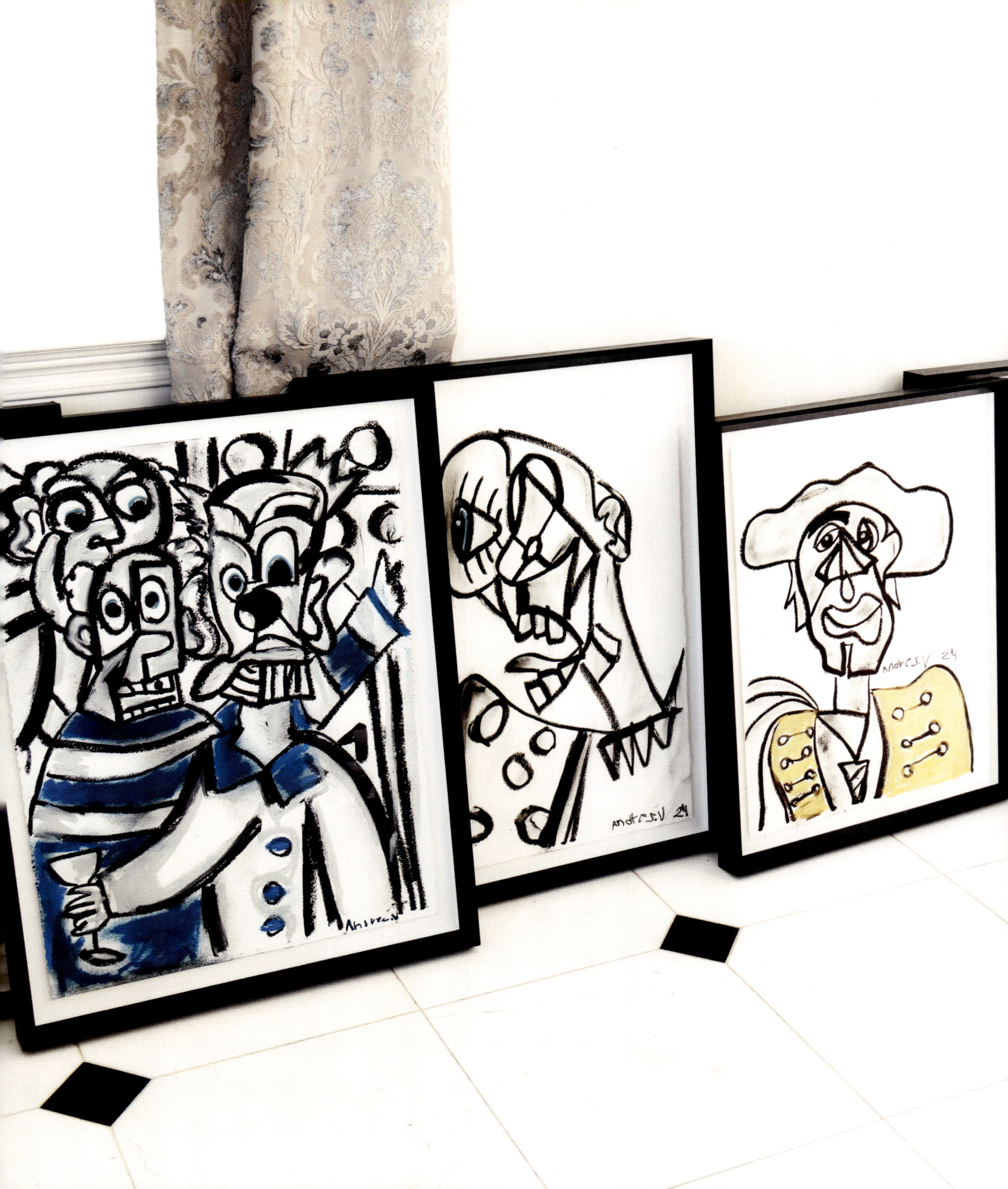

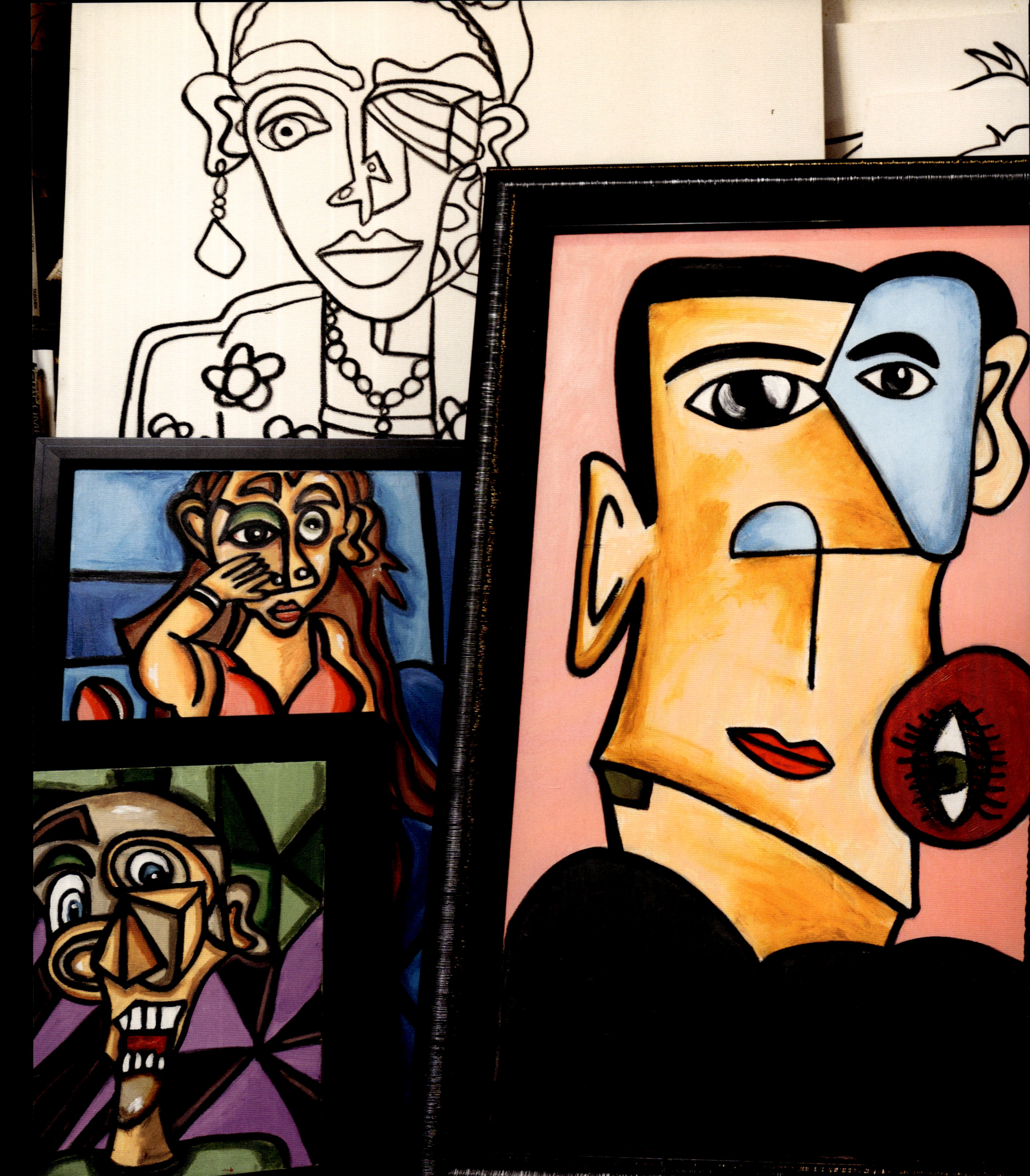

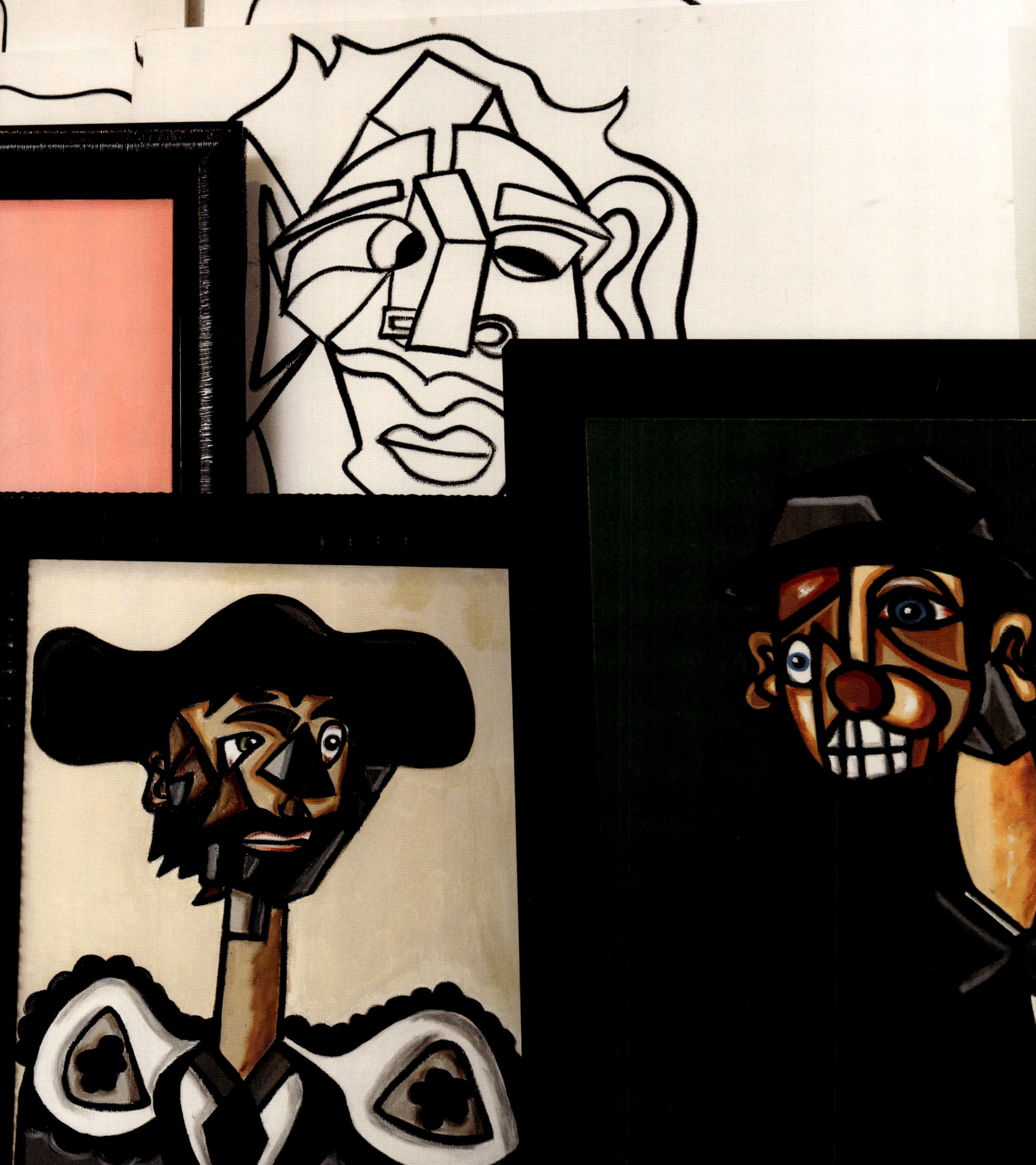

Museum Visits

One of Andres's earliest goals was to see the *Mona Lisa*, *Guernica*, and a Vincent van Gogh painting in person. Elsa recalls a checklist he wrote when he was five years old that included seeing these works. Meeting George Condo was also on the list. While he has yet to meet Condo, Andres can now happily claim that he has seen the *Mona Lisa*, *Guernica*, and many Van Gogh paintings.

During the fall of 2023, the Valencia family took a trip to Europe. They planned to visit as many museums as possible so Andres could see famous paintings up close. Getting to experience the *Mona Lisa* in person was "big for him," Elsa explains. "He wanted to see it because everybody kept telling him, 'It's not as big as you think it is.' So we took him to the Louvre in Paris to see it. He was so excited to visit there because he's read about how Picasso regularly went to the Louvre."

Andres wanted to visit the Louvre because it was where all the greats like Picasso went, including Modigliani. "It was my first time going to Europe, and I got to see the *Mona Lisa*, which was a dream come true," Andres says. "After we got back, I found an old bucket list I made in 2016. One of the things on it was to have my own art studio, and another was to see the *Mona Lisa*." Andres got to cross off both on the list. "It was very cool to see the *Mona Lisa* in person," he says. "It's such an iconic piece of art. People told me it was kind of small, but I did not expect it to be *that* small. I was still very impressed by it, and it's in the Louvre, which was my favorite museum we went to. I liked seeing all the other Da Vinci paintings too."

After visiting the Louvre, Andres got to explore the Musée Picasso in Paris to see hundreds of his paintings. The Valencias also traveled to Madrid, Spain, and visited the Museo Reina Sofía. There they saw Picasso's iconic painting, *Guernica*. It was very important for Andres to see this work, as he had read a great deal about it and wanted to have the chance to stand in front of it.

"When we walked into the room where *Guernica* is," Elsa says, "for some reason, there weren't a lot of people around." Andres couldn't believe he was finally seeing this incredibly famous painting by one of his favorite artists in person. "He wanted all of us to leave him alone so he could really live in that moment and take it all in. It's a huge painting, and there's so much to see. Andres stood there, and he got his little sketchbook out and started doing his thing while looking at Picasso's masterpiece for inspiration. I found this really interesting." Elsa wondered: *Is he copying Picasso? What is he doing?* "I think he was really inspired," she says. "We let him get on the floor and sketch and get into his creative groove. We stayed there with him, since we couldn't get Andres to leave the room. He wanted to live in that moment forever."

When the Valencia family took their Europe trip, Elsa tried to lay the ground rule that Andres was not going to be painting or making art on the trip. Instead, she hoped he could enjoy the museums and take in all the inspiration to apply to his work later on. This plan didn't quite work out.

Elsa says, "After every museum we went to, Andres was like, 'Can we please go get some canvases?'" At first, she didn't want to get canvases for him, because she knew it would be challenging to take them back home. But then Lupe had an idea: the canvases didn't have to be huge.

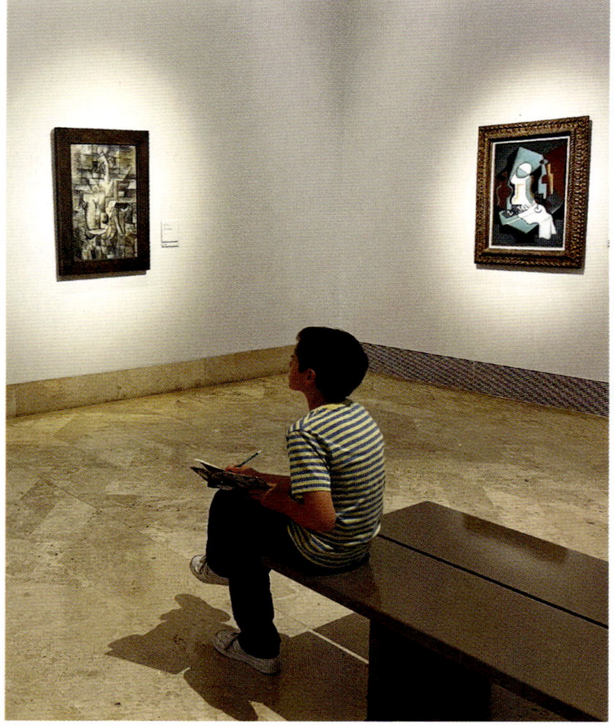

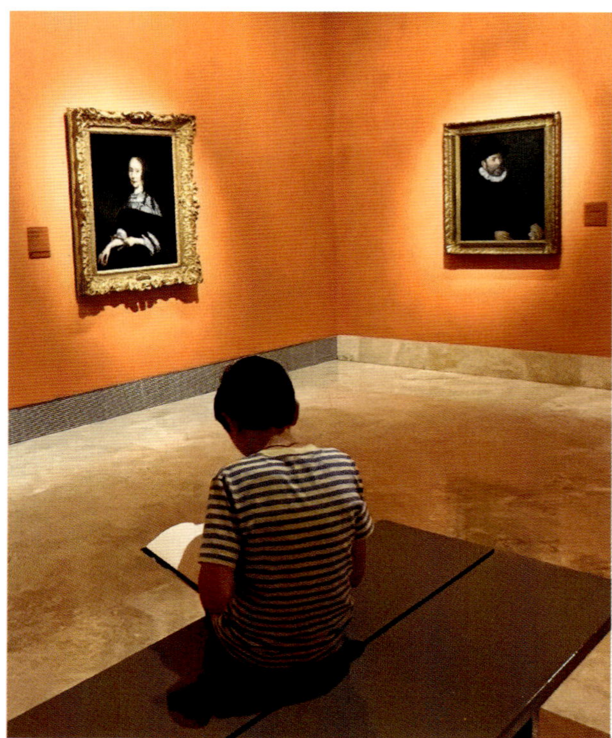

Above: Andres in two different gallery rooms at the Museo Carmen Thyssen in Málaga, Spain. **Opposite:** Andres creating new works in the family's hotel room after visiting museums in Paris during the summer of 2023. The painting (top left) is titled *Paris* (pg. 230).

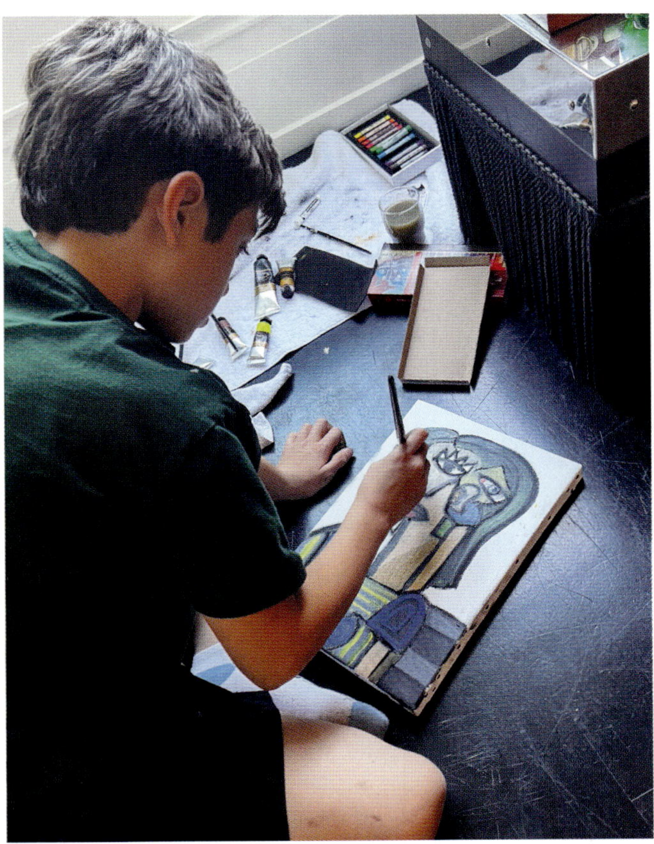

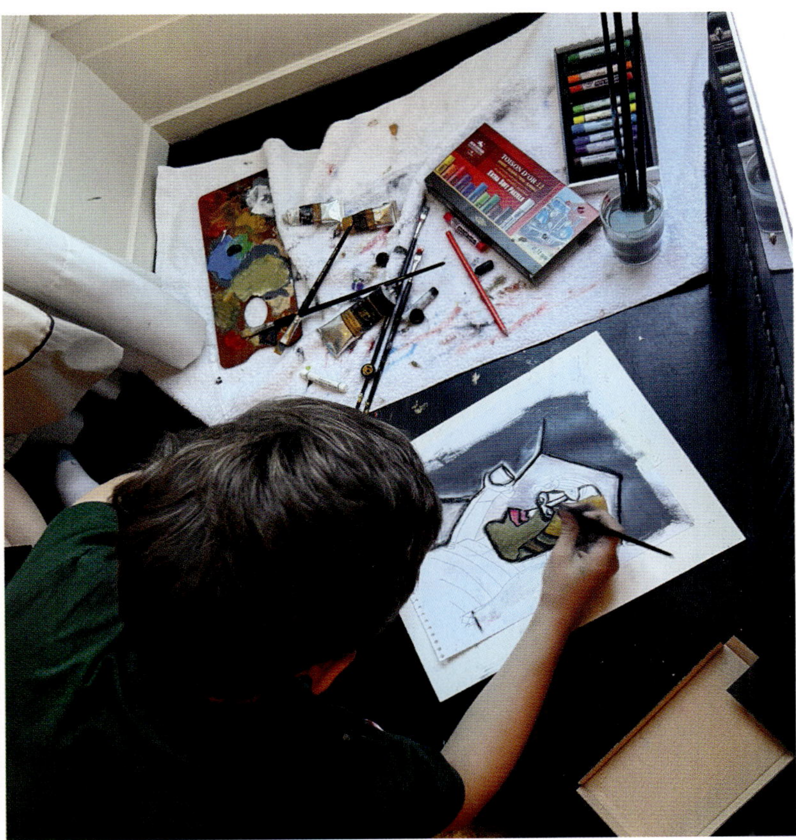

He went out and bought Andres several small canvases that could fit in a standard-size suitcase.

The family has also taken Andres to the Metropolitan Museum of Art in New York City, where he saw his first works by Vincent van Gogh. When he finally stood before one of Van Gogh's paintings, he was in a state of disbelief. While his sister and her friend grew impatient and were quickly ready to move on, Andres was content to sit in front of Van Gogh's paintings for as long as possible.

Andres has a lot of thoughts about classic pieces by well-known artists, as well as modern art by lesser-known names. But when he is asked if he likes one more than the other, he responds by saying, "Well, I like them all in different ways. Da Vinci's old paintings are just such great examples of what the old masters could do, and then the newer stuff is more about people expressing themselves, and they have more elements moving around and changing."

When the time came for Andres to go on his sixth-grade camping trip, he told Elsa he didn't want to go. He suggested another idea: "Can we please go to Los Angeles and visit museums there instead?" Andres was adamant about this, so Elsa eventually agreed, and the family traveled there and visited the Los Angeles County Museum of Art (LACMA) and a few other art museums in the city. Andres was especially excited to see the *Jean-Michel Basquiat: King Pleasure* exhibition in person, which featured over two hundred works by the artist. After visiting the museums, at the end of each day, Andres sketched new ideas in the car as the Valencias returned to their hotel.

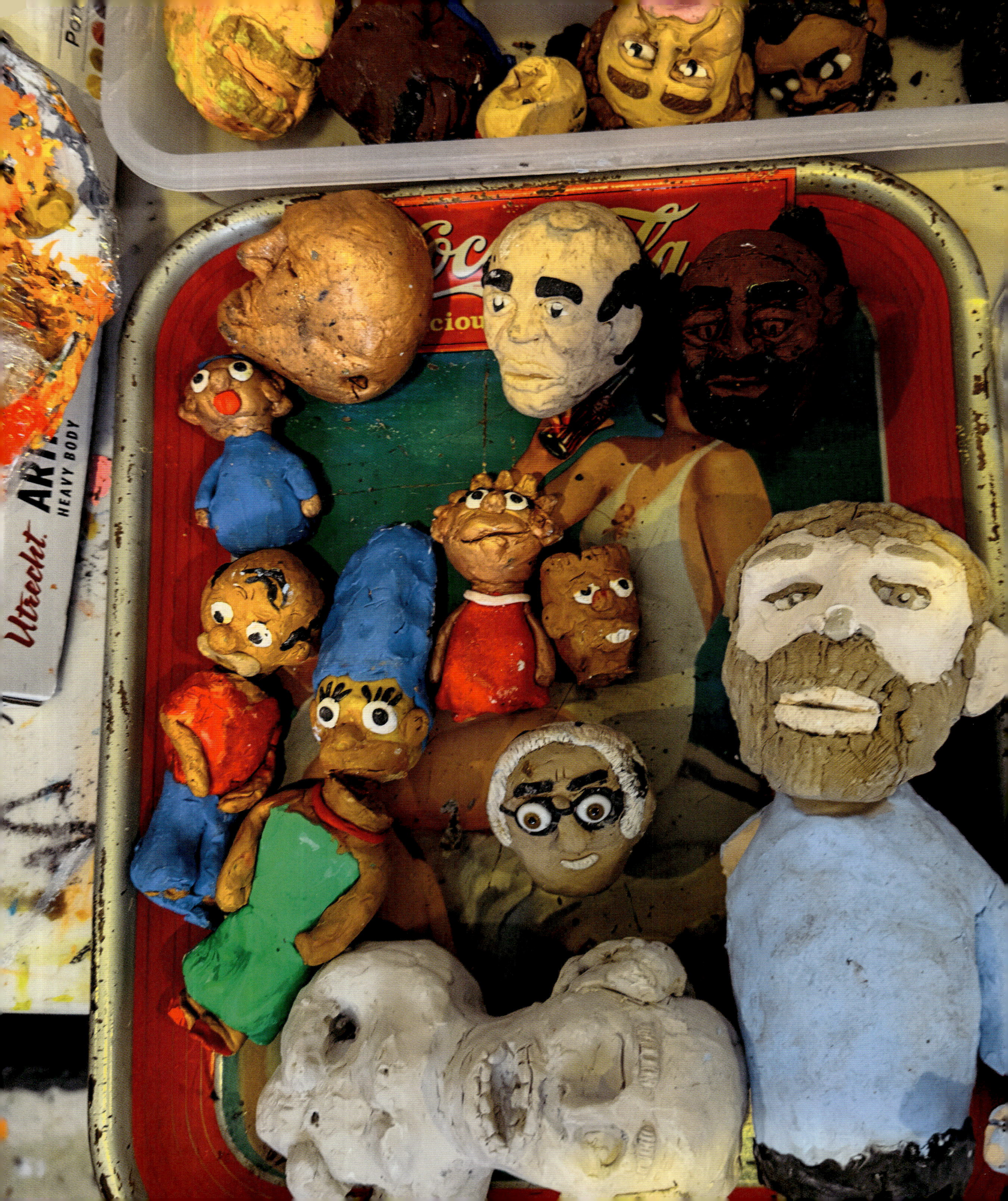

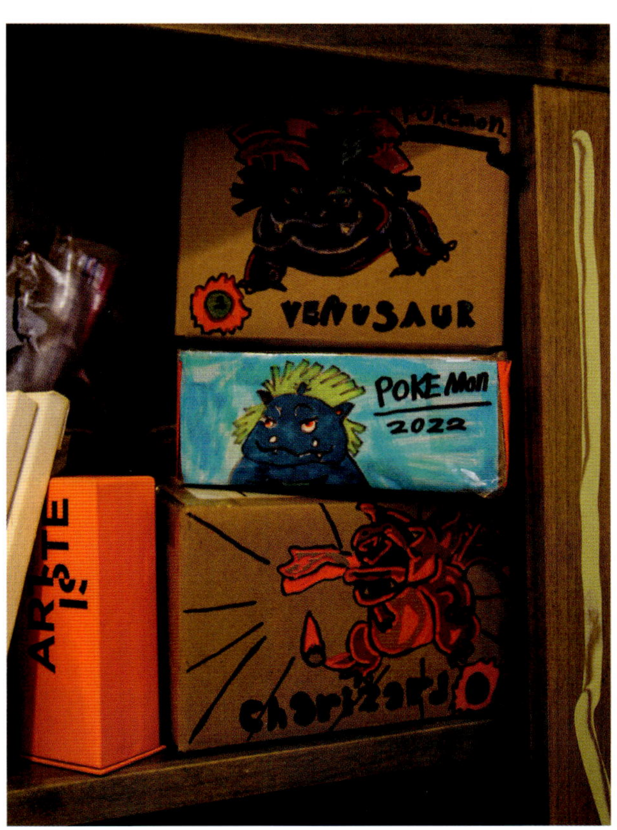

Above: A big fan of Pokémon, Andres has drawn some of his favorite characters on boxes to hold his cards.
Opposite: Andres has sculpted many clay figures, including *The Simpsons*.

Other Important Influences

While Andres is heavily influenced by other artists and their works, his creative process also pulls inspiration from many other places. He's a big fan of Pokémon, clowns, and Click N' Play army action figures. When Andres is asked about some of his favorite things, he says, "I like Pokémon because it's fun to get a good card out of a pack. I've actually drawn Venusaur too, since he's my favorite. My favorite TV show of all time is *The Simpsons* because it's funny."

Andres is a big music fan and often has music playing in his studio while he works. His father says, "I've learned a lot about music because of Andres. He went through a period where he was listening to a lot of Chuck Berry, the Beatles, and John Lennon. He's really into older music. He also likes Elvis, James Brown, and Prince. He tends to prefer older artists and songs. It's only recently that he started listening to some newer stuff." Andres says he likes listening to older music because "it's classic."

One of Andres's favorite living artists is Frankie Valli. When he heard Frankie Valli was coming to San Diego, he told Lupe they had to go see him perform. They bought tickets and got spots in the second row so they could be close to the stage. Lupe recalls the experience: "It seemed like Andres was the youngest person there. And then I was the second youngest person, and I'm fifty-two! Everybody else appeared to be much older. I think other people must have thought, *What is this kid doing here?* Andres was singing along since he knows all of Frankie's songs. He was having such a good time, and people were just looking at us like, 'This is strange.'"

Andres was even lucky enough to be allowed to head backstage and meet Frankie after the show. "Andres got to take some pictures with Frankie, and he got him to sign some old records too," Lupe says. "Andres had made me go out to an antique store before the show to find some old Frankie Valli records for this very purpose."

Collecting rare and antique objects is another one of Andres's passions. One of his favorite places to peruse is antique stores. He loves looking for unique treasures to add to his many collections. Among other things, Andres collects Mickey Mouse dolls from the 1930s, little toy monkeys from the circus, and old coins. "He's a collector at heart," Lupe says, "and this even applies to some modern items as well, since he also likes to collect Pokémon cards, especially rare ones."

When Lupe is asked if he thinks Andres has an old soul, he responds by saying, "Oh, absolutely, he's got an old soul. I mean, I don't really believe in it, but if I did believe in reincarnation, I'd say he came right out of the fifties, because I don't know any kid who wants to go to an antique store, who wants to go see Frankie Valli, and collect all these old things. It's like everything he does and loves is from fifty years ago."

In the film world, Andres enjoys historical stories the most. Lupe says, "He's watched every World War II movie, every Holocaust movie, every Civil Rights movie, and all the films that feature Picasso, Basquiat, and all the other painters and artists he enjoys." This includes both dramatic stories and documentaries. Andres enjoys watching movies based on real life. "He'll tell you all about some famous soldier whose life story he saw in a movie. That's the kind of stuff he likes."

"History is important to me," Andres says. "I like watching documentaries, because I want to learn. Wars are so bad, but I like to learn about the soldiers and what they did during these wars."

Andres is also a big fan of soccer and basketball. He even got to connect with the soccer player Sergio Ramos, who played sixteen seasons with Real Madrid. Sergio even reached out and said he wanted one of Andres's paintings. Andres recalls how this connection happened: "He said, 'I'm going to send you a jersey.' So he sent me a signed jersey, which I have framed now. Then I sent him a painting he really wanted. It was one of my bullfighter paintings that he liked." Andres enjoys painting the bullfighters, as they're some of his favorite figures in history. "They're like mascots for Spain," he says. "Their outfits are my favorite because they're really cool." If you pay attention to Andres's work, you will notice he has painted bullfighters many times, just as he has clowns, and some of these other important influences.

Opposite: Andres poses with his signed jersey from the soccer star, Sergio Ramos (top). Andres in his studio next to his bookcase (bottom). **Following:** Andres in his bedroom next to a painting and his collection of vintage toys at age eleven.

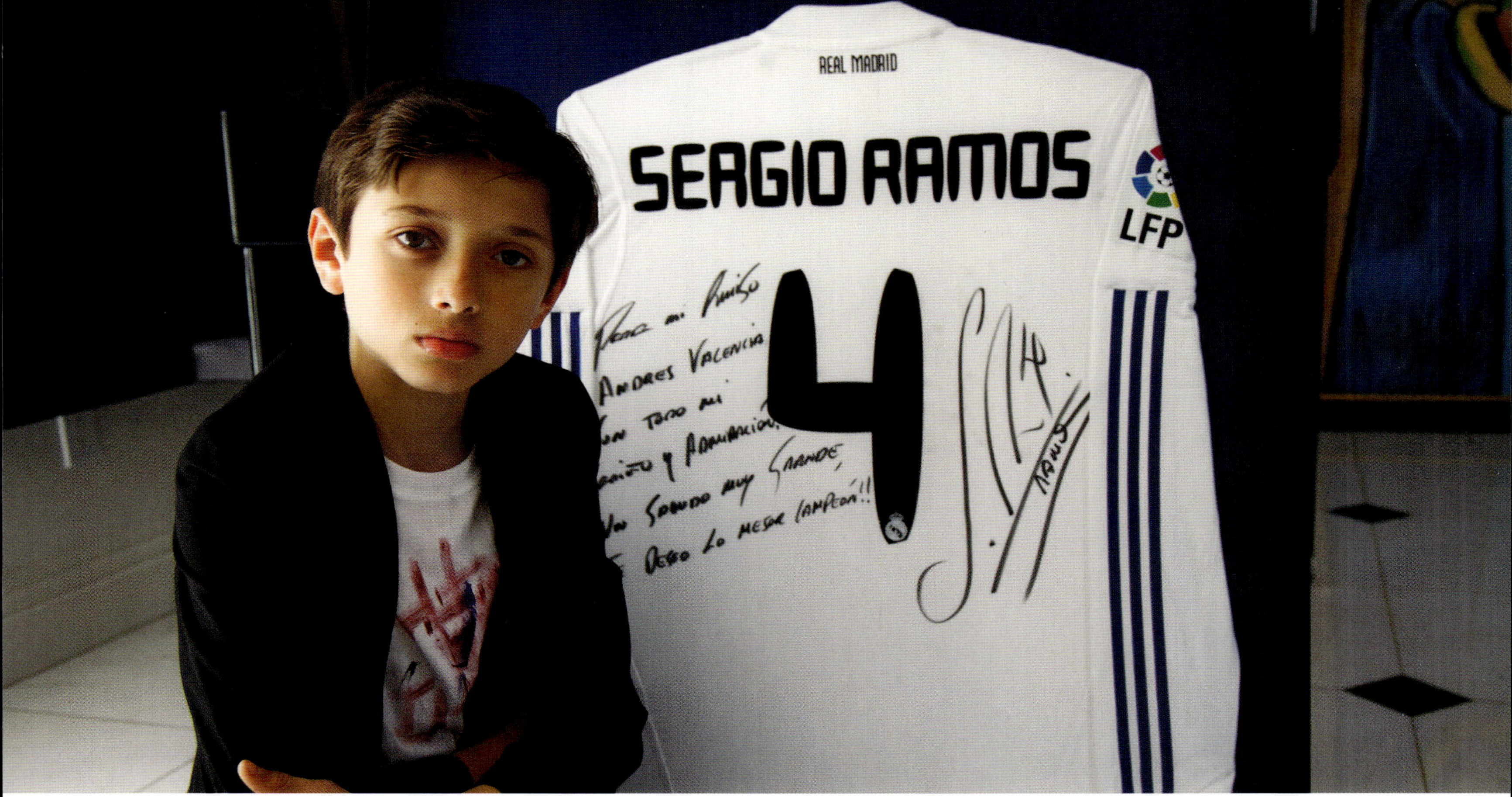

REAL MADRID
SERGIO RAMOS
LFP
4
Para mi amigo
Andres Valencia,
con todo mi
cariño y Admiracion,
un Saludo muy Grande,
te Deseo lo mejor Campeón!!
S. Ramos

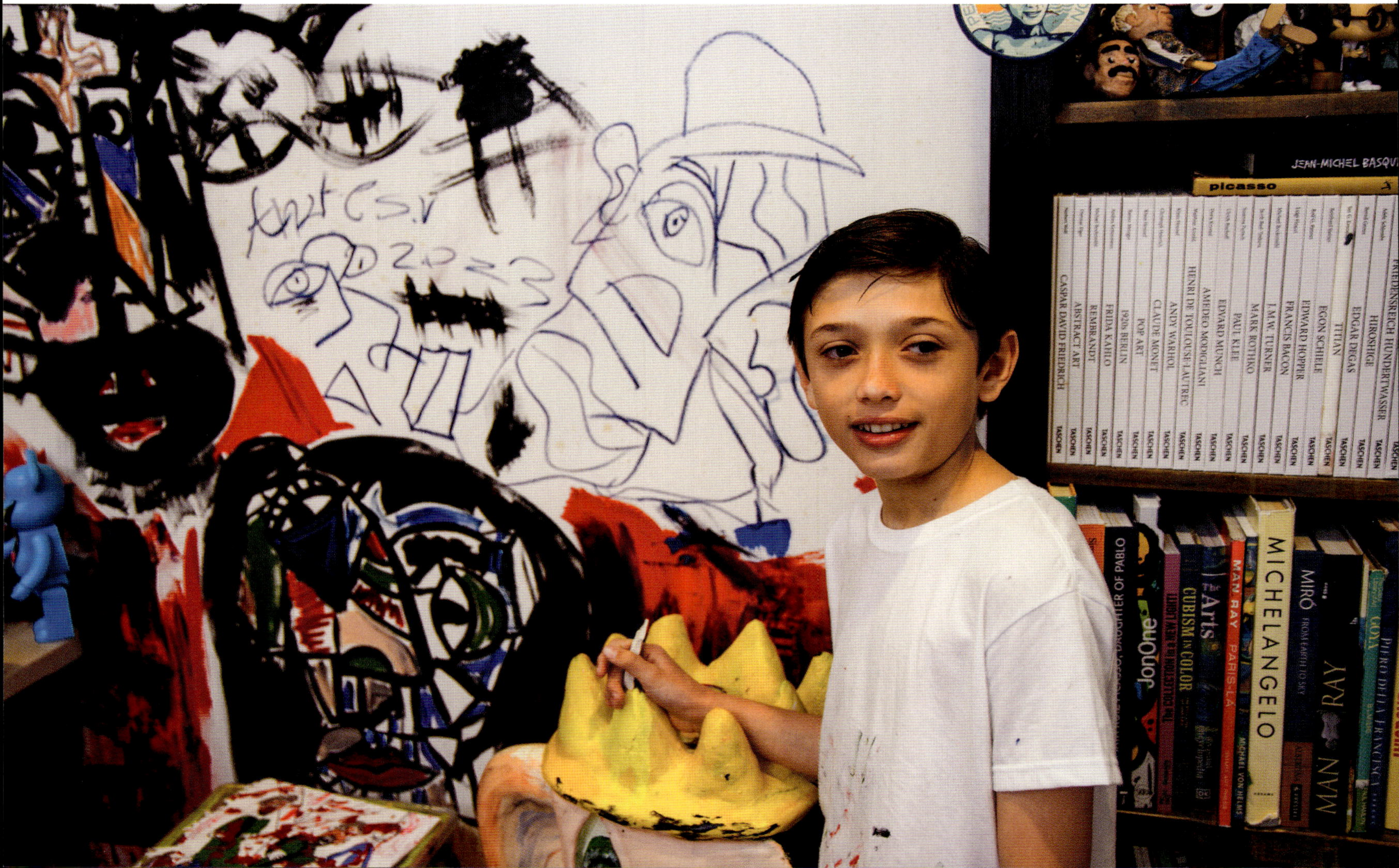

JEAN-MICHEL BASQUIAT
picasso
FRIEDENSREICH HUNDERTWASSER
HIROSHIGE
EDGAR DEGAS
TITIAN
EGON SCHIELE
EDWARD HOPPER
FRANCIS BACON
J.M.W. TURNER
MARK ROTHKO
PAUL KLEE
EDVARD MUNCH
AMEDEO MODIGLIANI
HENRI DE TOULOUSE-LAUTREC
ANDY WARHOL
CLAUDE MONET
POP ART
1920s BERLIN
FRIDA KAHLO
REMBRANDT
ABSTRACT ART
CASPAR DAVID FRIEDRICH
TASCHEN
DAUGHTER OF PABLO
JonOne
CUBISM IN COLOR
The Arts
MAN RAY PARIS-LA
MICHELANGELO
MIRÓ FROM EARTH TO SKY
MAN RAY
PIERO DELLA FRANCESCA

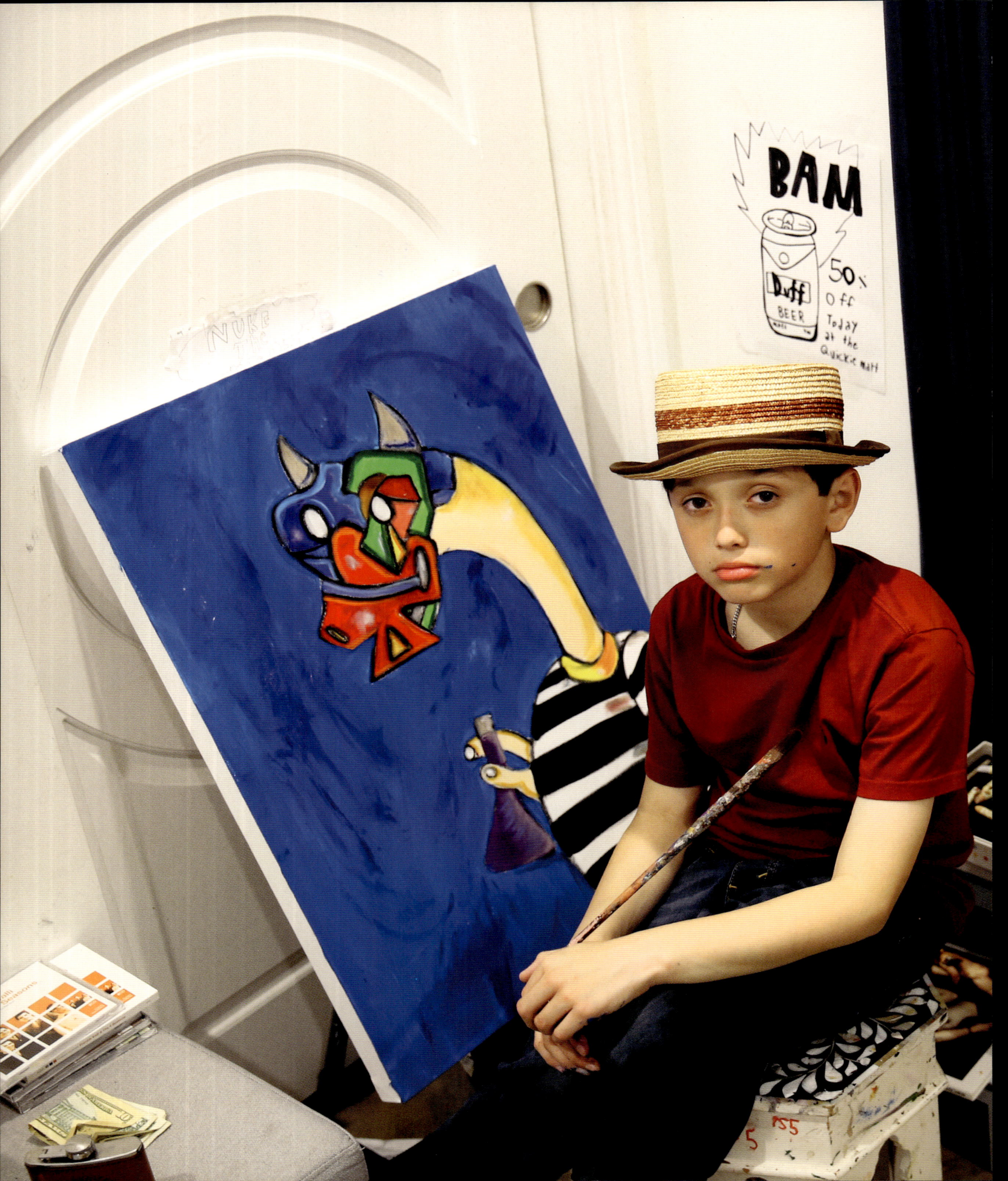

BAM
Duff
BEER
50%
off
Today
at the
Quikke Mart

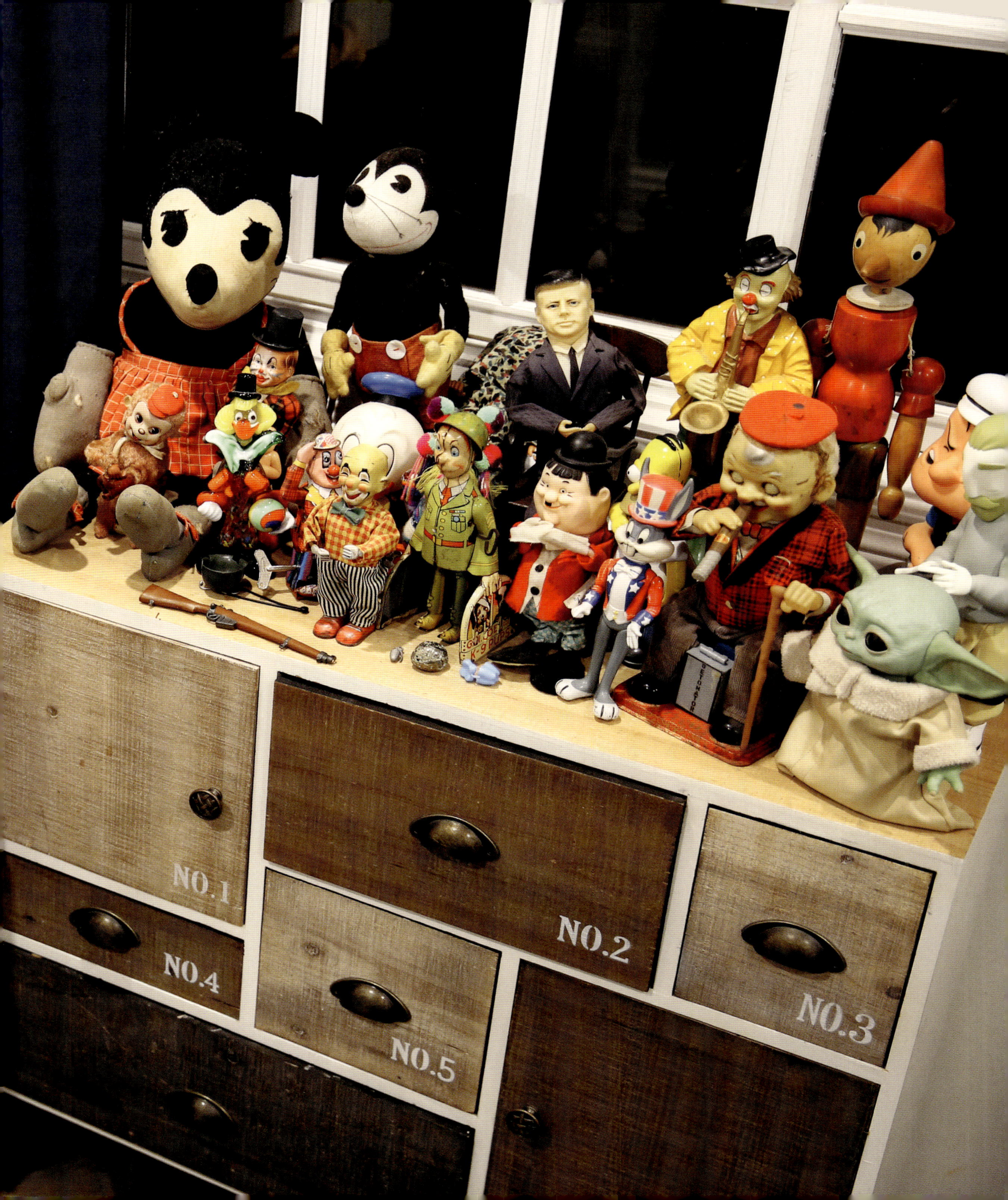

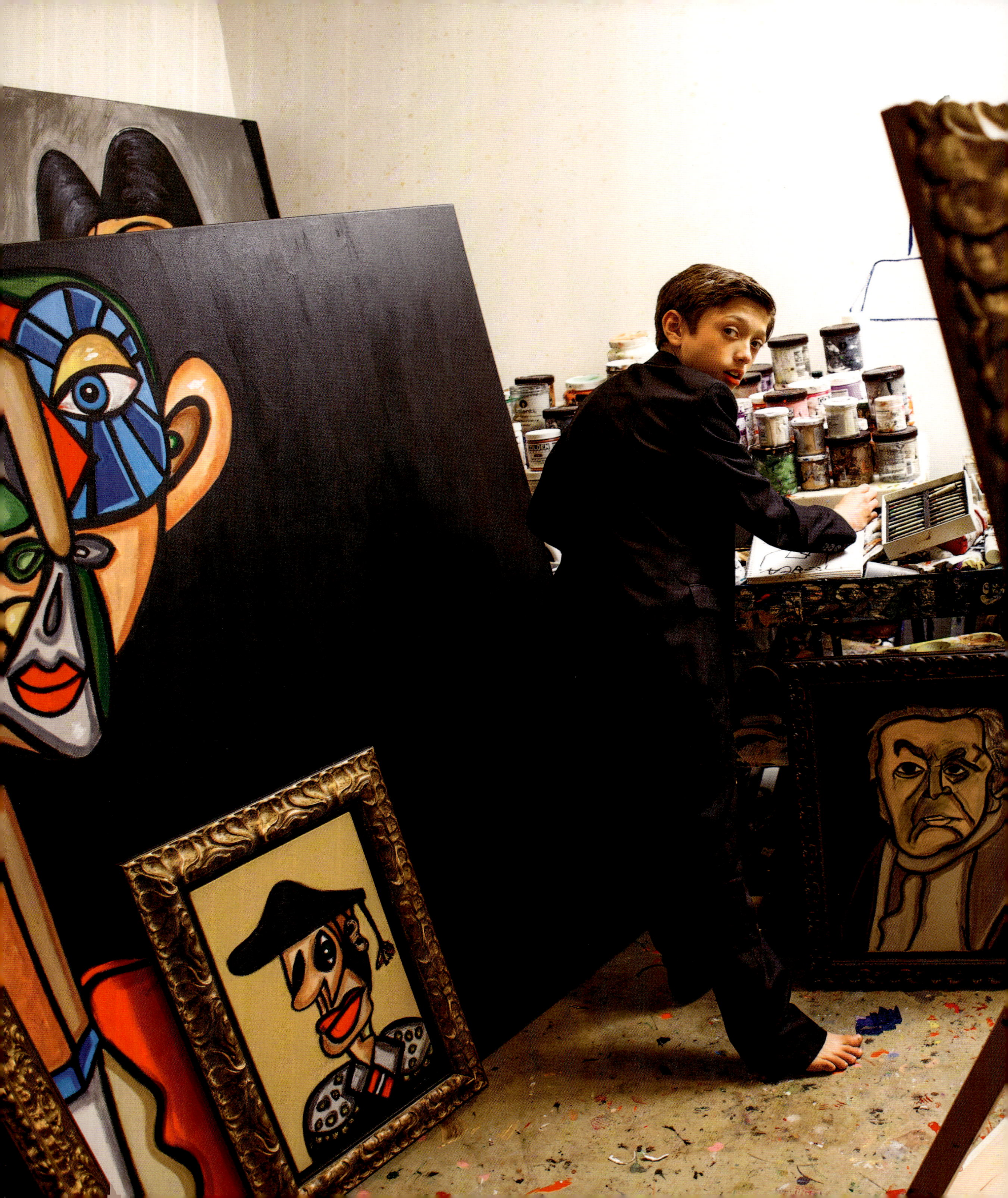

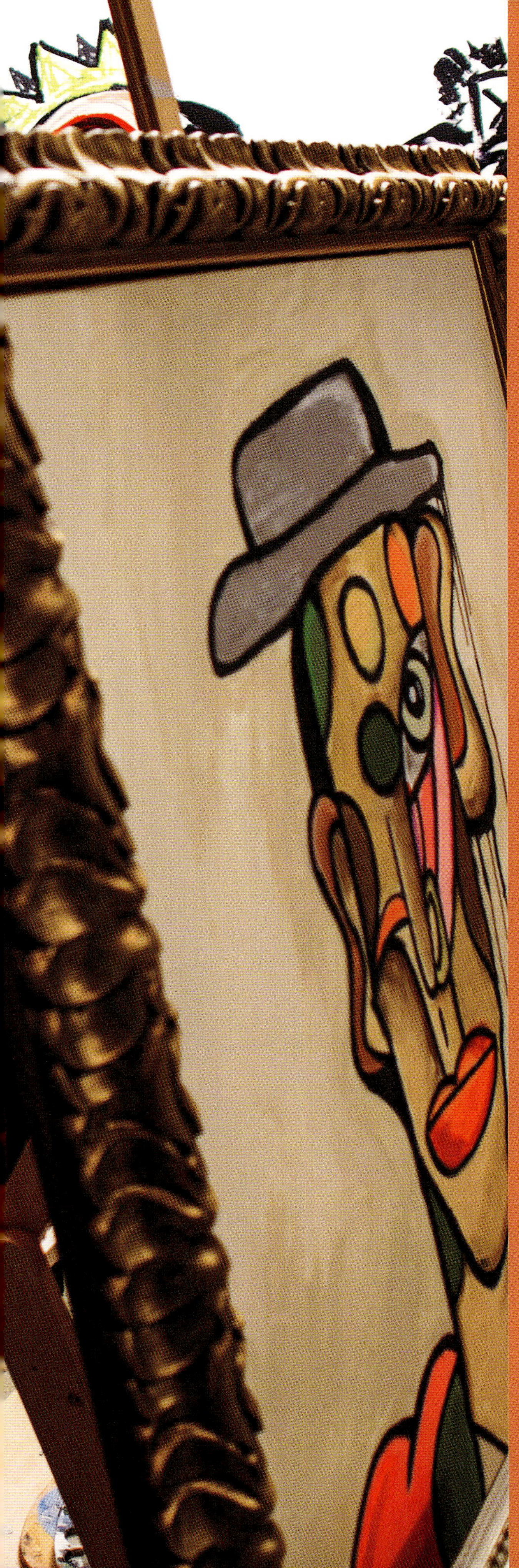

THE PROCESS

Every artist has their own process. Some approach a painting with planning and precision, others work from a place of instinct and inspiration. Andres is a spontaneous painter. He approaches each canvas as a blank slate, using it as a vessel to express his creativity. His fluid, unplanned painting style offers him an endless amount of variation and options for each abstract portrait. He very rarely plans out what he is going to paint before he brings his brush to the canvas. Instead, he allows his motions to lead his creative process in a free-flowing manner that is constantly evolving and changing in real time.

There are times when his paintings are informed by the spark of an idea, even if it is not fully formed. When he was as young as six, he often woke his mother in the middle of the night to ask, "Can I please go paint? I have an idea." Certain lightbulb moments like these still occur. Andres can be in the middle of a conversation or hanging out with his family when an idea comes, and he feels the urge to head downstairs to his studio to see how he can transform the idea into a physical painting.

"I think certain things do come to him more fully formed," Elsa says, "but not necessarily the full picture, because he'll say things like, 'I have an idea for this nose.'" For Andres, sometimes all he needs is the idea for a single defining feature around which to build the rest of a character.

Andres at work in his studio, March 2024.

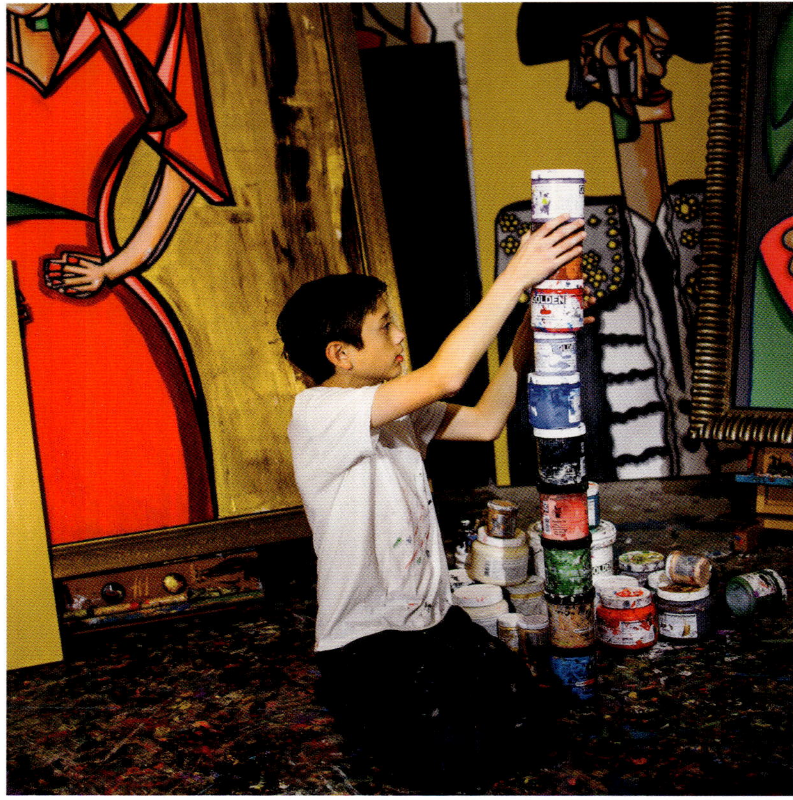

Being a Kid Comes First

Andres is a successful artist, but he is also a child, and the time he spends creating artwork in his studio is balanced with other typical childhood activities. He goes to school, studies music, takes piano lessons, and hangs out with his friends, just as other kids do. Elsa and Lupe encourage lots of outdoor time, so Andres can regularly be found outside, enjoying afternoons of carefree exploration. He and two of his friends often set up their GI Joes with their trucks, digging holes in the yard to create a course for their action figures to traverse, and sometimes even filling up the holes with water to make it more interesting. Andres is an active and busy kid, regardless of whether painting is factored in.

Andres is typically barefoot, even when he goes outside. Elsa has been known to say to him, "If you're stressed, try going outside and stand in the grass and see how it feels between your toes." Sometimes people make comments on the Instagram videos of Andres painting barefoot in his studio, saying things like, "Oh my God, why does he not have shoes on?" Elsa always has a quick response to this, saying, "Because you know what? It's amazing to let your bare skin touch paint, to be outside, to be running freely. Andres's feet usually have paint or dirt on them— sometimes both. I'm not even kidding. I do have to stop him and ask him to wash his feet. But I encourage him to play and exist barefoot as much as he wants to because it's so freeing."

Amid all this playing and outdoor childhood exploration, at the end of the day, Andres returns again and again to painting because he wants to paint. He never feels that he has to. And that is an important difference.

Above: Andres stacks containers of acrylic paint in his studio. **Opposite and Following:** Posing outside the Valencia family home on a sunny day, March 2024.

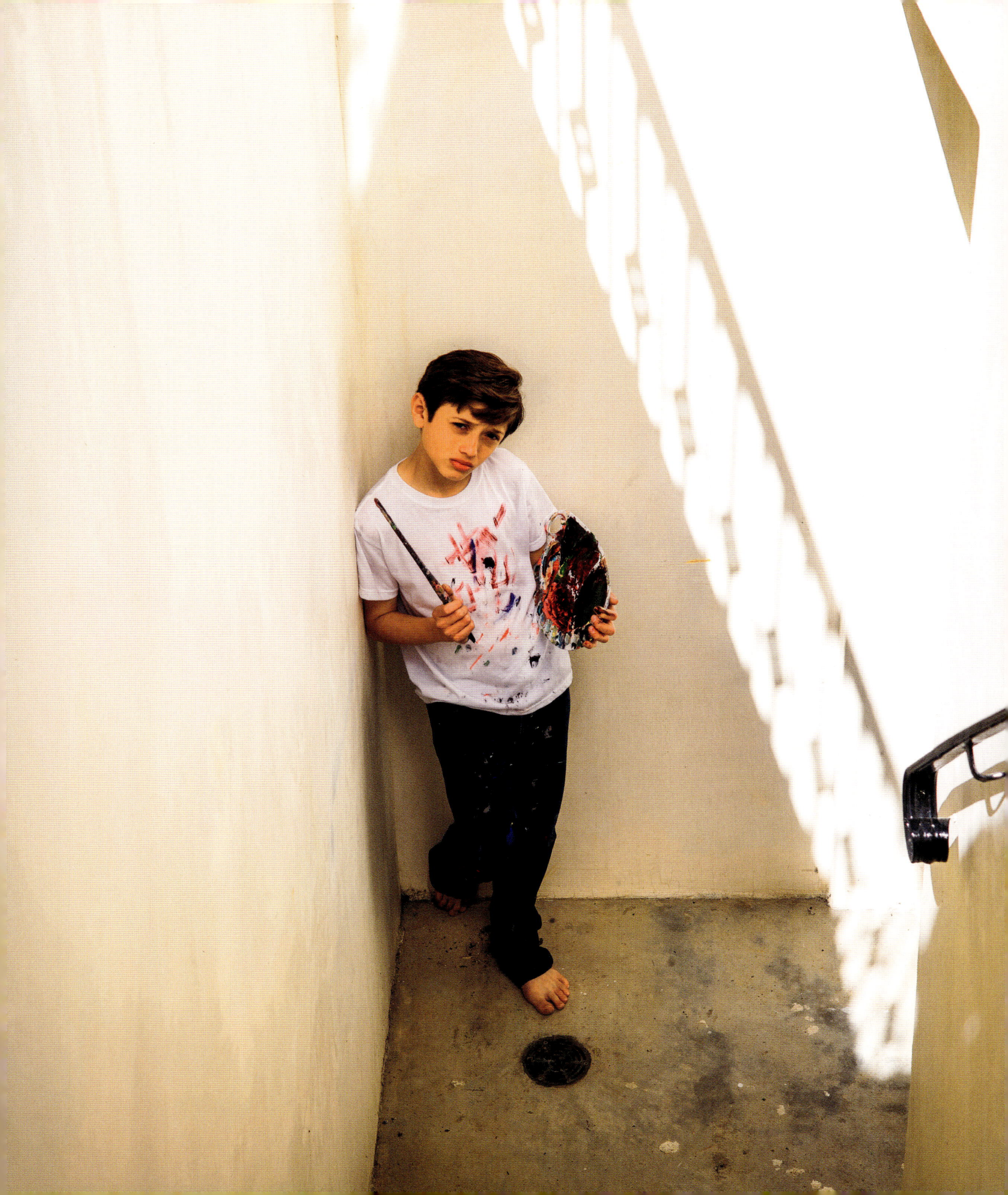

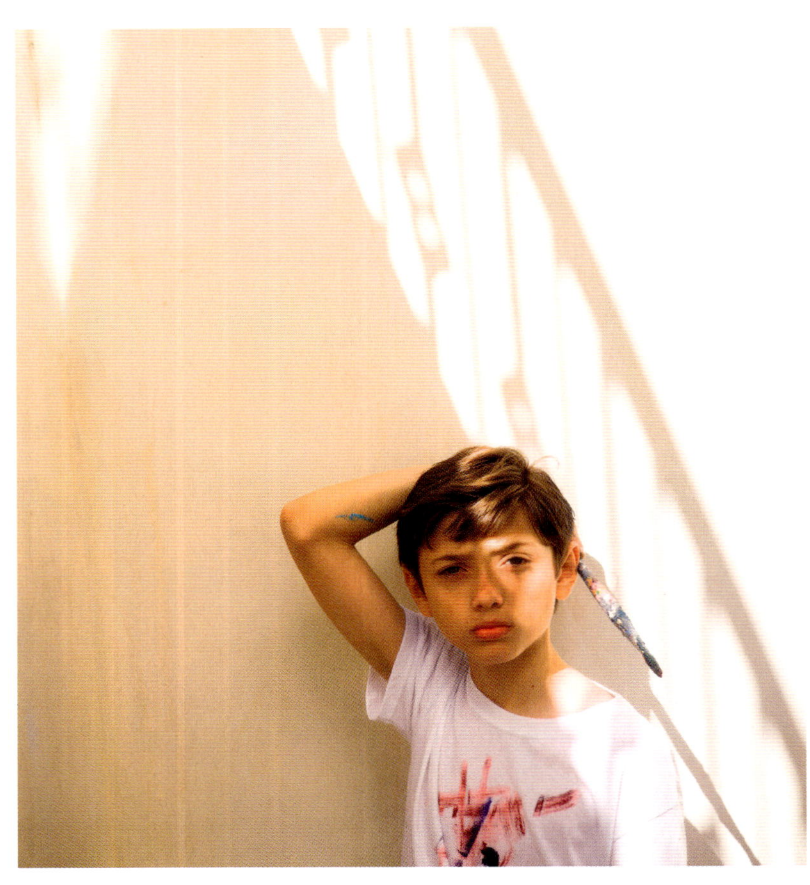

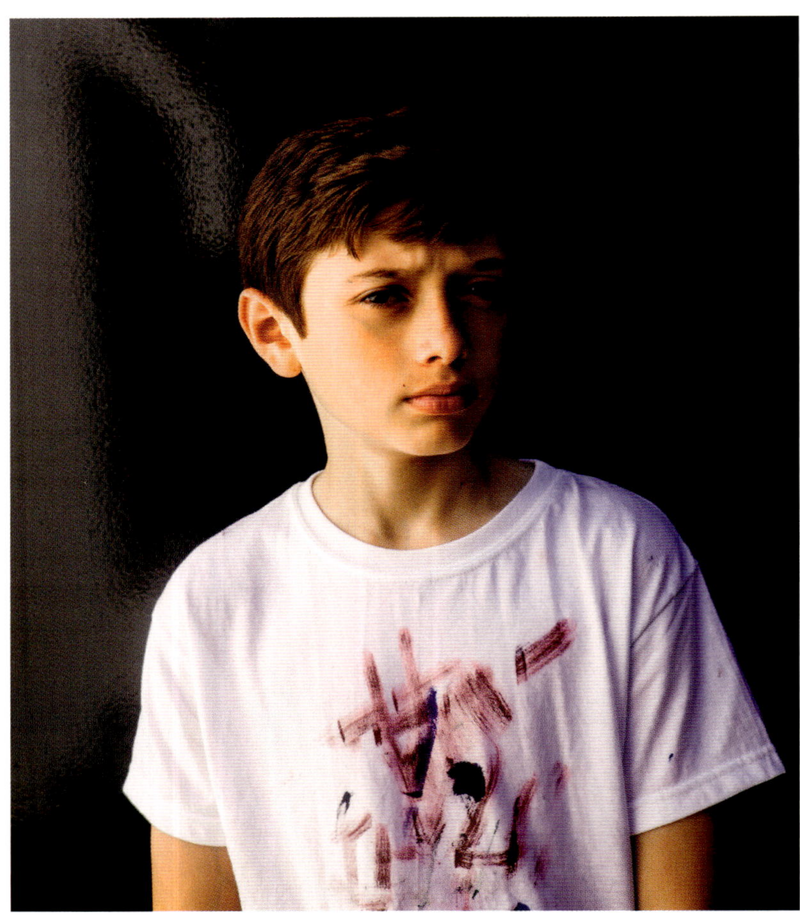

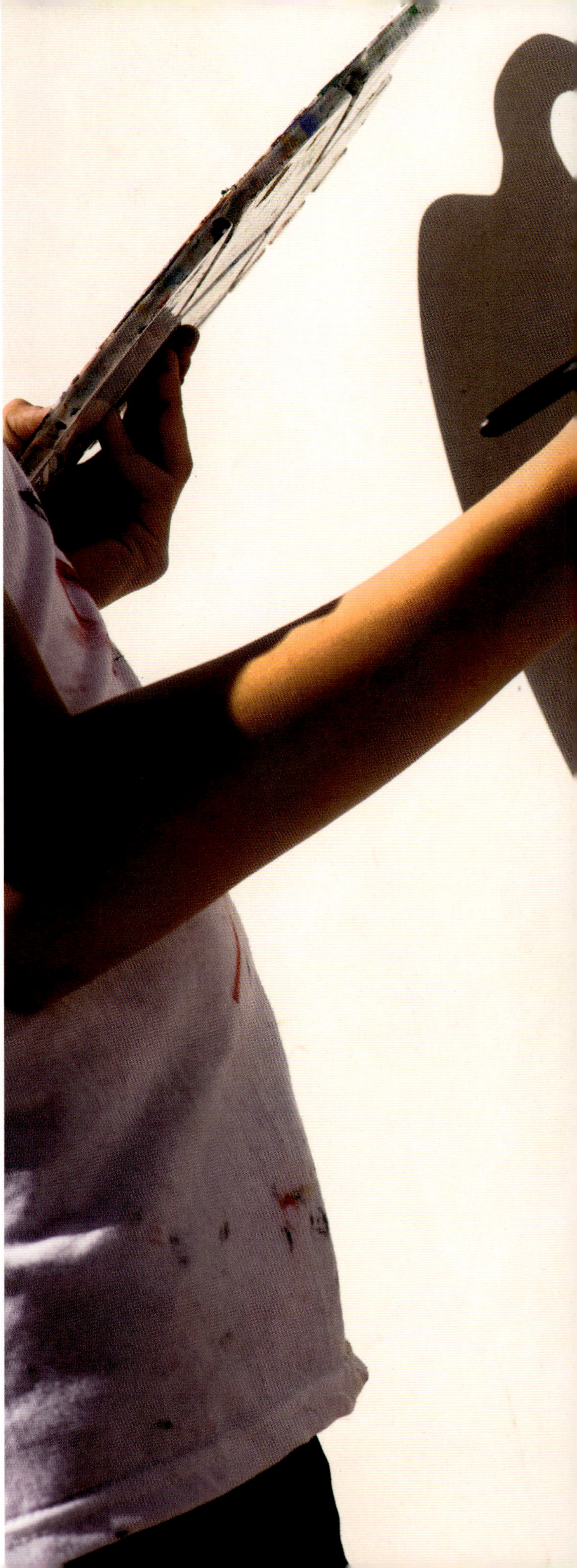

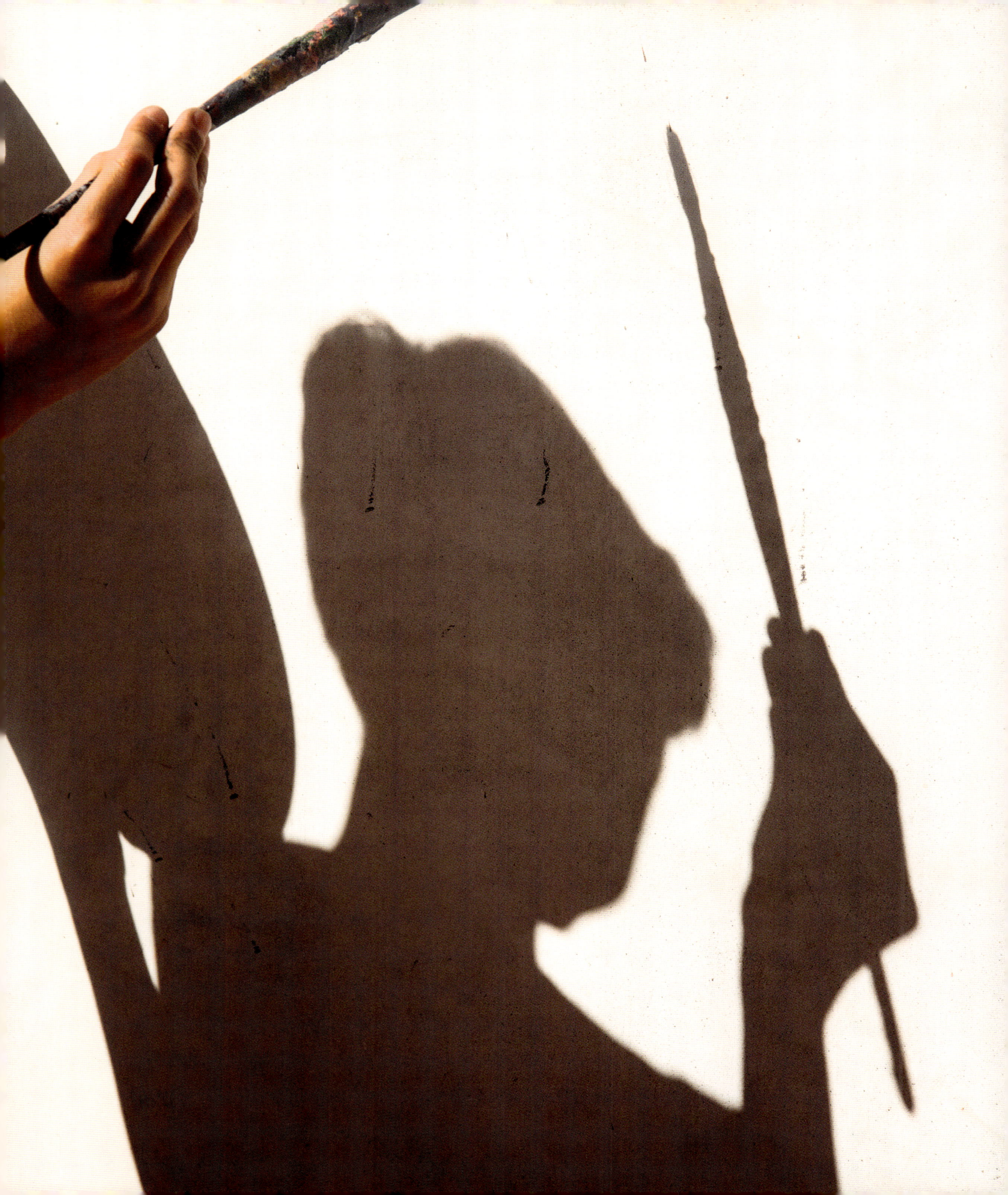

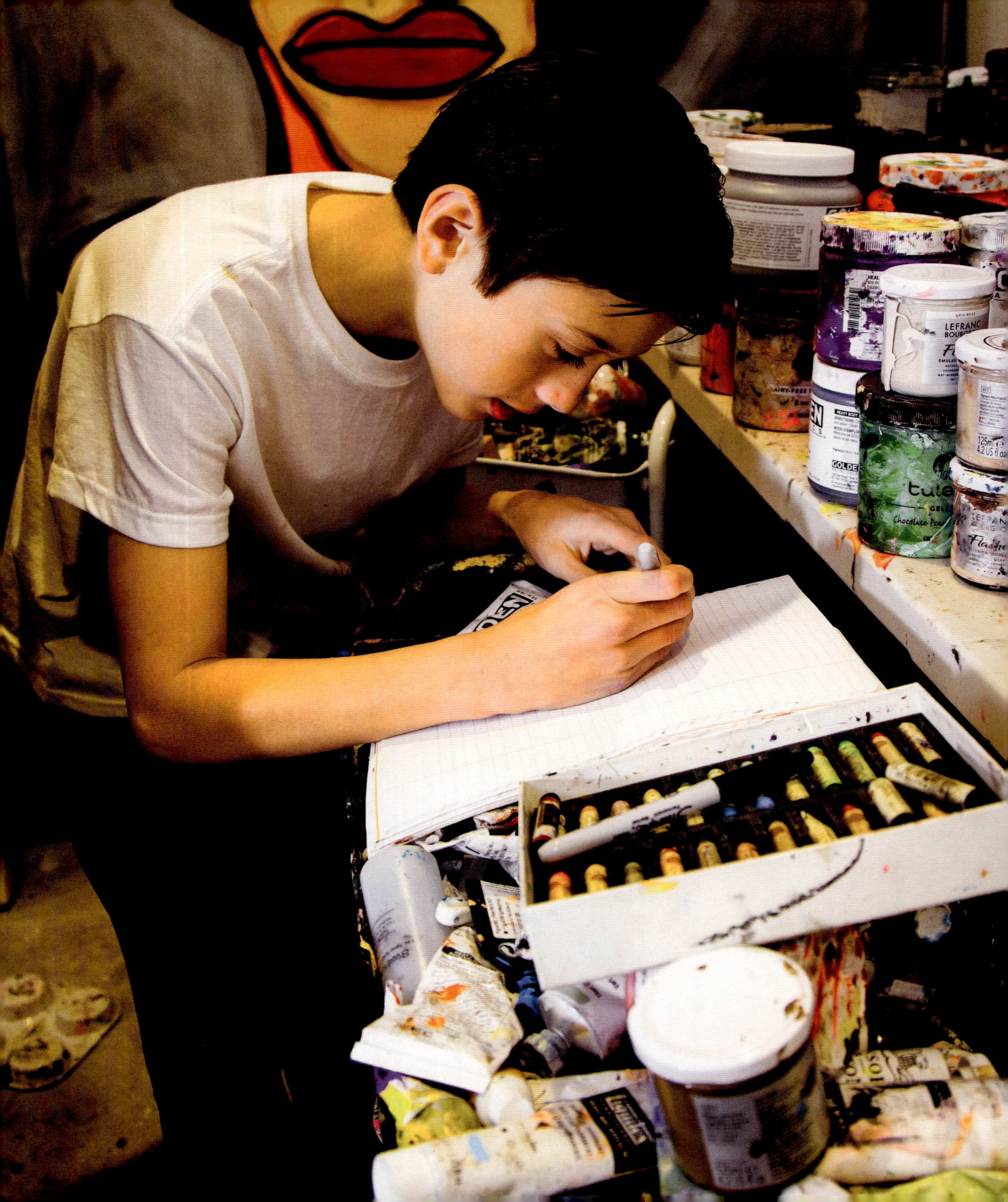

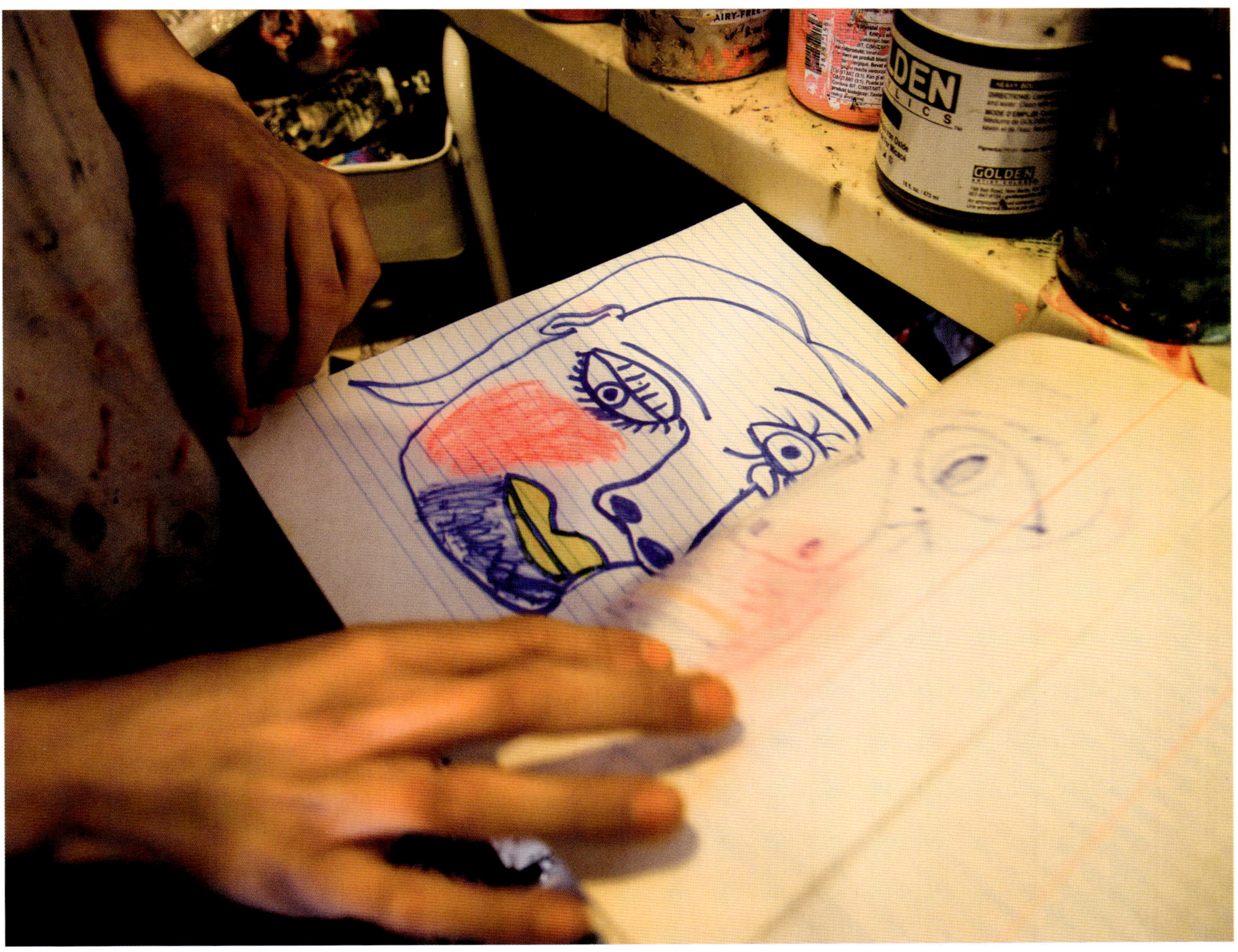

Sketching

Andres loves going to museums, and he can't help but be inspired by the art he sees when visiting a new collection. The ideas come to him in pieces, sometimes resulting in sketches he does on paper so he can practice and strengthen the concept before evolving it into a full piece on canvas. The sketches don't always directly translate from paper to canvas though, as Andres always keeps things spontaneous whenever he's adapting an earlier idea into something grander.

"For example," Elsa says, "if he sketches something on paper, and he likes how he did the hat, he'll say, 'For my next painting, I'm going to add this kind of hat.' But I have to tell you, it's never the same hat." Even if Andres notices the hat he puts on the canvas doesn't quite match the one he sketched, he won't ever erase it to try and make it look like the one he did before. He'll just keep moving forward. Elsa says, "It never comes out the same as the sketches, but it still comes out amazing."

Above: Andres shows off one of his sketchbooks, which is full of dozens of quickly drawn pieces. **Opposite:** Working on a new sketch in his studio, March 2024.

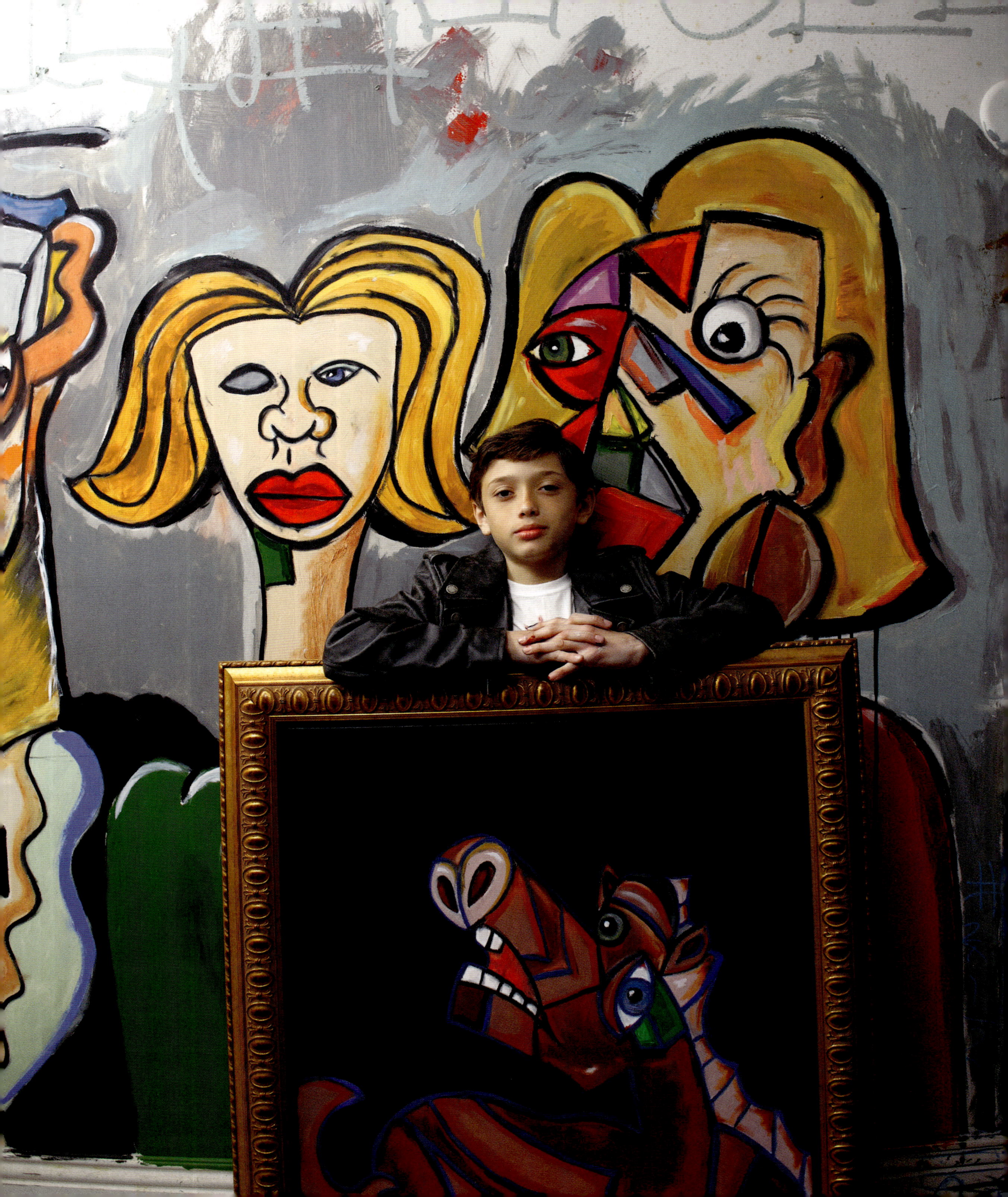

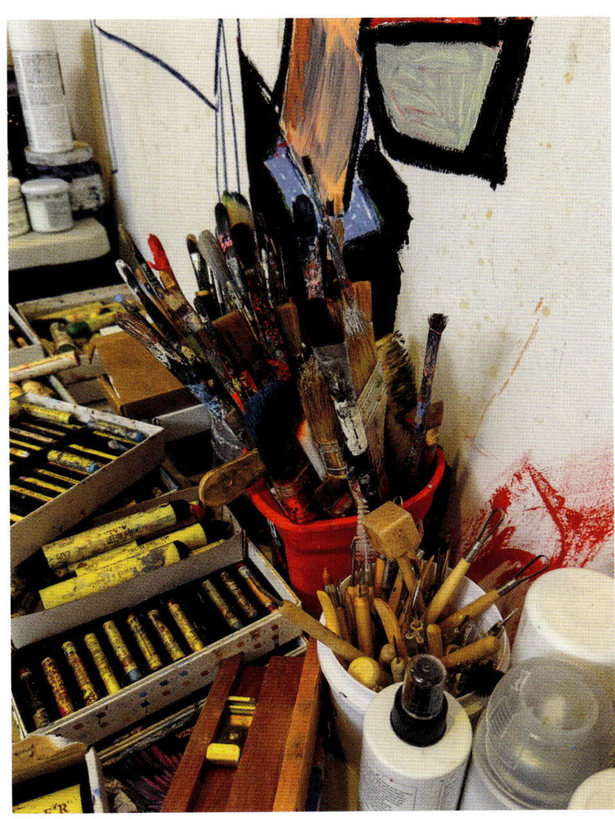

The Studio

The atmosphere of Andres's studio can sometimes be a bit chaotic, but it is clearly a space dedicated to creation, imagination, and freedom. There are paintings everywhere, both on canvas and directly on the walls. Some paintings are fully finished in bright shades of color, while others are still in progress or half-completed, with just the black outlines of oil pastel. Andres has dozens of paintbrushes, small containers of acrylic paint, things to sculpt with, sketch pads, art books, and anything else he might need at his disposal. His studio is the space where the magic happens. There is paint all over the floor, and nothing seems to be organized in any particular way. At the same time, it's a kind of organized chaos that gives him the liberty to explore in a safe, artistic space that is all his own.

The space that has become Andres's studio was originally meant to be a home theater in the Valencia family's basement. Previously, he would constantly paint in his bedroom and the living room, and after a while, it started to get out of control.

"There were racks and racks of paint littered all around," Elsa says. "My sofas were getting paint on them, canvases were everywhere, and when people came over, there was nowhere for them to sit. I was scrubbing the floors constantly, since paint was going all over the place. I kept thinking, *We can't live like this*. It was too much work to keep up with. So eventually, I just said, 'You know what? We should have him move down into the basement.'"

Since the plan to convert the basement into a movie theater wasn't going to happen for a while, Elsa decided it'd be better for everyone if he had a designated space down in the basement to work. She cleaned up Andres's painting supplies and moved his stuff downstairs. Andres was eight at the time. He had also pushed for the space to become his studio, as he knew it would be perfect for it.

Little by little, the Valencia family made the basement Andres's own creative space. It eventually evolved into fully being his designated painting studio. As Elsa explains, "It was so nice because I finally had places for everybody to sit down again in the living room, and I didn't have to be scrubbing my floors all the time anymore. Andres had all the space he needed downstairs to paint, especially since his canvases kept getting bigger and bigger."

Andres remembers it like this: "They said, 'Andres, you don't have to paint in the living room anymore.' This was good since I was getting a lot of paint on the floor. I had all my trays and all my big things upstairs, so there wasn't much room for all my paintings. I was so happy when they told me. It was always my dream to have my own art studio."

Andres enjoys painting whenever he has time and feels inspired. His studio is special to him, because it's a designated space in which to do what he loves best, and he's been able to curate it to fit his wants and needs. He's even painted a number of his abstract characters directly onto the studio's walls—much like two of his favorite artists, George Condo and Basquiat. "Since it's my room, I can do what I want," he says. "It doesn't matter if I get paint on the floor, and I'm allowed to draw on the walls. It's kind of every kid's dream." This is exactly what creative freedom looks like.

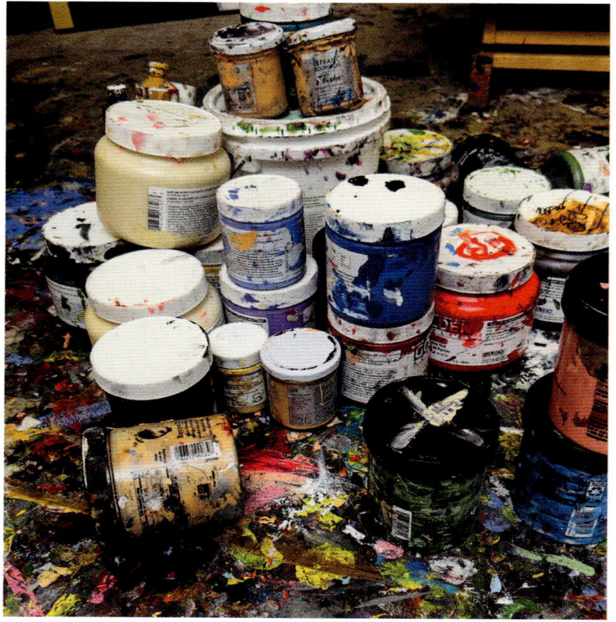

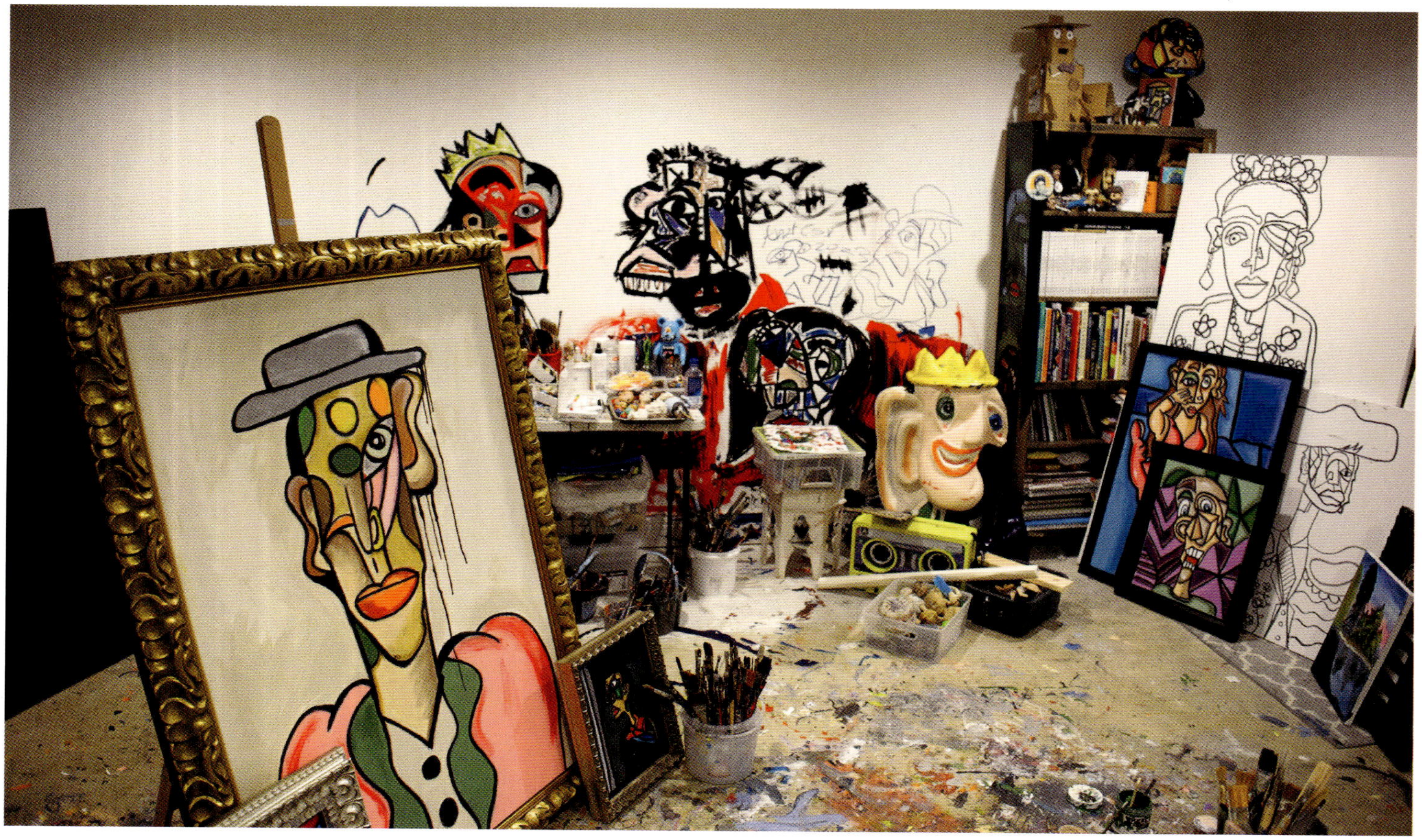

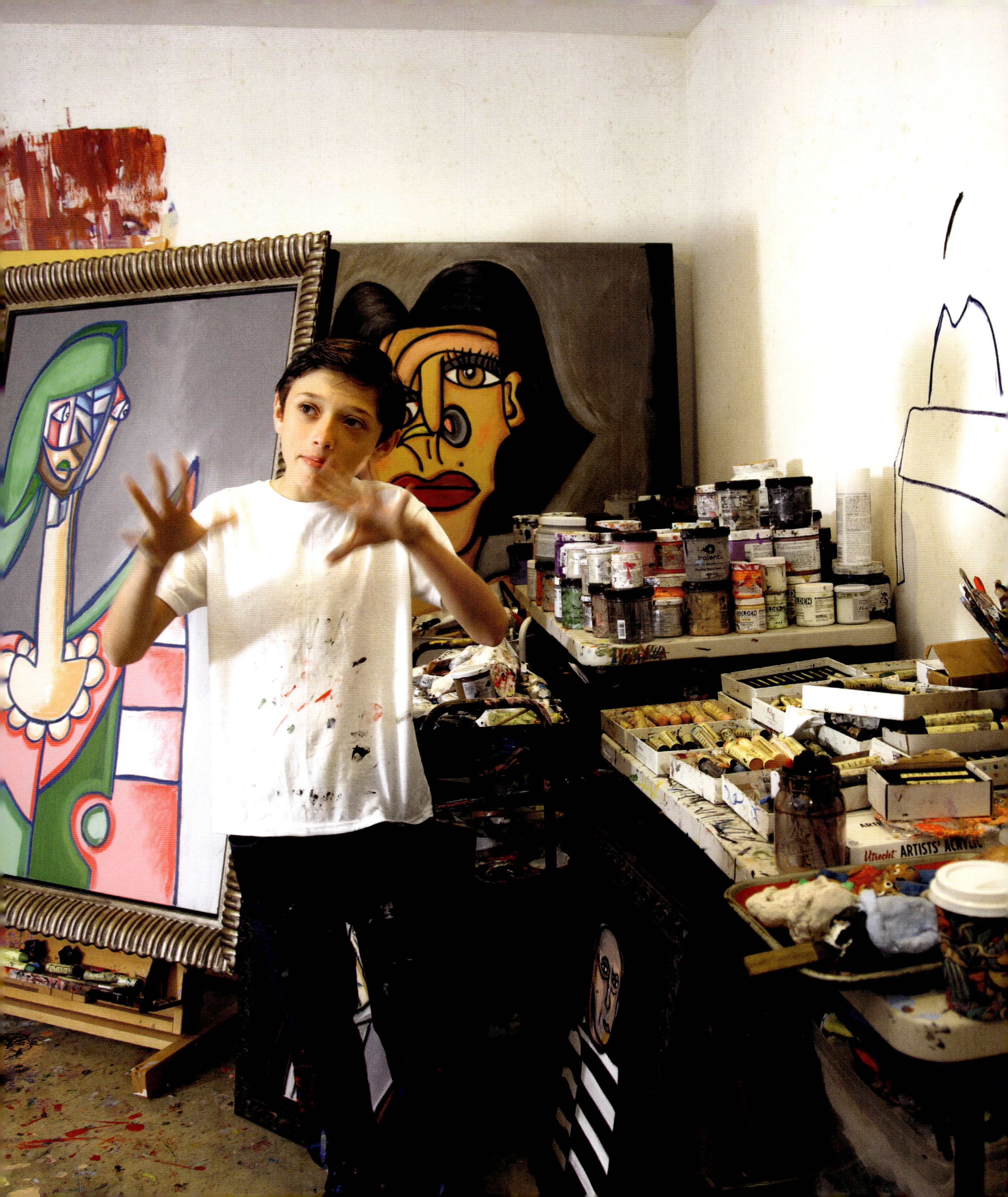

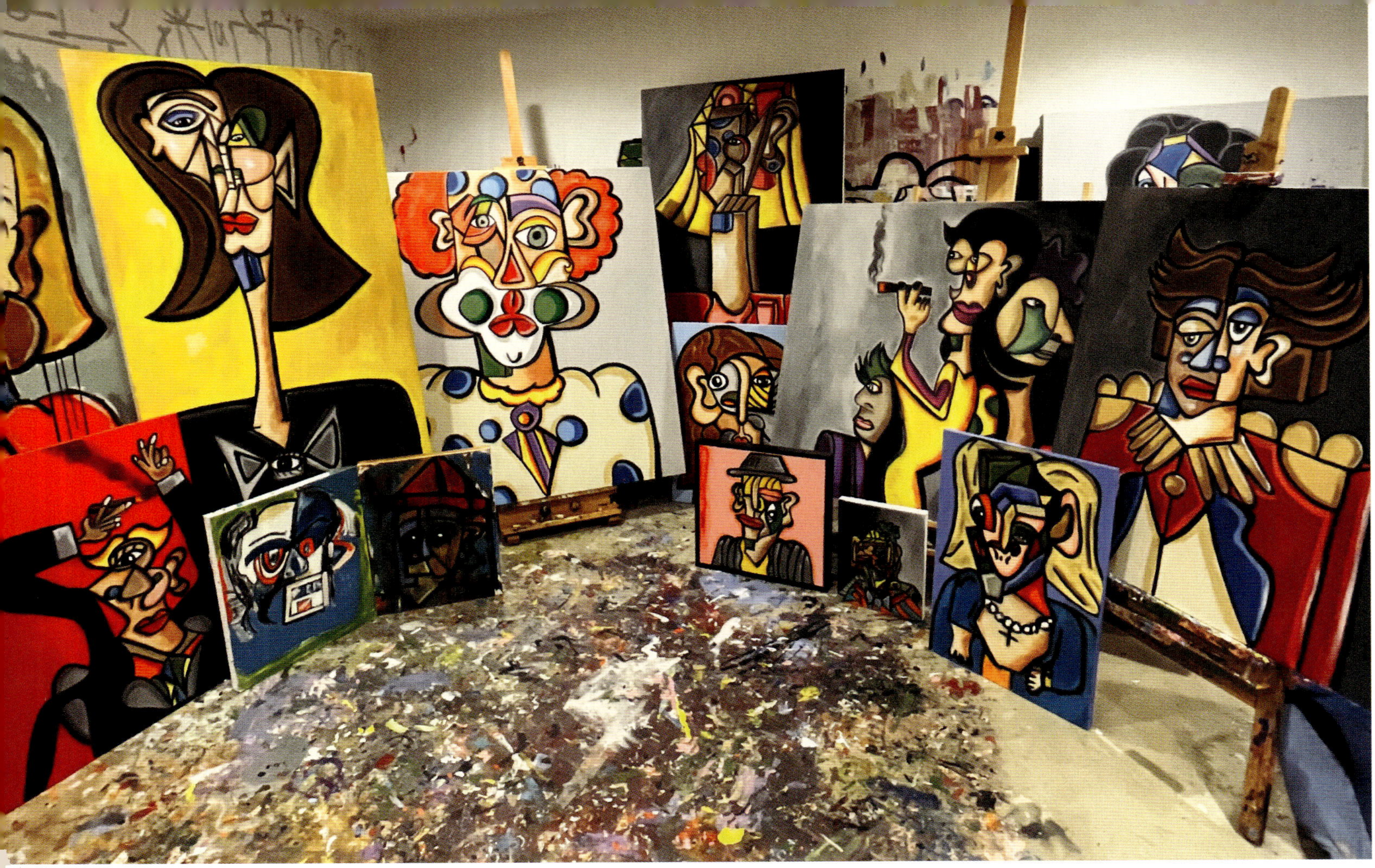

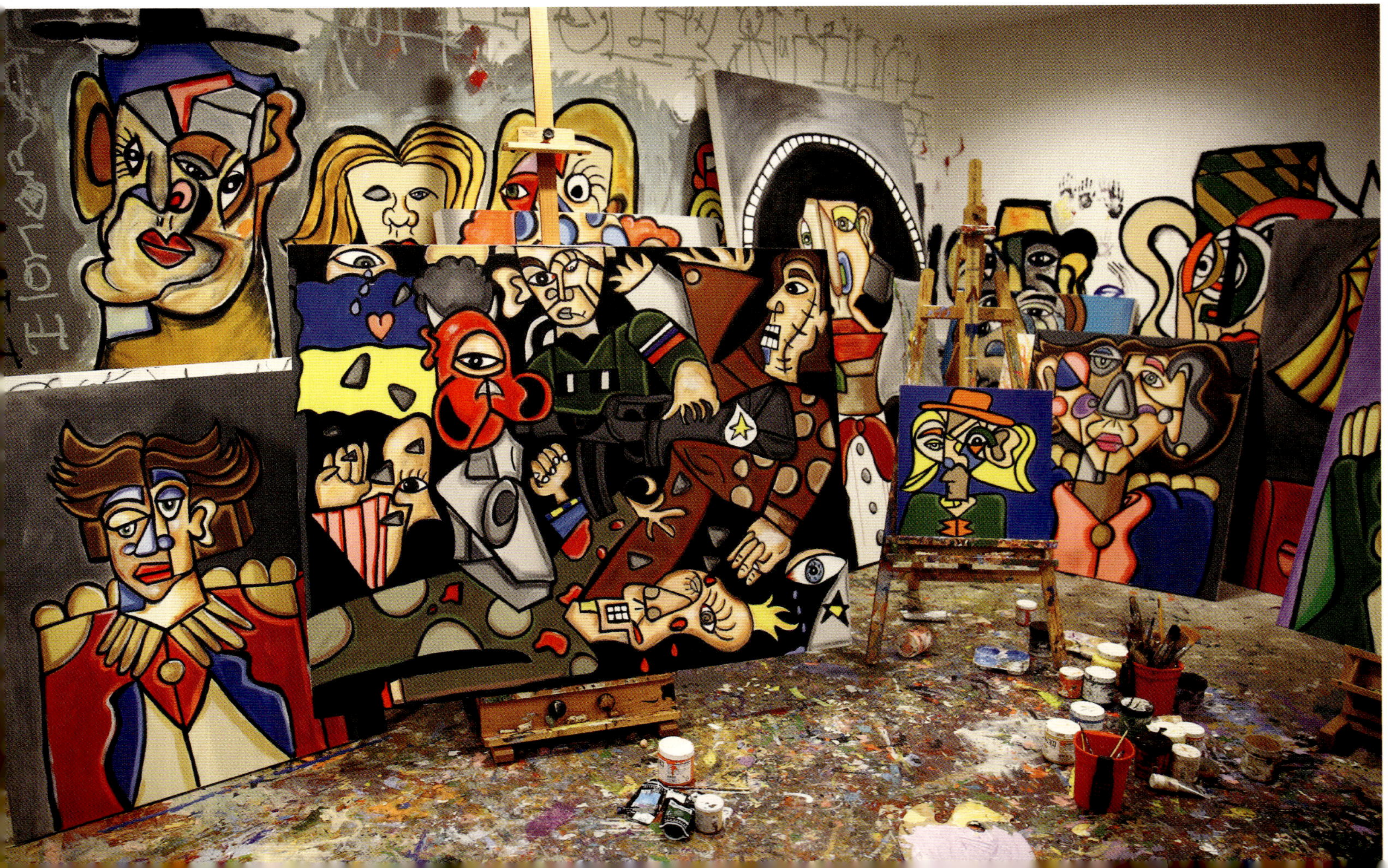

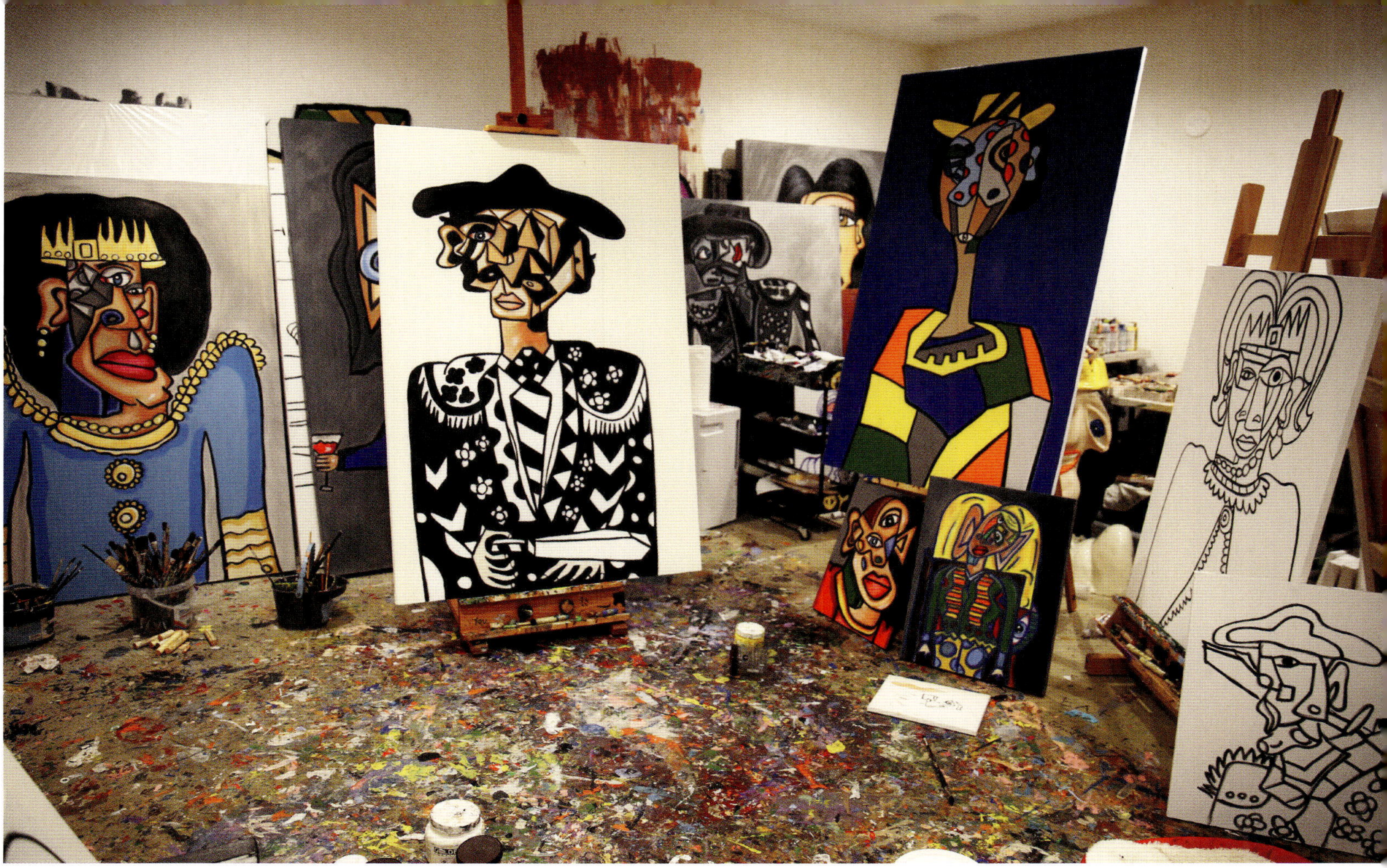

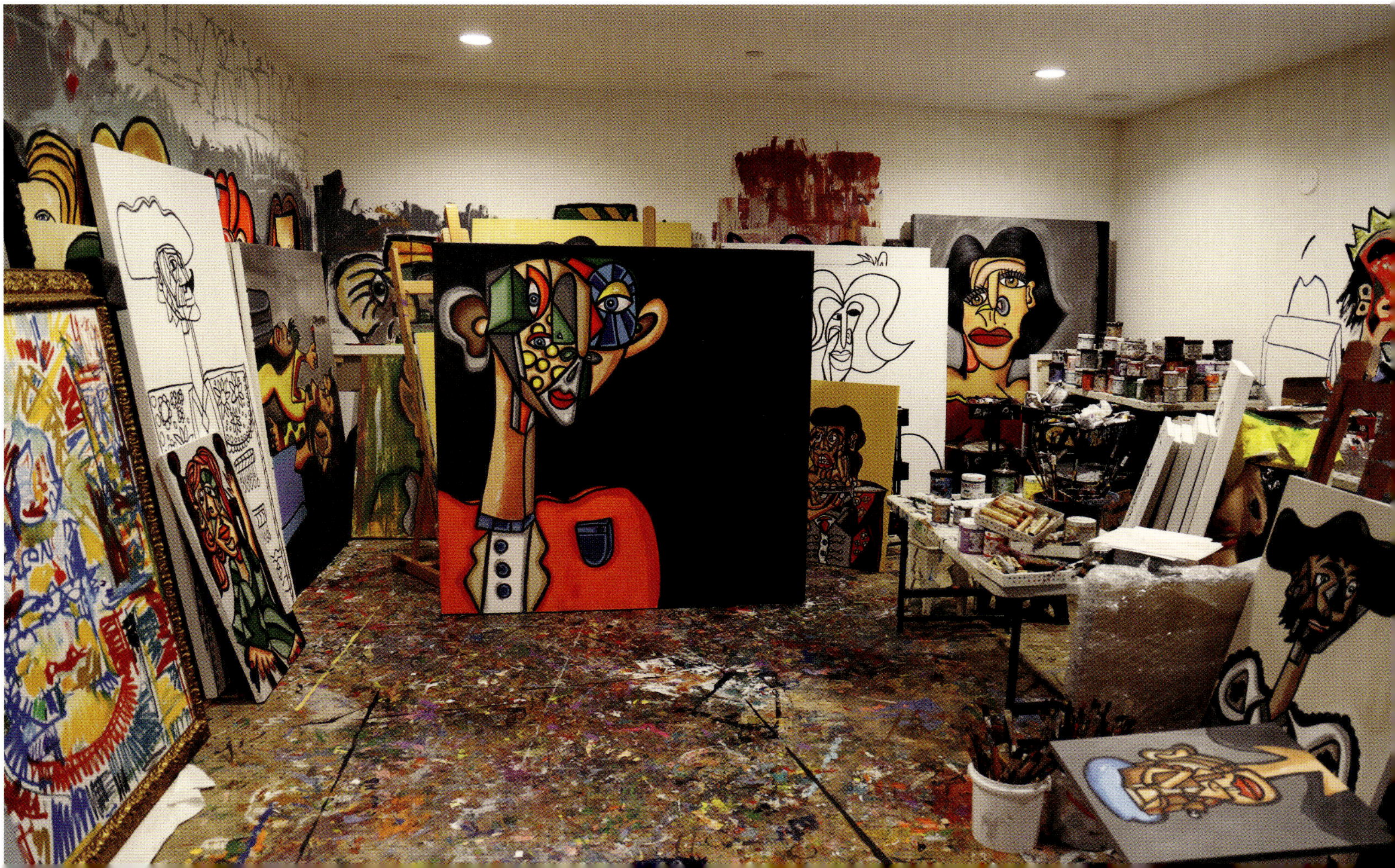

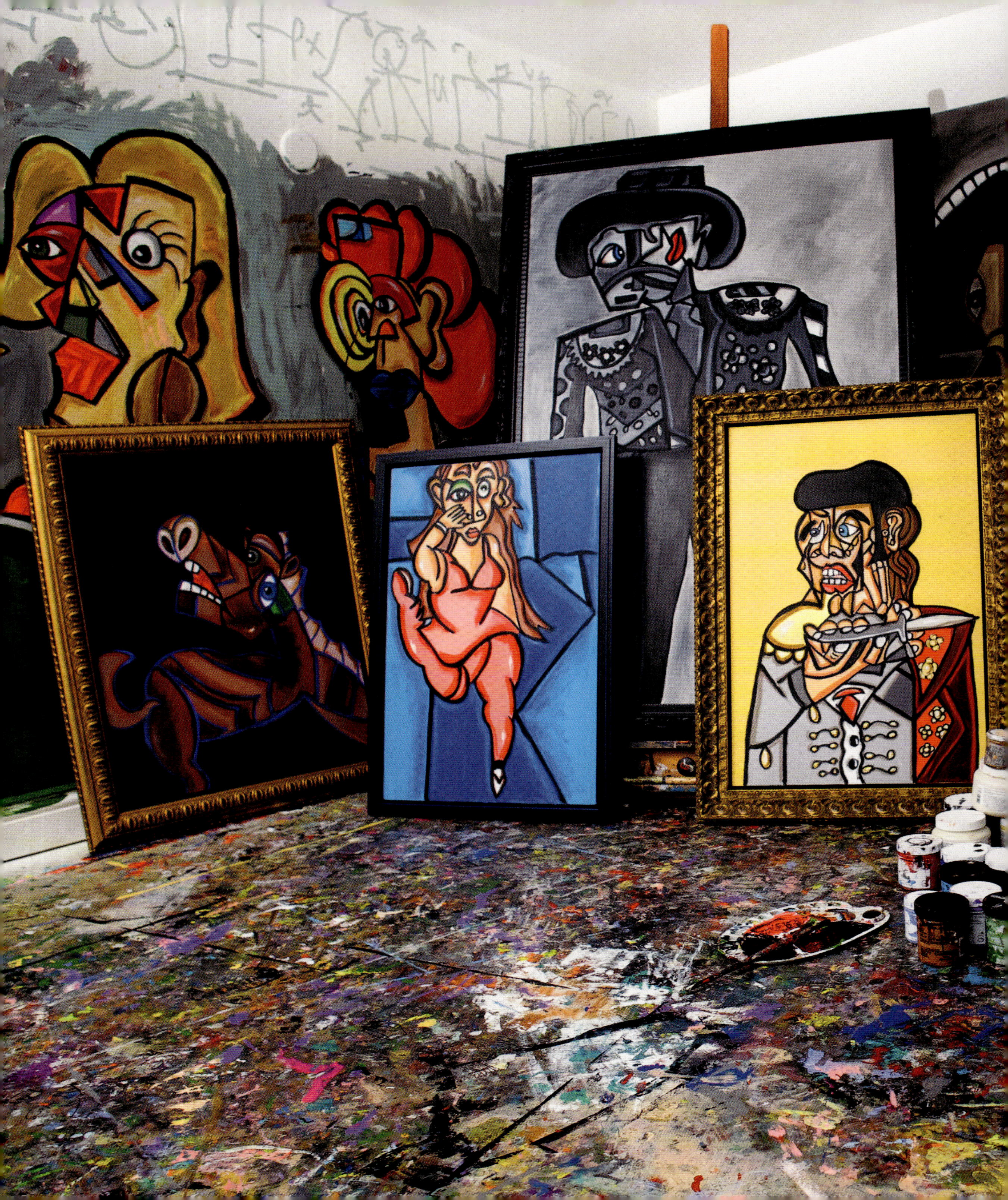

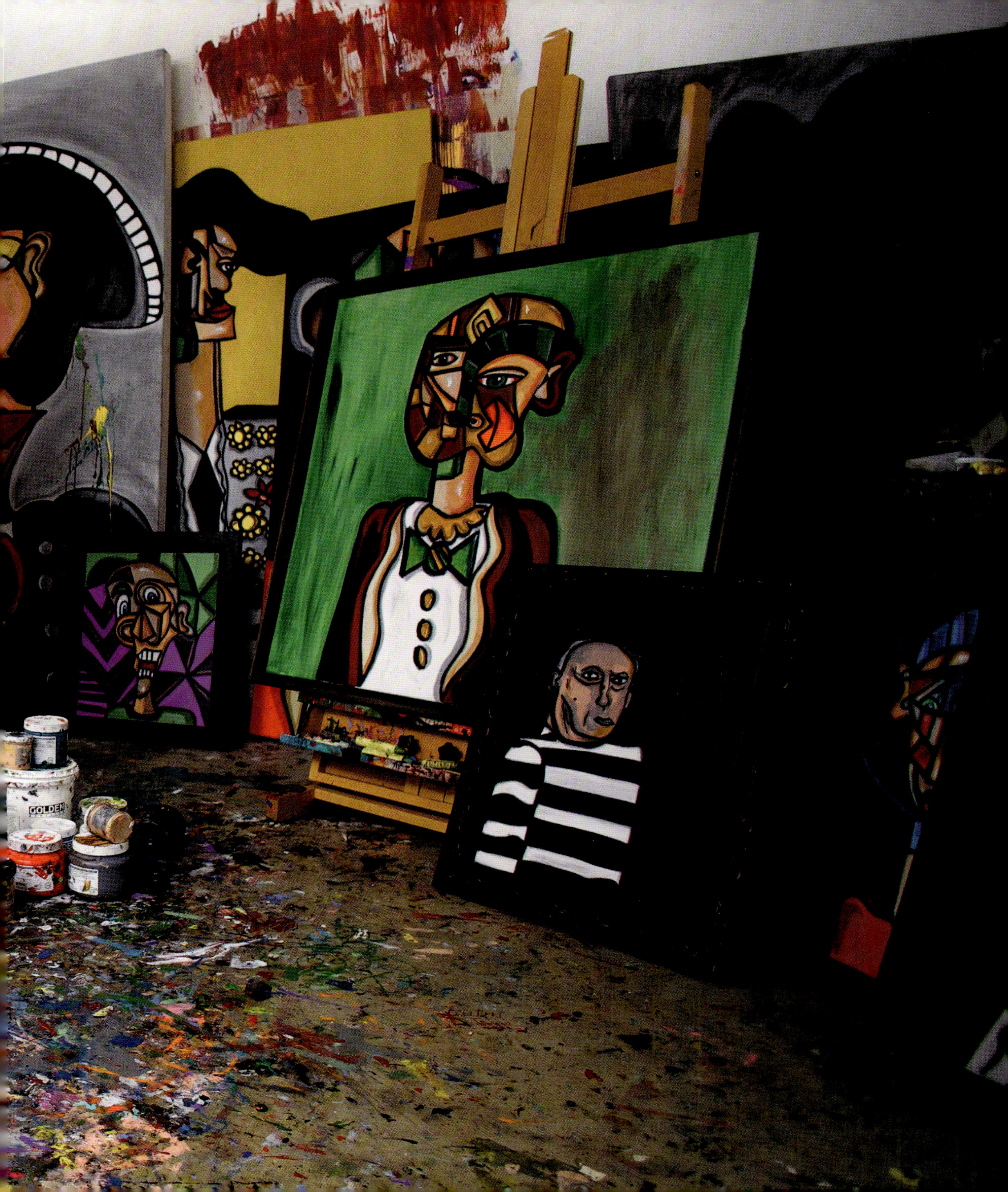

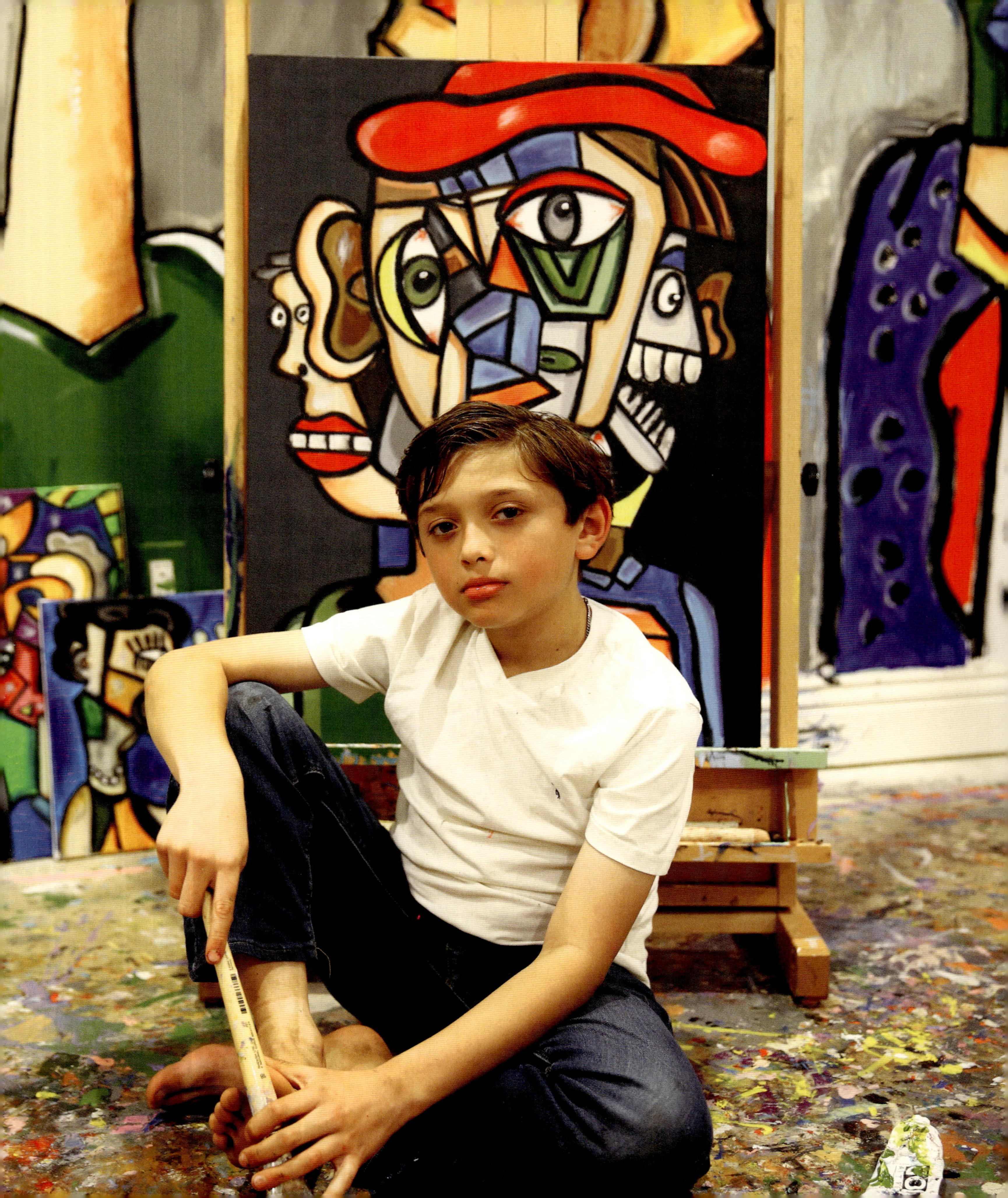

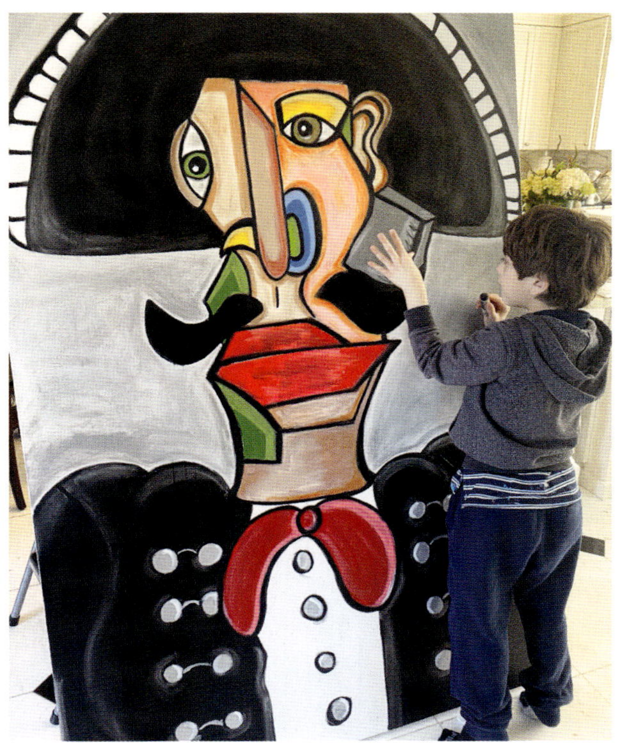

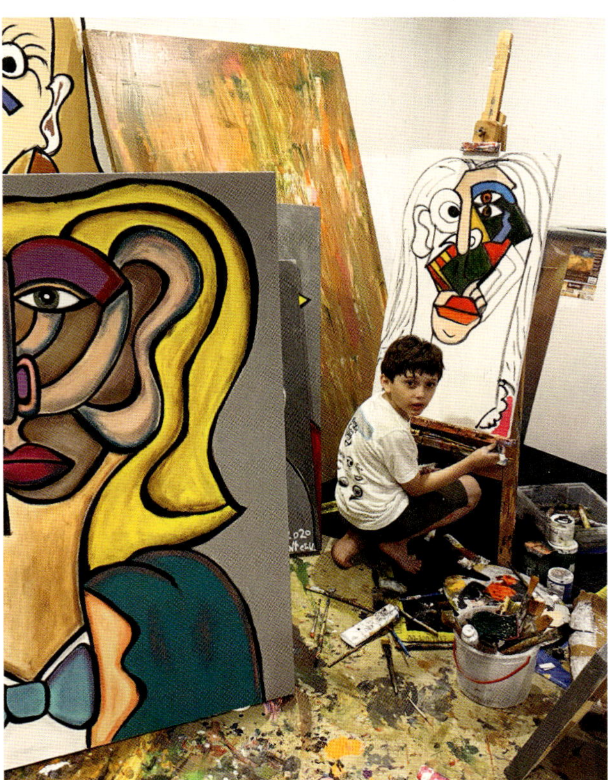

Above: Andres working on his painting *El Mariachi* (pg. 191) in December 2020, age nine (top). Working on *Adela* (pg. 178) in his studio, March 2021 (bottom). **Opposite:** Sitting in front of his painting *Many Opinions* (pg. 242), June 2023, age eleven.

Completing a Work

Since entering middle school, homework has begun to take up more of Andres's time, and he isn't able to paint every day. Still, he usually paints every other day on average. He typically does not work on one painting from beginning to end. Instead, he allows himself to move between pieces, even starting pieces he never finishes. He works on whatever grabs his attention and focus, sometimes returning to finish the pieces that call him back after he's set them aside for a while.

Andres's studio is filled with sketches he's never turned into larger pieces, as well as dozens of canvases that only have black-and-white outlines in oil pastel. These are works Andres drafted years ago, which he's still not found the inspiration to return to. When the moment is right, he'll come back to these unfinished pieces, sometimes months or even years after he began them.

In regard to why some of these canvases remain works in progress for long periods of time, Andres explains: "Sometimes I'll leave it and come back to it because I have another one I want to work on more. Then I'll come back a little bit later and finish it. I like working on what I'm most excited about."

There are instances where Andres finishes a painting in a shorter amount of time. This usually occurs when Andres is super excited about what he's creating. One of his bullfighter paintings came together this way, as Elsa recalls: "I think he sketched this one only two weeks or so before he decided to paint it on a canvas. He loved the sketch so much, so he told me, 'I just want to finish him now.' That's how he works. Sometimes he loves what he sketches from the start, and he decides to finish it right then. Other times, he sketches it and steps away. And later, he'll come back and be like, 'Oh wow, that's a really cool sketch. I want to get back to that.'" This kind of practice is a perfect example of what painting without rules means to Andres. He allows himself to follow his inspirations and inclinations without worrying or pressuring himself to complete a piece from start to finish.

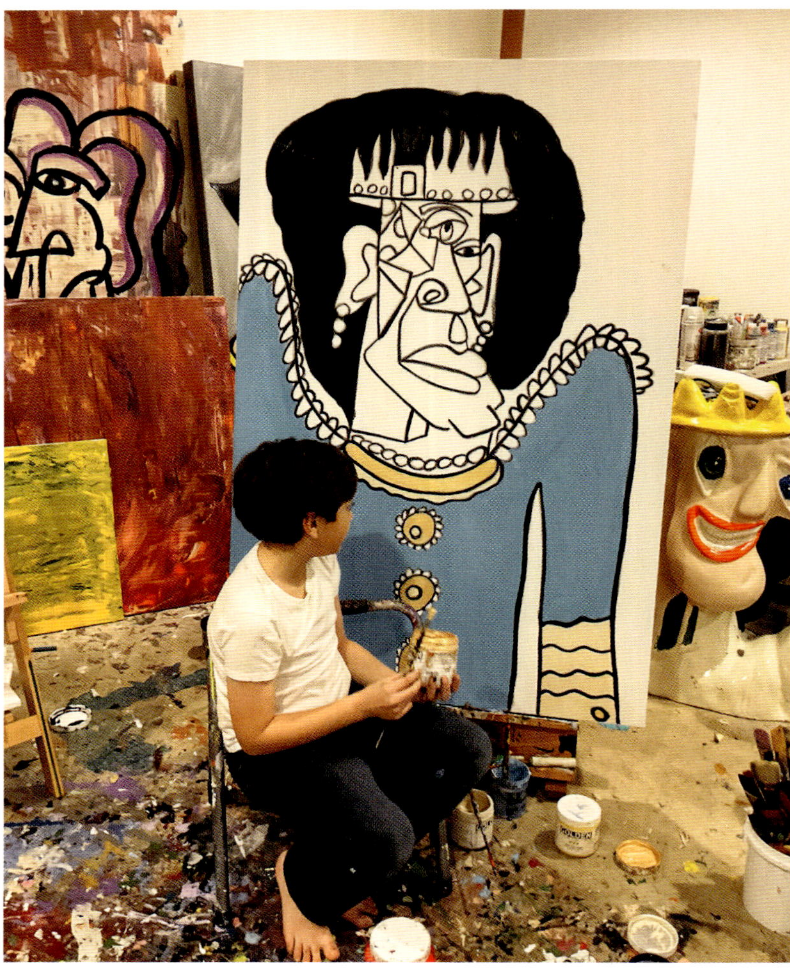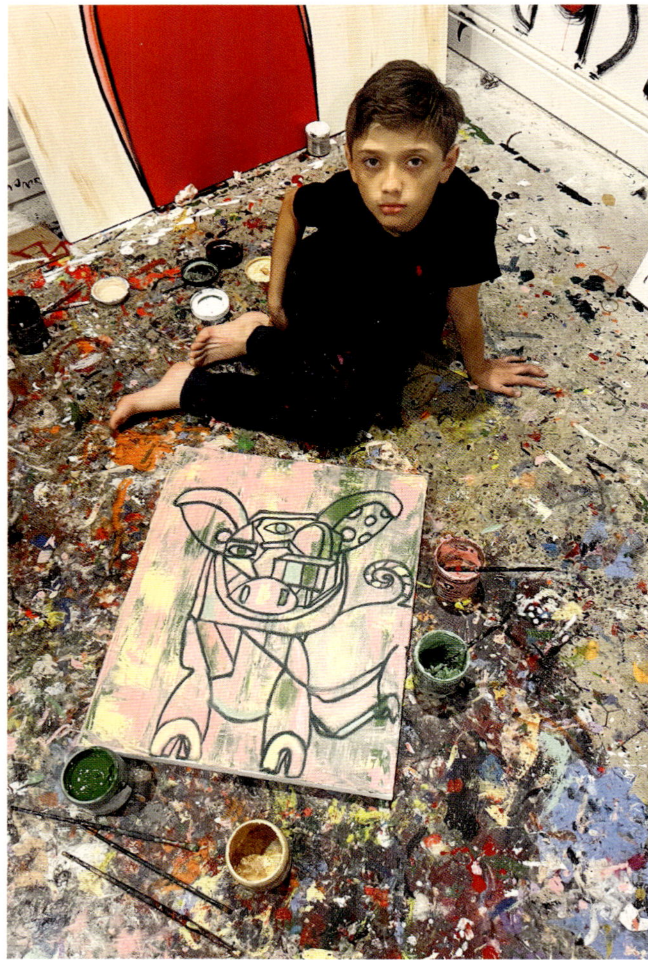

When Andres taps into this kind of excitement, it takes him about three days to complete a painting. The first day he sketches the subject, the second day he paints it, and then he waits for it to dry before going back on the third day to add in the shading. There are also rare occasions when Andres sketches something and finishes it within two hours from beginning to end, including painting. Typically, Andres enjoys painting in the evening the most, but he is willing to create any time he feels inspired.

Andres has completed so many works over the years that it's hard to know for sure just how many. Elsa estimates he has between three and four hundred paintings, not including sketches or unfinished works. Andres has made thousands of sketches. He keeps many of his sketchbooks in his studio, and he sometimes returns to them for inspiration. He also enjoys looking back at them to see how his art has progressed over time. The family has purposefully kept a number of his larger finished paintings, as there are certain pieces that neither Andres nor his parents ever want to part with. Elsa says they have twenty-five of his larger finished canvases, many of which are older pieces they'll never sell. A few of these paintings are hanging on the walls of the family home in San Diego, while others just sit on the floor of Andres's studio, leaning against one another and serving as backdrops while Andres continues to create new works.

Above: Andres working on *The Monarch* (pg. 204), January 2023 (left). Posing with one of his pig paintings, November 2023 (right). **Opposite:** The painting, *Natalia*, in progress, October 2023.

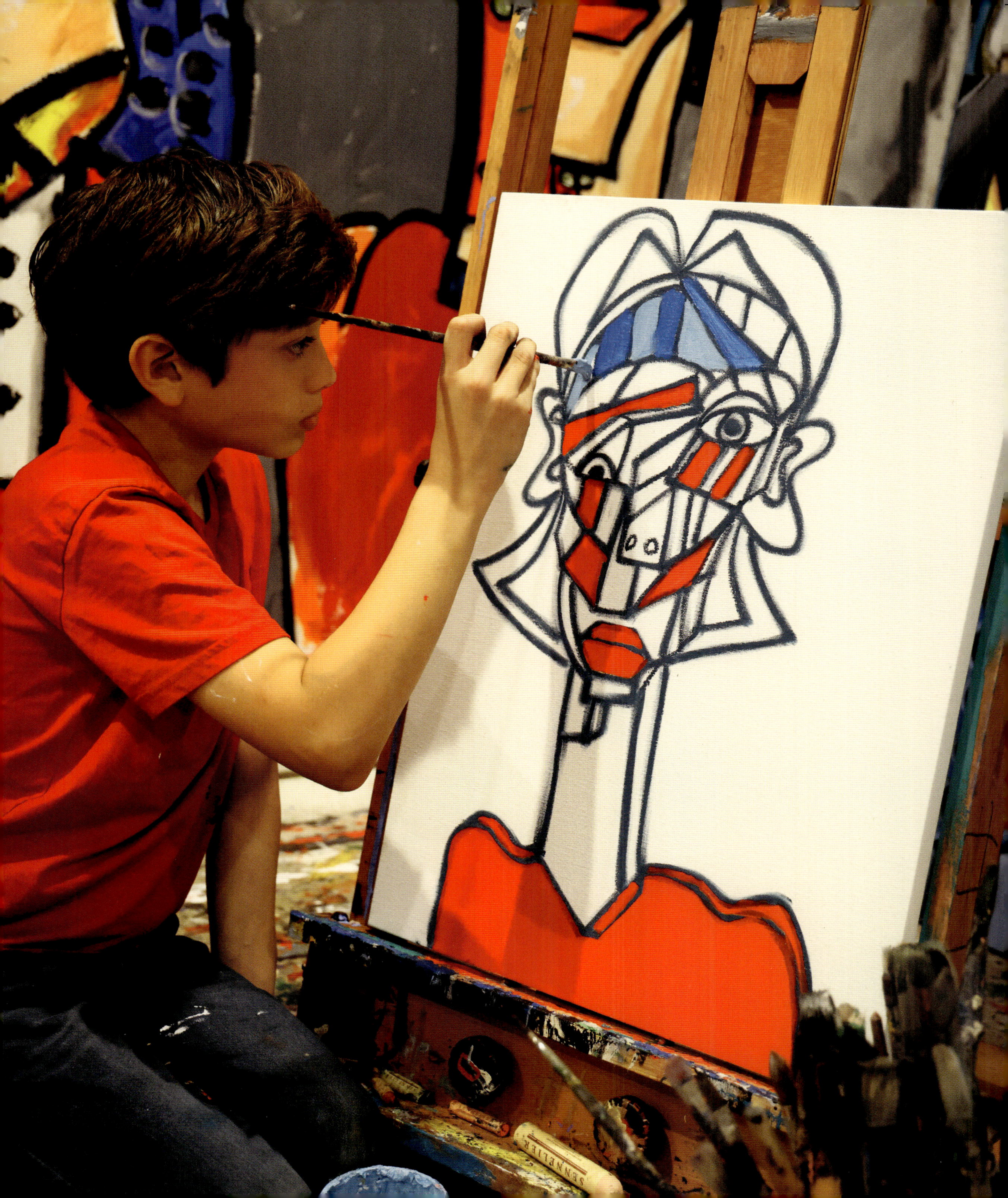

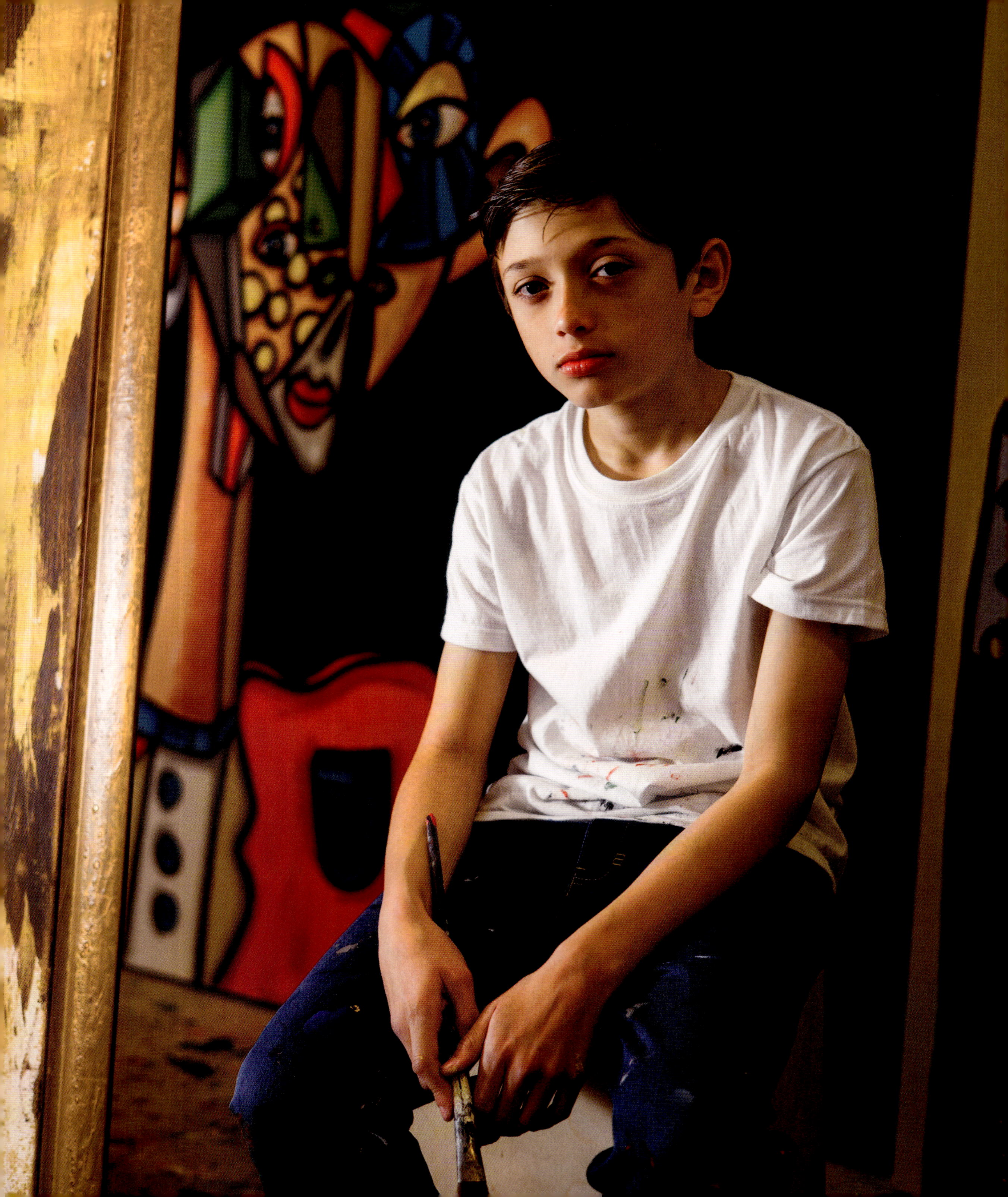

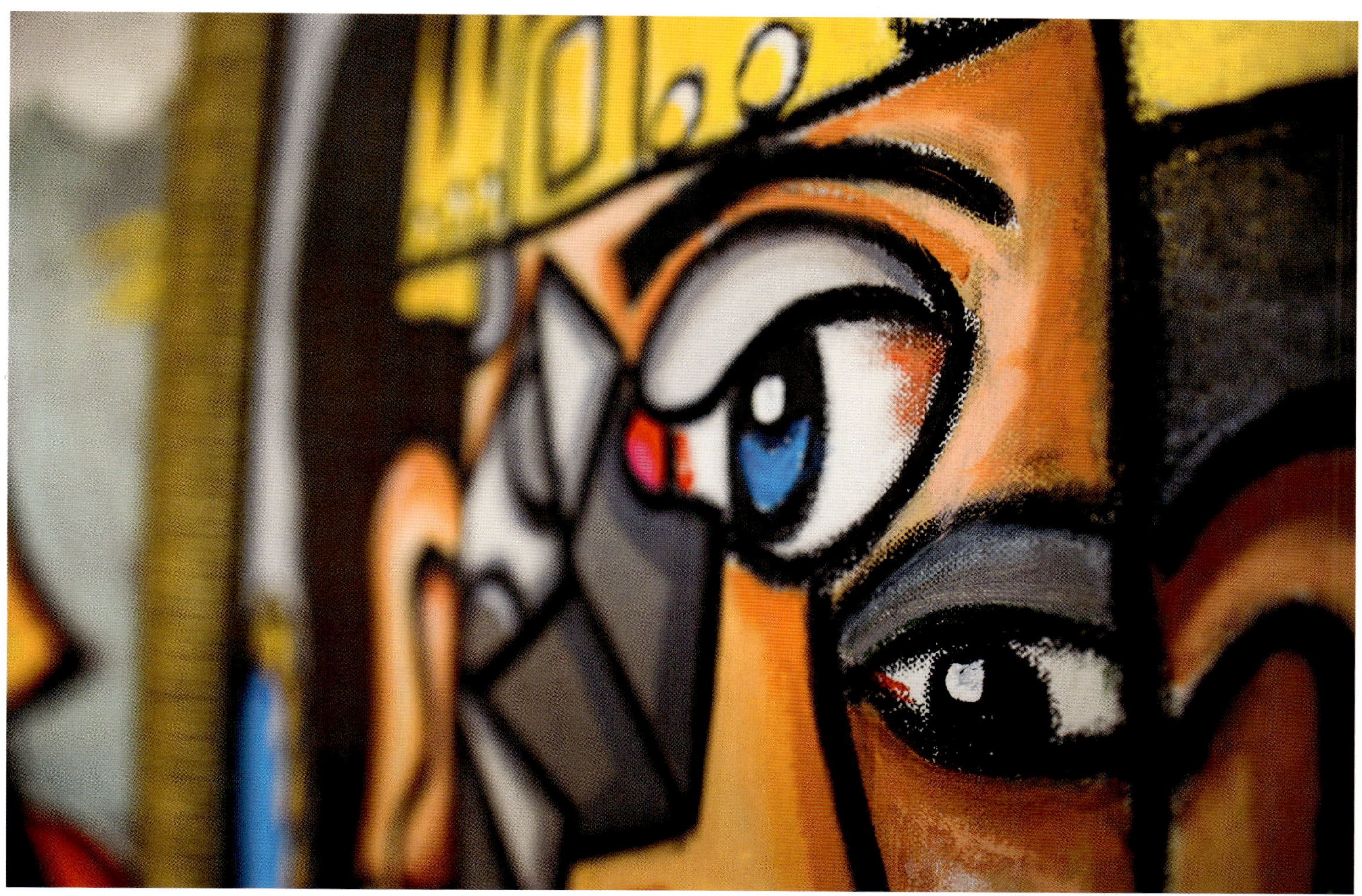

Style

Andres enjoys painting cubist portraits for many reasons, but one of the main draws is that he can maintain a consistent style across all the different colorful faces he creates. You can identify an Andres Valencia painting when you see one. At the same time, every portrait is unique.

"Andres tells us that he enjoys doing these kinds of disfigured characters," Lupe says. "He likes to create these faces that he has in his mind in his own way." Andres has also experimented with different things, like trying out landscapes similar to Bob Ross, along with paintings he's made in the style of Basquiat. "He knows he can do anything, because he's got the mind of an artist where he can do it if he wants to," Lupe says. "But I think he primarily sticks with cubism because that's what he enjoys the most."

Some people have said that Andres should try to learn how to paint realism instead of focusing on his abstract portraits, but Andres doesn't agree with this sentiment. "With abstract art, I feel like you can express yourself more than you can with realism," Andres says. "I've tried realism, and you always have to make sure you do this before you can do that. But with abstract art, you can just go for it and not have to worry about how it comes out. I like to go with the flow and not overthink it."

Above: Details of *The Monarch* (pg. 204). **Opposite:** Andres sits in his studio in front of the painting, *Minds in Motion* (pg. 258), March 2024.

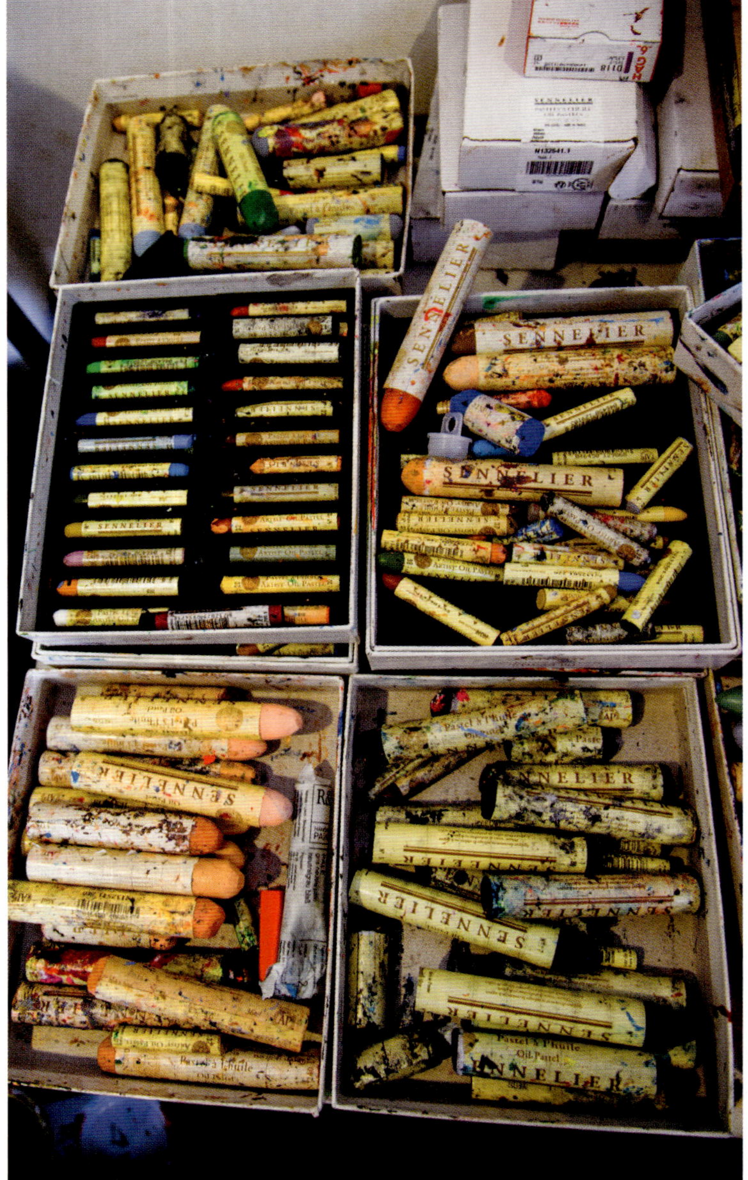

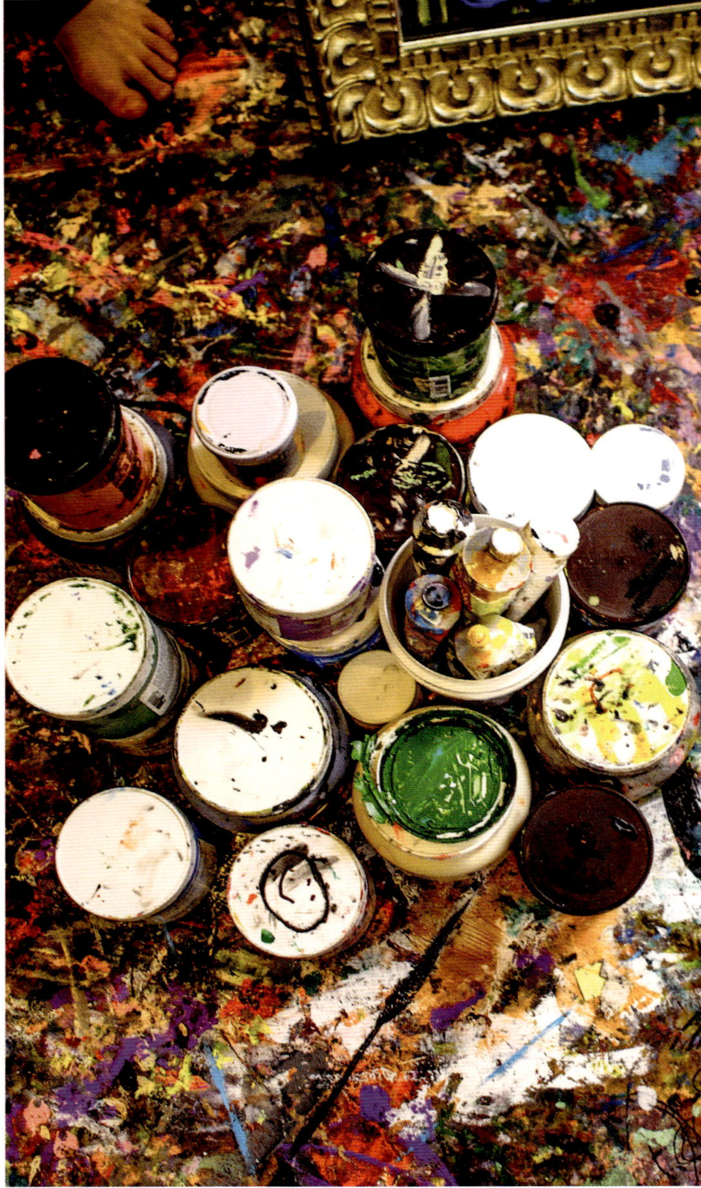

Mediums

Andres primarily works with oil pastel, acrylic paint, and canvas. These are his preferred mediums to express himself, and he especially loves oil pastels, explaining that "they're like butter" in their smoothness of applying fluid lines to canvas.

He begins a new piece by sketching the outline of his portrait with black oil pastel on a large, white canvas, finishing the character's outline before going back in with acrylic paint to add color and shading. "I like painting the best because it's just so calming to me," Andres says. "It also allows me to make really cool things." He has worked with oil paint on a few occasions and has created several sculptures out of clay, including many small heads, faces, and even a few Simpsons characters.

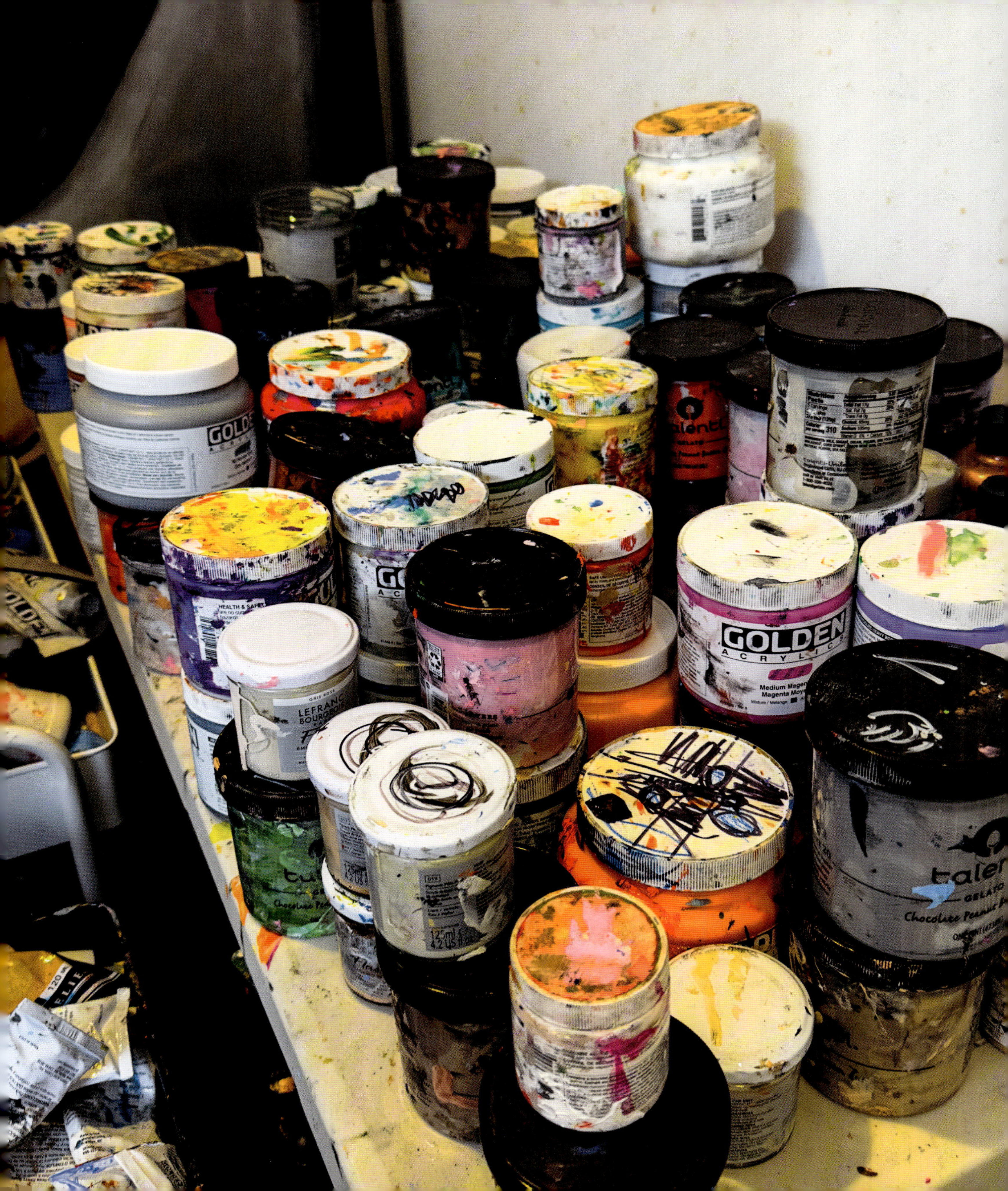

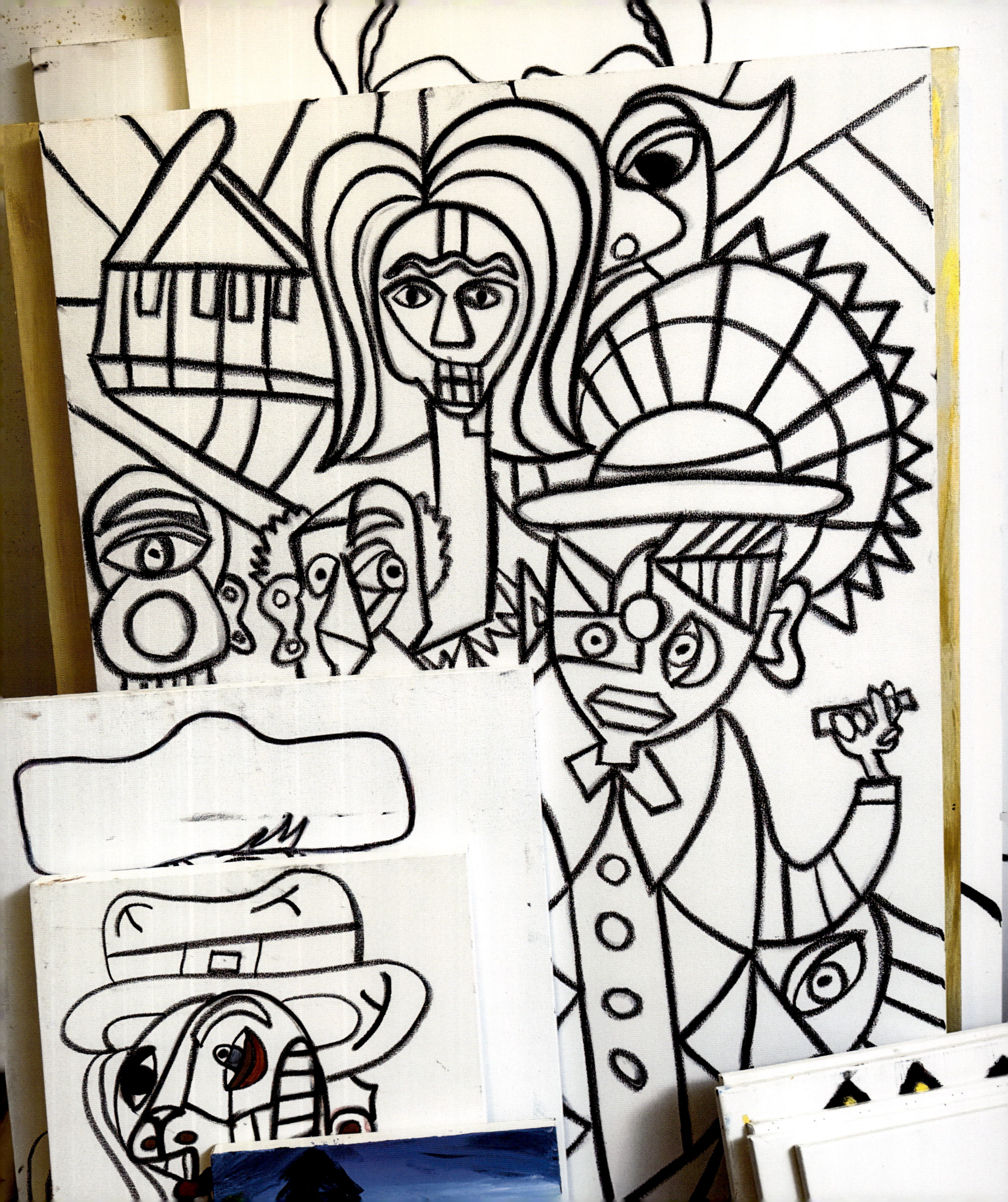

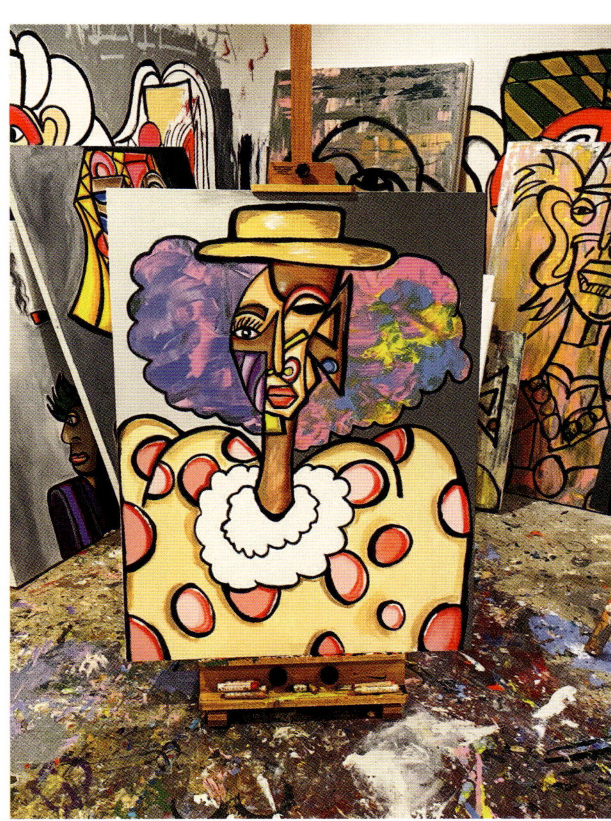

Canvases

Andres sometimes goes through a period where he does five or six small canvases in a row. Then suddenly, he's painting on a big canvas, and he'll continue working with several big canvases. Whether he wants to work with a small or large canvas often depends on his mood and what he feels like doing.

"When Andres first started working on big canvases, it was at the beginning of COVID," Lupe says. "I remember telling Elsa, 'I don't know how long we're going to be on lockdown. I don't know what kind of access we're going to have to materials.'" So Lupe went online and quickly bought a bunch of supplies: canvases, paints, brushes, and more. When Lupe went to pick them up, they were huge canvases, and he thought, *Oh my God. I didn't realize they were this big!* He didn't know what Andres was going to do with them—if he was going to be intimidated by these big canvases or not. "Elsa and I wondered, *What's going to happen now?*" Lupe says. "But as you can see in the videos of him painting, he's fearless. He just goes in. He's not afraid."

Andres was not fazed by the size of the canvases, and he regularly returns to paint on giant canvases that are sometimes even larger than he is. There are times he even has to use a step stool to reach the top of the canvas.

"When I see the canvas, it's up to my imagination to fill it," Andres says. "The bigger the canvas, the bigger point it's proving. And at first, sometimes people ask, 'Don't you ever get intimidated by the big canvas?' But for me, I just go for it." Andres is not afraid to express himself in whatever way he wants when the time comes to put the paintbrush to the canvas.

When Andres is asked what the difference is between working with big canvases versus creating something smaller, he explains, "To me, it's just a canvas. It's not about the size. It's just me putting down my ideas. It doesn't matter if it's a piece of paper, or it could even be a sticky note. I'm going to put down what's in my head and go for what I'm feeling." He is willing to create on any surface that will allow him to express his imagination.

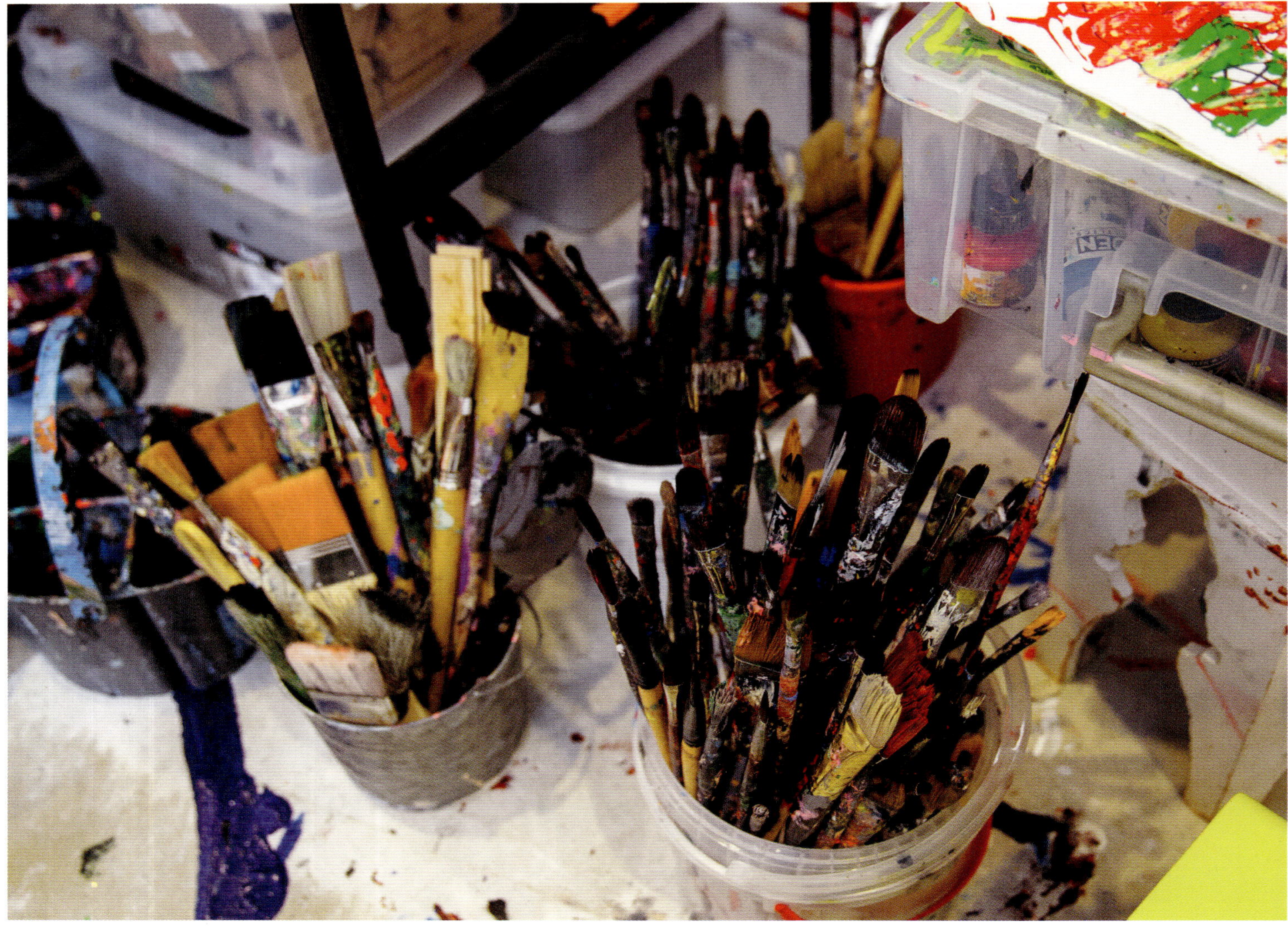

Art Supplies

Elsa and Andres typically buy his art supplies together now. Andres prefers to pick out the paint colors himself, and he tends to be very specific with the brushes he chooses. He feels the brushes very carefully with his fingers to see what he likes best before deciding which ones to purchase.

In the beginning, Elsa would buy him brushes, and he would say things like, "This is too soft. I don't like this." With a better understanding of what he likes, Elsa can now pick out brushes for Andres, but he still likes to go with her to get his supplies whenever possible. If he is about to start work on a bigger piece, Andres and Elsa will usually discuss what colors he is thinking of using so they can make sure he has the colors he needs.

Even planning ahead, sometimes Andres will use a color and realize it's not quite right. If he doesn't have the colors to create a new shade himself, they'll return to the store to get Andres exactly what he needs. Once he has the right paint in hand, Andres is able to continue working to bring his colorful vision to life.

Above: Andres's collection of paintbrushes. **Opposite:** Admiring one of his works in progress in the studio. **Following:** Andres posing in his studio, March 2024.

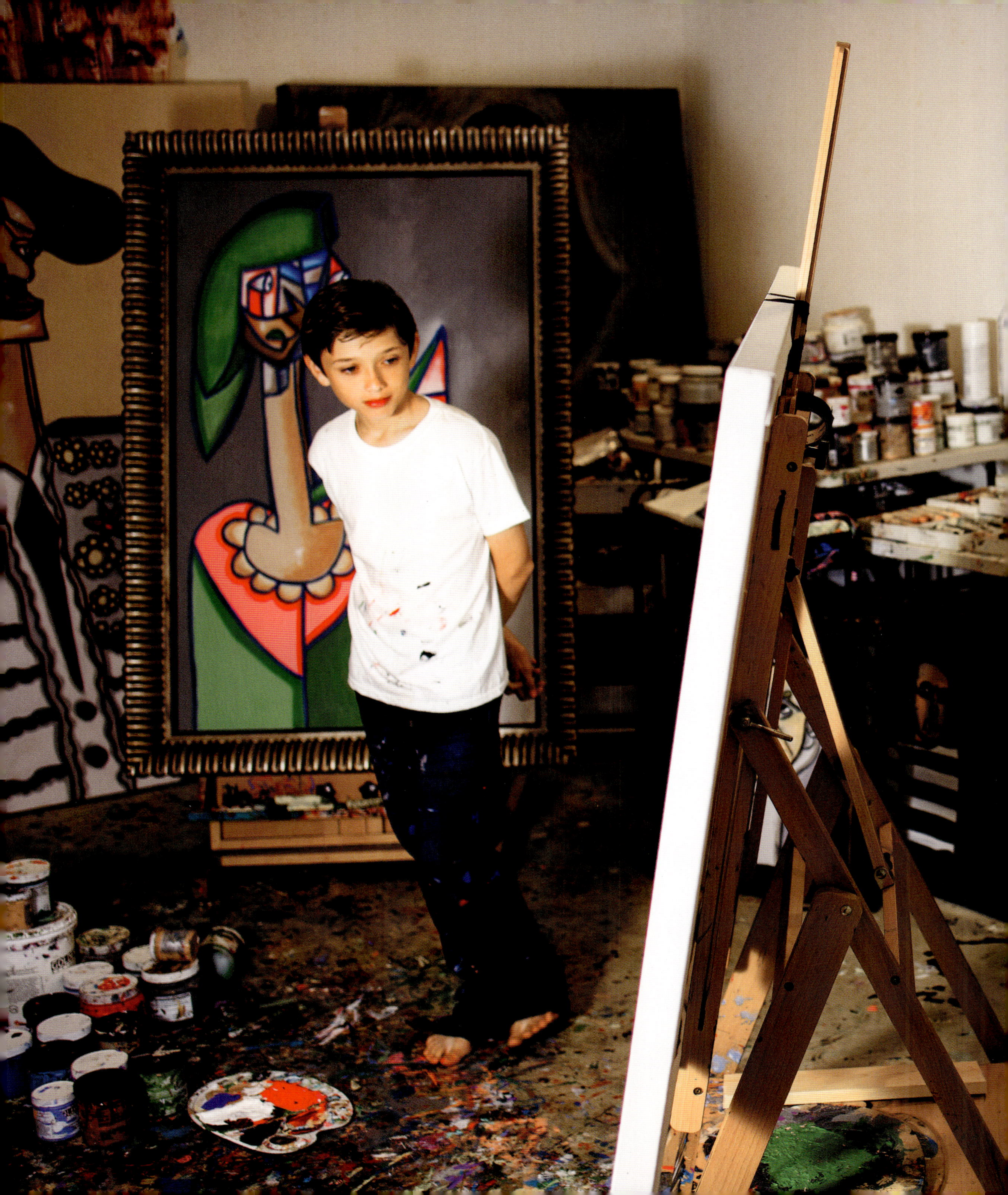

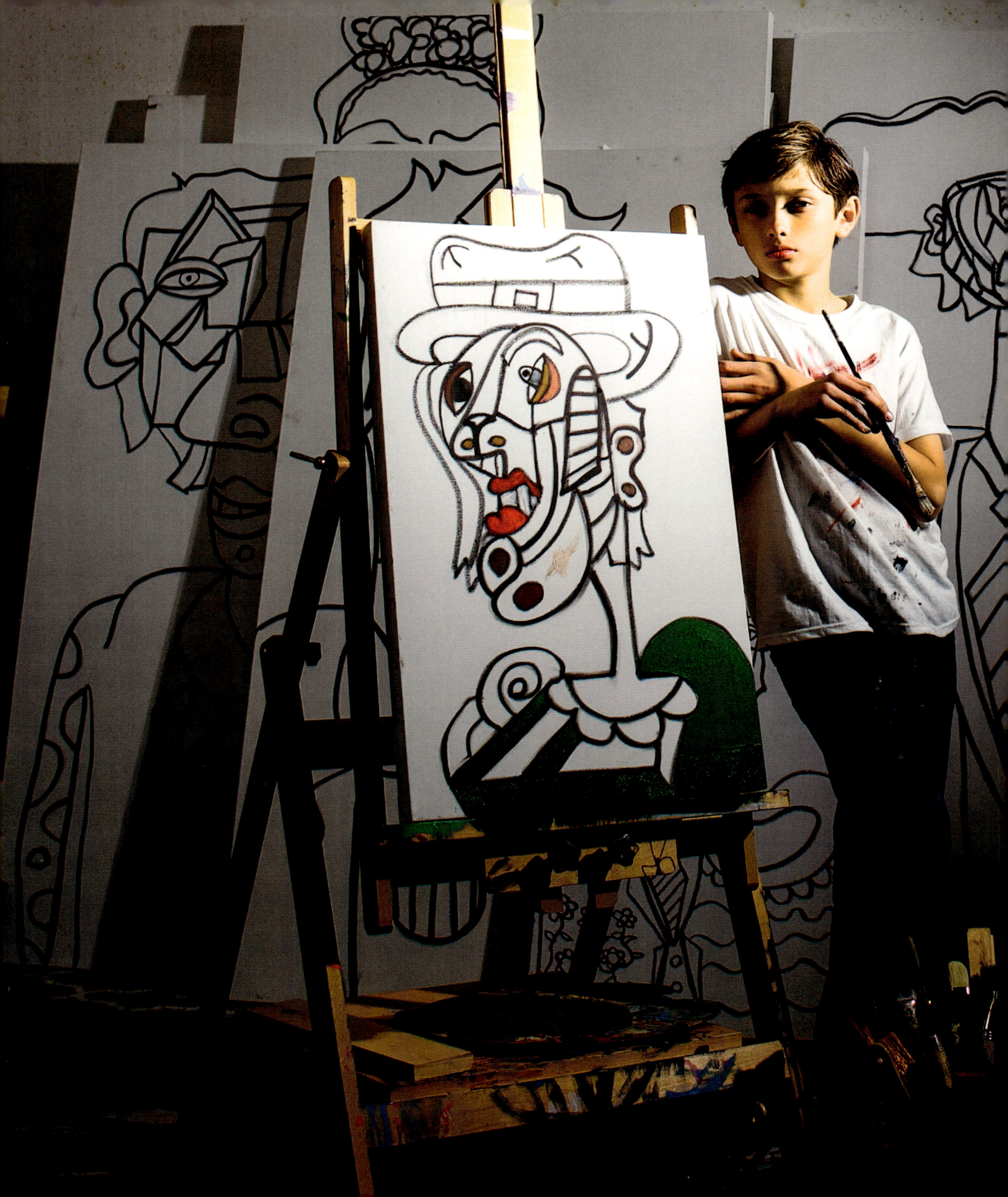

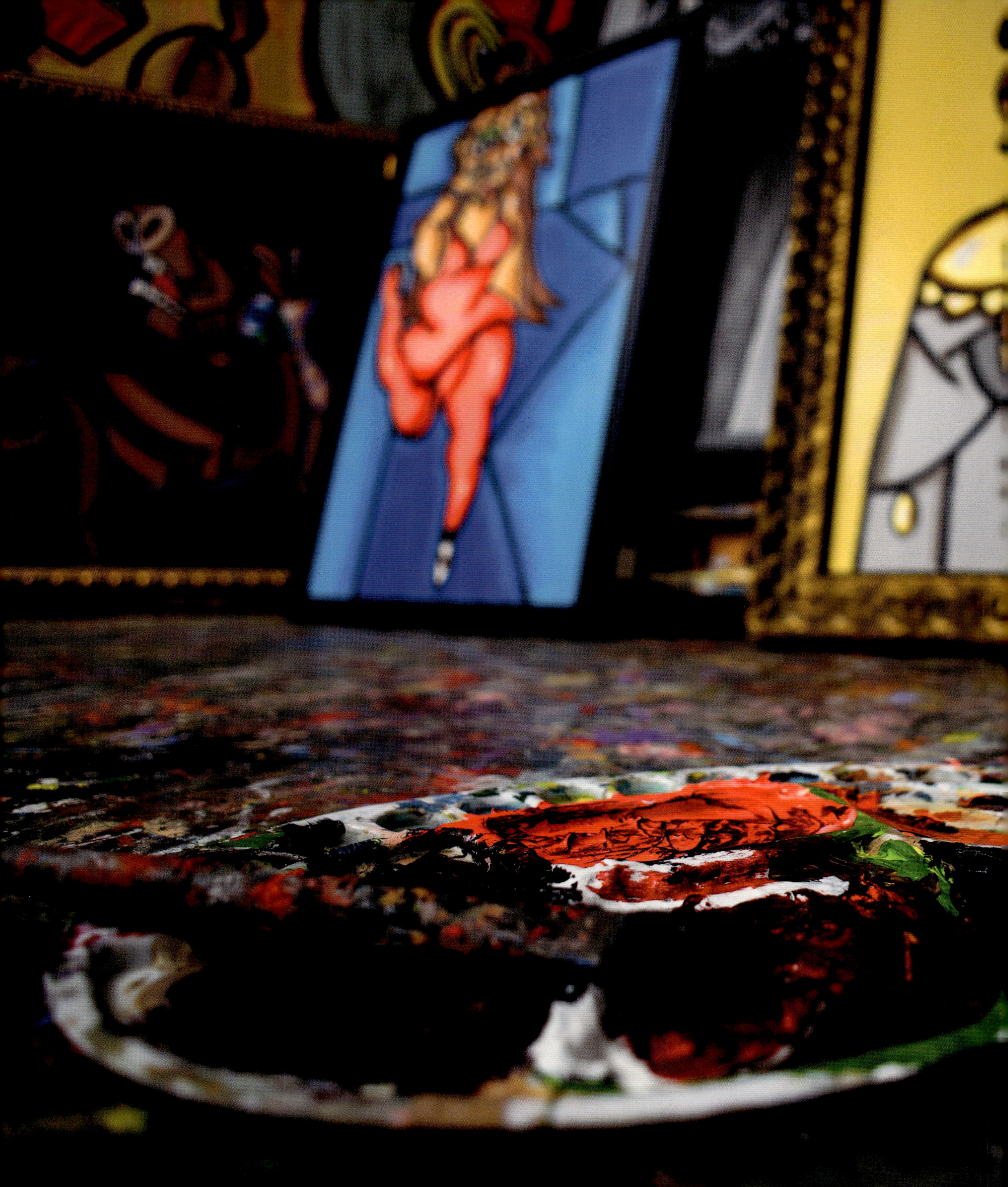

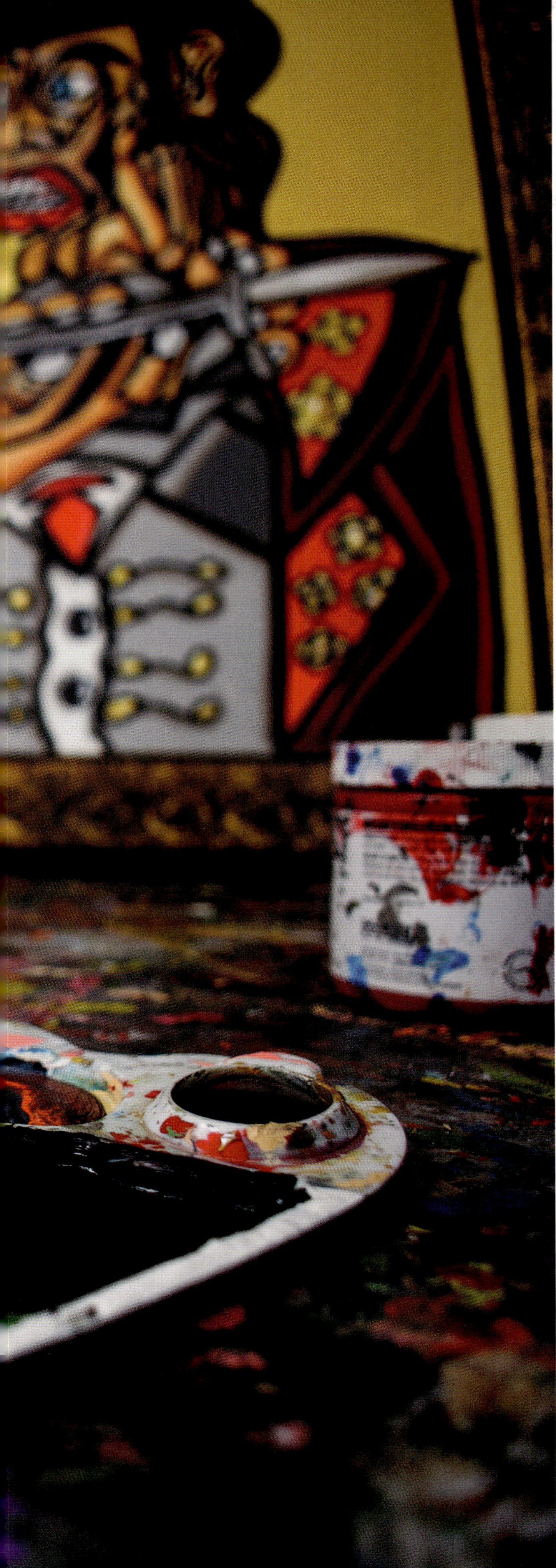

Color

Andres knows all about color theory. "He's really good at mixing and finding the colors he wants," Elsa says. "He works with the color wheel, and he's always looking at it for reference. The color wheel is his best friend." Andres has been known to say things like, "I like this color palette. The artist has mixed green and blue together, which works well." He'll recognize what colors pair nicely in other paintings and apply these lessons to his own work—pulling color inspiration from art books and other artists' paintings. Andres explains, "I look at the color wheel, and then I just go for it. Sometimes I might be inspired by the weather, like maybe I'll add a little bit of this yellow color because it's a sunny day."

Since Andres tends to use a lot of neutral colors, he always makes sure he has many different neutral hues at his disposal. If he becomes stuck on figuring out a color combo, he makes decisions to work through it. "Sometimes I'll just use a neutral color, because that's going to be safe."

His favorite color is blue. "Blue has always been my favorite color since I've known about color," Andres says. "It's just so nice." He also loves green and orange. These are the colors he uses most in his paintings, since he knows how to combine them in a number of interesting ways. Andres may start with one bold color, like green for the character's outfit, and then decide to do the background in another bright color, like yellow. He pictures in his mind what the color combinations may look like once applied to the canvas, and then he goes right in, adding them to the outline of the figure he's already put on the canvas with black oil pastel.

Composition

While Andres's paintings typically feature only one character, sometimes he creates a piece with multiple characters or faces. When asked how he decides to include one or several characters, he explains that it's random, "I'll start drawing one guy, and then I'll do a line or something, and I'll be like, well, this kind of looks like this could be this. So then I just start to add more, and then it just turns into something else and leads to me making another figure."

Andres isn't afraid to experiment with the way he paints his characters' body parts either. Long necks, crooked arms, and square shoulders can all be found in his work. His subjects are usually depicted from the waist up, but on rare occasions, the lower half of the body does come into the frame. Another common element found in his paintings is a decent amount of negative space around his characters. Sometimes this negative space is painted a bright color, while other times it is more neutral. The decision on how to shade the negative space often depends on how colorful the character is.

Opposite: Andres poses beside his paintings *Roberto* (pg. 263), *Sofía Vergara* (pg. 245), *Romero* (pg. 256), and *Lourdes* (pg. 227), March 2024.

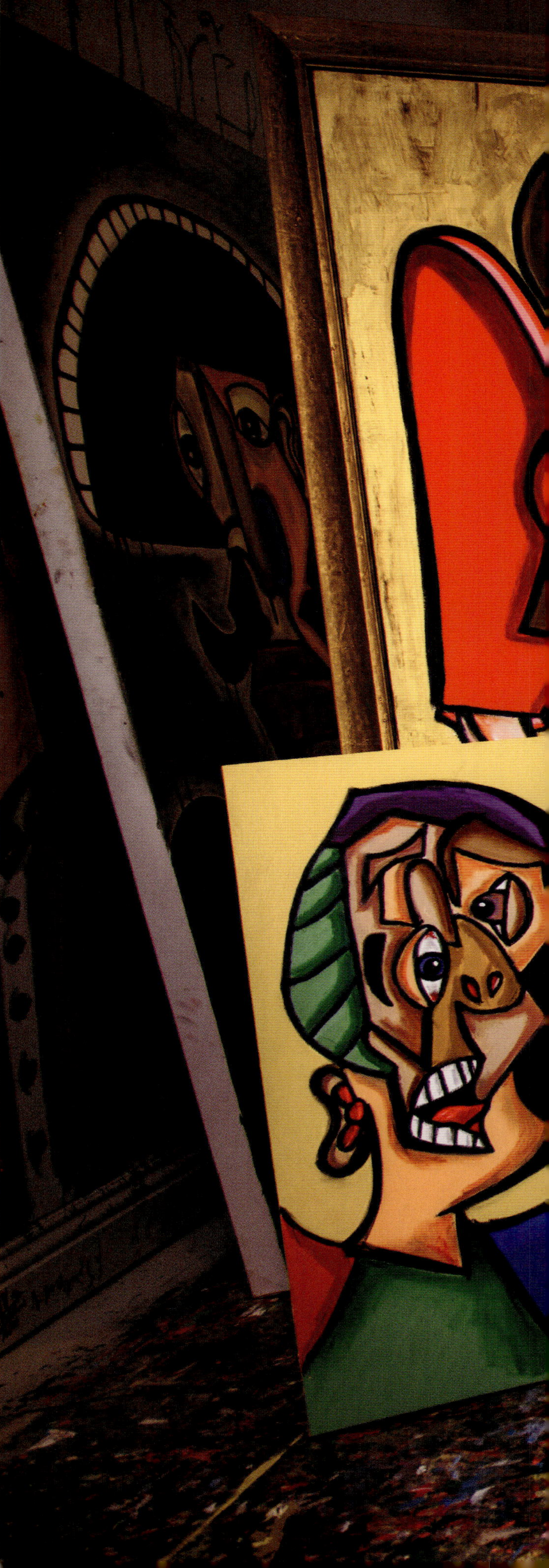

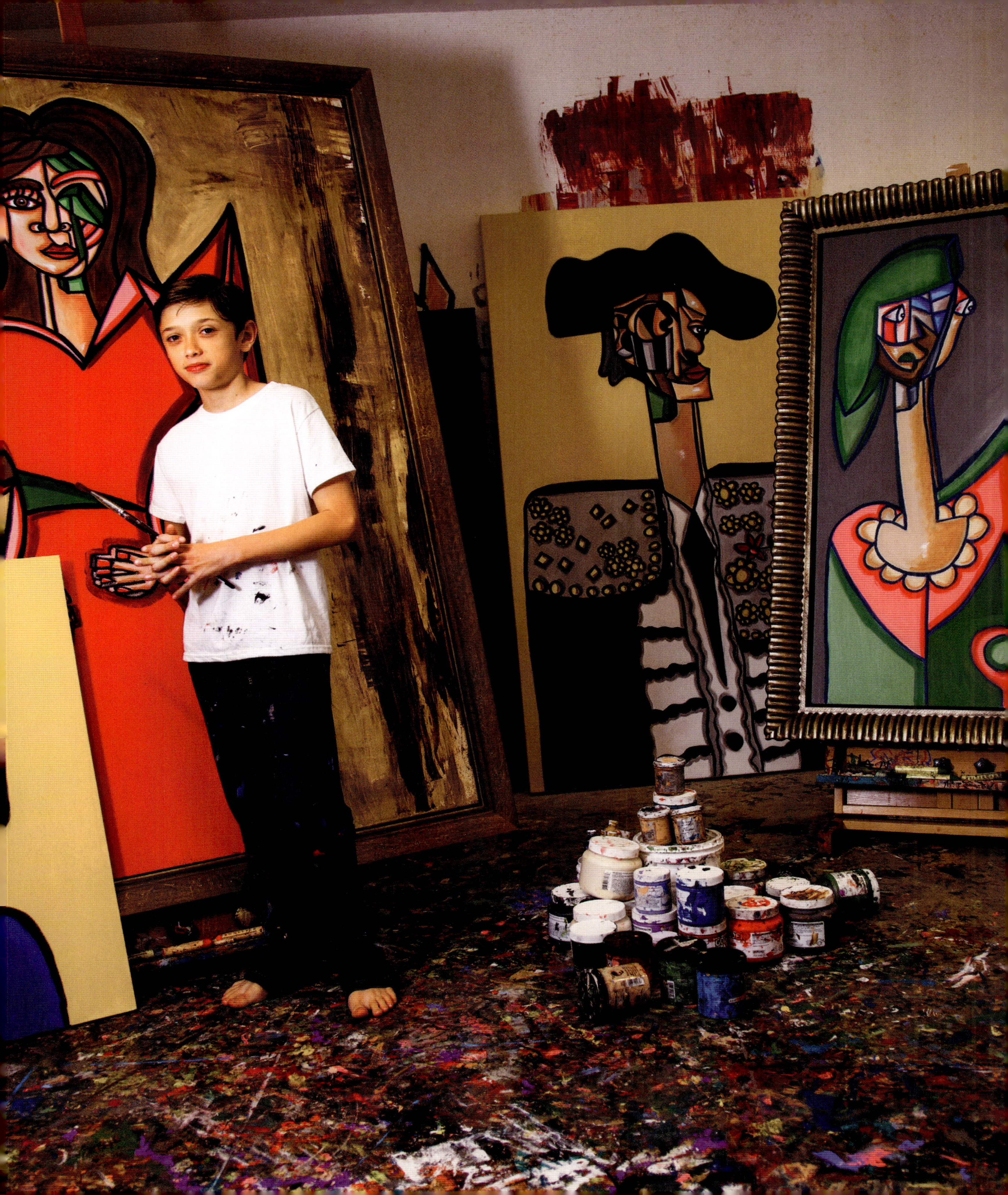

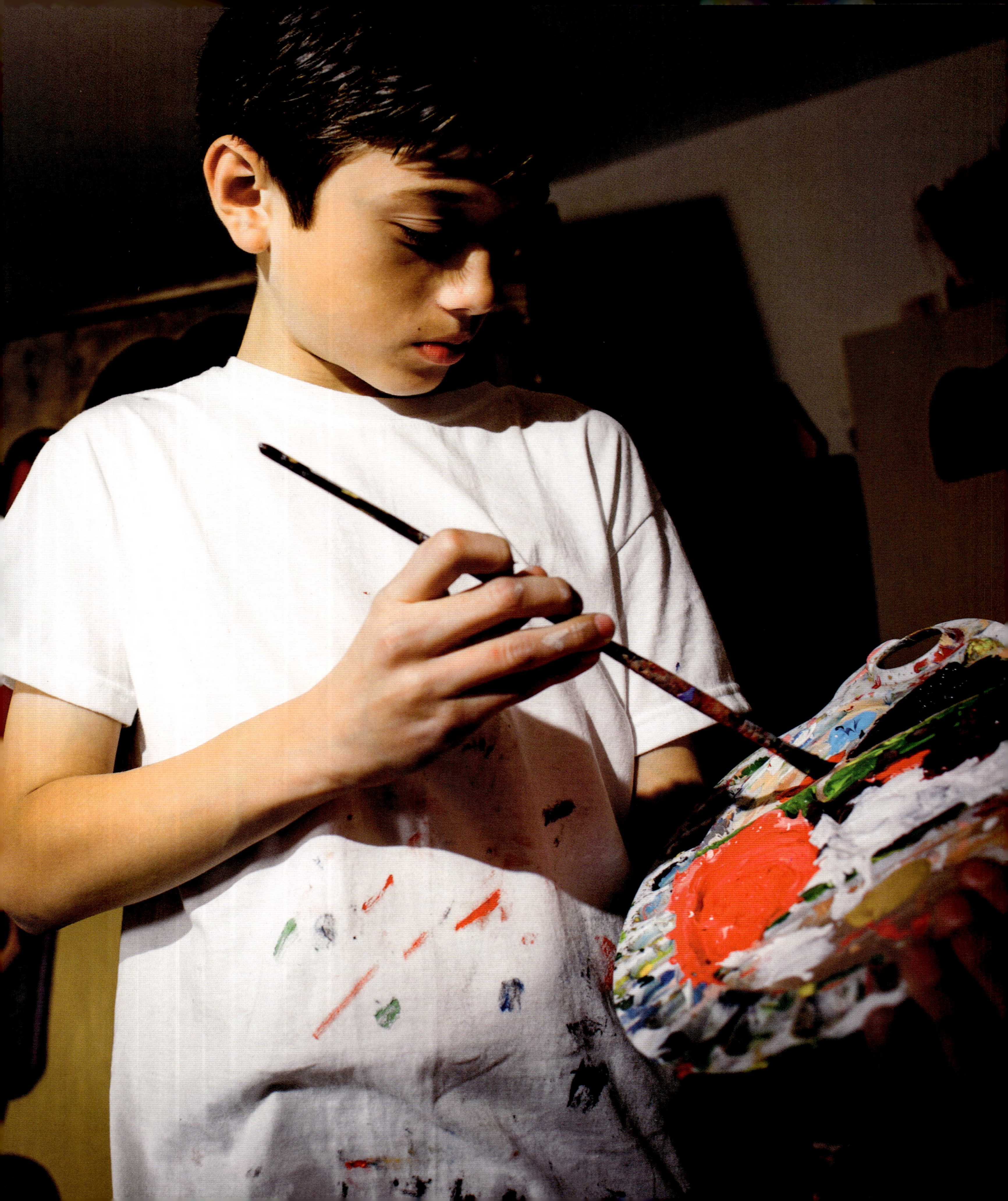

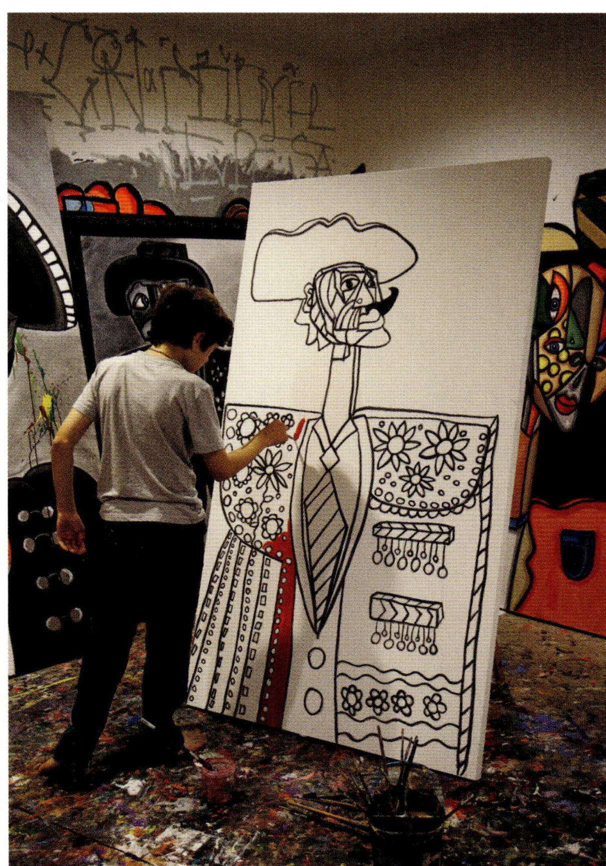

Recording Andres in Action

After Andres first started getting attention for his artwork, some people doubted he was the one creating his paintings. To combat this, Elsa decided to start filming him in action so people could see how he paints.

"I kept hearing people claiming that Andres wasn't the one making his art," Elsa says. "I couldn't believe it. People really thought me and Lupe were helping him." So, Elsa decided to start recording Andres to prove that he was doing it all on his own. She put a video up on Instagram, and people really enjoyed it. And then she continued doing it. "People were like, 'Thank you for showing us, this is amazing.'"

Once Elsa began posting these videos, she and Andres started a routine where Andres tells her when he has an idea and wants to go down to his studio to create. The idea can be something as singular as just a nose. It's typically not an idea for a whole painting. Elsa explains, "It's always like a hat or a hand or an eye. Lately it's been the eye a lot, so he'll say, 'I have an idea for an eye. Can you come down?' He tells me this because he knows I want to record it."

However, there are times when Andres wants to paint alone, without cameras present. Sometimes he tells Elsa he's going to paint in his room and that he doesn't want her to come in. She respects these wishes, as she never wants to interfere with his creative process. "There's been times where he'll close the door in his studio so he has privacy," Elsa says. "I'll hear the music playing, and I'll peek in and he'll tell me, 'I want to be alone. I don't want you to record me now.' And I respect that. So then I leave him to create and do his own thing. That's why we don't have a recording of every piece he creates, because some of them he makes alone."

Anyone with Instagram can see these videos of Andres creating art on his profile @andresvalenciaart. The videos are pieces of art themselves, as they show a time lapse of Andres sketching his abstract characters using oil pastel. Viewers can watch how he fluidly creates his unique cubist portraits in a sped-up style.

People from all around the world comment on Andres's Instagram posts and send him messages. His social media presence allows more and more people to see his art every day. As Lupe says, "We're very lucky to be living in a time where somebody like him can show the world the gift he has."

Through the videos Elsa records, people are able see Andres at work and learn what his process is like, starting with black oil pastel to sketch out the faces and torsos before filling in the outline with paint. By watching these videos, you get to appreciate the art as a finished piece when it's done, while also seeing how it came together. Viewers can watch Andres at work and see the fun he has in creating, time and time again.

Above: A still from one of the videos Elsa recorded of Andres painting in his studio. **Opposite:** Andres mixing colors on his palette, March 2024.

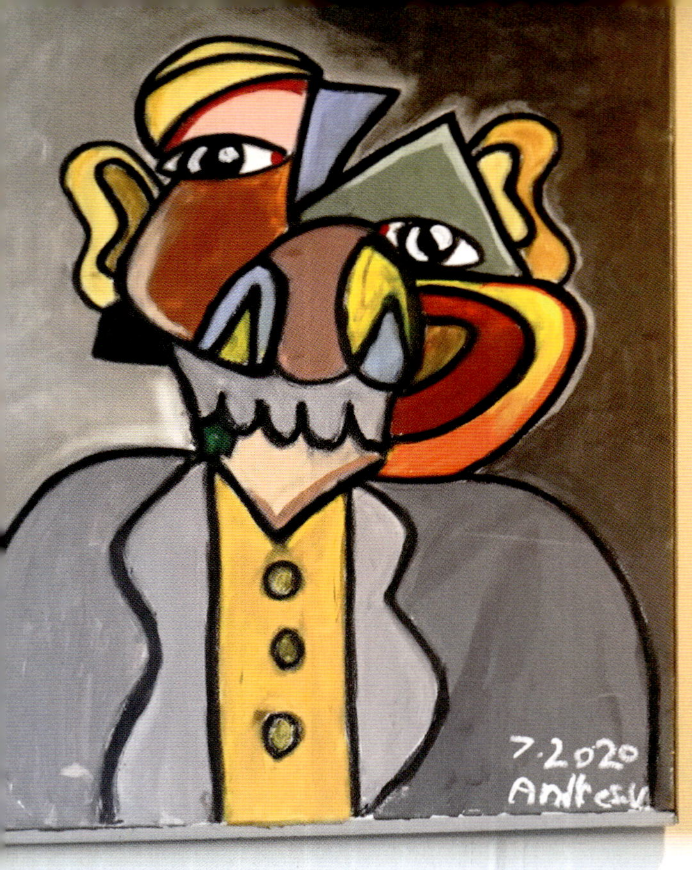
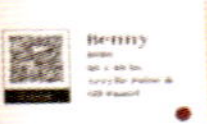
Benny
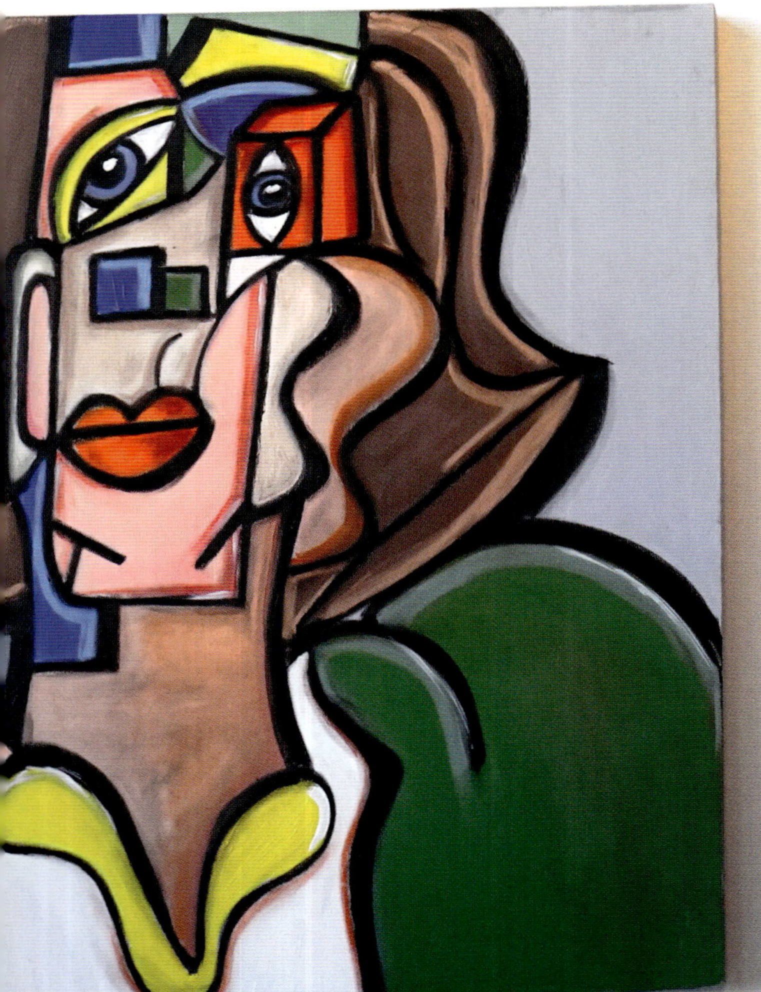
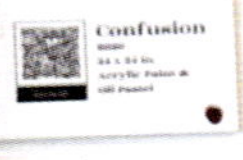
Confusion

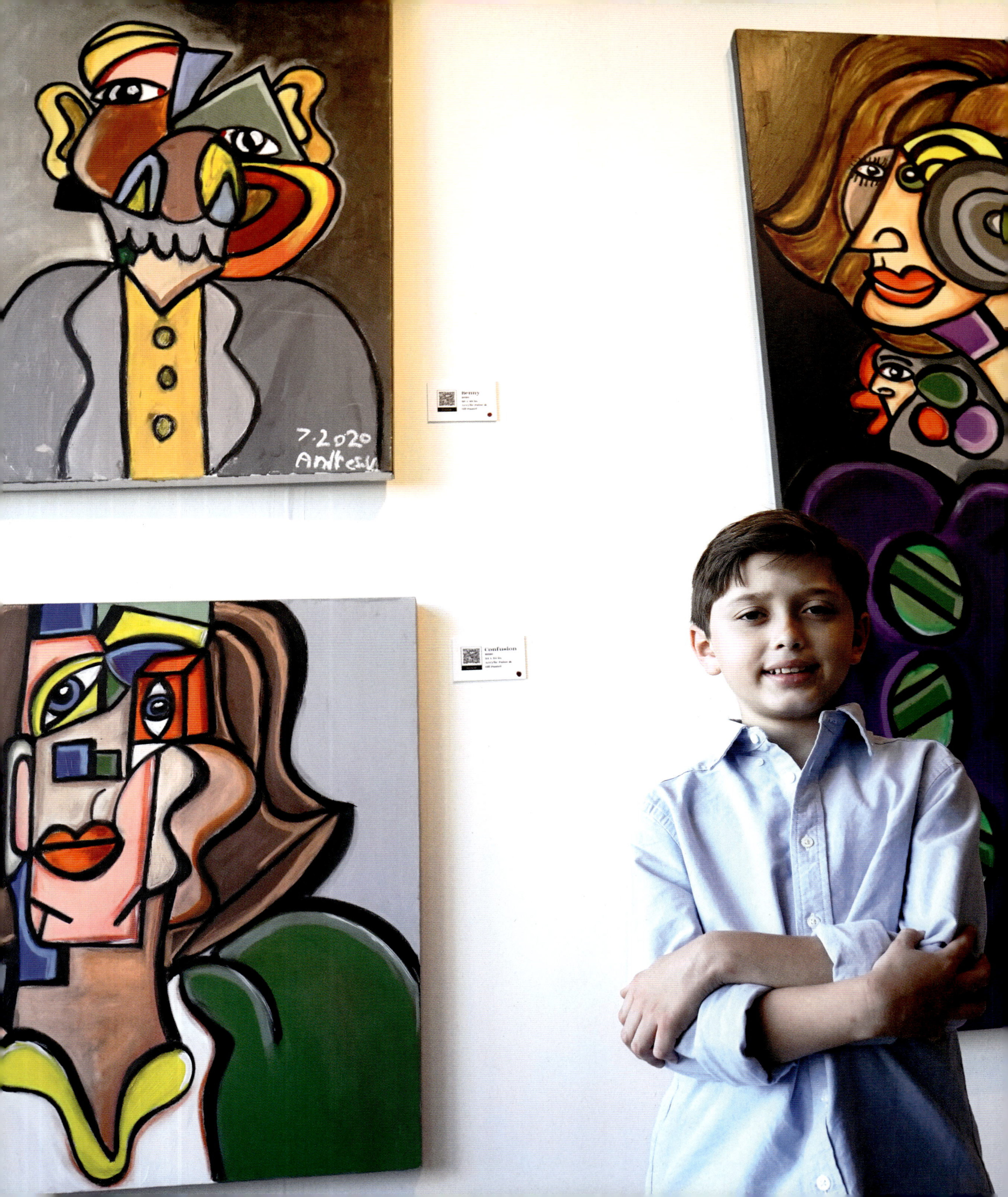

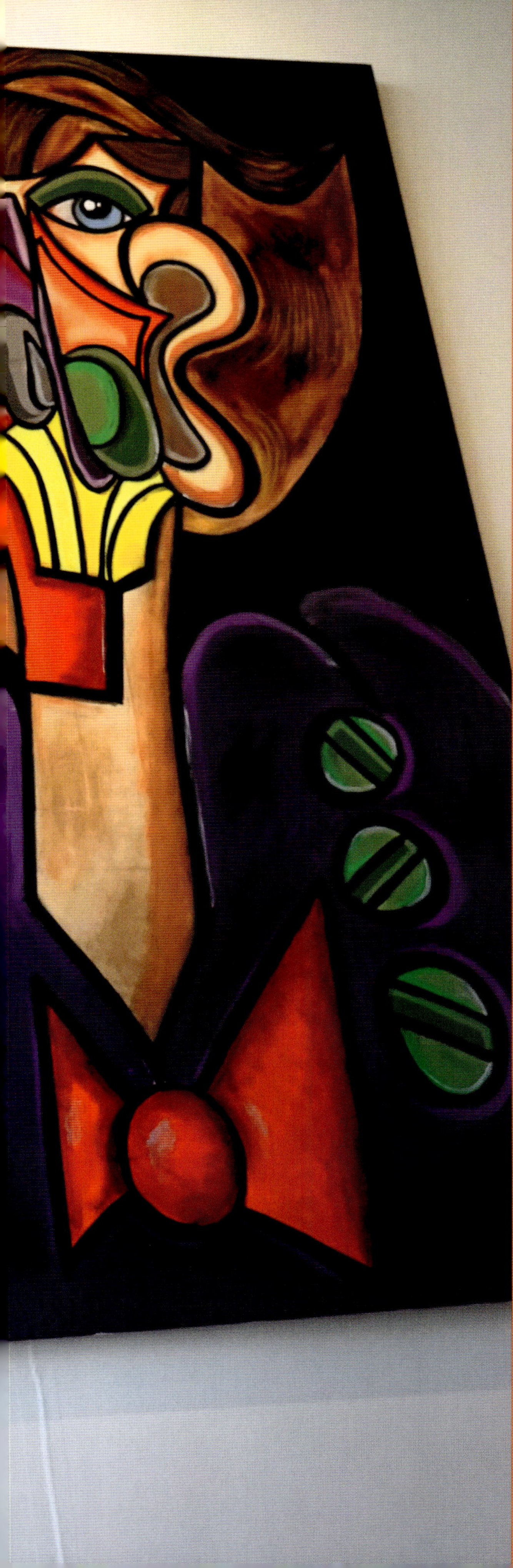

BREAKING BIG

Throughout Andres's time in first and second grade, whenever Elsa ran into the mothers of his classmates, they often got excited to speak with her about her son's artistic prowess. Not only were his fellow students noticing his talent, but parents in the community were also learning about it. Across the greater San Diego area, Andres began garnering attention. Word spread around the community, and people learned of his passion for painting. Andres even started selling small paintings to family friends for twenty dollars. This was only the beginning of Andres earning money for his work.

Andres stands in front of three of his paintings on display at Art Miami, December 2021, age ten. *Photo by Lynne Sladky, Associated Press.*

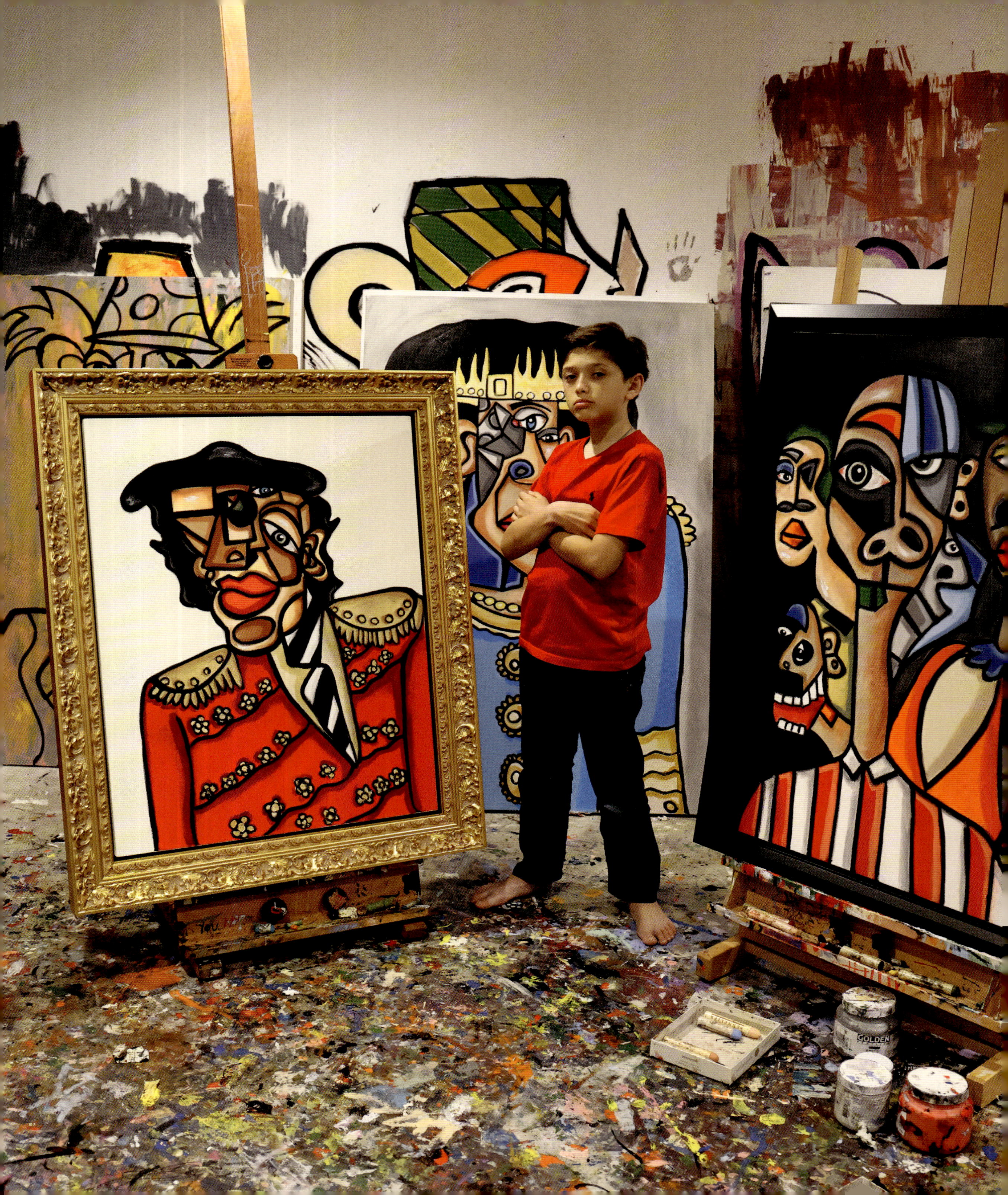

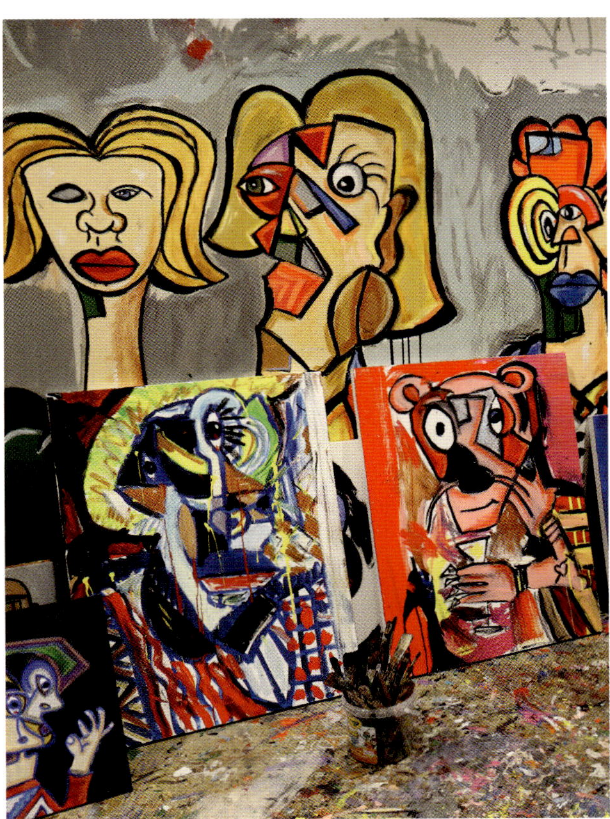

 Completed works leaning against his studio wall, August 2023. **Opposite:** Andres poses with paintings in his studio, September 2023. The painting in the gold frame is *Traje De Luces* (pg. 252).

Artistic Talent, Identified

One person who has been instrumental in championing Andres's artwork is Bernie Chase, a good friend of Lupe's and the founder of Chase Contemporary, a modern art gallery in the SoHo neighborhood of New York City. Bernie has known Andres since he was six years old and has witnessed Andres evolve from a child sketching for fun to painting more sophisticated pieces. "Andres was drawing on little pieces of paper whenever I came over, and I always liked seeing them," Bernie says. "In the beginning, it was just this little game we played where I asked him, 'Can I buy that?' And he'd sell some of his sketches to me." When Bernie first offered to pay for his work, Andres thought, "Wow, he must really want it since he's paying me so much. I was happy that he cared about my art."

Bernie has long been impressed by the way Andres paints. "His creativity comes from inside his belly and moves out through his arm without thinking. It's second nature," he says. "Whenever Andres wants to draw, there's magic going on in his mind, and then it just flows right out from his fingertips. It's always done the first round. He doesn't really plan. When he has a big canvas that he wants to work with, he just starts."

Bernie says that if you watch Andres draw or sketch, you'll notice he doesn't leave the canvas or the paper very often. "It's all very fluid," Bernie says. "I've been at the dinner table eating with him and the family, and we're not even talking about painting. Then he'll just leave, deciding he wants to go paint. He just goes straight to the canvas and gets to work, there's no practice." Nothing is more important for Andres than to follow the urge to create, regardless of when or where it arises, and Bernie has always been impressed with the way Andres prioritizes his art.

On Bernie's visit to San Diego in 2019, Lupe invited Bernie over to show him some of Andres's newer works. At first, Bernie couldn't quite believe Andres had created all these new, amazing paintings, or that they were created by a child at all. Bernie offered Andres a hundred dollars for one of his pieces, and Andres jokingly replied, "How about $5,000?" Bernie agreed to the price, and even started to write the check out to Andres for the amount before Elsa interrupted them and put a stop to it.

"During COVID," Lupe says, "Andres started painting big canvases that were thirty-by-forty-inches. When Bernie saw these, he wanted to buy one, but Elsa said, 'No, he's too little.' We didn't want to sell things at this point." Andres was selling sheets of paper with sketches on them and little things he'd made to friends and family, but nothing else. Bernie took a big interest in his work and tried to convince the family that it was serious art he wanted to sell. From then on, Andres had Bernie's full attention—he knew the work this young man was creating was something really special.

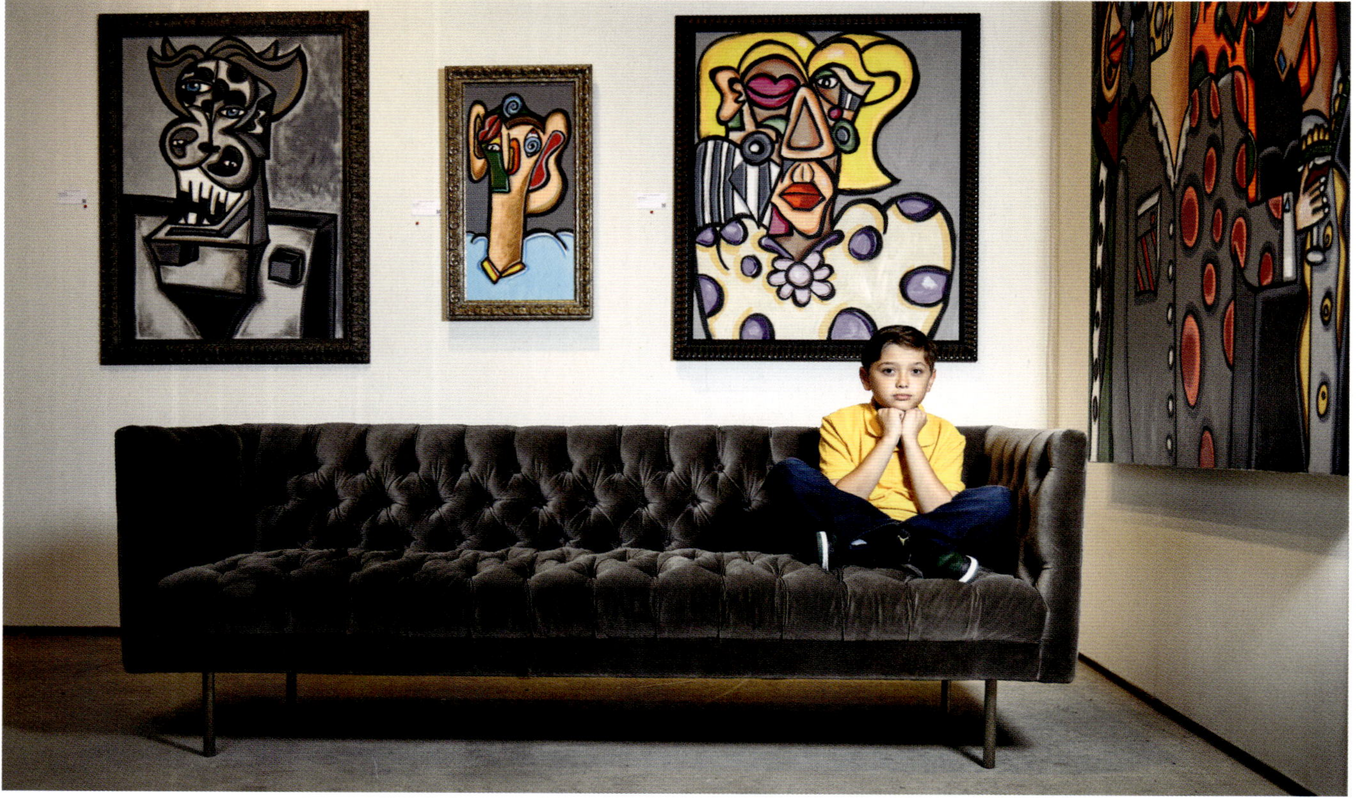

Andres's Work Goes on Display

At the end of summer 2021, Bernie asked Elsa if he could borrow ten of Andres's canvases. He wanted to put them on display in his gallery in New York to gauge other people's reactions to Andres's work. The family had not displayed any of Andres's artwork publicly or sold any of his canvases previously. Elsa felt very protective over her son and his paintings, so she was hesitant to allow Bernie to show Andres's paintings. Bernie was very persistent though, and eventually he convinced her. Shortly thereafter, Andres's paintings were shown in public for the first time at Chase Contemporary.

The Valencia family flew out to New York together to visit the gallery and see Andres's work on display. Lupe recalls the experience: "It was really amazing, truly incredible to see. We're like, 'Wow, his art is in a gallery in New York!' Andres couldn't believe it either."

This first showcase garnered a great response, and many people who visited the gallery inquired about purchasing Andres's artwork. Because of this, Bernie continued to ask if he could sell some of Andres's paintings, but Elsa remained firm, telling him no. Initially, people didn't even know they were created by a child artist. Bernie revealed Andres's age to the inquiring buyers, which only made them want to buy the paintings more, since they couldn't believe a young boy had created such incredible pieces. Still, Elsa held strong in her conviction not to allow the sale of Andres's paintings, but the positive reaction from the public was starting to convince her that perhaps she could allow some of Andres's paintings to be sold soon if the right opportunity came along.

Above: Andres sits on a sofa at Art Miami, with his paintings hung on the walls around him. **Opposite:** Andres studying his large painting *Venacube* (pg. 216). *Photos by George Kamper.*

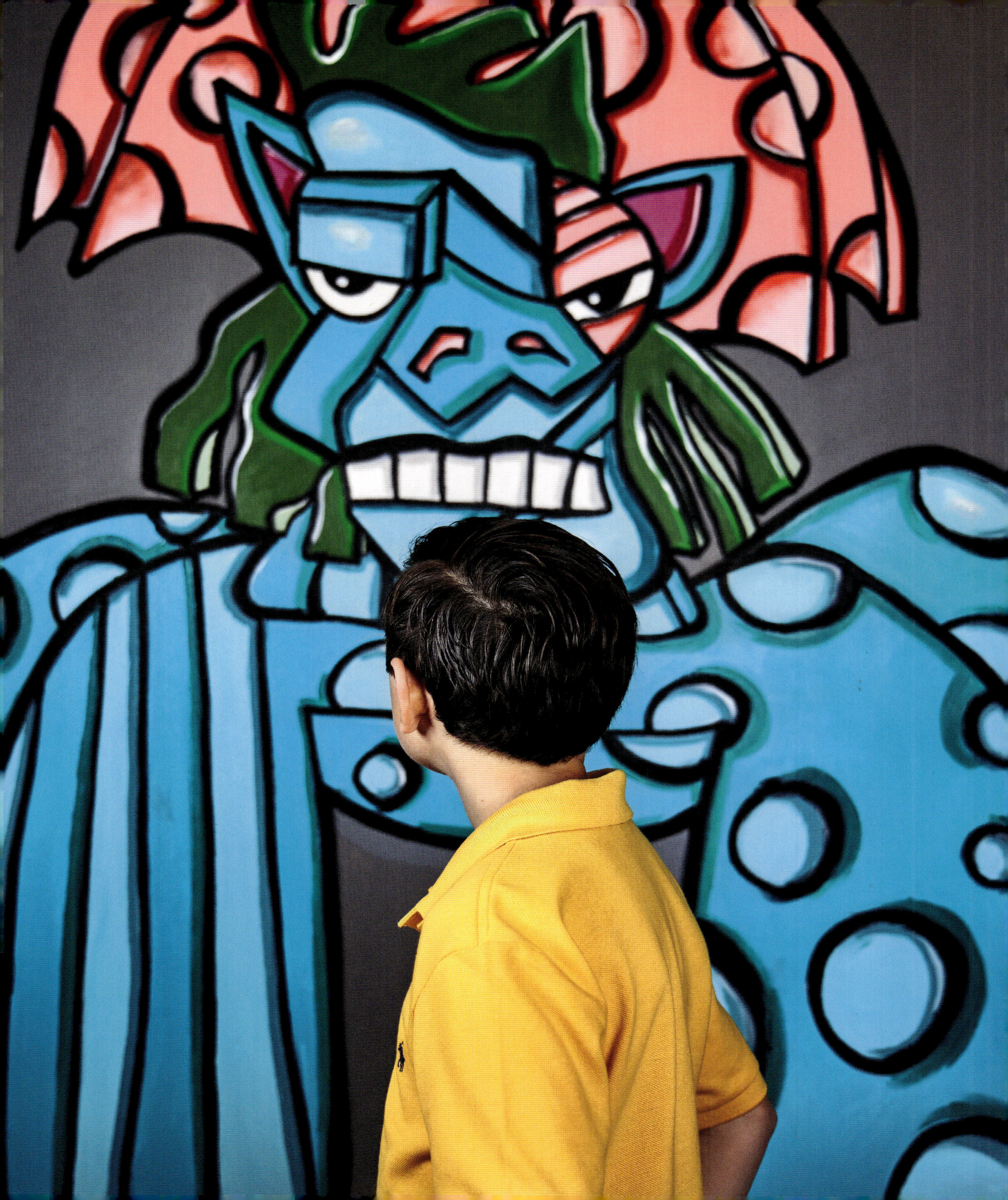

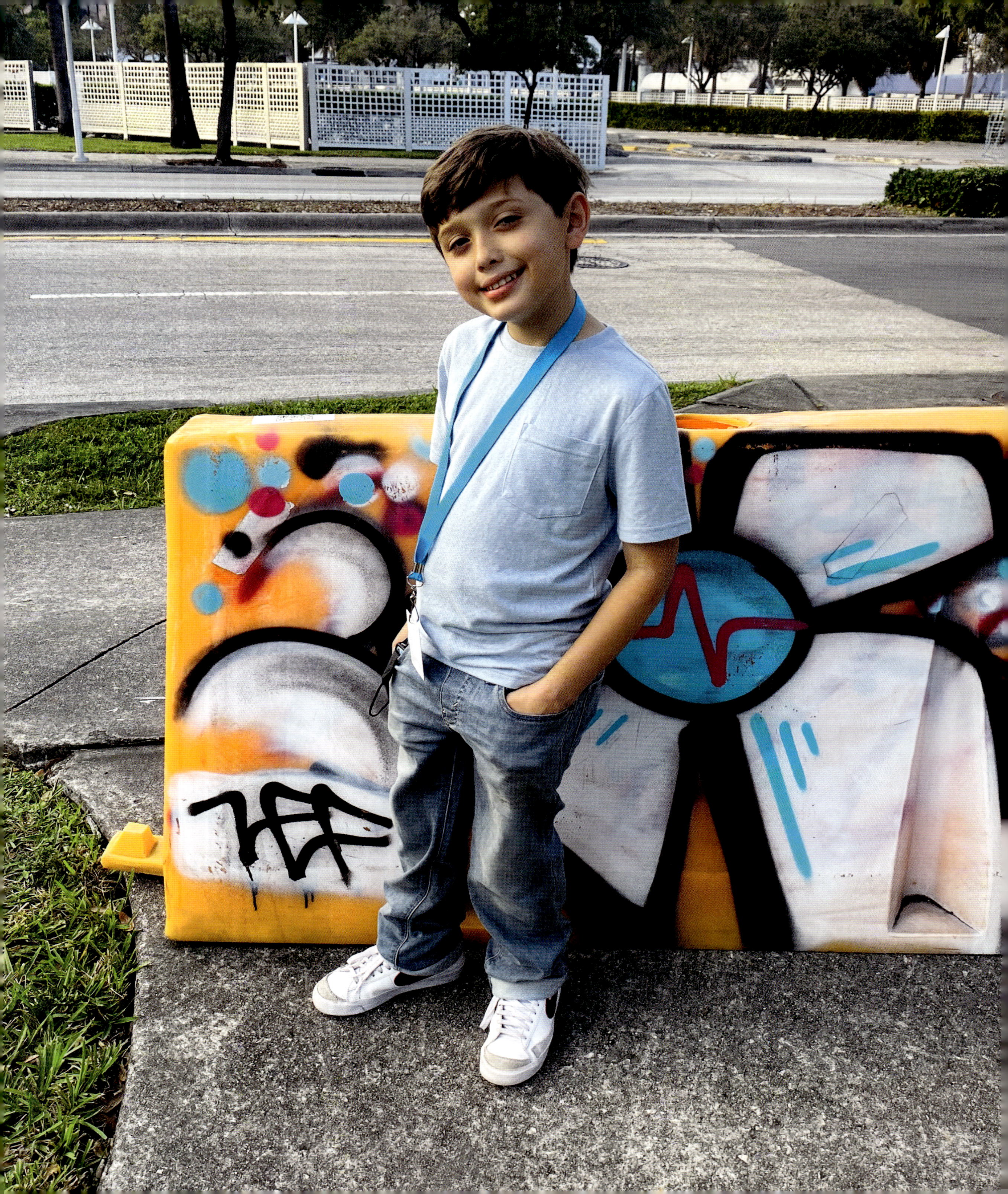

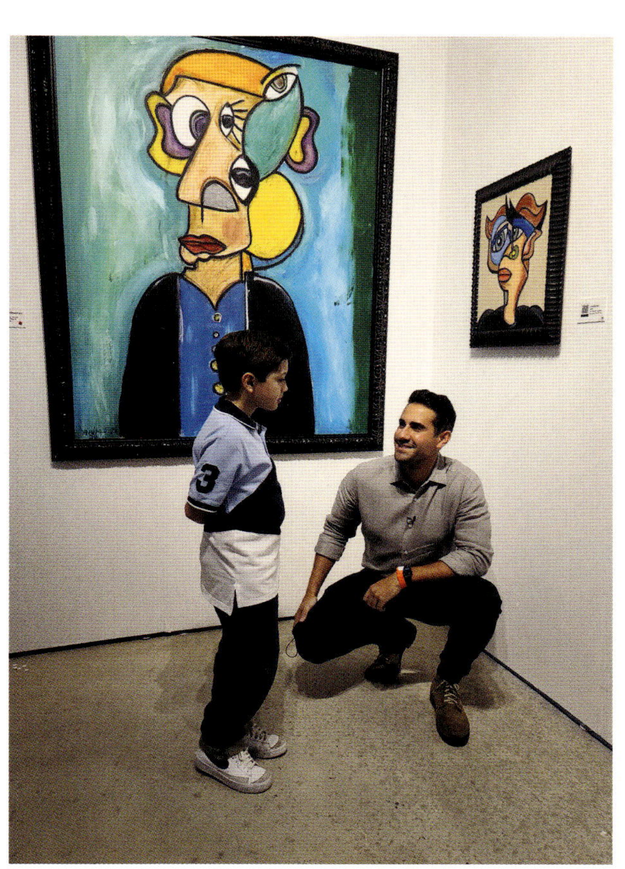

Above: Andres is interviewed at his booth by Victor Oquendo from *ABC News/Good Morning America*.
Opposite: Andres outside the Art Miami fair, ready to take on another day of creativity.

Art Miami

Not wanting to give up on selling Andres's paintings, Bernie contacted Nick Korniloff, the director of Art Miami, one of the biggest and most respected art fairs in the world. Bernie told Nick about Andres and how talented he was and proposed the idea of having Andres show some of his paintings at Art Miami.

Nick recalls the exchange: "Bernie approached me and said, 'What if I told you I had this amazing ten-year-old boy who is an incredible painter with an old soul? He listens to music from fifty years ago, and he paints in this really interesting way where his hand never leaves the canvas.'" Nick was skeptical at first. He wasn't sure someone so young would be able to showcase work on the same level as the other pieces featured. Nick explains, "We've worked with galleries that represent the estates of very well-established career artists. But the attendees also want to see what's new. So that's what the fair is always about, giving artists exposure and getting immediate feedback." When Bernie showed Nick examples of Andres's work, he was pleasantly surprised.

Nick admits he was a bit mesmerized when he first saw images of Andres's creations. He thought some of the paintings could hang on any wall at the art fair and that people would likely assume it was from an established artist. Nick found that Andres's art had the potential to develop into something very special and unique. "Once I agreed to show Andres's work at the fair," Nick shares, "I told Bernie, 'This is either going to be a tremendous success or a complete failure.'"

Bernie responded by saying, "Don't worry, this is going to work out. I promise you. It's the perfect time, right after the pandemic. It's a feel-good story. I've seen enough of his stuff to know he's multitalented."

Eventually, after several discussions, Nick gave Bernie the go-ahead to let Andres show at Art Miami, even giving him his own booth, which allowed him to list some of his paintings for sale. Because of the positive reaction Andres garnered at his first showcase at Chase Contemporary earlier in 2021, Elsa agreed to let her son show and list his paintings for sale at Art Miami.

A portion of the proceeds raised went to the Perry J. Cohen Foundation, named for the son of Nick's wife, Pamela. Perry was tragically lost at sea at age fourteen in 2015. The foundation supports the arts and marine and wildlife preservation and education. Since the fair had taken a year off in 2020 because of the pandemic, Nick believed art fans would enjoy seeing paintings from an inspiring young artist like Andres at the December 2021 fair—after all, it was a positive story folks could get behind.

Bernie and Nick decided not to do any pre-press ahead of the event. Instead, they simply hung Andres's canvases and let them speak for themselves. They wanted to keep the situation as neutral as possible to see how people would react. Even though the show didn't open until Tuesday, Nick gave Jane Woolridge, the head editor and arts writer for the *Miami Herald*, and some other members of the press a tour on the Sunday prior.

Once Nick led the tour near Andres's booth, one of the women asked about his work. Because Andres's paintings were big and bright, the booth really stood out and caught people's attention, even with its less prominent location. Nick told the reporters the pieces were created by a ten-year-old artist. They were surprised, quickly becoming even more interested in the artwork on display. Jane was especially impressed and told Nick she would have a writer come by later to report on Andres for the *Miami Herald*.

Andres's booth was located in an inconspicuous back corner, across from a coffee bar. And while Chase Contemporary was presenting Andres's pieces as part of their gallery offerings, they were not part of Bernie's main booth. "He was kind of out on an island by himself," Bernie says. But Andres's booth was next to Shepard Fairey's, the American contemporary artist and founder of OBEY Clothing, which allowed for Andres to meet and speak with Shepard.

Andres's work was on display at Art Miami and up for sale to the public for the first time. Together, the Valencias and Bernie Chase decided on the prices, and on the first night of the fair, Nick brought VIP attendees over to Andres's booth. Everyone appeared to appreciate the art a great deal, even before they realized it was created by a child. When people learned Andres's age, the excitement over his work only grew.

"People couldn't believe it," Lupe says. "They thought it was incredible that all these paintings were made by a ten-year-old. I think people were kind of shocked." A two-minute video of Andres painting was also playing on a loop at his booth, allowing anyone who stopped by to see how Andres creates.

Nick came up with the idea of having Andres paint at the art fair in person, so those in attendance could witness the child prodigy in action firsthand. He believed such a display would further convince some of the skeptics that Andres had in fact made all the paintings on his own. Elsa talked to Andres about the idea to make sure he was comfortable putting himself in the spotlight, and he agreed. Andres did a live collaboration with the artist Bradley Theodore, where hundreds of people watched them paint and create right in front of them.

By the second day of the show, all seventeen paintings the Valencias had brought for Andres's booth had been sold. But that didn't stop people from checking out Andres's work, with dozens of requests

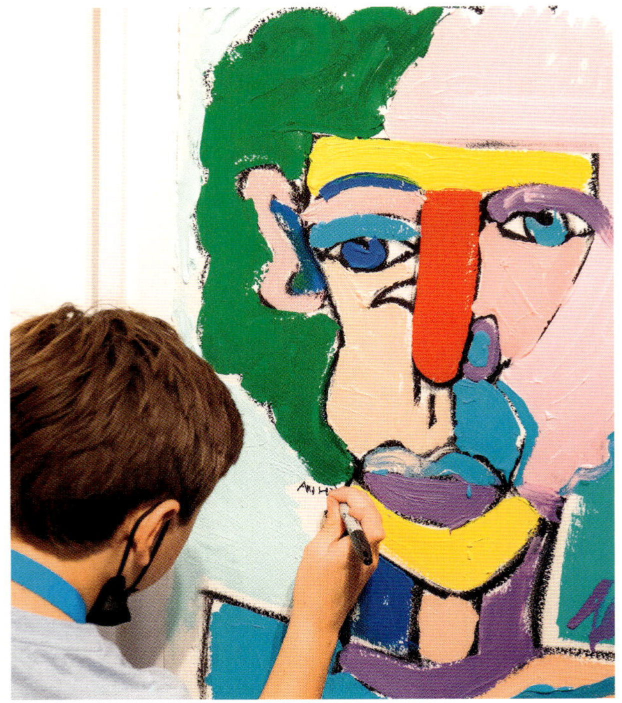

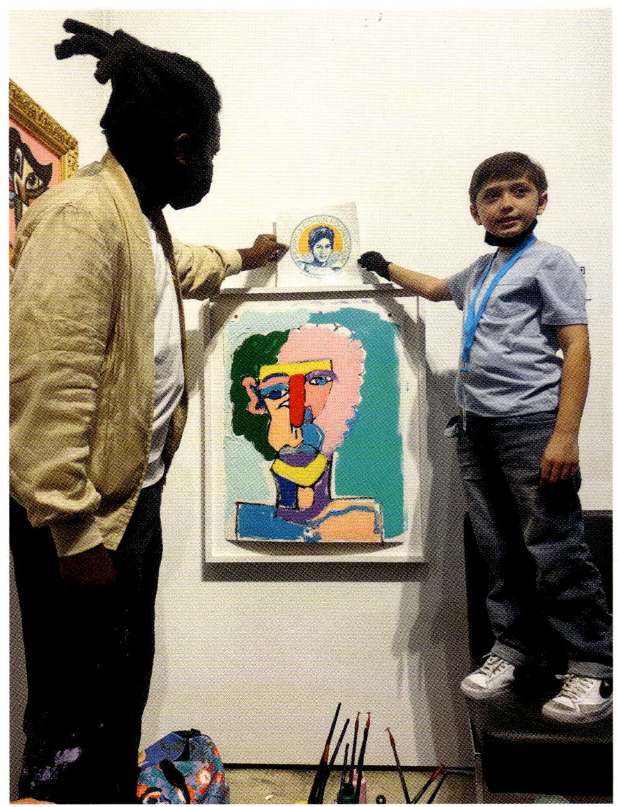

Above: Andres puts the final touches on a piece (top). With the artist, Bradley Theodore, holding the logo for the Perry J. Cohen Foundation above the painting (bottom). **Opposite:** An Art Miami visitor holds a catalog about Andres and his art.

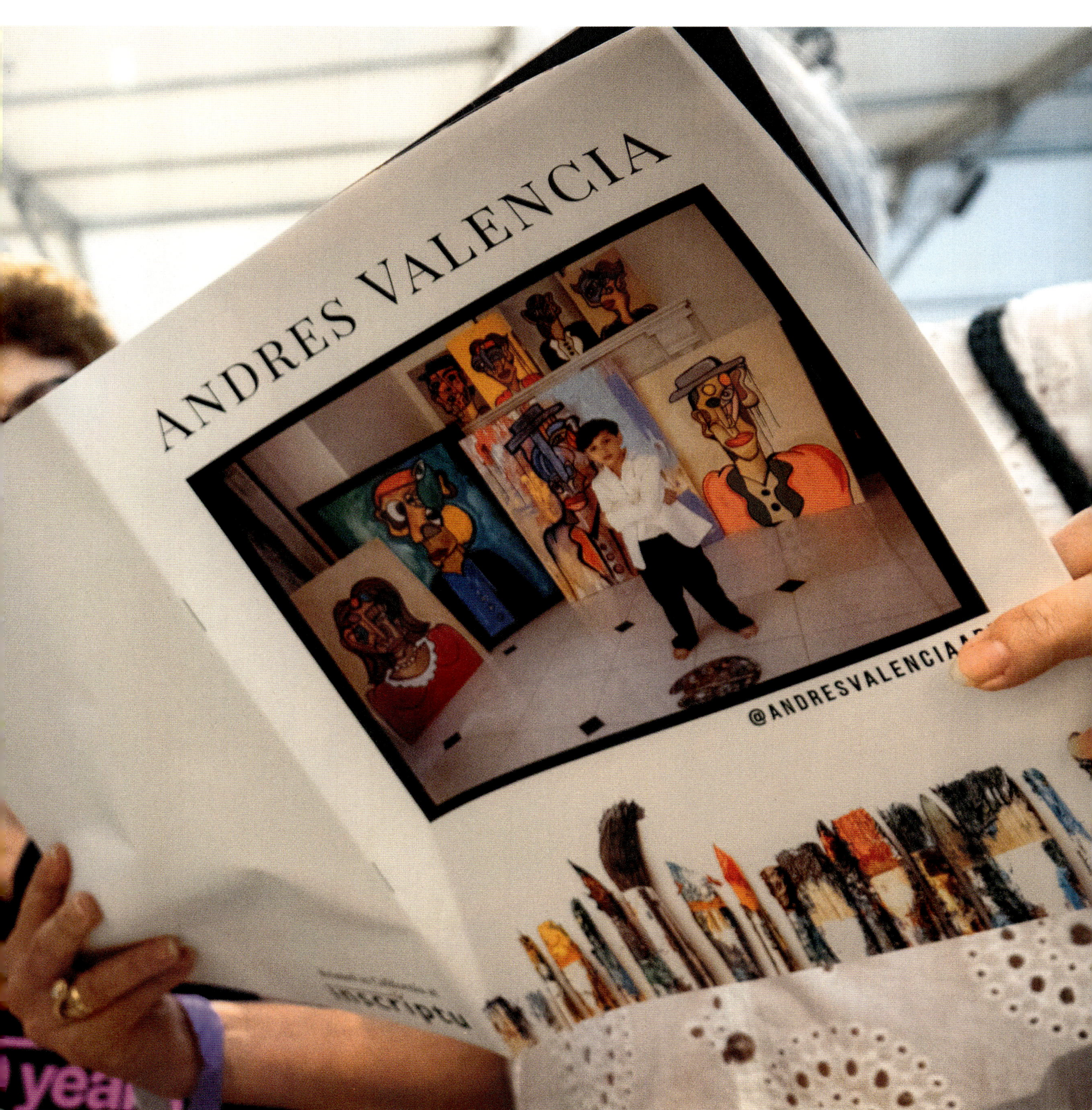
ANDRES VALENCIA
@ANDRESVALENCIA

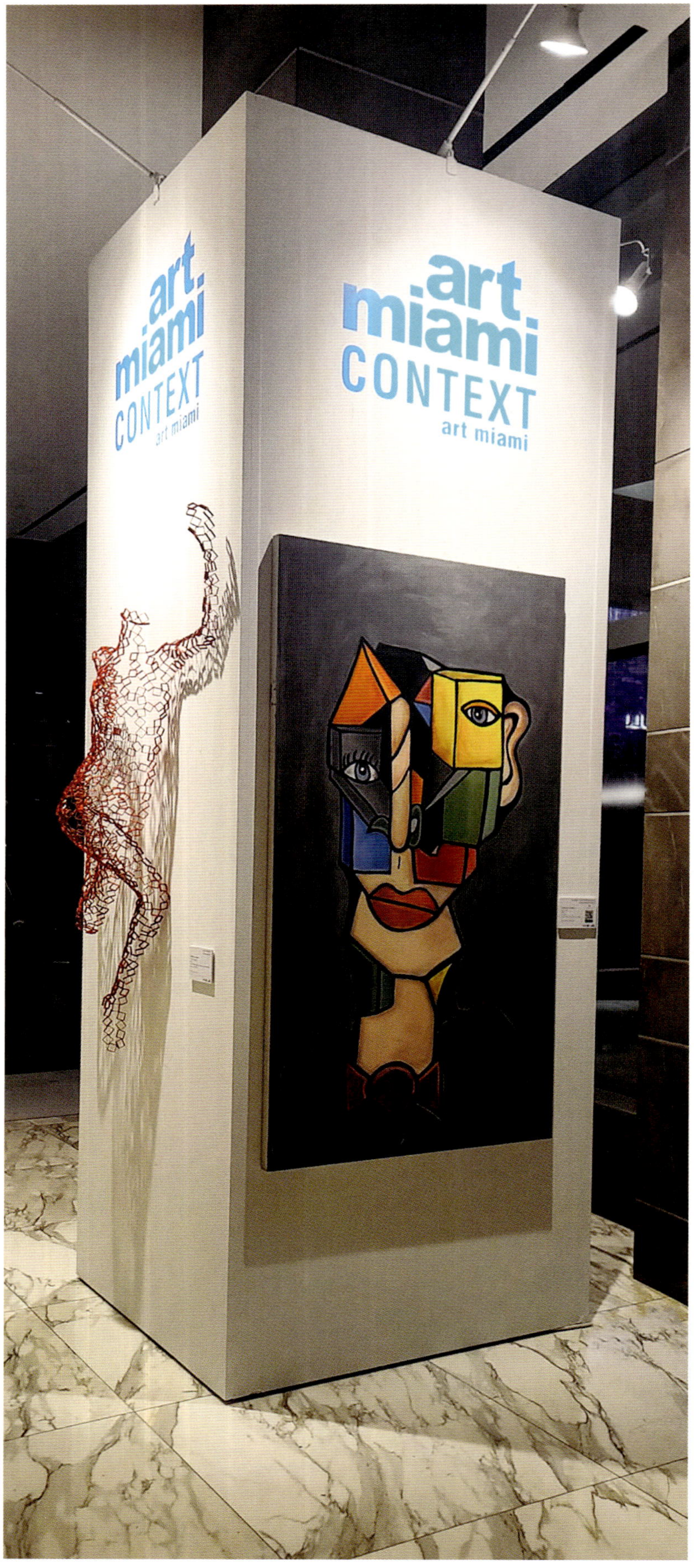

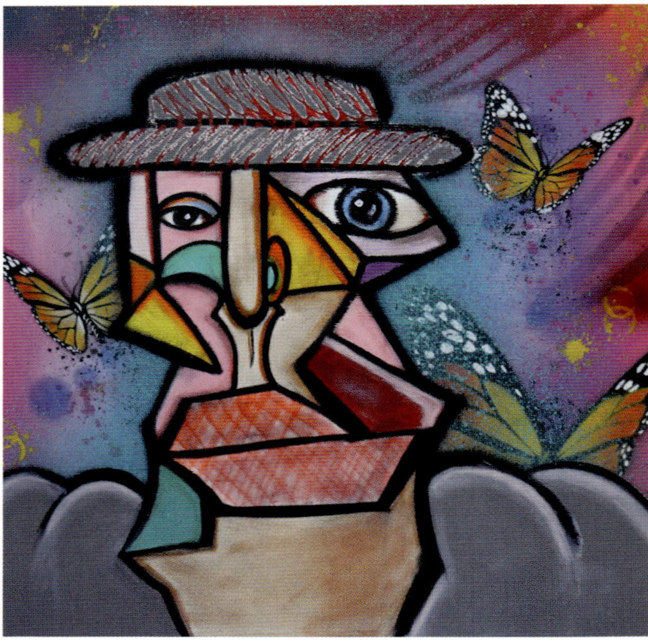

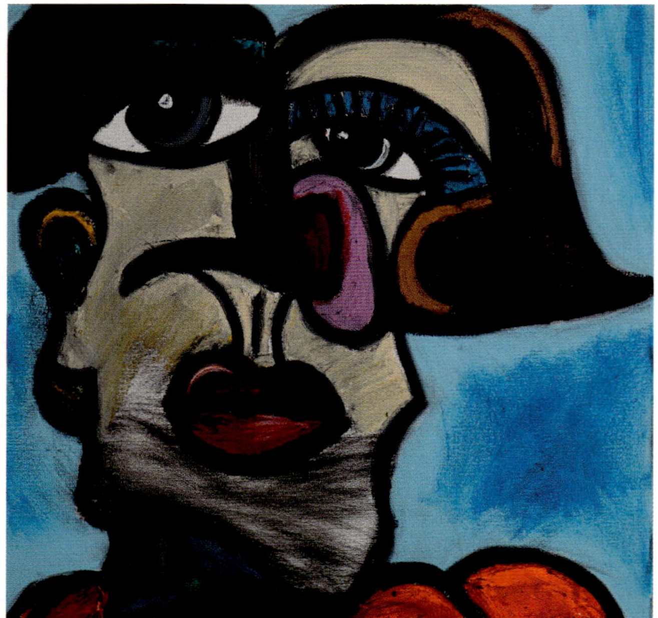

THE SEVENTEEN PAINTINGS
SOLD AT ART MIAMI:

Abraham the Clown, 2021 | 30 × 22 in (pg. 168)

Alexandra, 2020 | 48 × 36 in (pg. 157)

Amelia, 2021 | 24 × 18 in (pg. 175)

The Bachelor, 2020 | 20 × 16 in (pg. 137)

Benny, 2020 | 40 × 30 in (pg. 138)

Confusion, 2020 | 34 × 34 in (pg. 152)

George, 2020 | 24 × 18 in (pg. 144)

Gloria, 2021 | 20 × 20 in (pg. 108, bottom)

Juliette, 2020 | 20 × 16 in (pg. 138)

King and Queen, 2021 | 29 × 41 in (pg. 174)

Lady in Pink, 2021 | 36 × 36 in (pg. 179)

Lenny, 2021 | 36 × 30 in (pg. 183)

Lucky, 2021 | 72 × 36 in (pg. 173)

Marilyn, 2021 | 48 × 48 in (pg. 165)

The Menace, 2021 | 72 × 48 in (pg. 181)

Pepino the Clown, 2020 | 36 × 36 in (pg. 152)

Untitled, 2021 (Risk Rock and Andres Valencia collaboration piece) | 40 × 40 in (pg. 108, top)

from people who wanted to buy something leaving their names and information. Catalogs featuring other pieces by Andres were laid out on the booth's tables so people could see examples of works not brought to the fair.

During Art Miami, *Good Morning America* contacted the Valencias and asked if Andres could be on the show. Lupe and Elsa agreed to let him be featured, resulting in a two-and-a-half-minute segment that included interviews with both Andres and Elsa talking about the art he was displaying at the fair and the reaction it was getting. Andres was also on the front page of the *Miami Herald* that week, and many other outlets stopped by his booth over the five days of the fair to interview him.

While people online had already started to notice Andres and his immense talent from the Instagram account Elsa was running, Art Miami was his first big break. It was there that he was really discovered, and where serious people in the art world started to notice he was someone special. With all the media attention, interviews, and coverage on Andres being the youngest artist to ever show at the fair, plus all the paintings he'd brought selling quickly, the attention only compounded. His Instagram following started to grow exponentially from that point on, giving him an impressive platform to continue sharing his art.

Nick has organized many exhibitions with well-known and established artists who have long histories in the art market. These artists are featured in major collections with pre-promotion to bring attention to their work and to allow for more success at the fair. "But for Andres," Nick says, "we just let things happen. His work being featured at Art Miami was the most organic experience I've seen in my entire career. The attention all came about naturally with the most amount of energy and positivity. It was a great response." The Valencia family couldn't have asked for a better introduction into the spotlight for Andres as a serious, respected, and highly sought-after artist.

Opposite, clockwise from left: Andres's painting *Ms. Cube* (pg. 182) on display in the hallways of Art Miami, December 2021; *Untitled* collaboration piece with Risk Rock; the painting *Gloria*. Right: Andres being interviewed by Lisa Petrillo from *CBS News* at Art Miami.

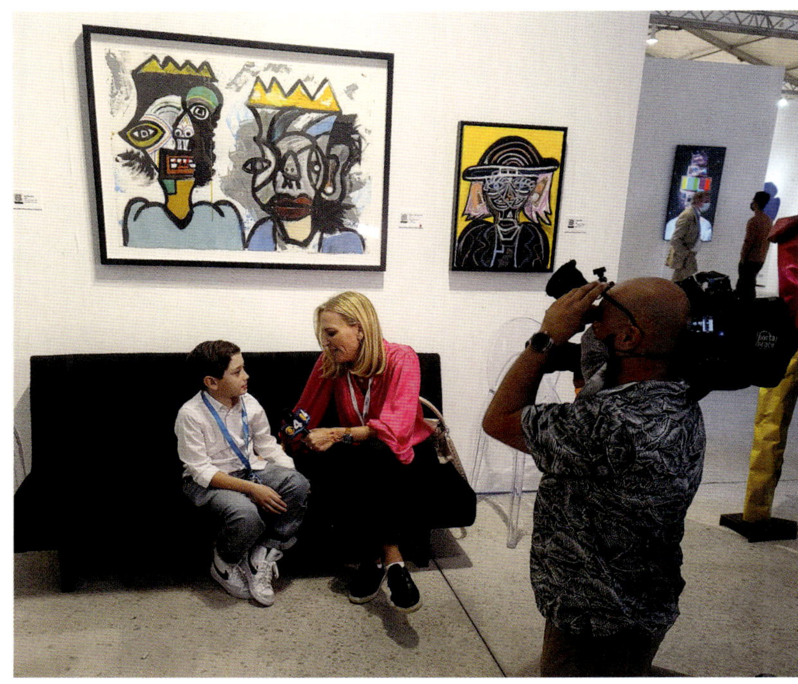

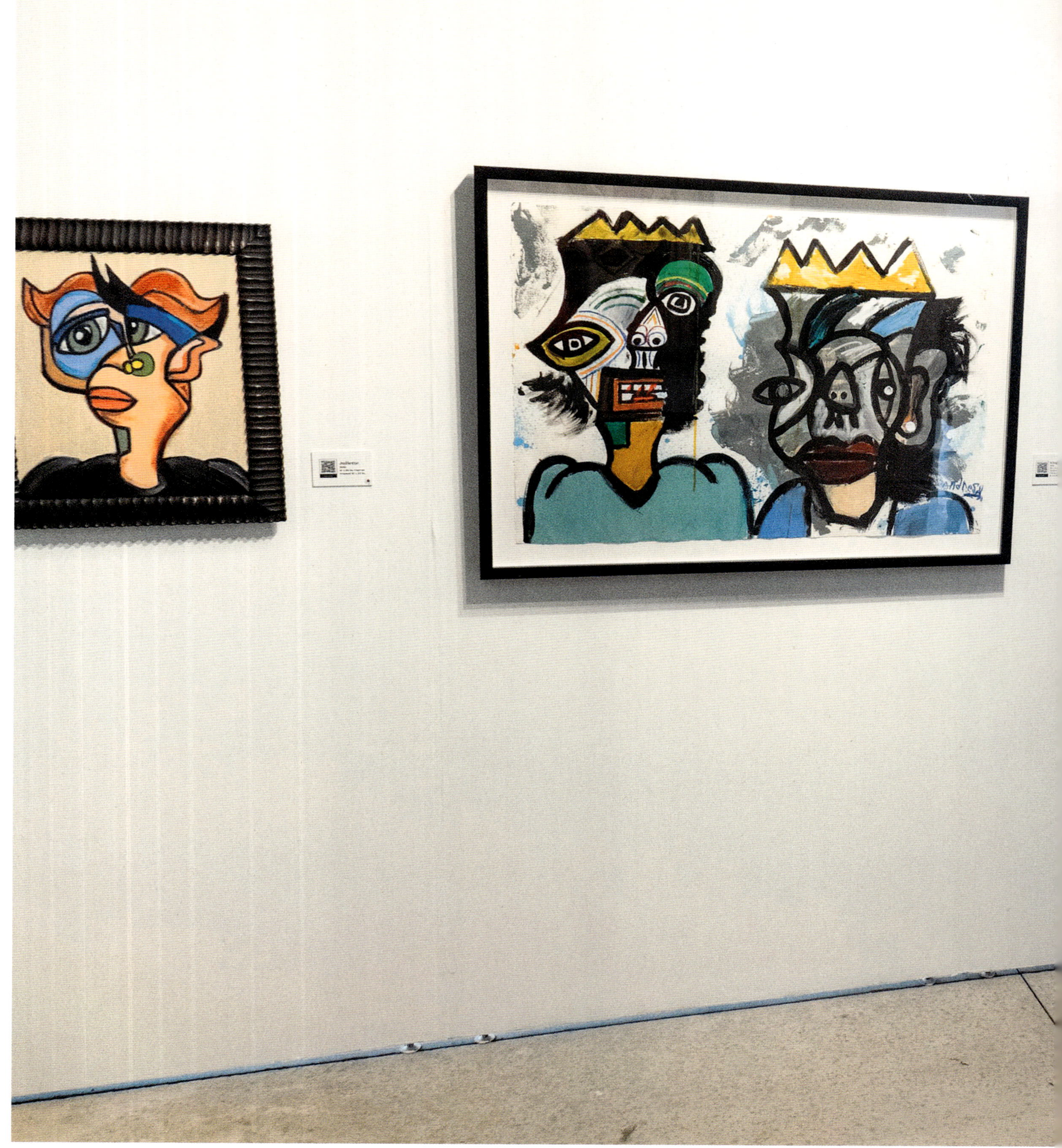

Attendees at Art Miami gather in the space beside Andres's booth, December 2021.

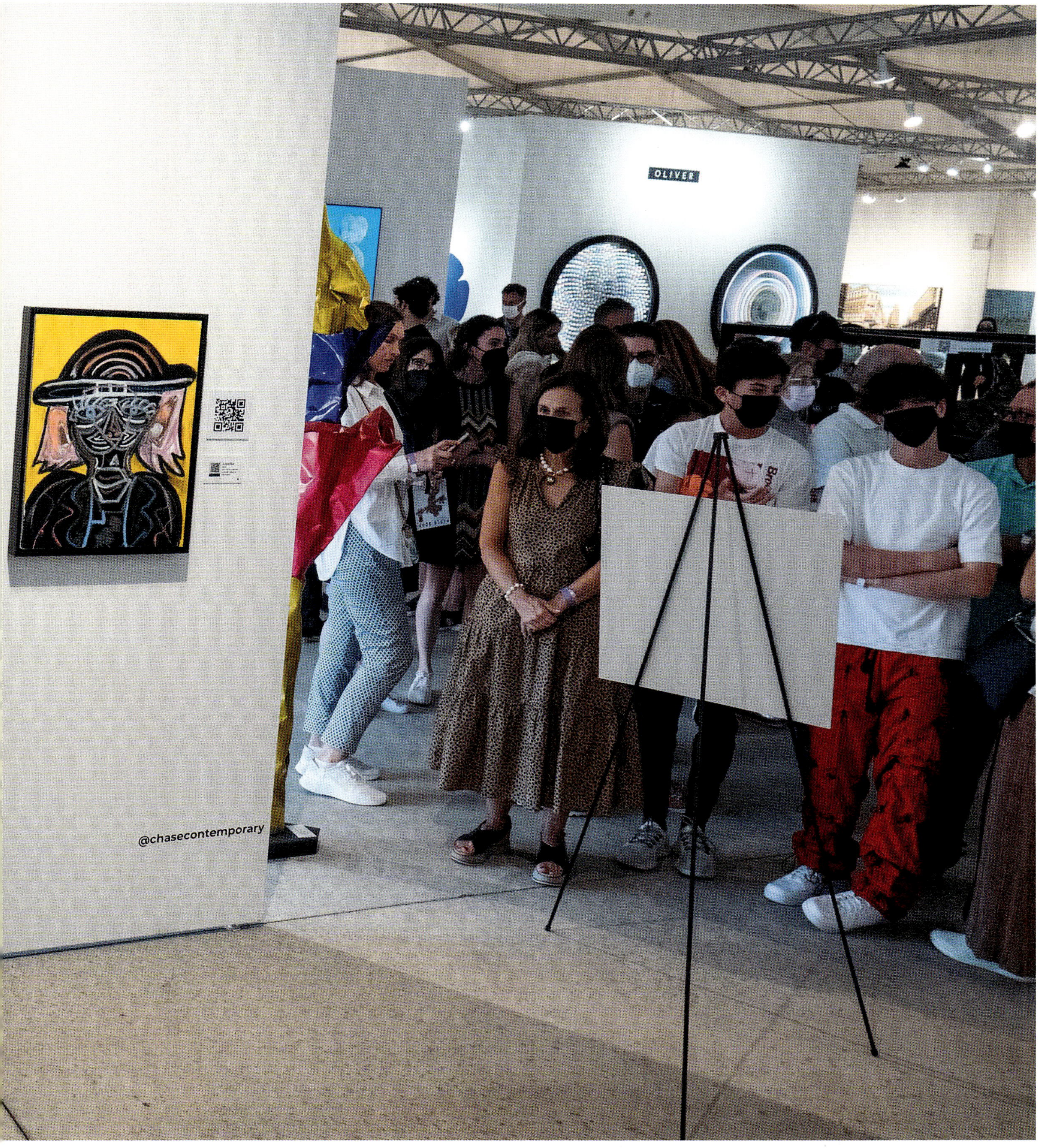
OLIVER
@chasecontemporary

Celebrity Fans

Andres's artwork has many different celebrity fans in addition to everyday art lovers and collectors. One of the first celebrities to buy an Andres Valencia painting was Colombian actress and serious art collector Sofía Vergara, who purchased a piece at Art Miami. She then posted about the painting on her Instagram story to her millions of followers, which was a huge deal for Andres and his art career. That purchase, the post from Sofía, and the publicity that came with it added to the other media attention Andres received at Art Miami.

While Sofía was the first major celebrity to buy a piece from Andres, there were other notable individuals who purchased an Andres Valencia painting at Art Miami as well, including Jessica Goldman Srebnick, CEO of Goldman Global Arts and the lead curator of Wynwood Walls, the outdoor art park in Miami, which showcases graffiti and street art. When Jessica bought her piece, she went over to Andres's booth and spent a lot of time talking to him. She even invited him to visit Wynwood Walls to spray paint a wall, which Andres did a few days later.

"Andres was kind of like a little celebrity himself," Nick says, "as there were times where he kind of got mobbed at the show. Collectors kept coming back to buy another piece. People were doubling down. Jon Bon Jovi and his wife, Dorothea, are friends of ours and fans of the fair, and they wanted to meet Andres. I brought them over to Andres's booth, and they spent time with him. They looked at his work and talked to him about it, which was pretty amazing. It was just a good vibe all around."

Andres also met Brooke Shields, who visited his booth and took pictures. Channing Tatum also visited and took photos, although Andres, who was already gone for the day, didn't get to meet him. In addition to the pieces purchased at Art Miami, other big names, including Sergio Ramos, Karol G, Eugenio López Alonso, Michael Strahan, Tommy Mottola, Thalía, and BTS singer V also own paintings by Andres.

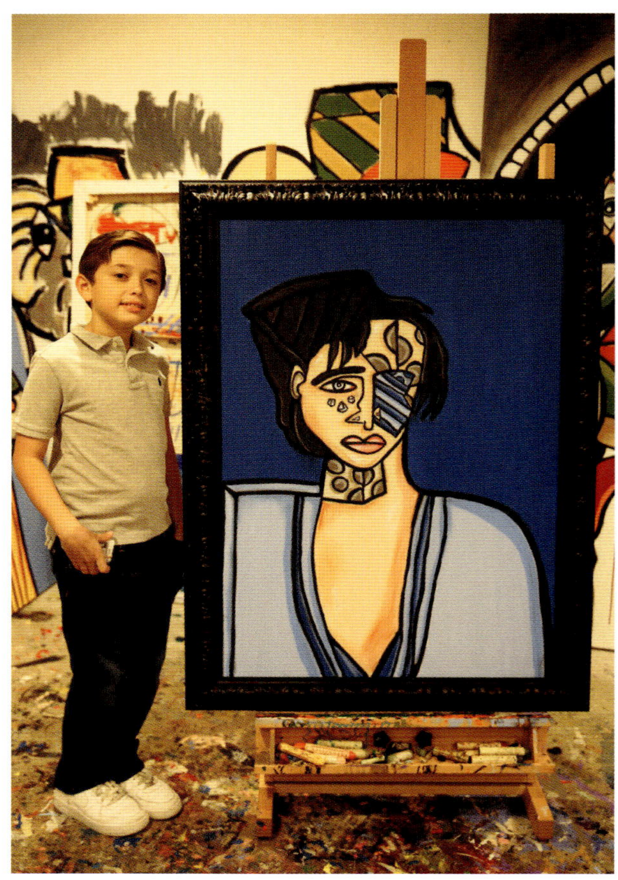

Above: Andres stands beside the painting he created for the BTS singer, *V* (pg. 221). **Opposite, clockwise from top left:** Brooke Shields and Andres at Art Miami in 2021; Sergio Ramos with the painting *Traje De Luces* (pg. 252); Jon Bon Jovi with the painting *Fred 1* (pg. 162); Andres and Karol G with the painting *Mademoiselle* (pg. 194); Sofía Vergara with the painting *The Bachelor* (pg. 137); Andres with Jon Bon Jovi pointing to his painting *Invasion of Ukraine* (pg. 199) at Art Miami, 2022.

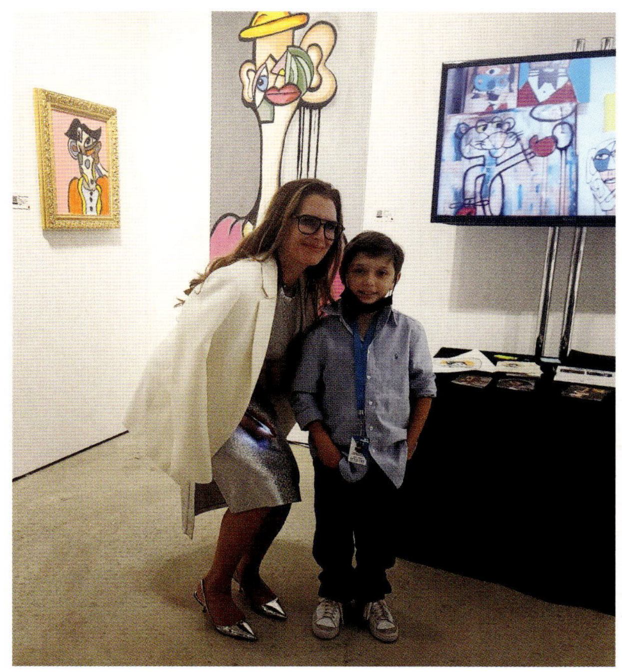

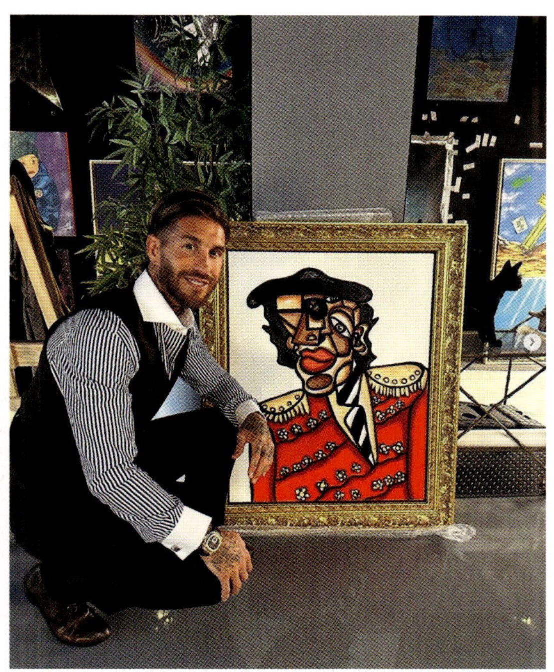

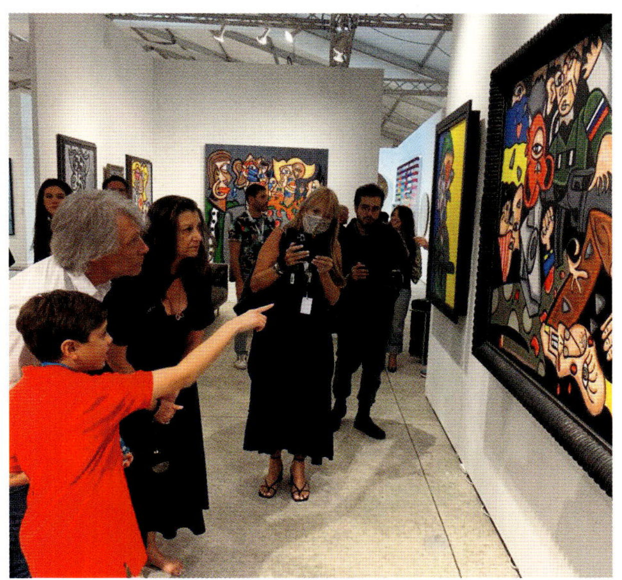

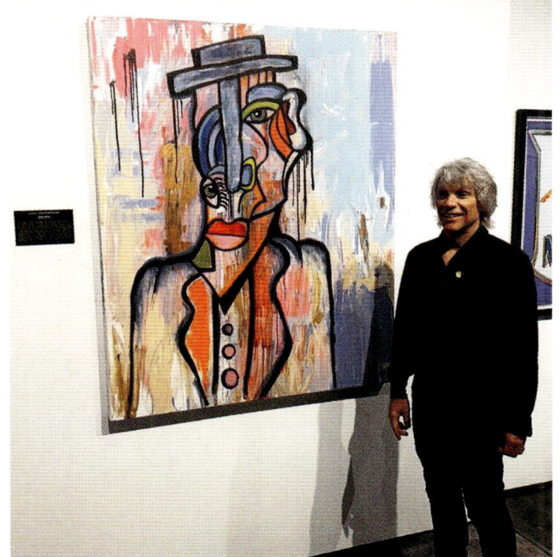

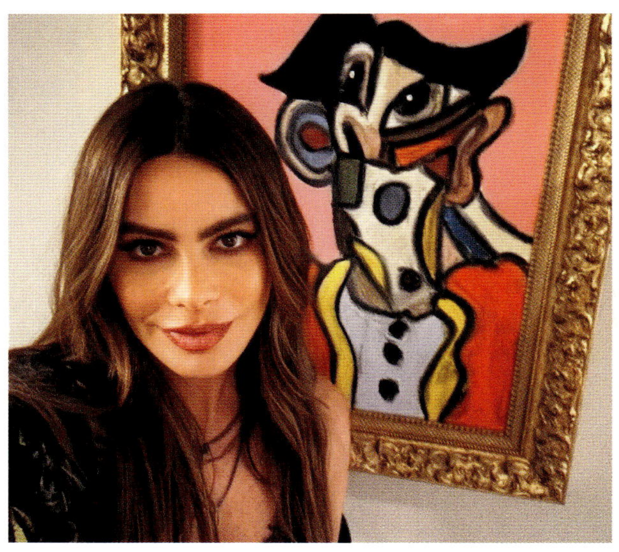

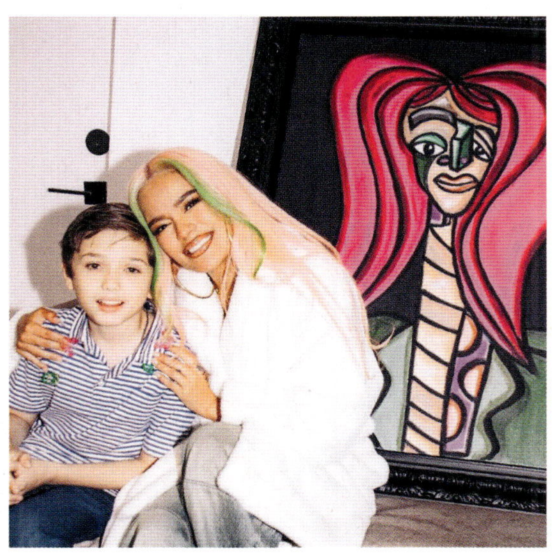

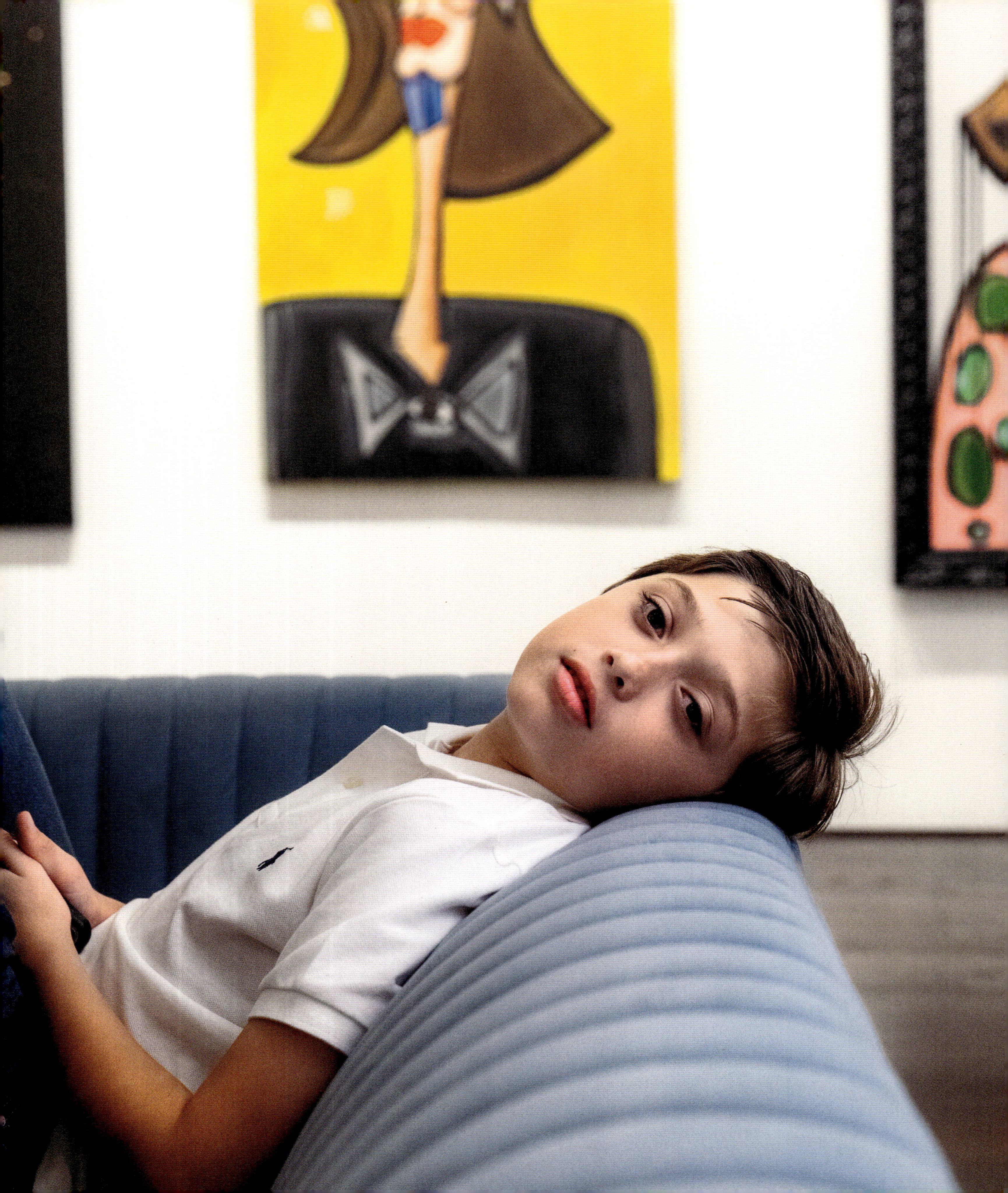

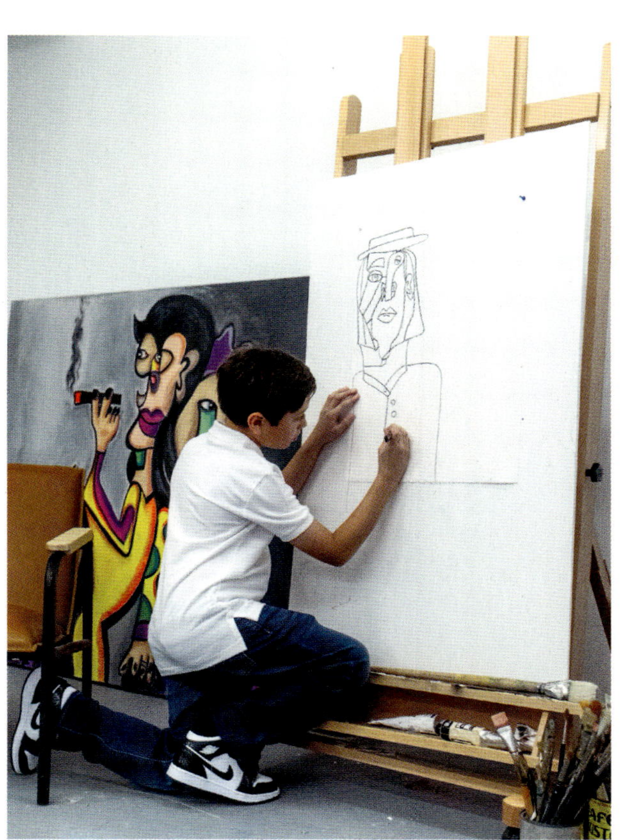

All Eyes on Andres

Everyone close to Andres, and even Andres himself, seems to think of his career as having two main parts: before Art Miami and after Art Miami. His debut at the art fair in December 2021 is without a doubt what led to much of the success that followed.

"Even before Art Miami," Lupe says, "when Andres started painting on big canvases, I would watch him and really believed he was extremely talented." Lupe loved everything Andres did. He was amazed at the artwork his son created and realized he was going to be a big artist. "He's really special," Lupe says. "I knew in my mind and my heart that there was something different and unique about him." So when Andres went to Art Miami, Lupe said it was nerve-wracking because they didn't know how others were going to react to him and his work at first. Still, Lupe had a feeling other people were going to like Andres's style. "I just had no idea the extent of what was going to happen there," Lupe says. "It exceeded our expectations. I was hoping we'd sell some pieces, and we could start building his career little by little. I obviously had no clue how big this opportunity would turn out to be for Andres." Lupe credits Bernie and Nick for believing in him. "They always considered him to be a real artist and took a chance with him."

Of the experience, Nick says, "The whole week was probably the most joyful experience I ever had in relation to producing an art fair, because so many people were happy. People were finally taking their masks off at this point of the pandemic and enjoying being in a public space where they could see art up close. And all the attention Andres got, I don't think it could ever be re-created."

Even though Andres was only ten at the time, both Elsa and Lupe made sure to continuously check in with him to see how he was feeling about all the attention he was getting. Andres didn't express any concern. Instead, he was excited that his paintings were making people happy. Andres helped decide which paintings to list for sale at the art fair. Sometimes when he completes a piece, he tells his parents he doesn't want it to be sold, and they always respect these requests.

Some artists work their whole lives and never make it to Art Miami. Yet Andres made it to the well-known artist showcase when he was just ten years old. While Lupe doesn't think Andres fully understood the significance at the time, he's very smart and still knew it was a big deal.

Even after Andres has found so much early success, Elsa and Lupe work very hard to make sure their son stays grounded. "We try to make sure he still knows he's a little boy," Lupe says. "We let him do little boy things and never say anything like, 'Now you're an adult worker here.' One of the main things we try to accomplish is to let him be who he is. We never force him to do anything."

Elsa says she got scared when posts about Andres started going viral in Miami. "All of a sudden," she says, "I was getting phone calls while I was in the hotel room with Andres from friends and family in California who saw him on the news." Elsa's sister sent a video of her watching Andres on TV. Elsa put her phone down and called Lupe, who was still at the booth. She told him, "You need to come back to the hotel room now." He returned right away to talk to Elsa. Meanwhile, Andres was on the floor, playing with vintage 1960s GI Joes, which he'd found at a shop in Miami. Elsa took Lupe to the other room and sat him down. She said, "Please promise me that we will not force Andres to do anything he doesn't want to do.'" He immediately responded, "I promise." That was the moment Elsa really started worrying about all the attention Andres was getting and the pressure it might put on him. "I never thought it would go where it was going," she says. "I never expected any of this. That's why now, I'm very careful about what we say yes to. I've said no to a lot of opportunities because I want to protect Andres. This is a difficult industry. He's a little boy, and it can be scary, because people are always going to talk about his work."

When Andres started receiving so much attention for his artwork, Elsa's main concern was what people were going to say, including potential criticism. To prepare Andres, she had a discussion with him, explaining that sometimes people might have negative opinions about his art. They discussed how Picasso had many critics. Over the years, Andres has heard many people say they don't like Picasso or that they don't consider cubism to be "real art." Yet Andres loves Picasso, and during these talks with his mother, he responded by telling her about how Picasso had a long and successful career, to which Elsa responded, "Exactly. So you have to learn not to let the negative comments stop you from doing what you love."

Through it all, Andres remains positive. As Elsa explains, "I've never heard him say anything negative. He always says, 'I'm a hard worker. I work hard at my art.'" She encourages him to keep working hard and continue developing his craft, even if negative comments make their way to his ears.

The attention Andres has received for his art makes him grateful and proud. "I hope I can motivate other people," he says, "especially other kids my age, so they know they can create and make things and not just play video games. I think it's cool people know me even though I'm young, and that they like my art. They know I work hard on it. I'm so happy to sell my paintings. I'm not emotionally attached to them because I can always make another one."

Andres is one of the few living artists who's been able to sell individual paintings for six-figure sums, an impressive feat that inspires both pride and gratitude in the young creator. "I'm very proud of myself," he says. "It all came from hard work, going down to the studio, and

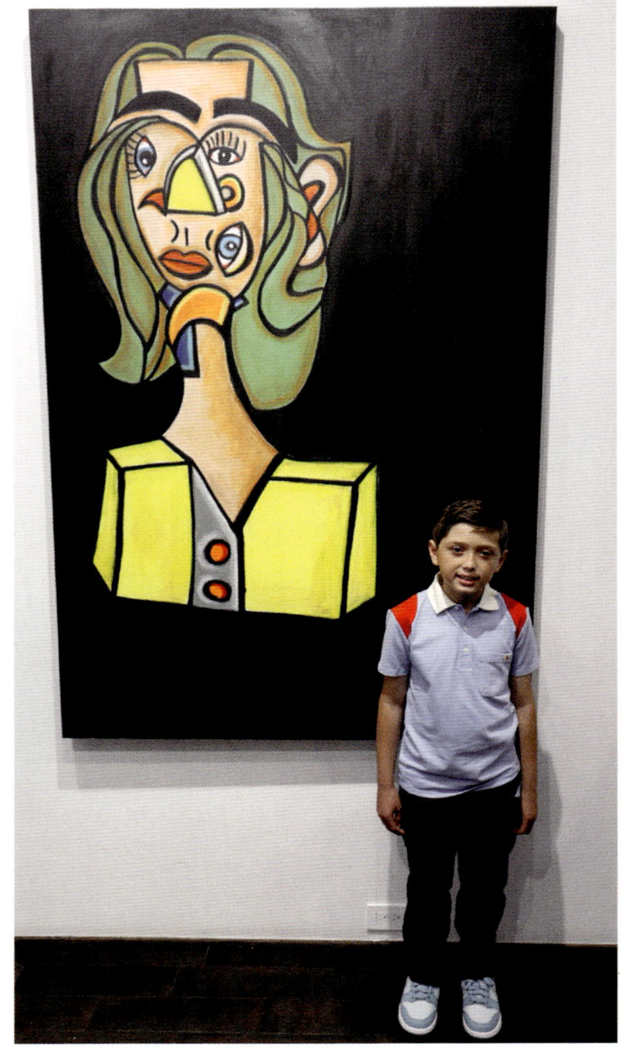

Above: Andres standing before his painting, *Donna* (pg. 180) on display at Chase Contemporary, June 2022.
Opposite: Andres being interviewed at his *No Rules* show.

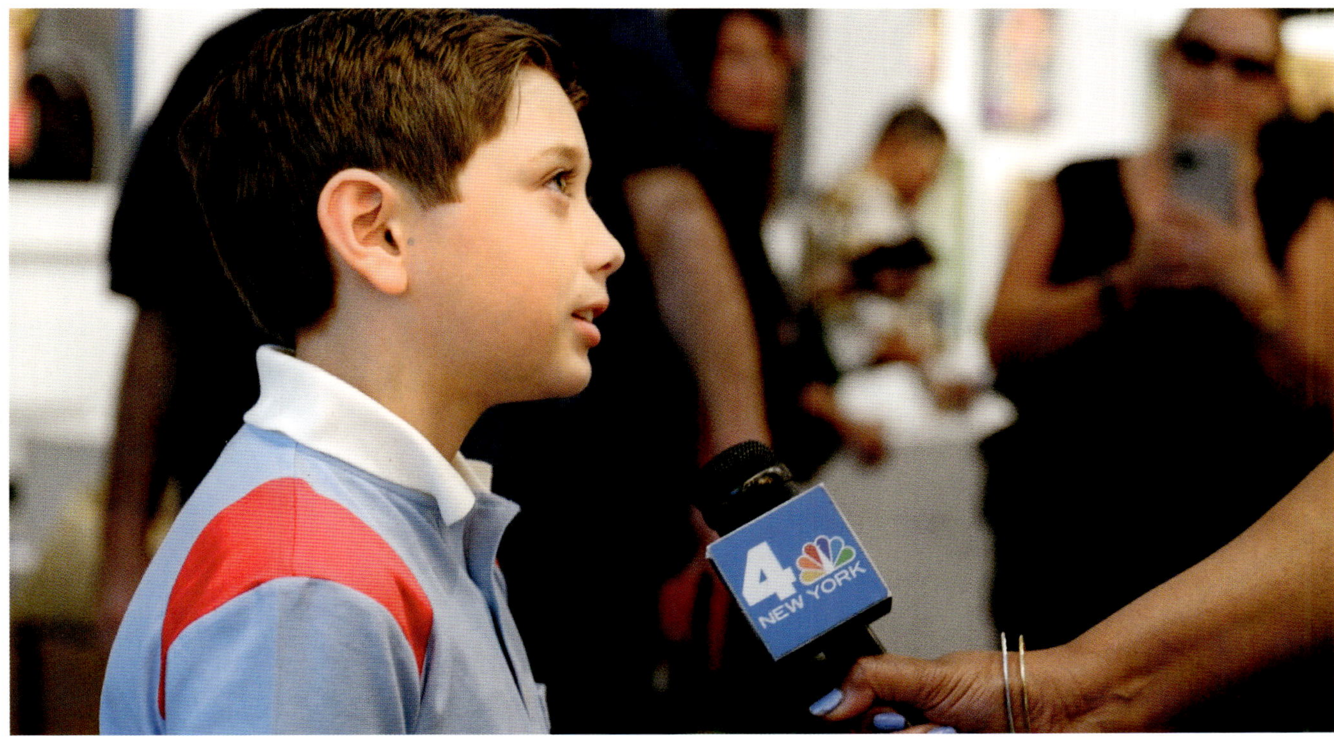

working. It doesn't just come out of nowhere. I'm very grateful for it too. It doesn't happen to a lot of people." As remarkable as the prices he's been able to fetch for his paintings are, Andres is more excited about being taken seriously as an artist. People have called him a child prodigy, and when asked what he thinks of this, Andres replies, "I think they're kind."

Lupe and Elsa always ask Andres for his permission before they ever sign him up to do anything publicly. When a media outlet requests an interview, they always check in with him before committing to it. If Andres ever says no, that's the end of the story, and they decline the interview. His parents don't make him do anything he doesn't want to do. They never try to convince him or change his perspective. They are fully respectful of his decisions, which is incredibly important when raising a young creative.

After the success of Art Miami and all the media attention Andres received, Bernie started to get several phone calls from other parents who wanted him to represent their children and get their artwork shown at Art Miami too. As Bernie explains, "We've had people from Europe and all over the US send me examples of their kids' work and even videos of them creating something. They try to convince me to show their stuff. It still happens today. But Andres is special. You can't replicate his talent."

Nick sums it up best when thinking about who Andres is as an artist, why he has received so much attention, and what's next: "Andres is a young boy who's got some amazing talent. He's truly an artist inside and out. If you get to talk to him, you can tell he's a caring kid. And his parents are very astute and understanding that he is a young child with this special talent. They don't want to do anything that will burn him out." Andres is just beginning his artistic career, and while he has already found great success, there's much more still to come.

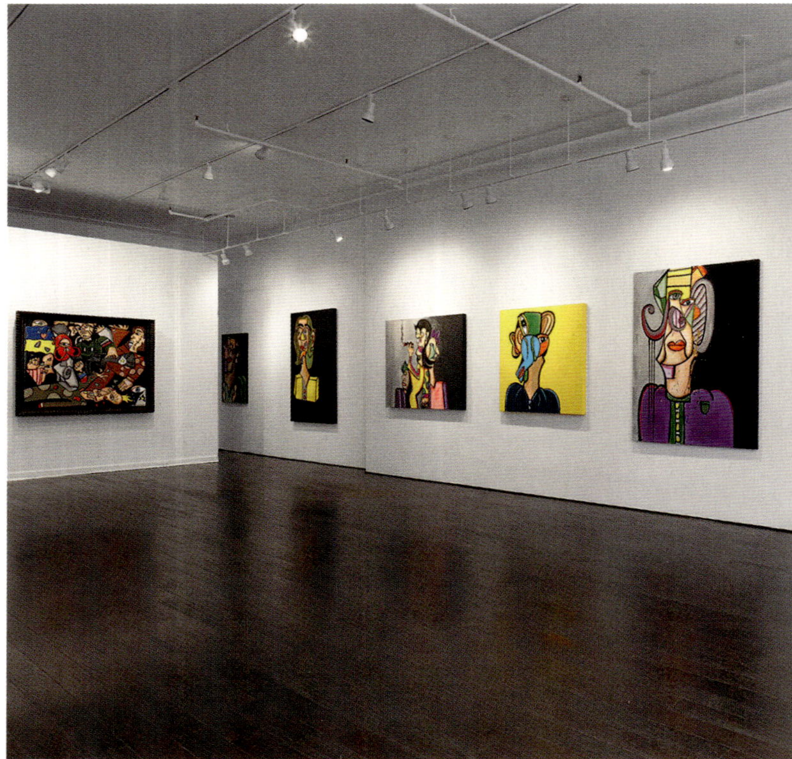

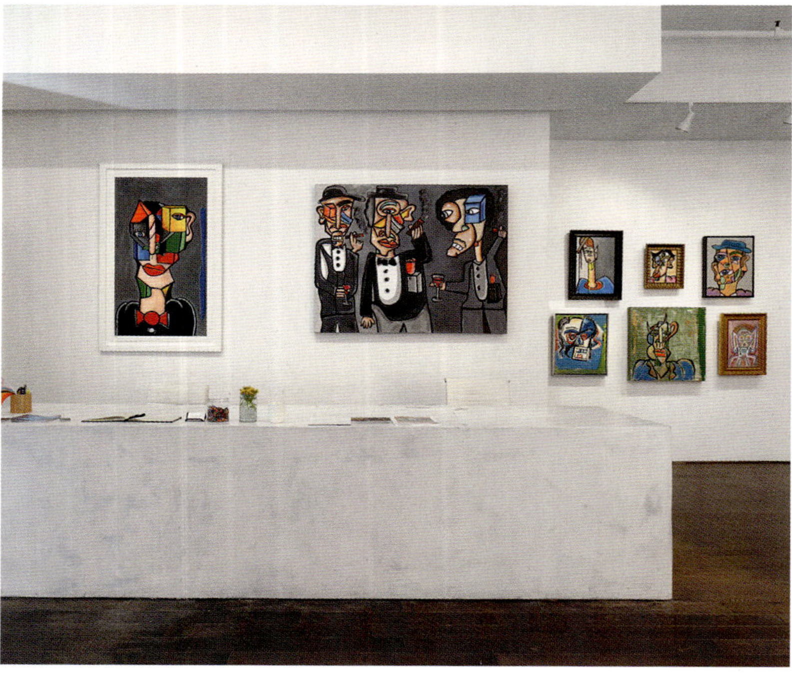

The *No Rules* Show

In July 2022, Andres had his first solo exhibition at the Chase Contemporary gallery in SoHo. The show was titled *No Rules*. All thirty-six of his paintings on display were sold, each fetching anywhere from $50,000 up to $125,000.

THE THIRTY-SIX PAINTINGS SOLD AT THE *NO RULES* SHOW:

Alberto the Clown, 2021 | 60 × 36 in (pg. 177)

Alex, 2022 | 20 × 20 in (pg. 196)

Ana, 2021 | 24 × 24 in (pg. 166)

Blue Madness, 2021 | 72 × 48 in (pg. 187)

Bob, 2022 | 20 × 20 in (pg. 197)

Captain, 2022 | 20 × 20 in (pg. 197)

Carlo, 2021 | 24 × 16 in

The Commander, 2022 | 48 × 36 in (pg. 202)

Dalila, 2021 | 68 × 51 in (pg. 188)

Donna, 2021 | 72 × 48 in (pg. 180)

El Payaso Loco, 2021 | 36 × 36 in (pg. 185)

Homage to Basquiat 2, 2021 | 11 × 8.5 in (pg. 43)

Jim, 2020 | 14 × 11 in (pg. 136)

John Lennon and Yoko Ono, 2022 | 60 × 36 in (pg. 210)

Julio, 2021 | 24 × 18 in

Karla, 2022 | 42 × 35 in (pg. 209)

La Payasita, 2022 | 48 × 36 in (pg. 213)

The Law Man, 2020 | 24 × 18 in (pg. 137)

The Lieutenant, 2022 | 42 × 35 in (pg. 201)

Lucy, 2021 | 72 × 36 in (pg. 178)

Mary, 2021 | 30 × 20 in (pg. 164)

Master Warrior, 2021 | 30 × 30 in (pg. 167)

Max the Clown, 2022 | 60 × 48 in (pg. 214)

Mono, 2021 | 51 × 36 in

Olga, 2021 | 48 × 36 in (pg. 171)

Paula, 2022 | 36 × 30 in (pg. 209)

The Professor, 2020 | 54 × 40 in (pg. 160)

Richard, 2022 | 20 × 20 in (pg. 196)

Roger, 2020 | 40 × 36 in (pg. 163)

The Royals, 2021 | 46 × 70 in

Sara, 2021 | 40 × 40 in (pg. 184)

The Scientist, 2020 | 48 × 48 in (pg. 155)

The Three Punks, 2021 | 48 × 60 in (pg. 179)

Tom and Jenny, 2022 | 48 × 68 in (pg. 219)

Toni, 2022 | 36 × 28 in (pg. 218)

Tony, Joe, and John, 2022 | 48 × 60 in (pg. 219)

Above: Andres's work on display for *No Rules* at Chase Contemporary in New York City. **Opposite:** Andres surrounded by show attendees (top). Another photo of his work on display for the show (bottom).

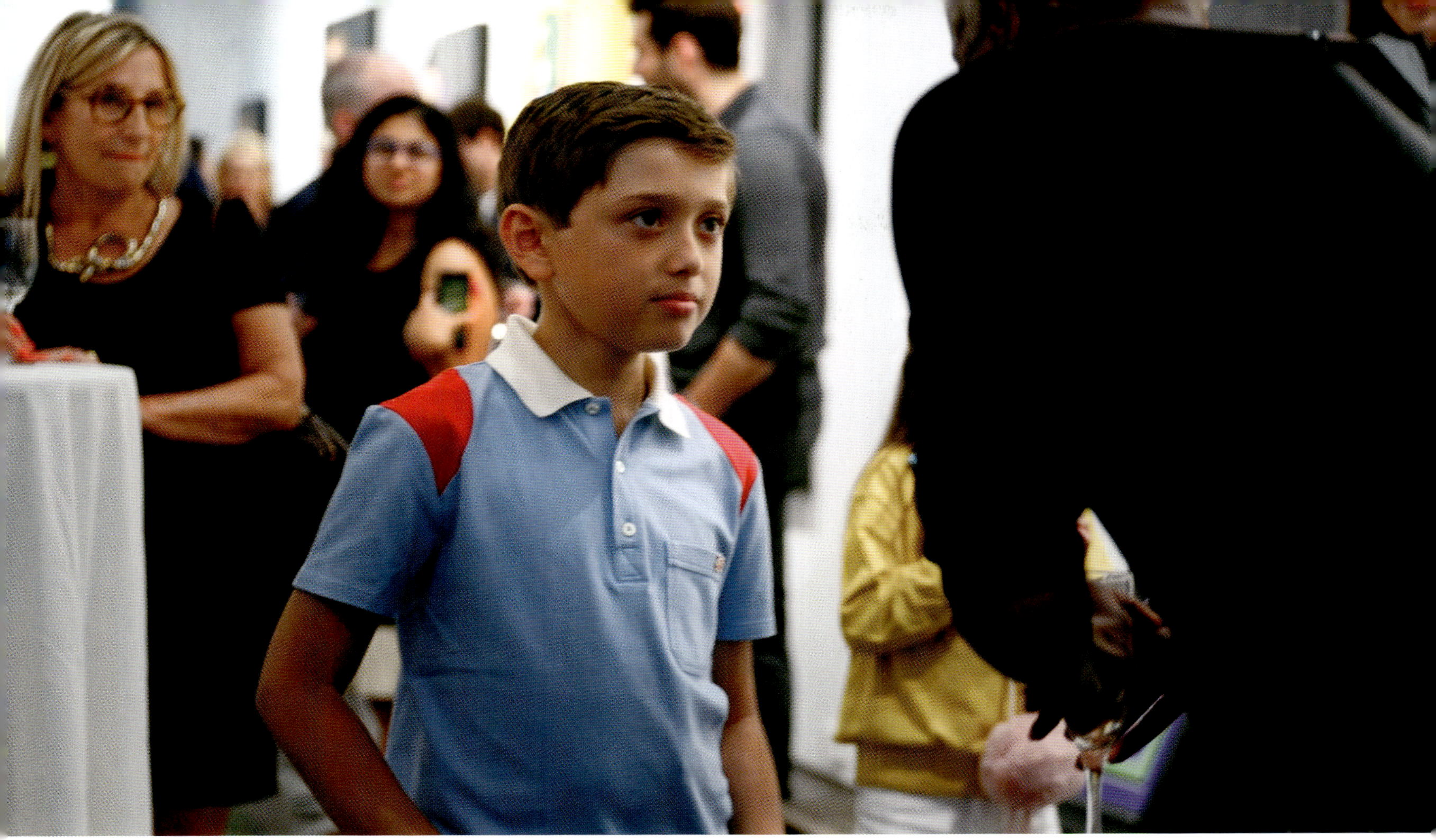

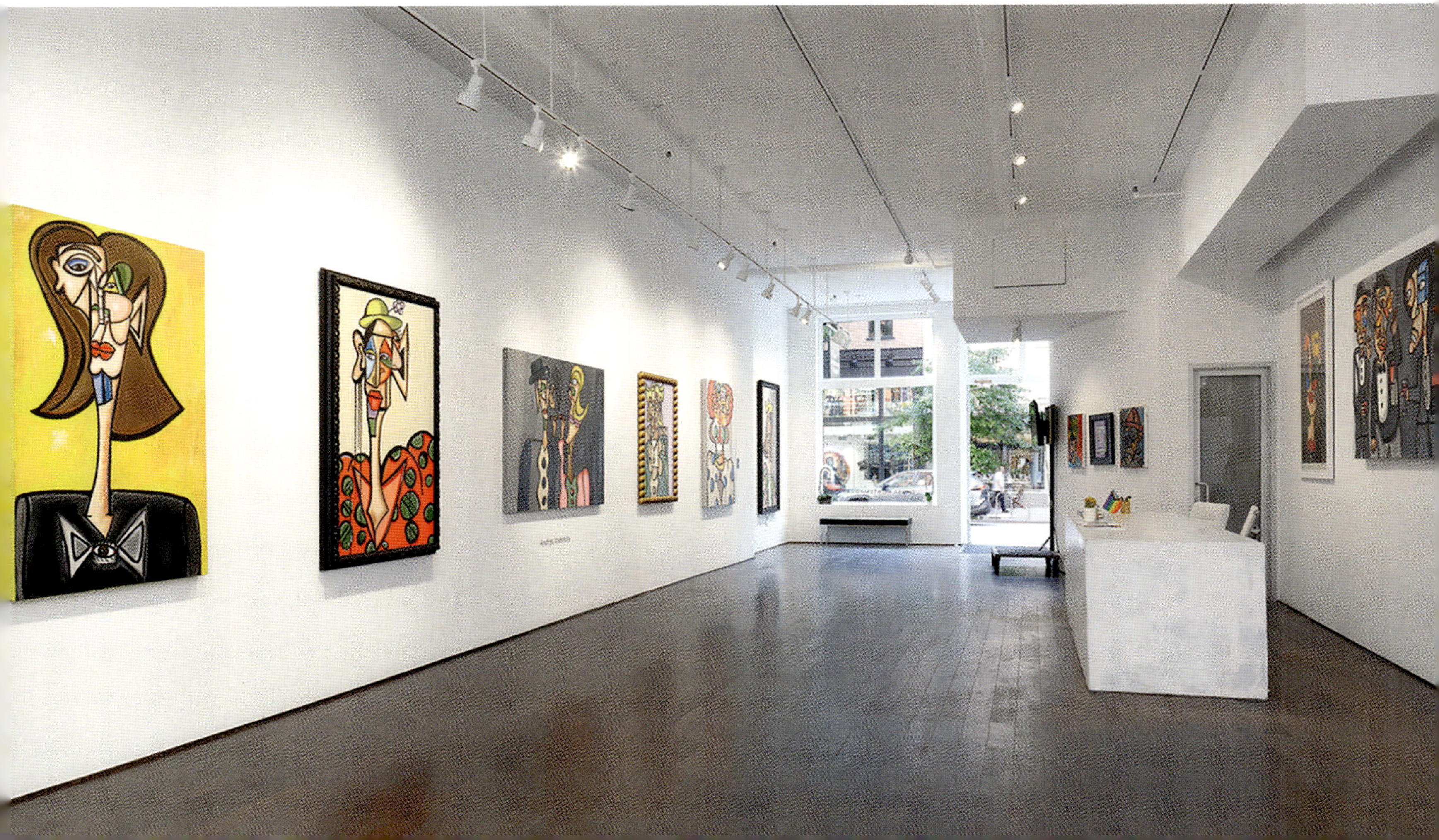

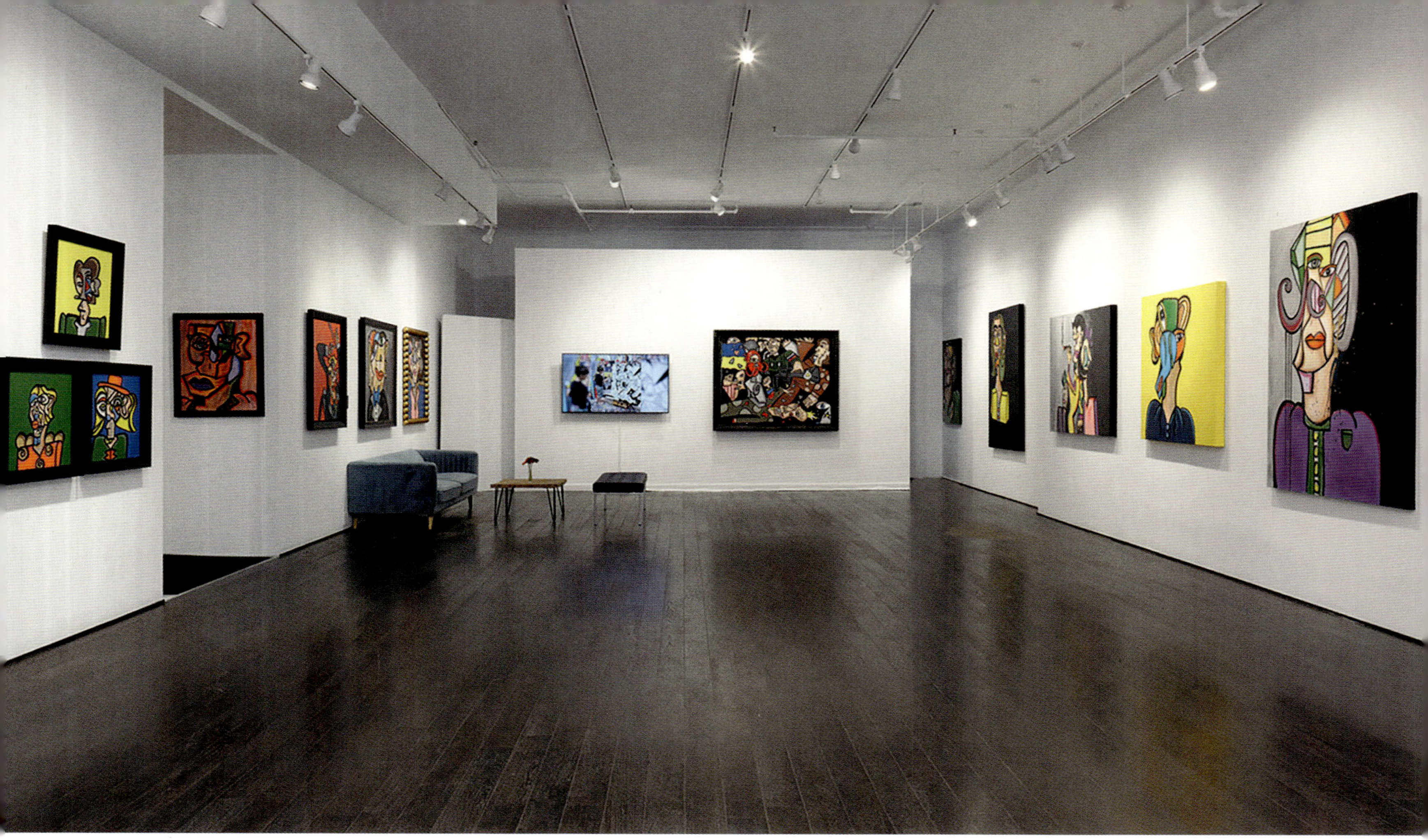

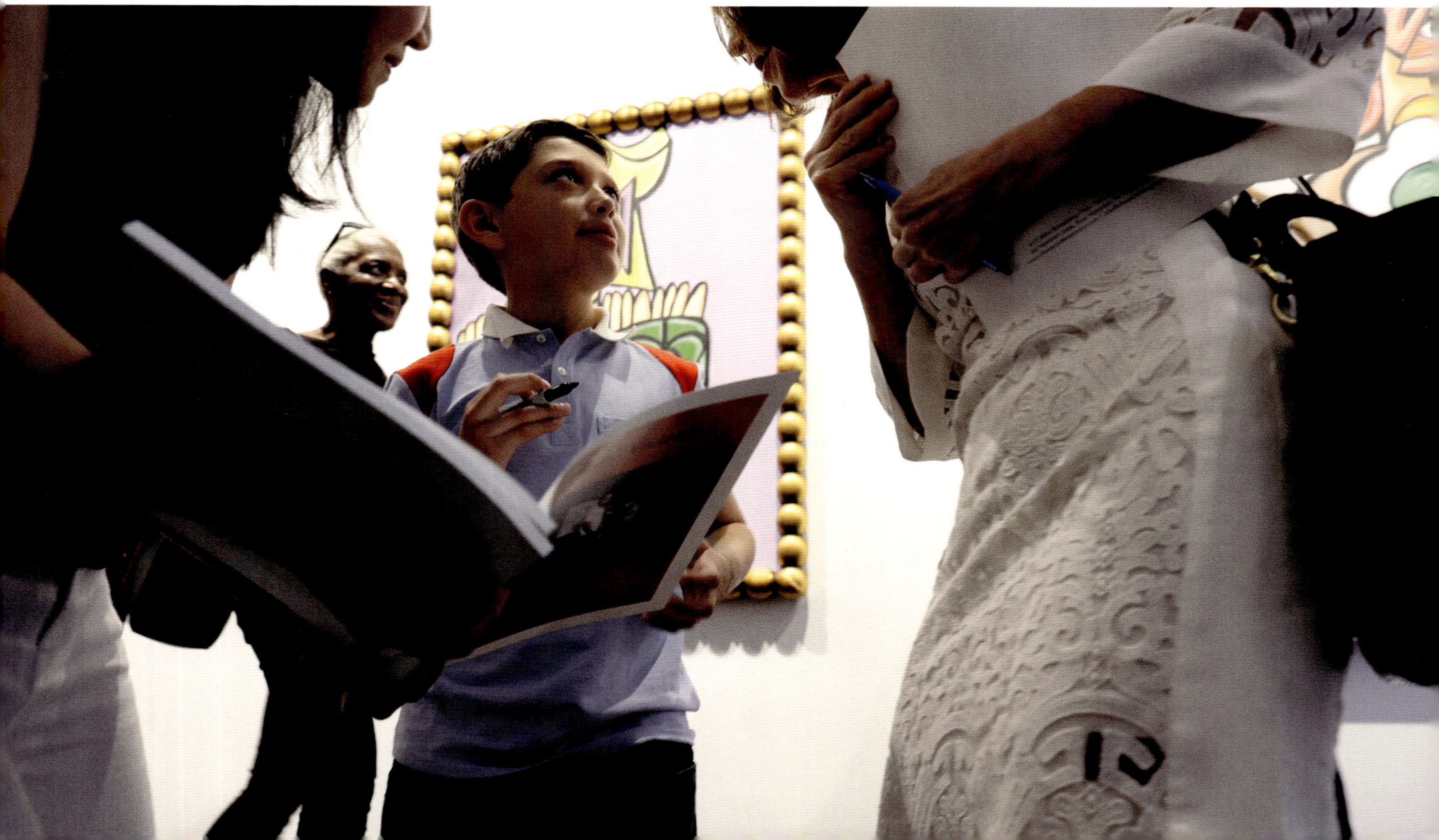

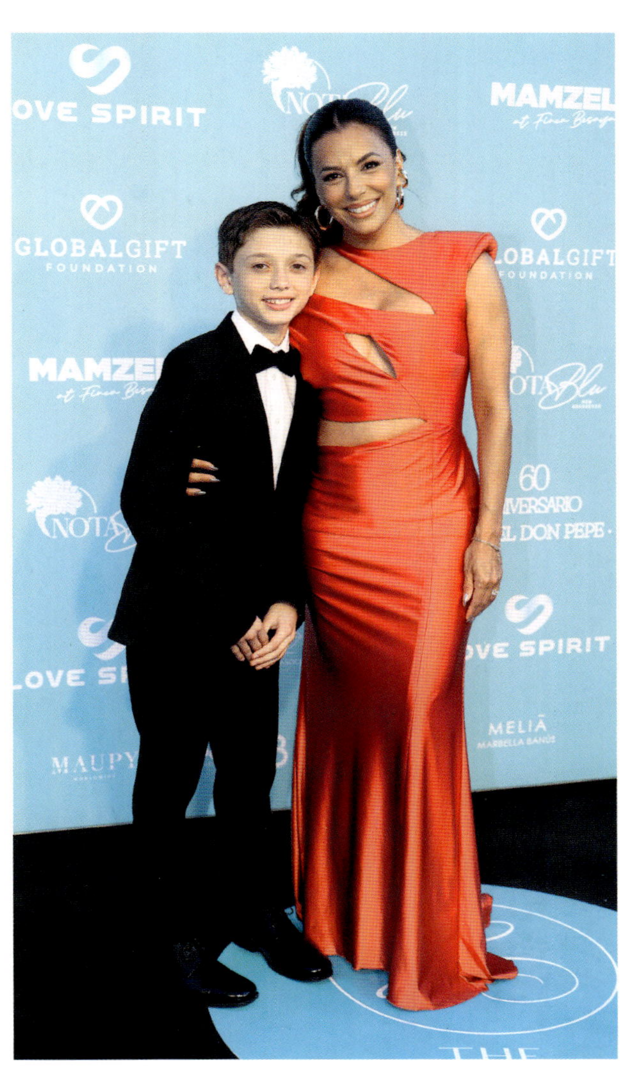

Above: Andres and Eva Longoria at The Global Gift Gala, July 2024. **Opposite:** Paintings hanging at Chase Contemporary (top). Andres signs his autograph at the *No Rules* show in 2022 (bottom).

Auctions & Giving Back

The first piece Andres had up for auction was *Ms. Cube* (pg. 182), which sold for $159,000 at Phillips in Hong Kong. This painting was auctioned alongside works by Kaws, Banksy, Anish Kapoor, and one of Andres's main influences and favorite artists, George Condo. A portion of the proceeds for the painting's sale went to Box of Hope, a charity that aids underprivileged children living in Asia.

Another painting called *Maya* (pg. 208), named after Picasso's daughter, went for $230,000 in Capri, Italy, at a charity gala in July 2022 that benefited UNICEF. The Valencia family has also donated proceeds from Andres's paintings to the AIDS charity group amfAR.

Lupe shares more insight on these charitable donations: "When Andres started selling his art and making money, we felt really blessed. It was important to us to give back, so we spoke with Bernie about donating money to different charities." Bernie connected the Valencias to Andy Boose, founder of AAB Productions—an international event-production and fundraising company—who helped them partner with amfAR and other organizations. Together, they donated Andres's paintings to raise money for charity at events in Capri, Venice, and St. Barts. Since the family started donating portions of Andres's sale proceeds, they have given over a million dollars to different charitable organizations.

When Andres created his painting inspired by the suffering of people in Ukraine, the family decided they wanted to do something to help those in the war-torn country. Lupe contacted Wladimir Klitschko, the Ukrainian boxer and founder of the Klitschko Foundation, to tell him about Andres's art and their hope to use it to generate funds for those who were negatively affected by Russia's invasion. They decided to make a limited print run of the painting to raise money. One hundred percent of the proceeds from the sales of the *Invasion of Ukraine* (pg. 199) prints, amounting to over $200,000, were donated to support children in the war-torn country through the Klitschko Foundation.

In July 2024, Andres and his family attended The Global Gift Gala in Marbella, Spain, which was organized by Maria Bravo and Eva Longoria, co-founders of the Global Gift Foundation. Andres donated his painting, *Sebastian* (pg. 254) for auction at the event, which went on to raise $151,000 for charity.

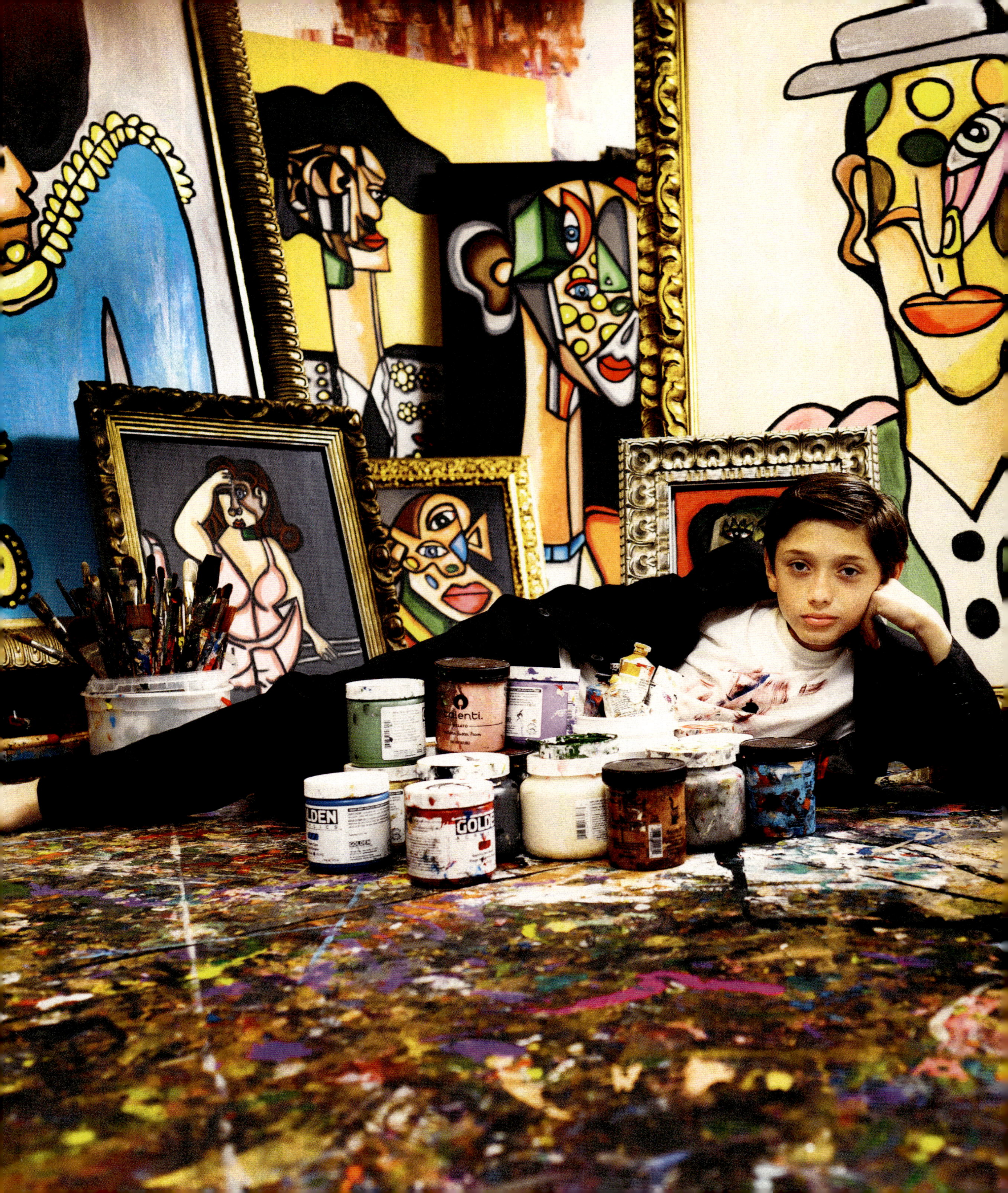

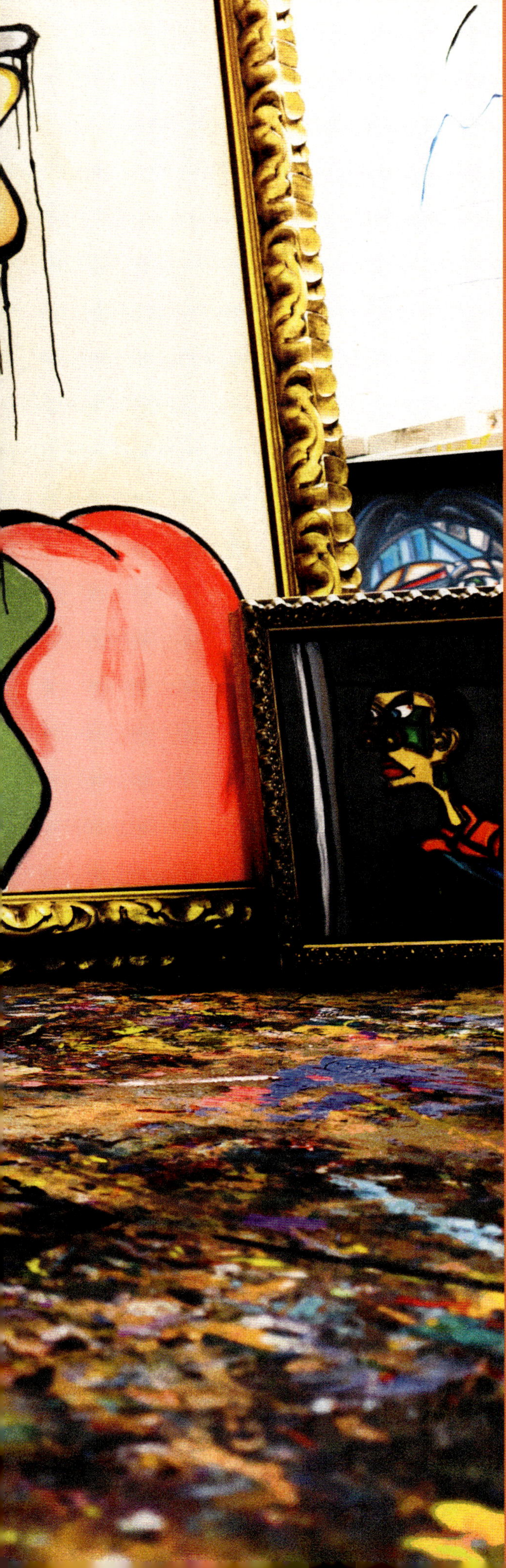

LOOKING AHEAD

While Elsa and Lupe will encourage Andres to keep creating as long as he wants to, they are also very protective of him. They want to make sure he has as normal a childhood as possible. "My son is an artist," Elsa says, "but he is, above all, a child. We want him to go to school, play the piano, learn to read and write in Spanish, and hang out with his friends." Finding the right balance for Andres can sometimes be tricky, but luckily, he has parents who have his best interests at heart and who can help him navigate the unique path he is on.

Andres on the floor of his studio, March 2024.

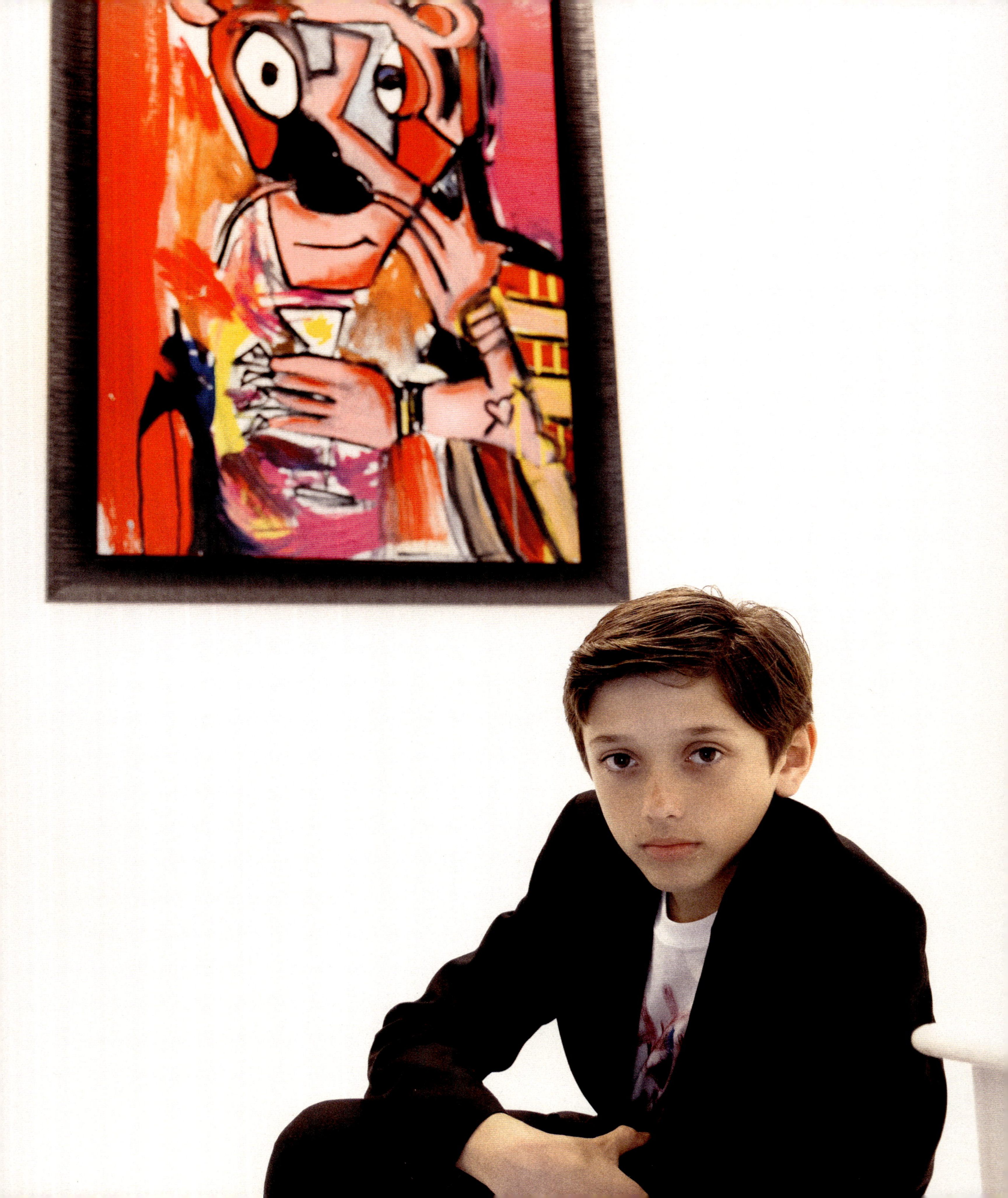

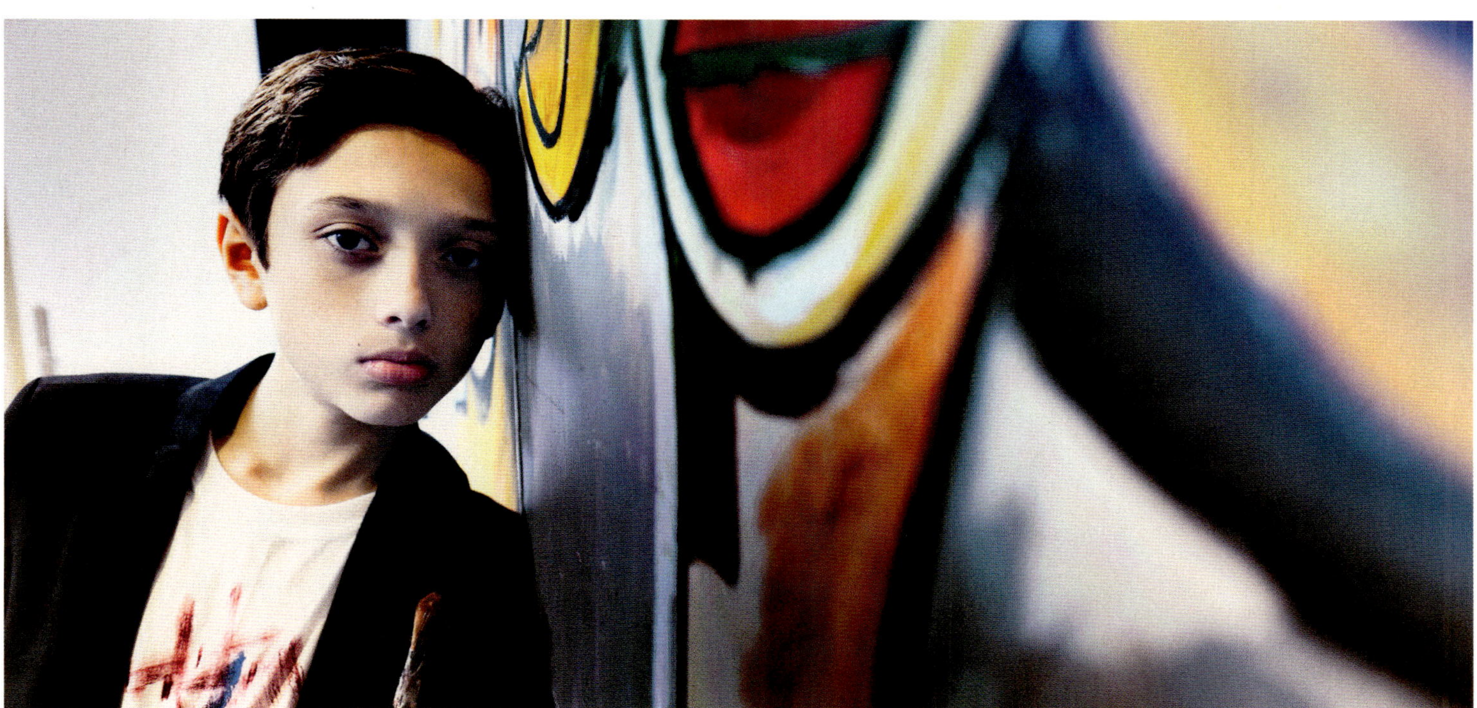

The Future

Andres has one main goal for the future: to continue being an artist. "That's what he wants to do forever," Lupe says. "He's even mentioned going to art school in Paris."

While some have commented that Andres's popularity and success in the art world may be temporary, Elsa feels it's important not to focus on the negative comments. The family is very focused on the present, and they work hard so Andres can enjoy the simple act of painting for what it is. They try not to put any pressure on him and never set specific expectations for the future of his artistic career. Andres does talk about what he wants to do in the future, though, and has shared many of his ideas with his parents. "He's told me he wants to go to school in Europe for art," Elsa says. "When I ask him why Europe, he says, 'I just want to see what else is out there. I want to see different processes.'"

Andres has also told Elsa he wants to sculpt more and learn more about what it takes to create large sculptures. There is a school in Florence, Italy, that specifically focuses on both portraiture and sculpture, and it has caught Andres's attention as something that could be a good fit for him.

Finding art teachers and classes for Andres closer to home in San Diego has been a challenge. "I've asked four different teachers from various art schools here who do private lessons, and none of them would take Andres on," Elsa explains. "They've all told me no, they think he's too young for it."

Elsa has only been able to get Andres into a sculpting class. He was the sole child in attendance. She also joined the class, as that was the only way the program would admit him. "I would love for Andres to be able to learn other techniques," Elsa says, "but at his age, it's been hard to expose him to much more, because people don't want to take him on as a

Above: Andres leans against the wall of his studio, where he has many faces painted. **Opposite:** Posing in the stairwell which leads to his basement studio. The painting *Pink Panther 2* (pg. 228) hangs behind him.

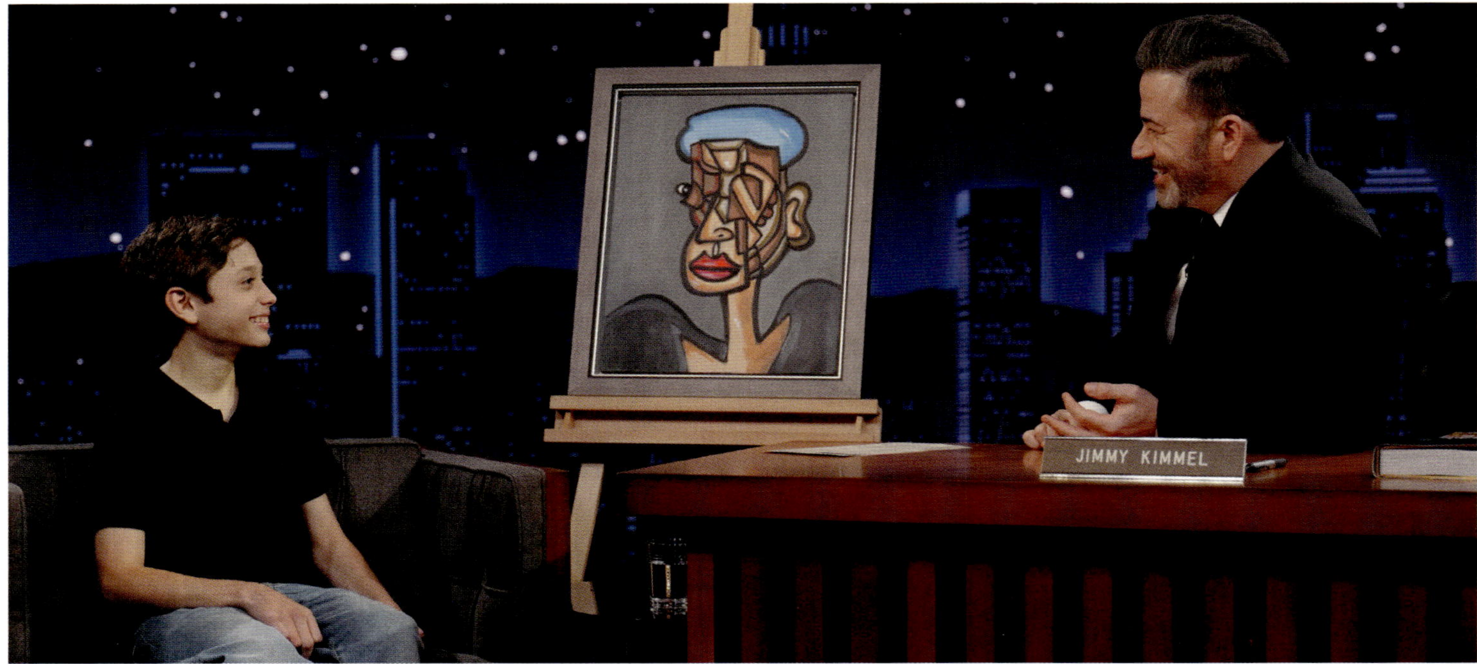

student. But I hope he can evolve with his artwork. I think him learning more and really seeing what else is out there will be amazing for him and his development as an artist."

Andres has been exploring other mediums, including making videos of clay figures using stop-motion animation. He enjoys working with clay as a secondary medium, but when asked if he thinks he will ever work more with other mediums besides paint, he responds, "Well, I do like clay, but if I had to compare it to painting, I'd rather just stick with that. It's my favorite, and I know a lot about it." While he's been hesitant to paint realistic portraits in the past, Andres began experimenting with realism for two paintings in 2024, including *William Adolphe Bouguereau* (pg. 265) and *Cardinal Camillo Astali Pamphili* (pg. 265).

Looking ahead to what may come next, Andres says, "I always love to try new things with my art, of course, because you never know, maybe you'd like it. But so far, I really like what I do. I would love to keep being an artist, and I would like to see myself evolve in the future." He dreams of having one of his paintings hanging in the Louvre but would also be thrilled to have any of his paintings displayed next to his premier inspiration, Pablo Picasso. Having his artwork shown somewhere in Asia also excites him a great deal. He cites the countries of Japan and Korea specifically as the two places at the top of his wish list.

If another child were to ask Andres for advice on how to become a good artist or painter, he would share the following: "I would tell them to just be an artist. You have to work hard, put your art first, and never give up. None of this came overnight. You have to put in the work. There have been times where I don't sell paintings, and there have been times where it's been harder, but I keep going, and then at the end, it works out." Andres is so passionate about painting and the pieces he creates. He believes in his art and in himself, which is another main factor that has led him to such great success.

JIMMY KIMMEL INTERVIEW

Andres was interviewed by Jimmy Kimmel on *Jimmy Kimmel Live!* on May 30, 2024. The nine-minute segment featured Andres and Jimmy in conversation as they discussed his paintings, how he started creating, his artistic process, and the success he's found selling his paintings for six-figure sums. Andres's playful sense of humor was apparent, as he drew laughs from those in the studio. This book was also announced during the interview, as Jimmy held up a copy of *Painting Without Rules* to show the audience.

The paintings displayed during the interview included *El Mariachi* (pg. 191), *Rich Old Lady* (above, which Kimmel named and now owns), *Frida Kahlo* (pg. 238), *Benito* (pg. 260), and *El Caballode Picasso* (pg. 233).

Above: Andres being interviewed on *Jimmy Kimmel Live!*, May 30, 2024. **Opposite:** Andres and Jimmy Kimmel. *Photos by Randy Holmes, Disney.* **Following:** Andres's studio, March 2024.

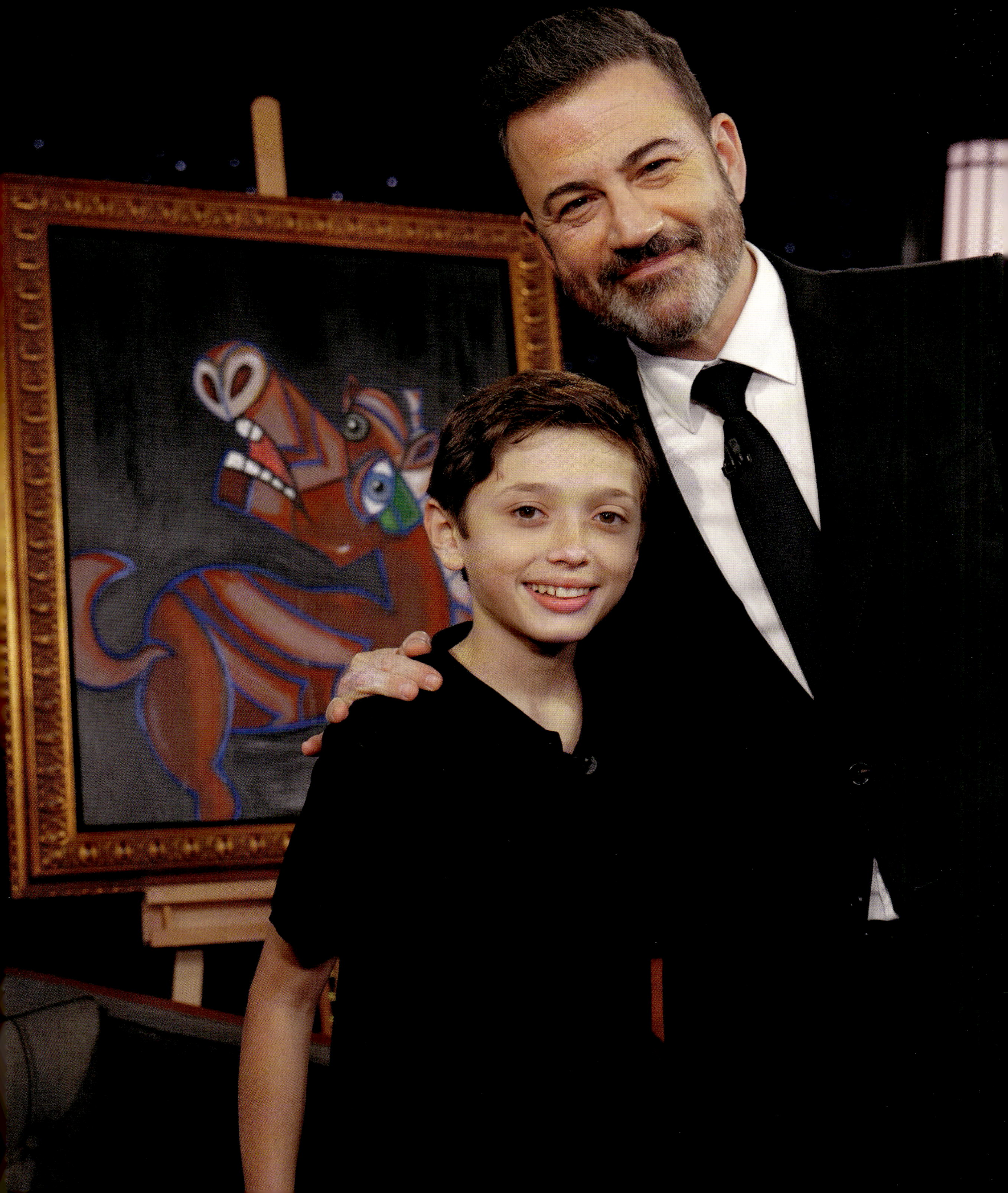

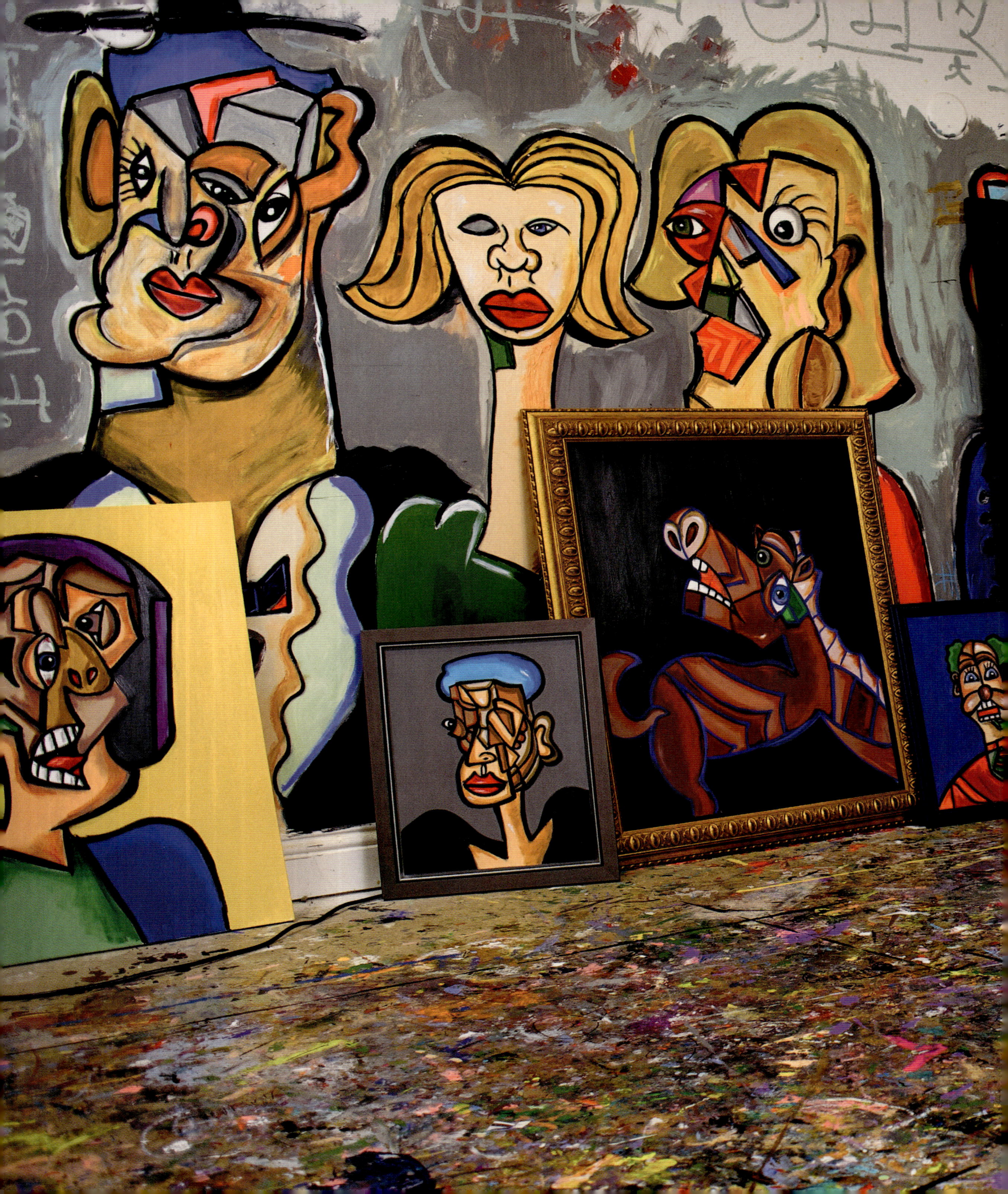

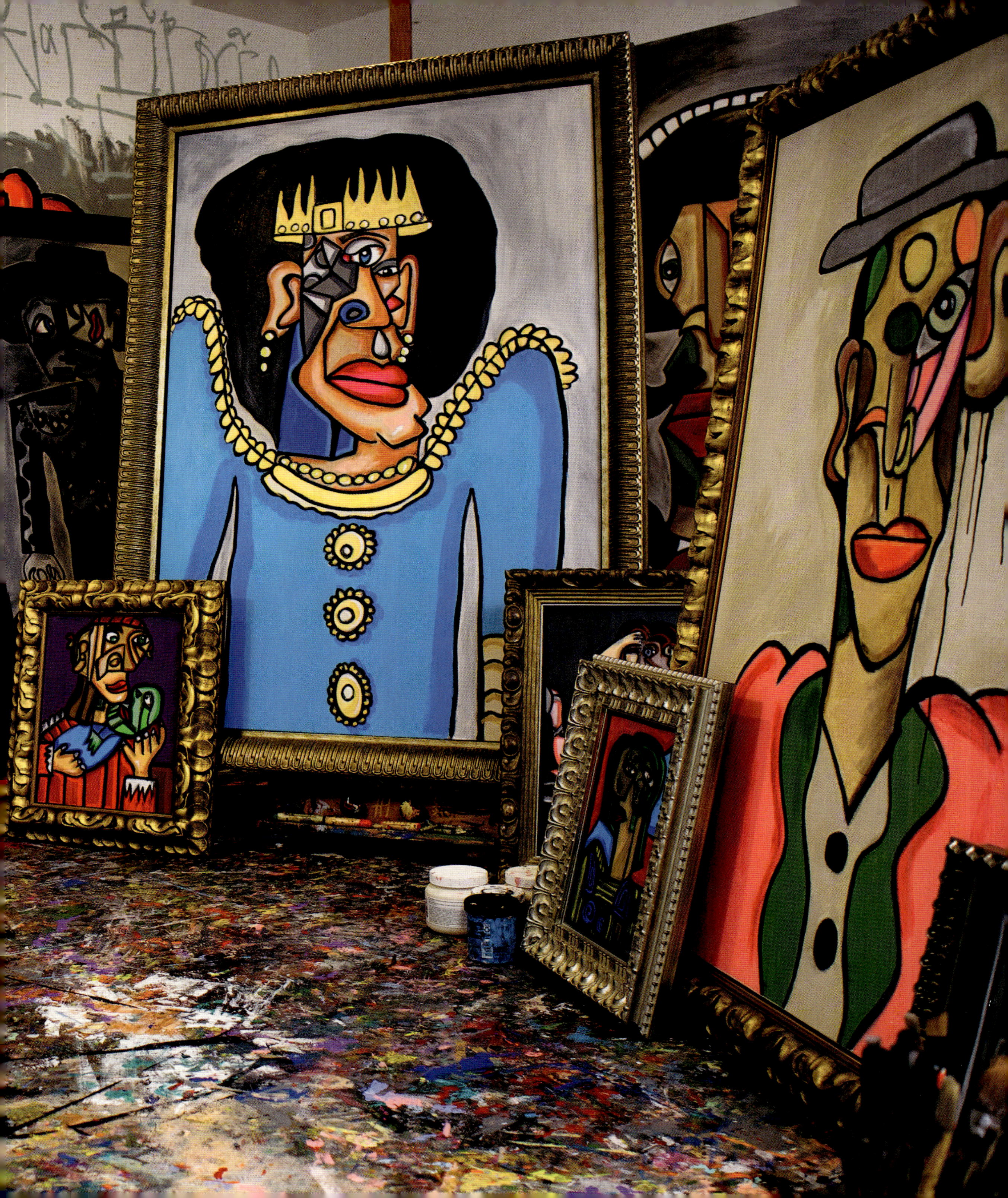

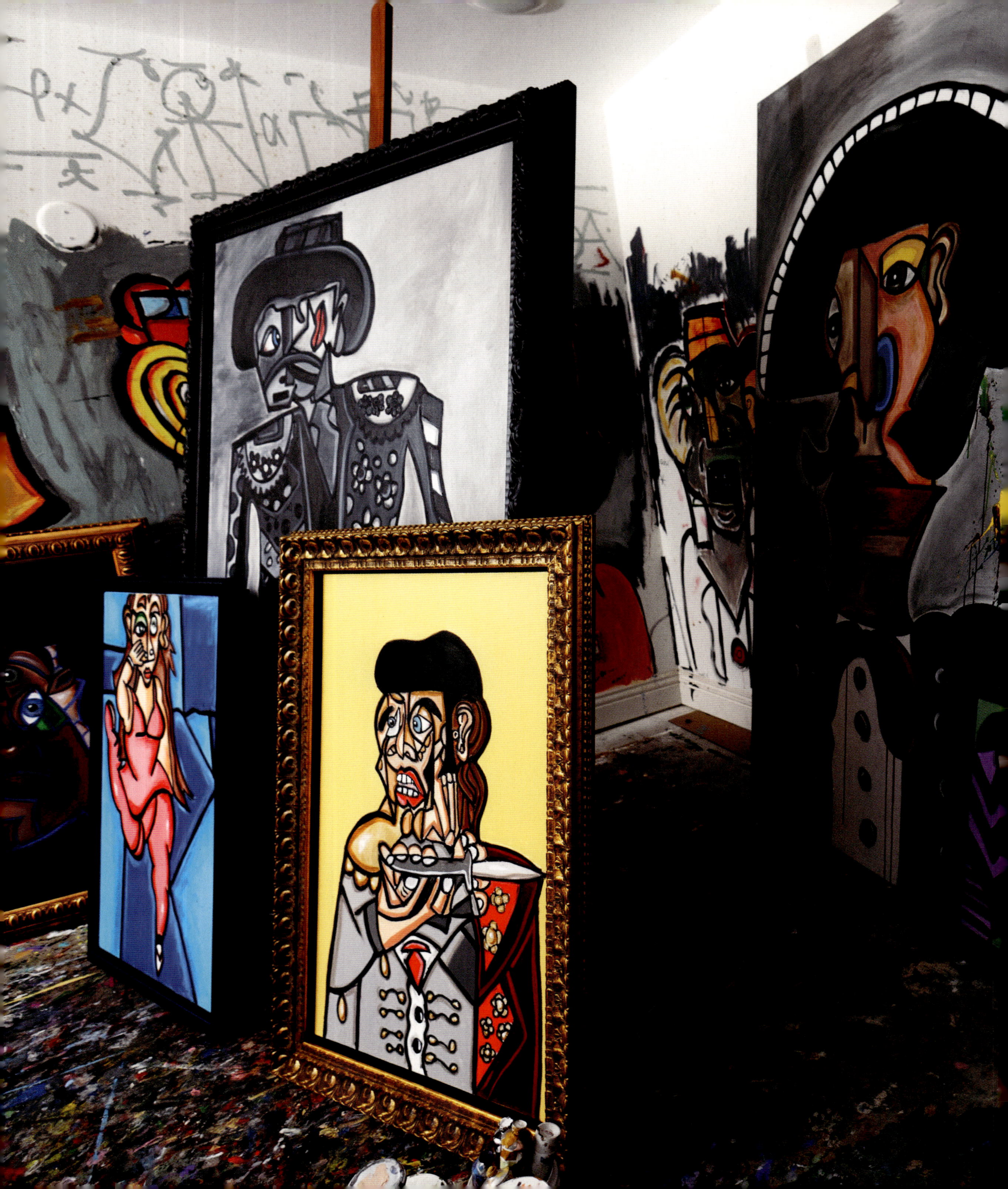

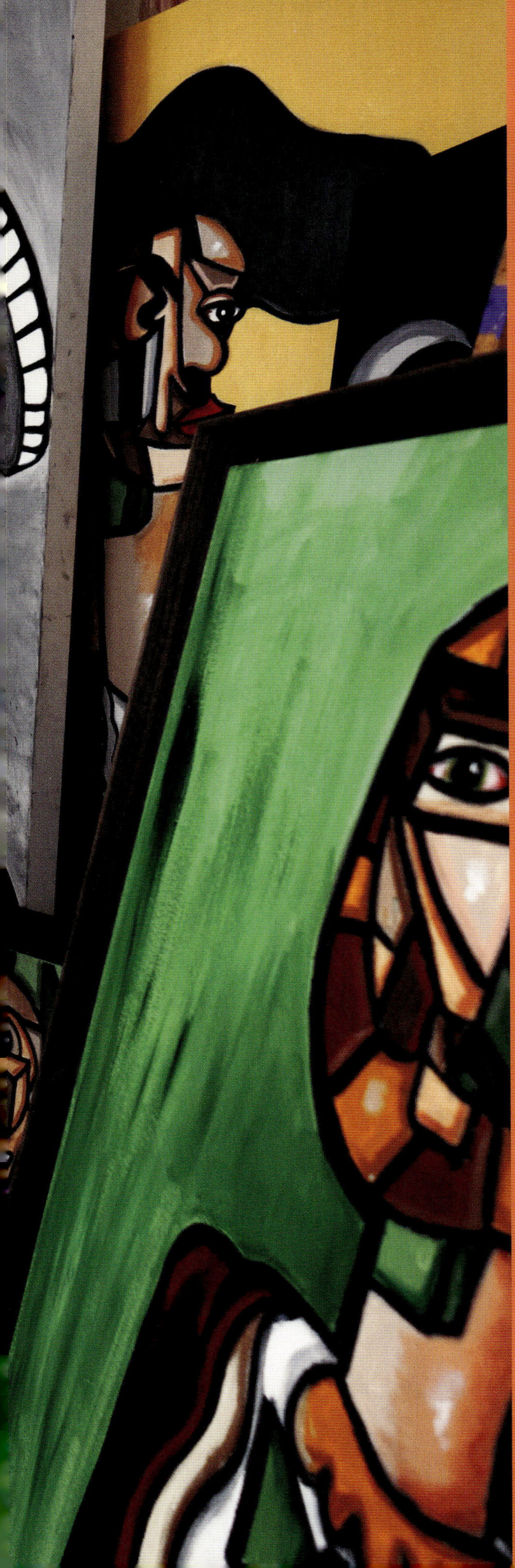

PART 6

THE PAINTINGS

Since the age of five, Andres has been an artist. He doesn't remember a time when he wasn't sketching, painting, or creating in some fashion. Like many other children, his earliest works were drawings of stick figures and other simple sketches. He constantly used his imagination to create something new. When he began painting on canvas, his talent really started to develop as he found his passion guiding a paintbrush. Andres explains that his favorite part of painting is how it looks at the end. "When I'm done," he says, "it makes me feel like I've accomplished something."

For such a young man, he has accomplished more than many artists do in their lifetimes, already having sold over a hundred of his paintings to art collectors around the world. By using vivid colors, intricate facial compositions, large canvases, and quick brush strokes, Andres has created unique, abstract portraits of characters again and again.

The paintings on the pages that follow are organized in chronological order and are meant to showcase the evolution of Andres's painting style over the years. While the paintings featured here are not fully exhaustive, they do include Andres's favorite and most important pieces, offering an immersive look at the original works created by this immensely talented artist.

A collection of Andres's paintings in his studio, March 2024.

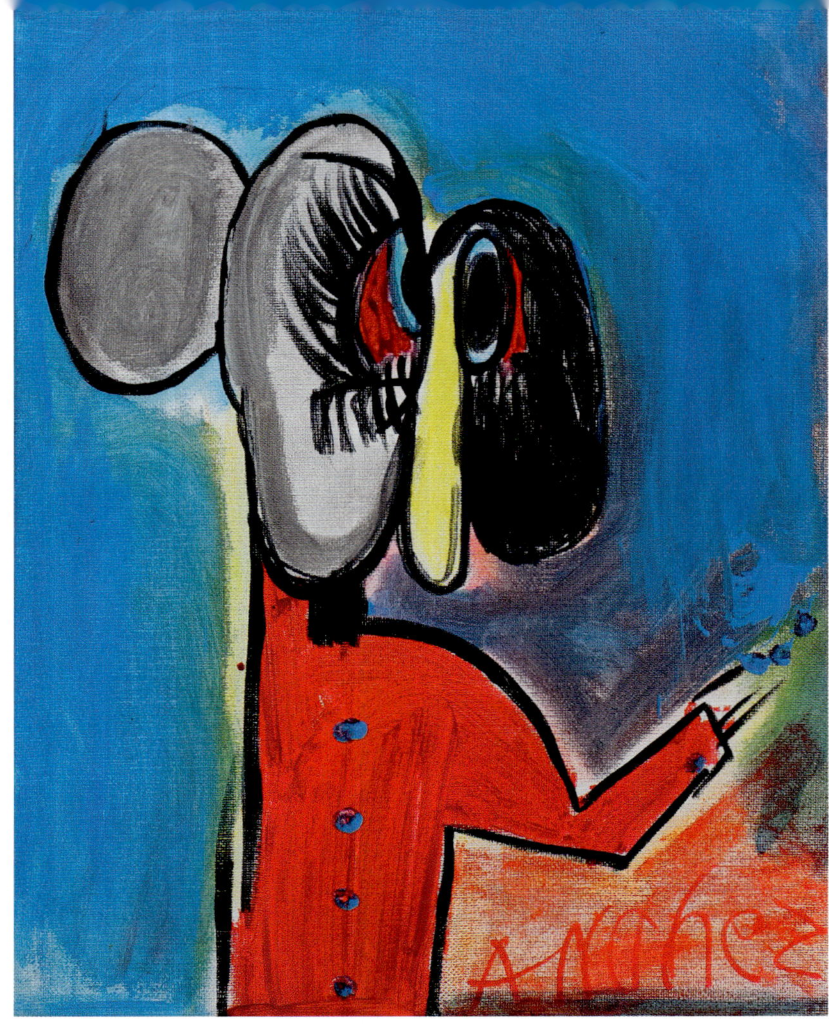

Wild Mouse, 2018 │ acrylic and oil pastel on canvas, 14 × 11 in

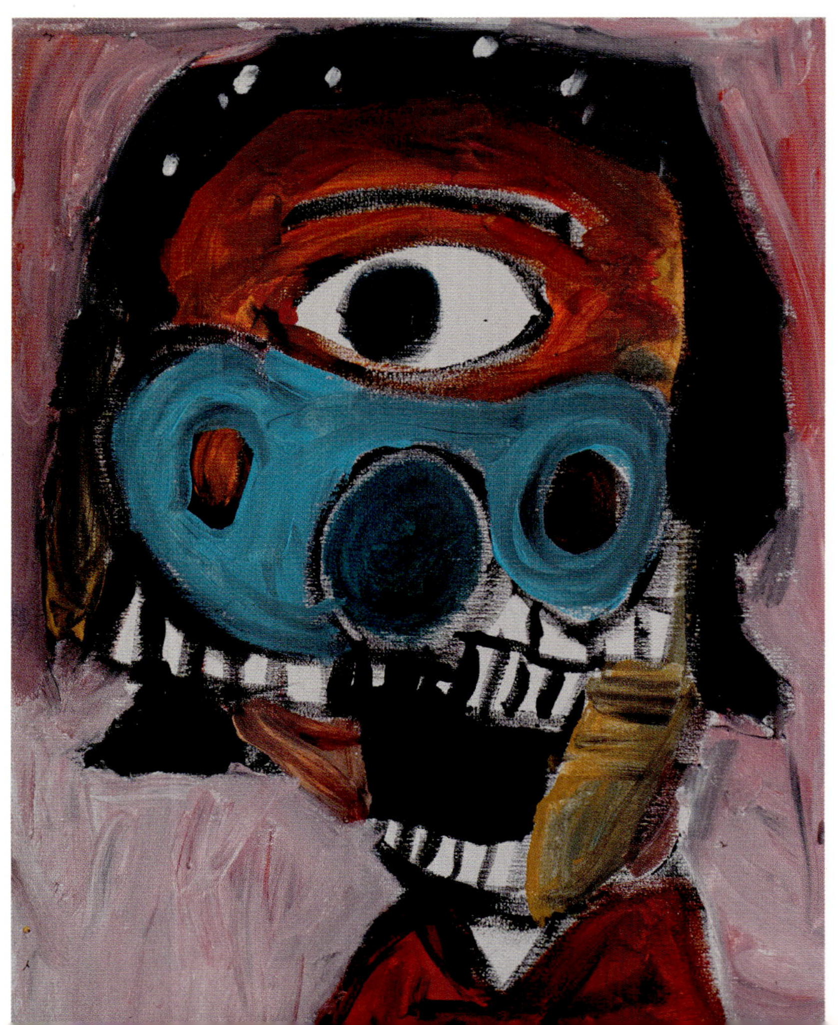

Smiling Peter, 2019 │ acrylic and oil pastel on canvas, 18 × 12 in

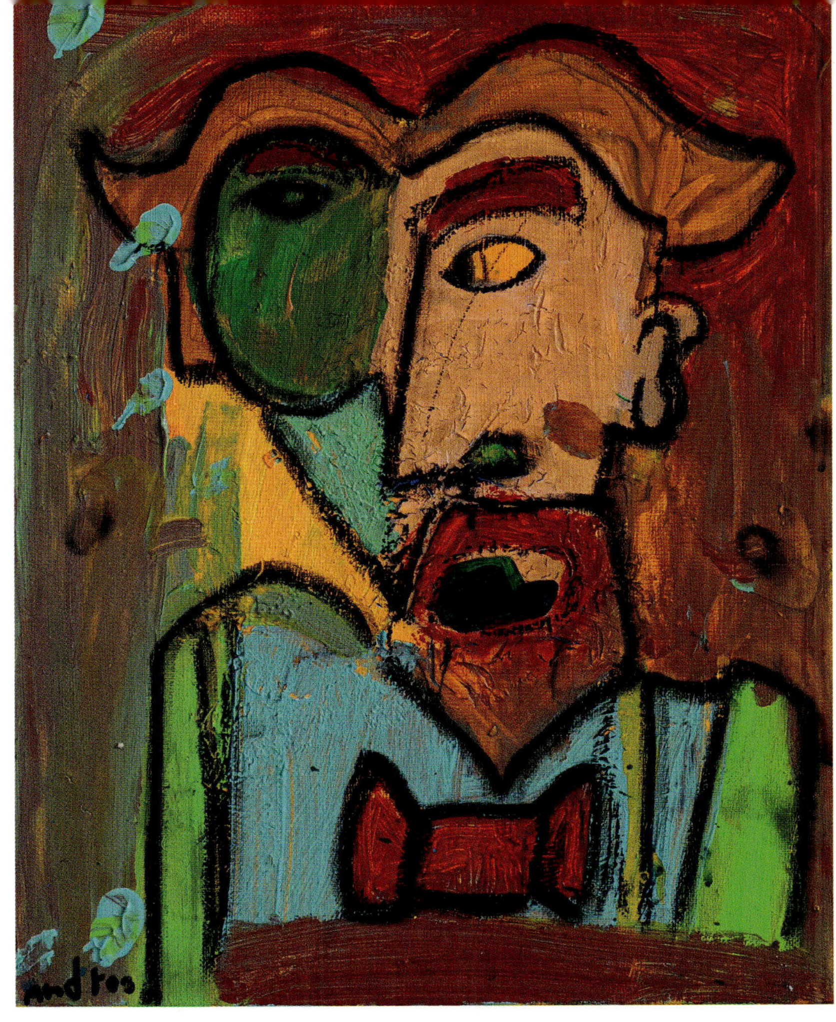

Dennis, 2019 | acrylic and oil pastel on canvas, 14 × 11 in

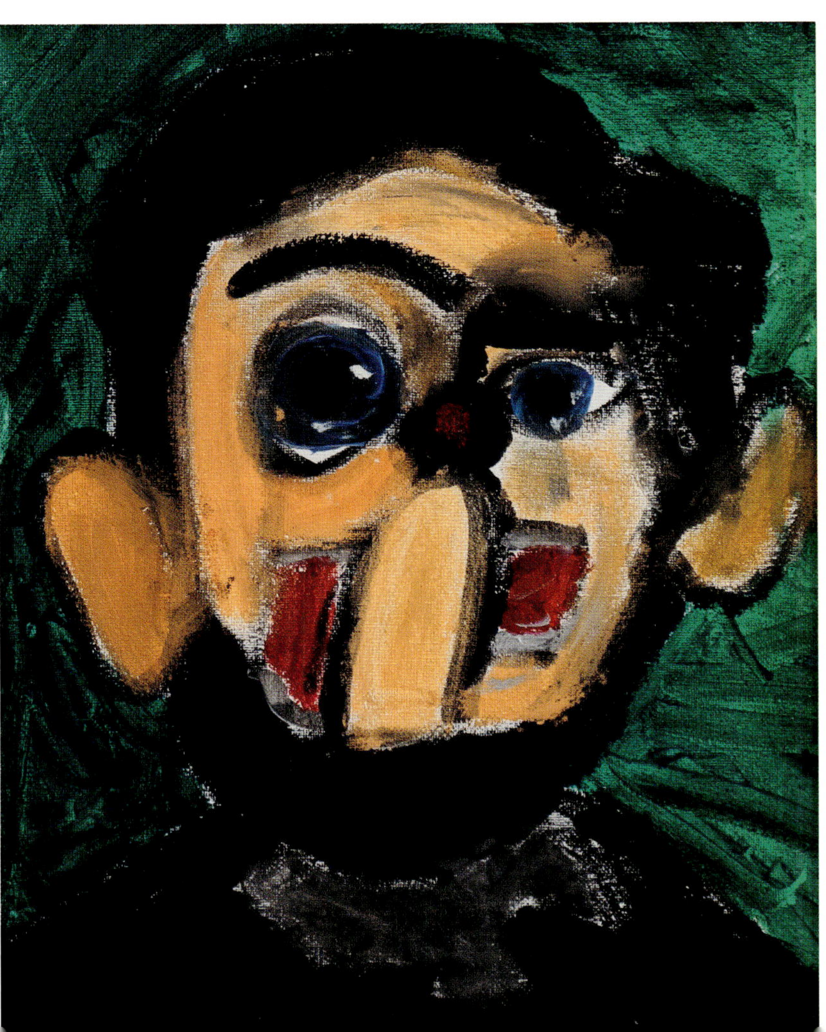

Lincoln, 2019 | acrylic and oil pastel on canvas, 14 × 11 in

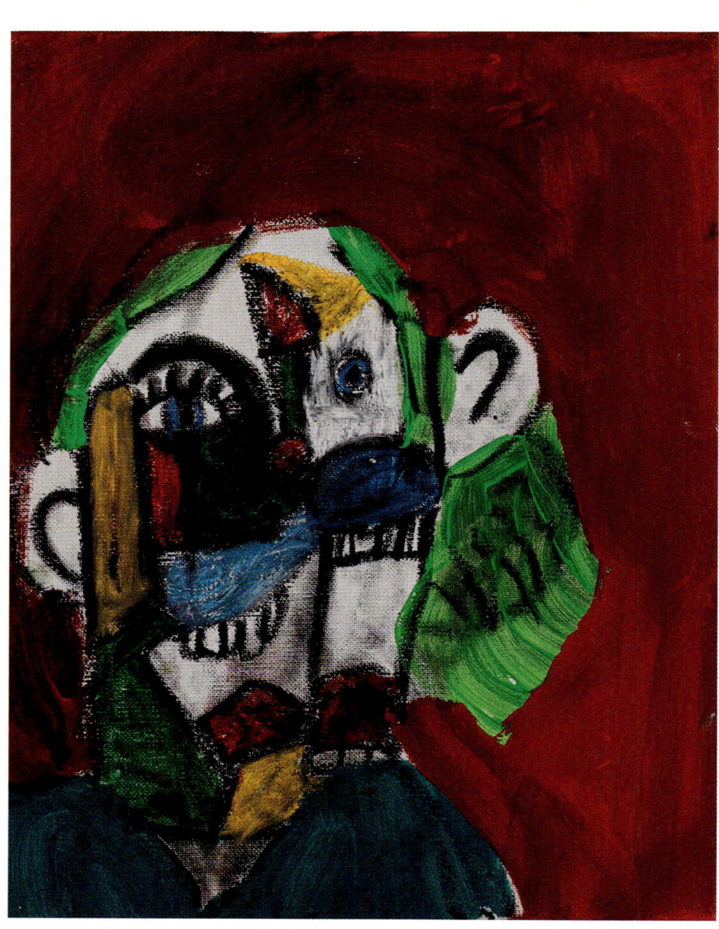

Homage to George Condo, 2019 | acrylic and oil pastel on canvas, 14 × 11 in

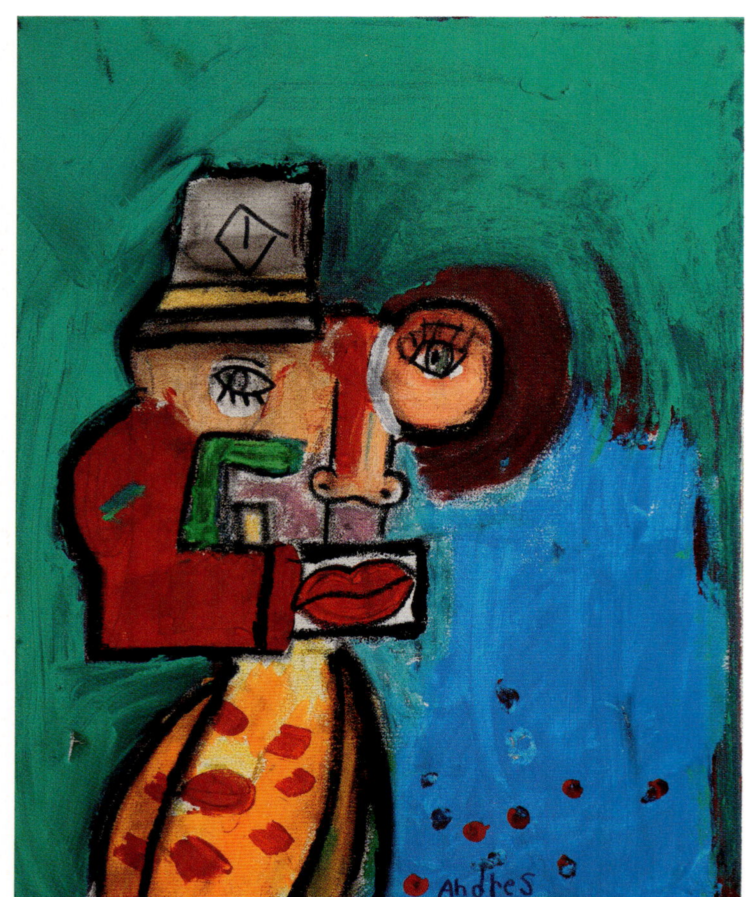

Red Lips, 2019 | acrylic and oil pastel on canvas, 20 × 16 in

Distorted Man, 2019 | acrylic and oil pastel on canvas, 14 × 11 in

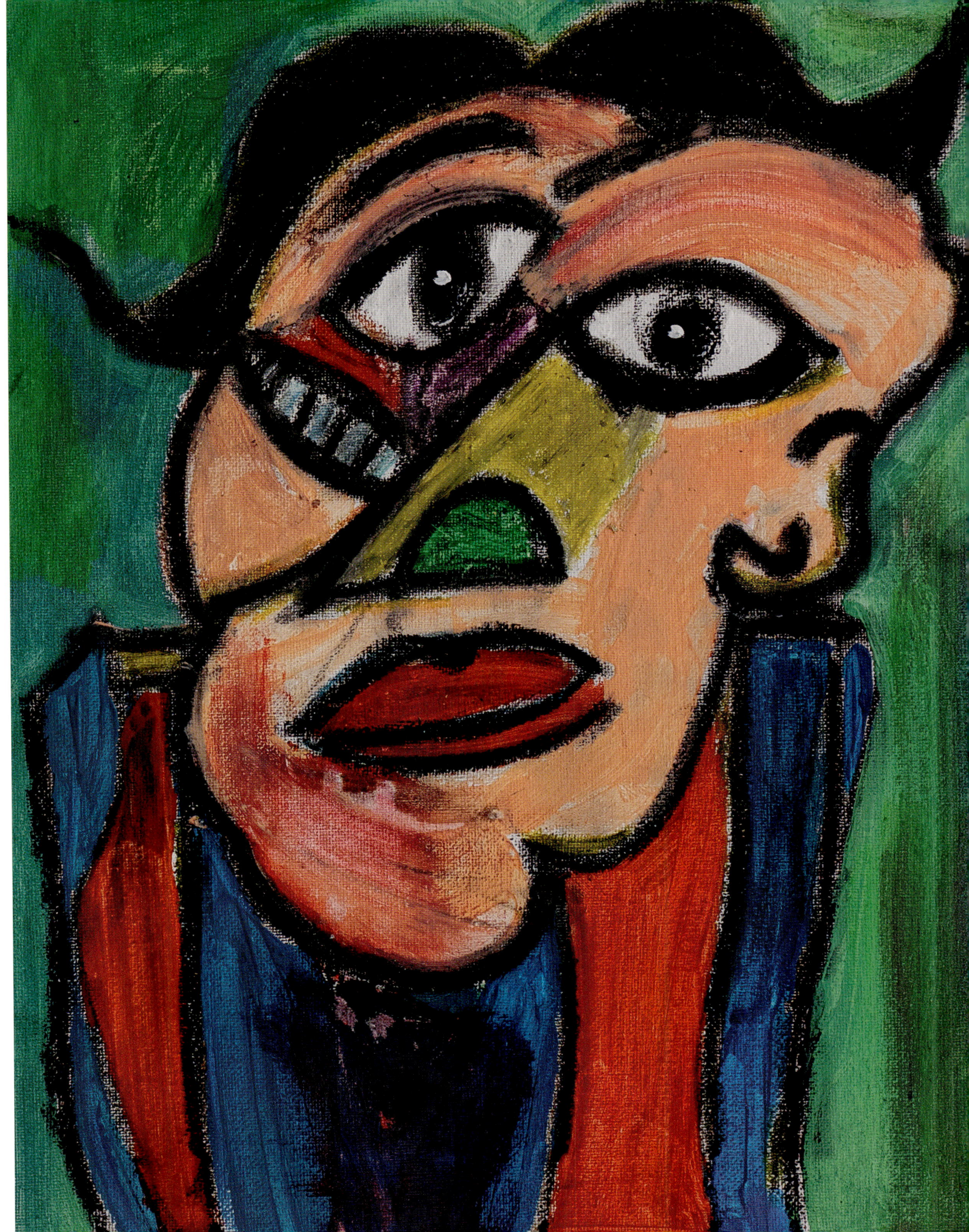

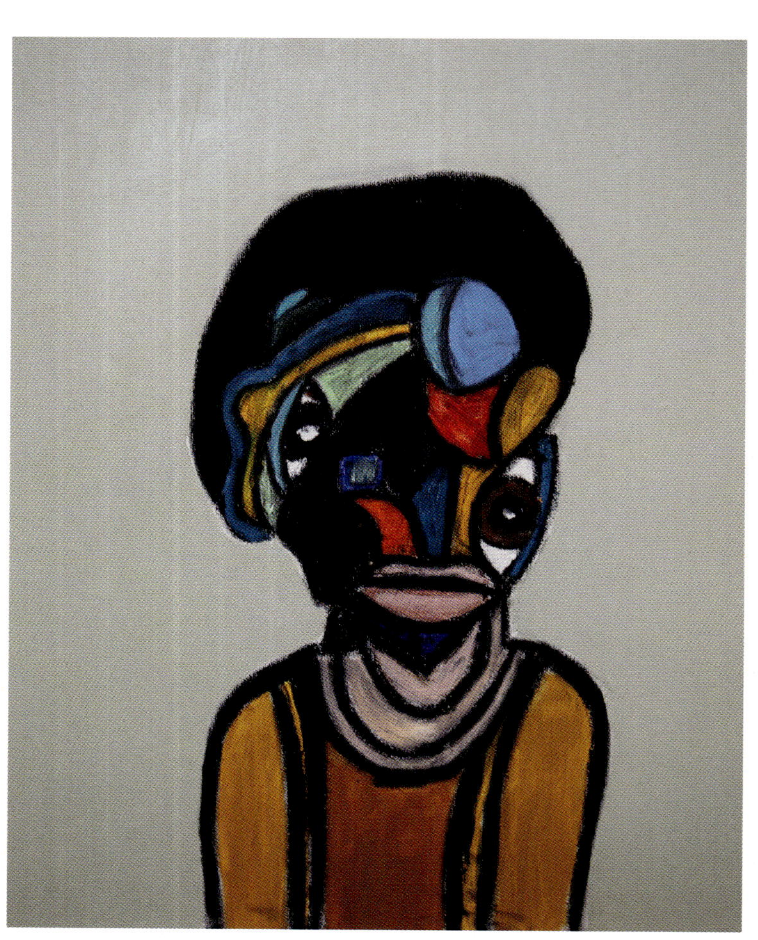

The Flawless, 2020 | acrylic and oil pastel on canvas, 20 × 16 in

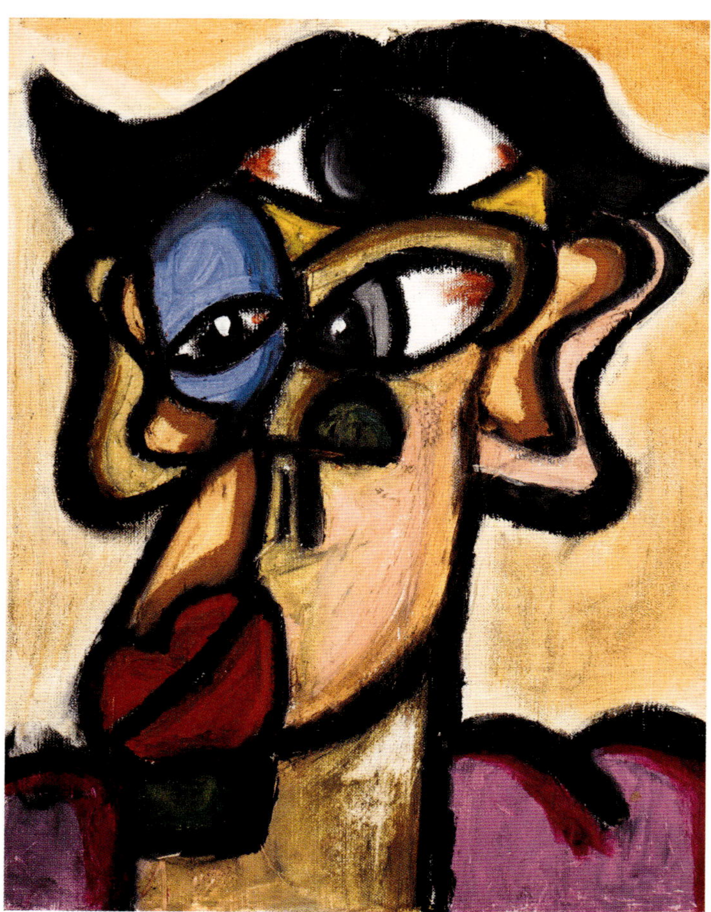

Jim, 2020 | acrylic and oil pastel on canvas, 14 × 11 in

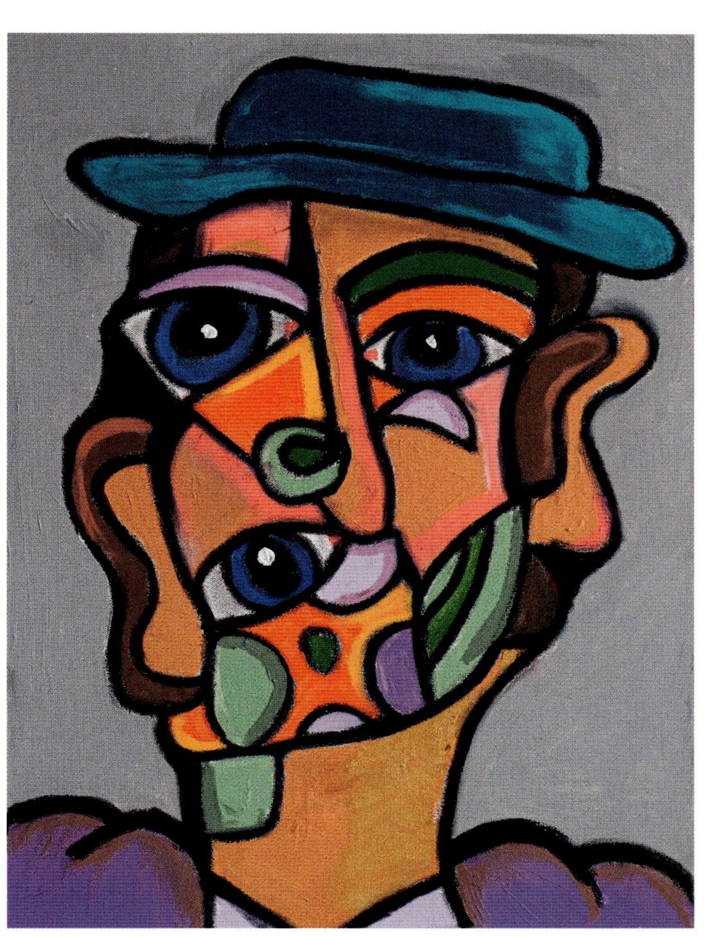

The Law Man, 2020 | acrylic and oil pastel on canvas, 24 × 18 in

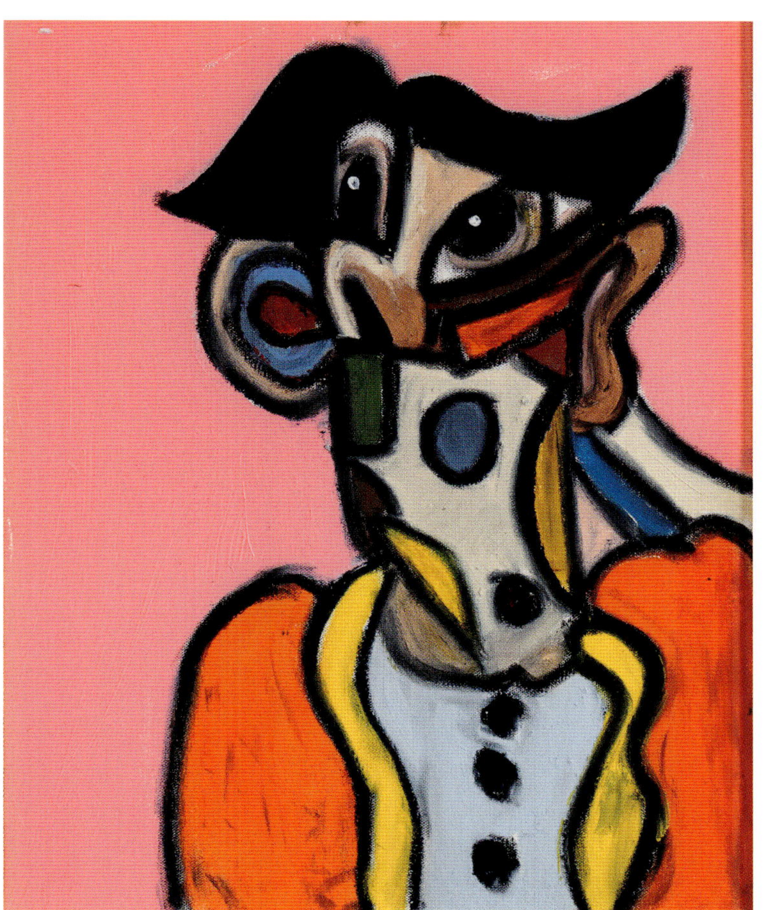

The Bachelor, 2020 | acrylic and oil pastel on canvas, 20 × 16 in

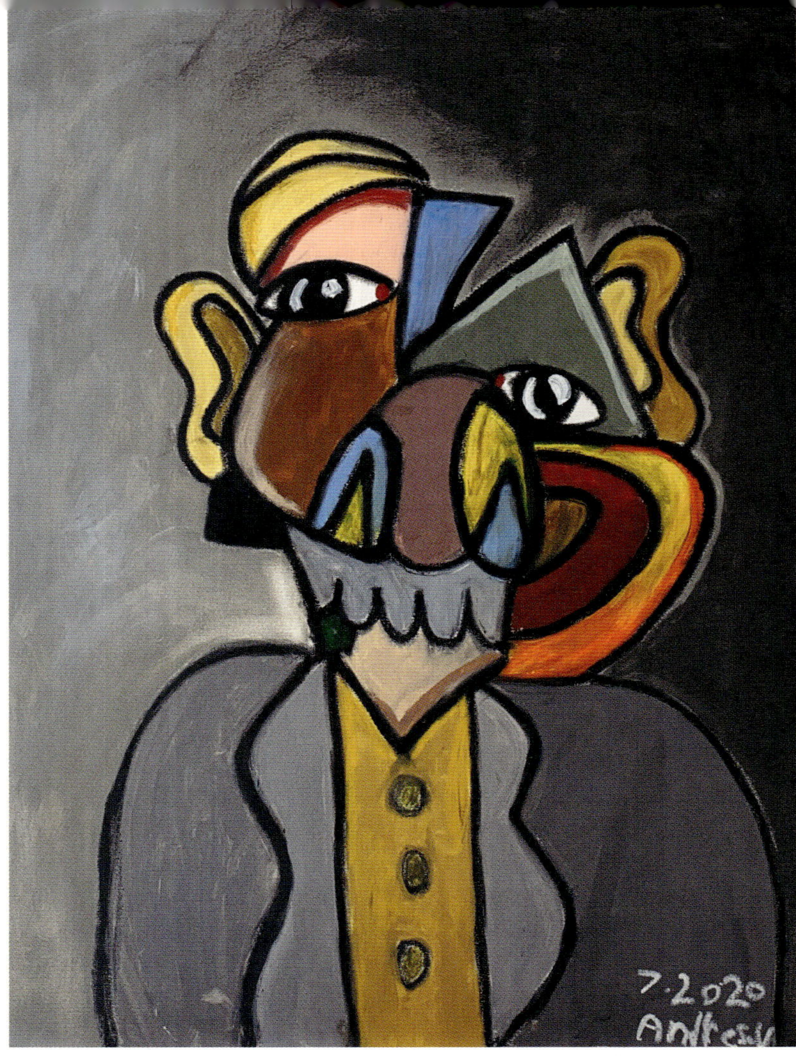

Benny, 2020 | acrylic and oil pastel on canvas, 40 × 30 in

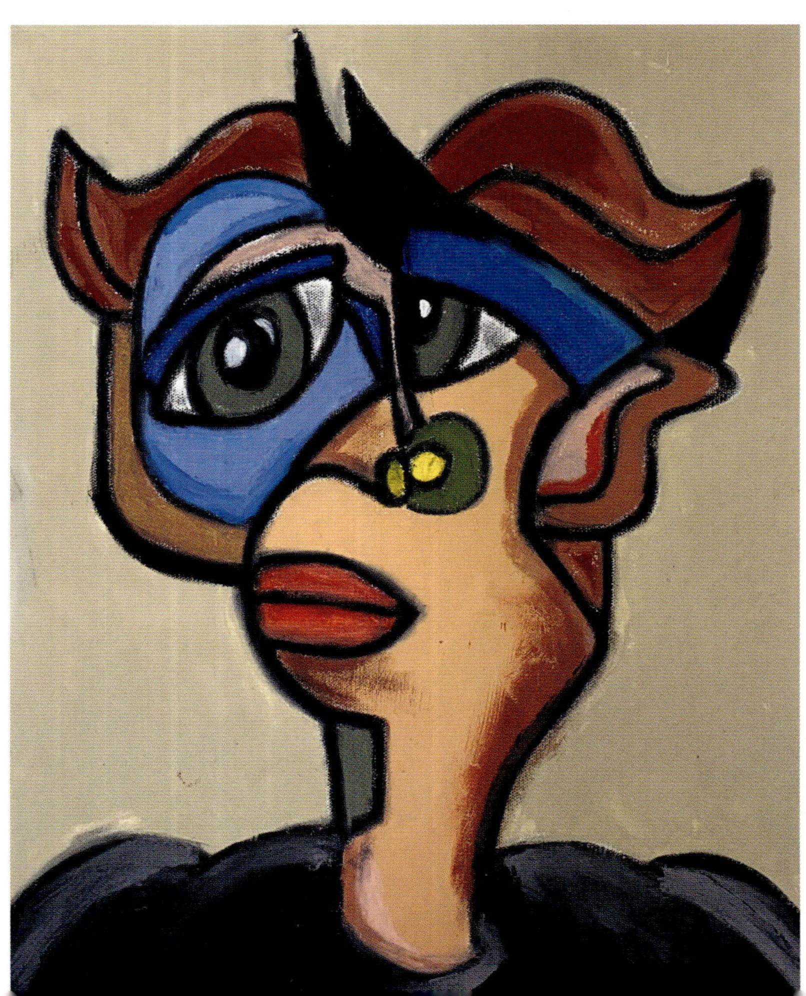

Juliette, 2020 | acrylic and oil pastel on canvas, 20 × 16 in

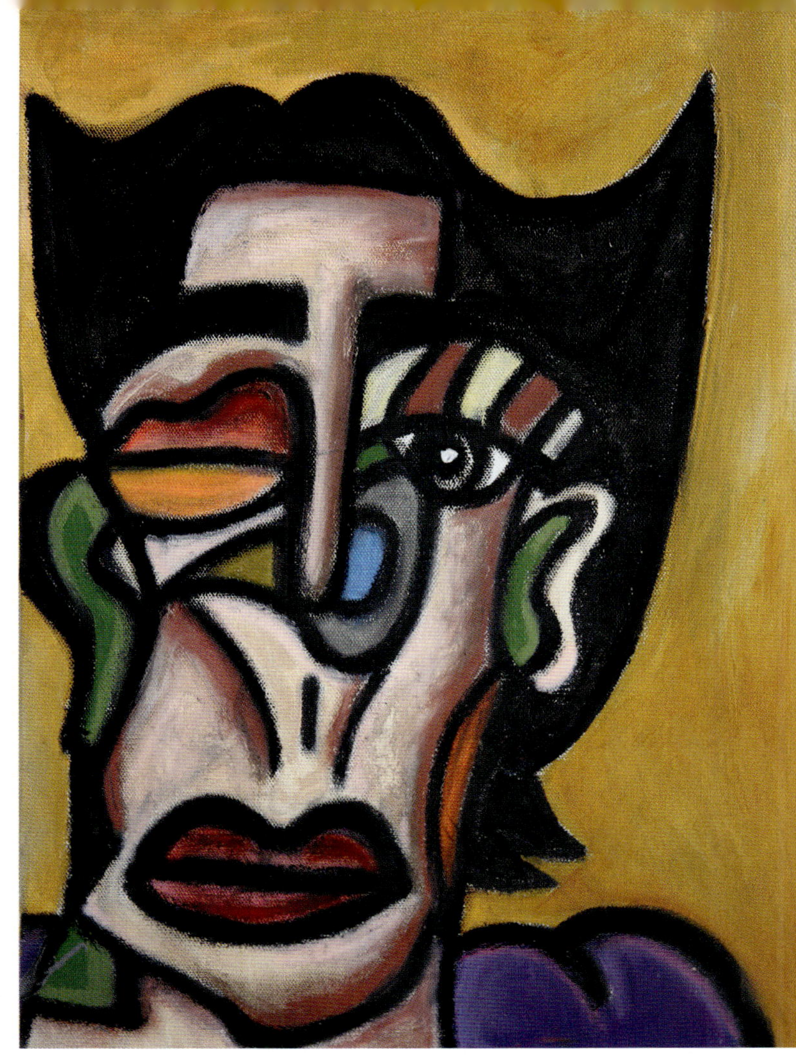

Fred 2, 2020 | acrylic and oil pastel on canvas, 18 × 14 in

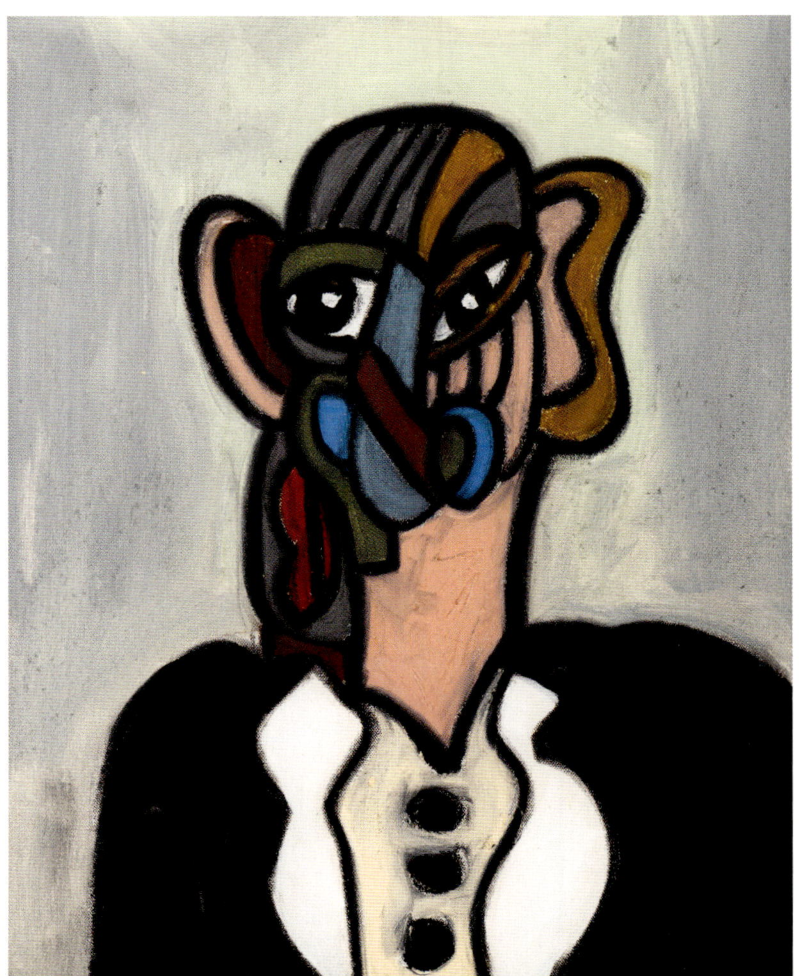

The Dealer, 2020 | acrylic and oil pastel on canvas, 24 × 18 in

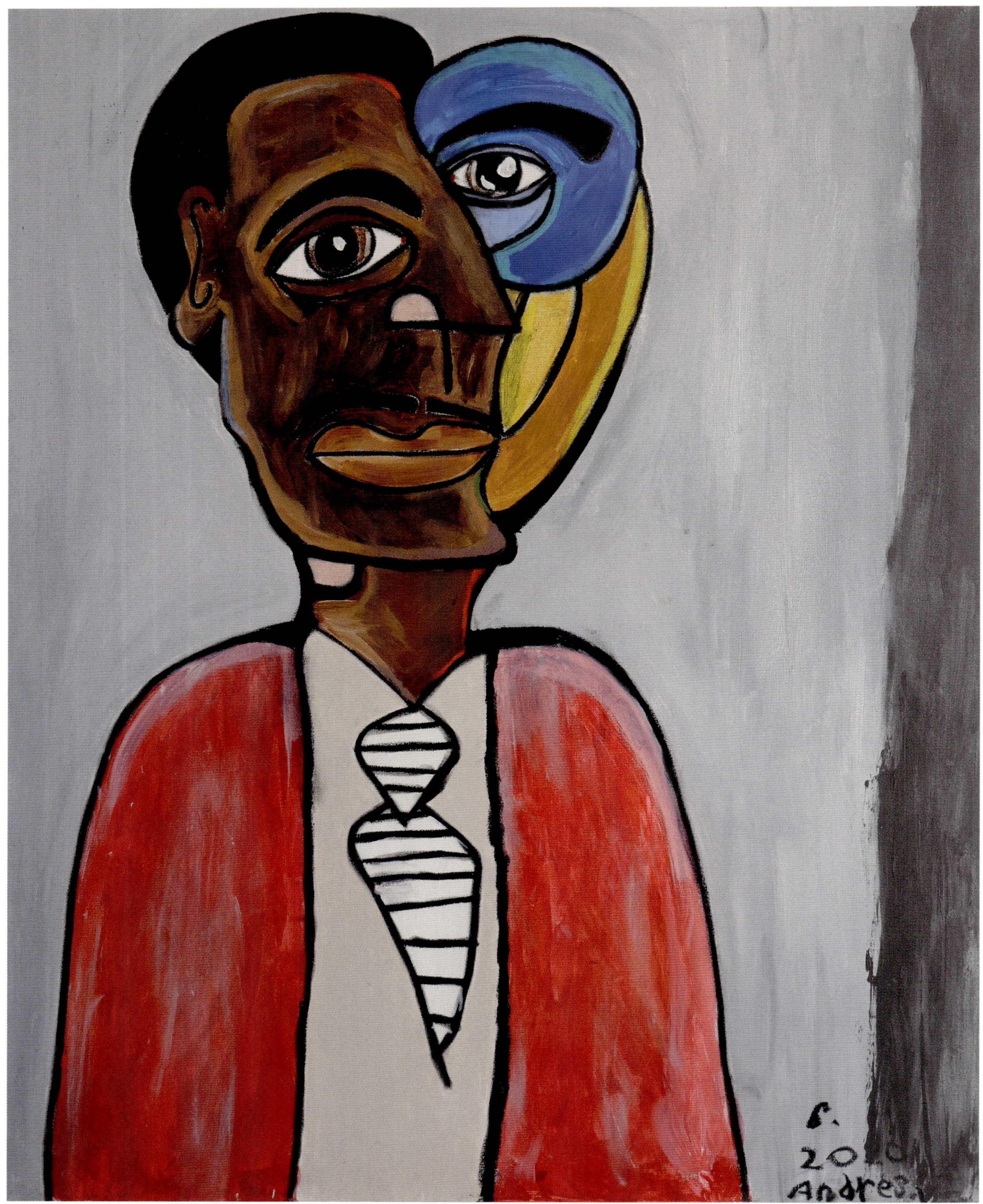

Fats Domino, 2020 | acrylic and oil pastel on canvas, 60 × 48 in

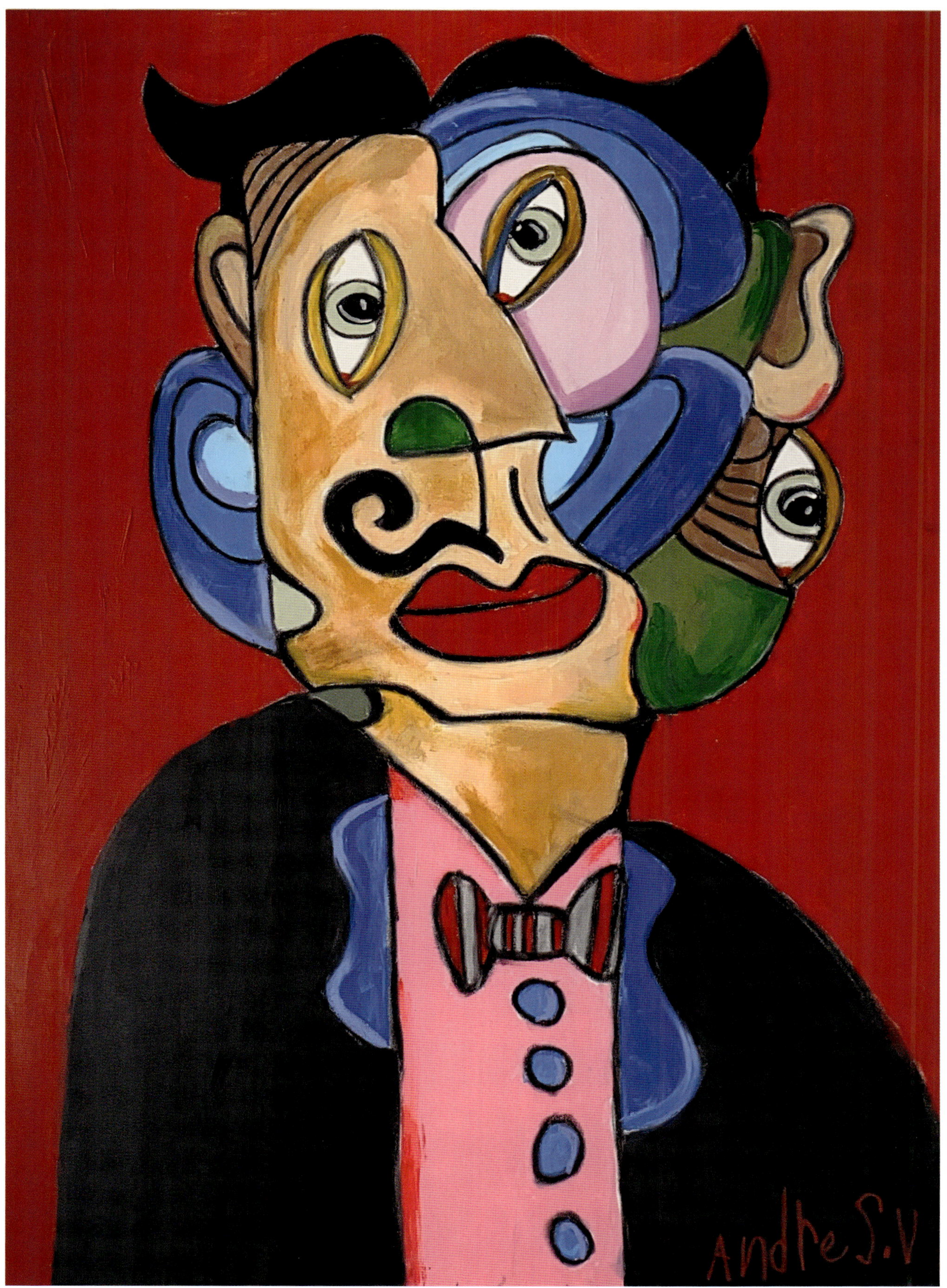

Salvador Dalí, 2020 | acrylic and oil pastel on canvas, 48 × 41 in

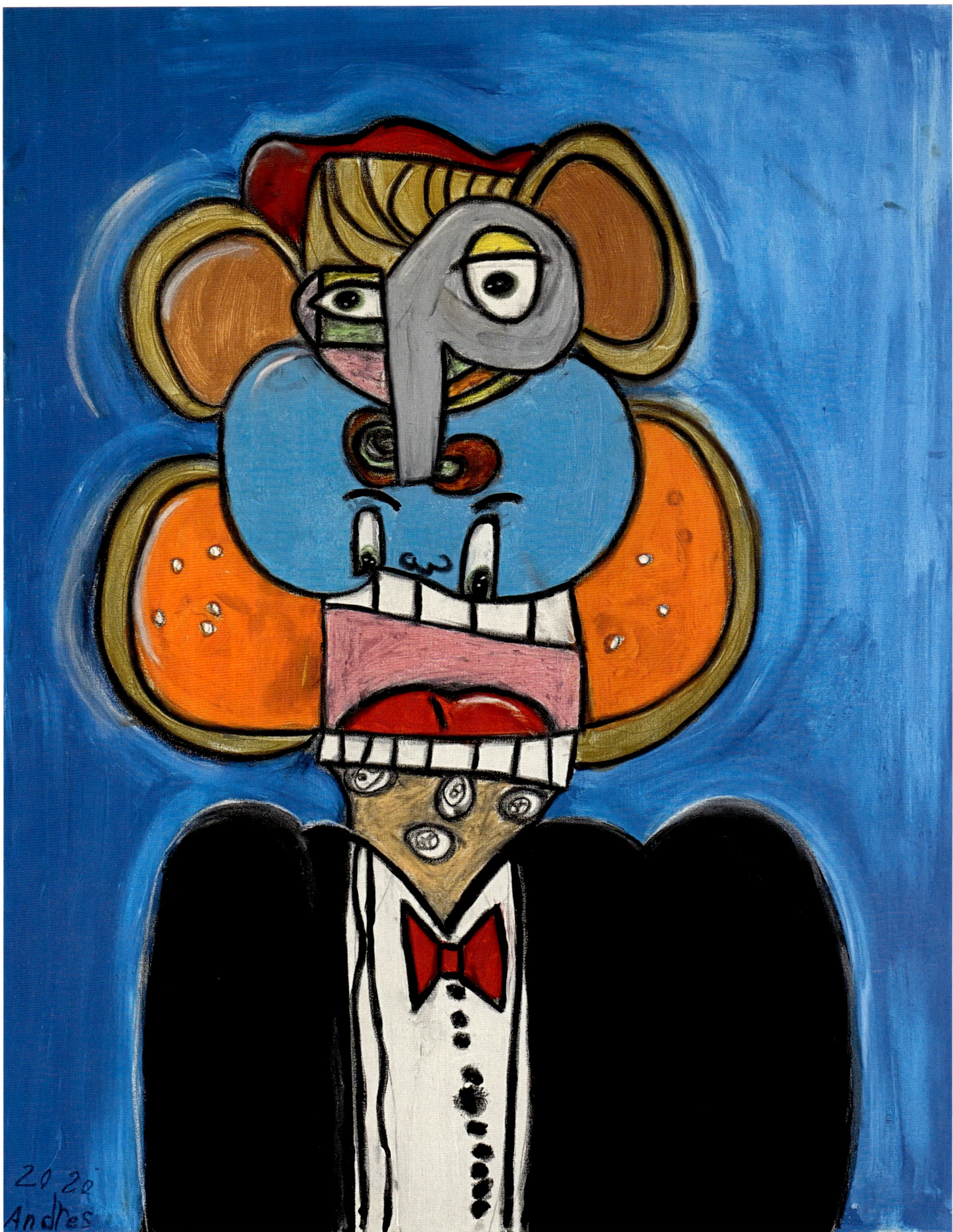

Elephant Man, 2020 │ acrylic and oil pastel on canvas, 48 × 36 in

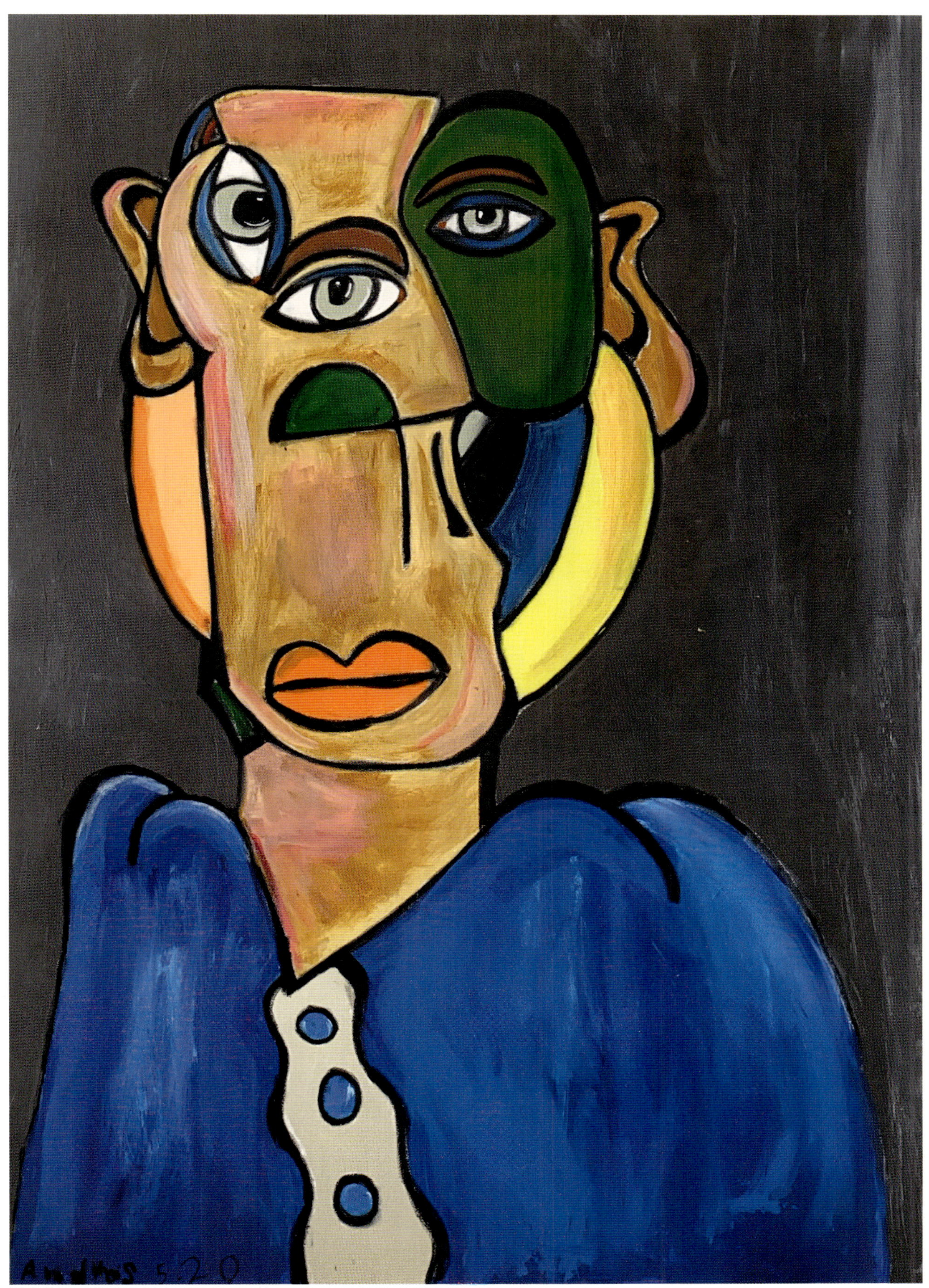

Warrior, 2020 | acrylic and oil pastel on canvas, 60 × 48 in

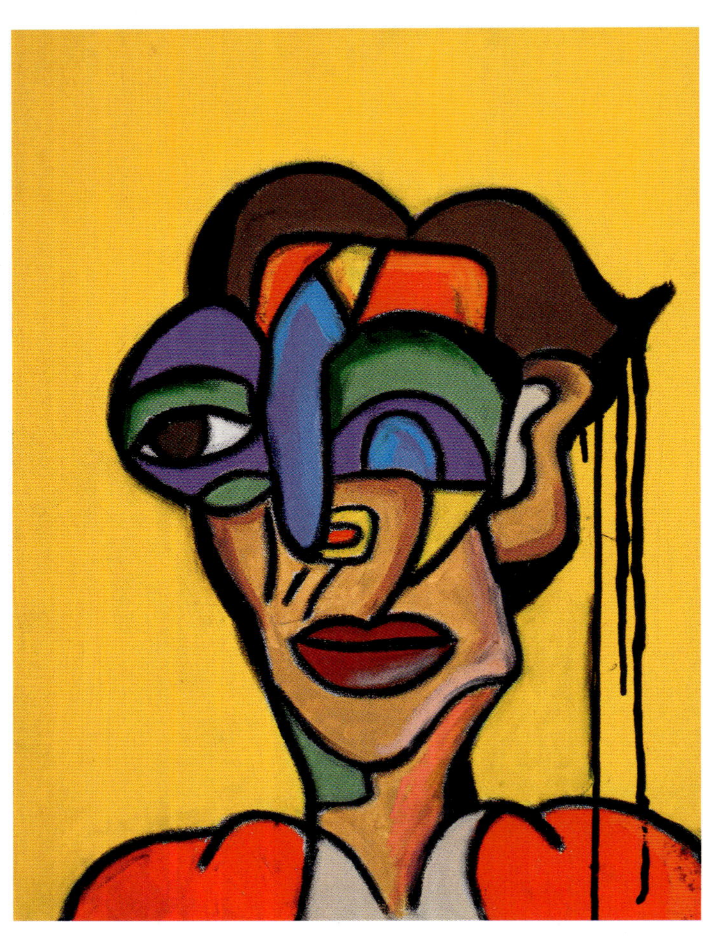

George, 2020 | acrylic and oil pastel on canvas, 24 × 18 in

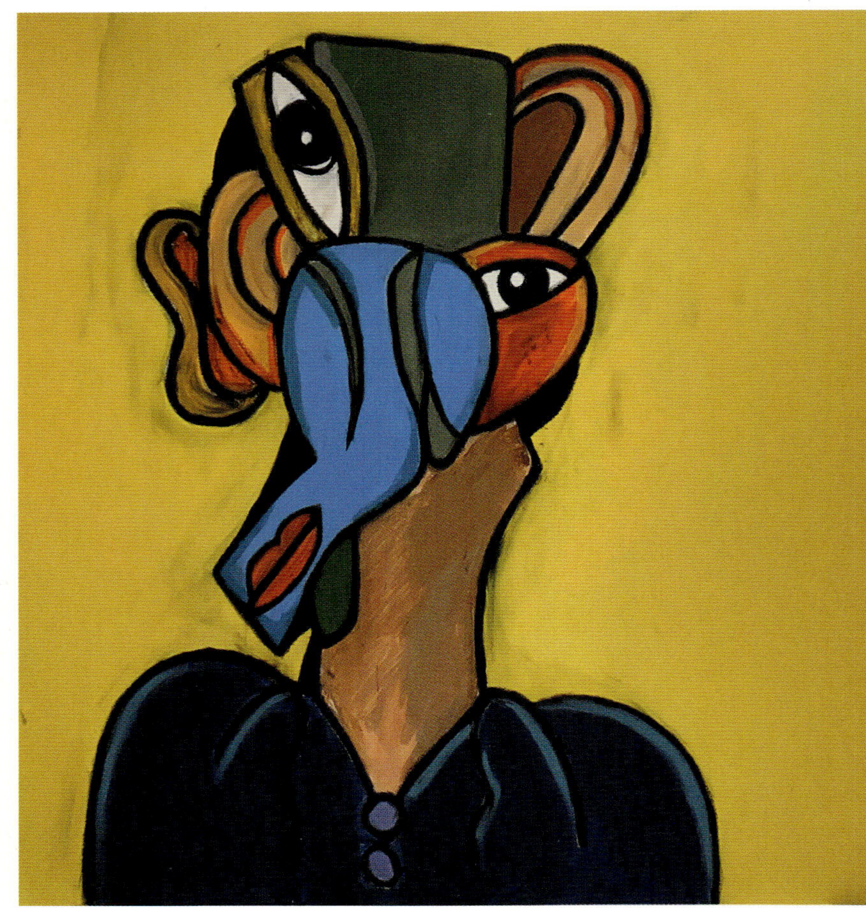

The Director, 2020 | acrylic and oil pastel on canvas, 48 × 48 in

El Payaso, 2020 | acrylic and oil pastel on canvas, 51 × 36 in

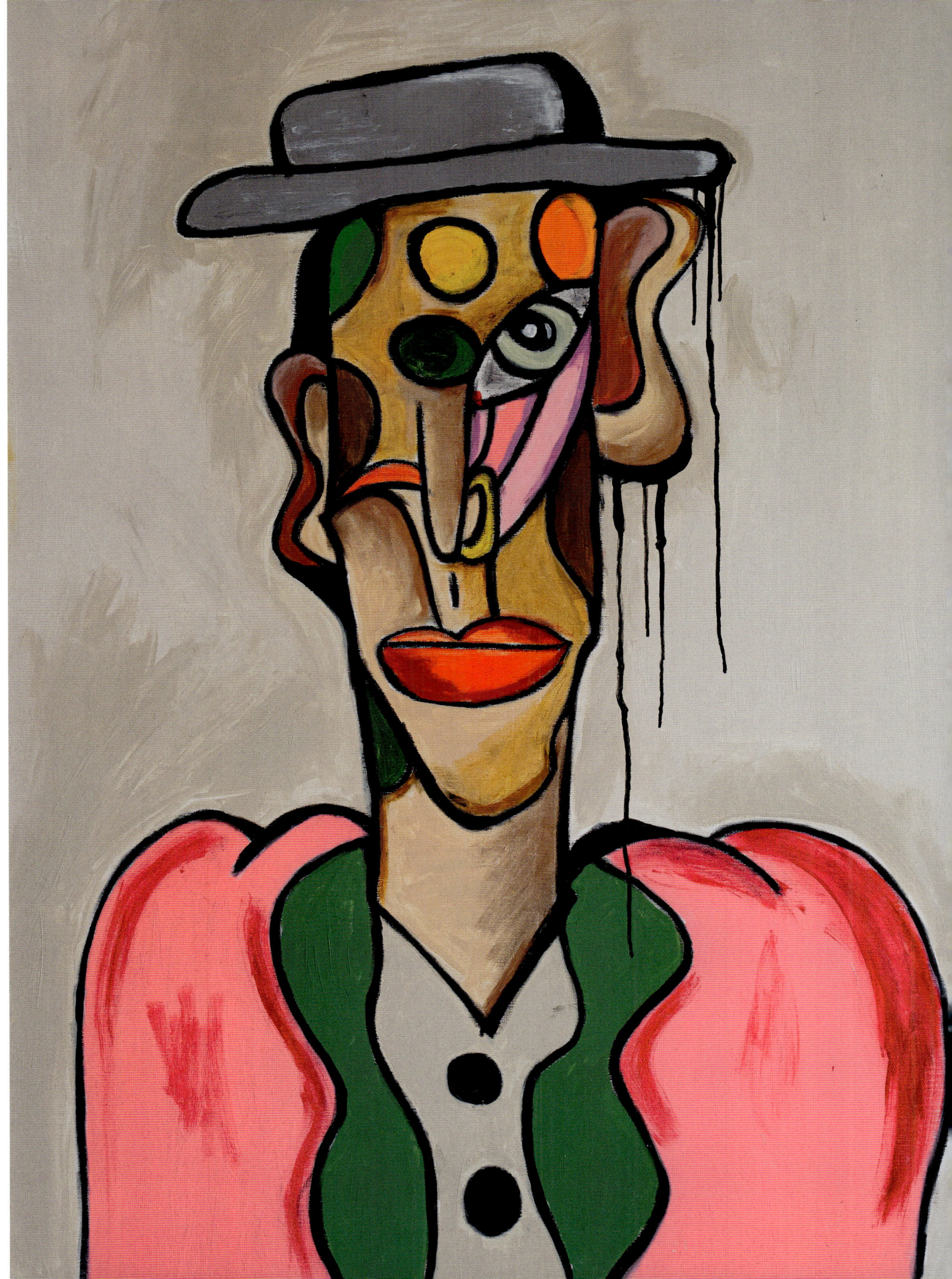

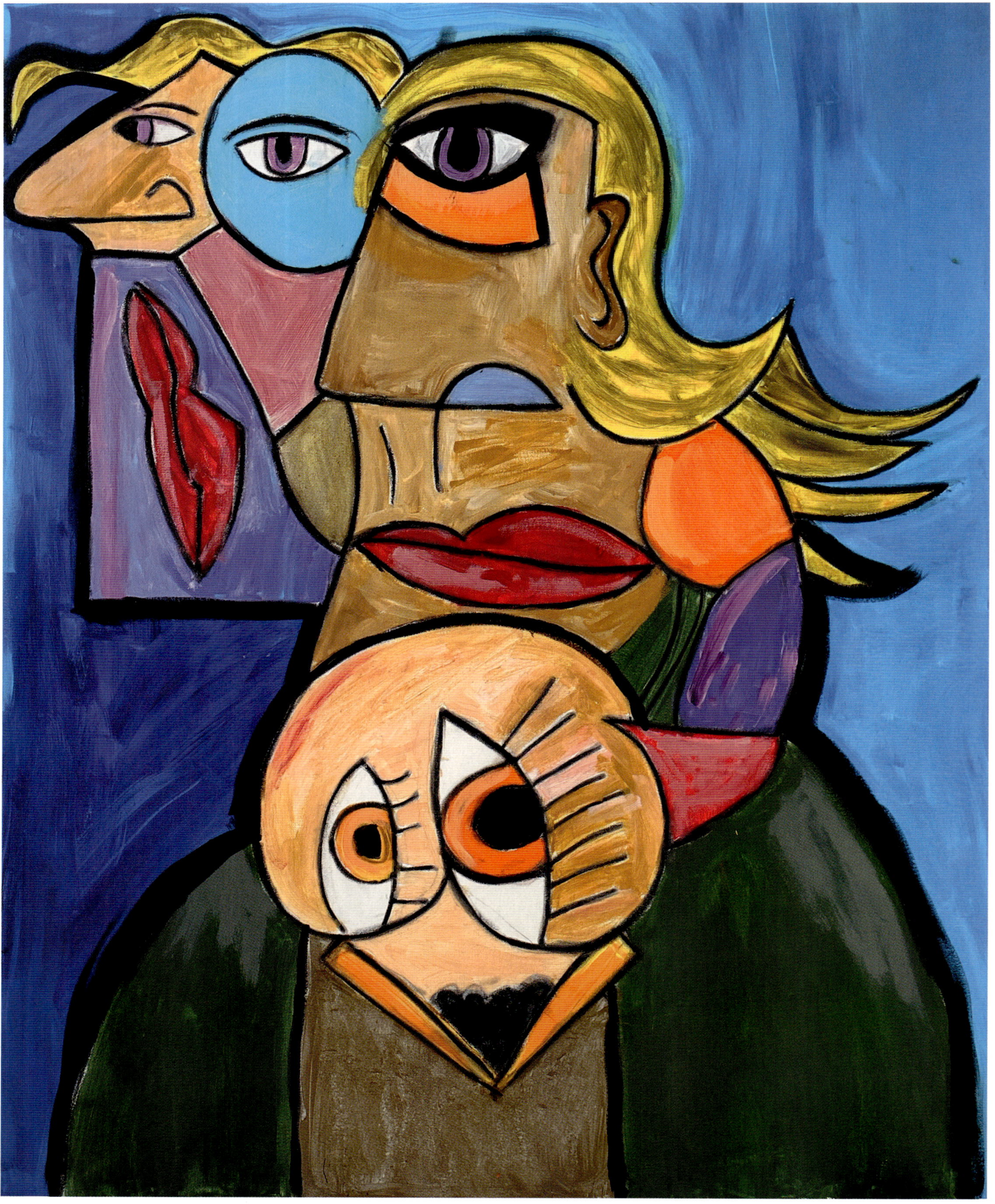

Faces, 2020 | acrylic and oil pastel on canvas, 60 × 48 in

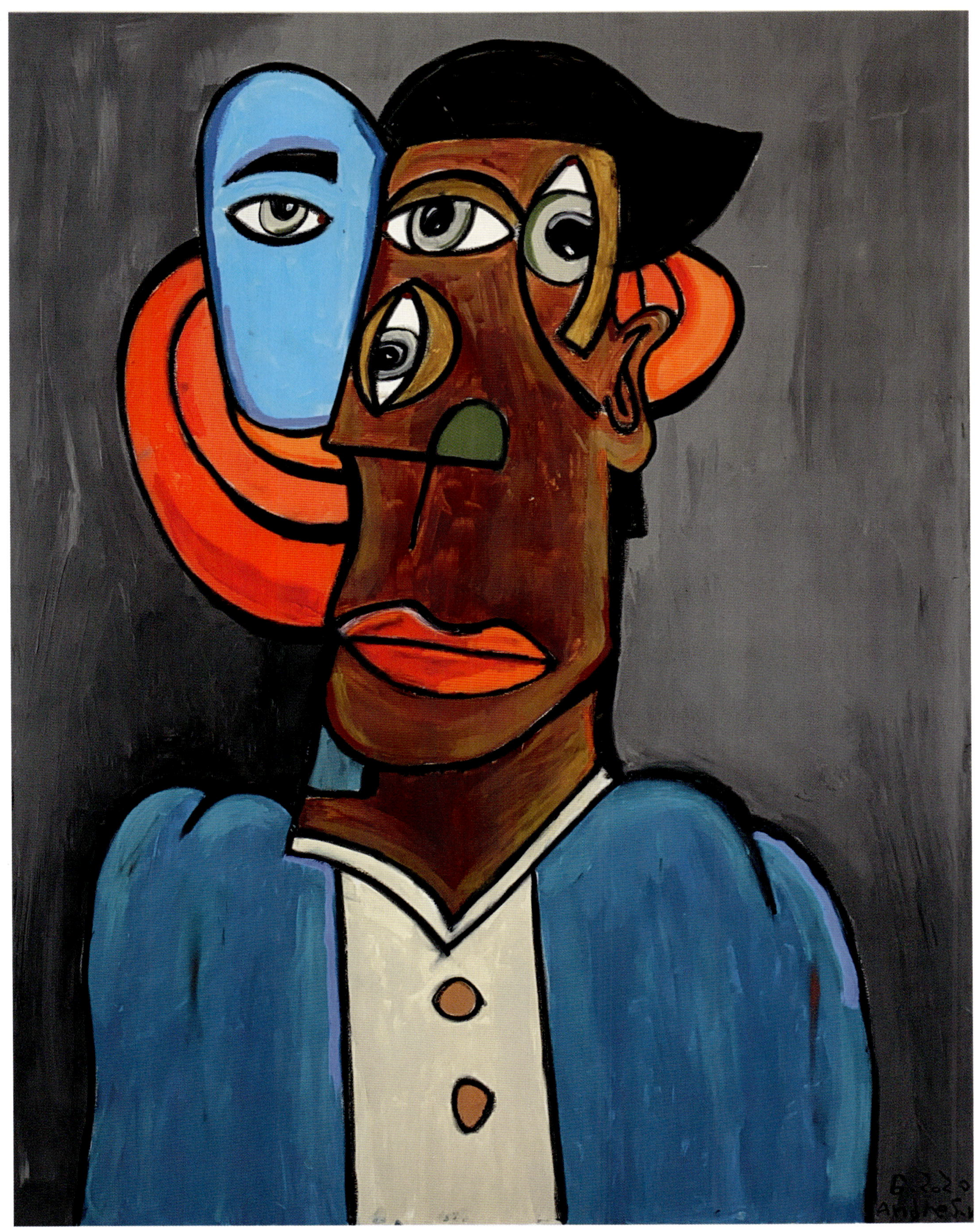

The Musician, 2020 | acrylic and oil pastel on canvas, 60 × 48 in

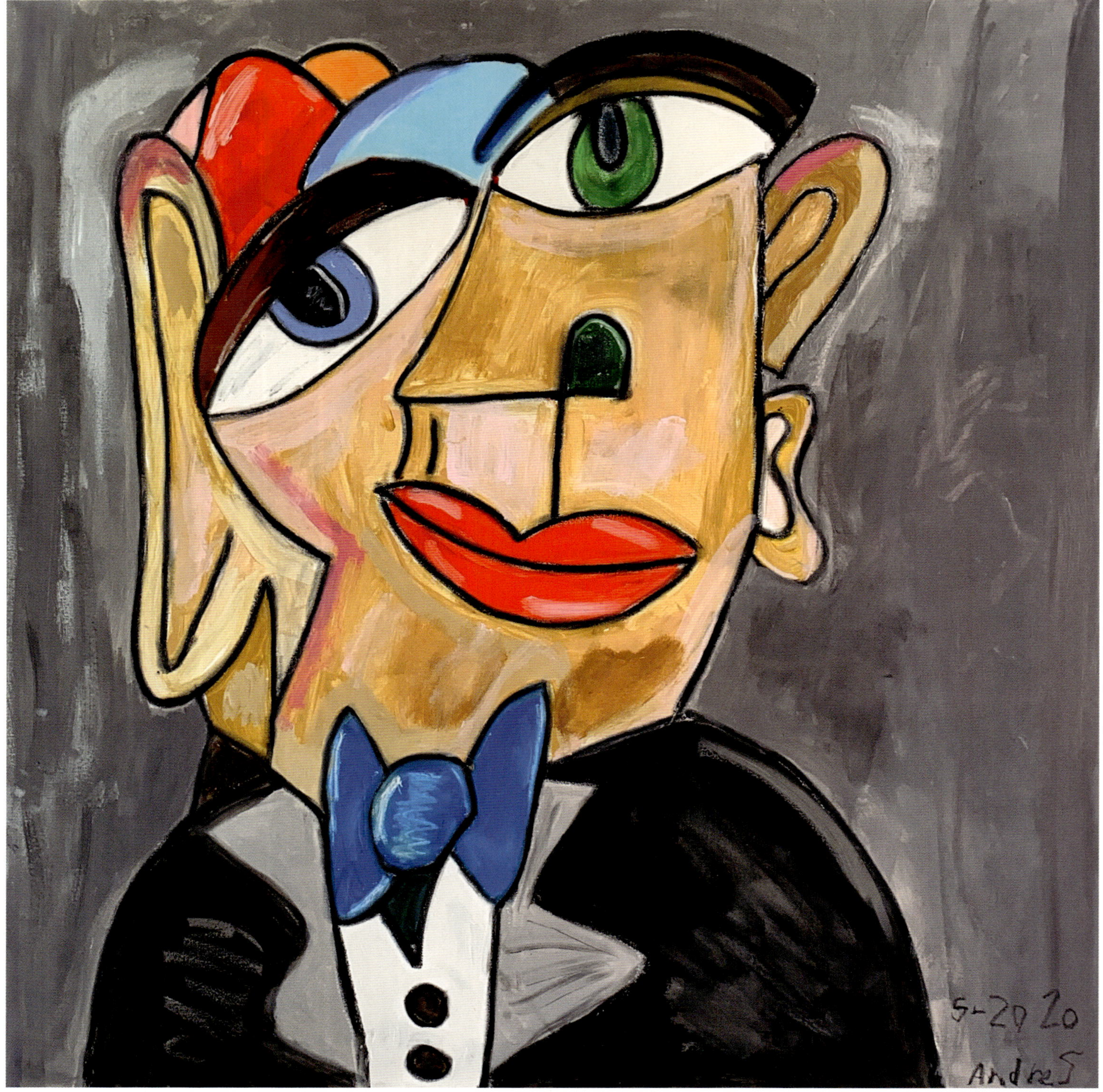

The Judge, 2020 | acrylic and oil pastel on canvas, 40 × 40 in

The Farmer, 2020 | acrylic and oil pastel on canvas, 60 × 40 in

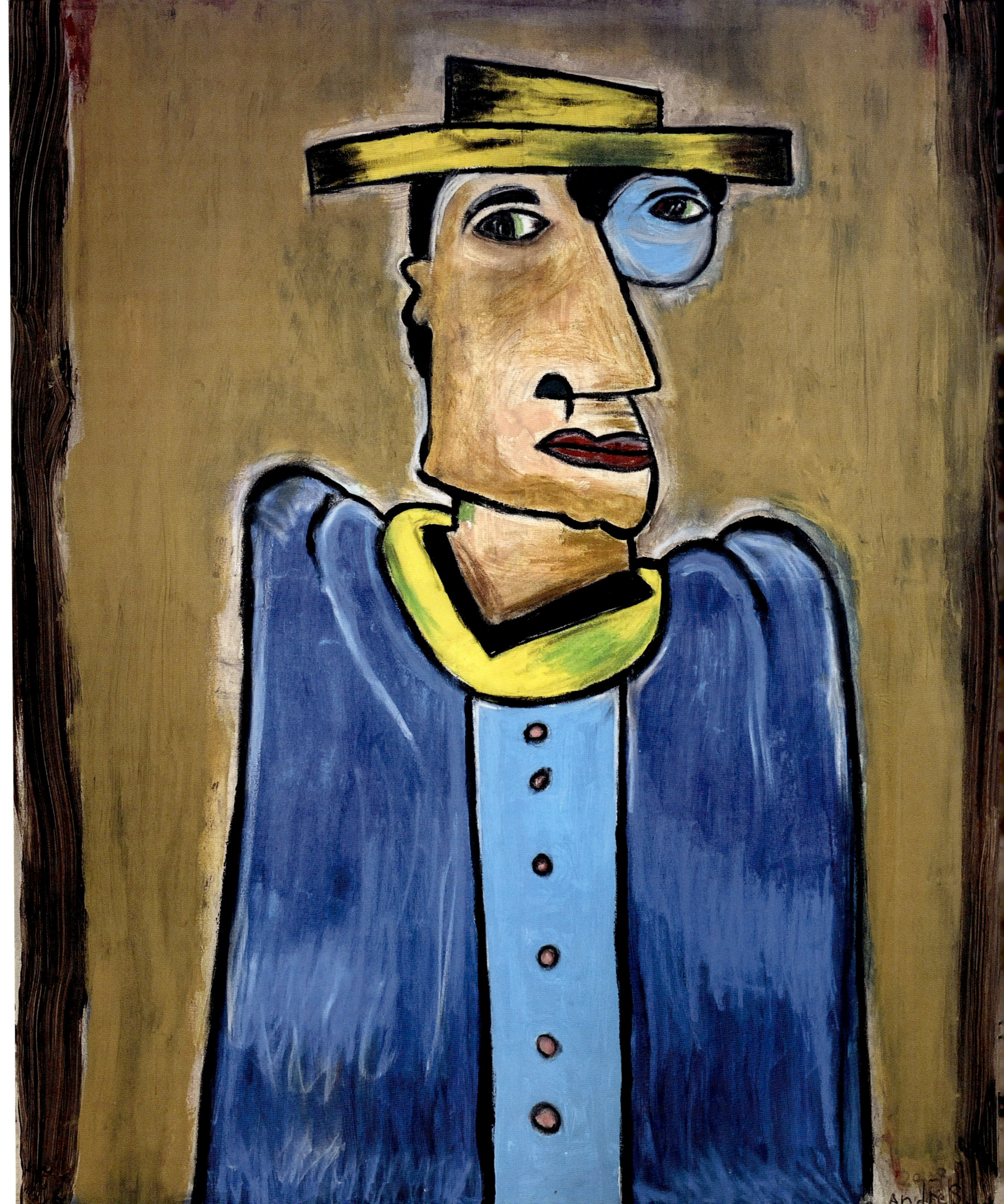

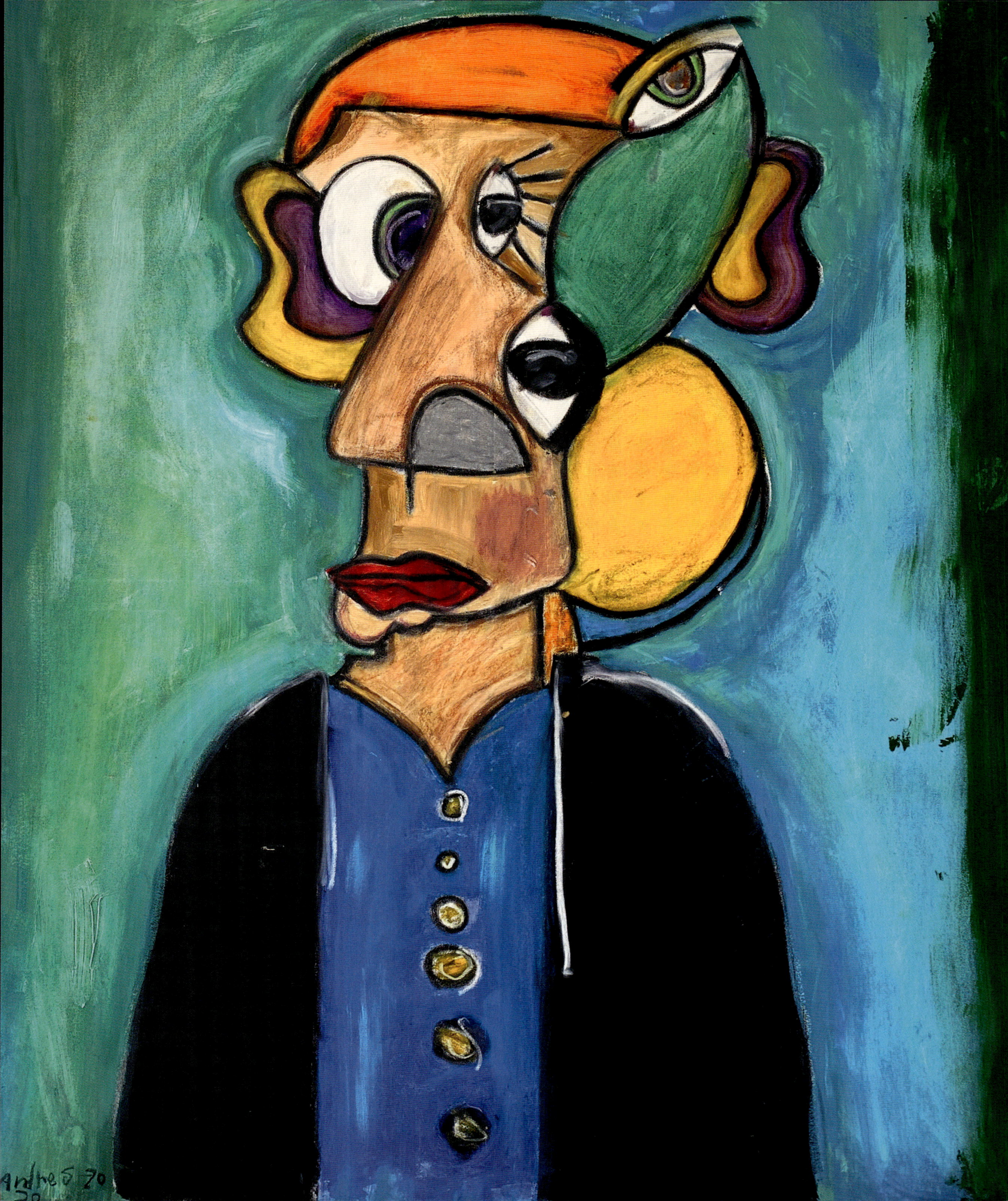
Andres 70

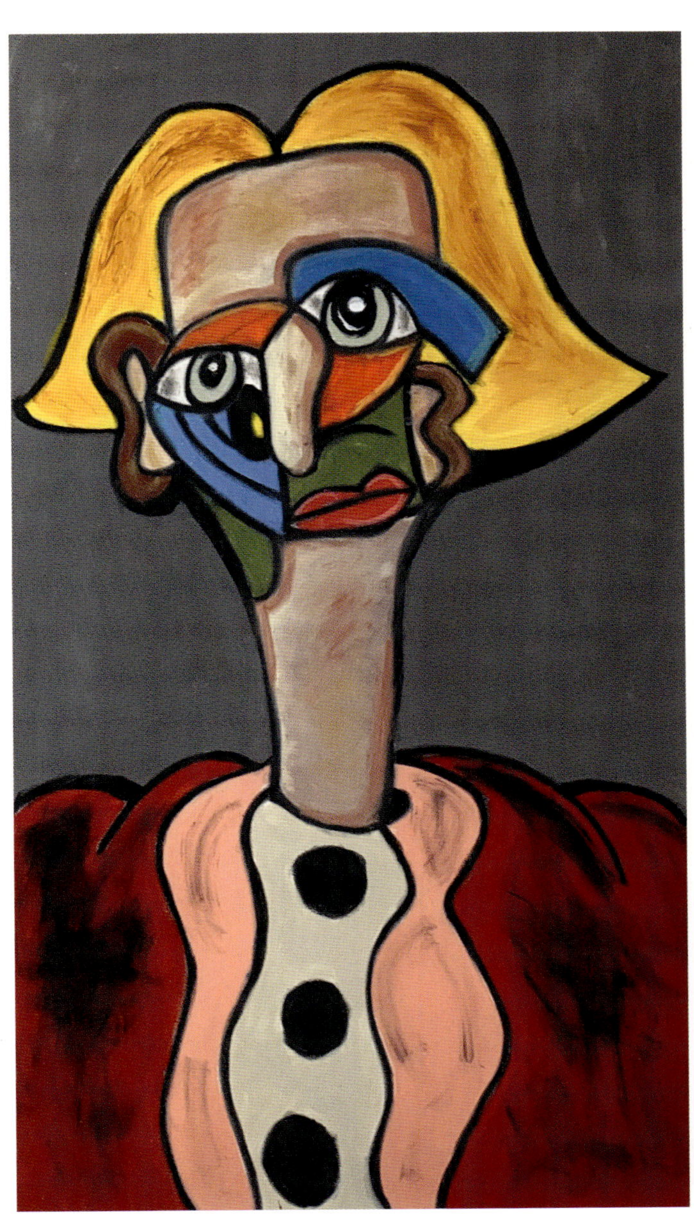

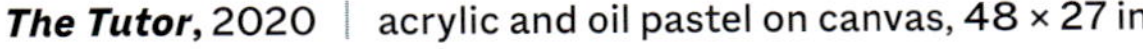

The Tutor, 2020 | acrylic and oil pastel on canvas, 48 × 27 in

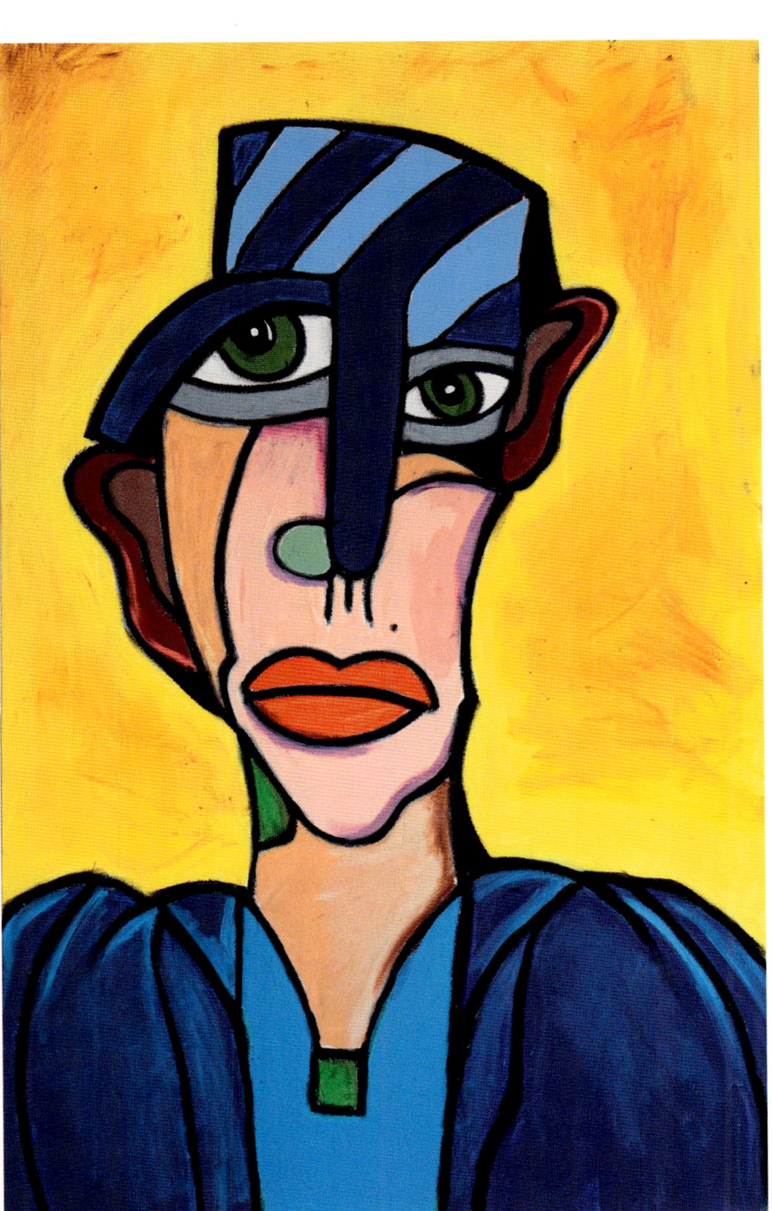

Sofia, 2020 | acrylic and oil pastel on canvas, 48 × 30 in

The Observer, 2020 | acrylic and oil pastel on canvas, 60 × 48 in

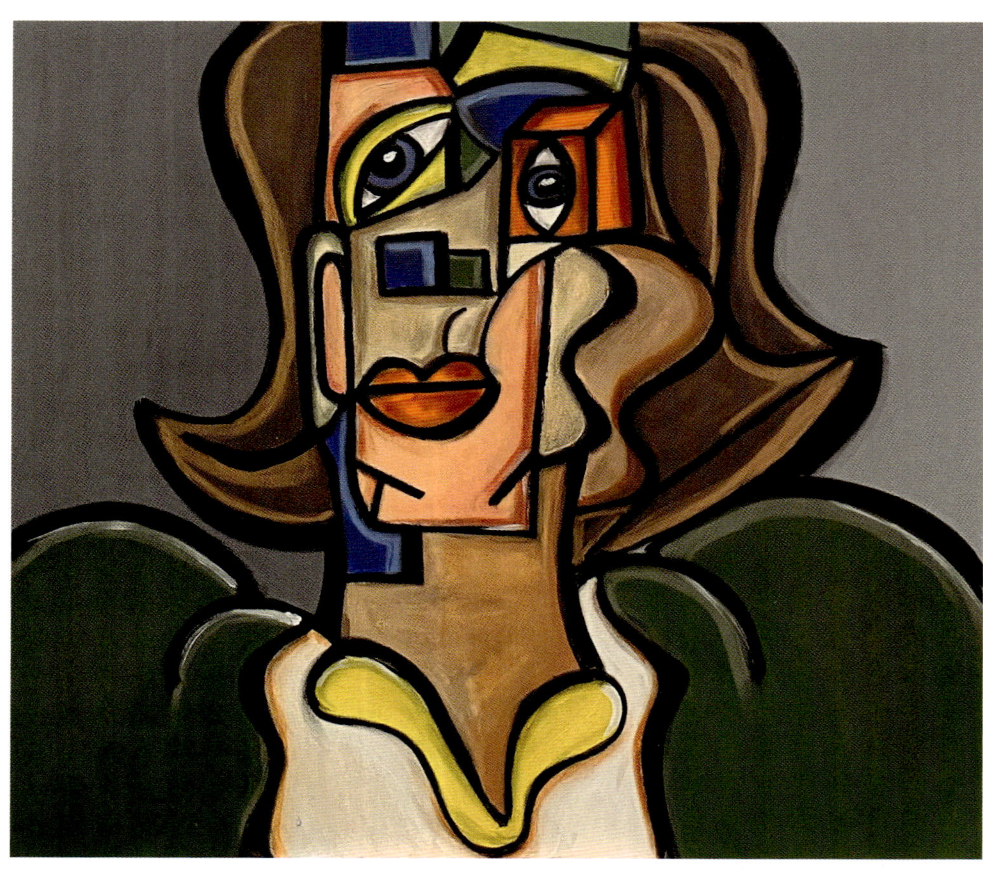

Confusion, 2020
acrylic and oil pastel on canvas, 34 × 34 in

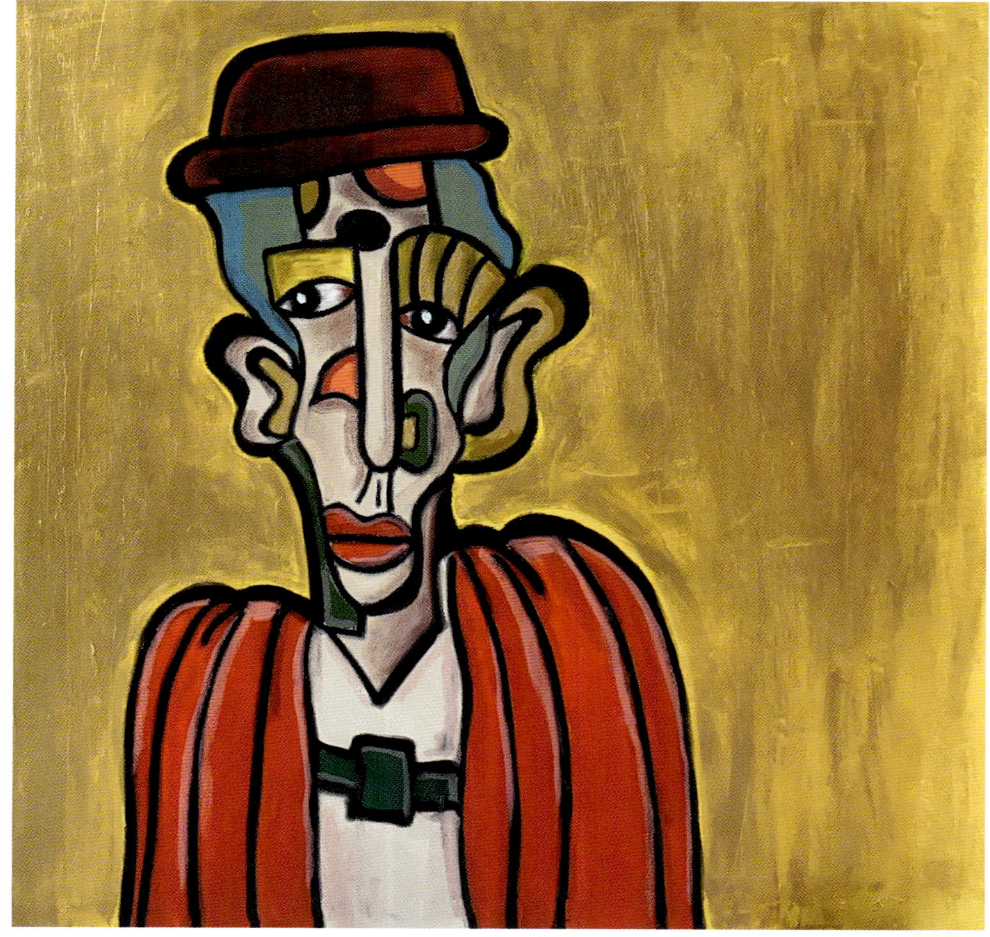

Pepino the Clown, 2020
acrylic and oil pastel on canvas, 36 × 36 in

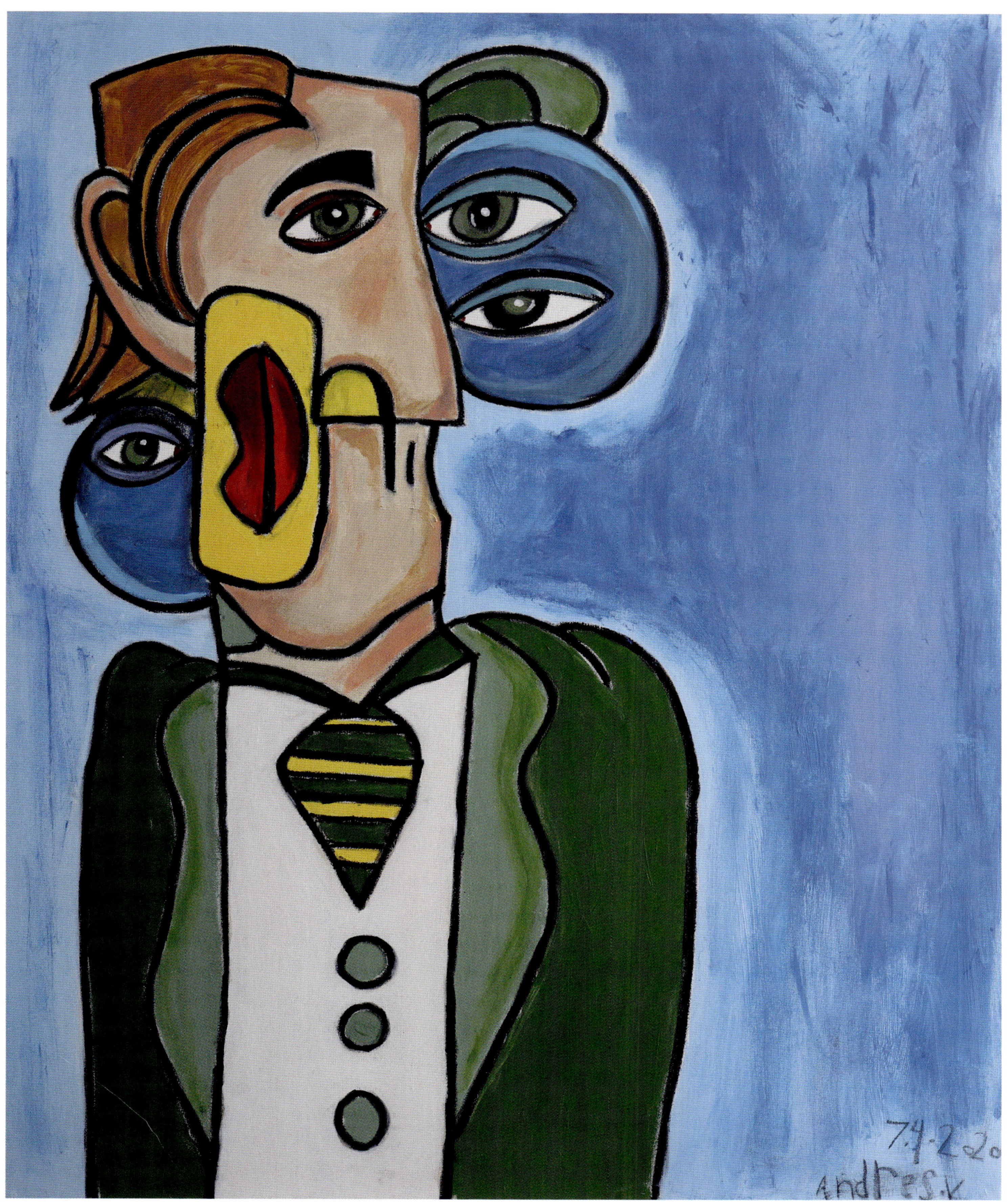

The Banker, 2020 | acrylic and oil pastel on canvas, 60 × 48 in

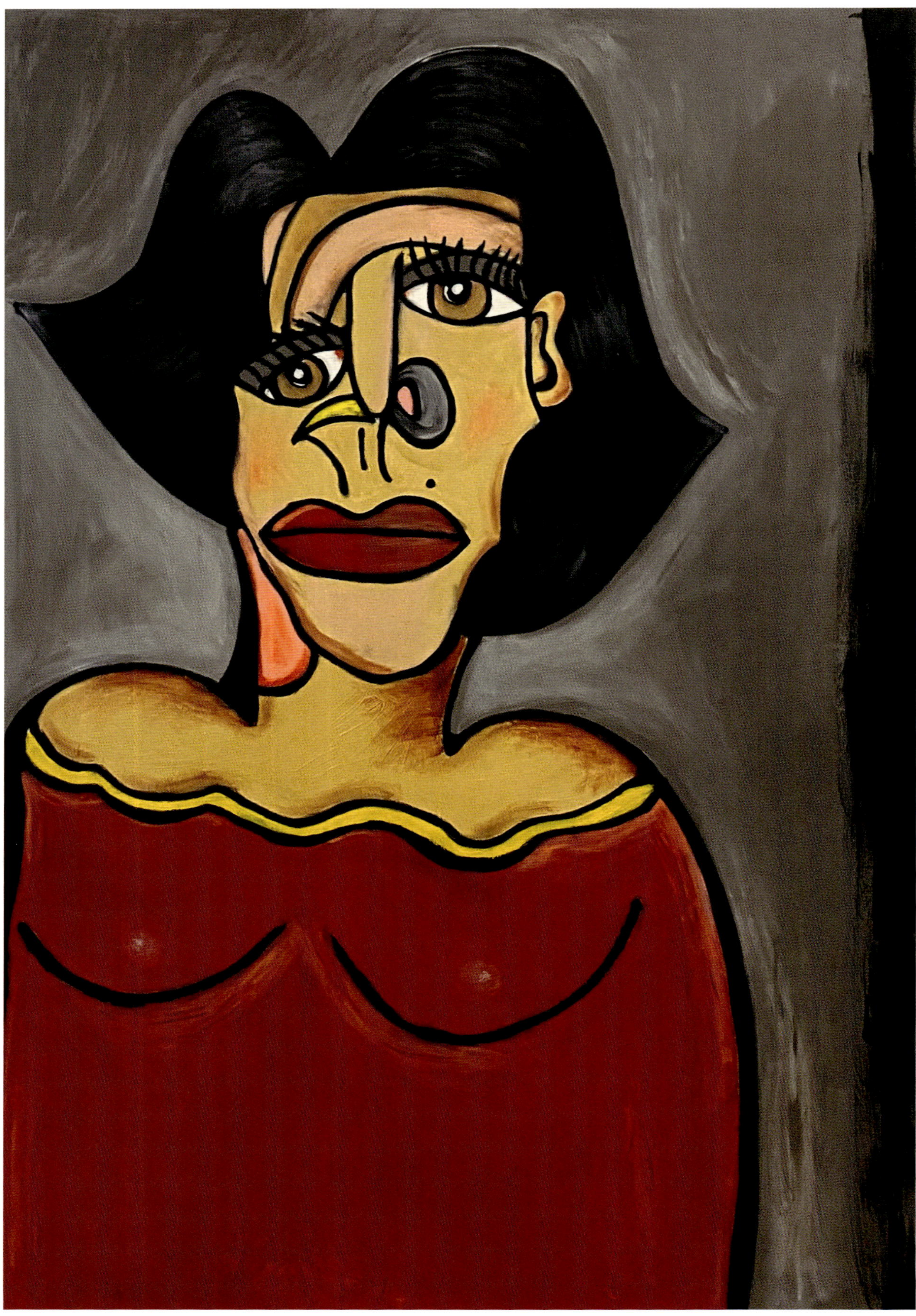

Maria, 2020 | acrylic and oil pastel on canvas, 72 × 48 in

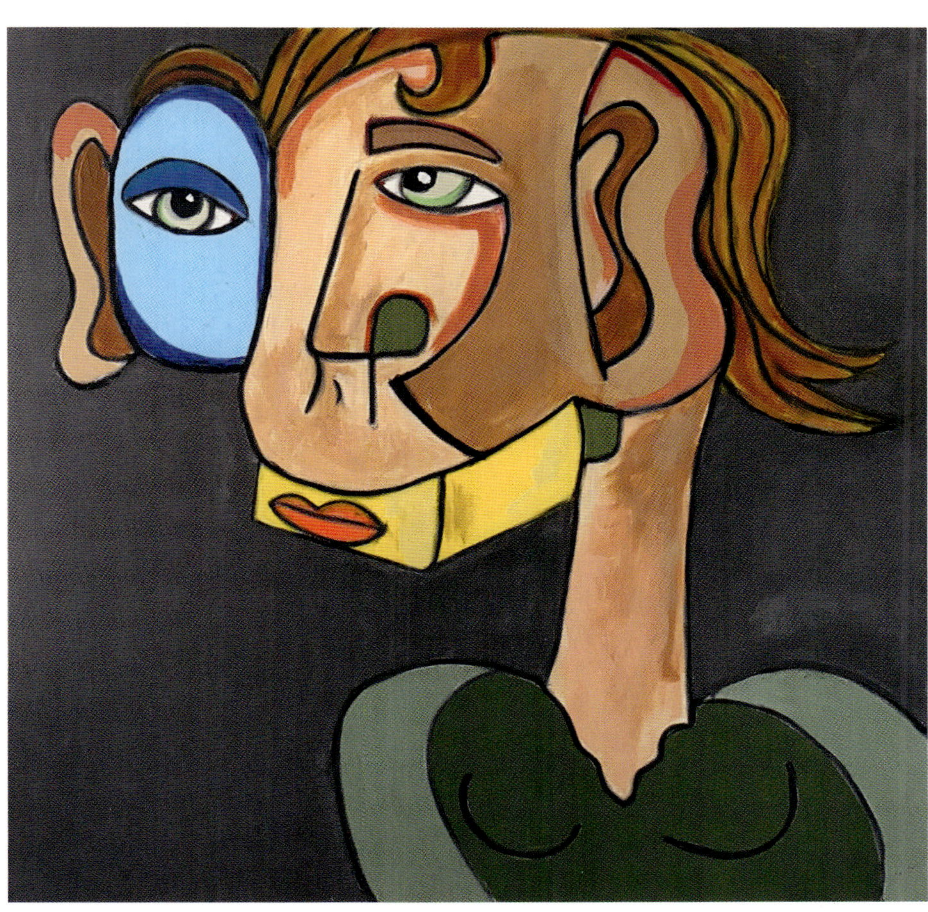

Katalina, 2020
acrylic and oil pastel on canvas, 48 × 48 in

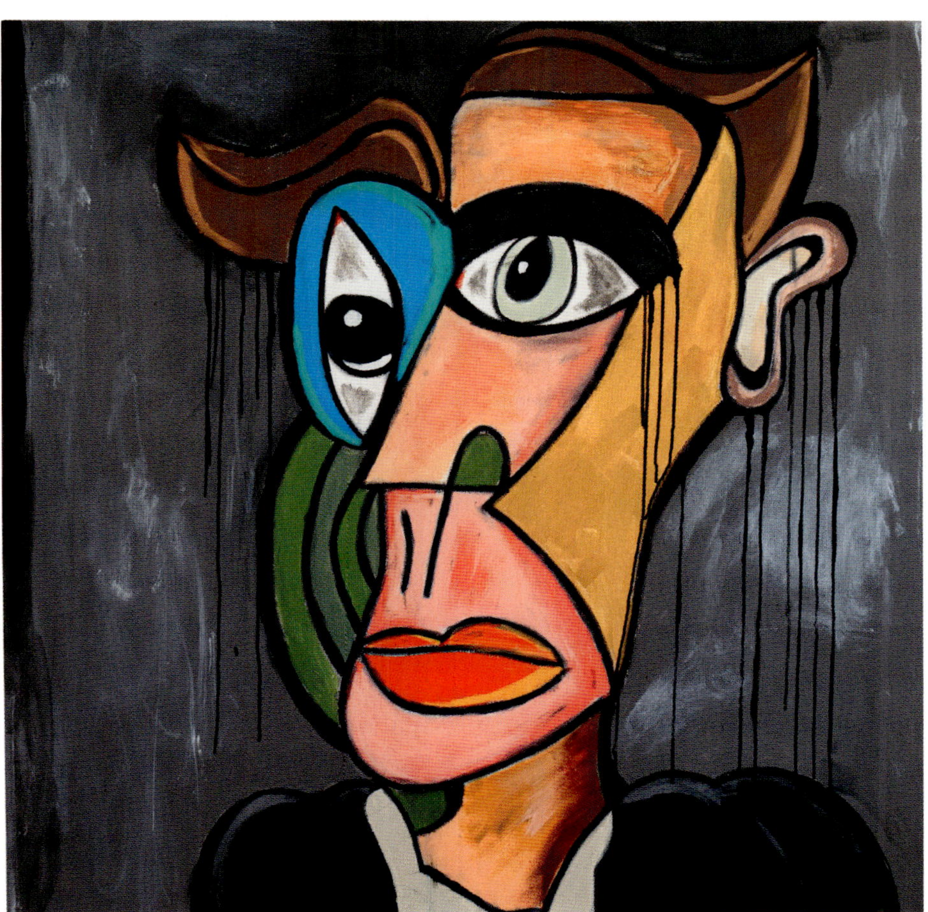

The Scientist, 2020
acrylic and oil pastel on canvas, 48 × 48 in

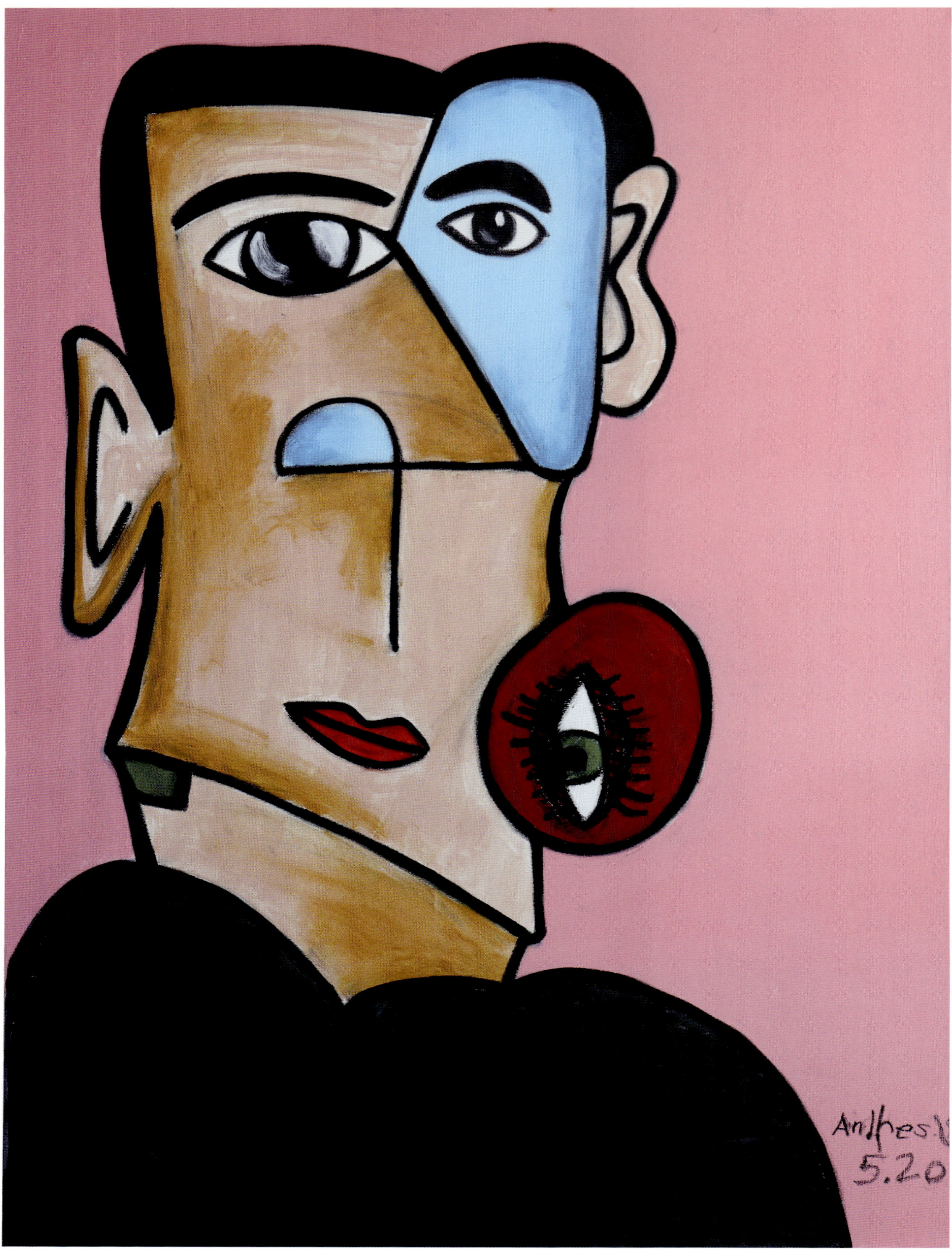

Mr. Pink, 2020 | acrylic and oil pastel on canvas, 48 × 36 in

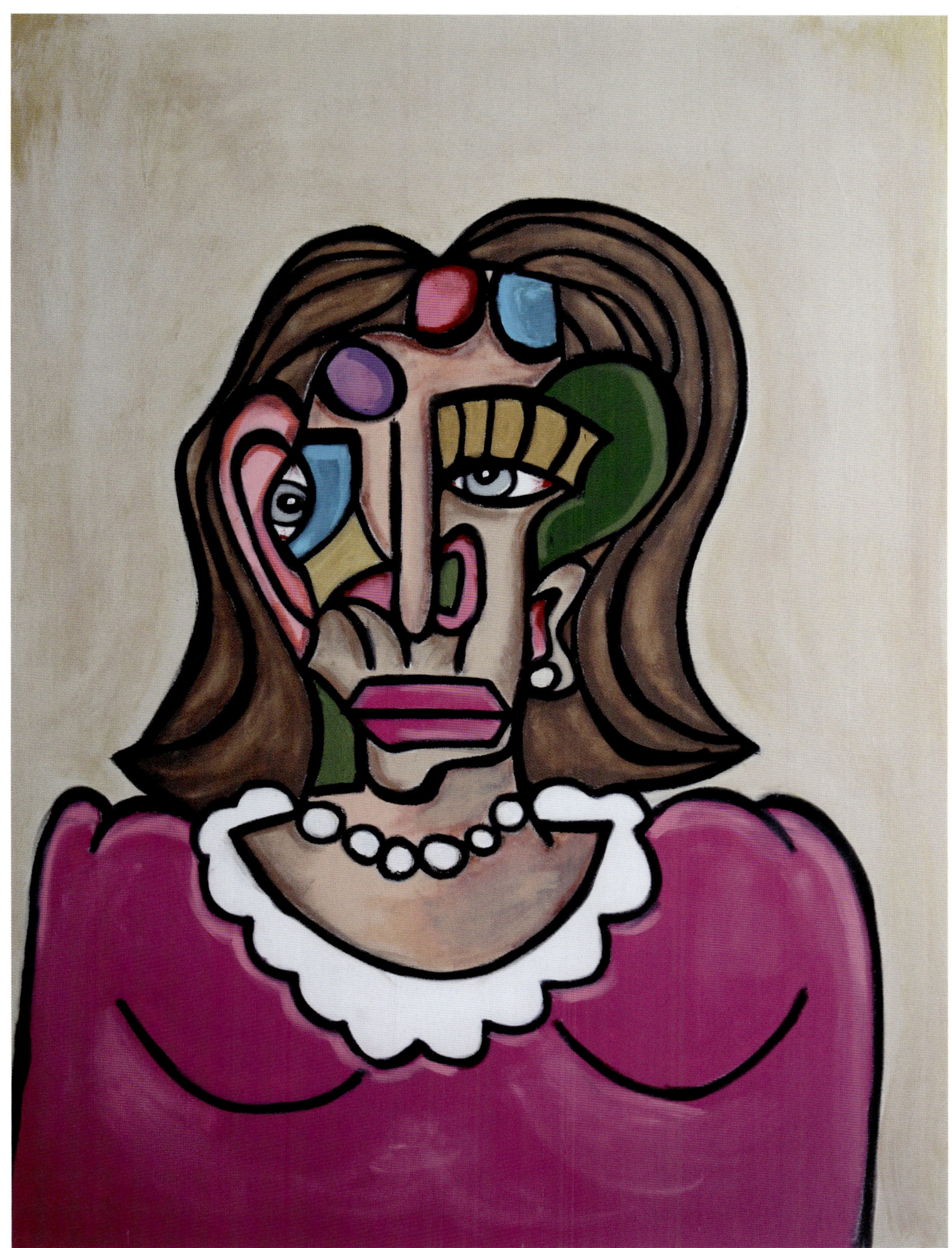

Alexandra, 2020 | acrylic and oil pastel on canvas, 48 × 36 in

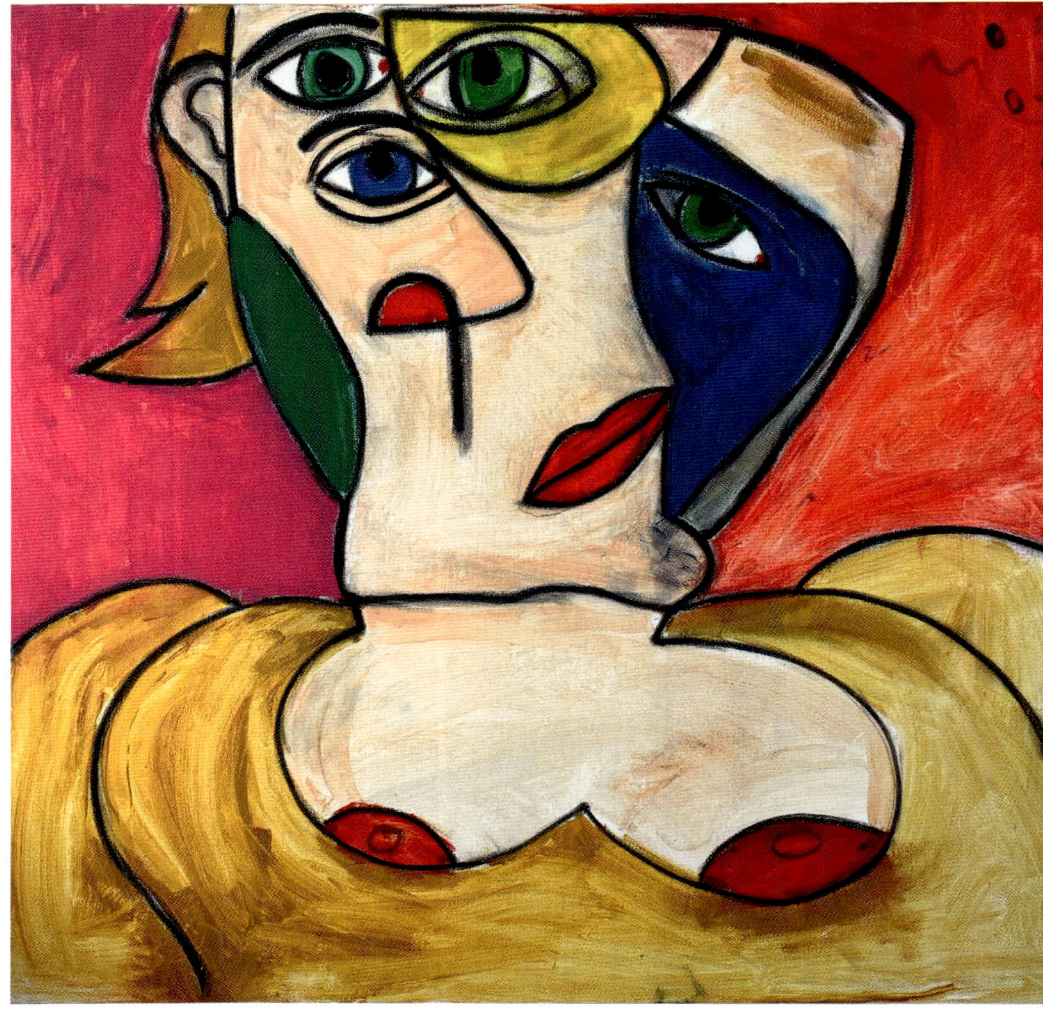

Pink, 2020
acrylic and oil pastel on canvas,
40 × 40 in

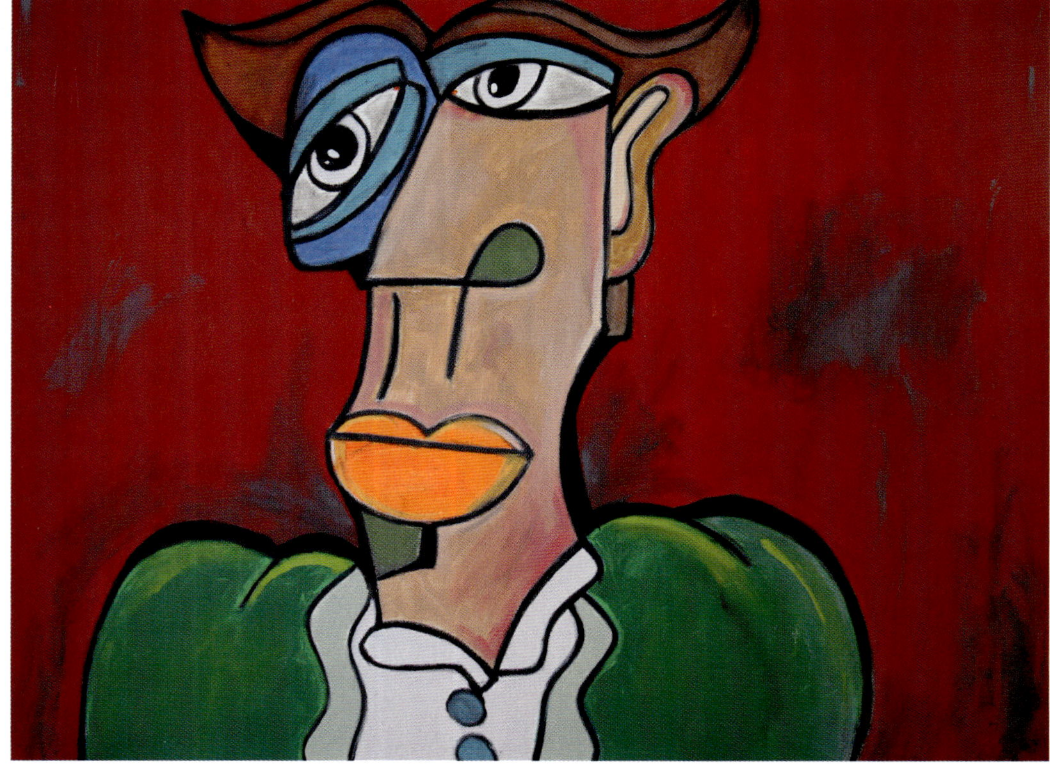

Sir Monarch, 2020
acrylic and oil pastel on canvas,
48 × 60 in

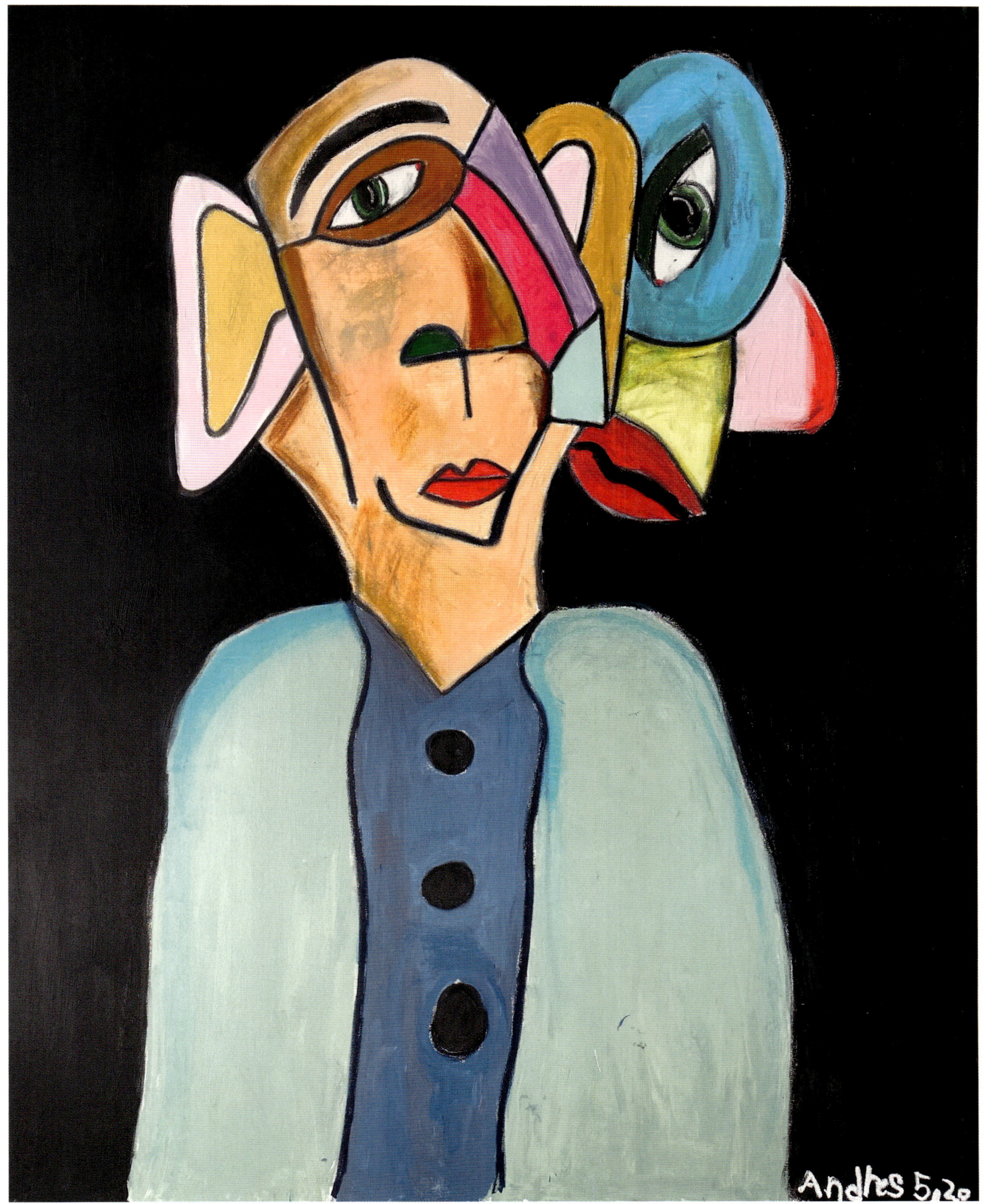

Paul McCartney, 2020 | acrylic and oil pastel on canvas, 60 × 48 in

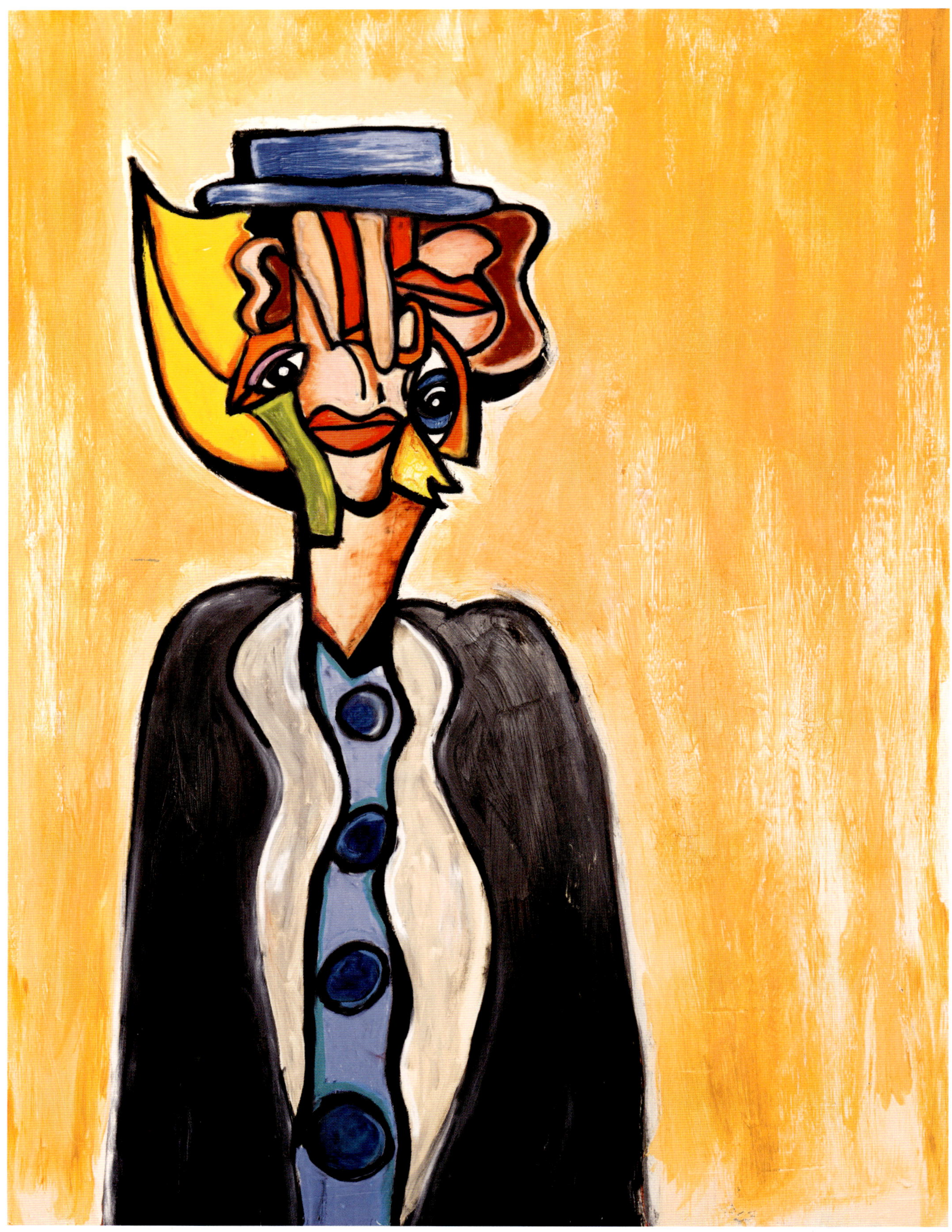

The Professor, 2020 | acrylic and oil pastel on canvas, 54 × 40 in

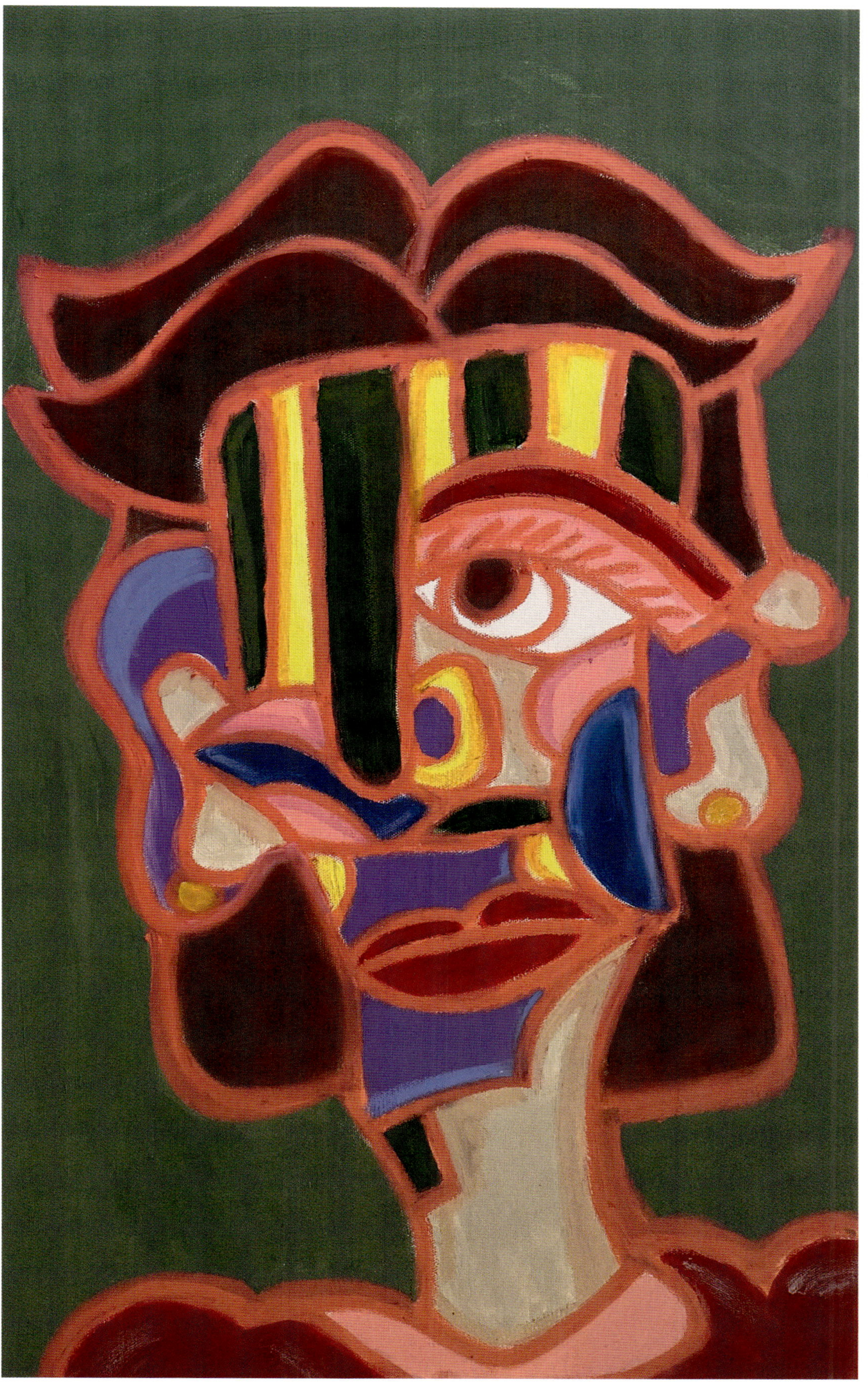

Alcirita, 2020 | acrylic and oil pastel on canvas, 26 × 15 in

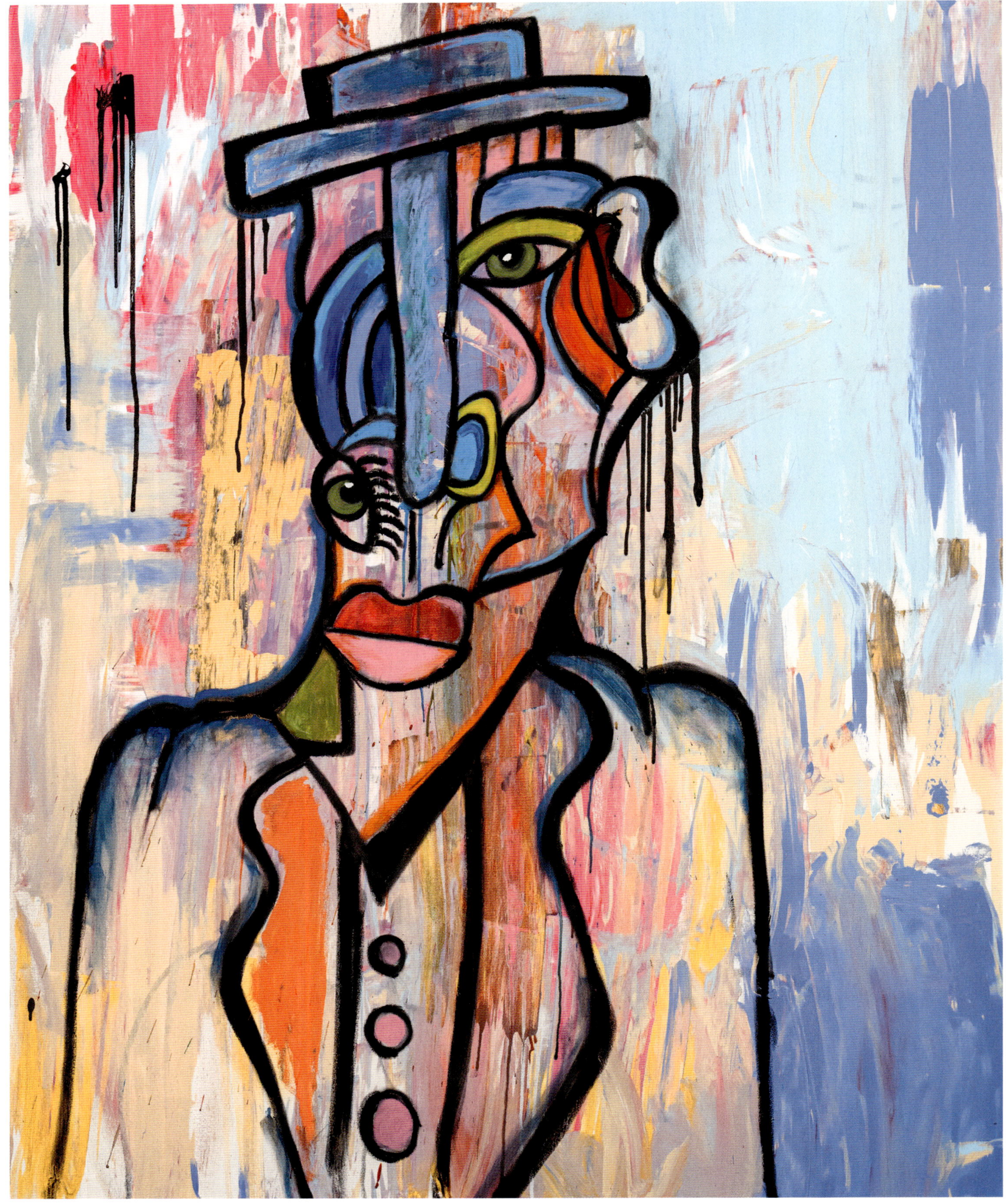

Fred 1, 2020 | acrylic and oil pastel on canvas, 60 × 48 in

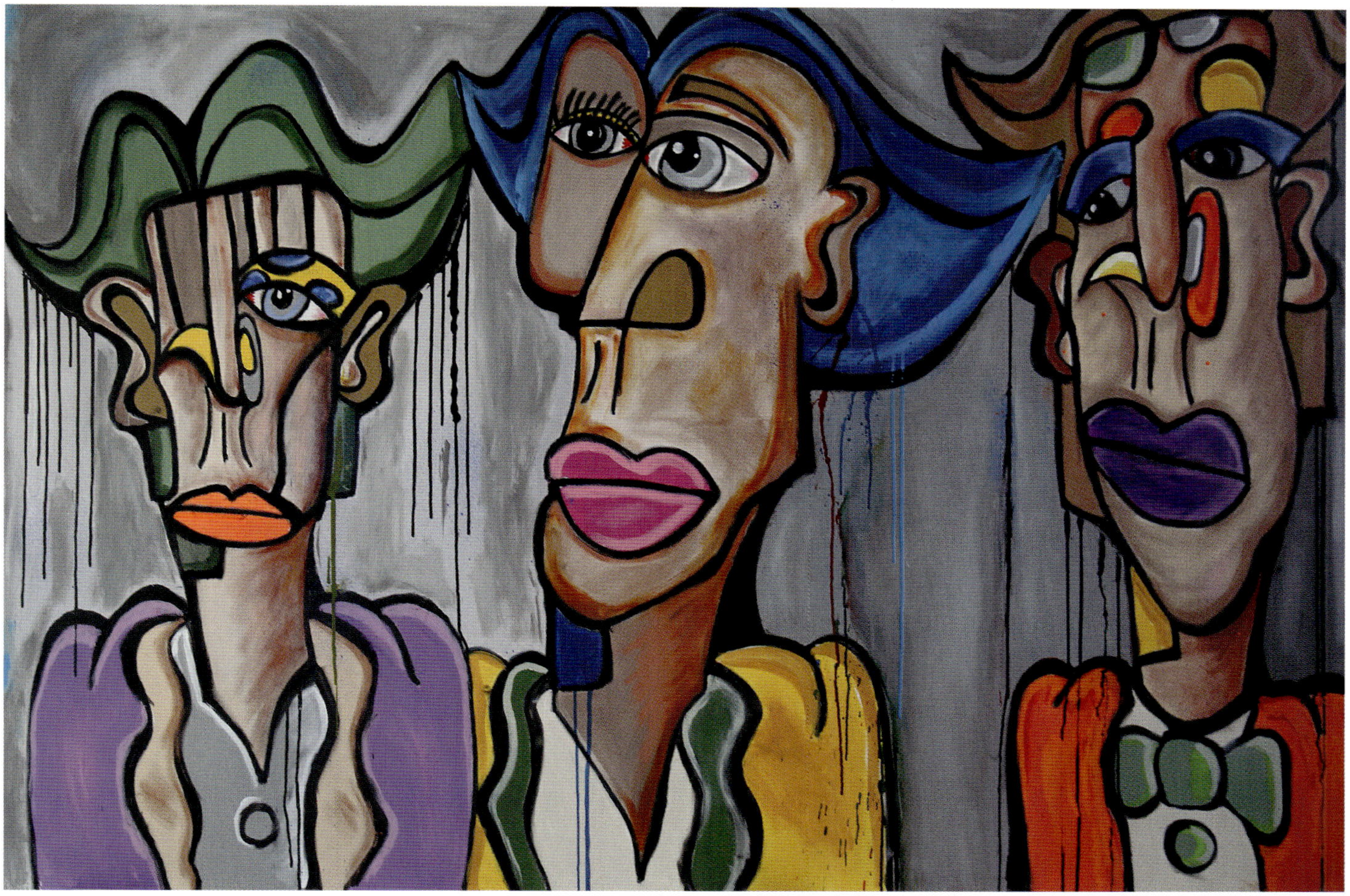

The Three Amigos, 2020 | acrylic and oil pastel on canvas, 50 × 76 in

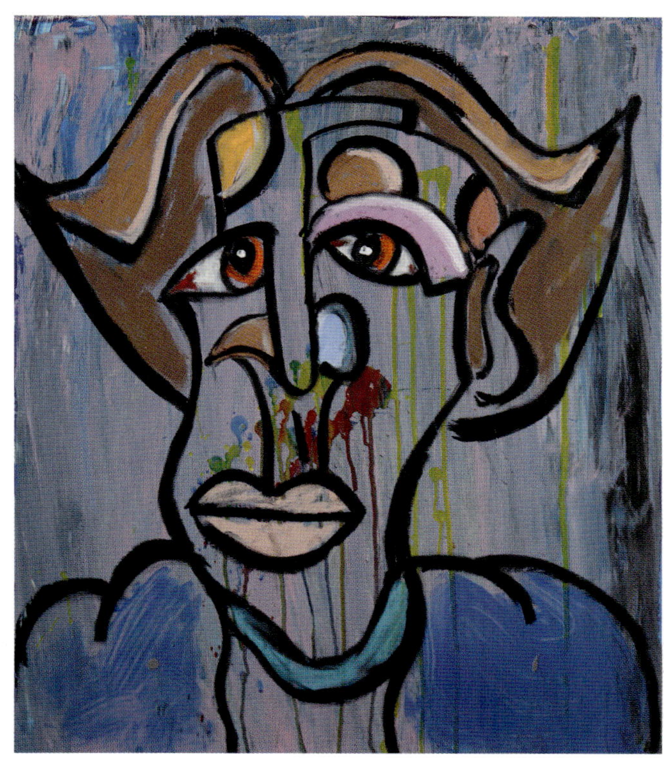

Sam, 2020 | acrylic and oil pastel on canvas, 30 × 24 in

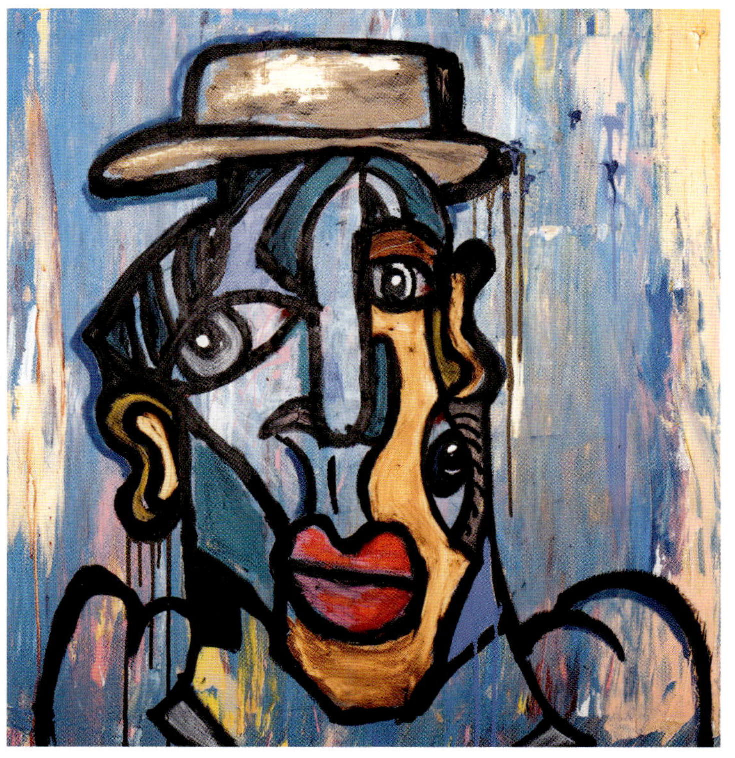

Roger, 2020 | acrylic and oil pastel on canvas, 40 × 36 in

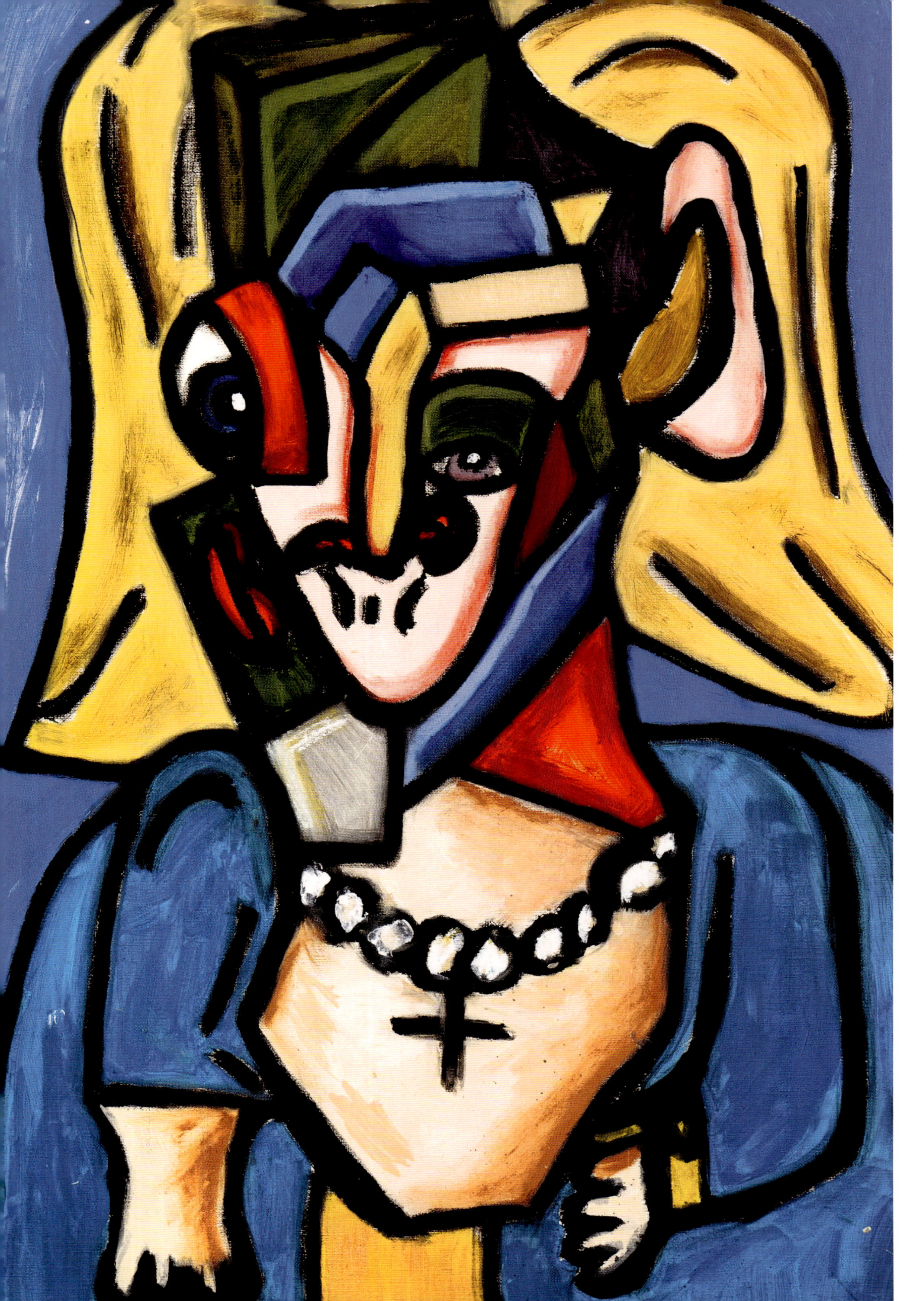

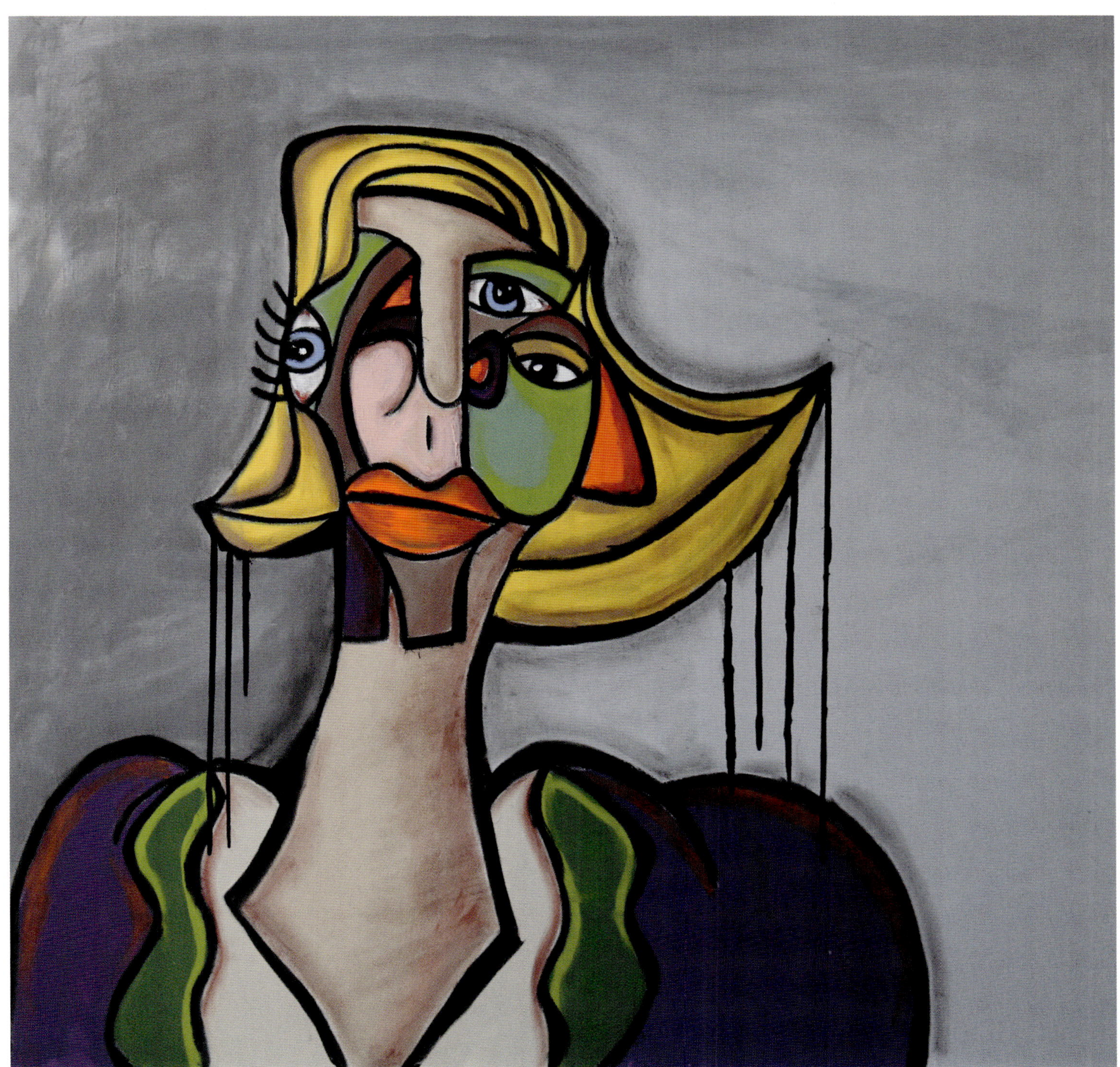

Marilyn, 2021 | acrylic and oil pastel on canvas, 48 × 48 in

Mary, 2021 | acrylic and oil pastel on canvas, 30 × 20 in

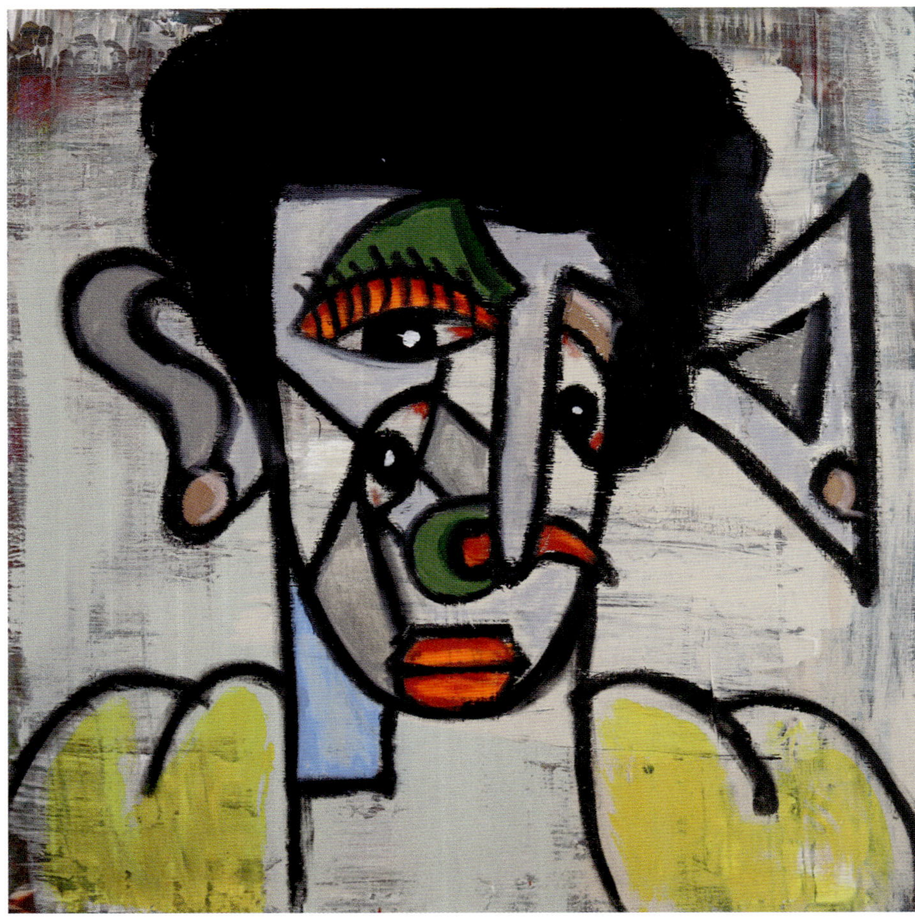

Aretha Franklin, 2021
acrylic and oil pastel on canvas, 30 × 30 in

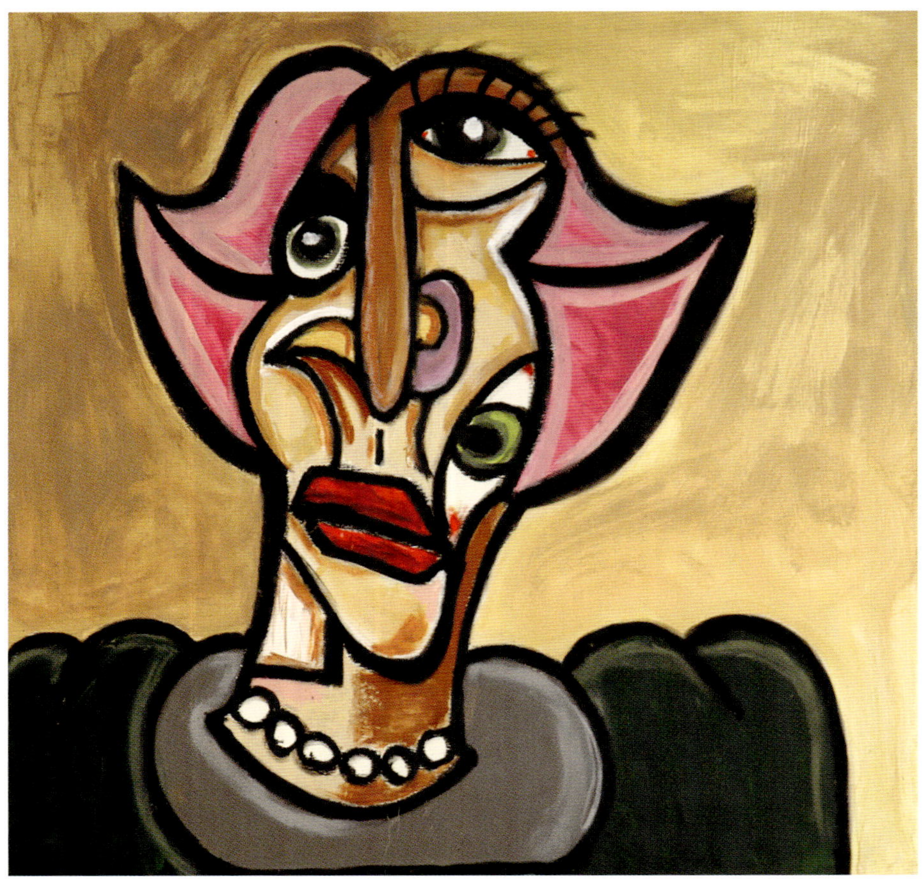

Ana, 2021
acrylic and oil pastel on canvas, 24 × 24 in

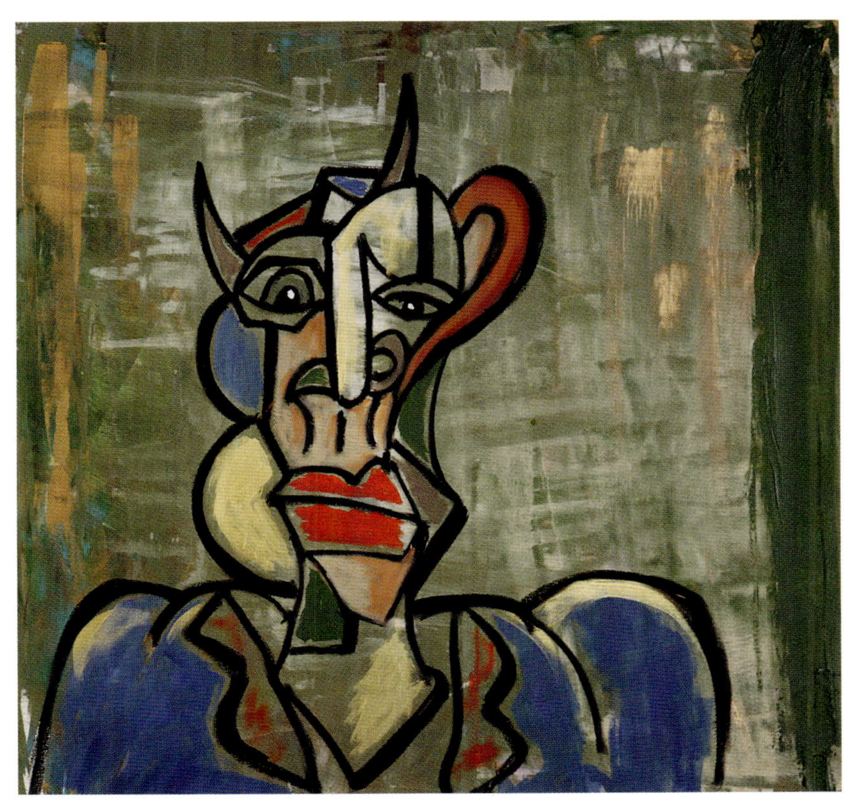

Master Warrior, 2021
acrylic and oil pastel on canvas, 30 × 30 in

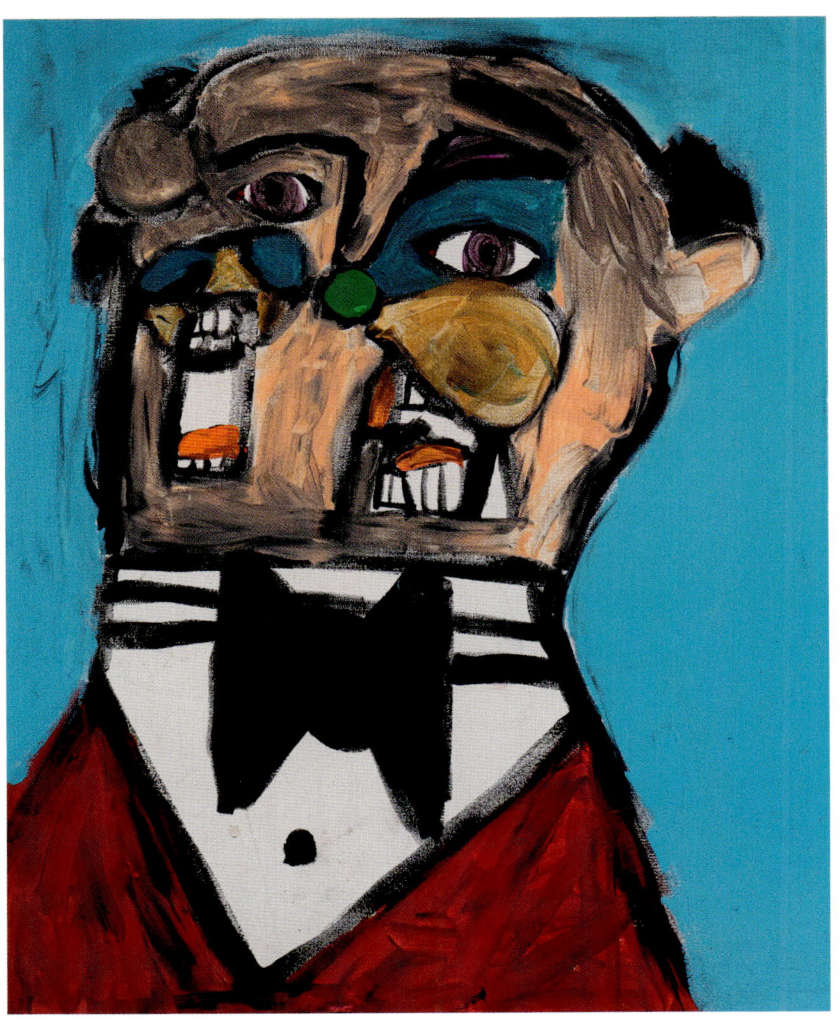

Homage to George Condo, 2021
acrylic and oil pastel on canvas, 28 × 22 in

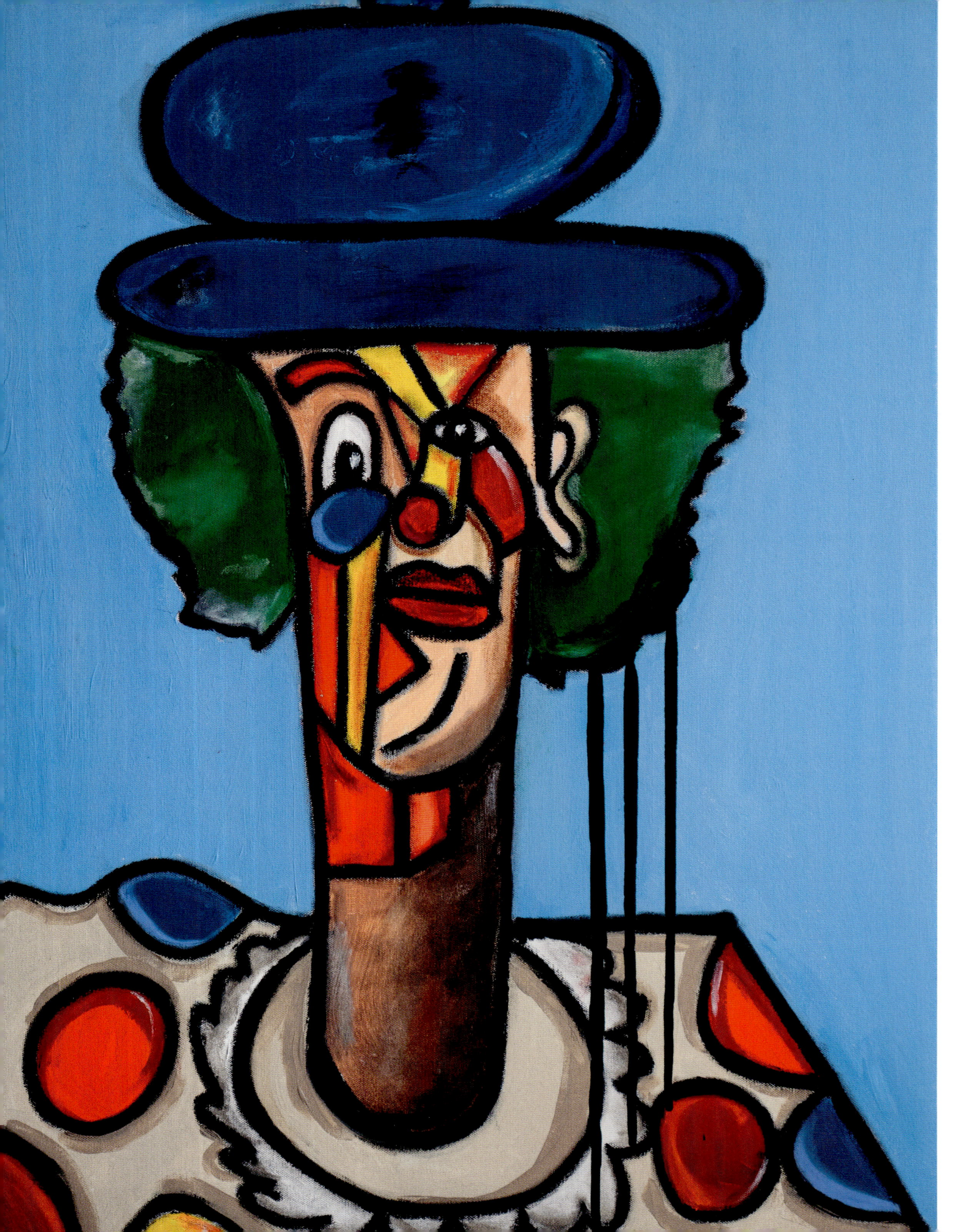

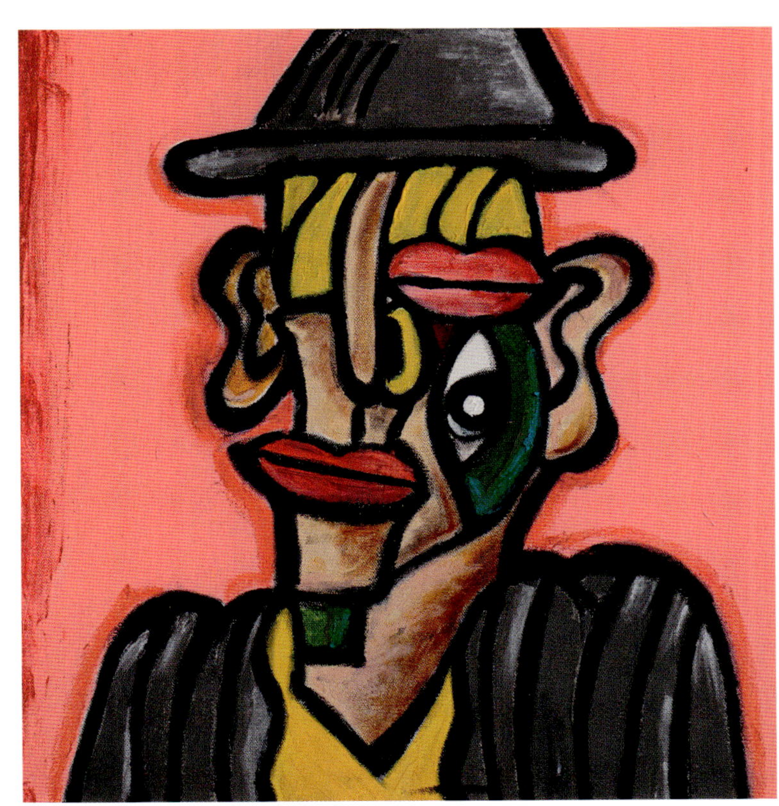

The Visionary, 2021
acrylic and oil pastel on canvas, 20 × 20 in

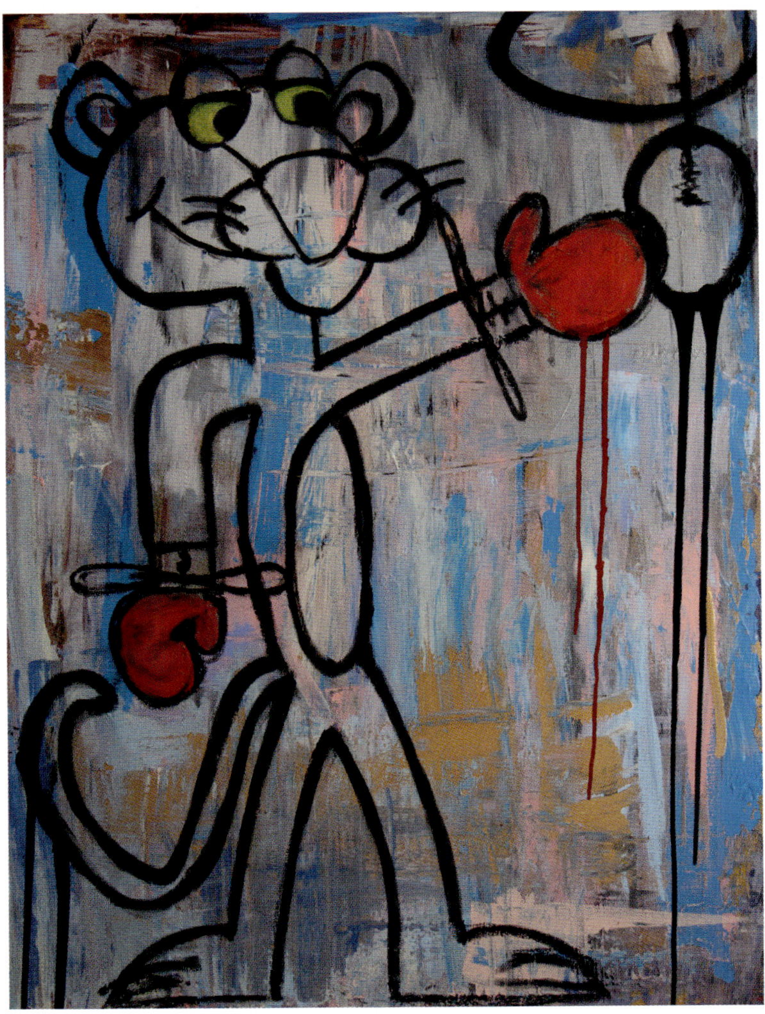

Abraham the Clown, 2021
acrylic and oil pastel
on canvas, 30 × 22 in

Pink Panther 1, 2021
acrylic and oil pastel
on canvas, 48 × 36 in

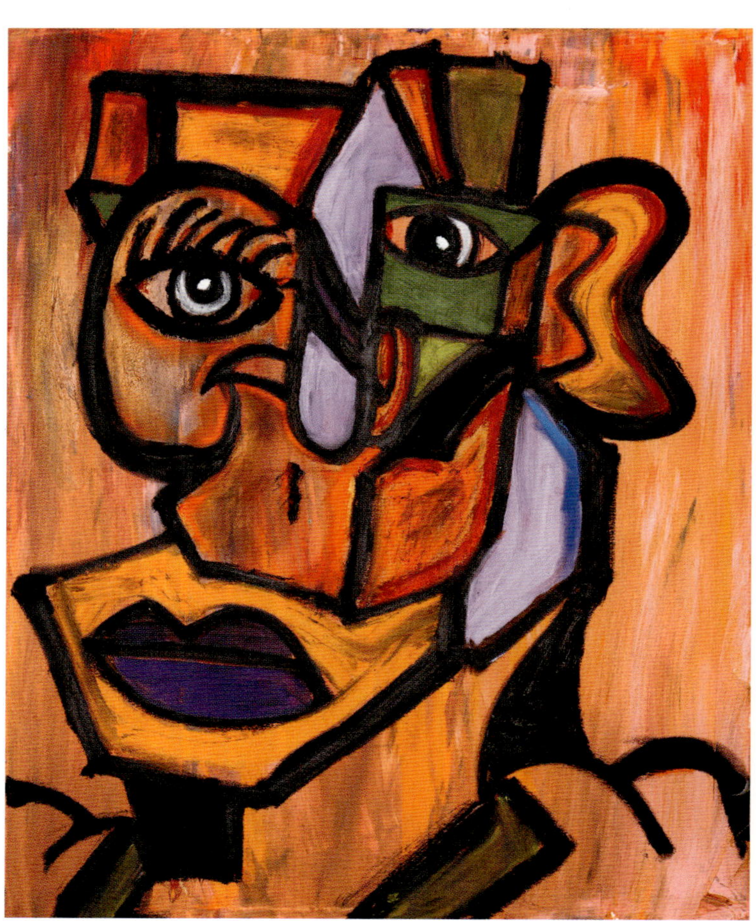

The Orange Cube, 2021 │ acrylic and oil pastel on canvas, 30 × 24 in

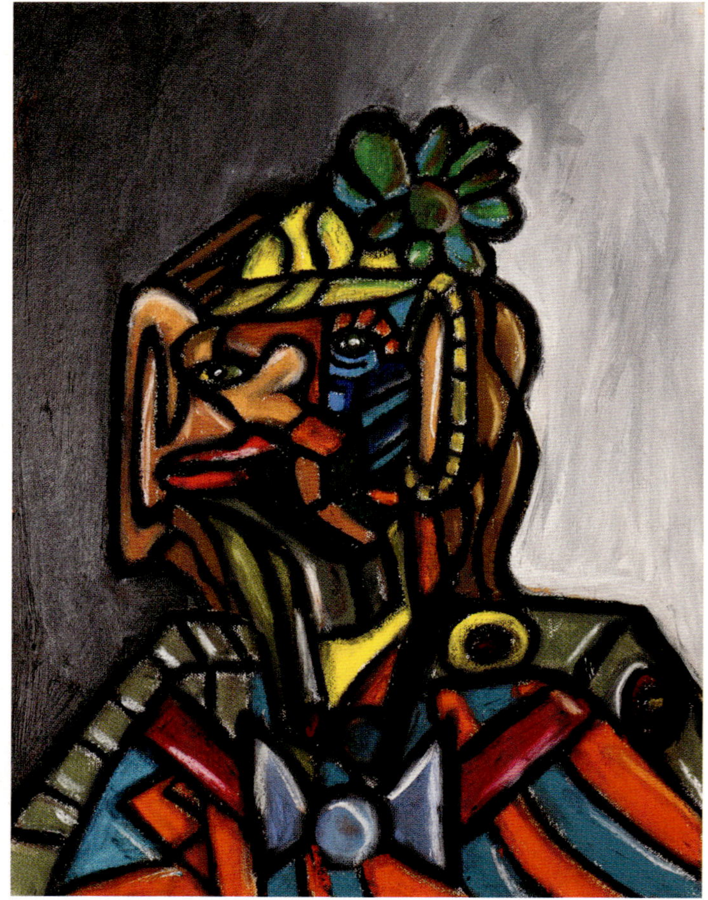

Lucia, 2021 │ acrylic and oil pastel on canvas, 16 × 12 in

Olga, 2021 │ acrylic and oil pastel on canvas, 48 × 36 in

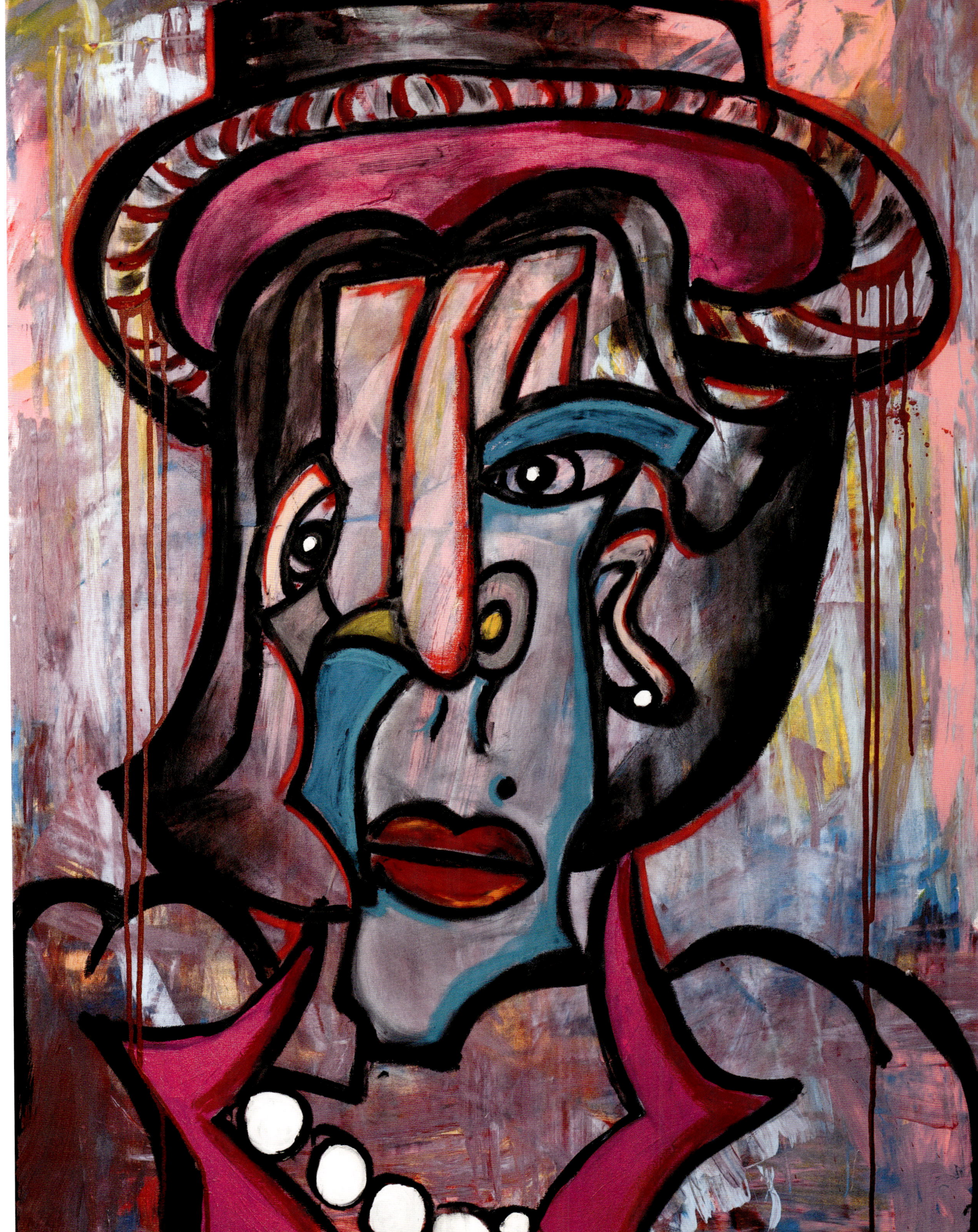

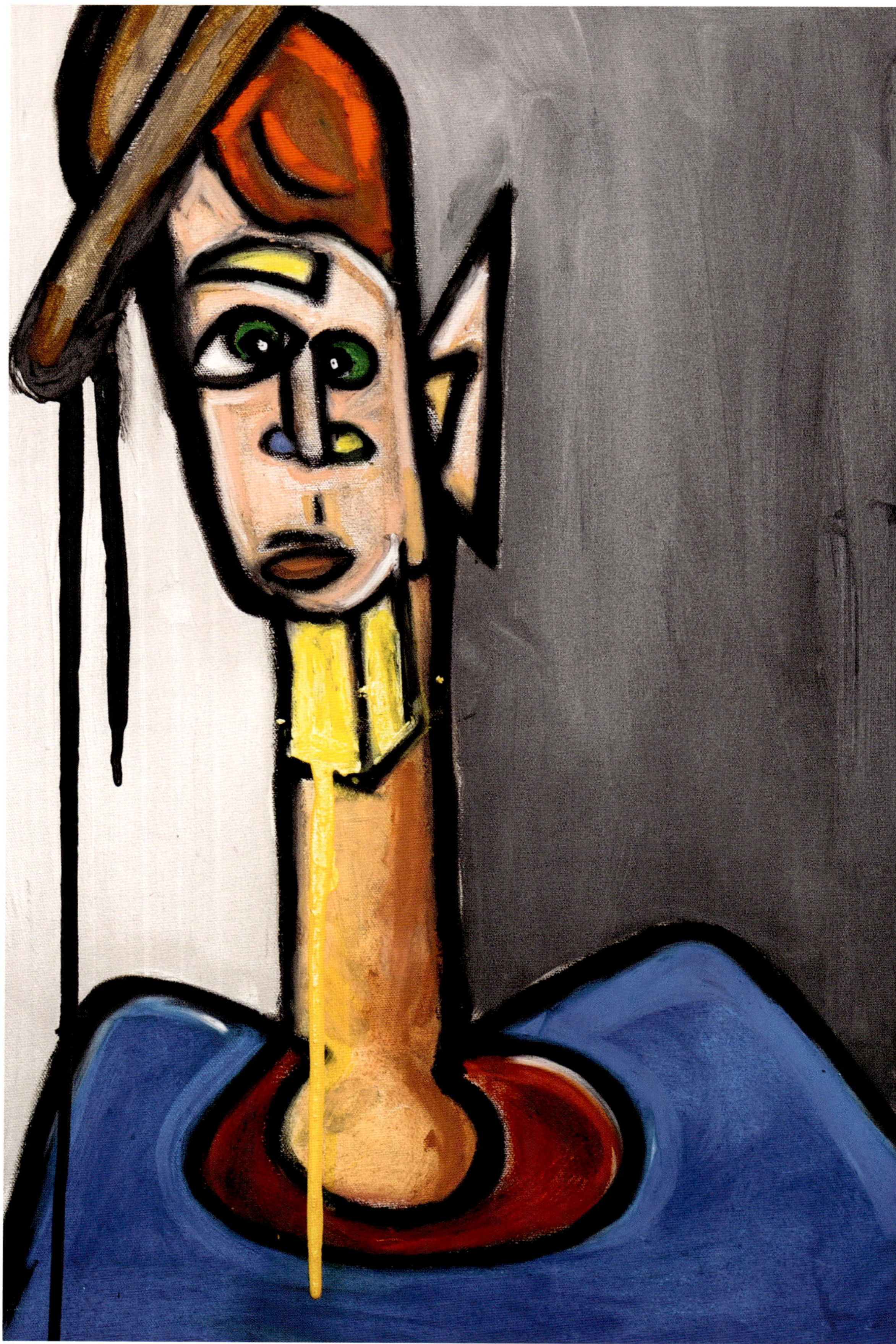

Child, 2021 | acrylic and oil pastel on canvas, 24 × 16 in

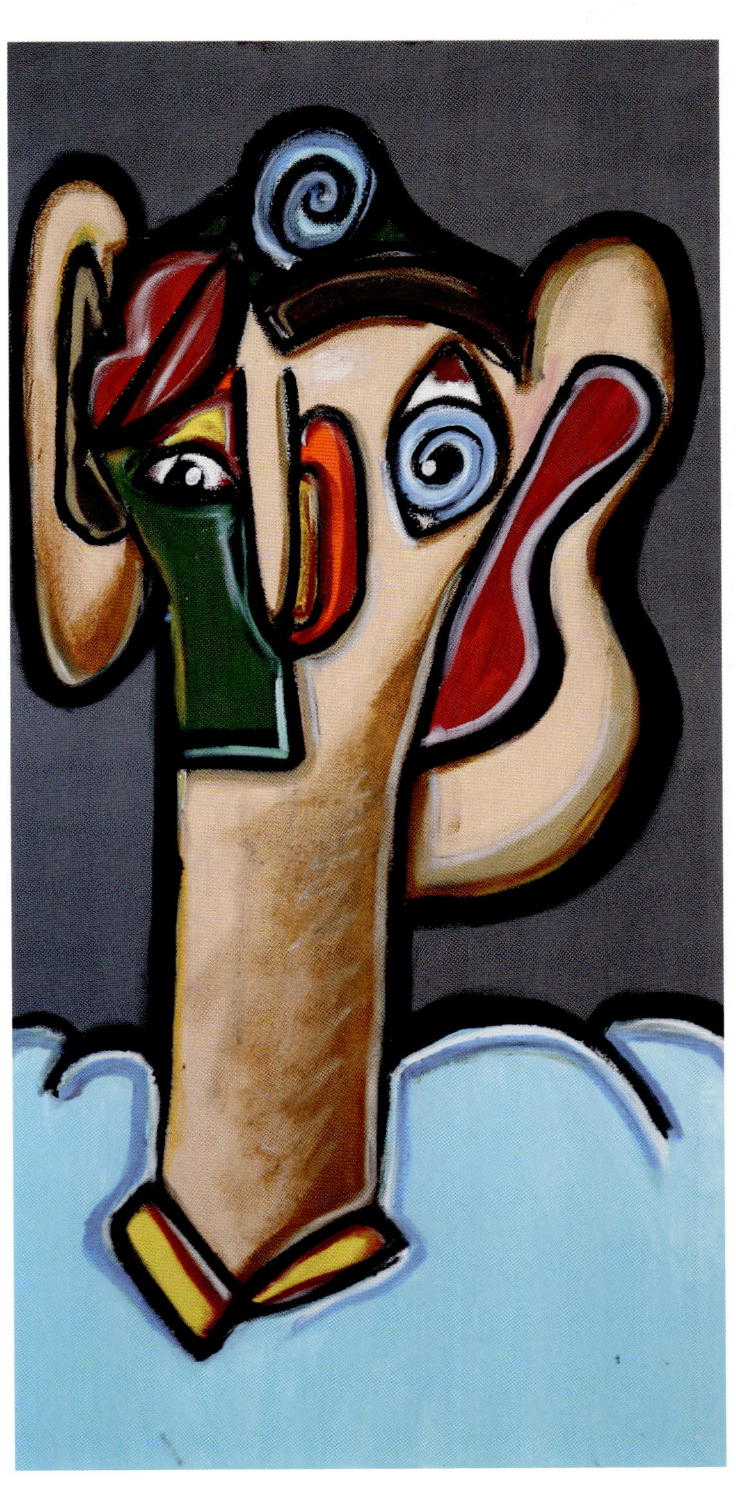

Willis, 2021 | acrylic and oil pastel on canvas, 30 × 15 in

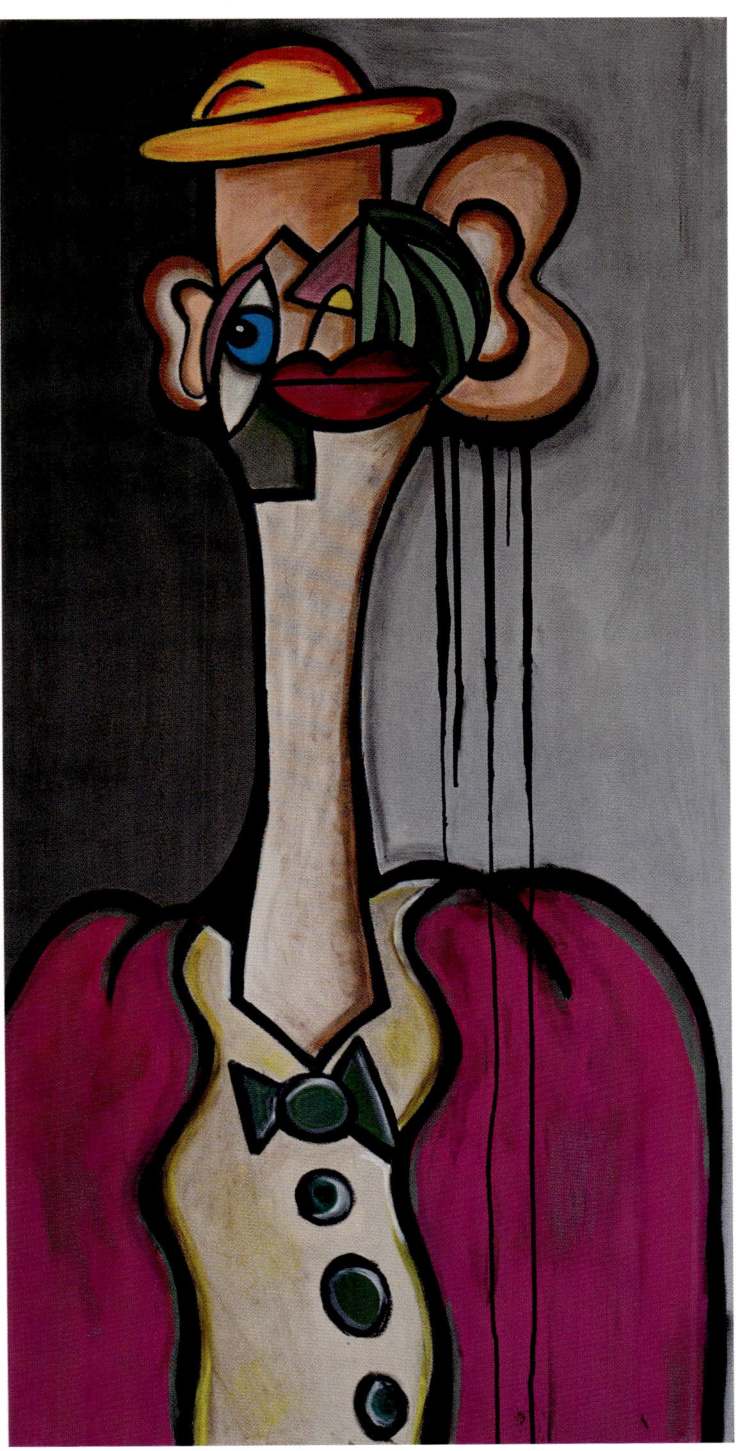

Lucky, 2021 | acrylic and oil pastel on canvas, 72 × 36 in

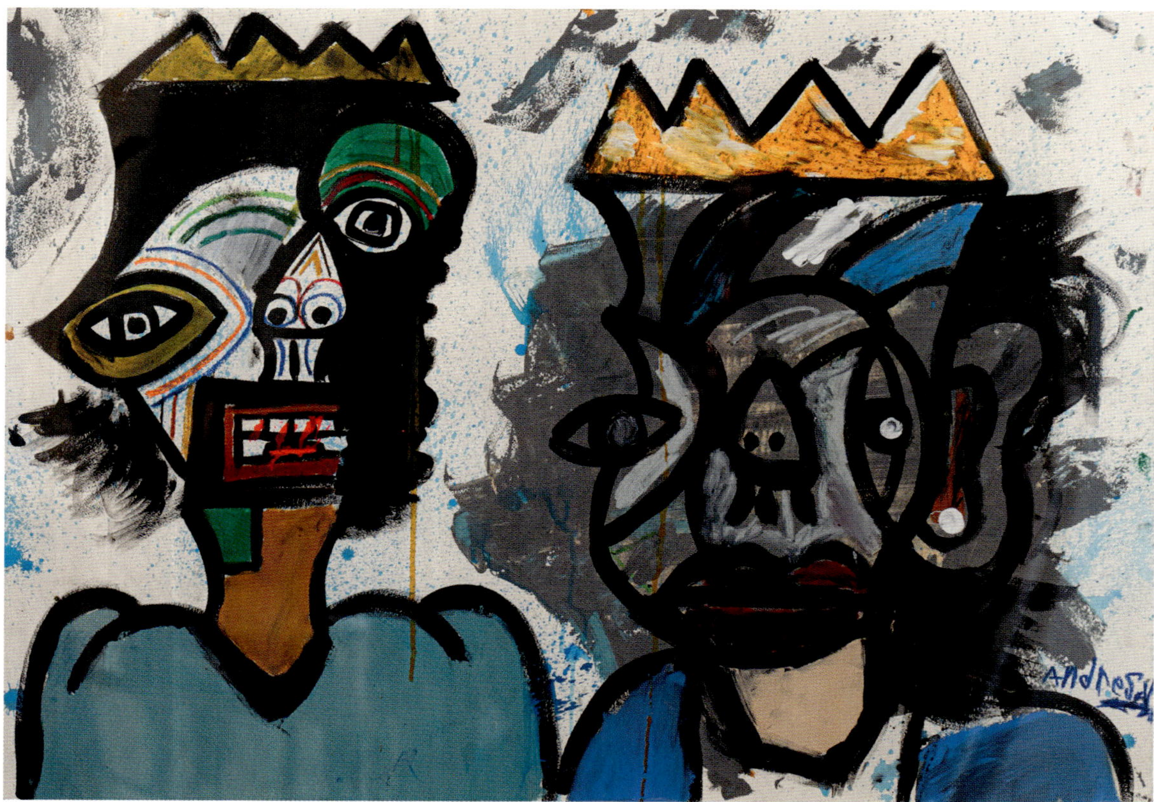

King and Queen, 2021 | acrylic and oil pastel on canvas, 29 × 41 in

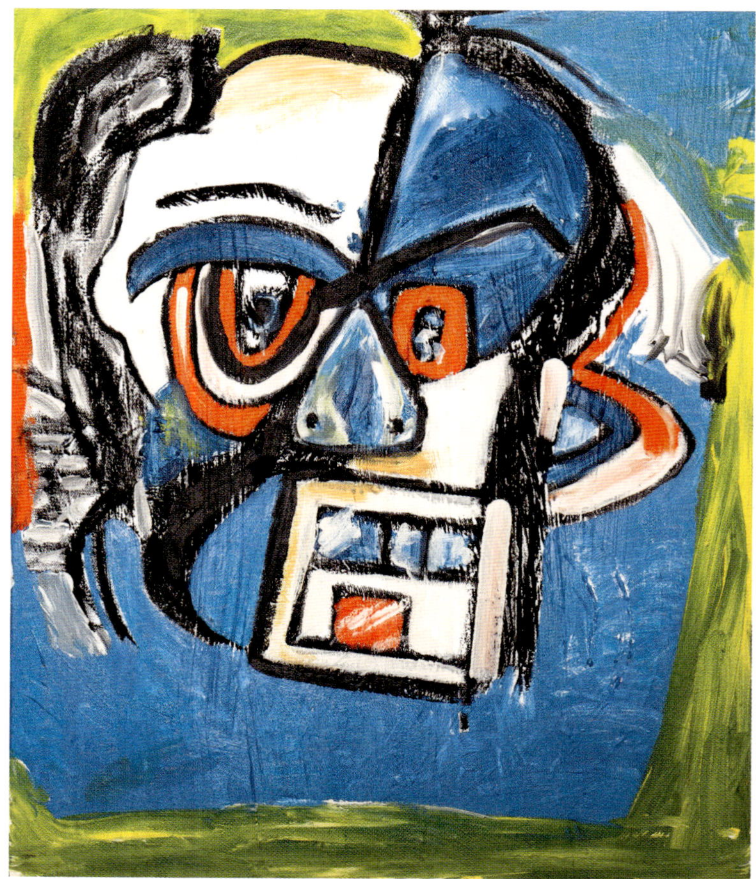

Homage to Basquiat, 2021 | acrylic and oil pastel on canvas, 24 × 20 in

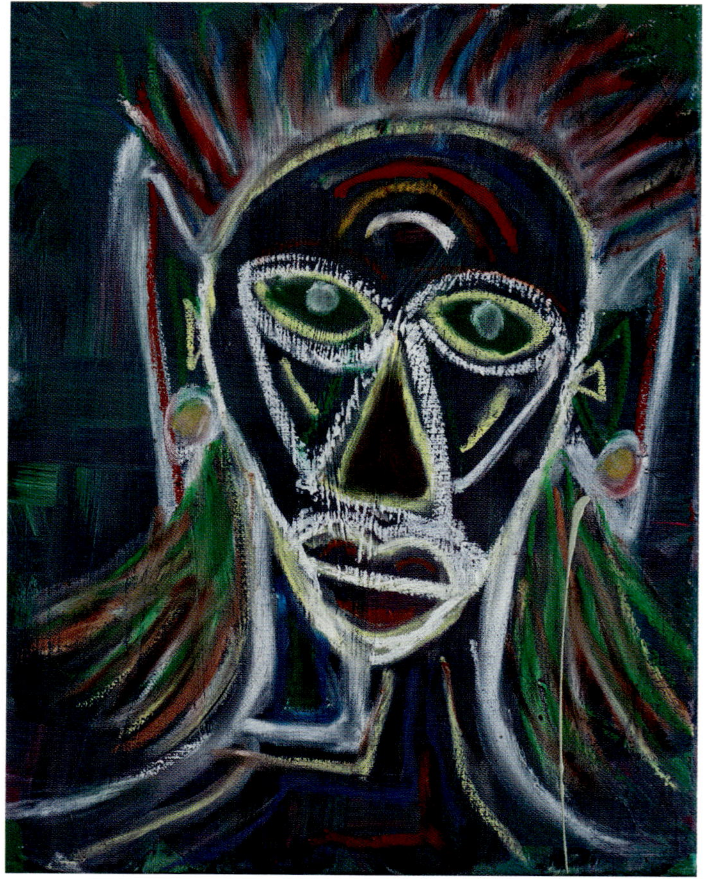

The Ghost Boy, 2021 | acrylic and oil pastel on canvas, 18 × 12 in

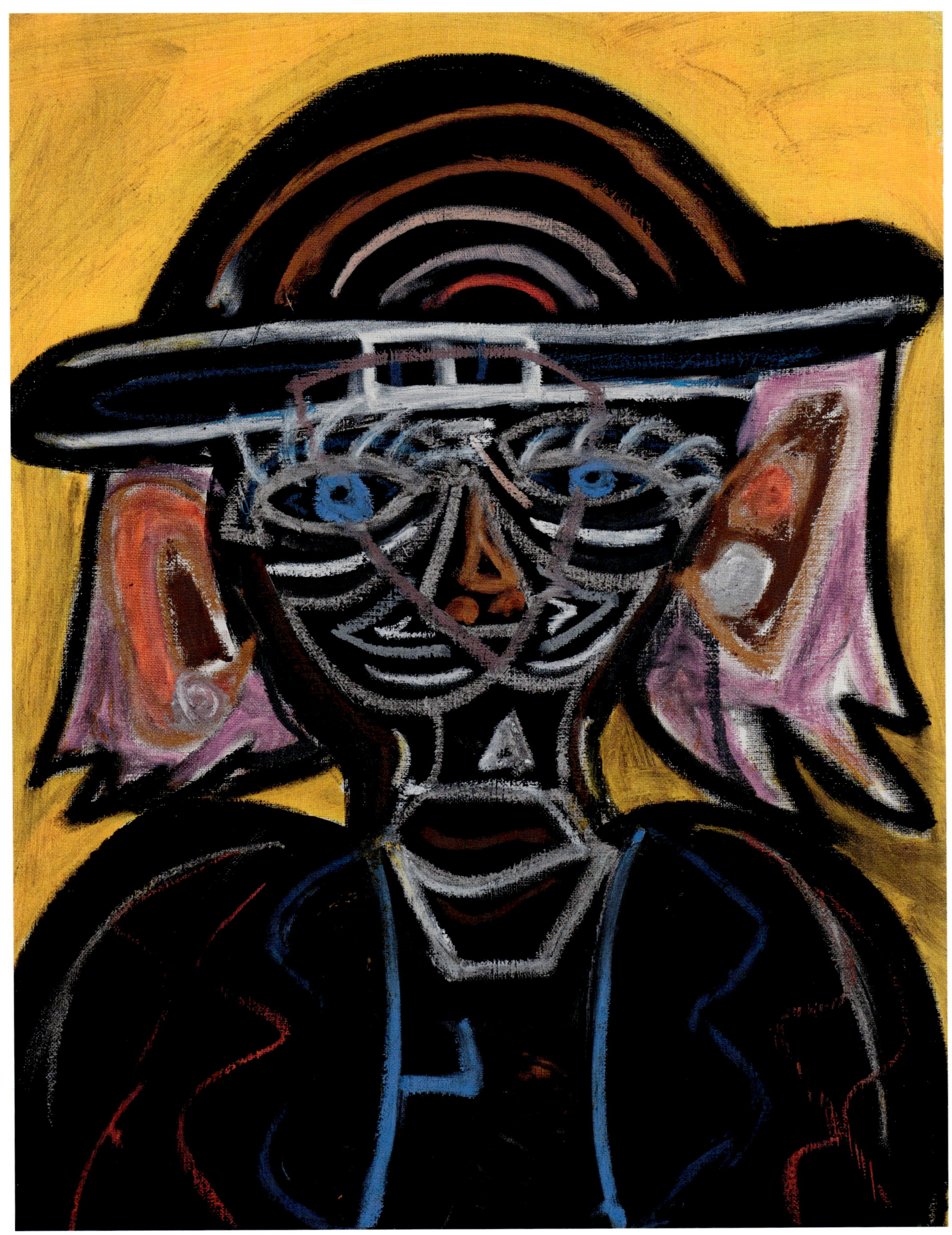

Amelia, 2021 | acrylic and oil pastel on canvas, 24 × 18 in

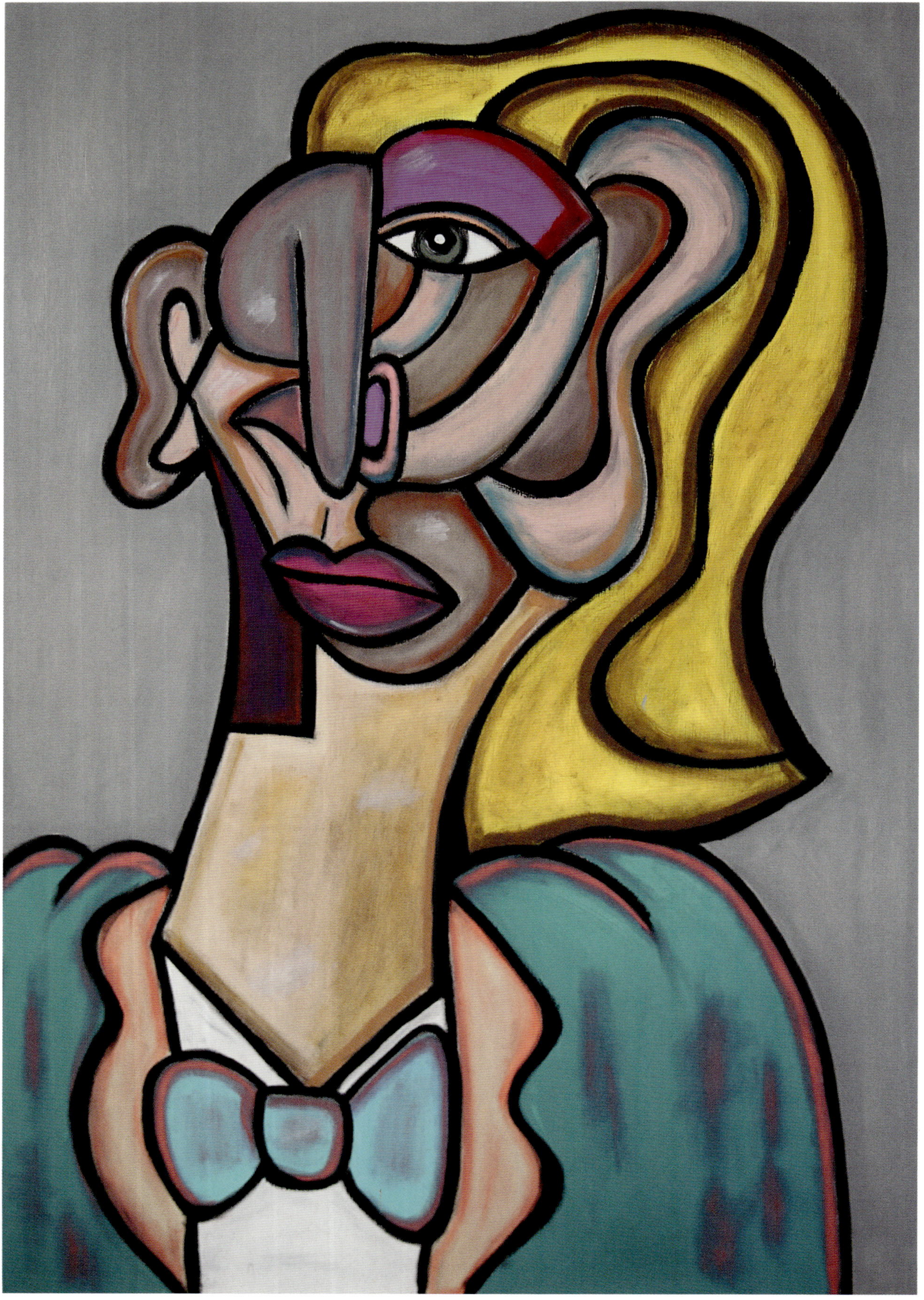

Lady, 2021 | acrylic and oil pastel on canvas, 51 × 36 in

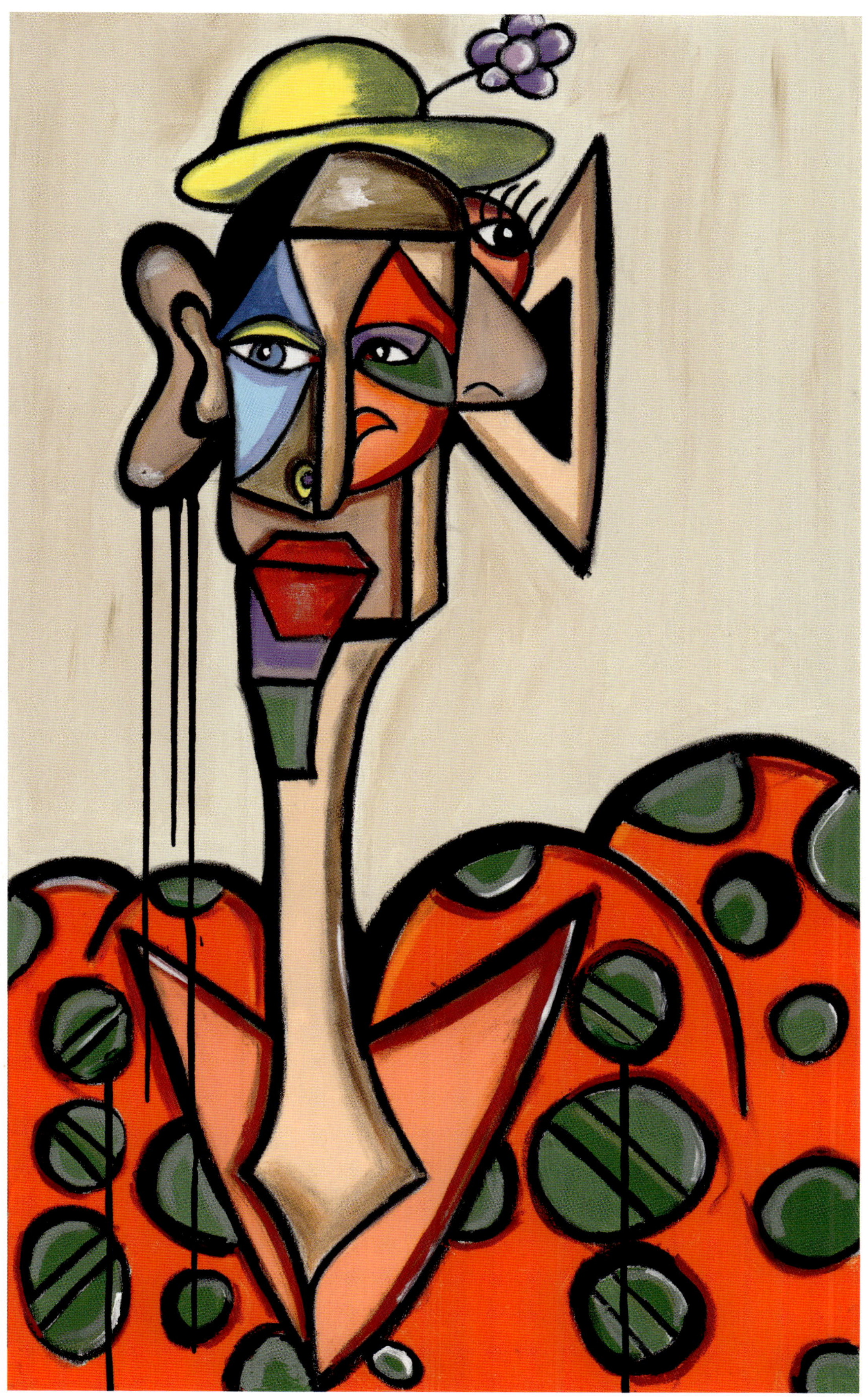

Alberto the Clown, 2021 | acrylic and oil pastel on canvas, 60 × 36 in

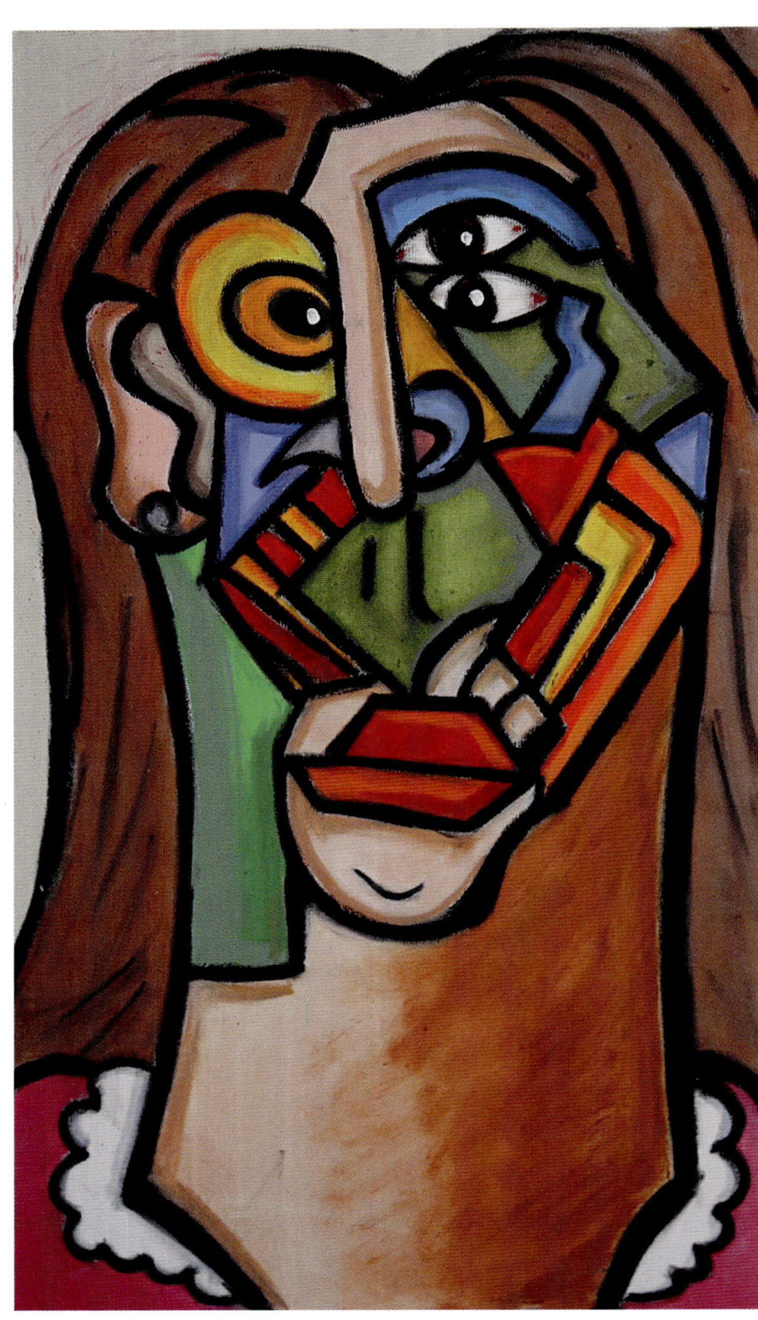

Adela, 2021 | acrylic and oil pastel on canvas, 36 × 20 in

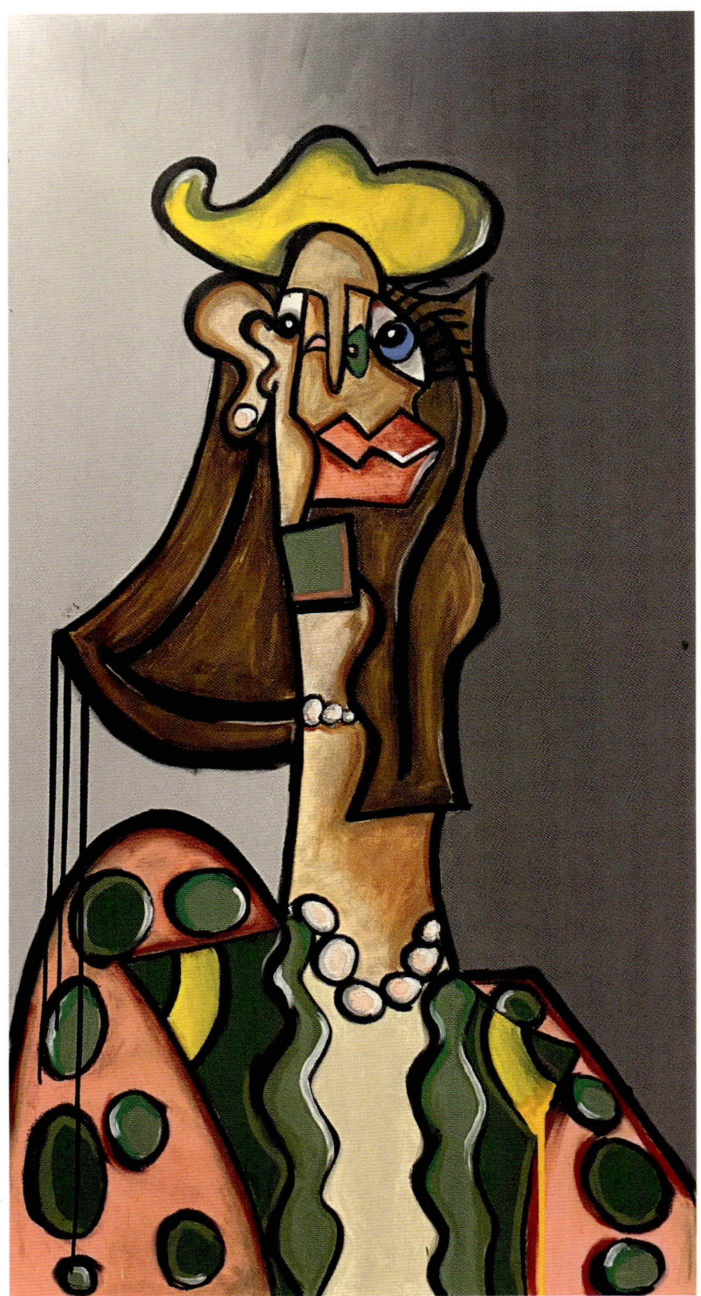

Lucy, 2021 | acrylic and oil pastel on canvas, 72 × 36 in

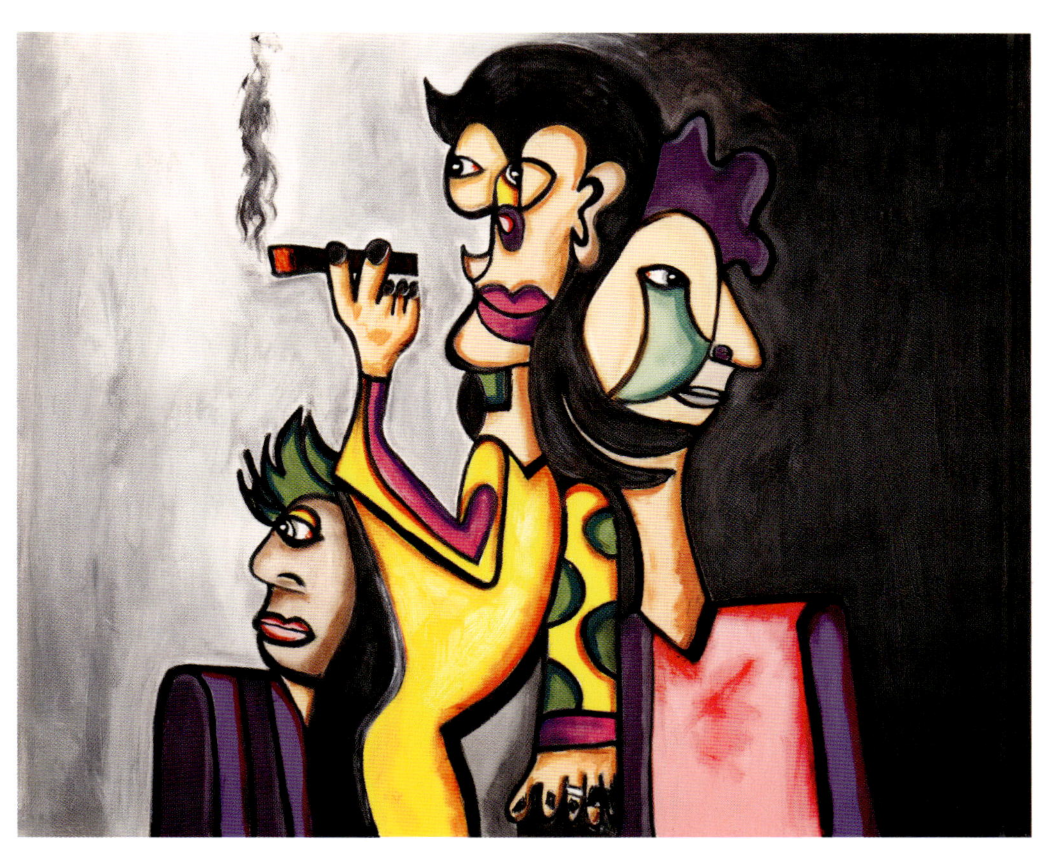

The Three Punks, 2021
acrylic and oil pastel on canvas, 48 × 60 in

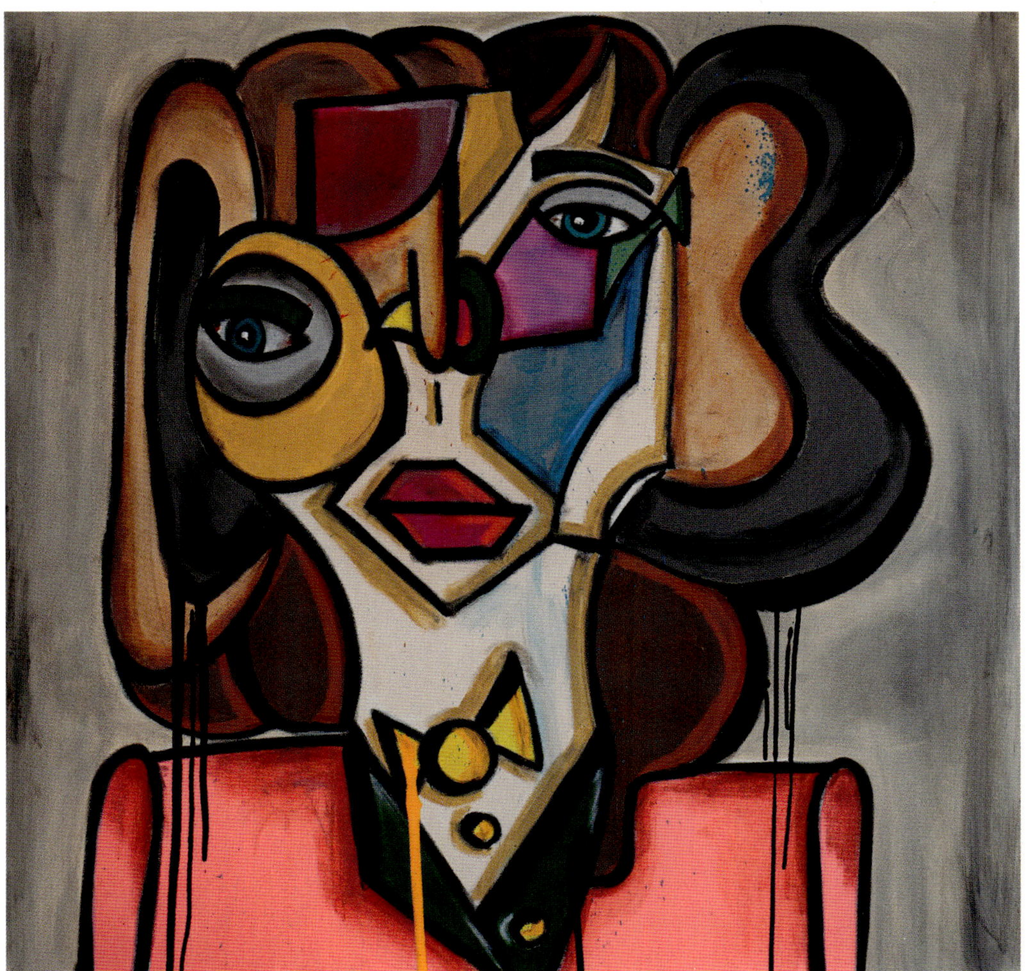

Lady in Pink, 2021
acrylic and oil pastel on canvas, 36 × 36 in

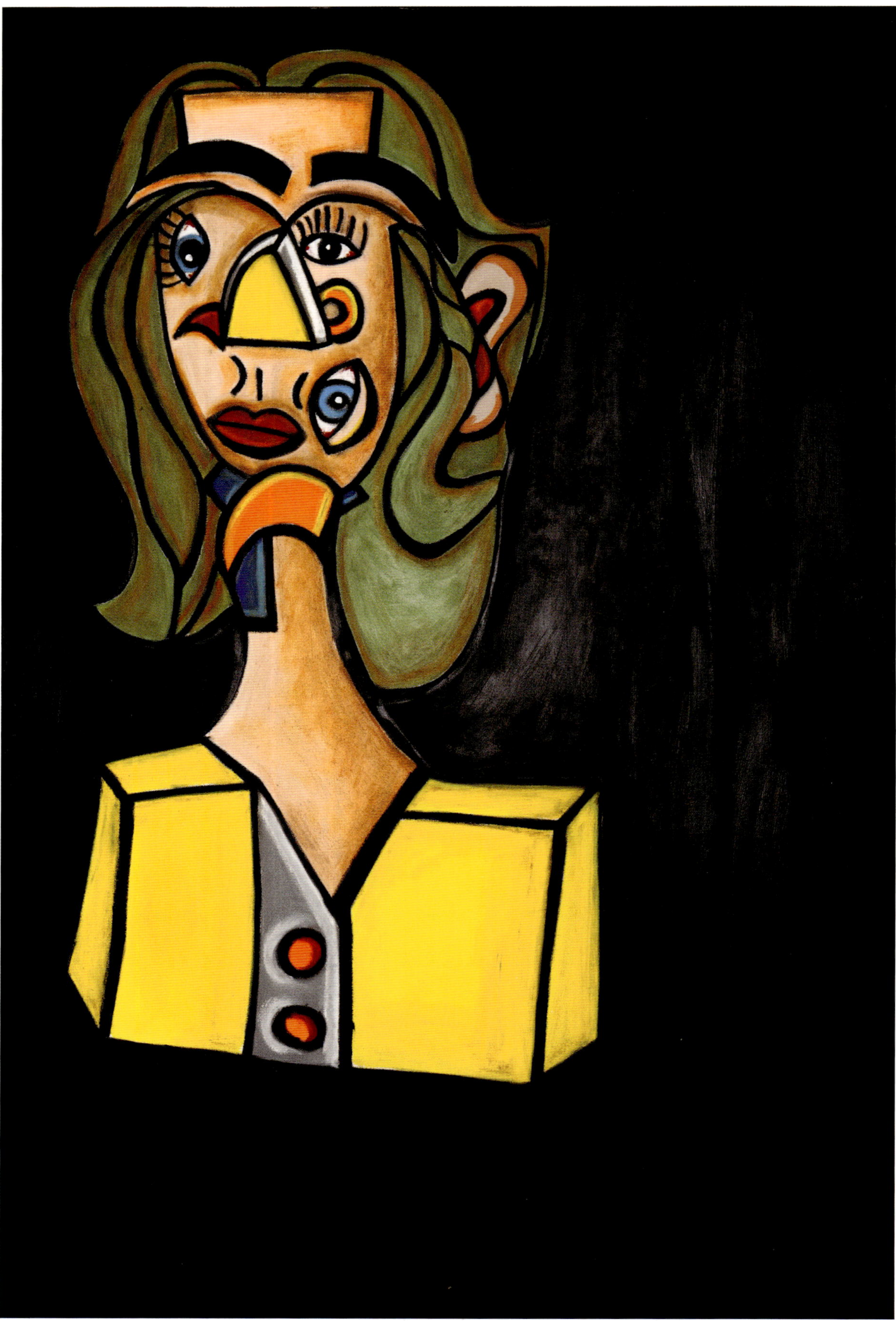

Donna, 2021 | acrylic and oil pastel on canvas, 72 × 48 in

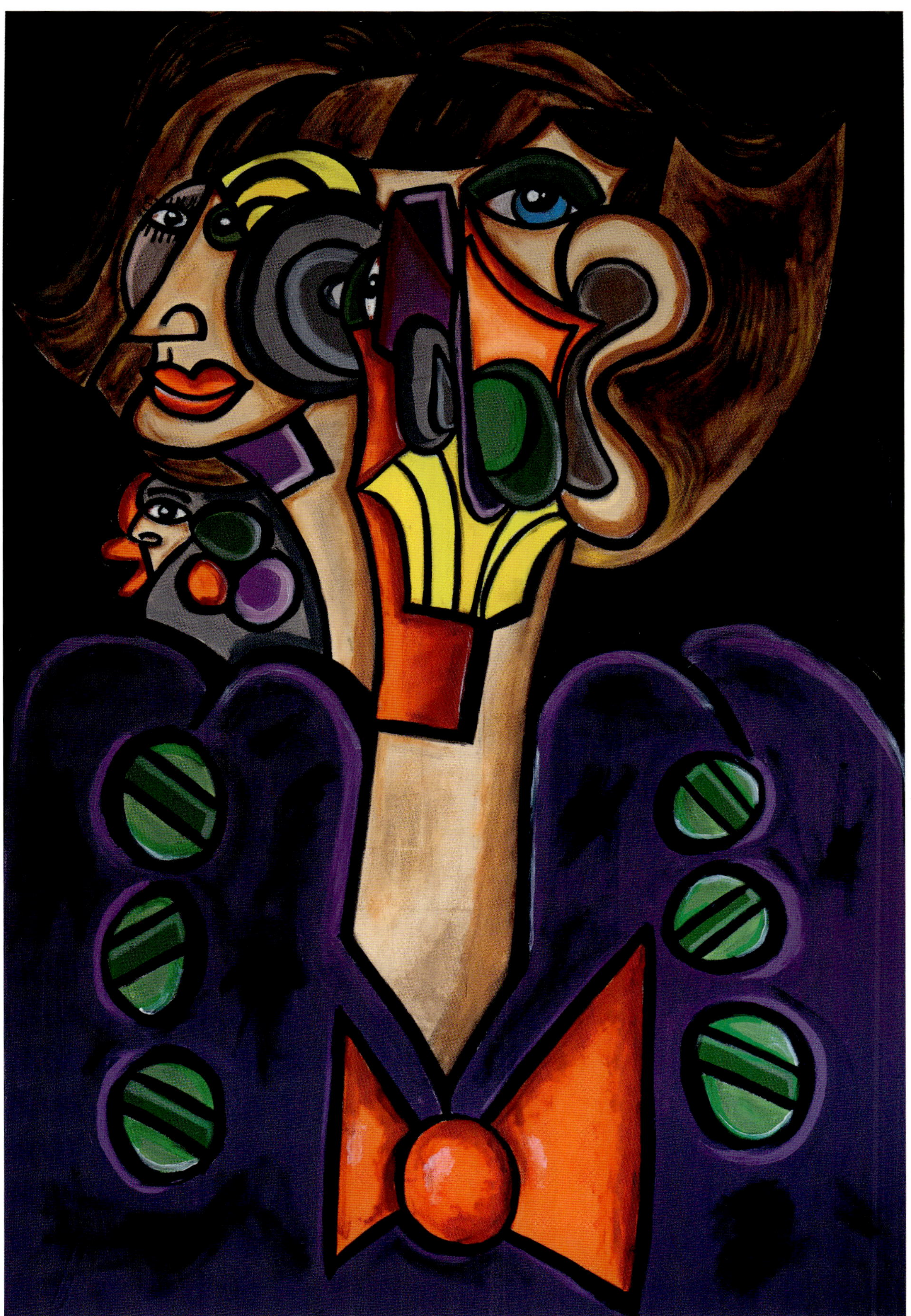

The Menace, 2021 | acrylic and oil pastel on canvas, 72 × 48 in

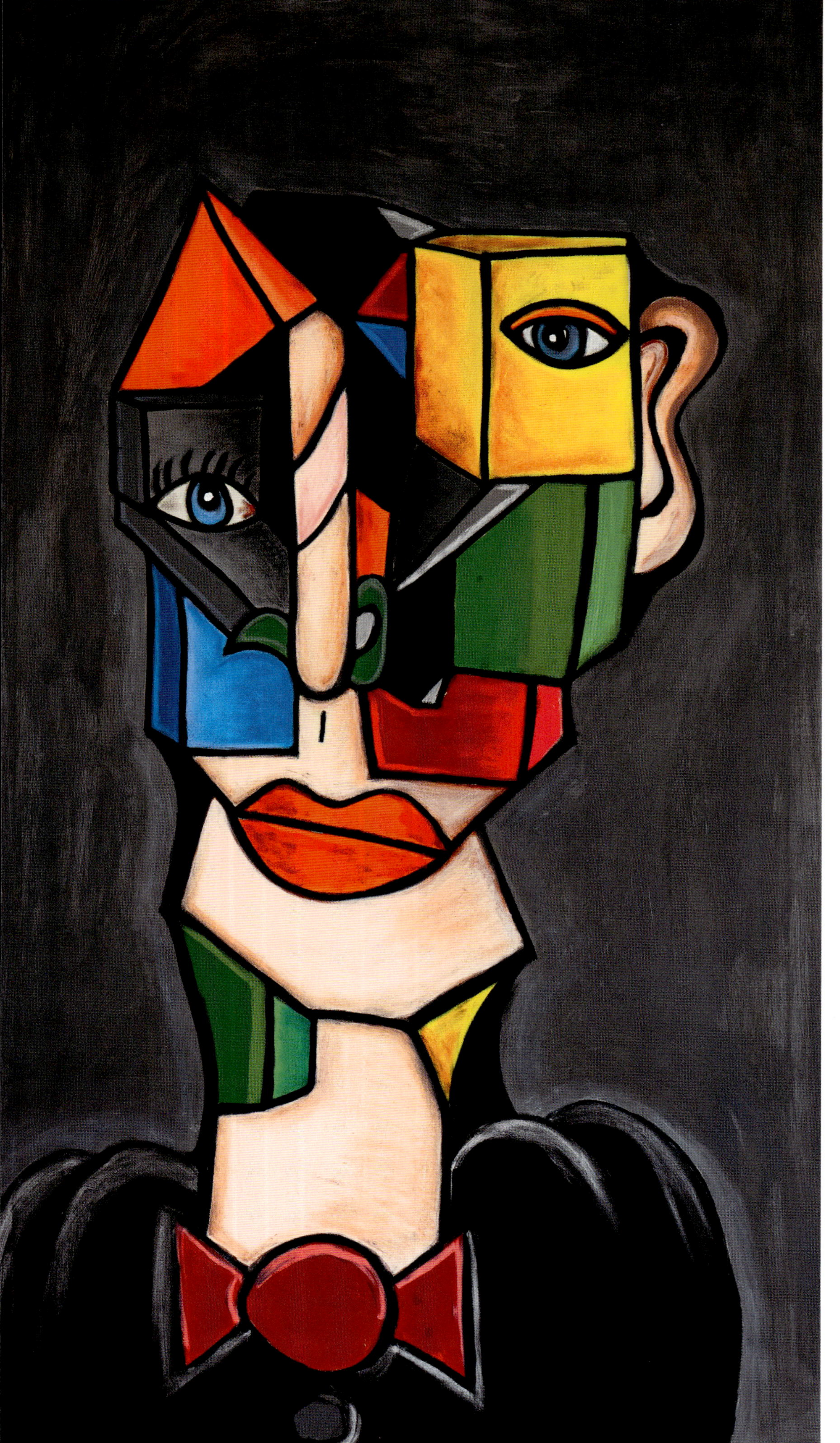

Ms. Cube, 2021
acrylic and oil pastel on canvas, 72 × 40 in

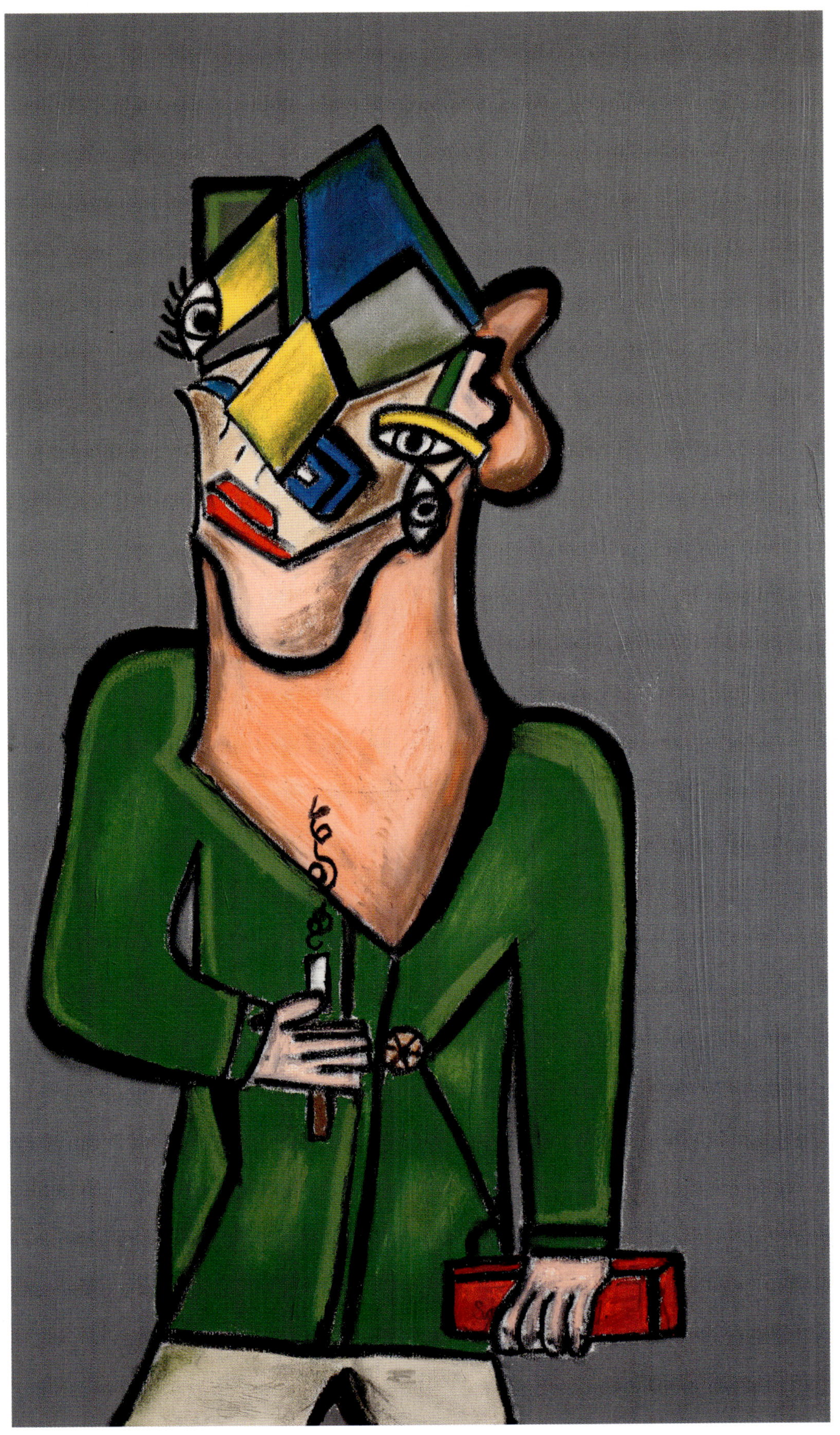

Lenny, 2021 | acrylic and oil pastel on canvas, 30 × 20 in

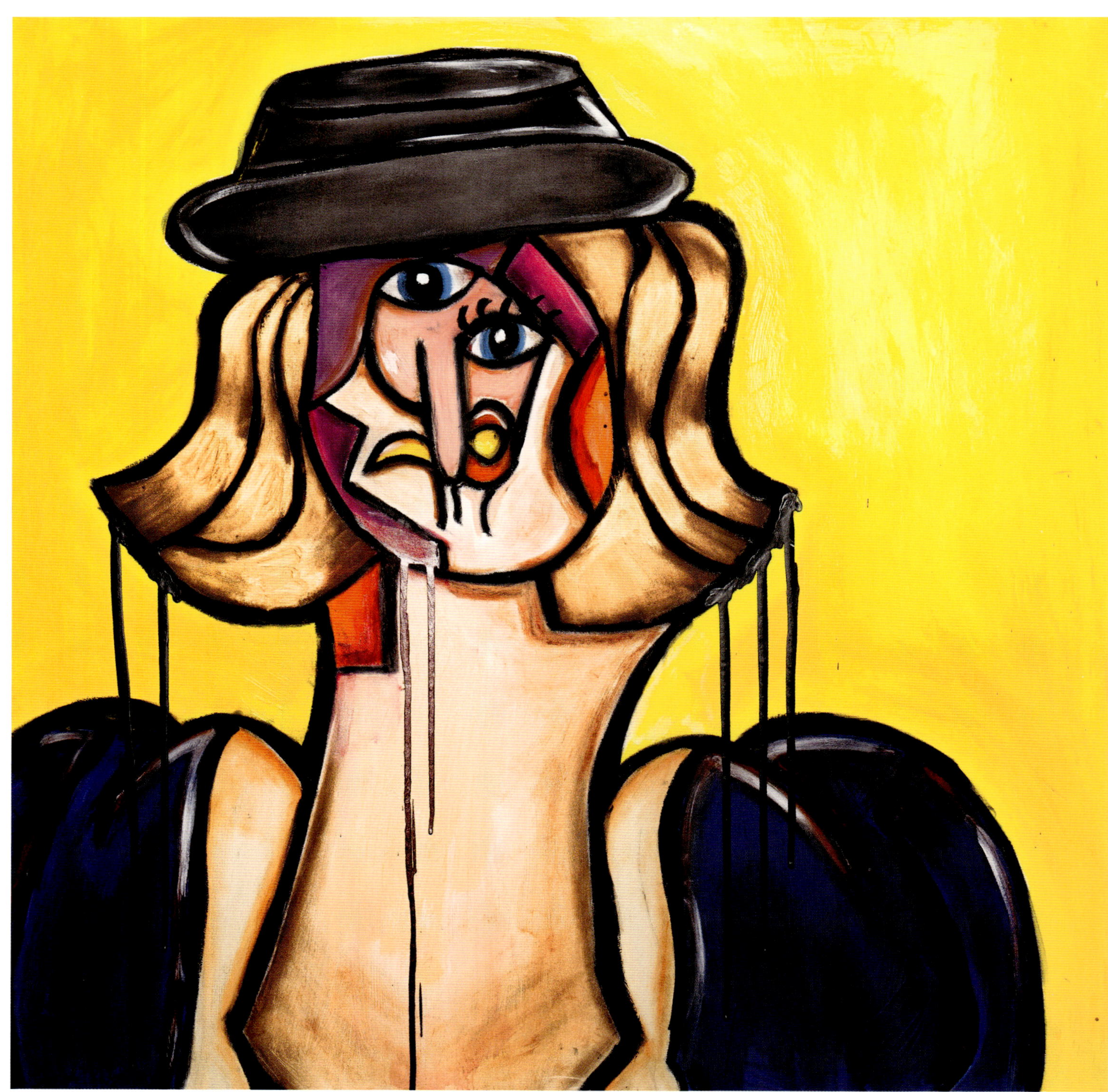

Sara, 2021 | acrylic and oil pastel on canvas, 40 × 40 in

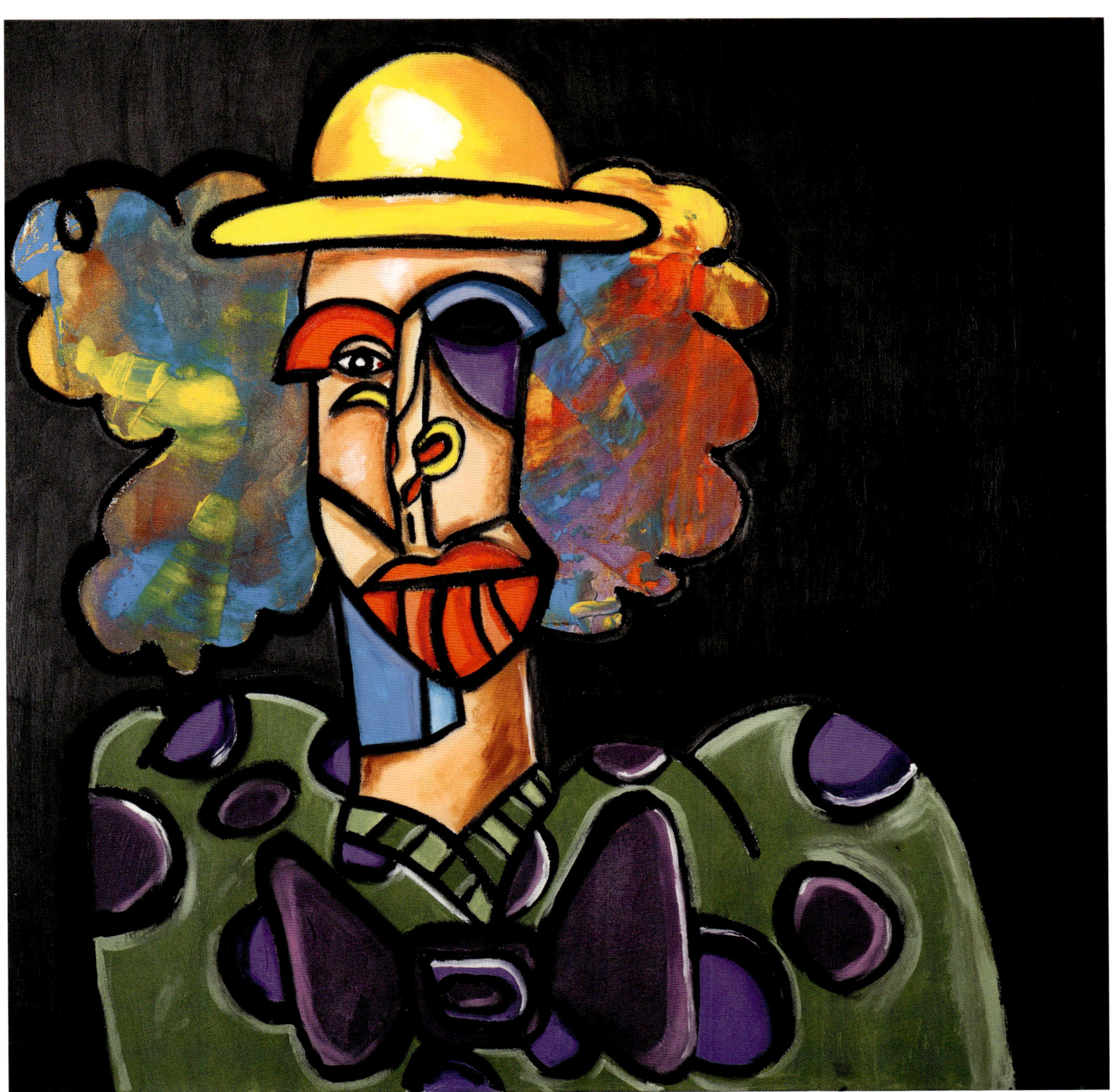

El Payaso Loco, 2021 | acrylic and oil pastel on canvas, 36 × 36 in

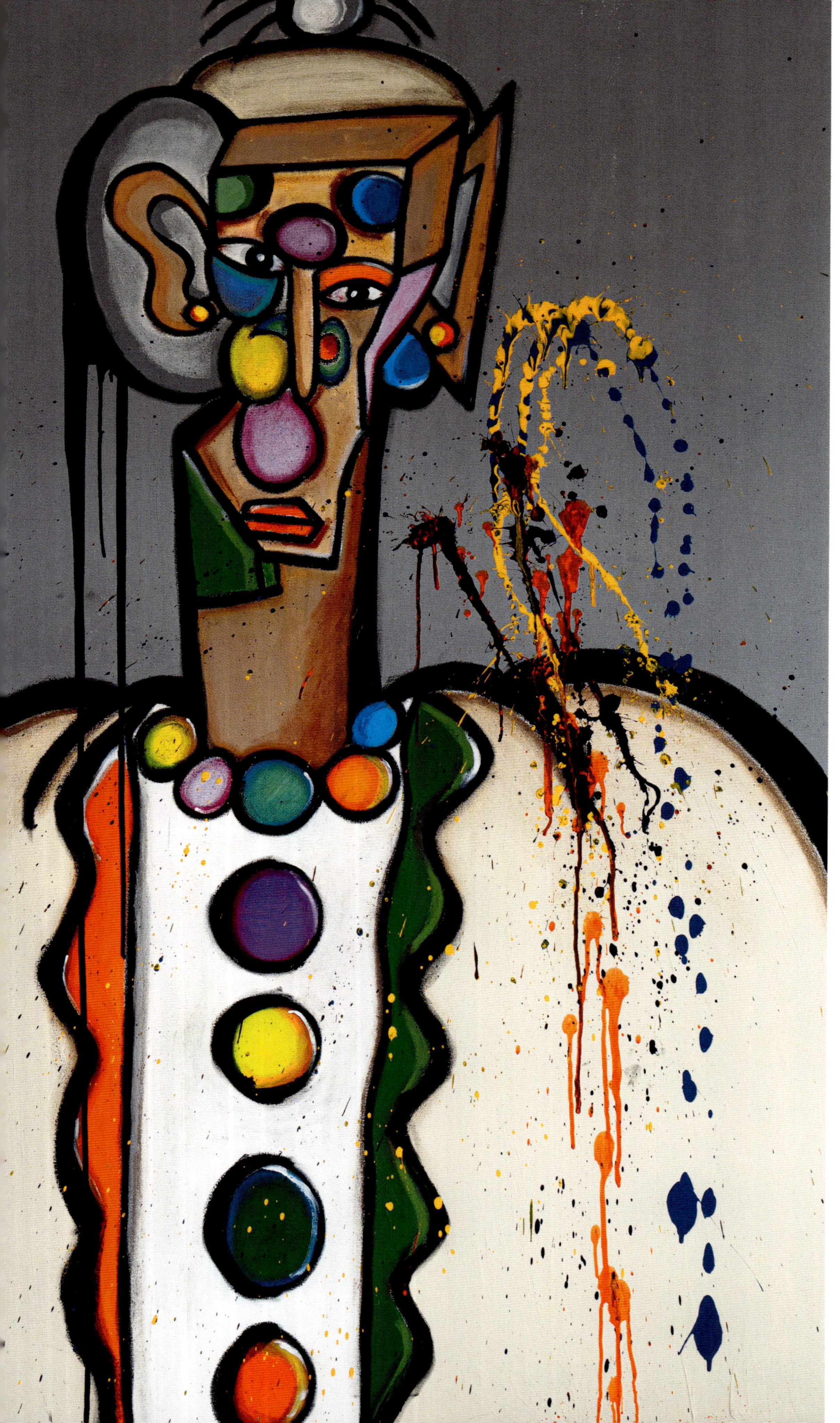

Gesture the Clown, 2021
acrylic and oil pastel
on canvas, 70 × 40 in

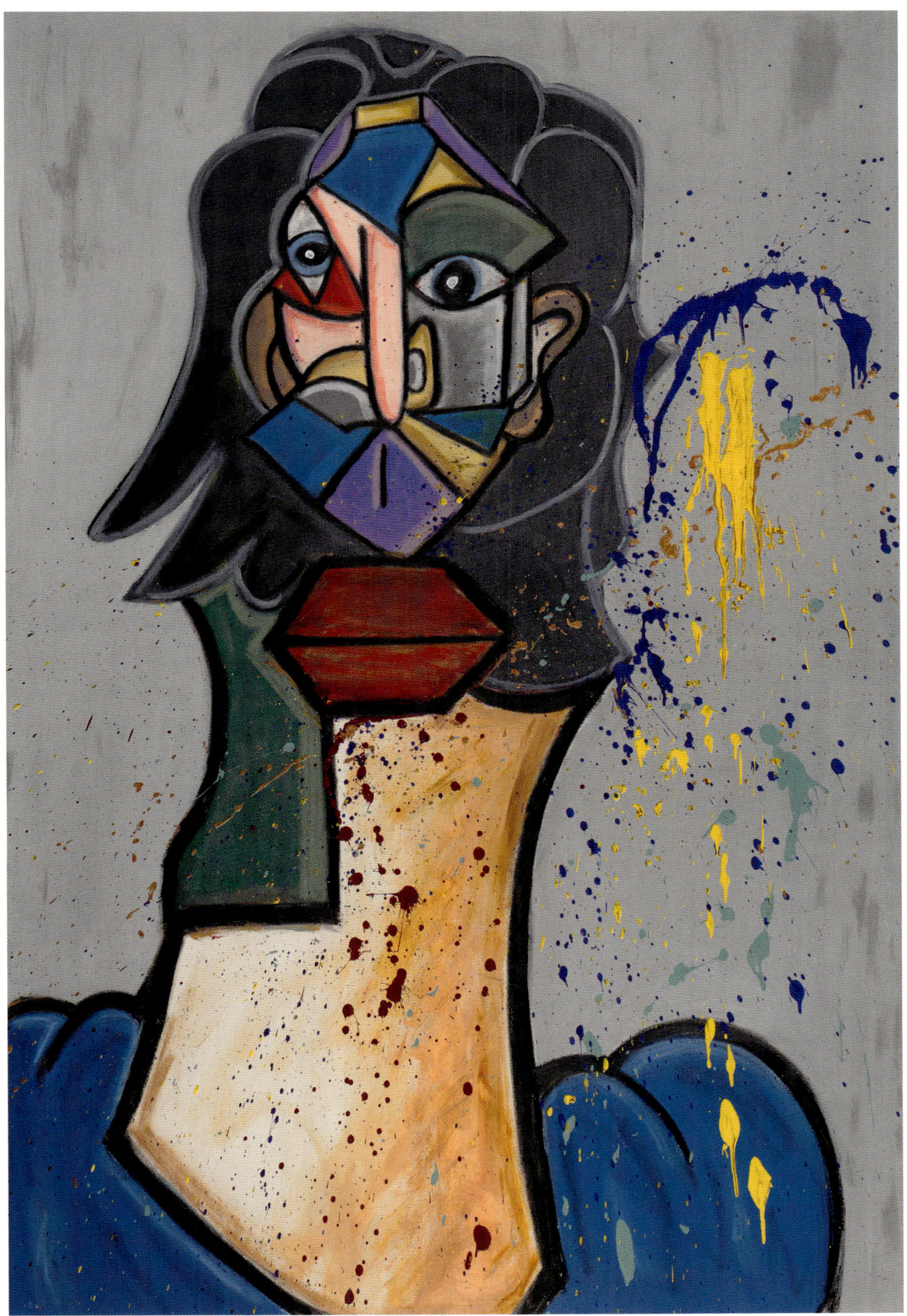

Blue Madness, 2021 | acrylic and oil pastel on canvas, 72 × 48 in

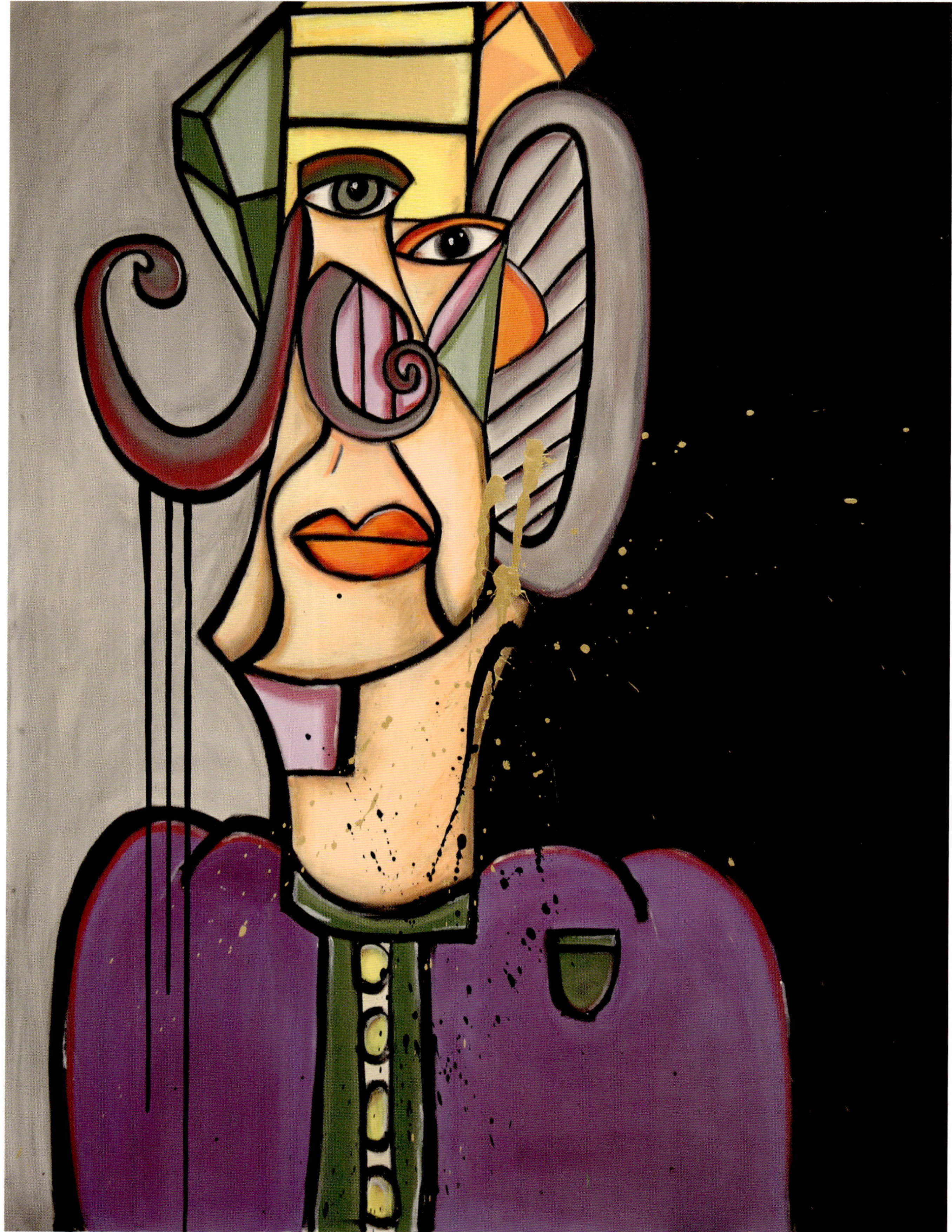

Dalila, 2021 | acrylic and oil pastel on canvas, 68 × 51 in

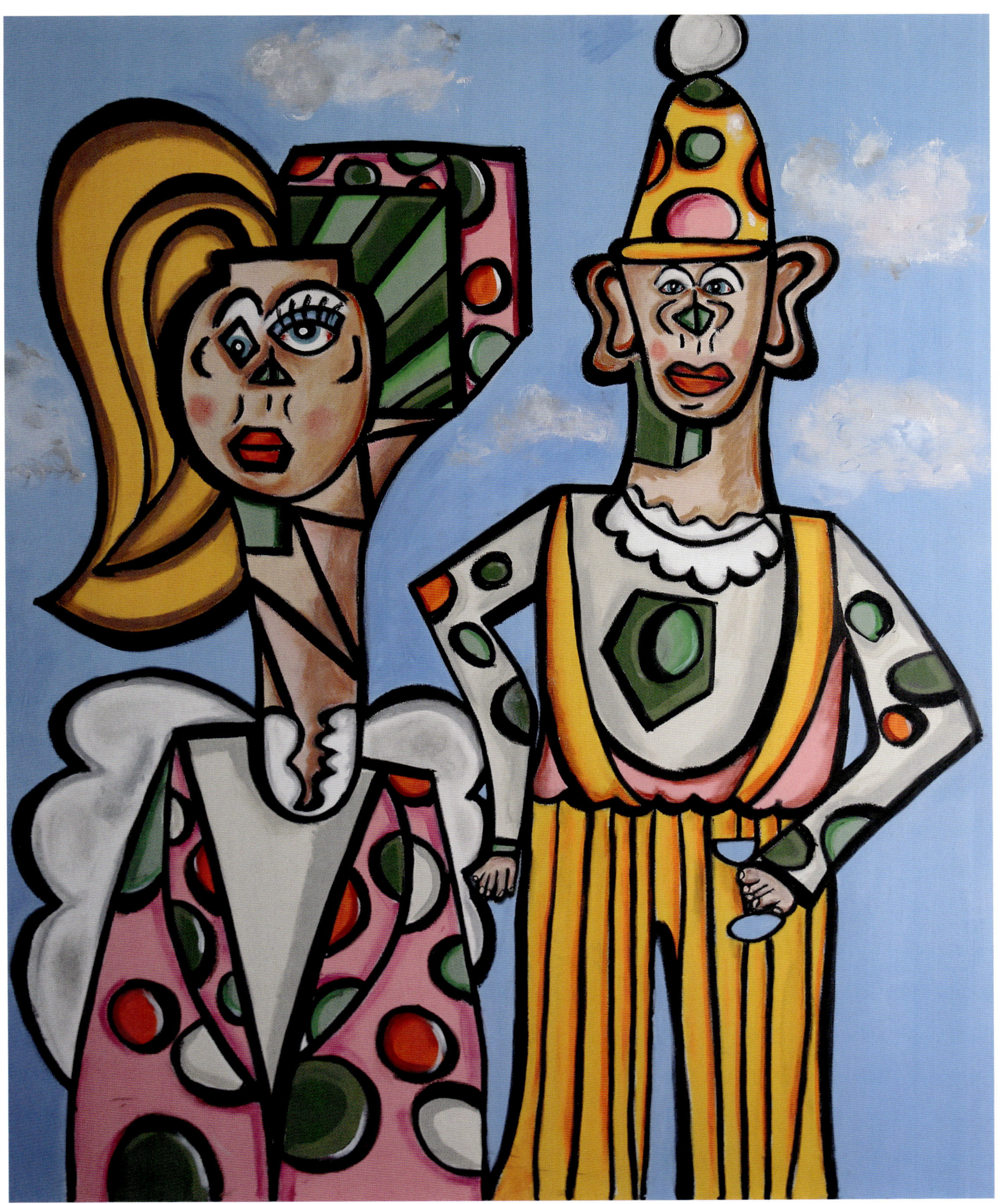

Birthday Clowns, 2021 | acrylic and oil pastel on canvas, 70 × 57 in

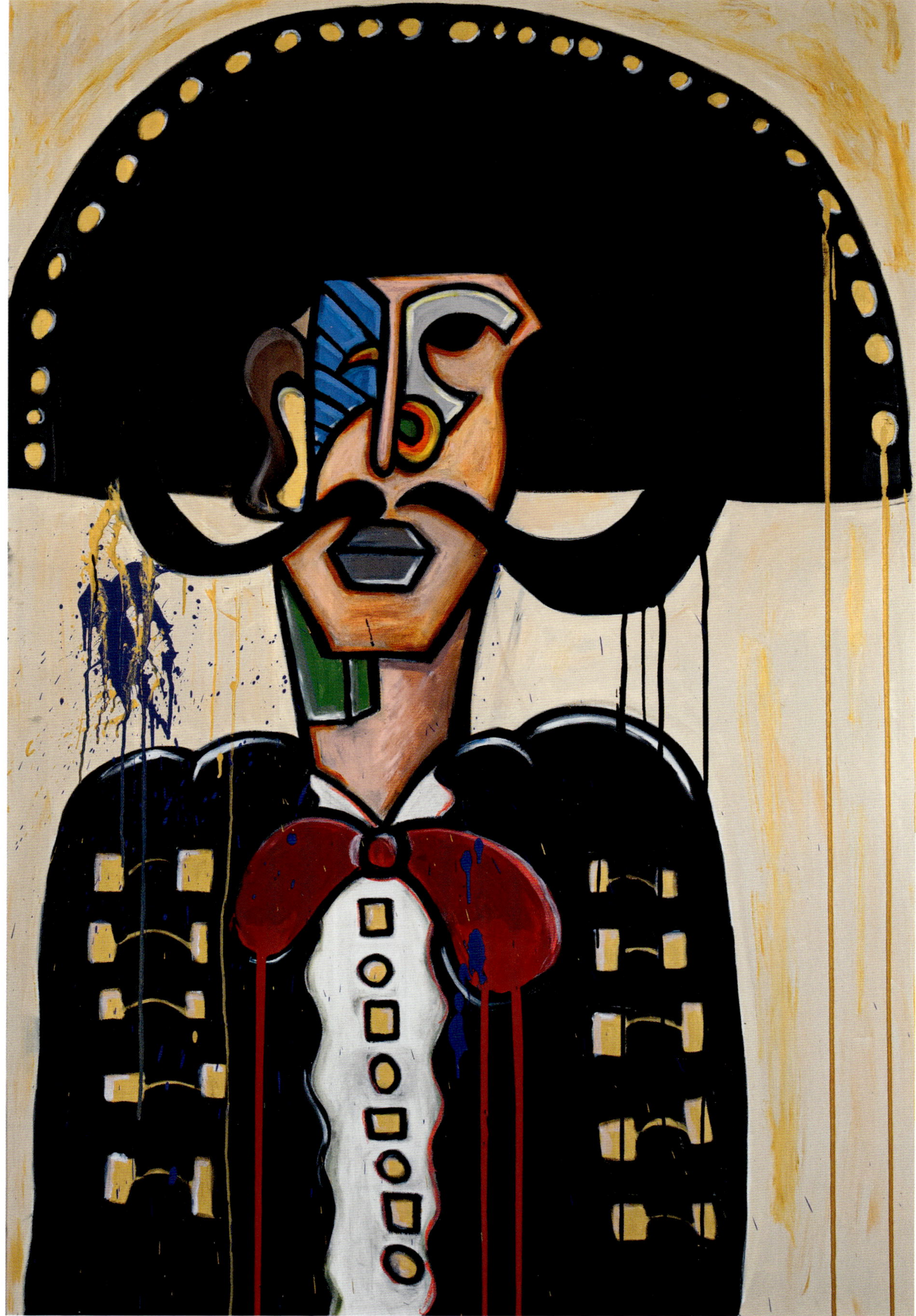

El Mariachi Loco, 2021 | acrylic and oil pastel on canvas, 72 × 48 in

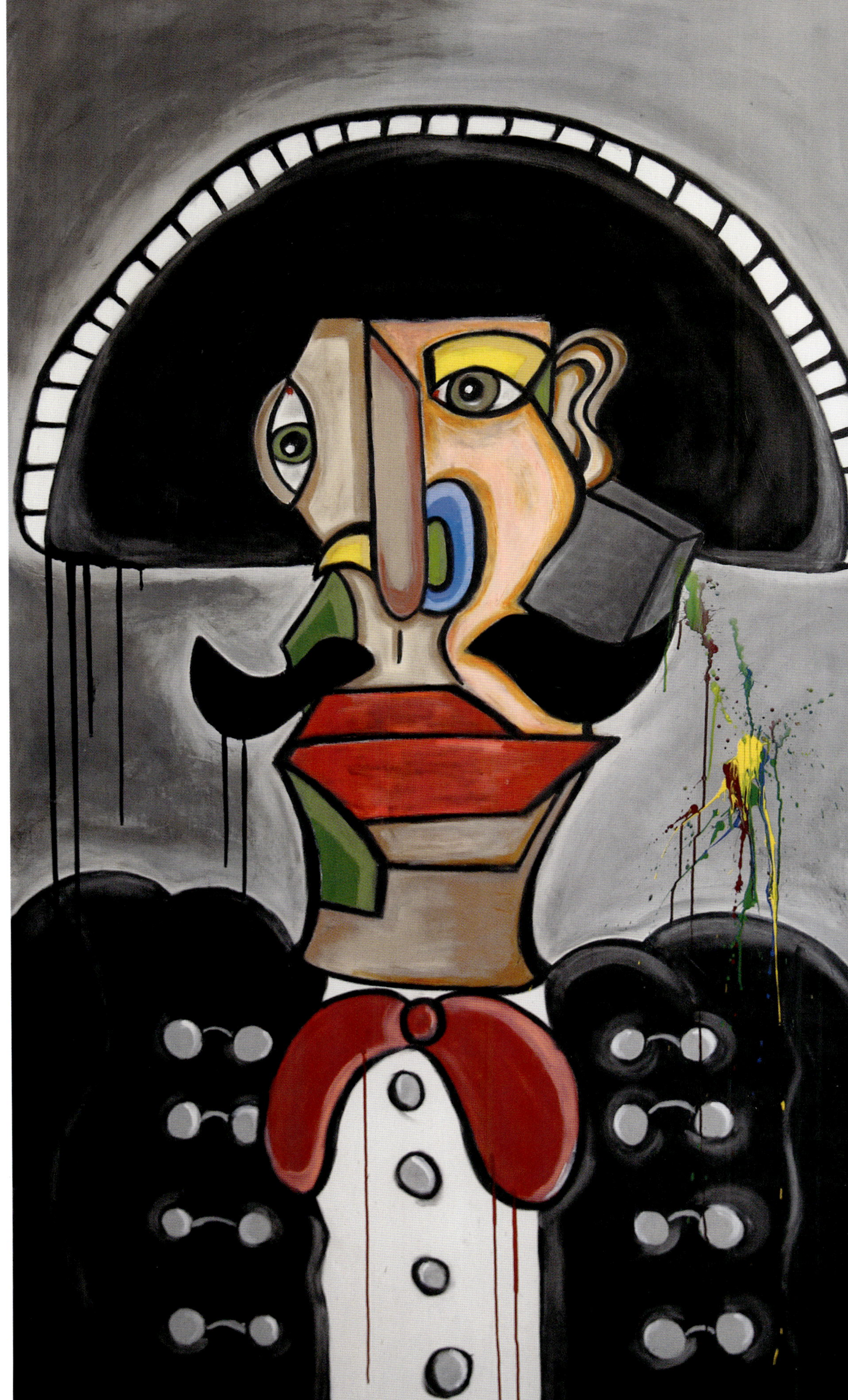

El Mariachi, 2021
acrylic and oil pastel
on canvas, 84 × 48 in

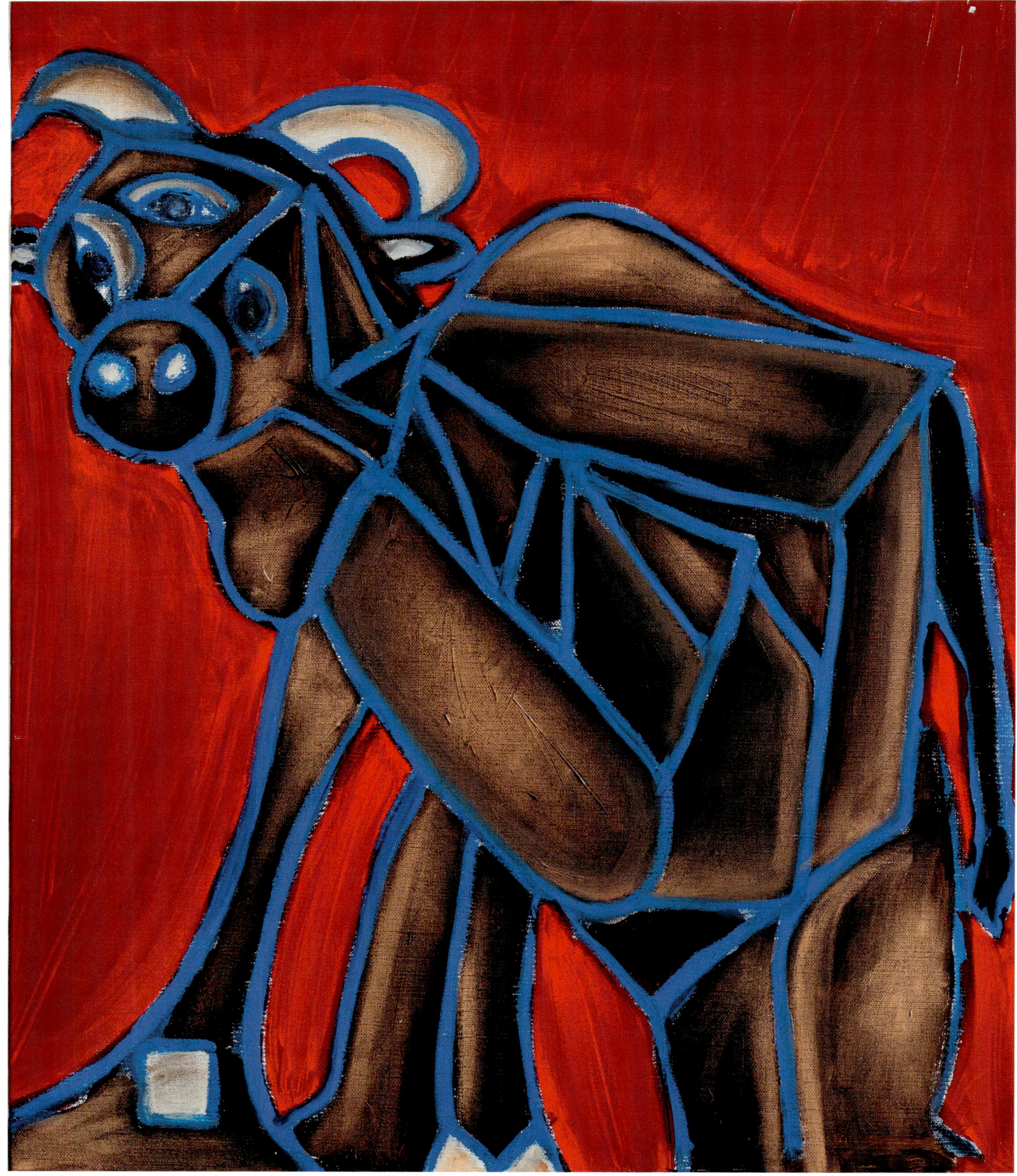

El Toro, 2021 | acrylic and oil pastel on canvas, 24.5 × 20 in

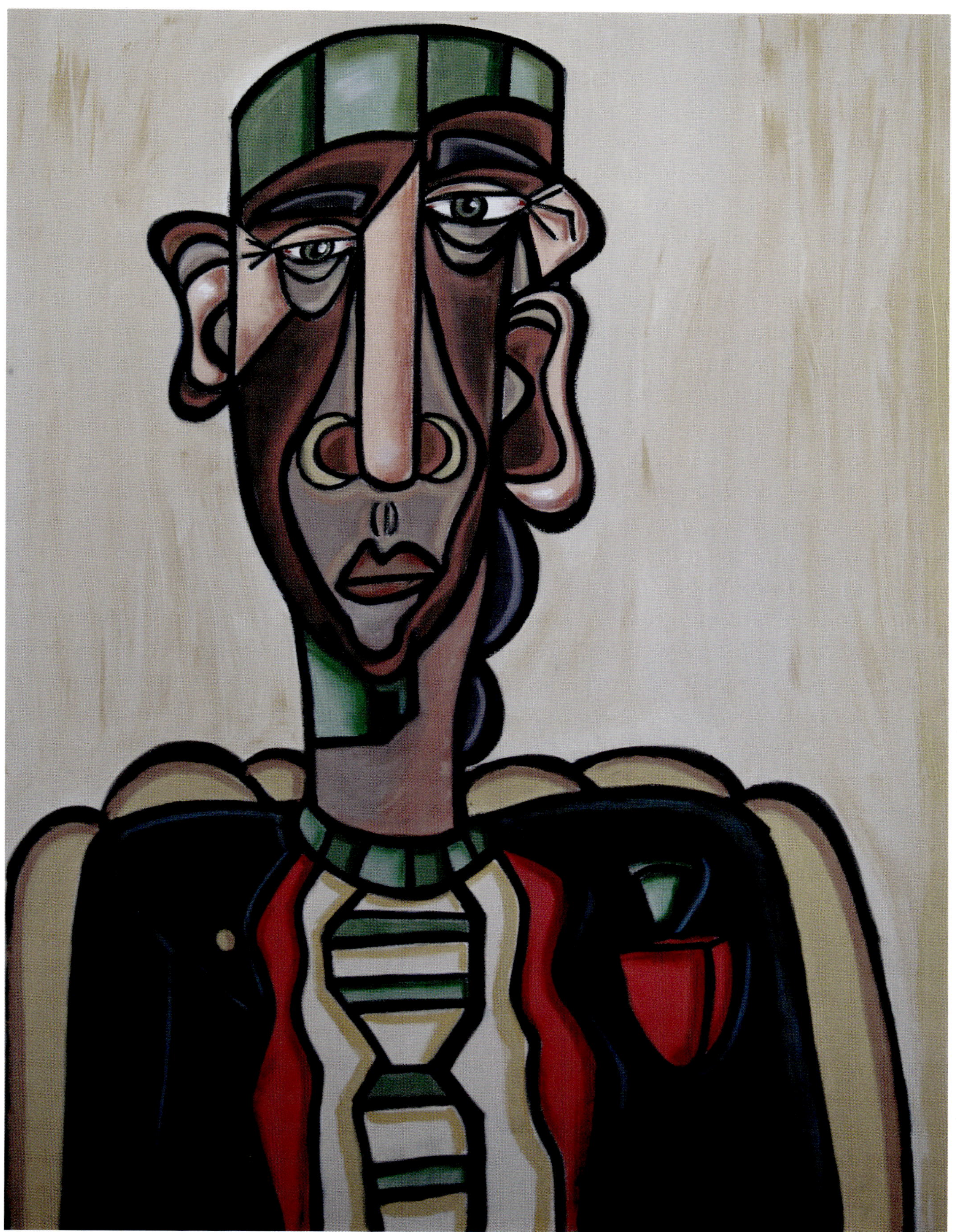

The Poet, 2022 | acrylic and oil pastel on canvas, 48 × 36 in

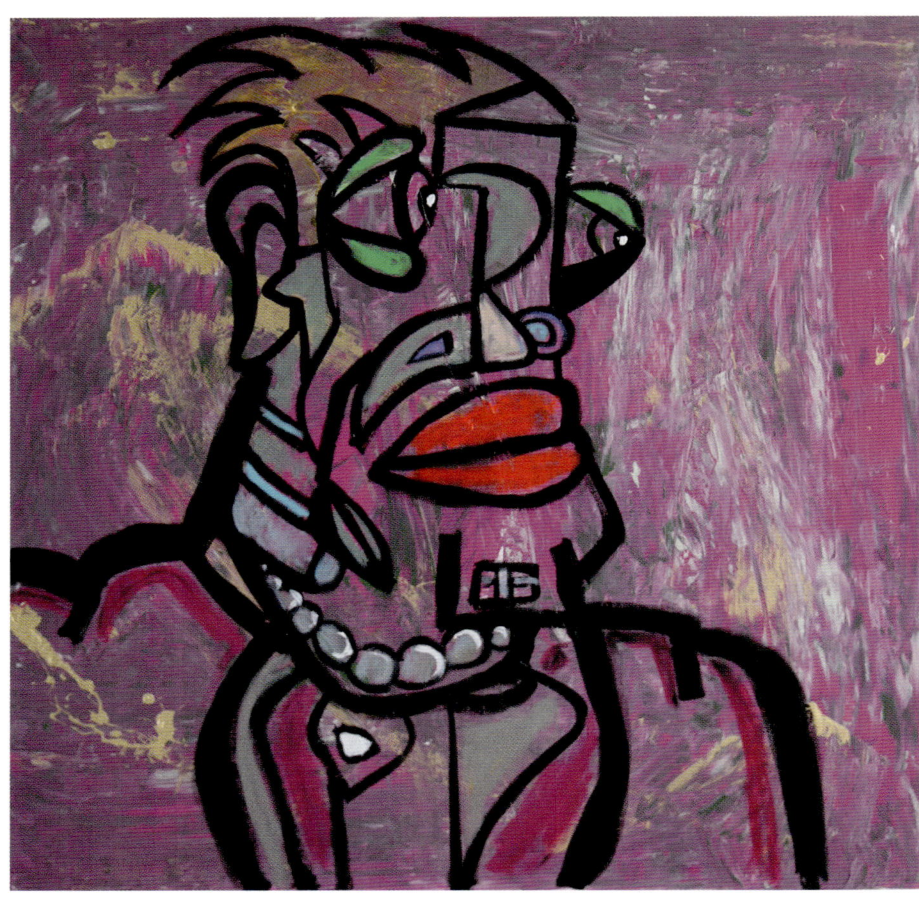

Bernard, 2022
acrylic and oil pastel on canvas, 42 × 42 in

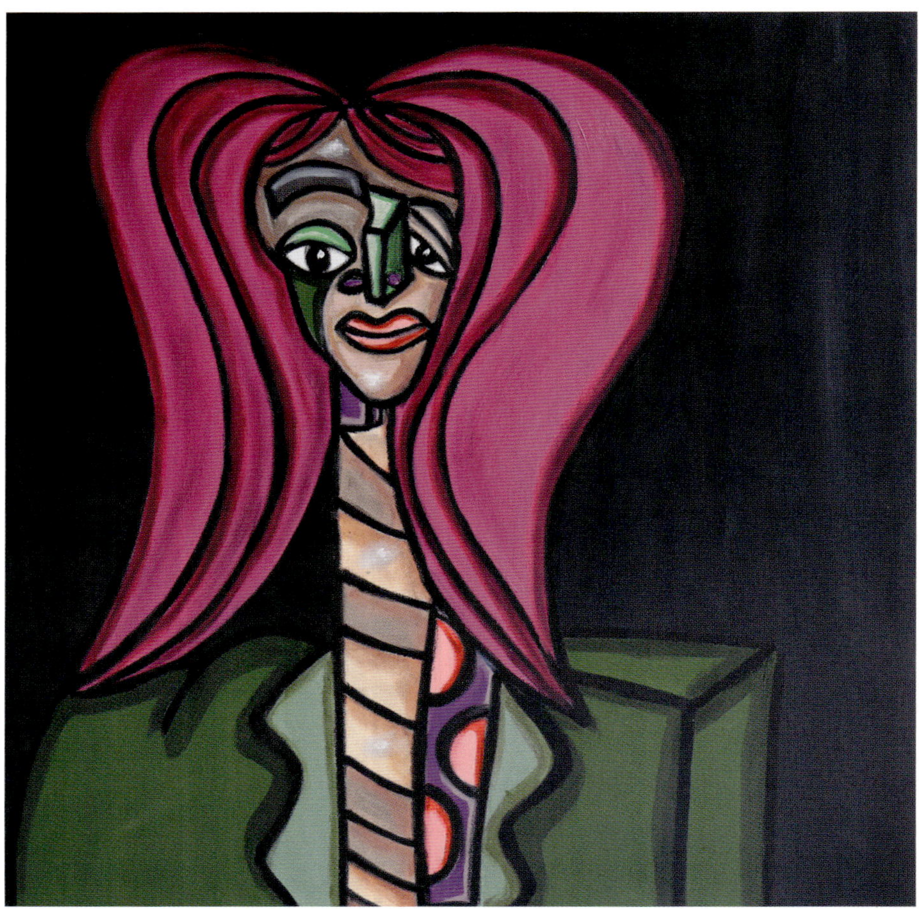

Mademoiselle, 2022
acrylic and oil pastel on canvas, 40 × 40 in

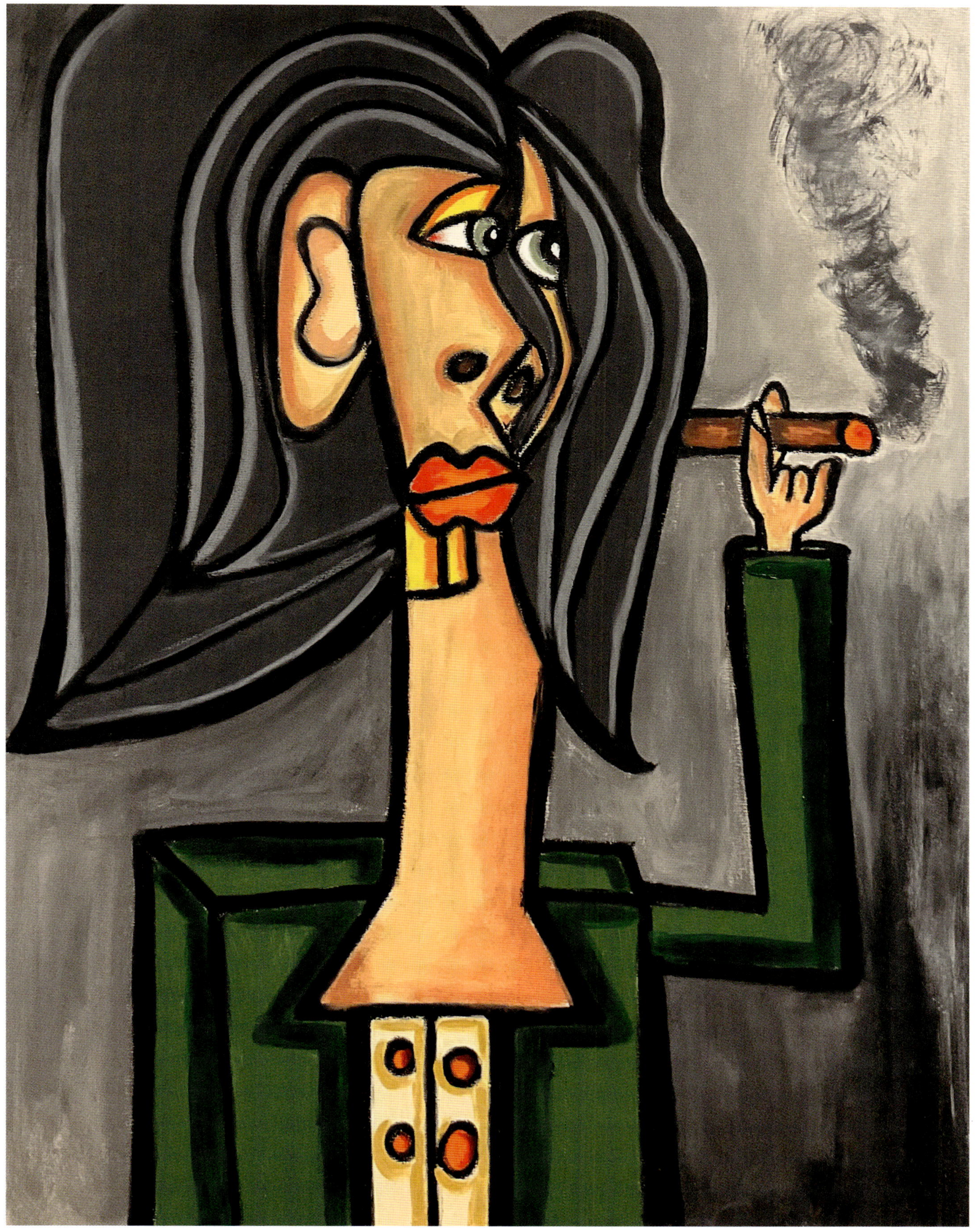

Marina, 2022 | acrylic and oil pastel on canvas, 40 × 30 in

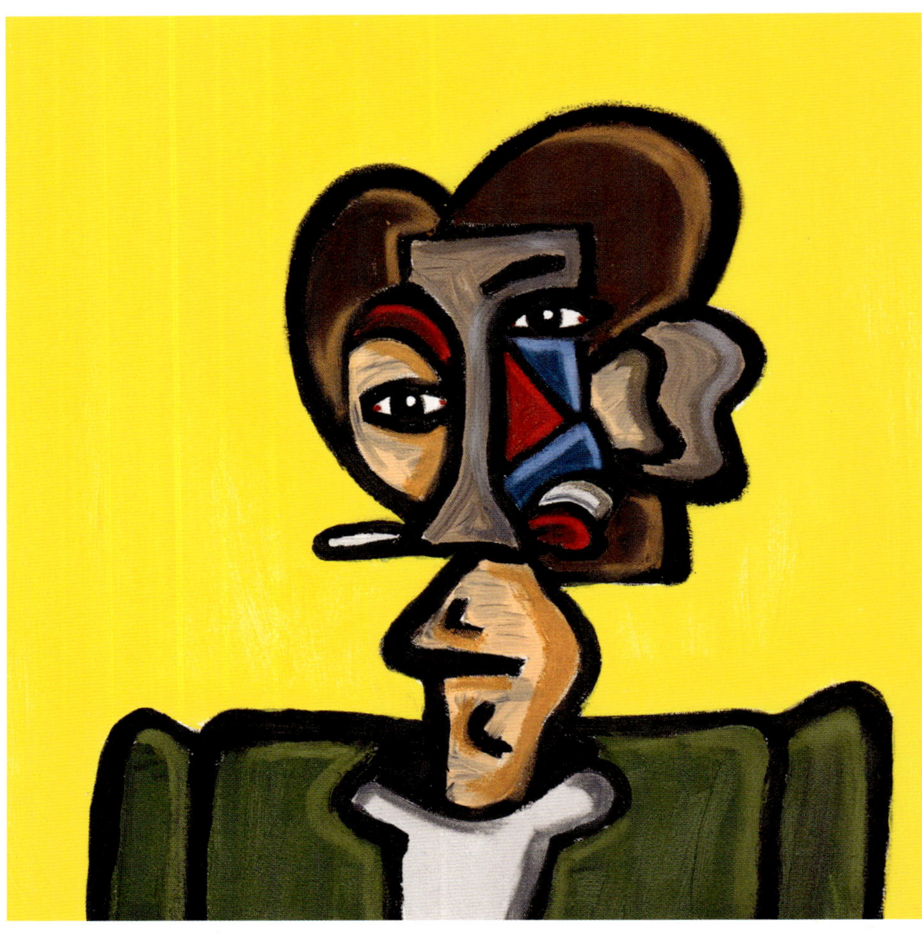

Richard, 2022
acrylic and oil pastel on canvas, 20 × 20 in

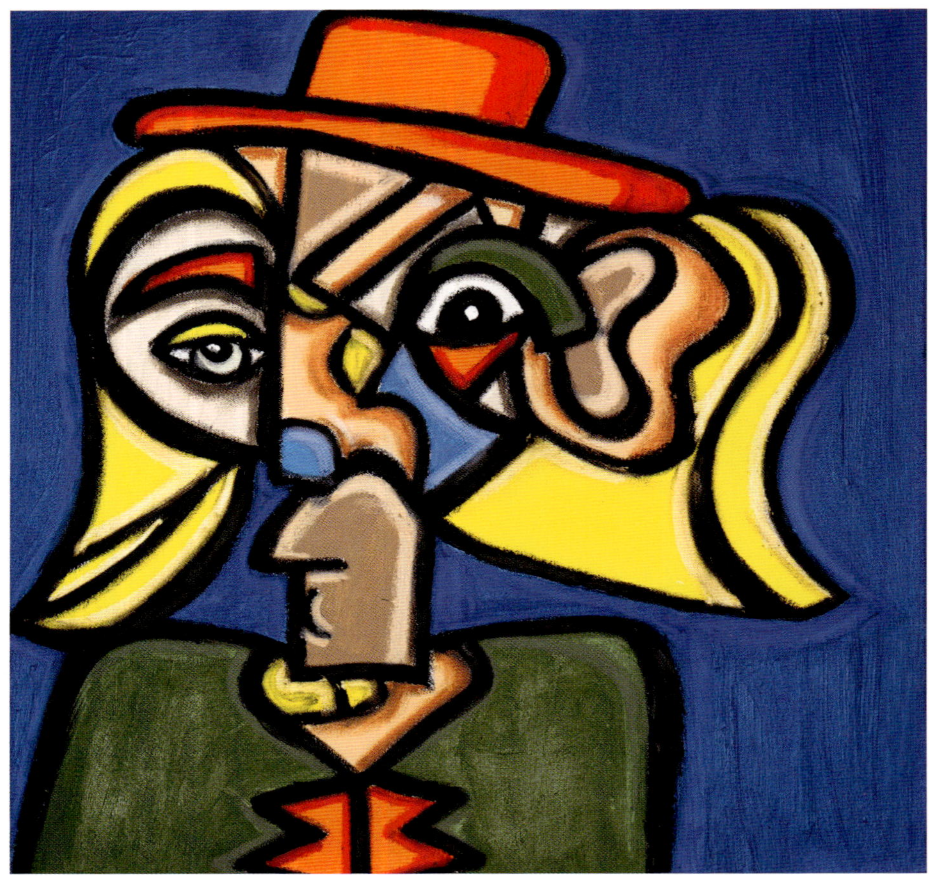

Alex, 2022
acrylic and oil pastel on canvas, 20 × 20 in

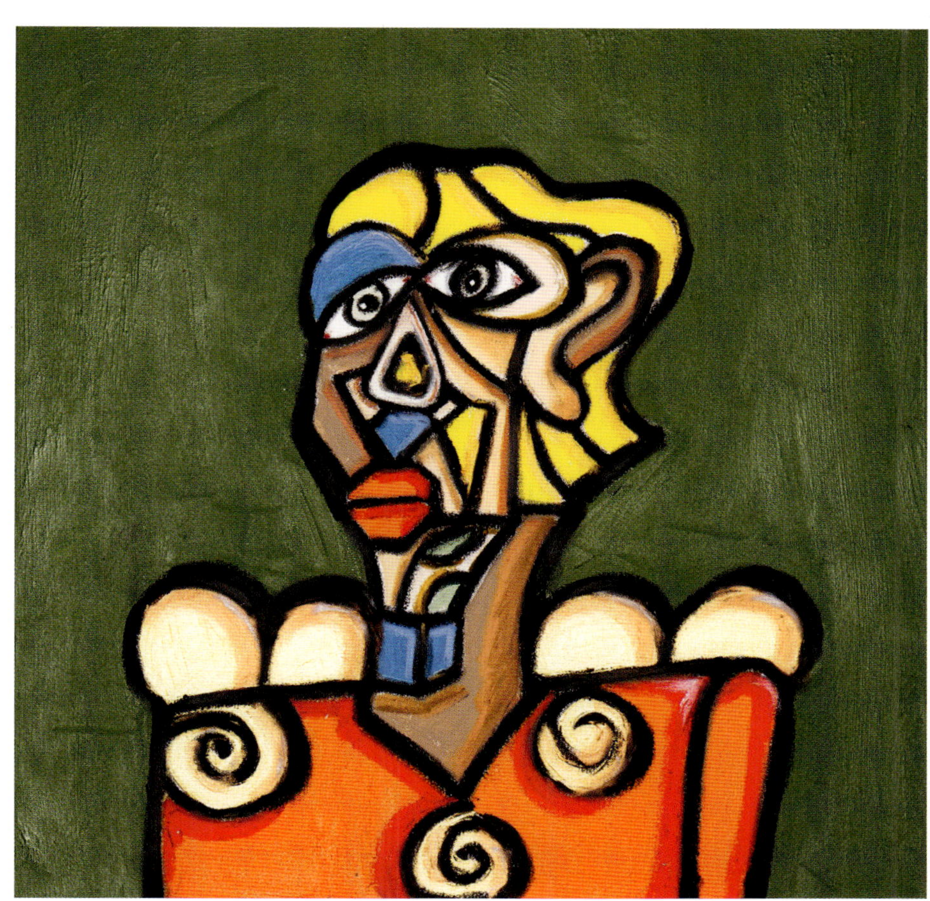

Captain, 2022
acrylic and oil pastel on canvas, 20 × 20 in

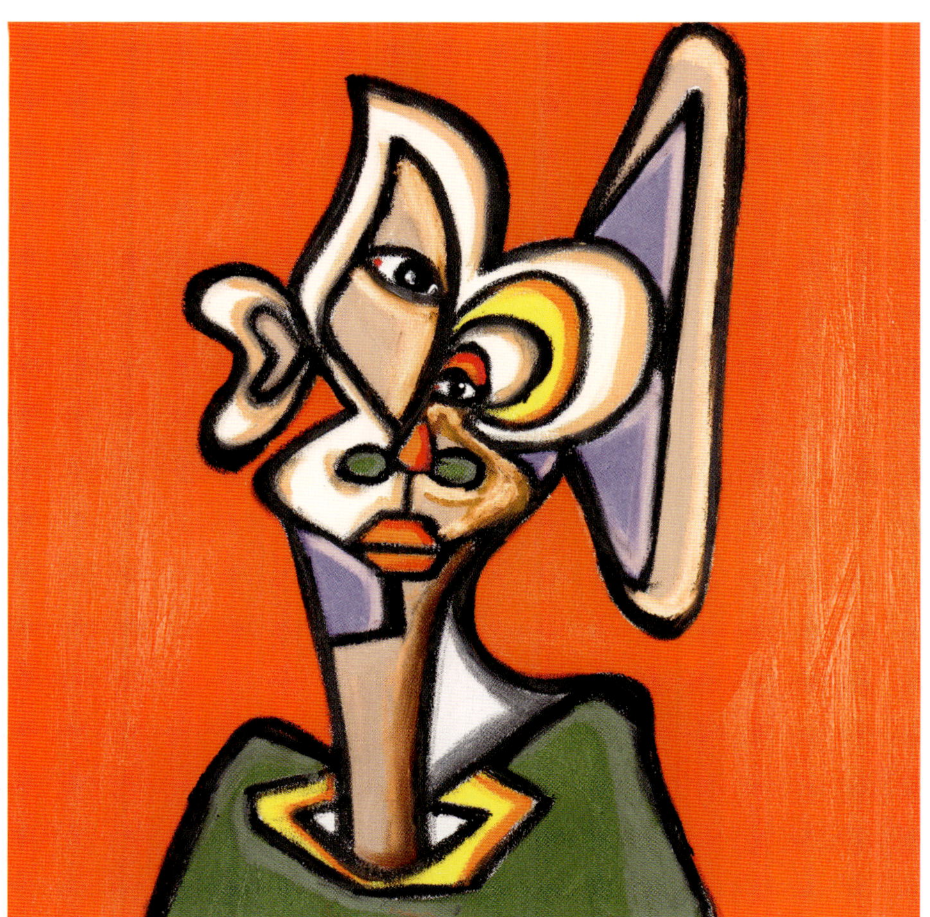

Bob, 2022
acrylic and oil pastel on canvas, 20 × 20 in

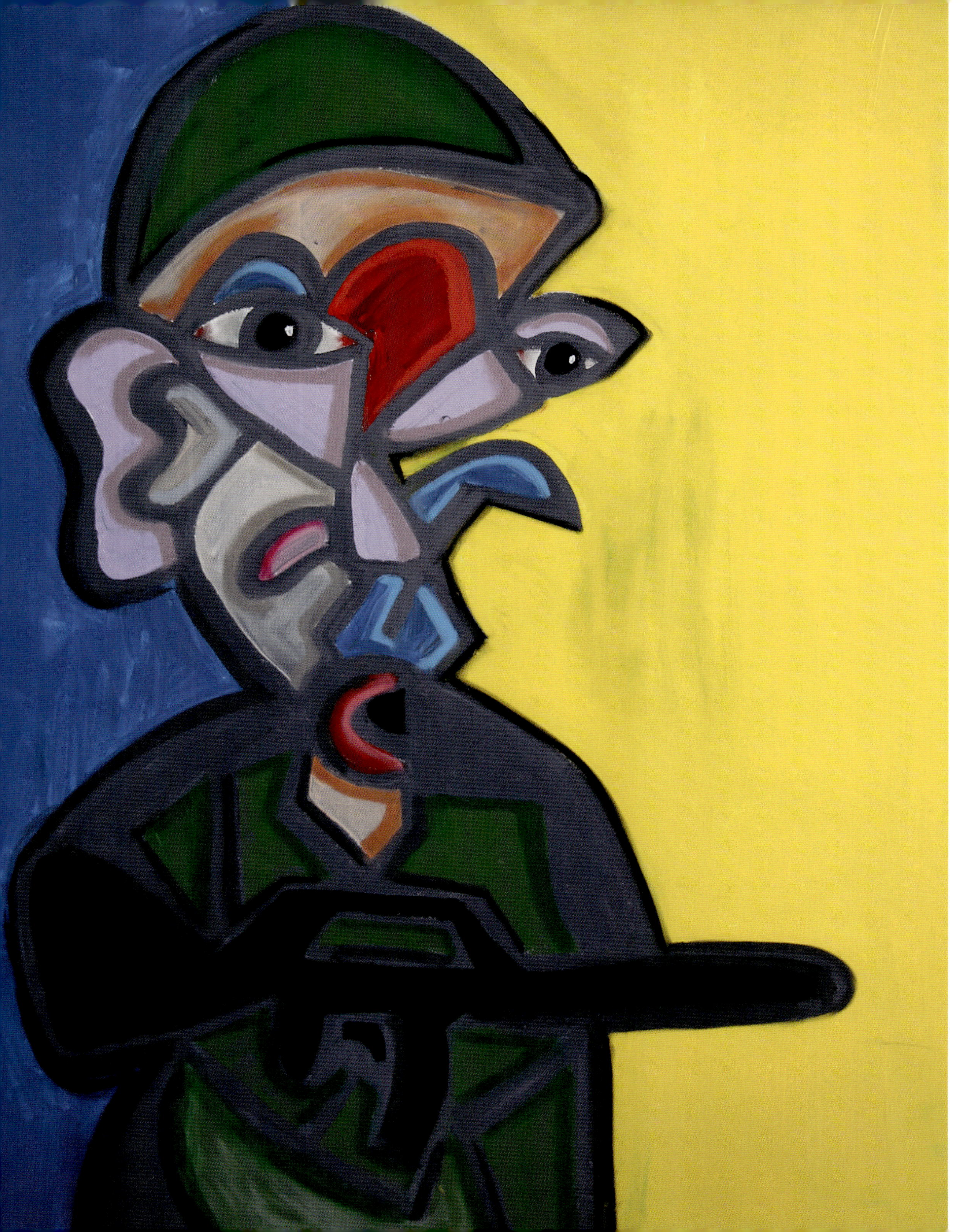

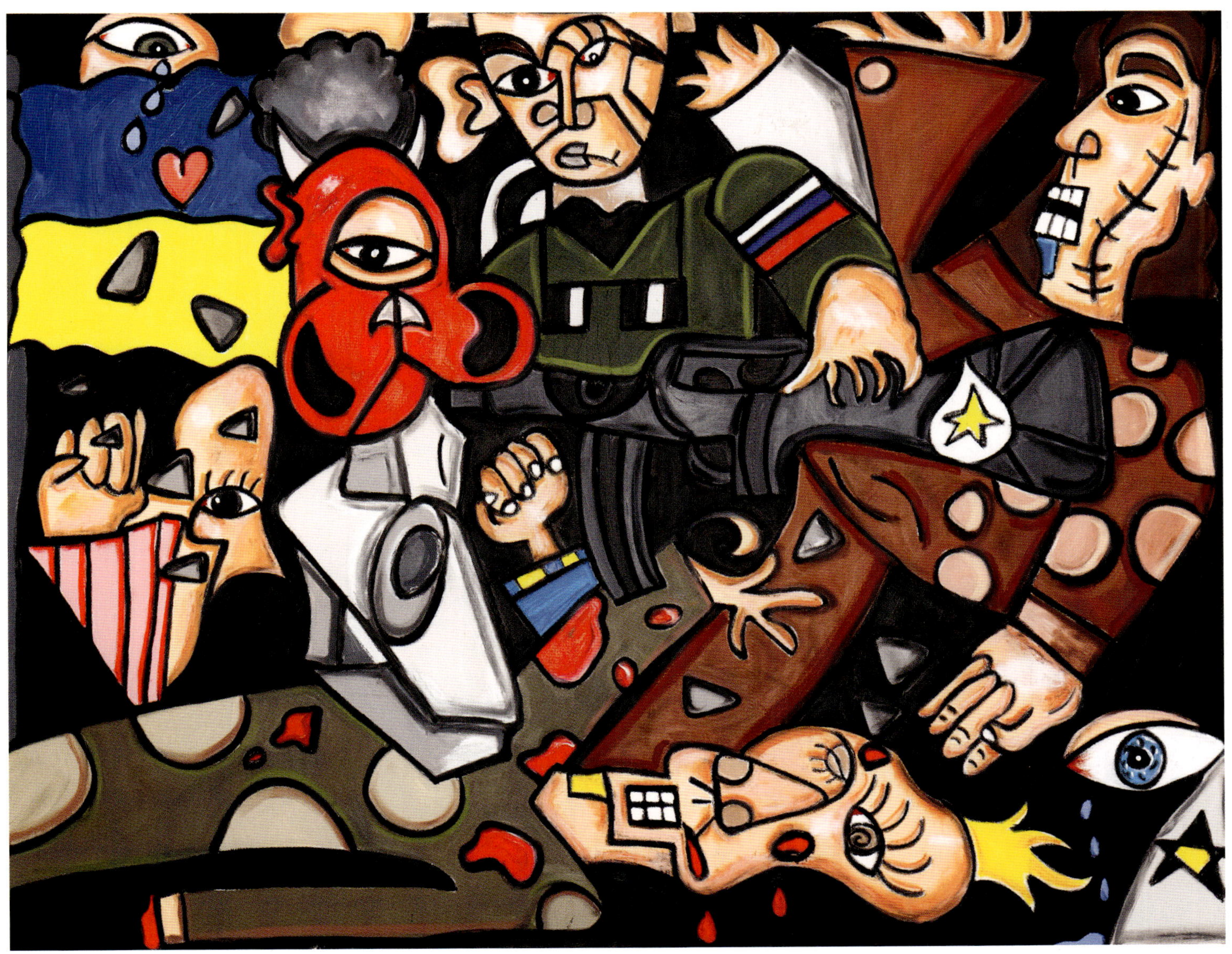

Invasion of Ukraine, 2022 | acrylic and oil pastel on canvas, 30 × 36.8 in

Ukrainian Soldier, 2022 | acrylic and oil pastel on canvas, 48 × 36 in

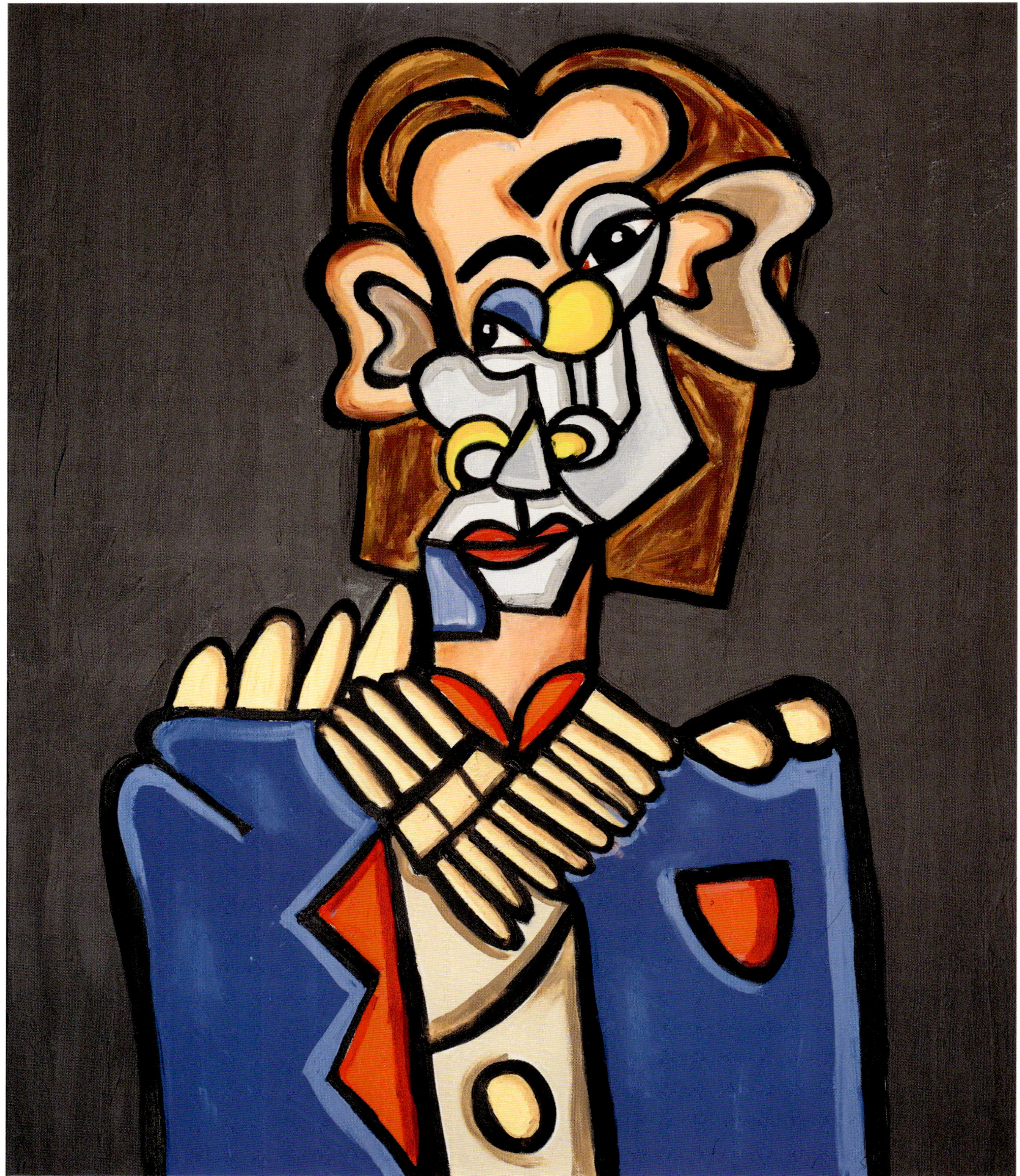

The Sergeant, 2022 | acrylic and oil pastel on canvas, 42 × 35 in

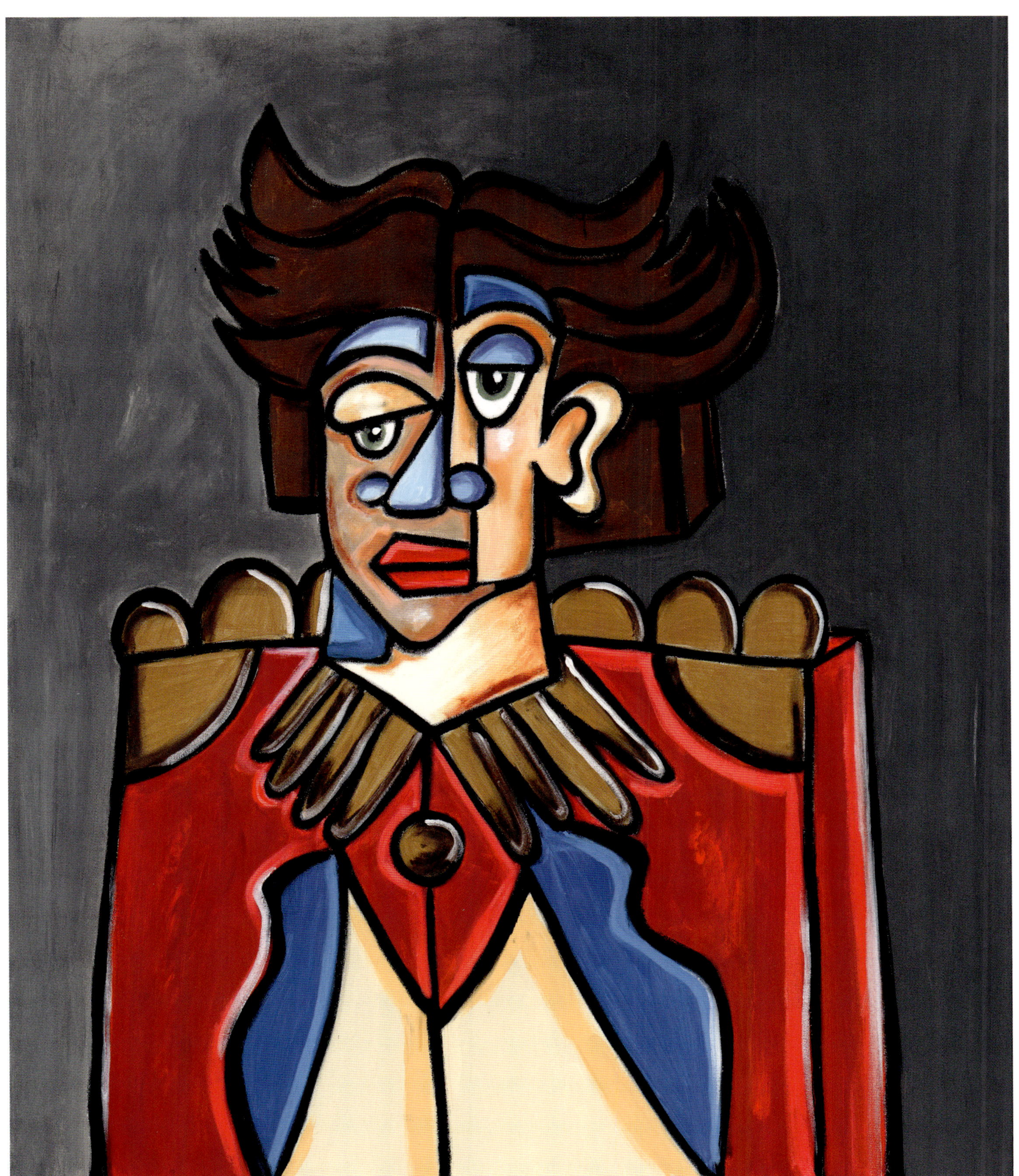

The Lieutenant, 2022 | acrylic and oil pastel on canvas, 42 × 35 in

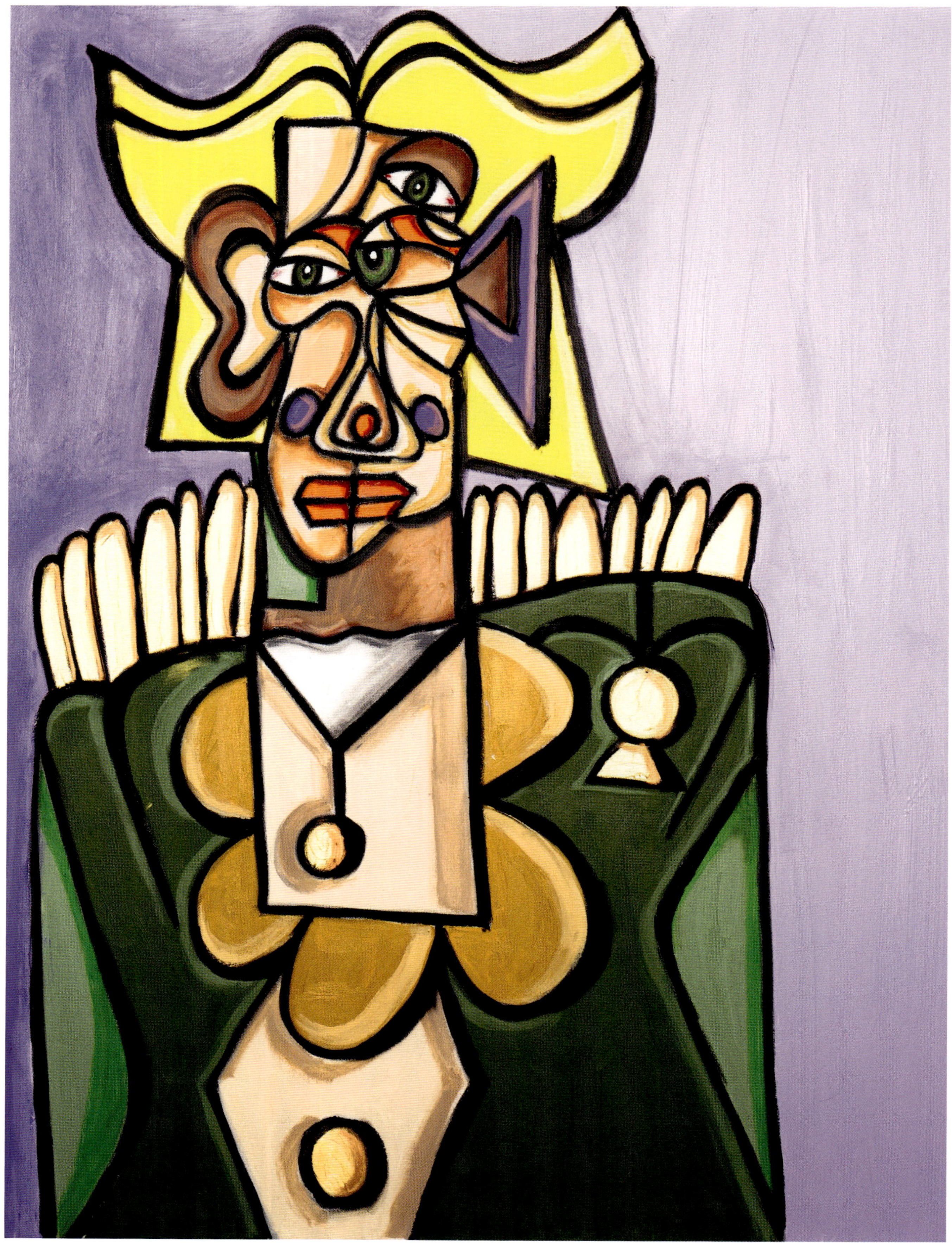

The Commander, 2022 | acrylic and oil pastel on canvas, 48 × 36 in

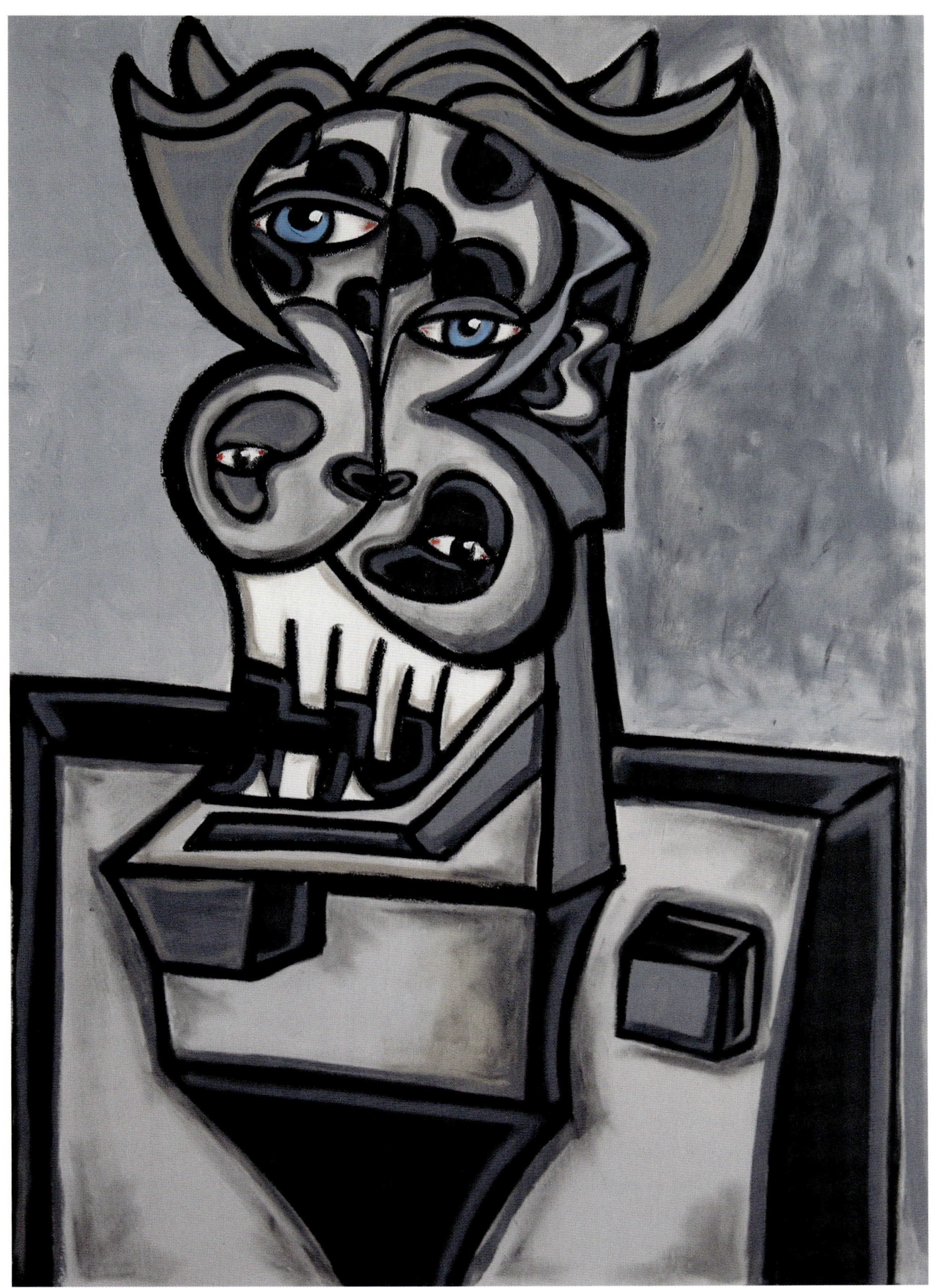

The Samurai, 2022 | acrylic and oil pastel on canvas, 42 × 30 in

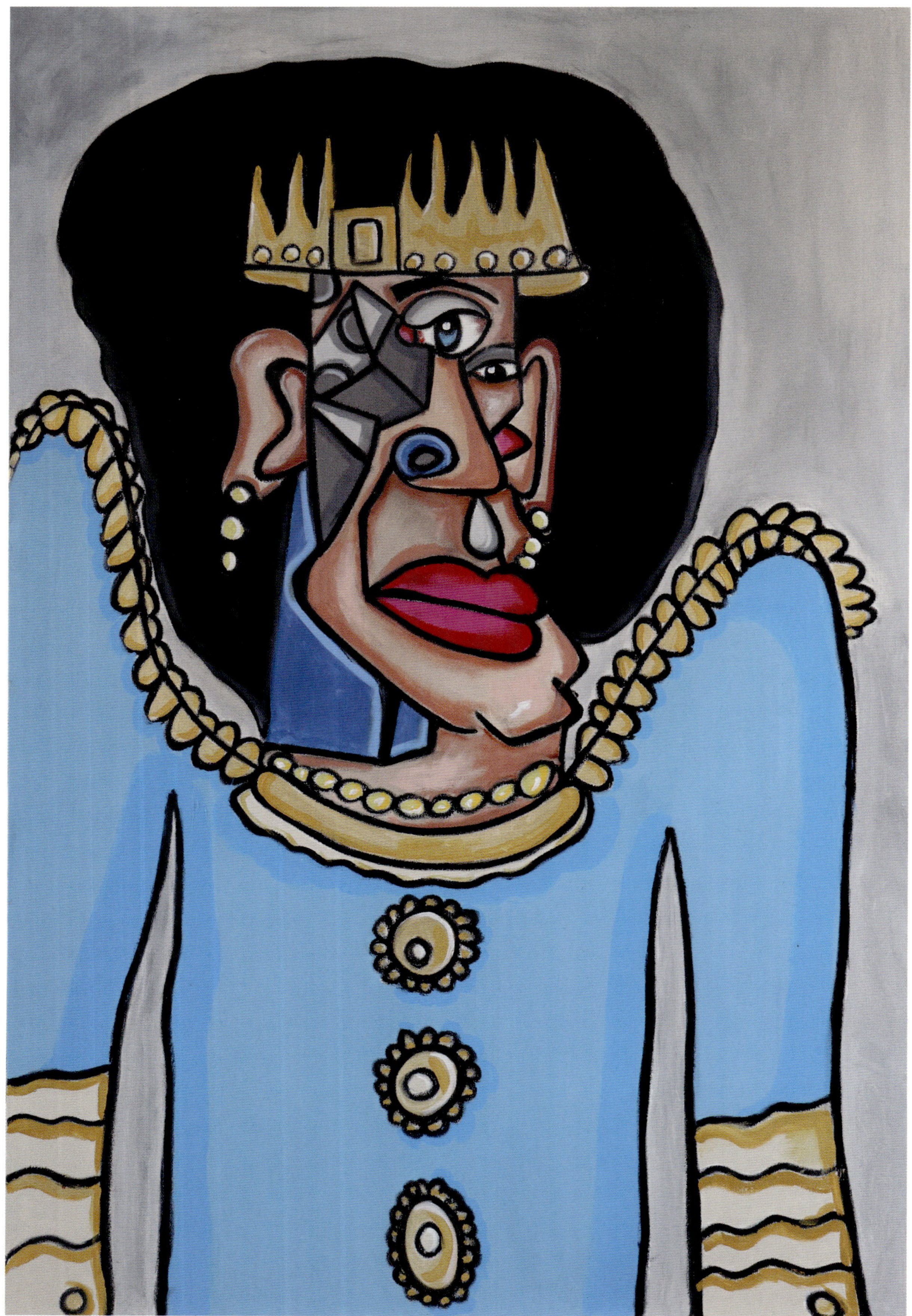

The Monarch, 2022 | acrylic and oil pastel on canvas, 60 × 40 in

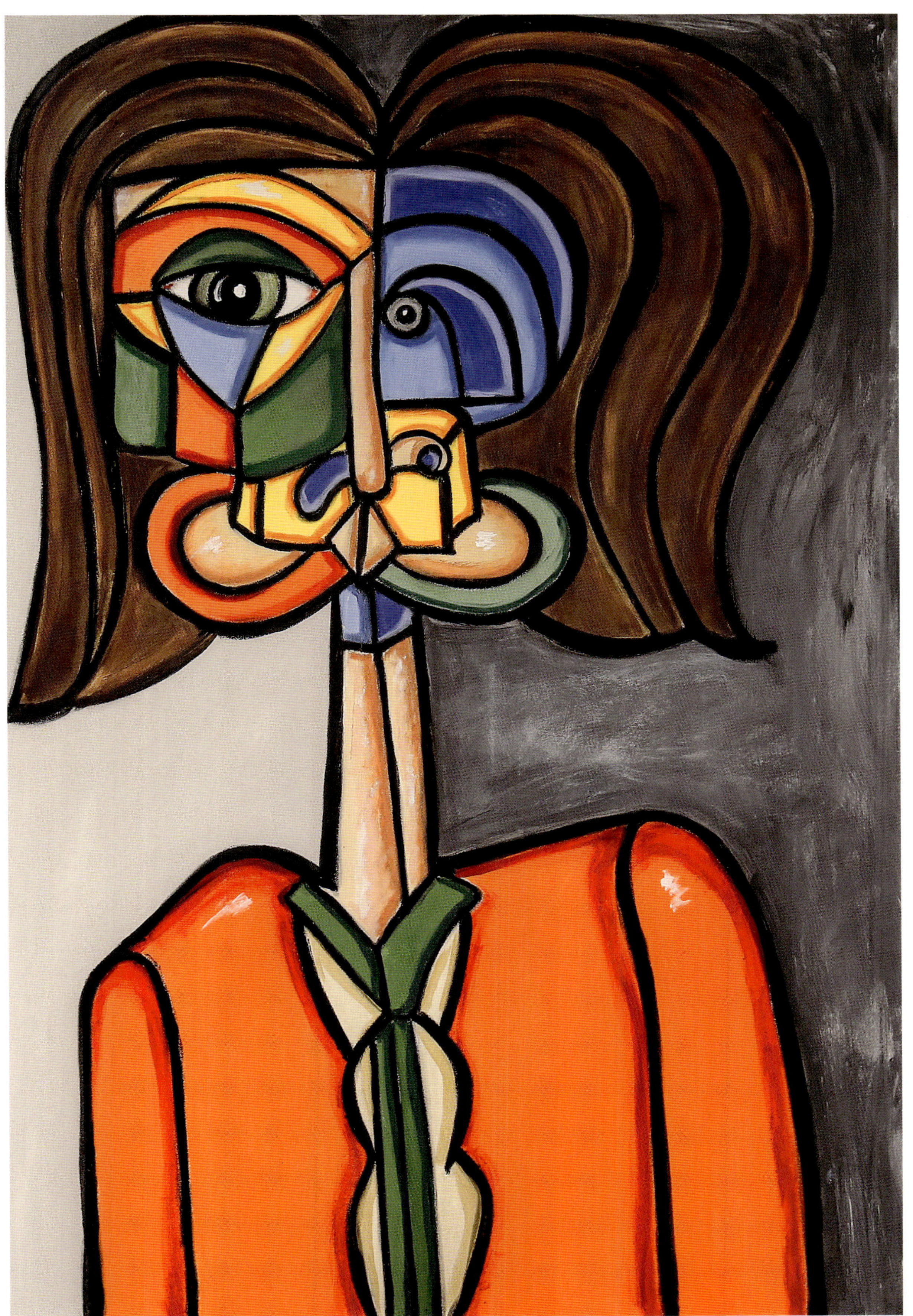

Daisy, 2022 | acrylic and oil pastel on canvas, 54 × 36 in

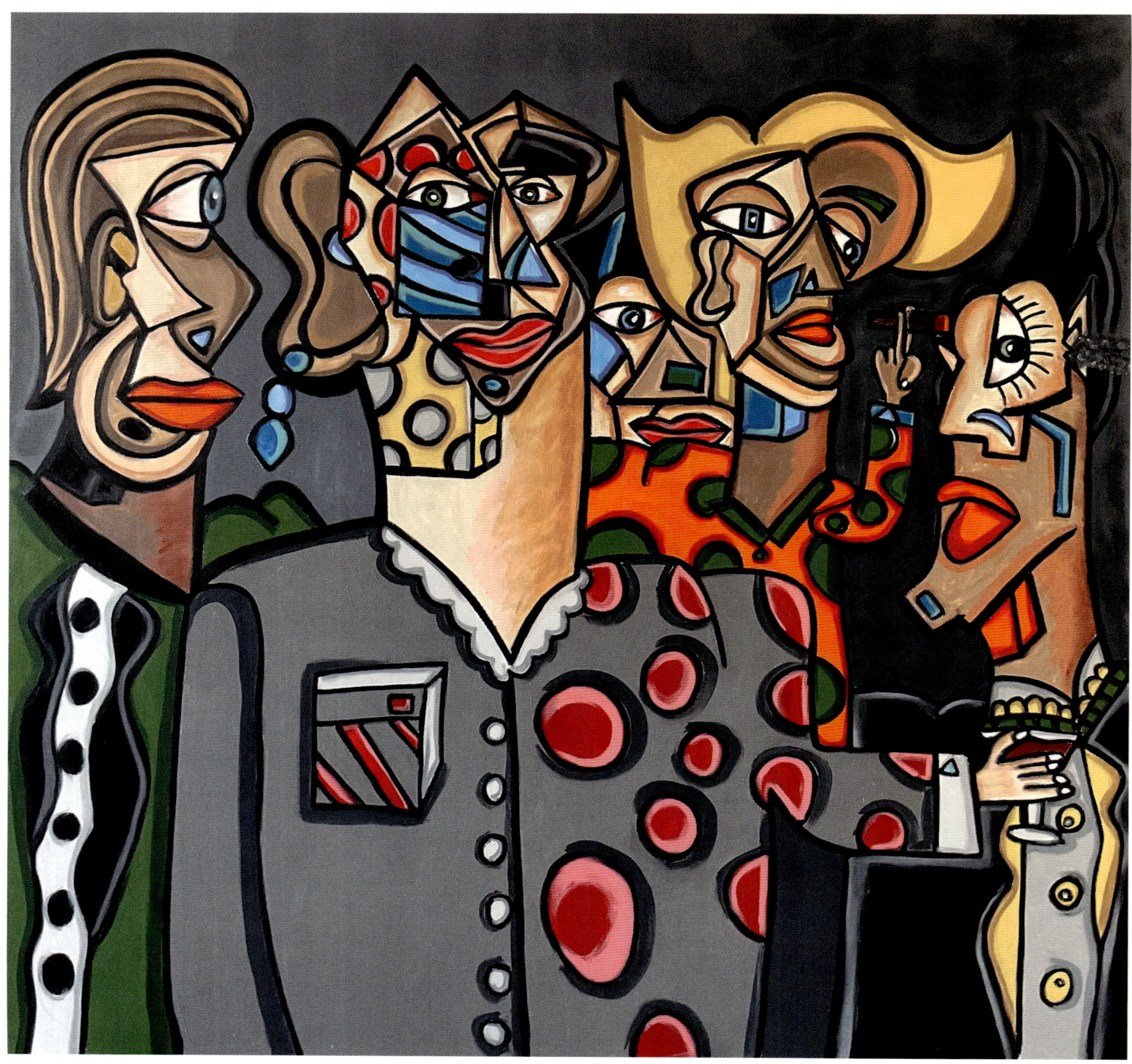

The Outsiders, 2022 | acrylic and oil pastel on canvas, 72 × 72 in

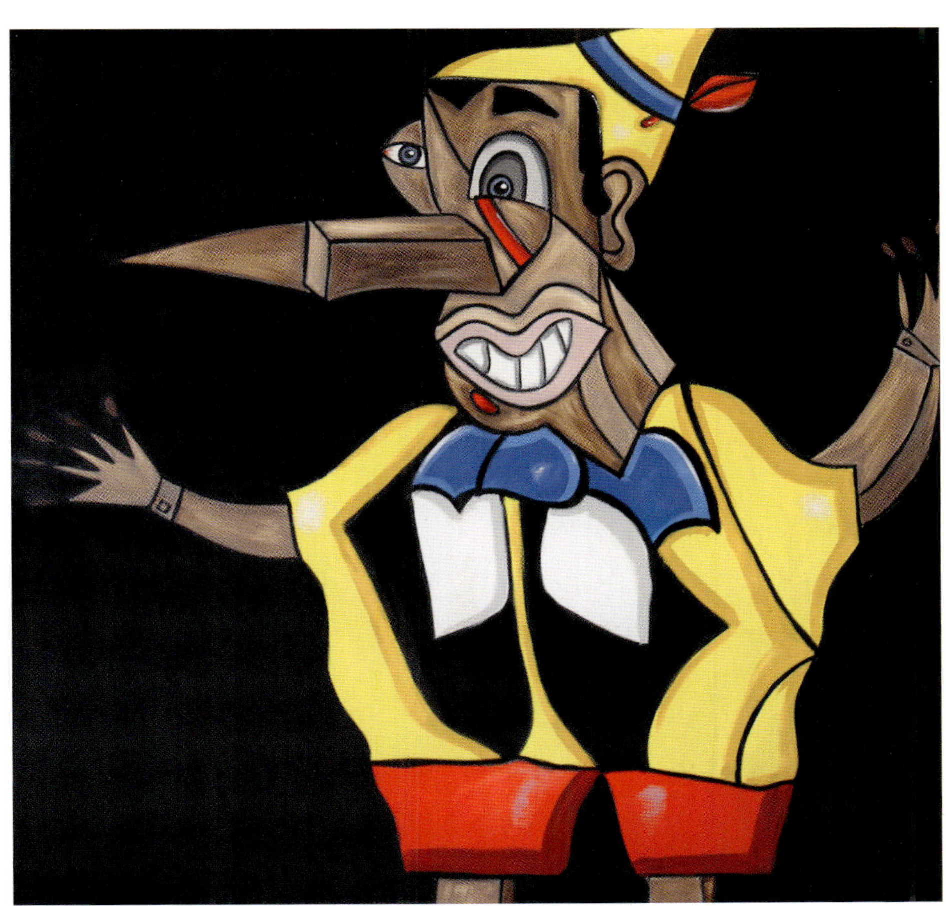

Pinocchio, 2022
acrylic and oil pastel on canvas, 72 × 72 in

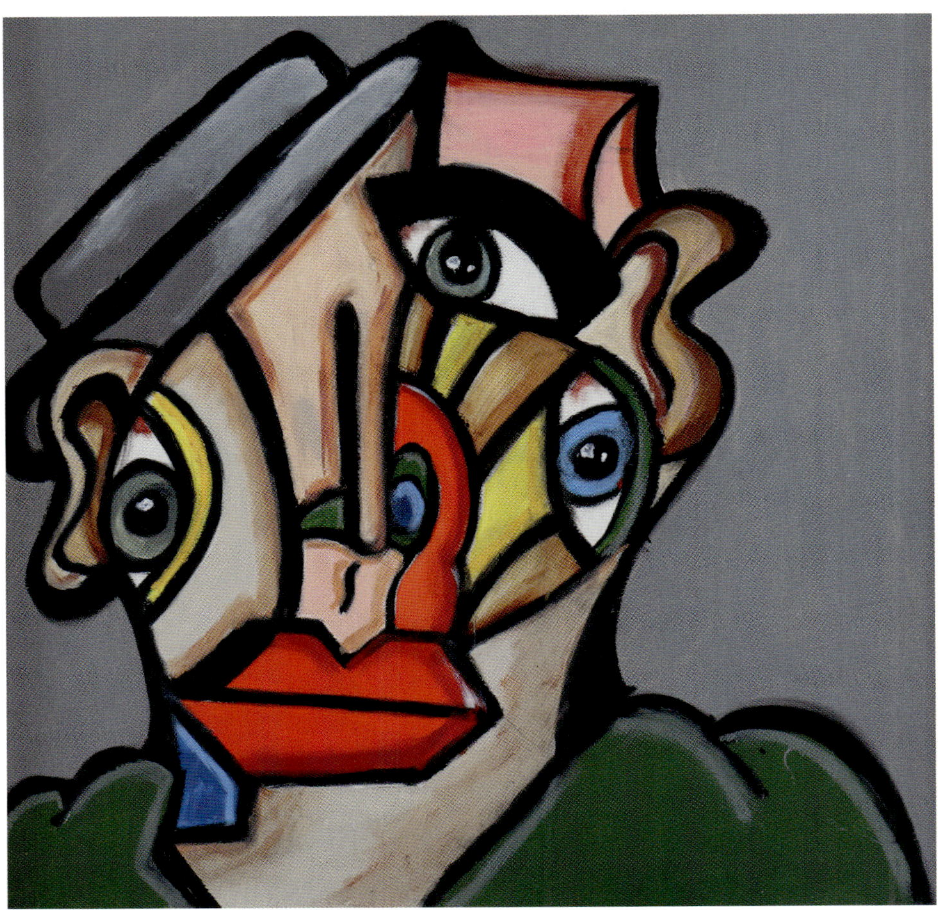

Mr. Skipper, 2022
acrylic and oil pastel on canvas, 24 × 24 in

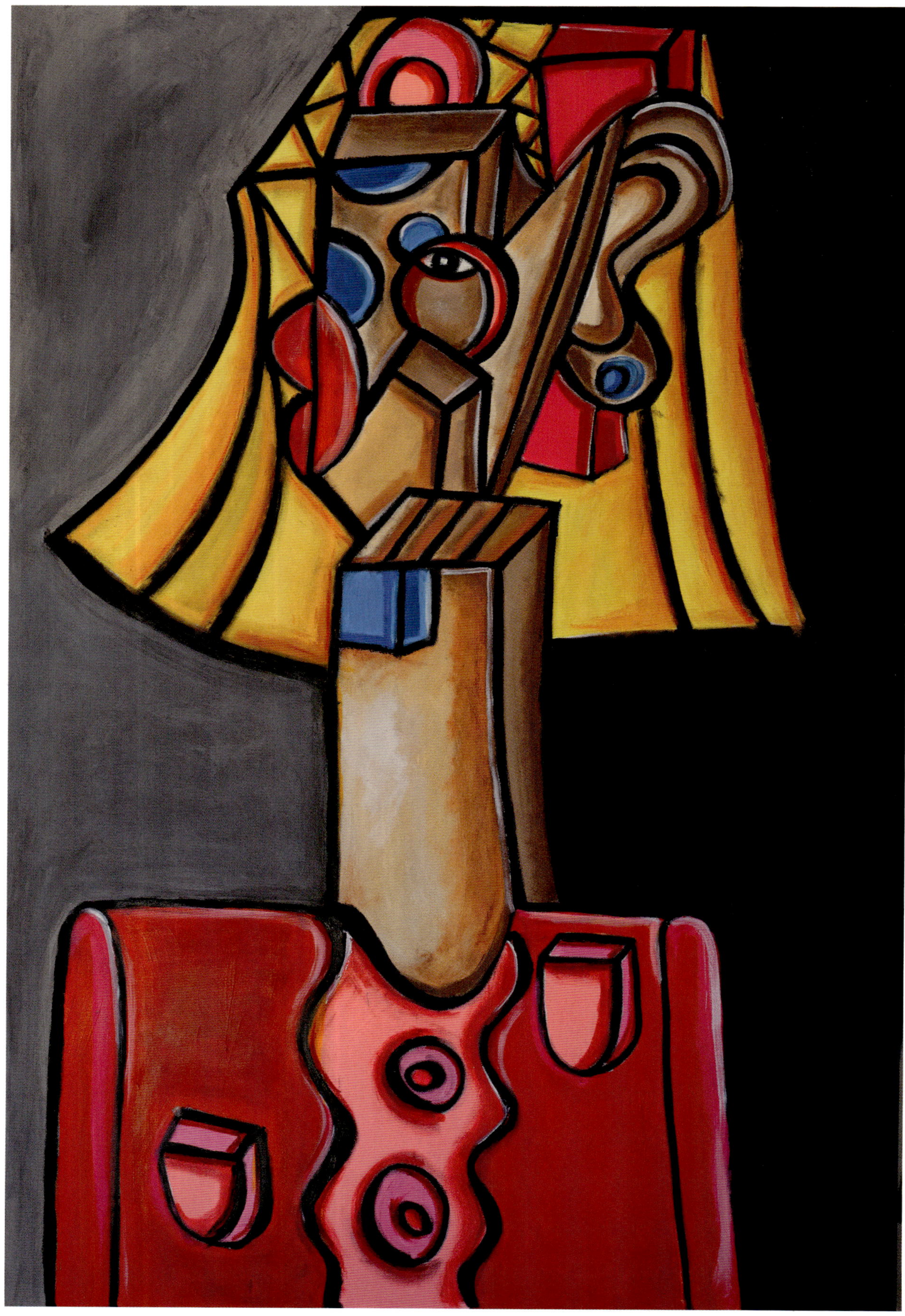

Maya, 2022 | acrylic and oil pastel on canvas, 60 × 40 in

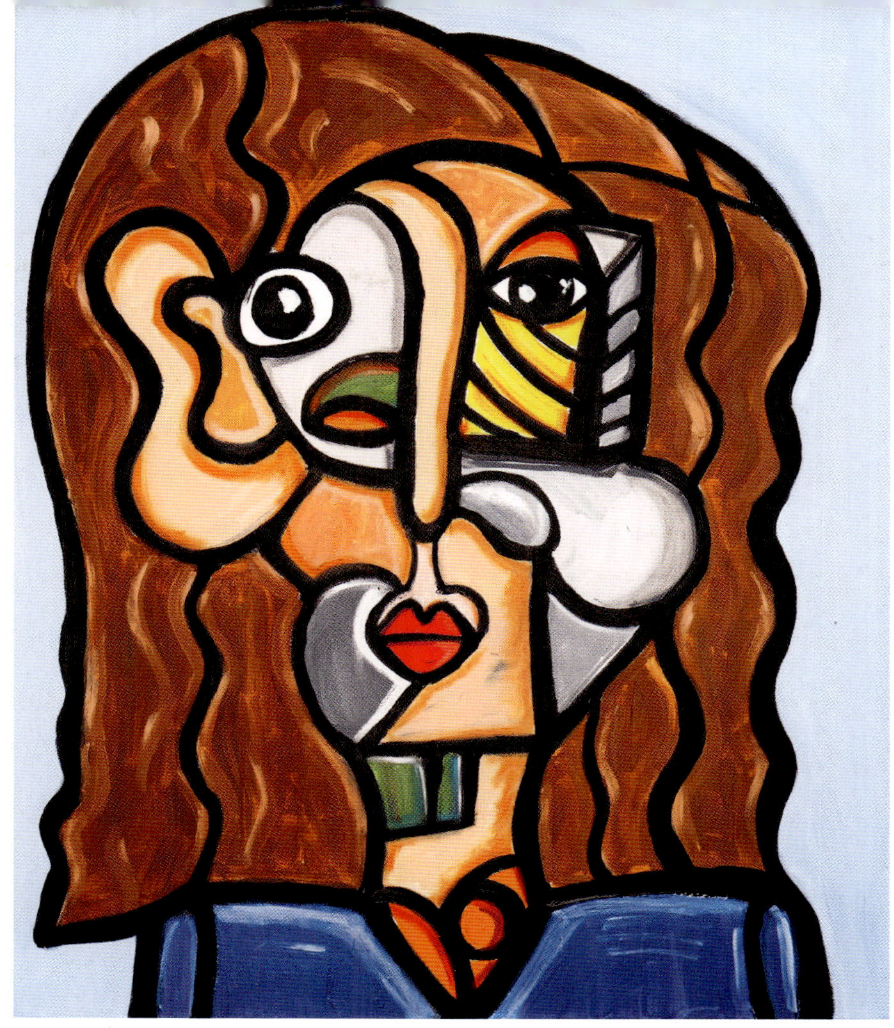

Karla, 2022 | acrylic and oil pastel on canvas, 42 × 35 in

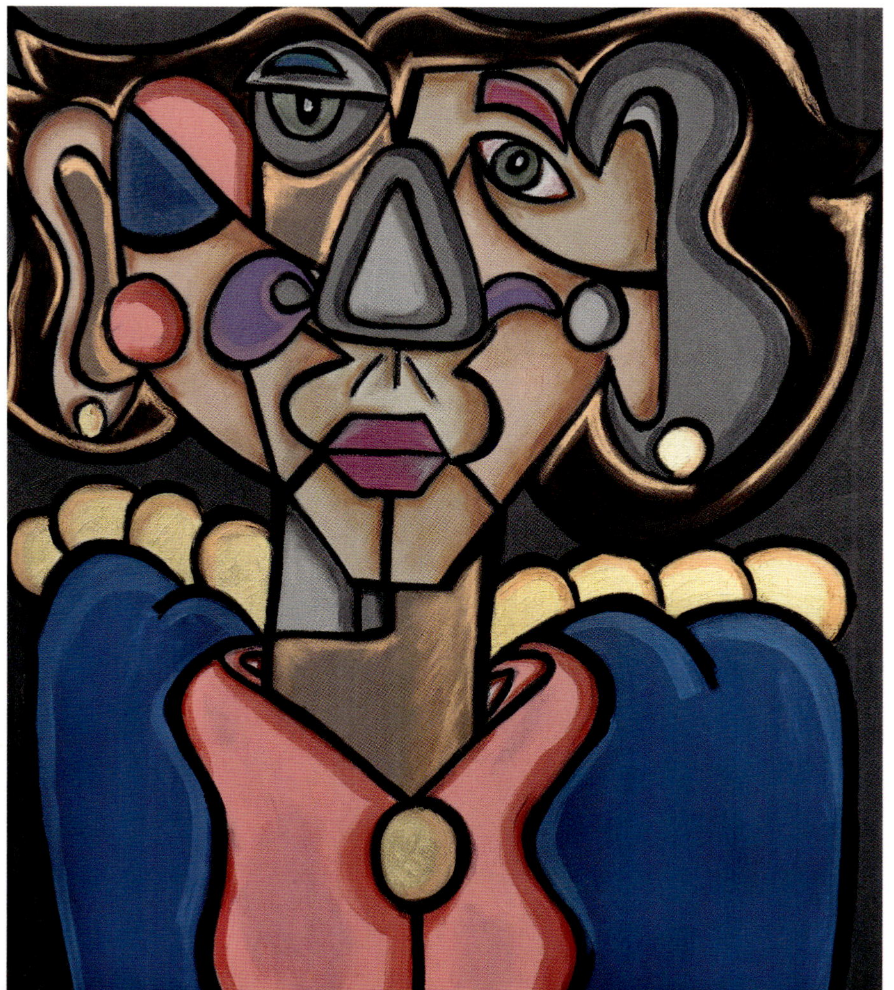

Paula, 2022 | acrylic and oil pastel on canvas, 36 × 30 in

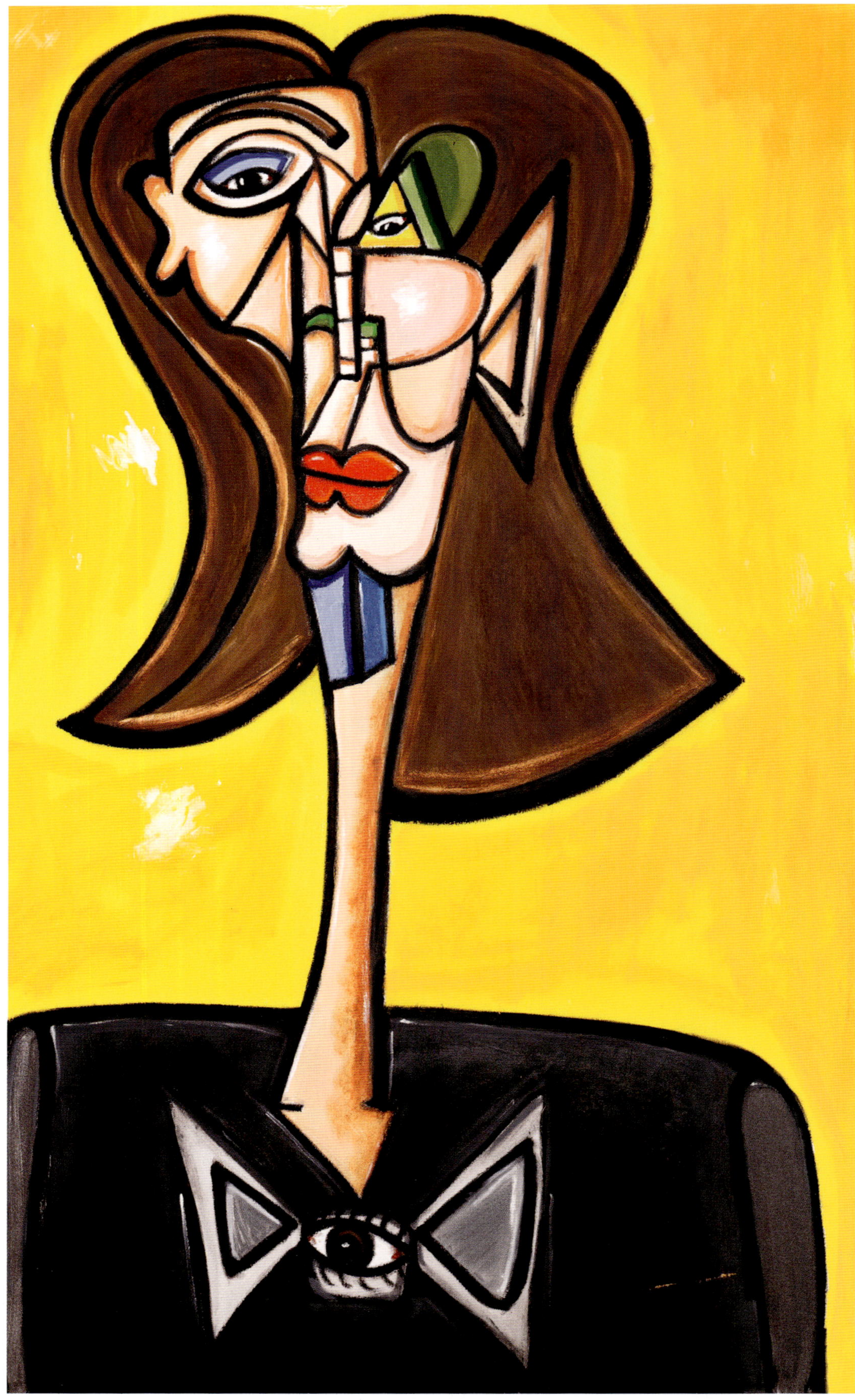

John Lennon and Yoko Ono, 2022 │ acrylic and oil pastel on canvas, 60 × 36 in

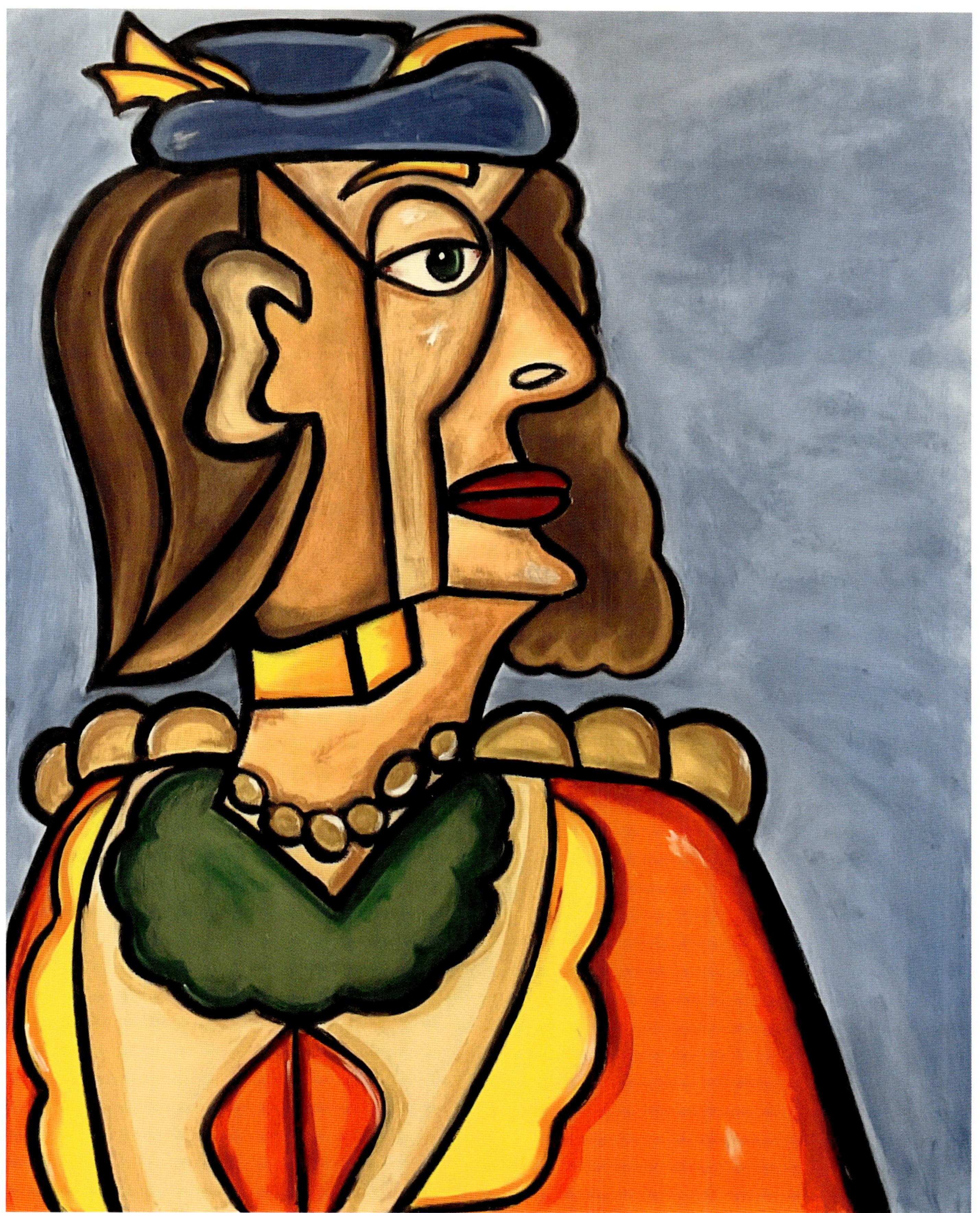

Woman, 2022 | acrylic and oil pastel on canvas, 40 × 30 in

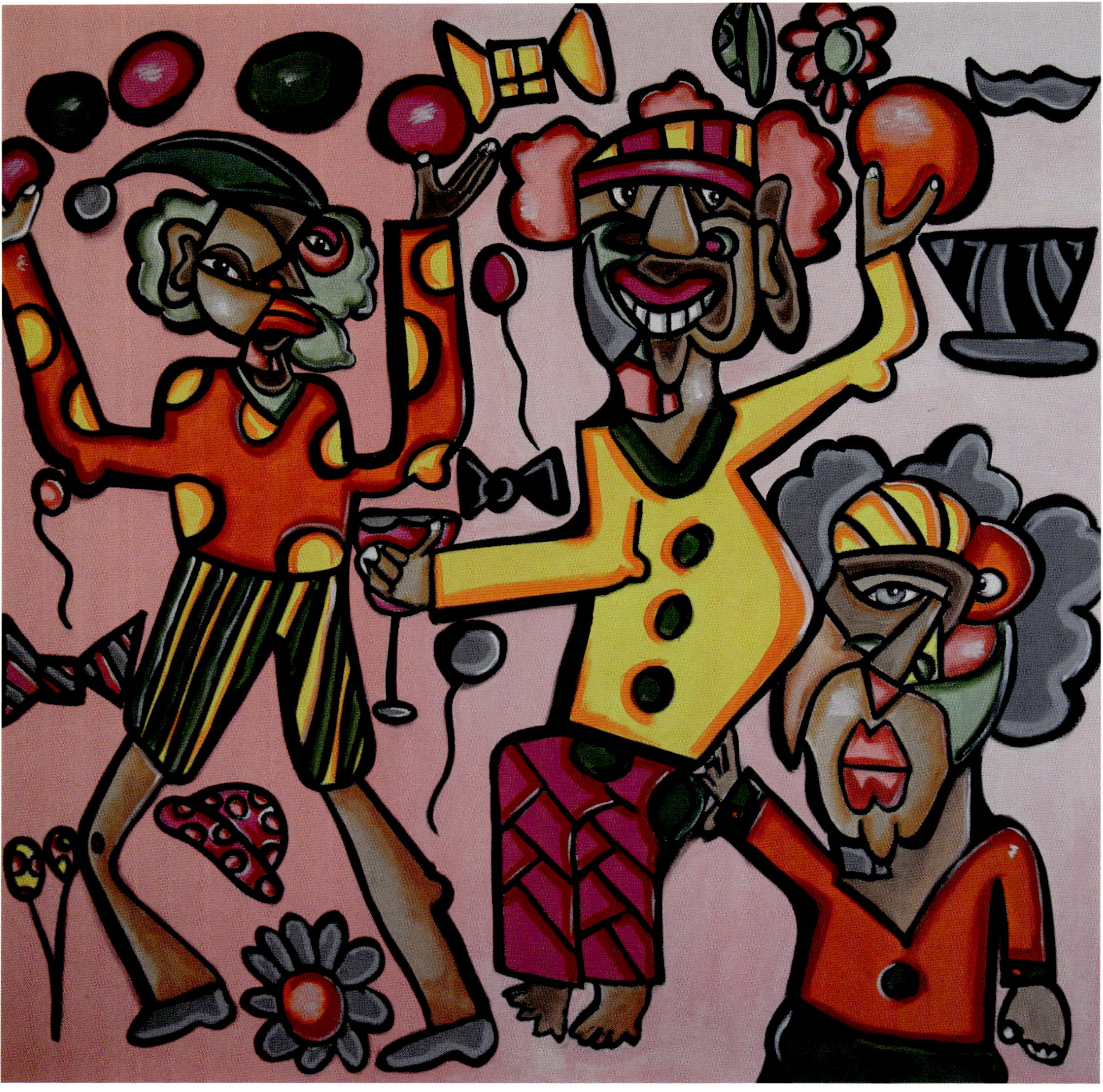

Happy Clowns, 2022 │ acrylic and oil pastel on canvas, 60 × 60 in

La Payasita, 2022 │ acrylic and oil pastel on canvas, 48 × 36 in

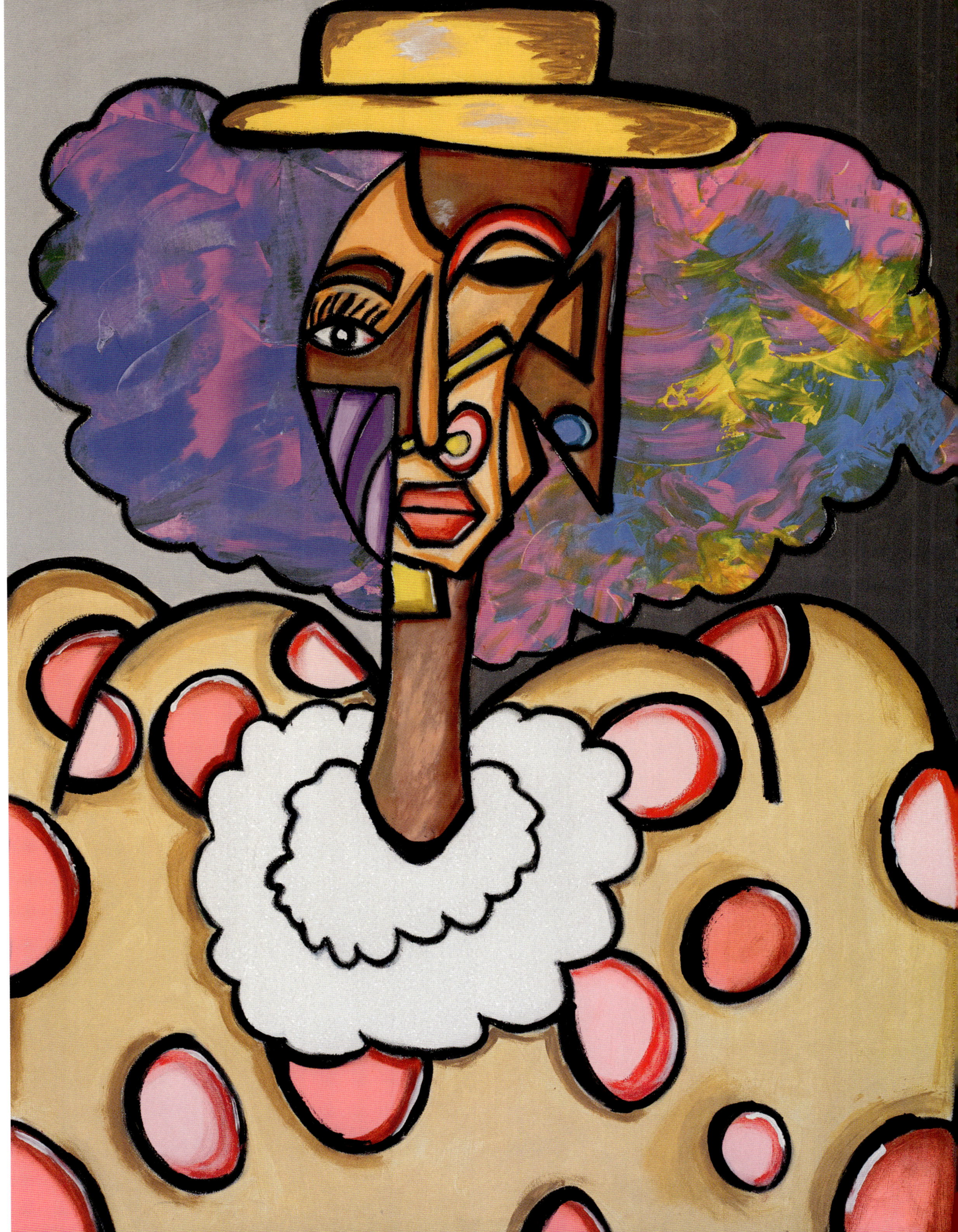

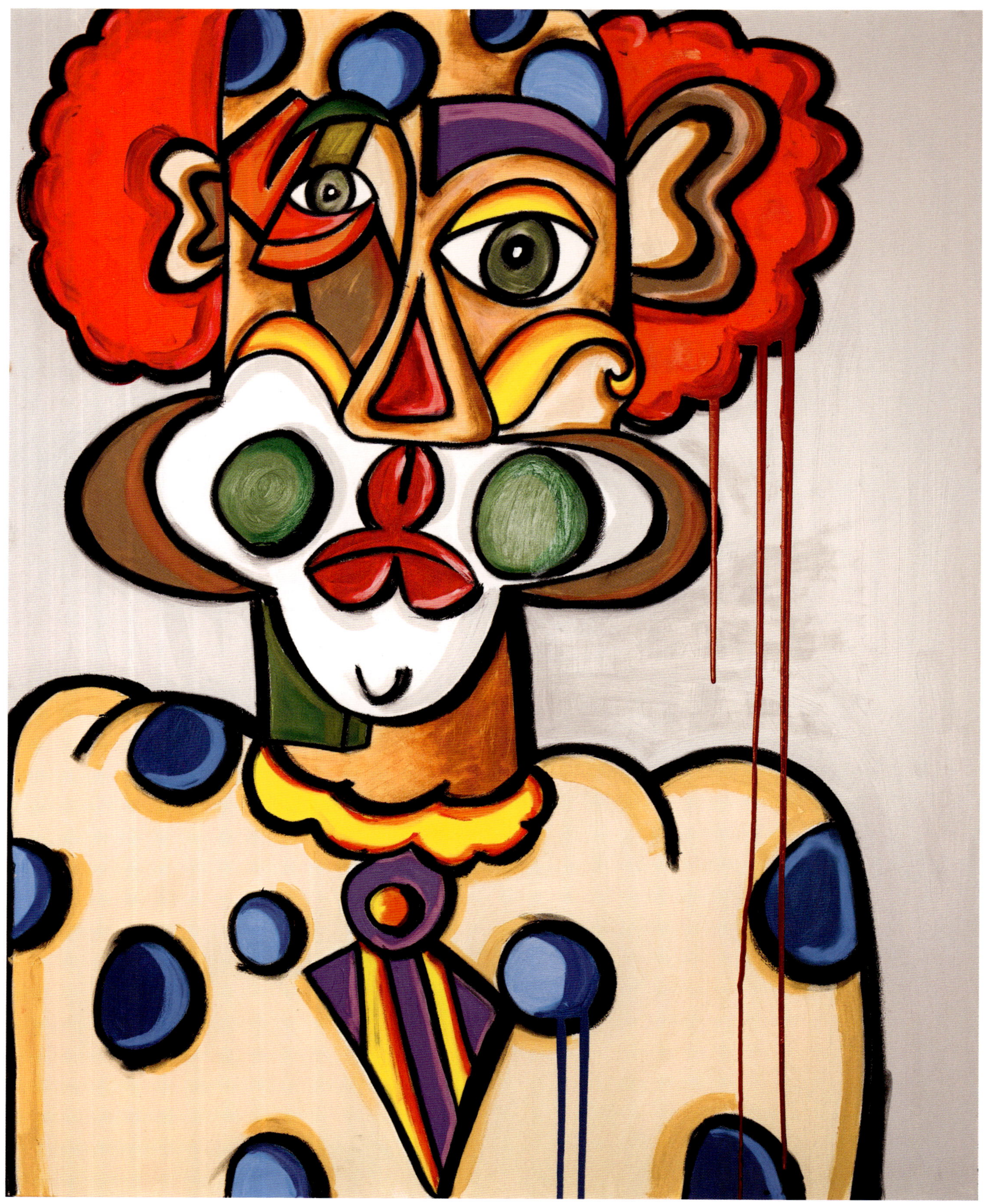

Max the Clown, 2022 | acrylic and oil pastel on canvas, 60 × 48 in

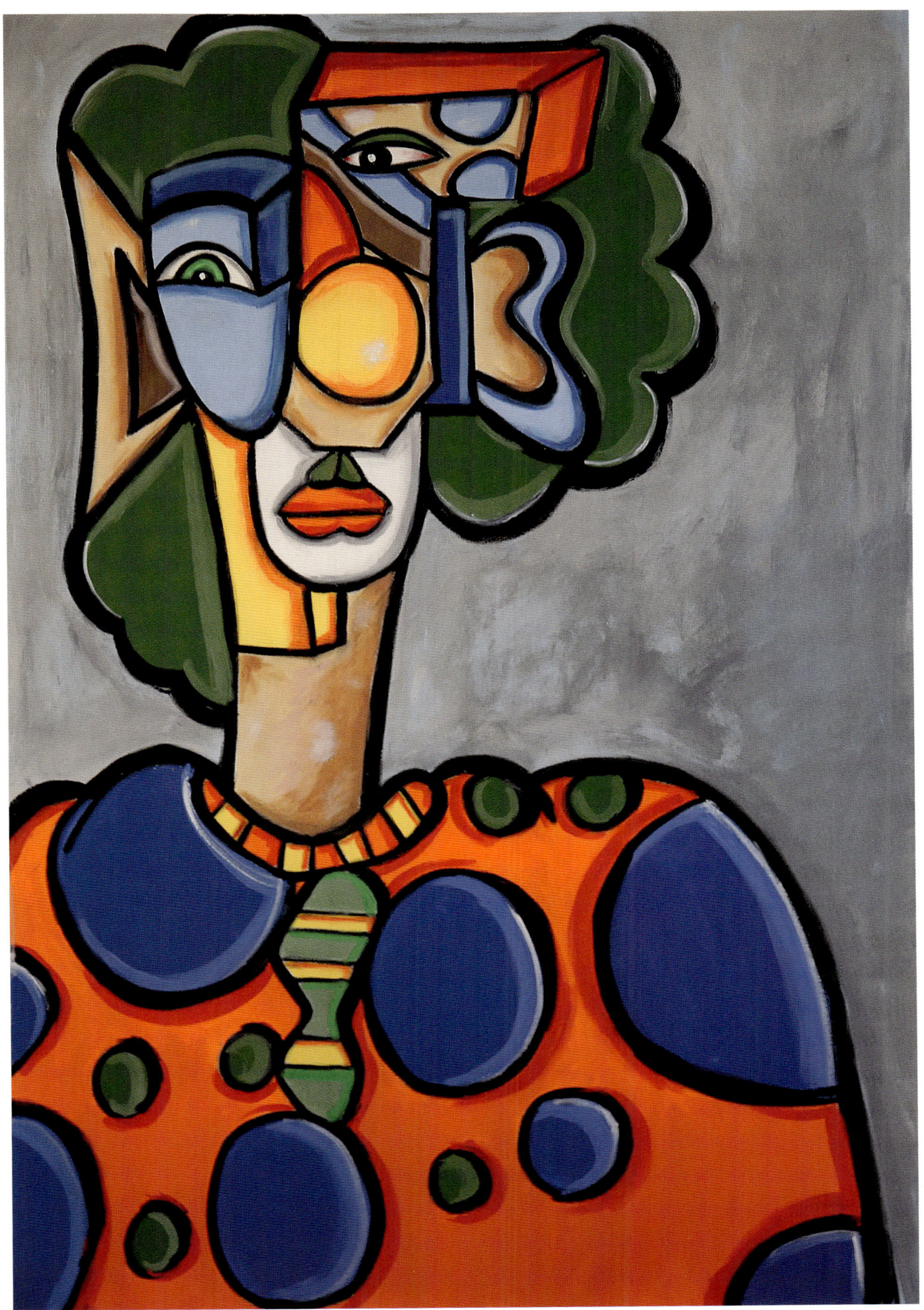

Diego, 2022 | acrylic and oil pastel on canvas, 60 × 40 in

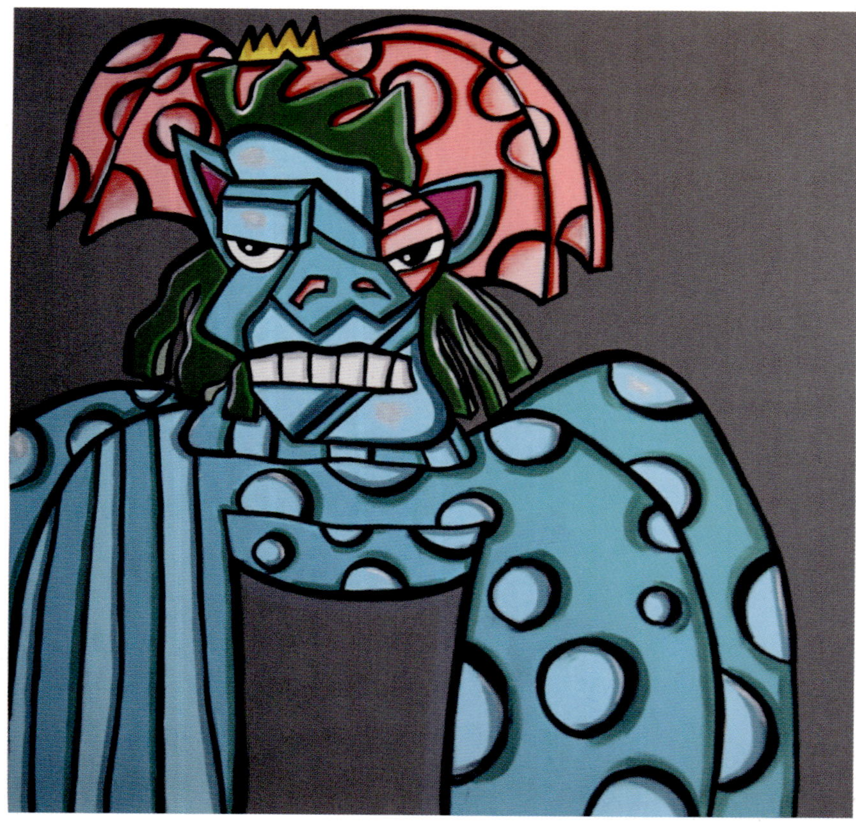

Venacube, 2022
acrylic and oil pastel on canvas, 60 × 60 in

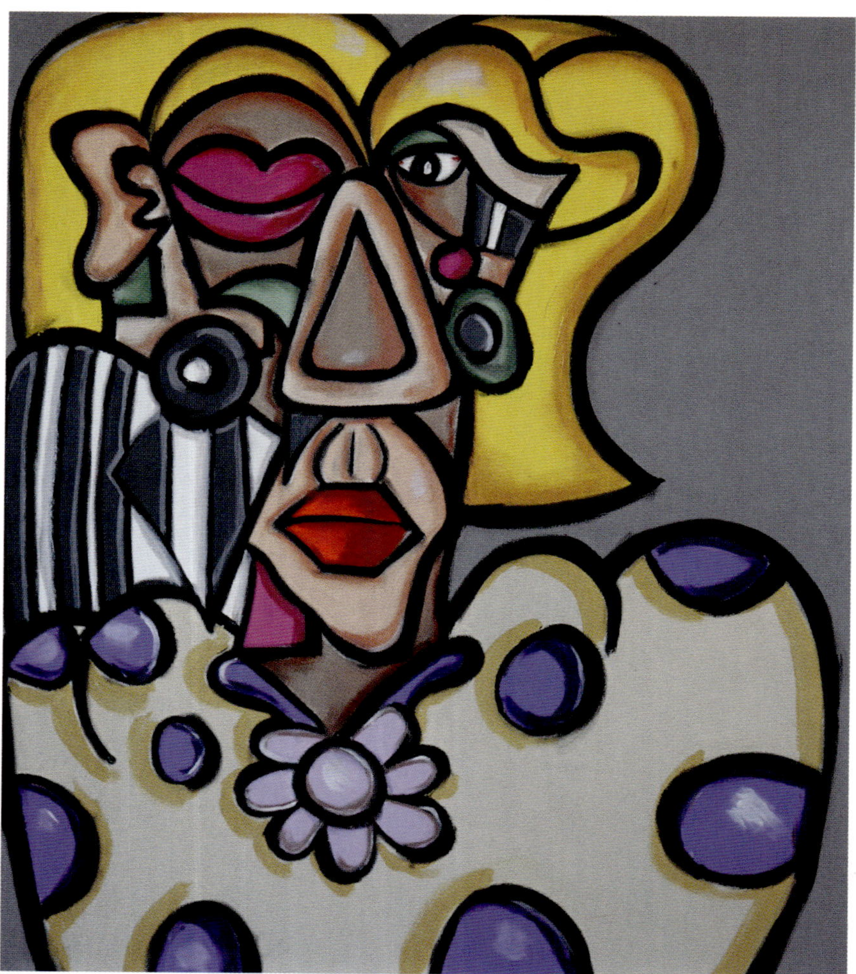

Valentina, 2022
acrylic and oil pastel on canvas, 42 × 35 in

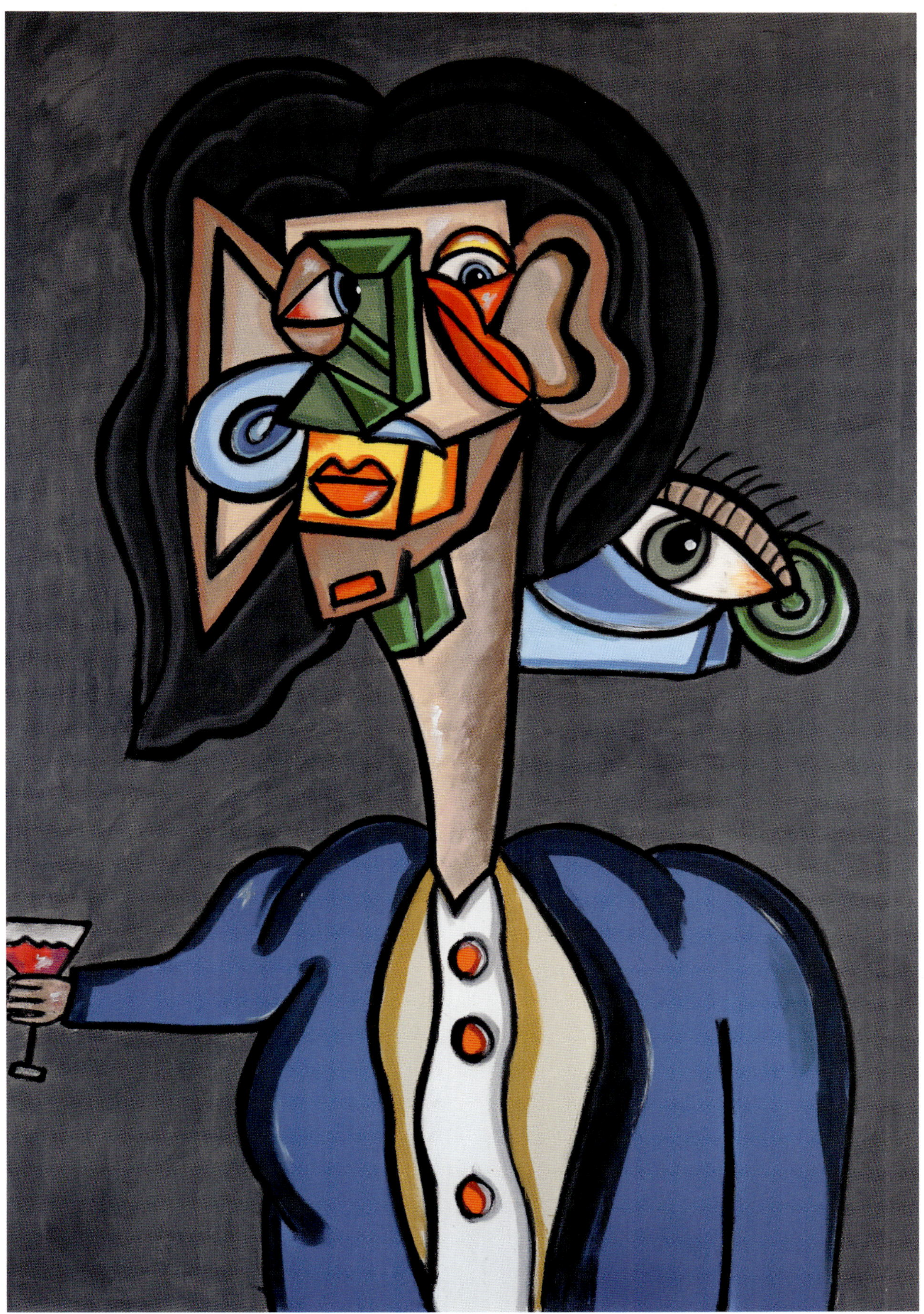

Alex and Alexa, 2022 | acrylic and oil pastel on canvas, 72 × 48 in

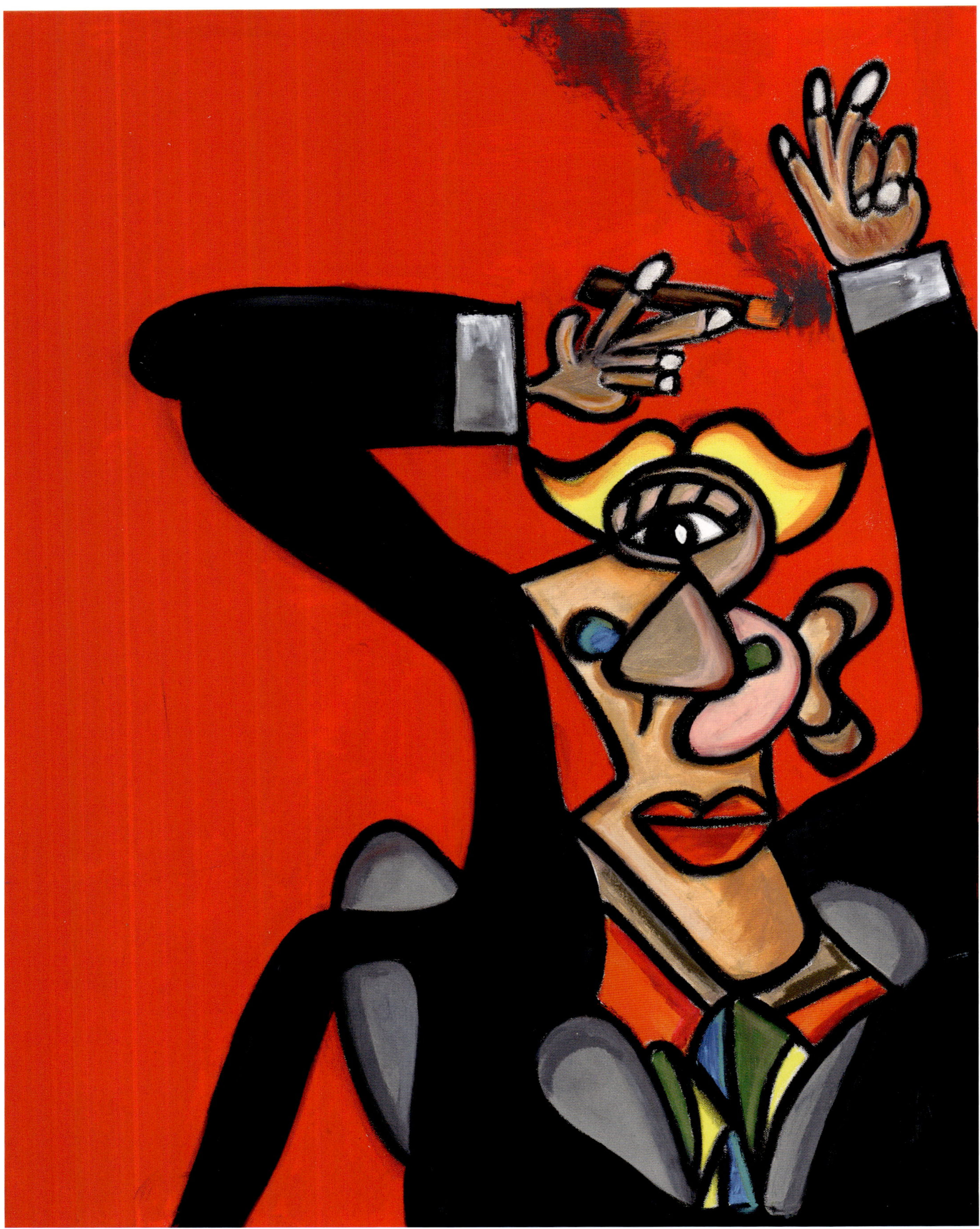

Toni, 2022 | acrylic and oil pastel on canvas, 36 × 28 in

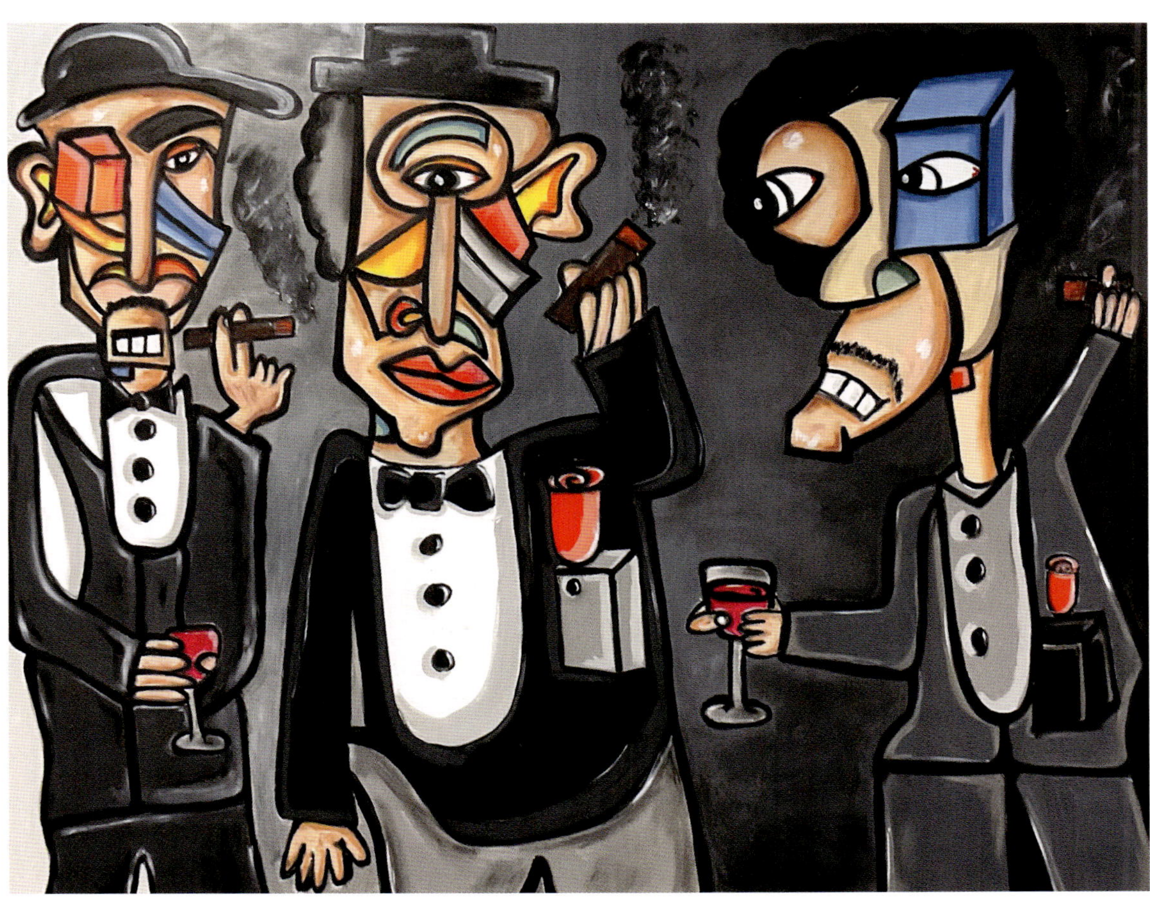

Tony, Joe, and John, 2022 | acrylic and oil pastel on canvas, 48 × 60 in

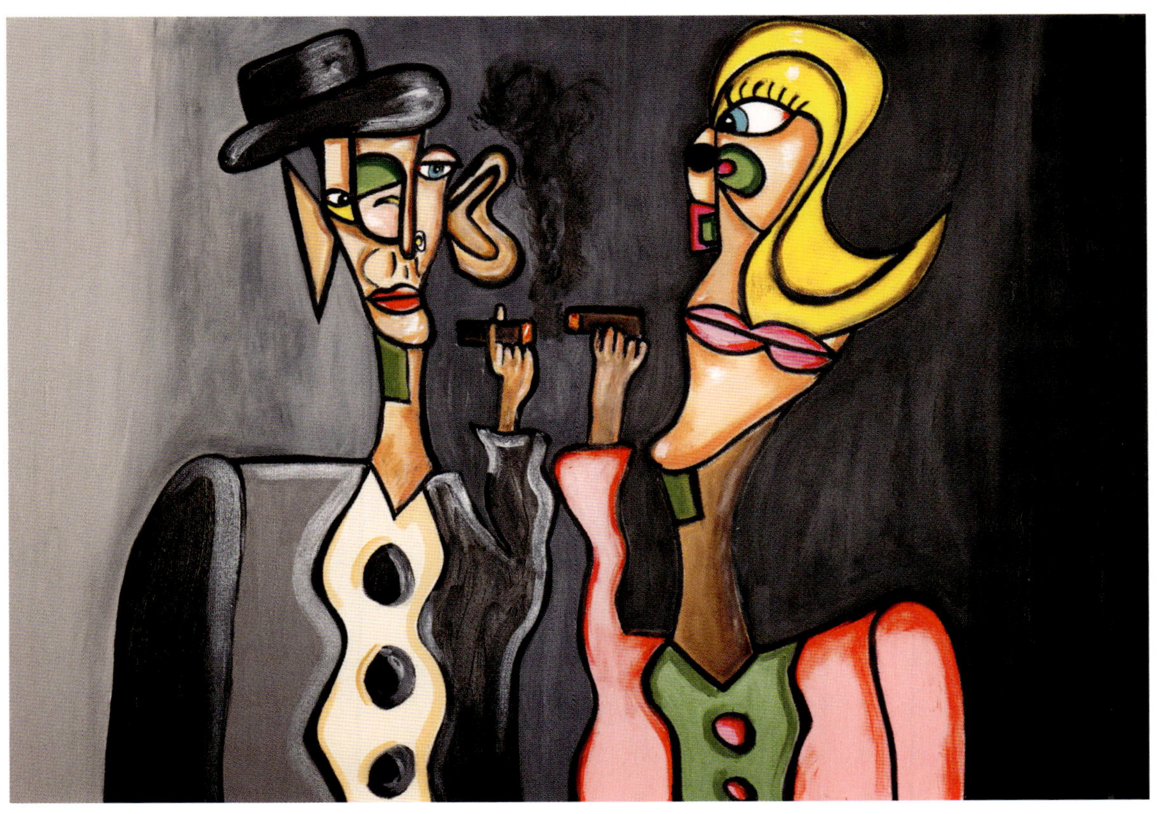

Tom and Jenny, 2022 | acrylic and oil pastel on canvas, 48 × 68 in

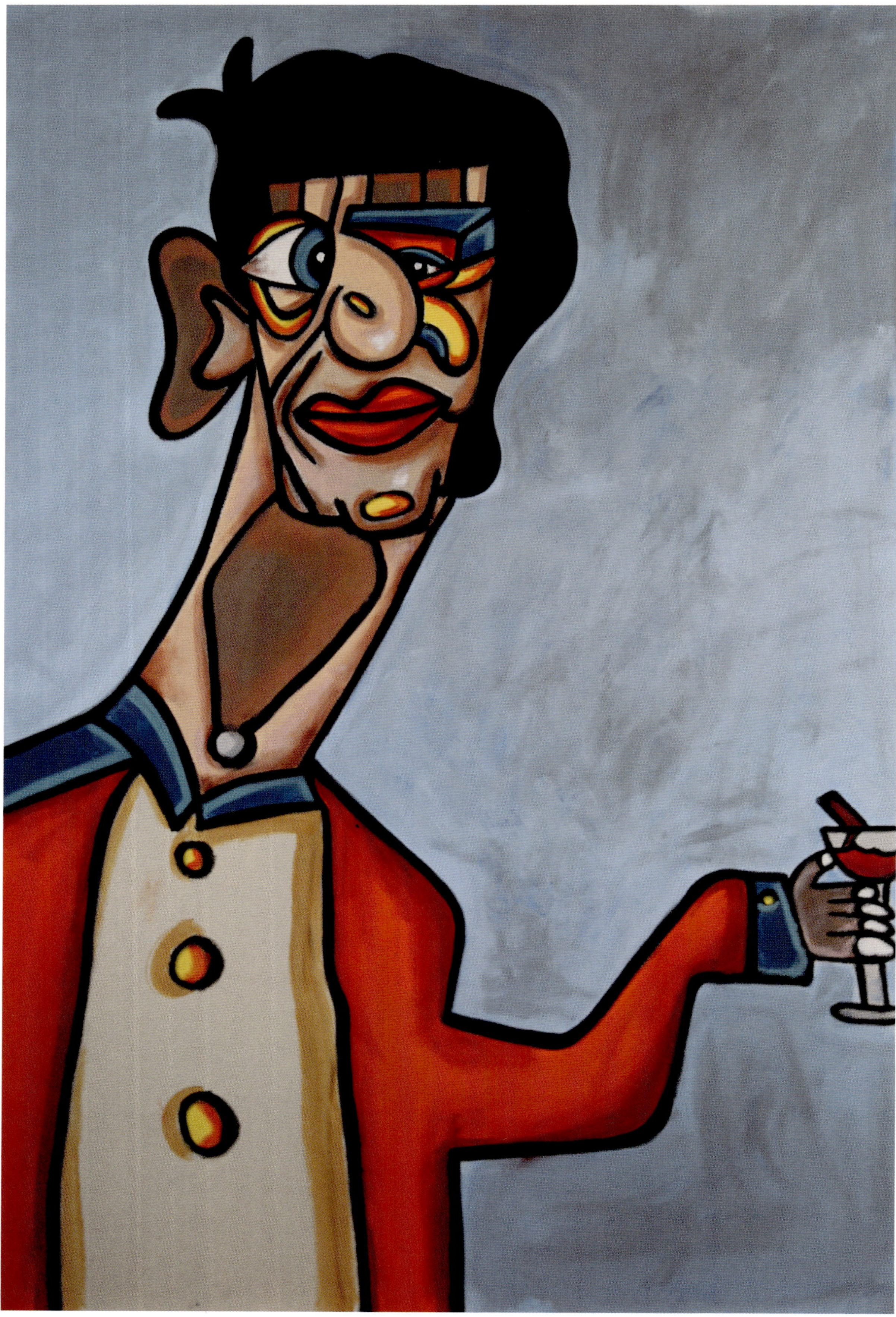

Arnold, 2022 | acrylic and oil pastel on canvas, 60 × 40 in

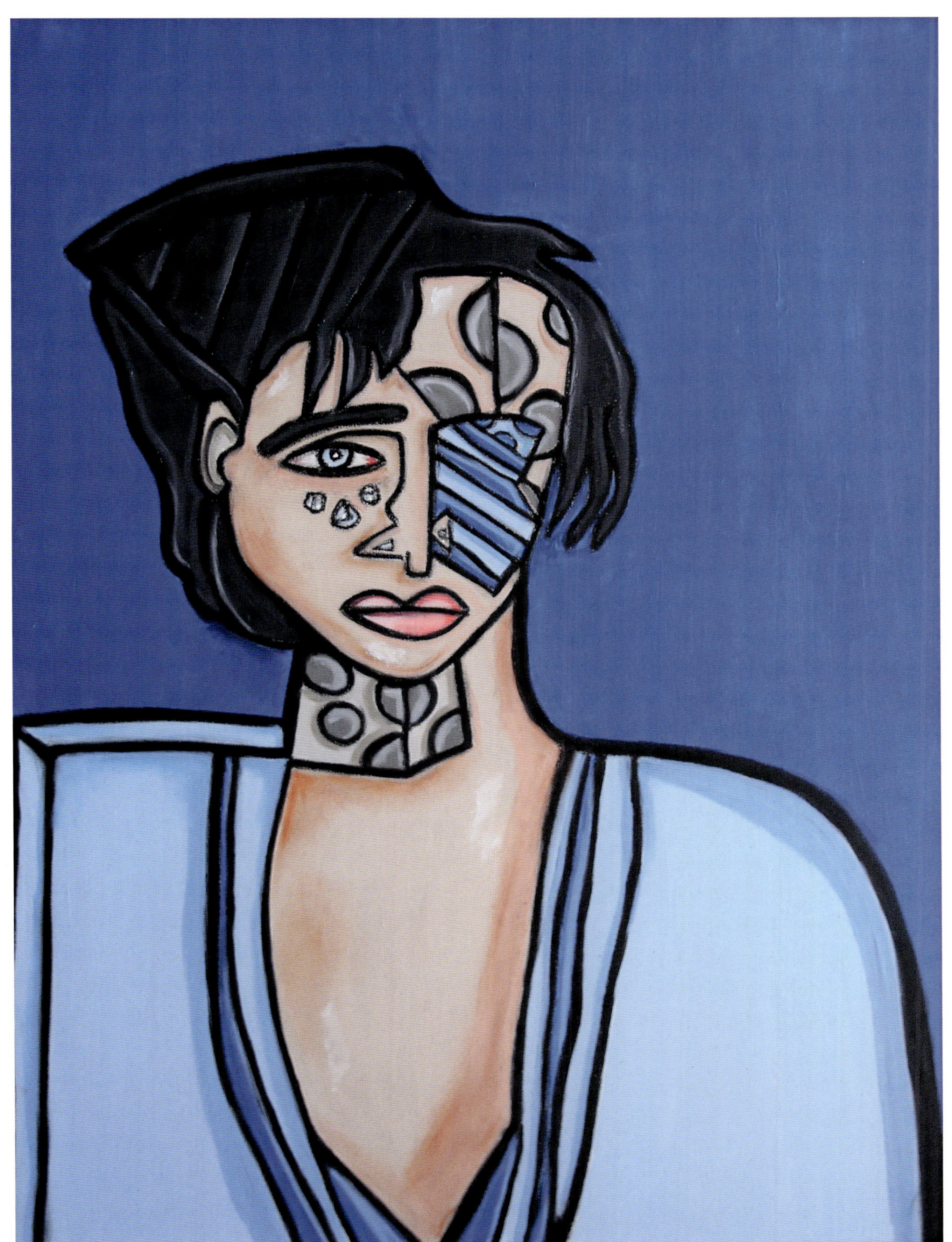

V, 2022 | acrylic and oil pastel on canvas, 42 × 30 in

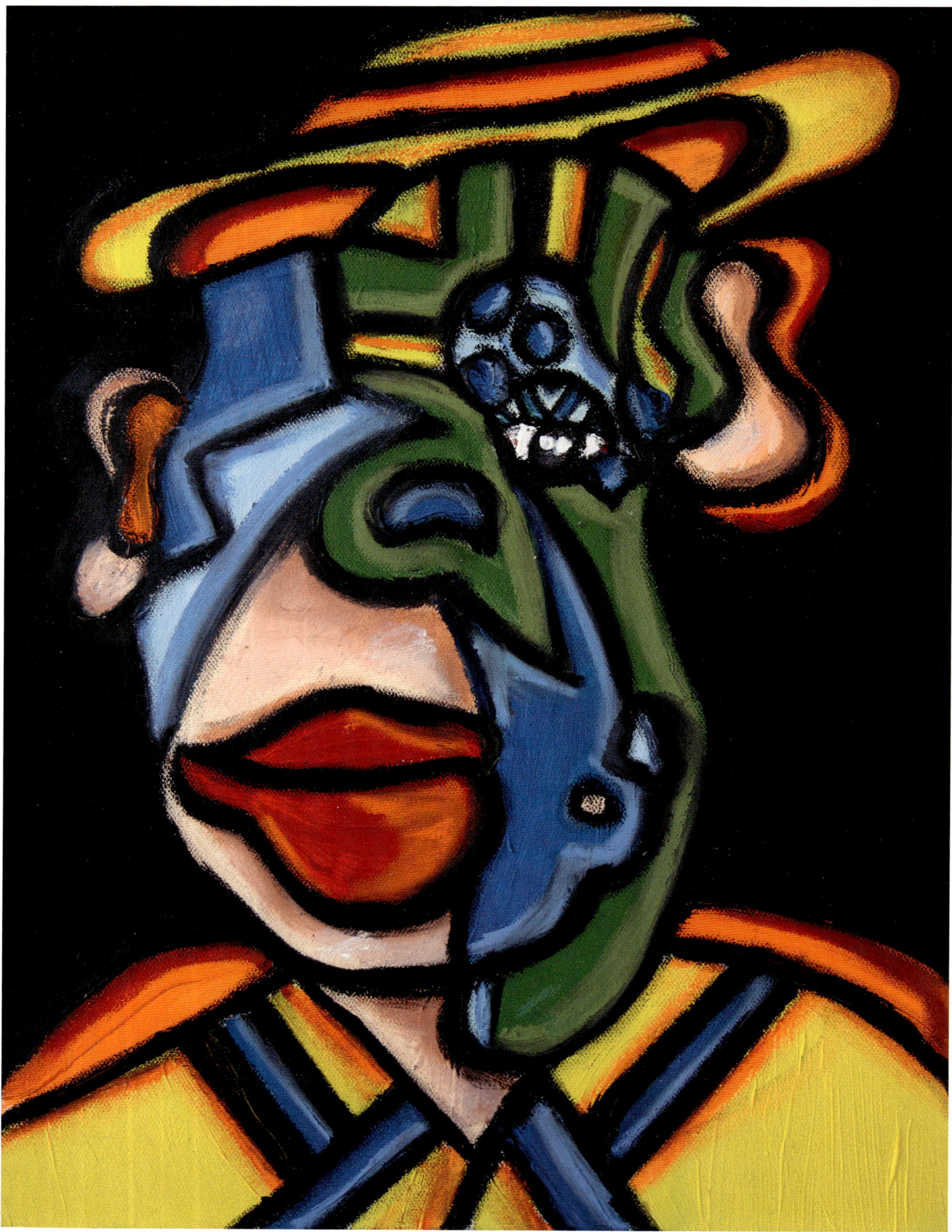

Peter, 2023 | acrylic and oil pastel on canvas, 16 × 12 in

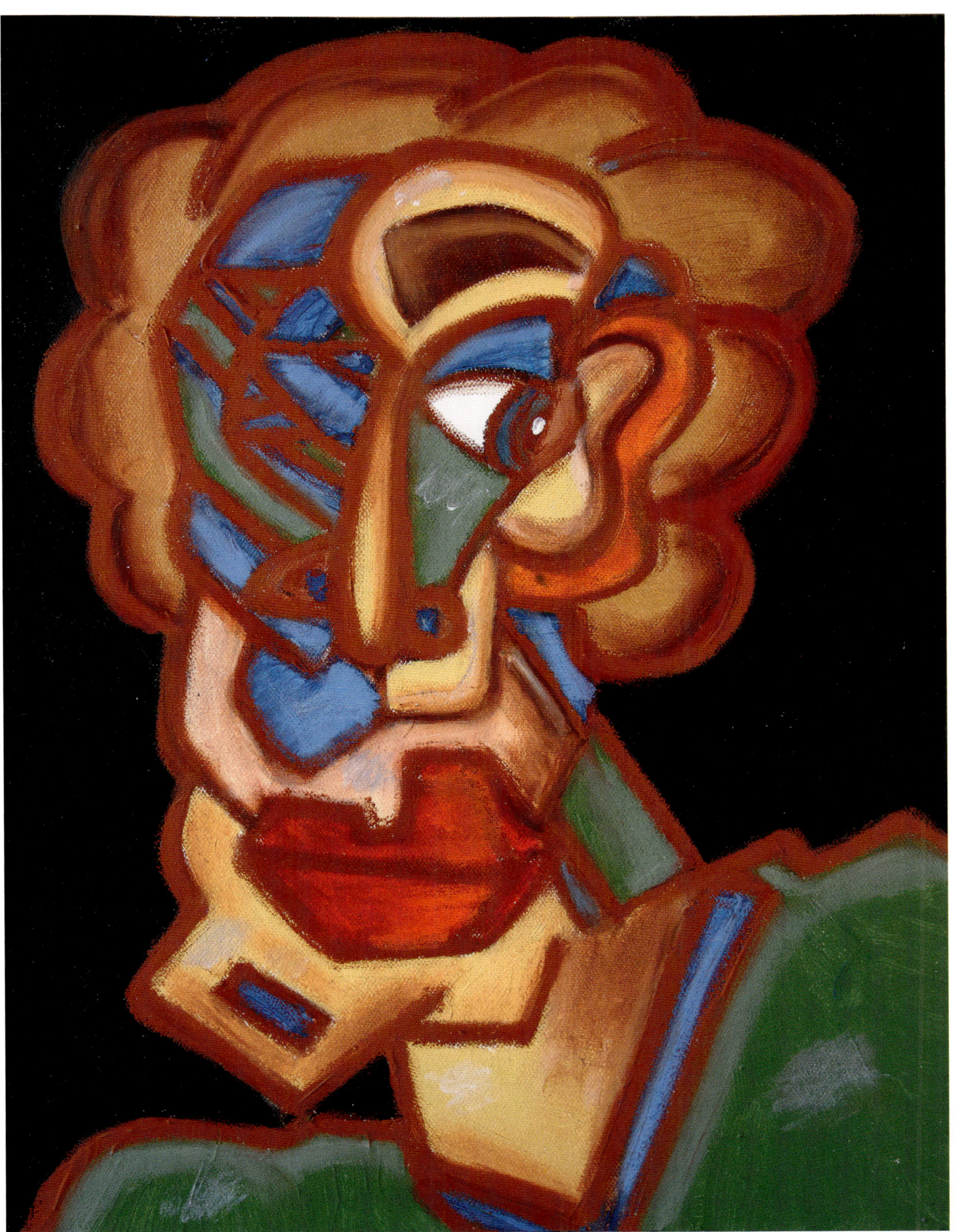

Jewel, 2023 │ acrylic and oil pastel on canvas, 16 × 12 in

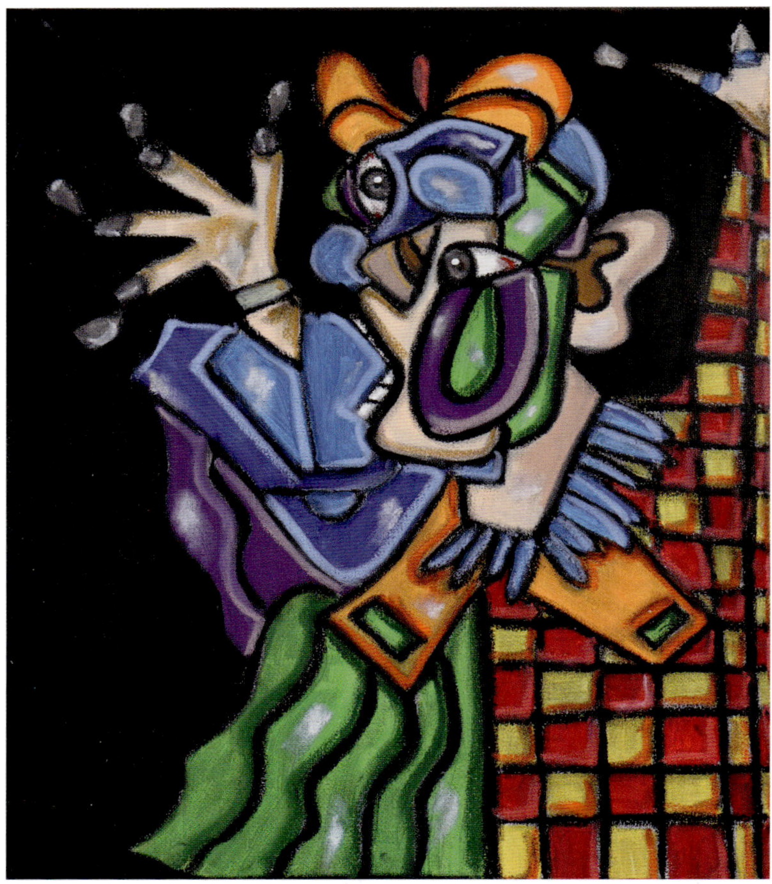

Eddy, 2023
acrylic and oil pastel on canvas, 20 × 16 in

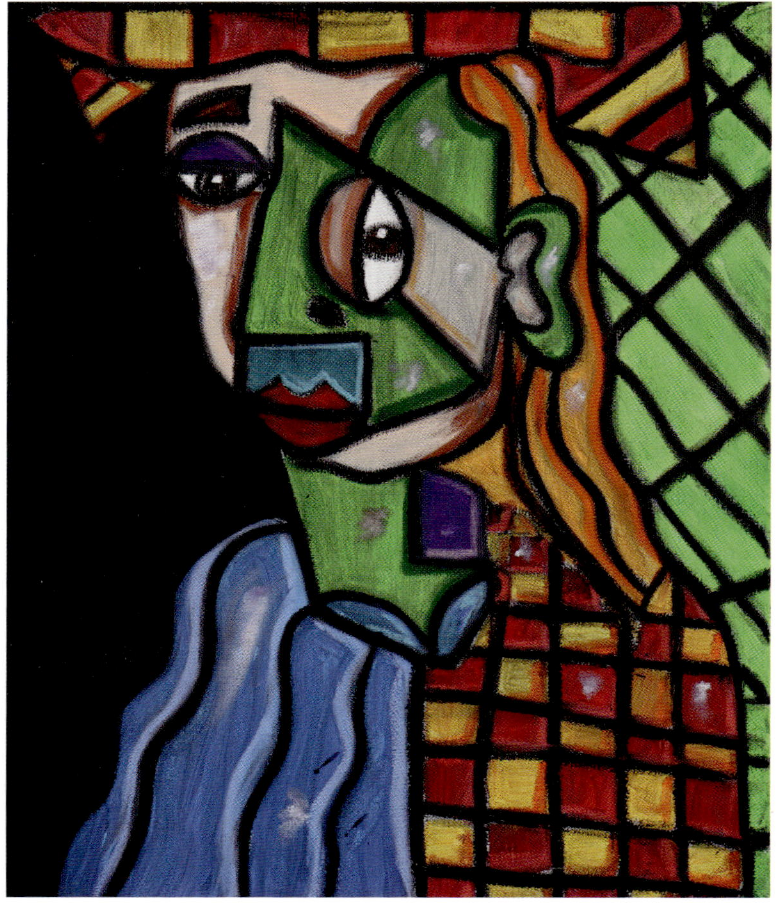

Elsa, 2023
acrylic and oil pastel on canvas, 20 × 16 in

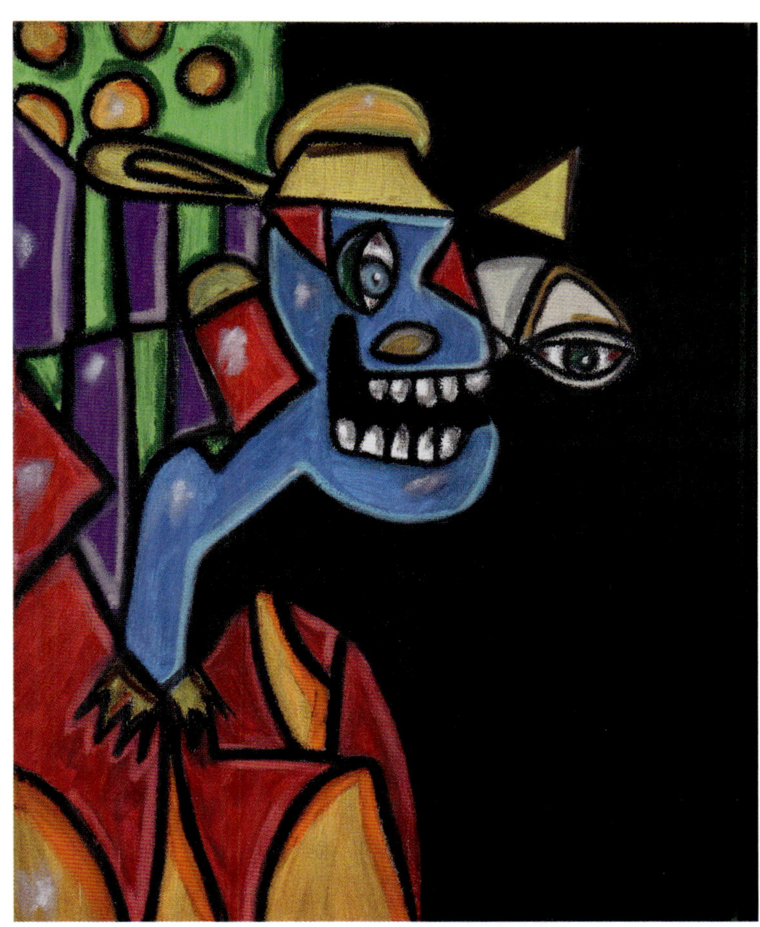

Jasper, 2023
acrylic and oil pastel on canvas, 20 × 16 in

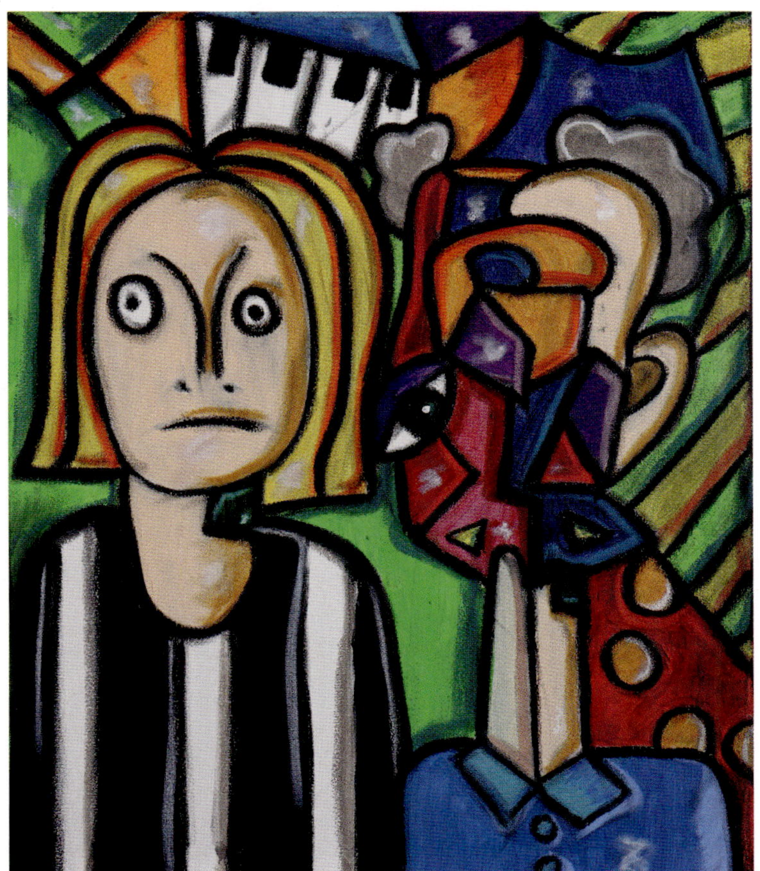

Los Pianistas, 2023
acrylic and oil pastel on canvas, 20 × 16 in

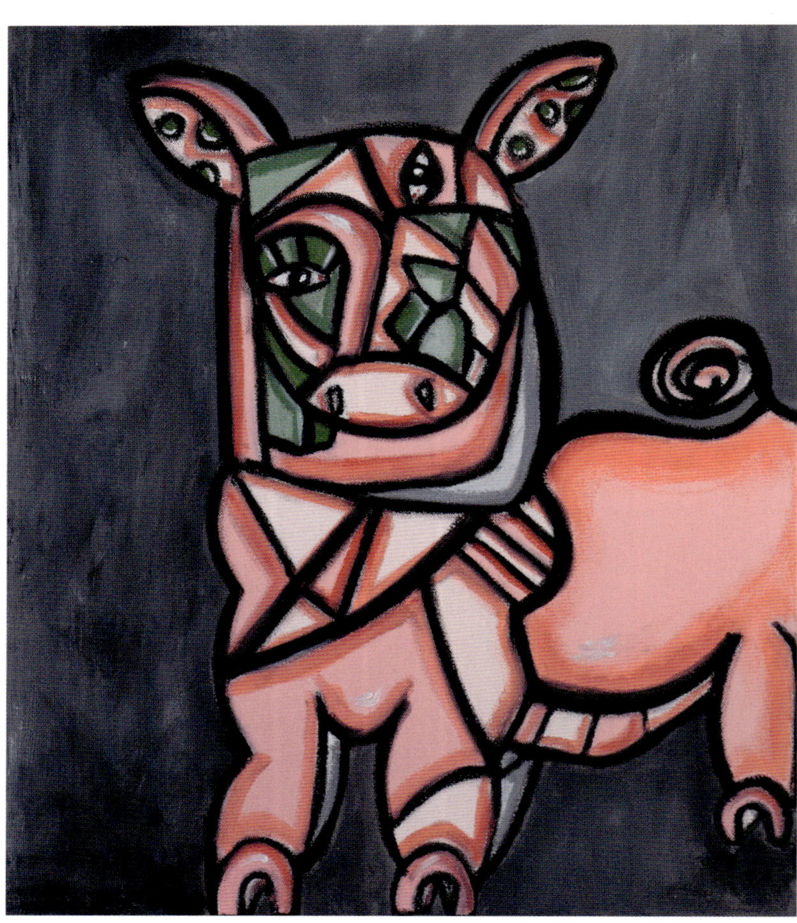

Lupita, 2023 | acrylic and oil pastel on canvas, 24 × 20 in

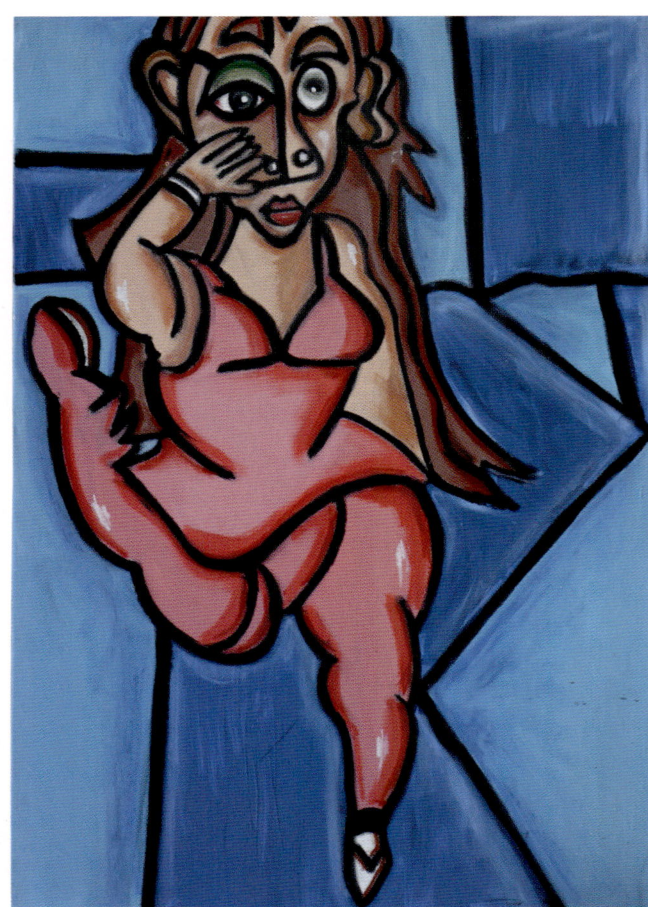

Amalia, 2023 | acrylic and oil pastel on canvas, 36 × 24 in

Lourdes, 2023 | acrylic and oil pastel on canvas, 50 × 31 in

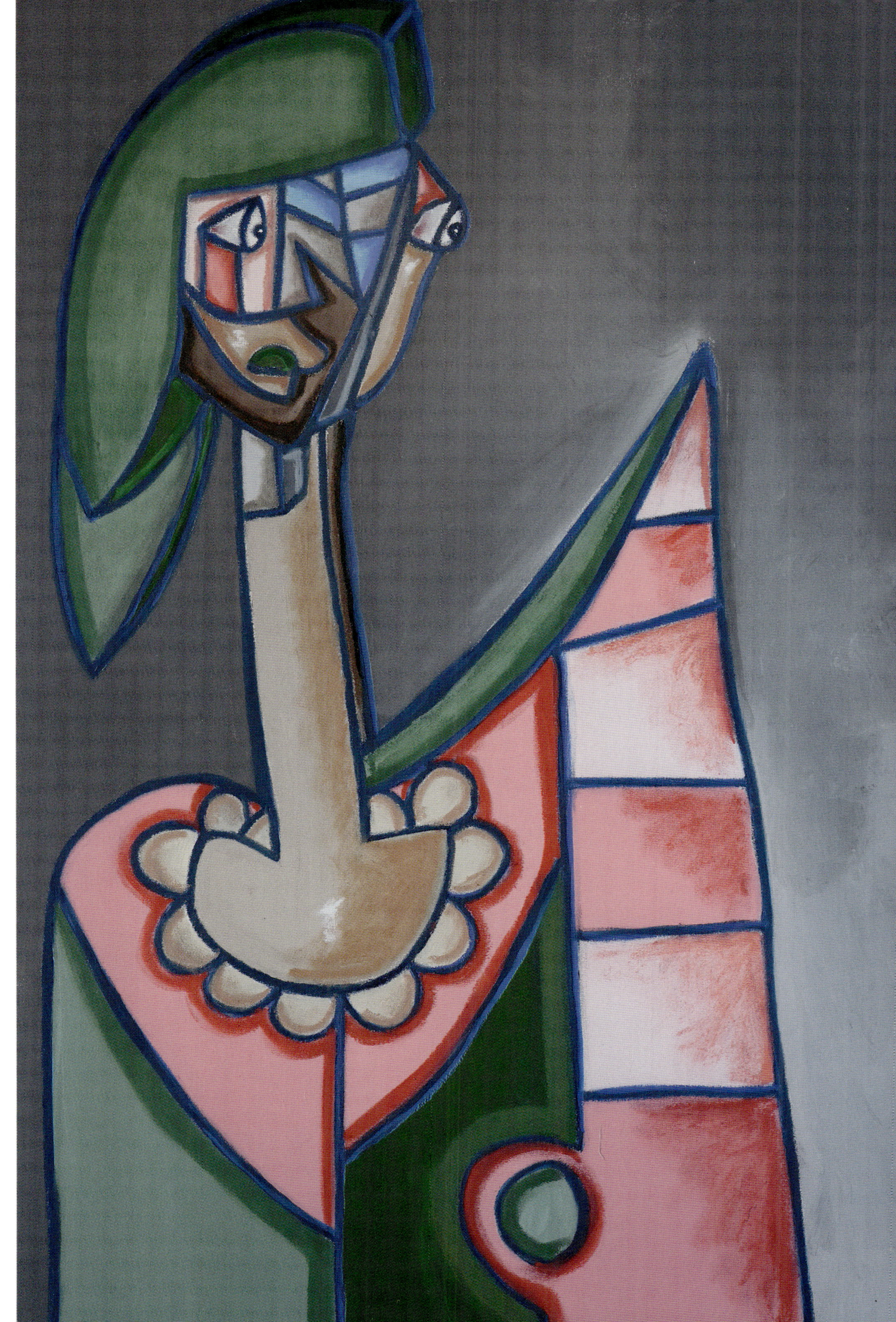

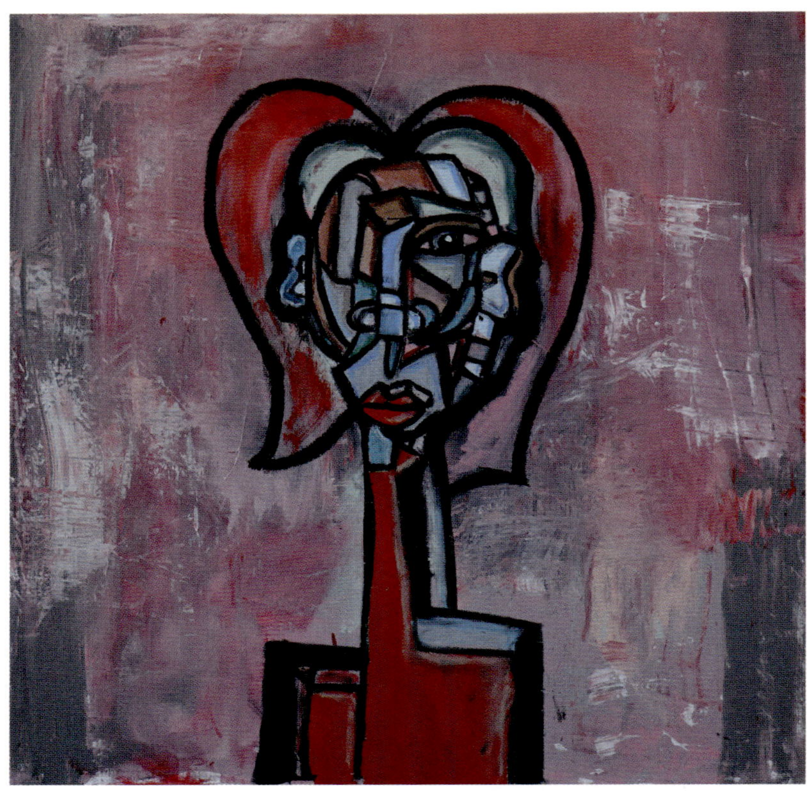

Amor, 2023
acrylic and oil pastel on canvas, 40 × 40 in

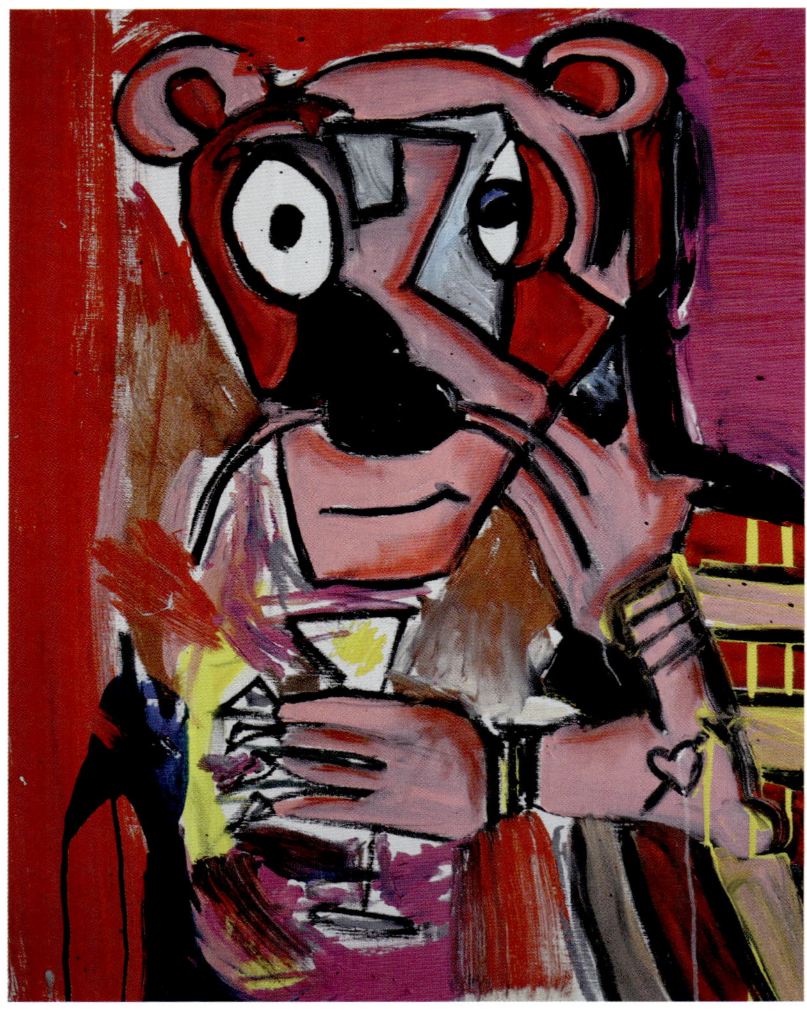

Pink Panther 2, 2023
acrylic and oil pastel on canvas, 40 × 30 in

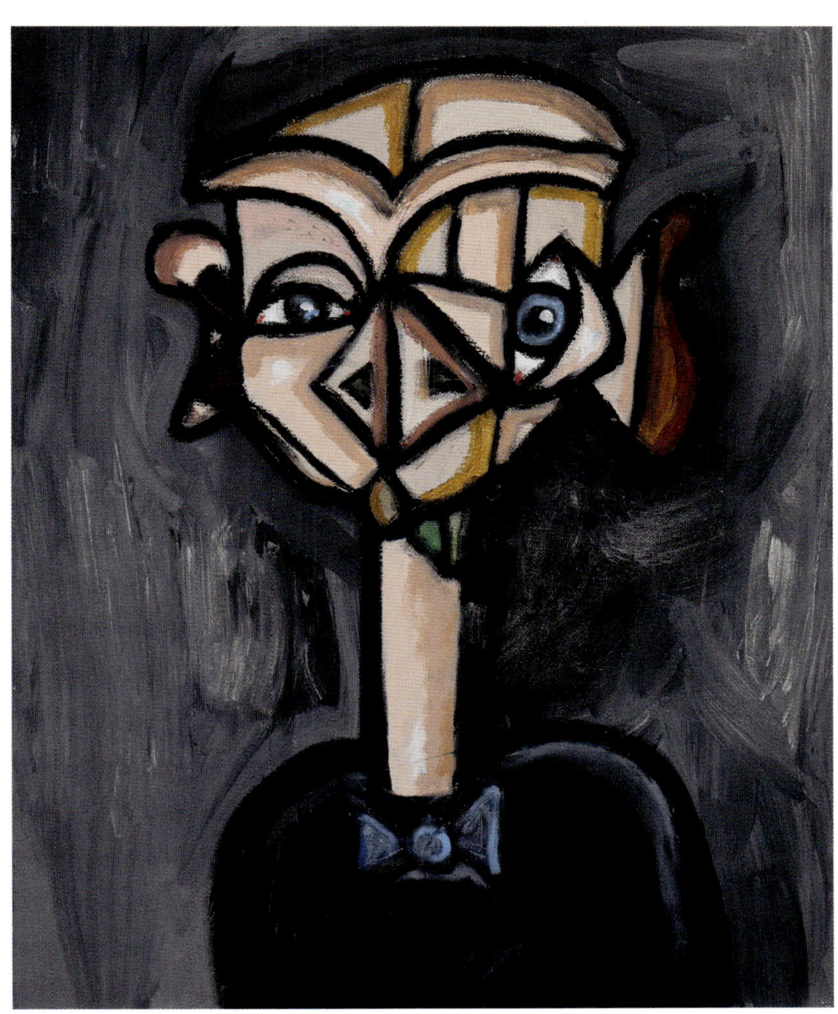

Frankie, 2023
acrylic and oil pastel on canvas, 20 × 16 in

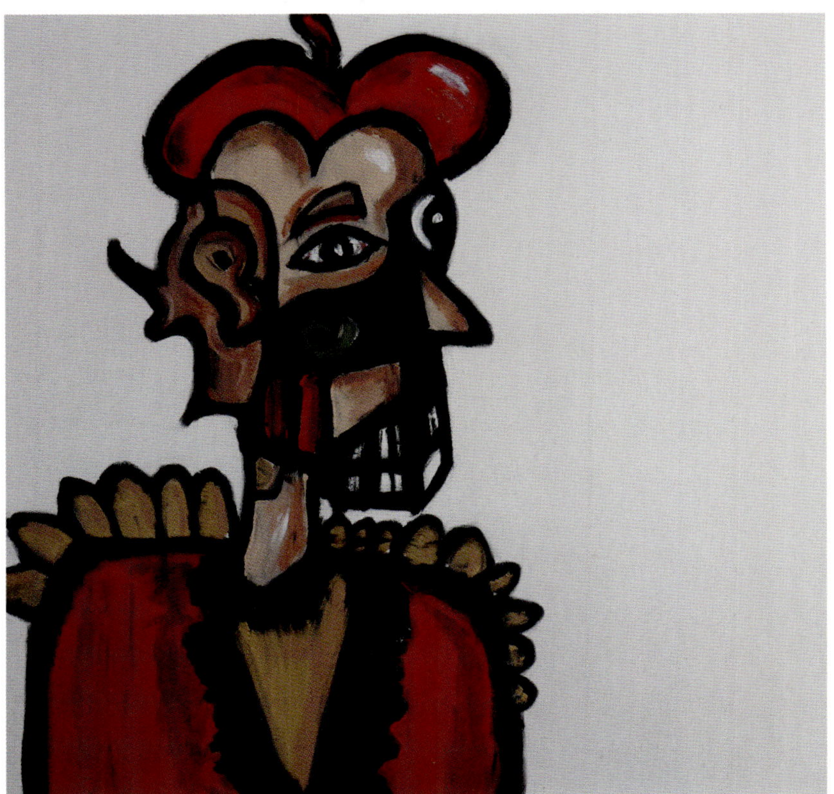

El Gran Torero, 2023
acrylic and oil pastel on canvas, 30 × 30 in

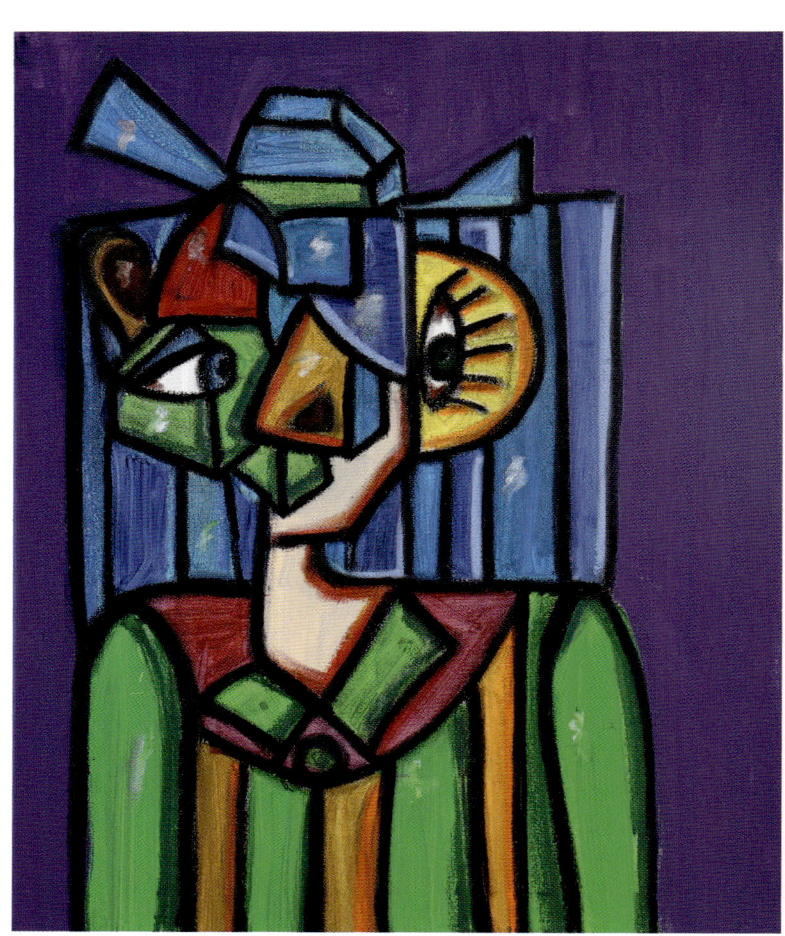

Nina Cube, 2023 | acrylic and oil pastel on canvas, 20 × 16 in

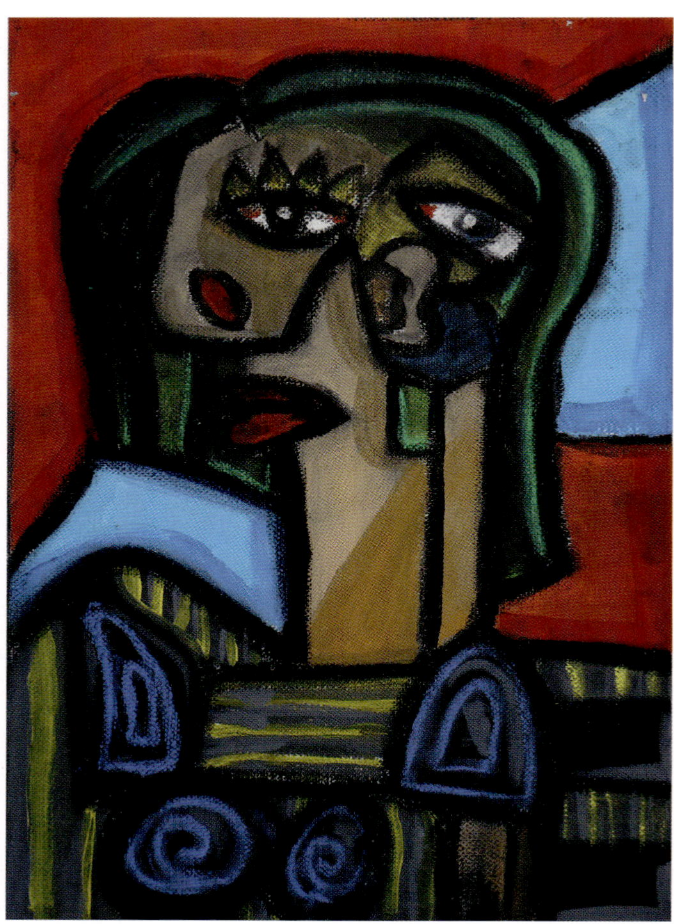

Paris, 2023 | acrylic and oil pastel on canvas, 14 × 9.5 in

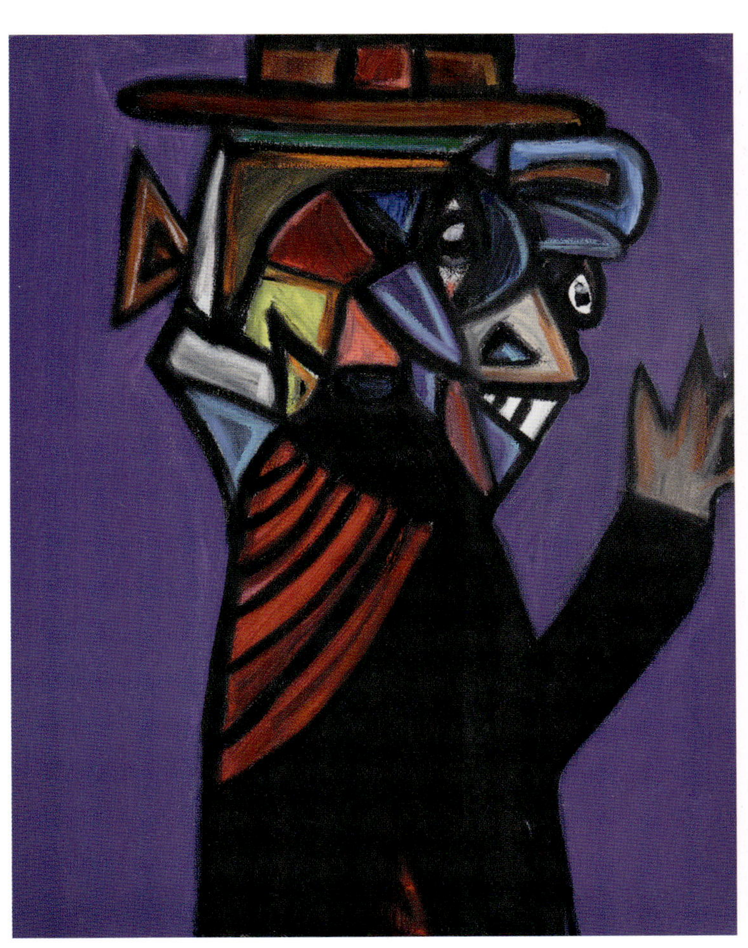

Robert, 2023 | acrylic and oil pastel on canvas, 20 × 16 in

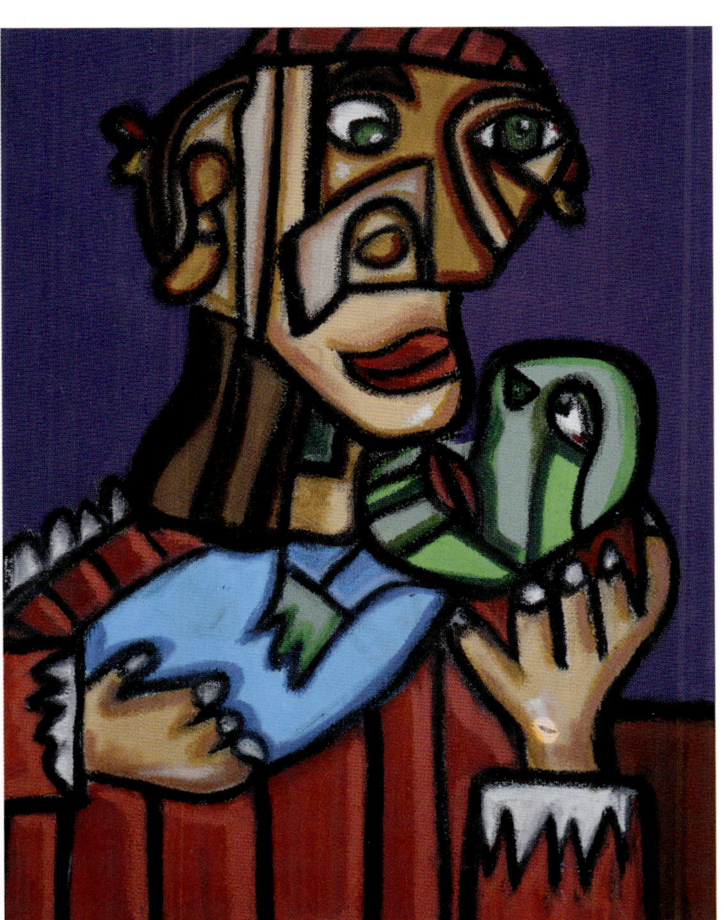

Mama and Baby, 2023 | acrylic and oil pastel on canvas, 18 × 14 in

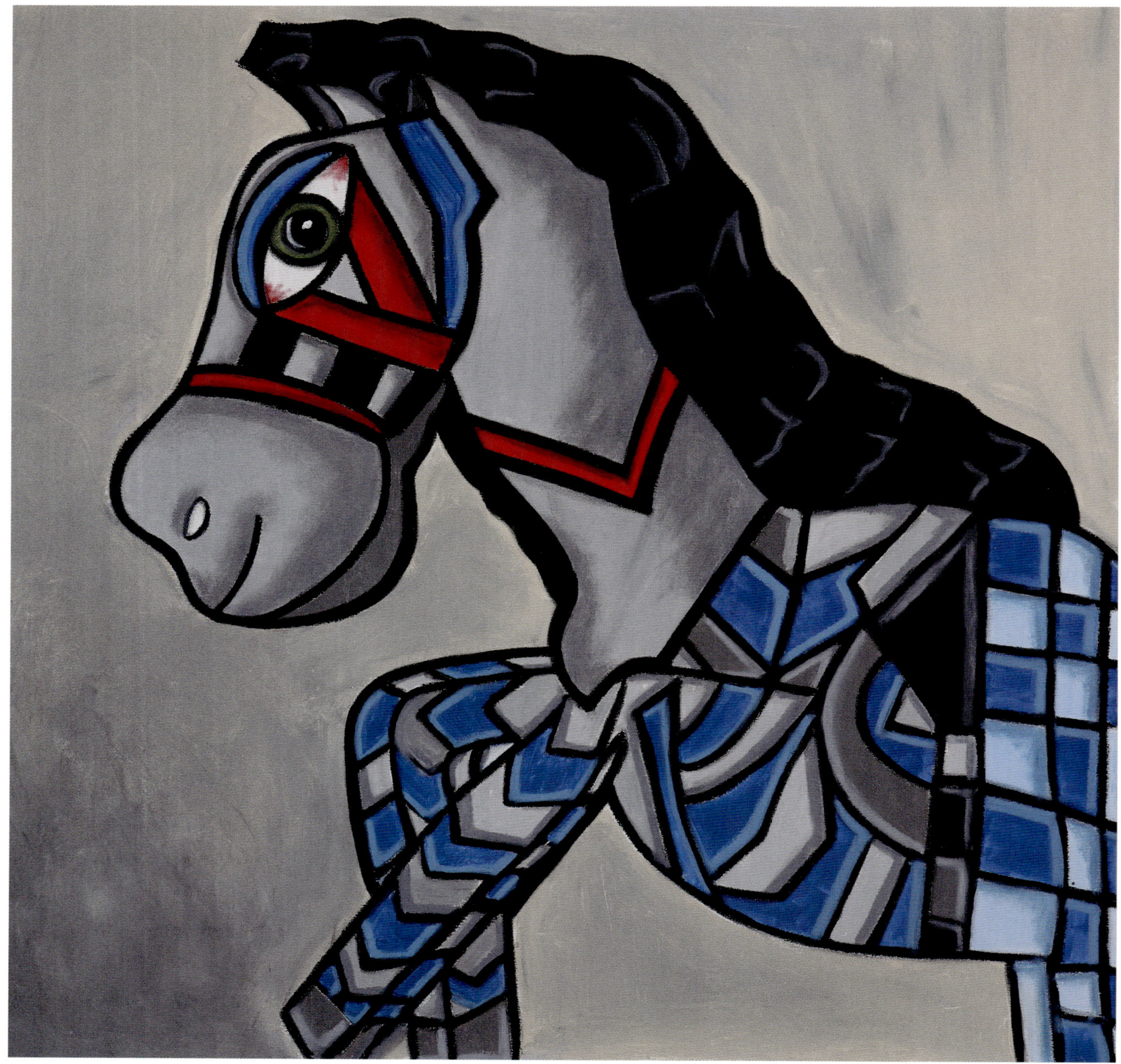

Caballo Azul, 2023 | acrylic and oil pastel on canvas, 40 × 40 in

El Caballode Picasso, 2023 | acrylic and oil pastel on canvas, 36 × 28 in

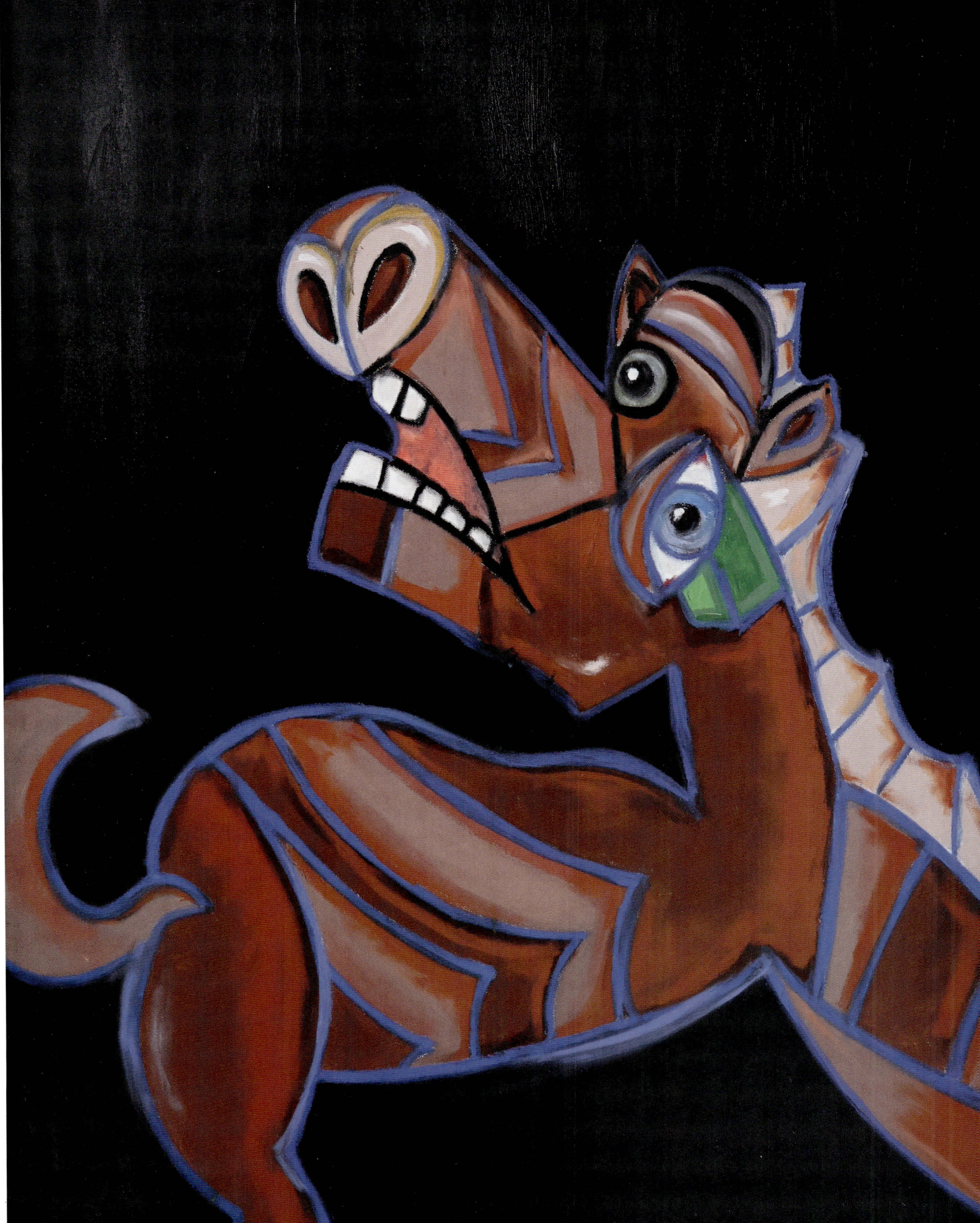

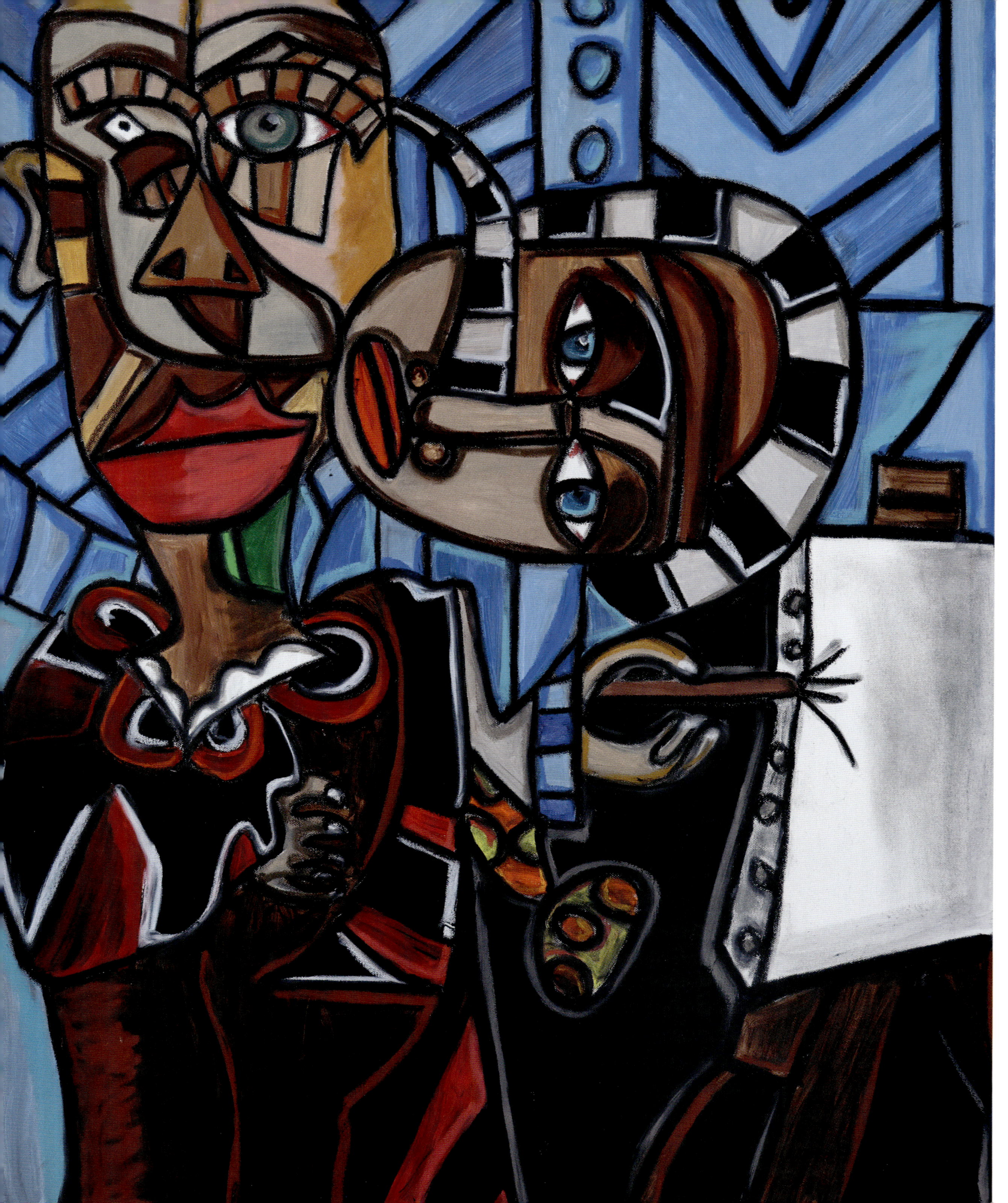

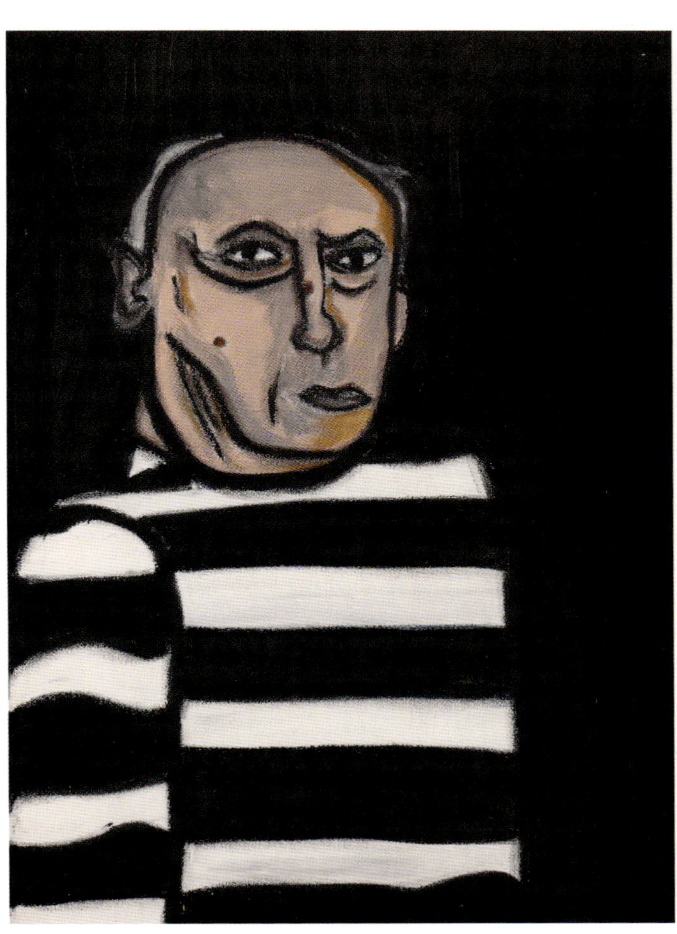

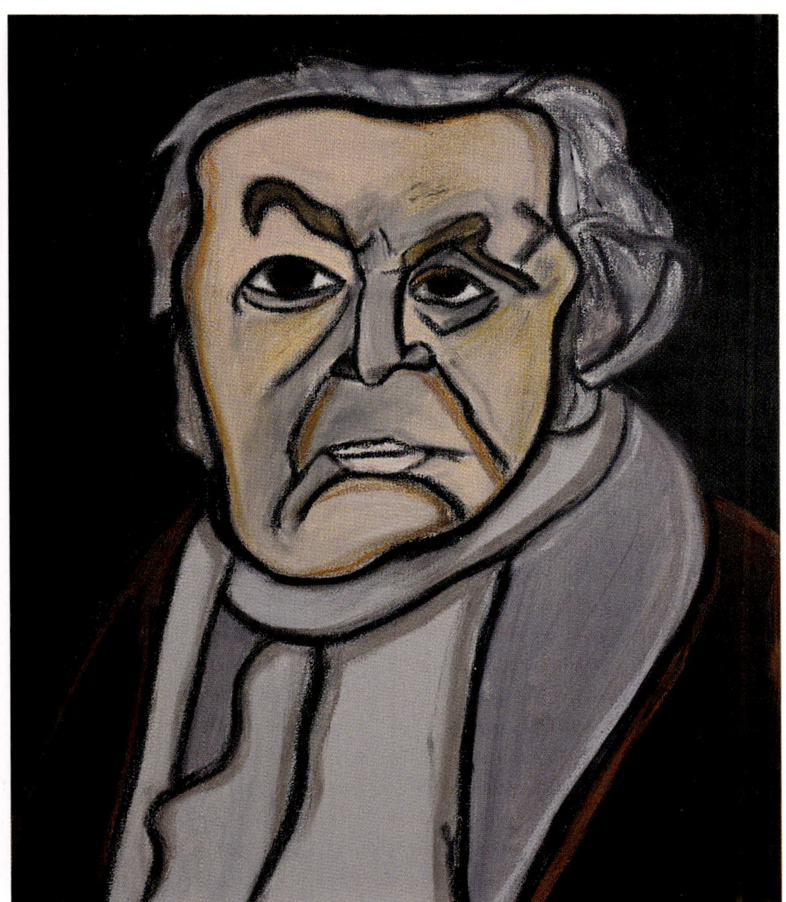

Pablo Picasso, 2023 | acrylic and oil pastel on canvas, 20 × 16 in   ***Francisco de Goya,*** 2023 | acrylic and oil pastel on canvas, 20 × 16 in

Picasso Thinking and Painting of a Woman—Jaqueline, 2023 | acrylic and oil pastel on canvas, 36 × 28 in

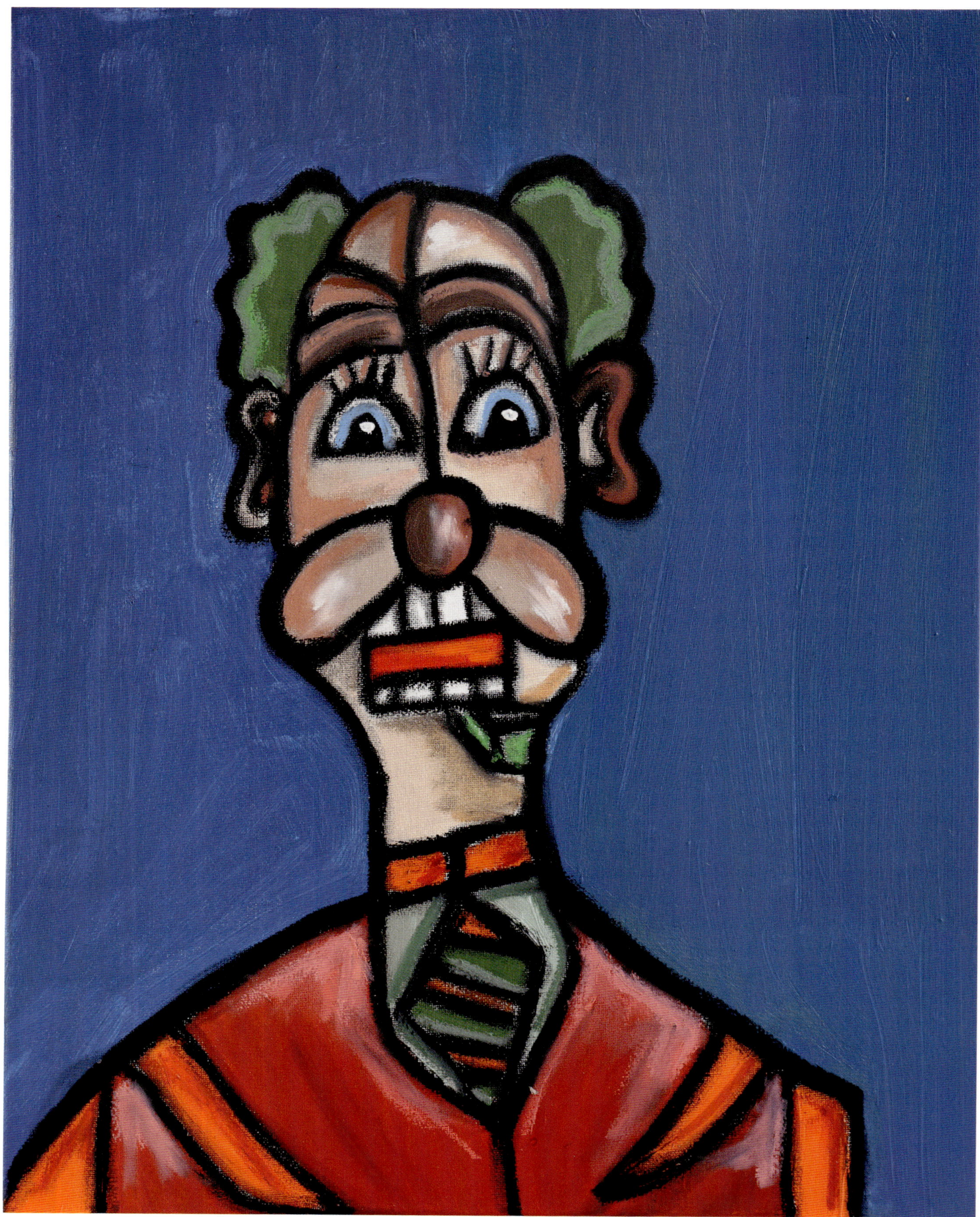

Tommy, 2023 | acrylic and oil pastel on canvas, 20 × 16 in

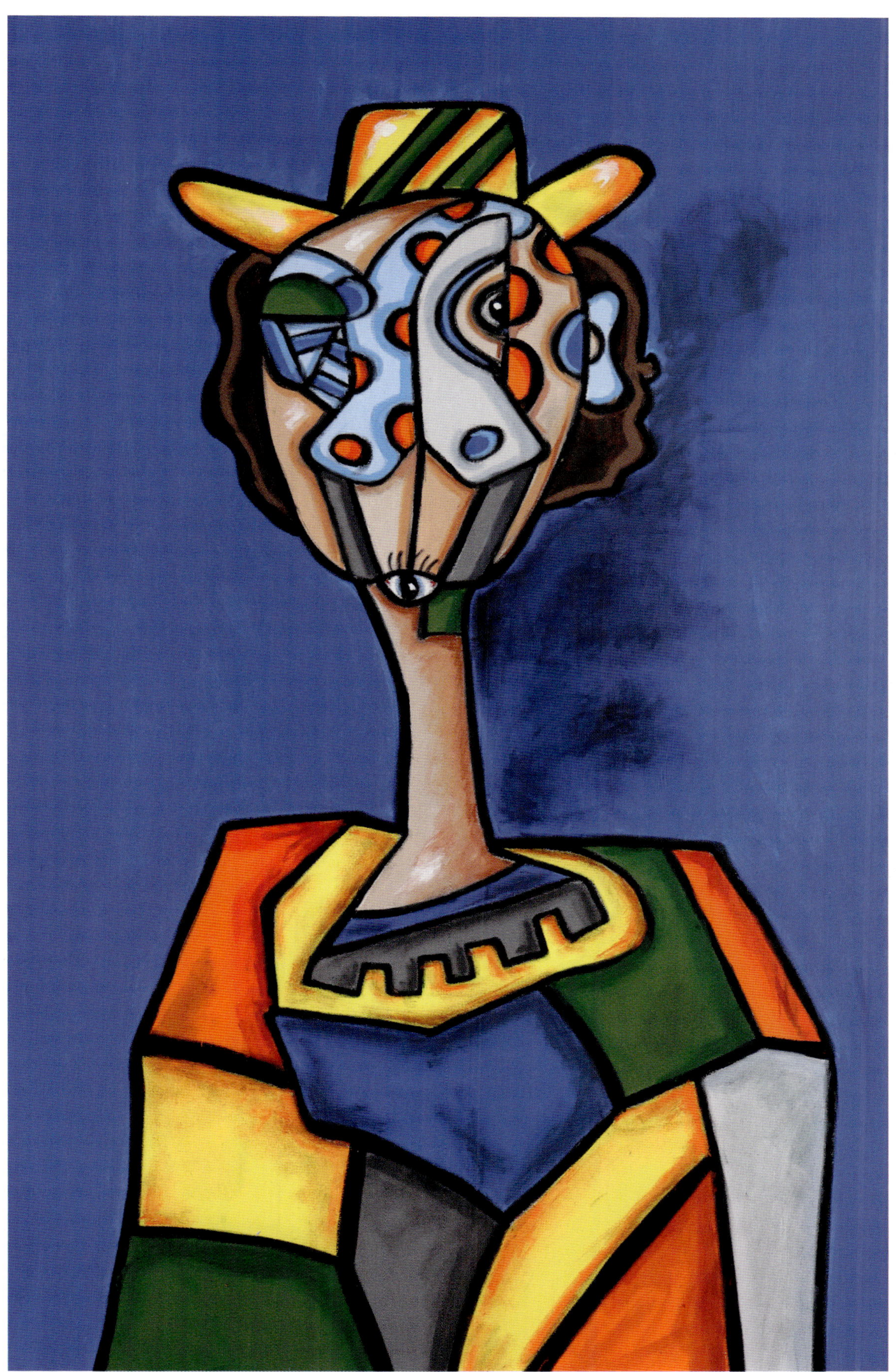

The Cowboy, 2023 | acrylic and oil pastel on canvas, 60 × 36 in

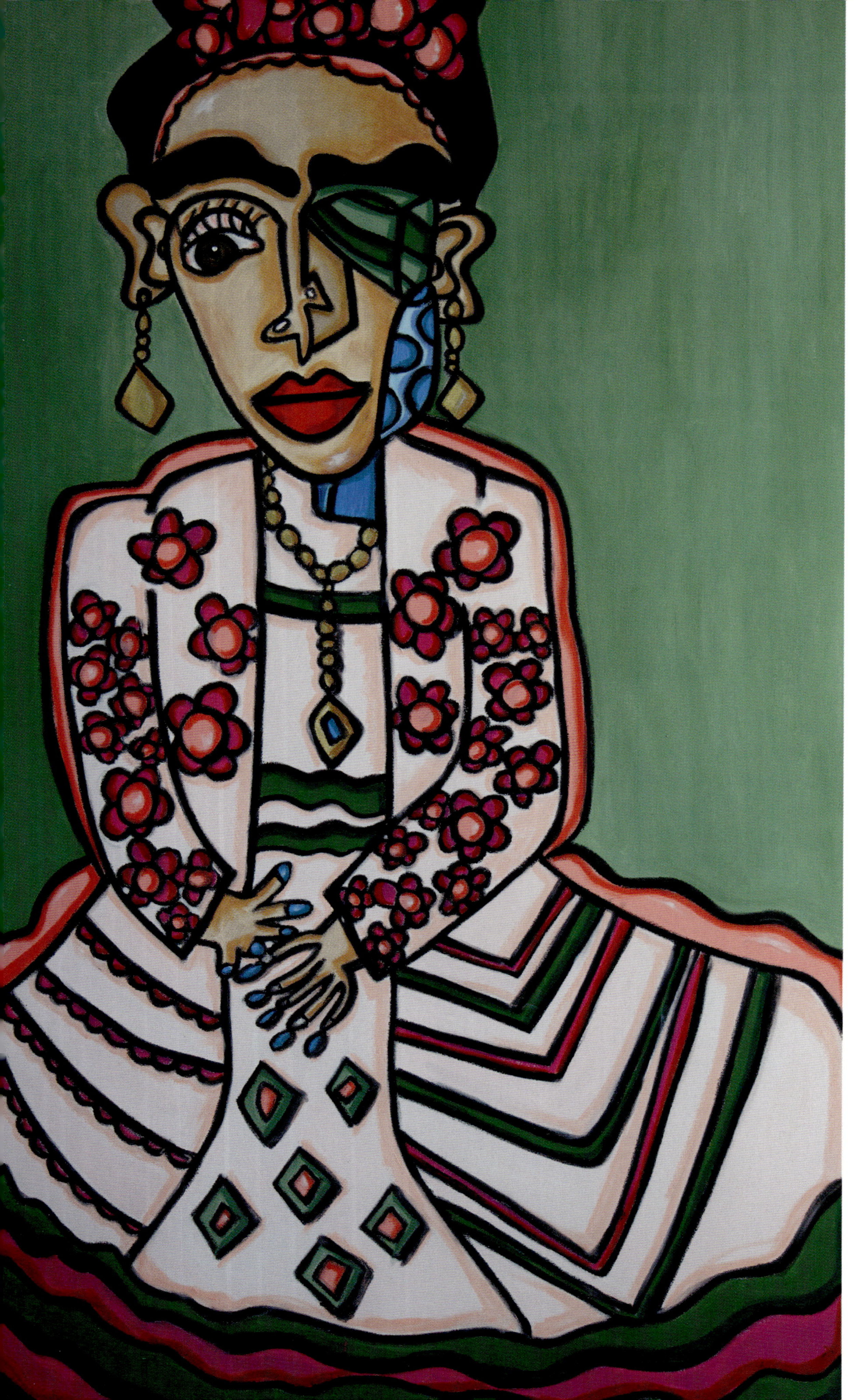

Frida Kahlo, 2023
acrylic and oil pastel
on canvas, 70 × 40 in

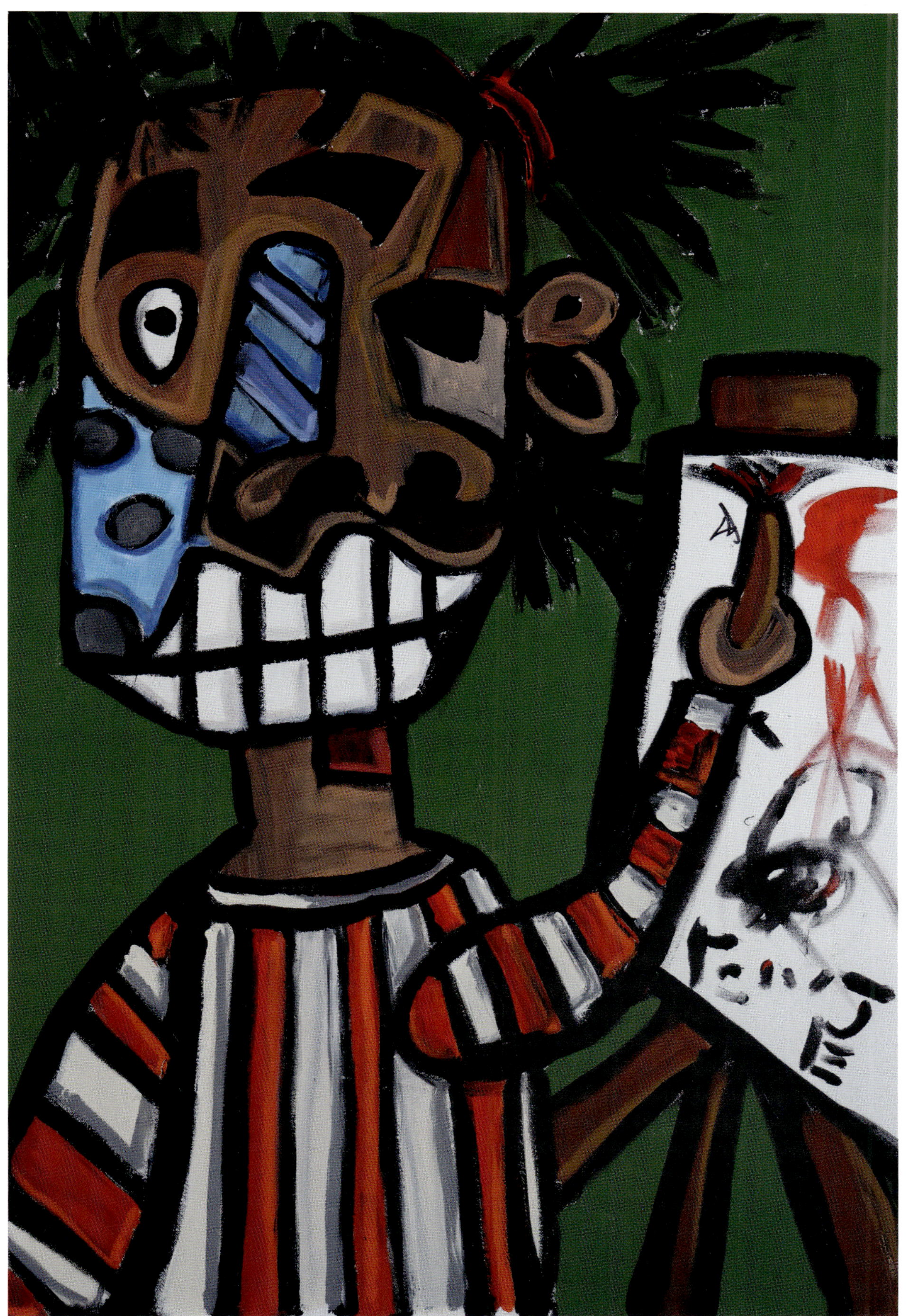

Jean-Michel Basquiat, 2023 | acrylic and oil pastel on canvas, 36 × 24 in

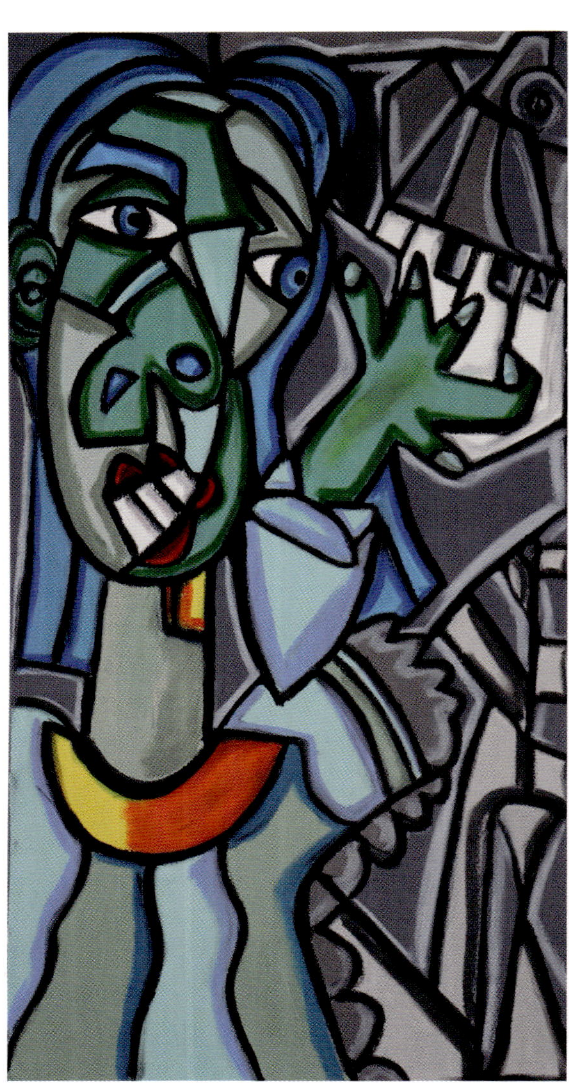

Marisa, 2023 | acrylic and oil pastel on canvas, 36 × 18 in

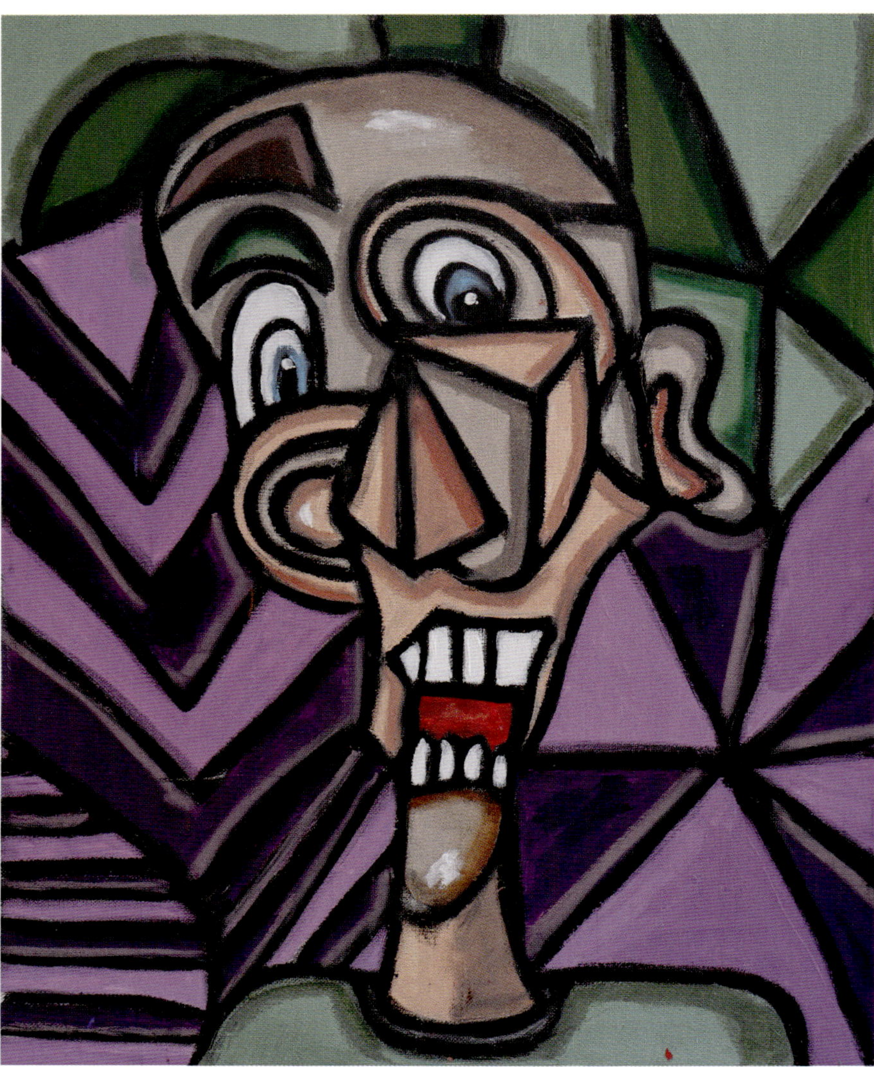

Cosmic, 2023 | acrylic and oil pastel on canvas, 20 × 16 in

Lady Cube, 2023 | acrylic and oil pastel on canvas, 40 × 30 in

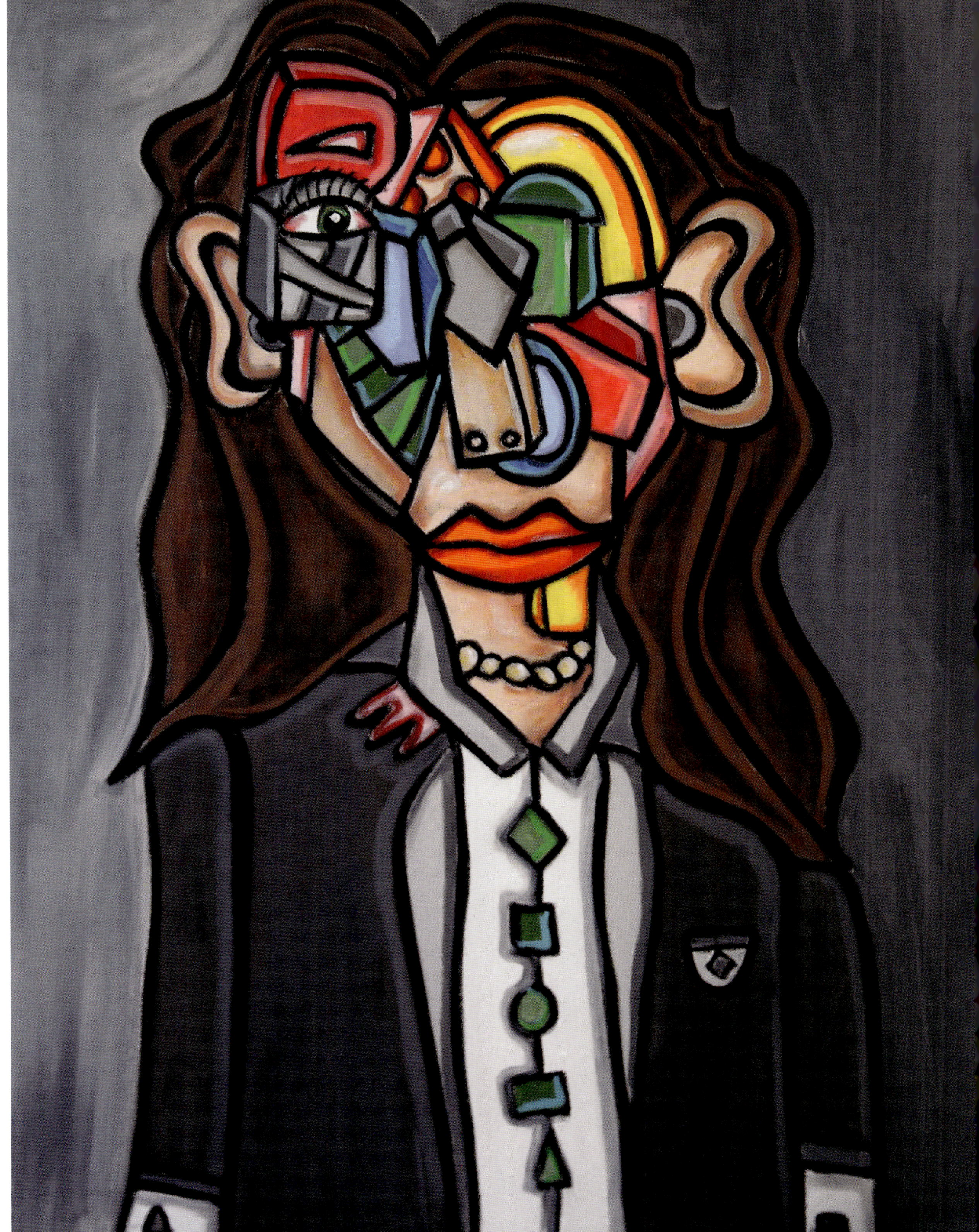

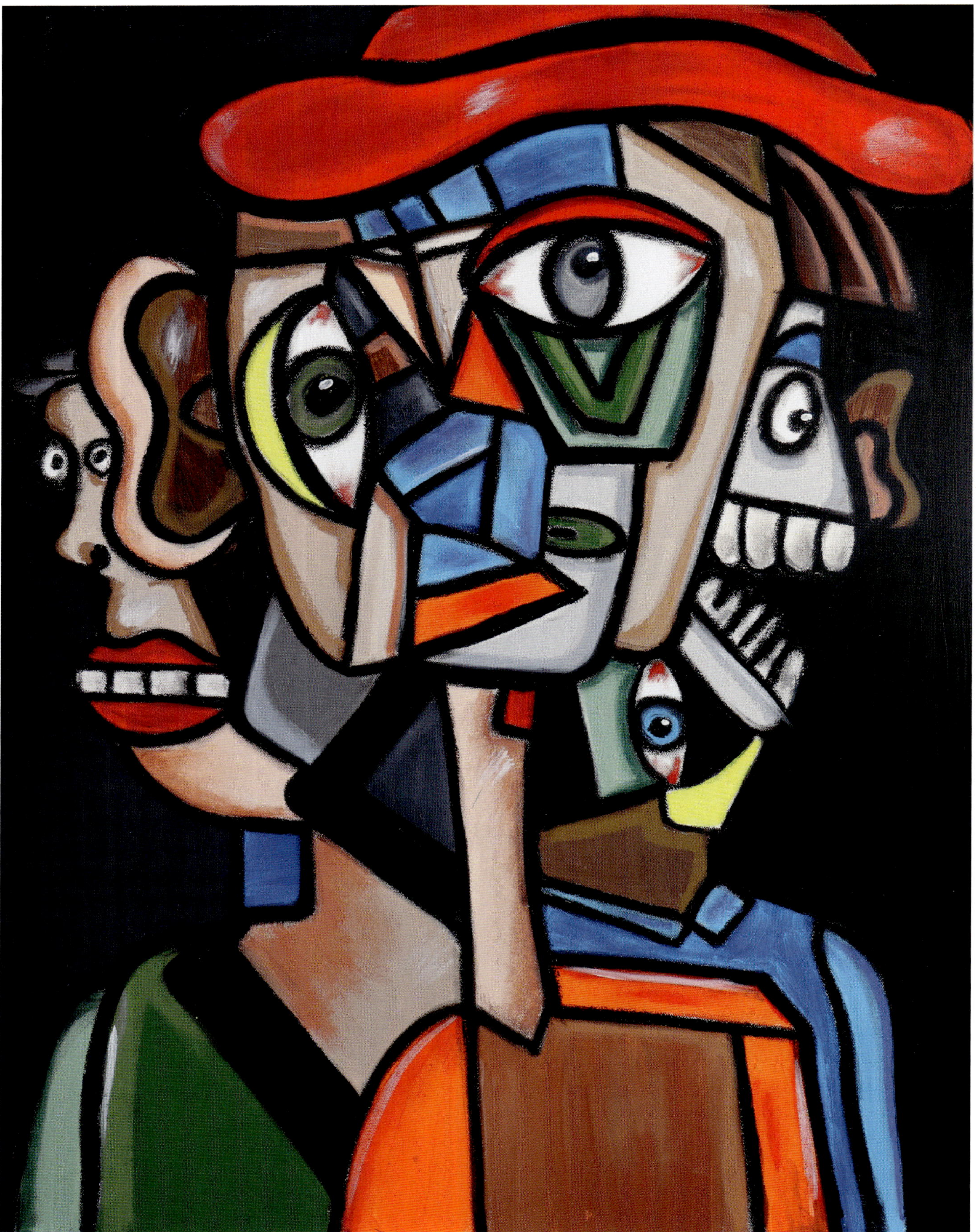

Many Opinions, 2023 | acrylic and oil pastel on canvas, 30 × 22 in

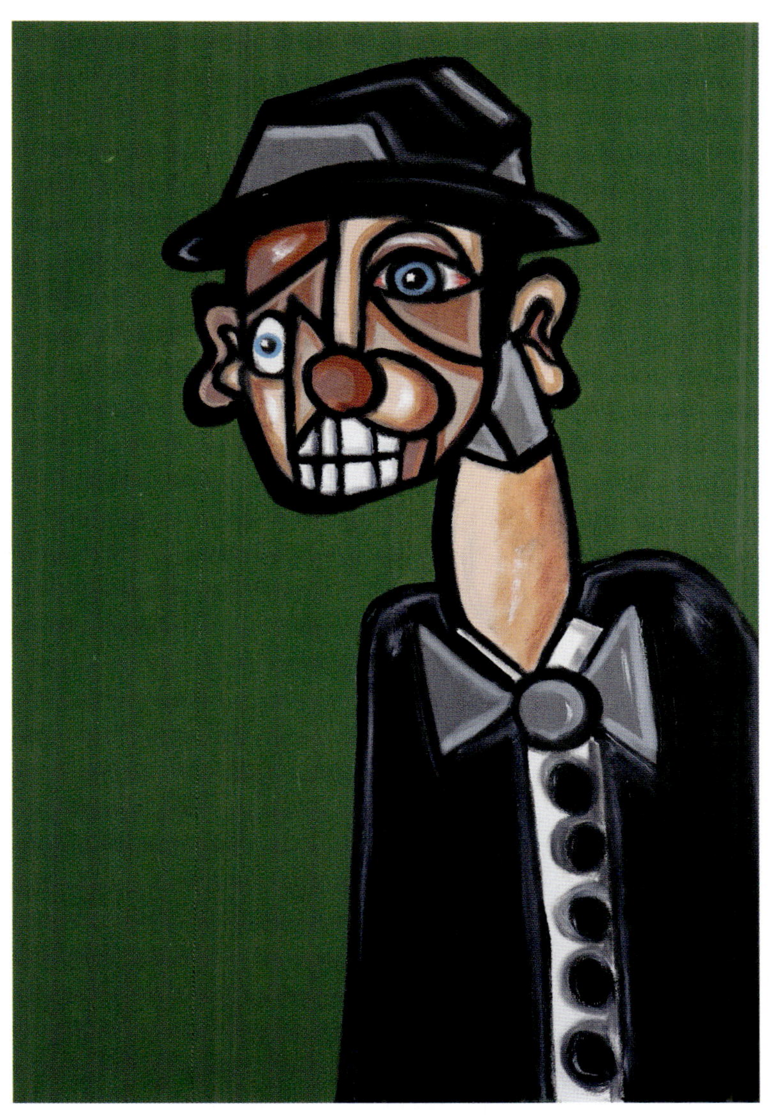

Joe, 2023
acrylic and oil pastel on canvas, 36 × 24 in

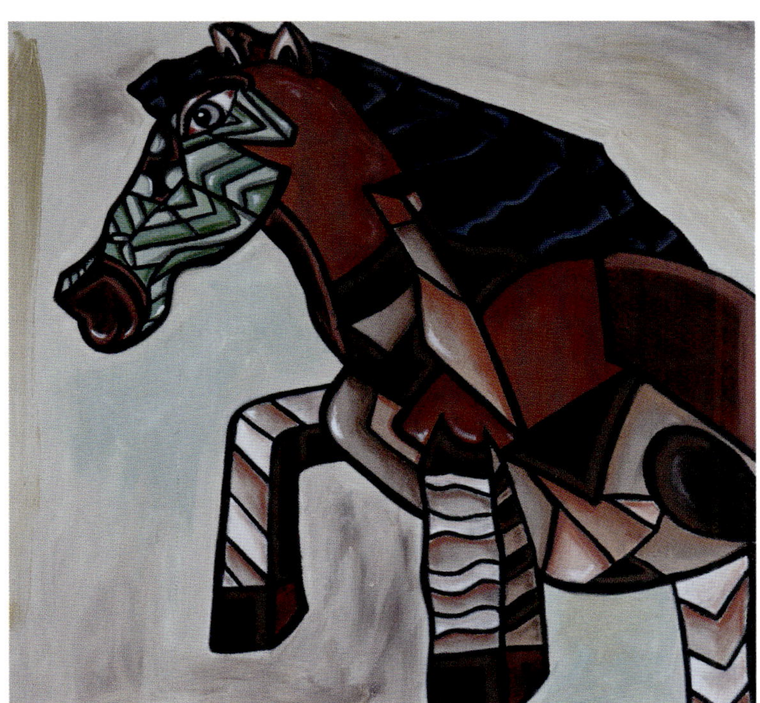

Caballo Fino, 2023
acrylic and oil pastel on canvas, 40 × 40 in

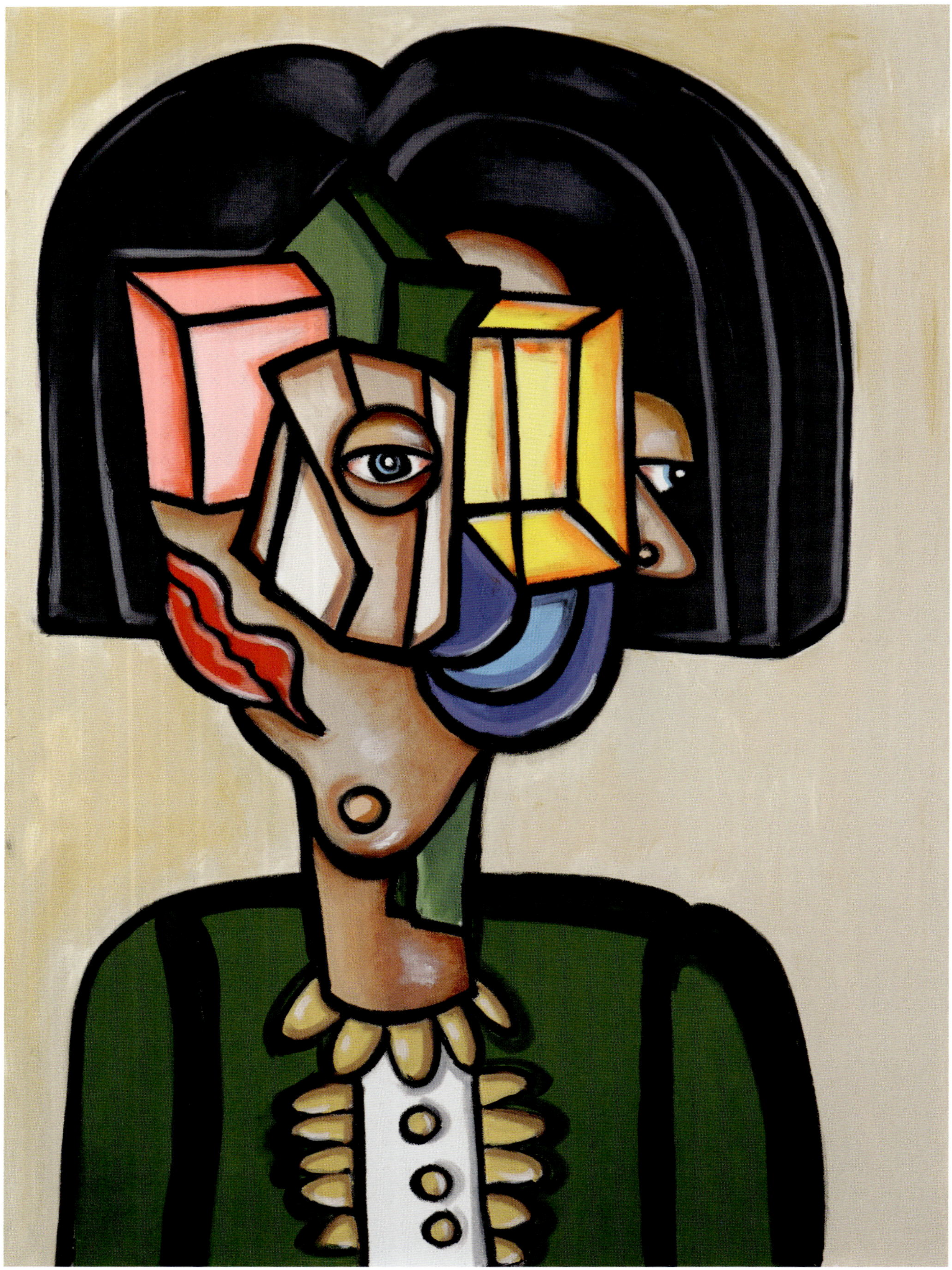

Caroline, 2023 | acrylic and oil pastel on canvas, 42 × 30 in

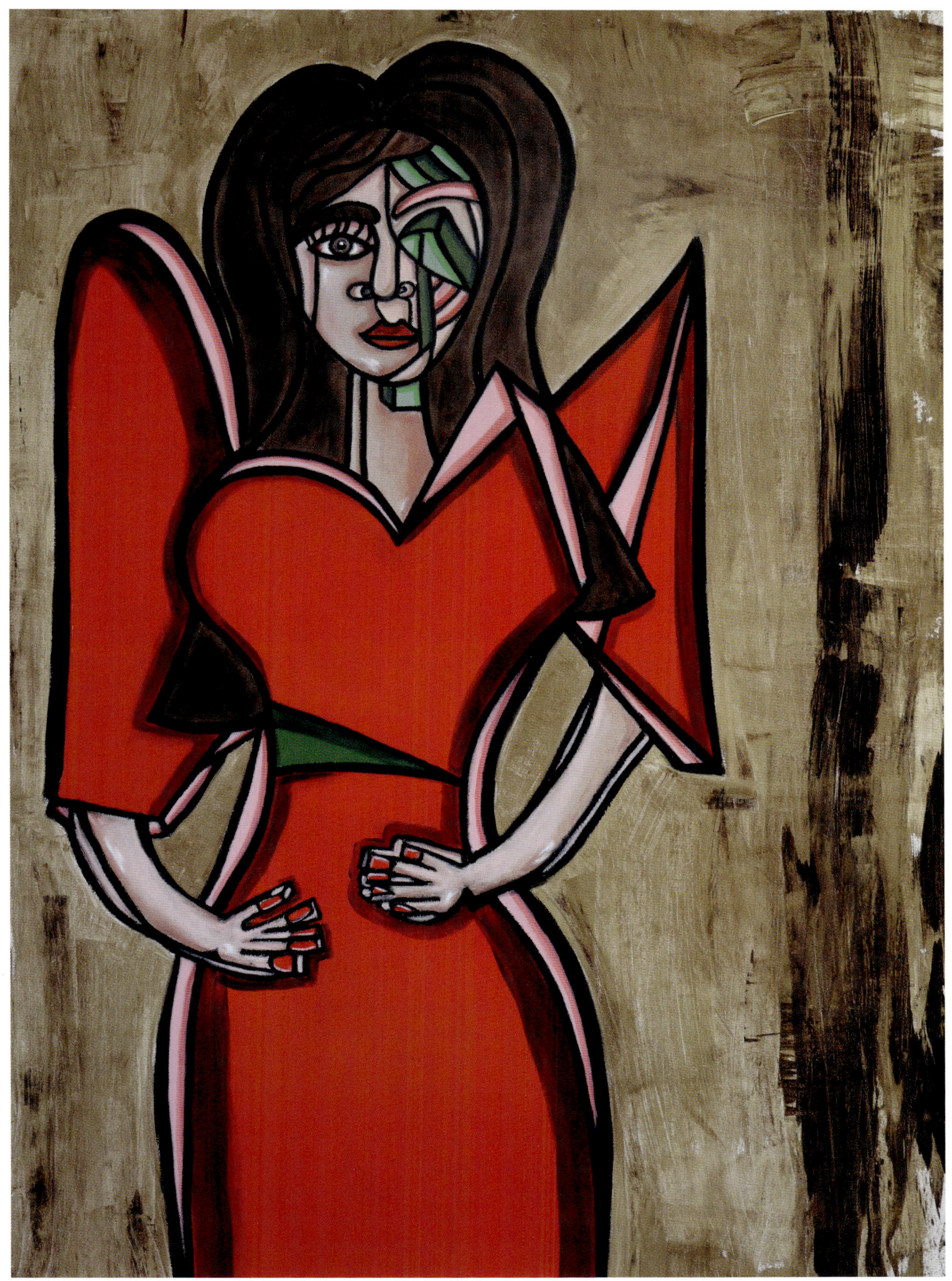

Sofía Vergara, 2023 | acrylic and oil pastel on canvas, 69 × 48 in

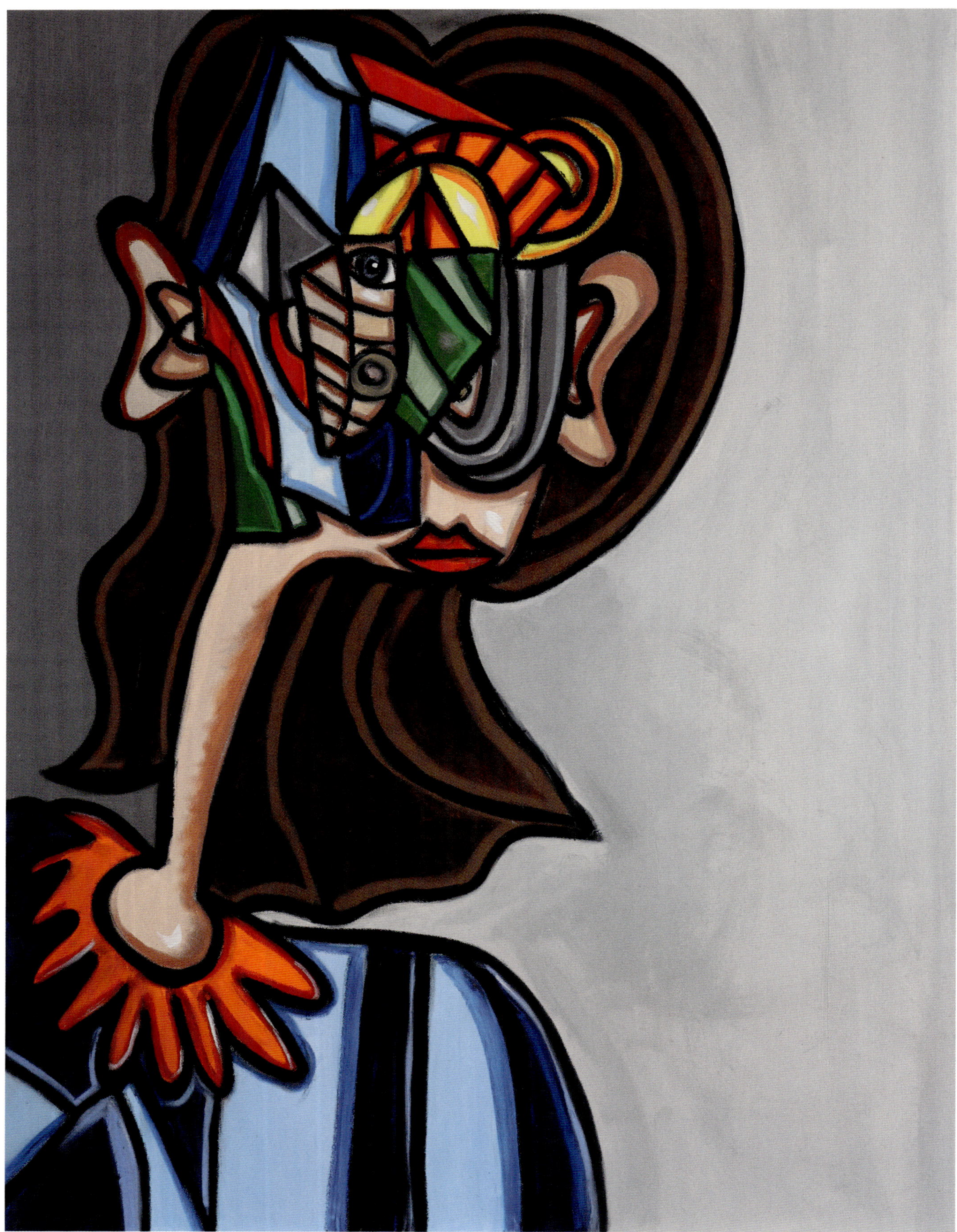

Divina, 2023 │ acrylic and oil pastel on canvas, 40 × 30 in

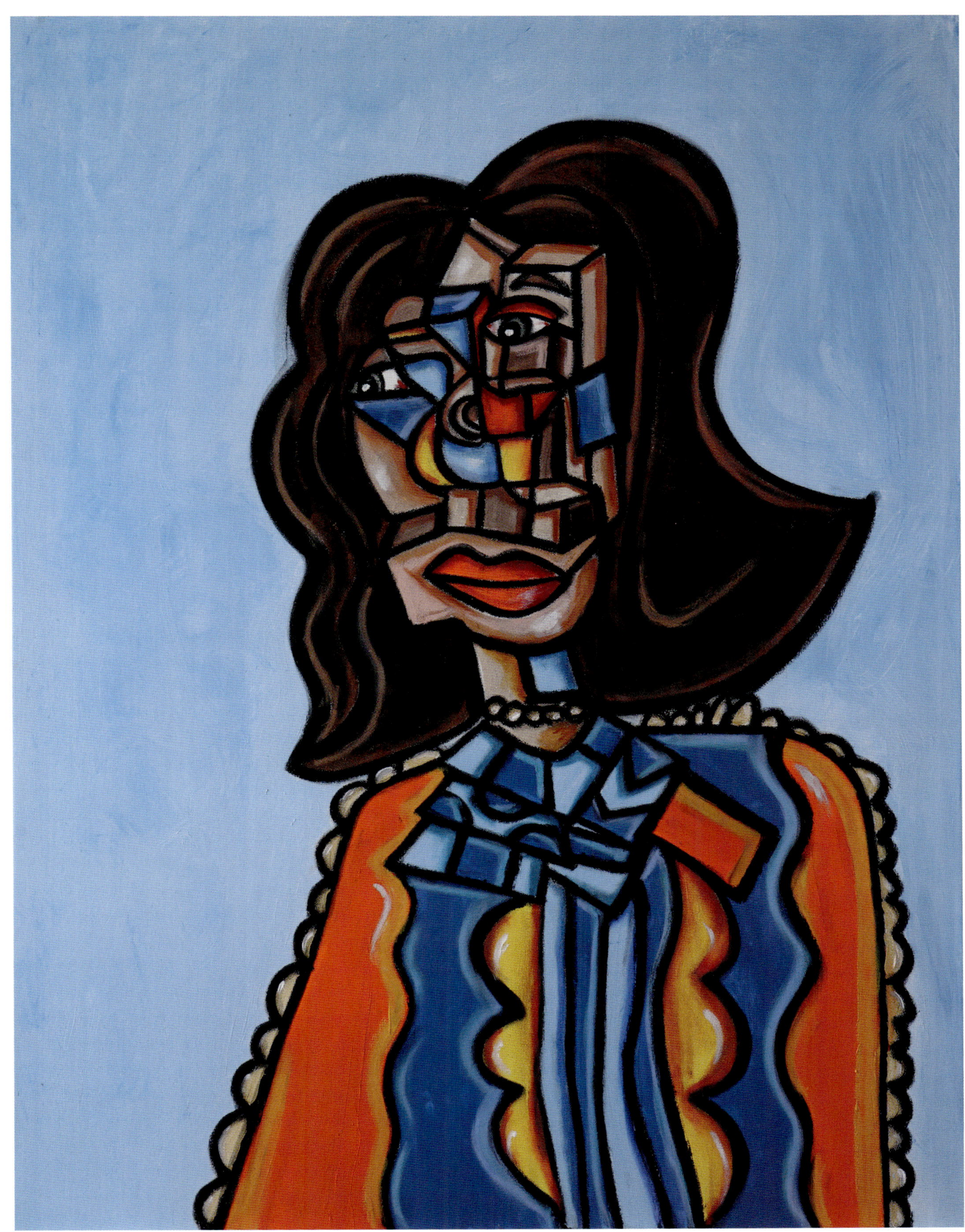

Society Lady, 2023 | acrylic and oil pastel on canvas, 40 × 36 in

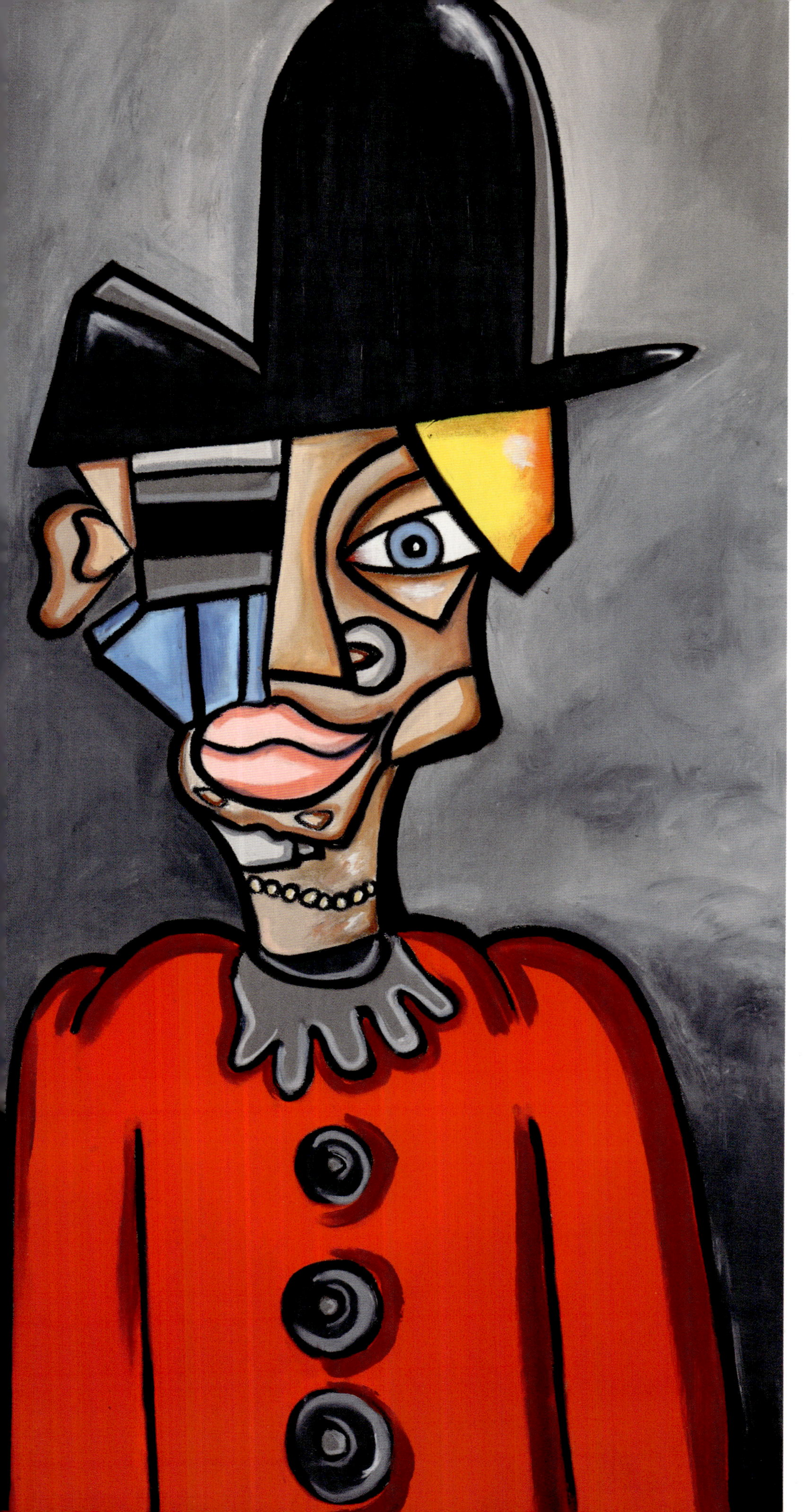

Otto, 2023
acrylic and oil pastel on canvas, 60 × 30 in

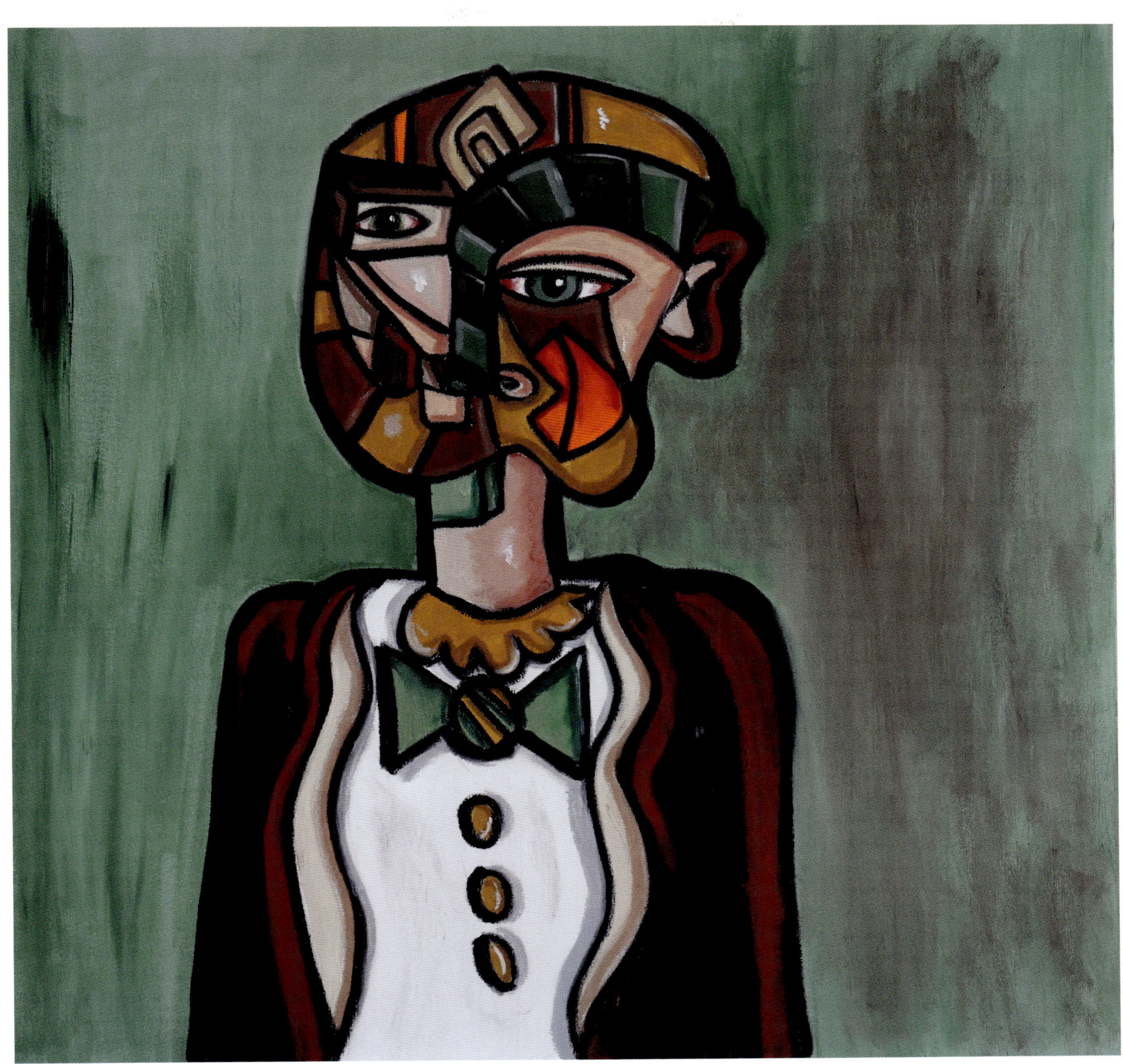

Master Mind, 2023 │ acrylic and oil pastel on canvas, 36 × 36 in

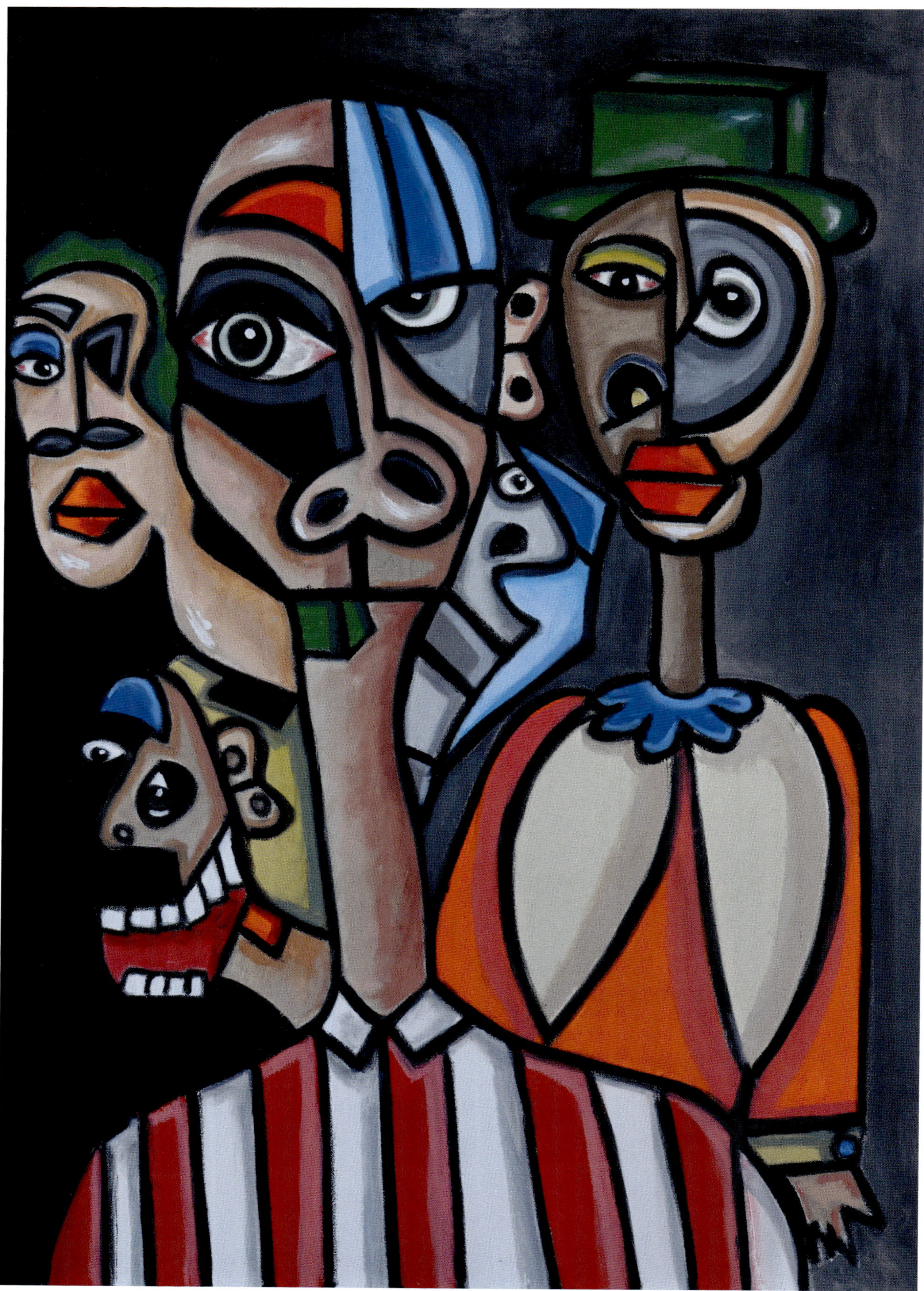

The Family Portrait, 2023 | acrylic and oil pastel on canvas, 42 × 30 in

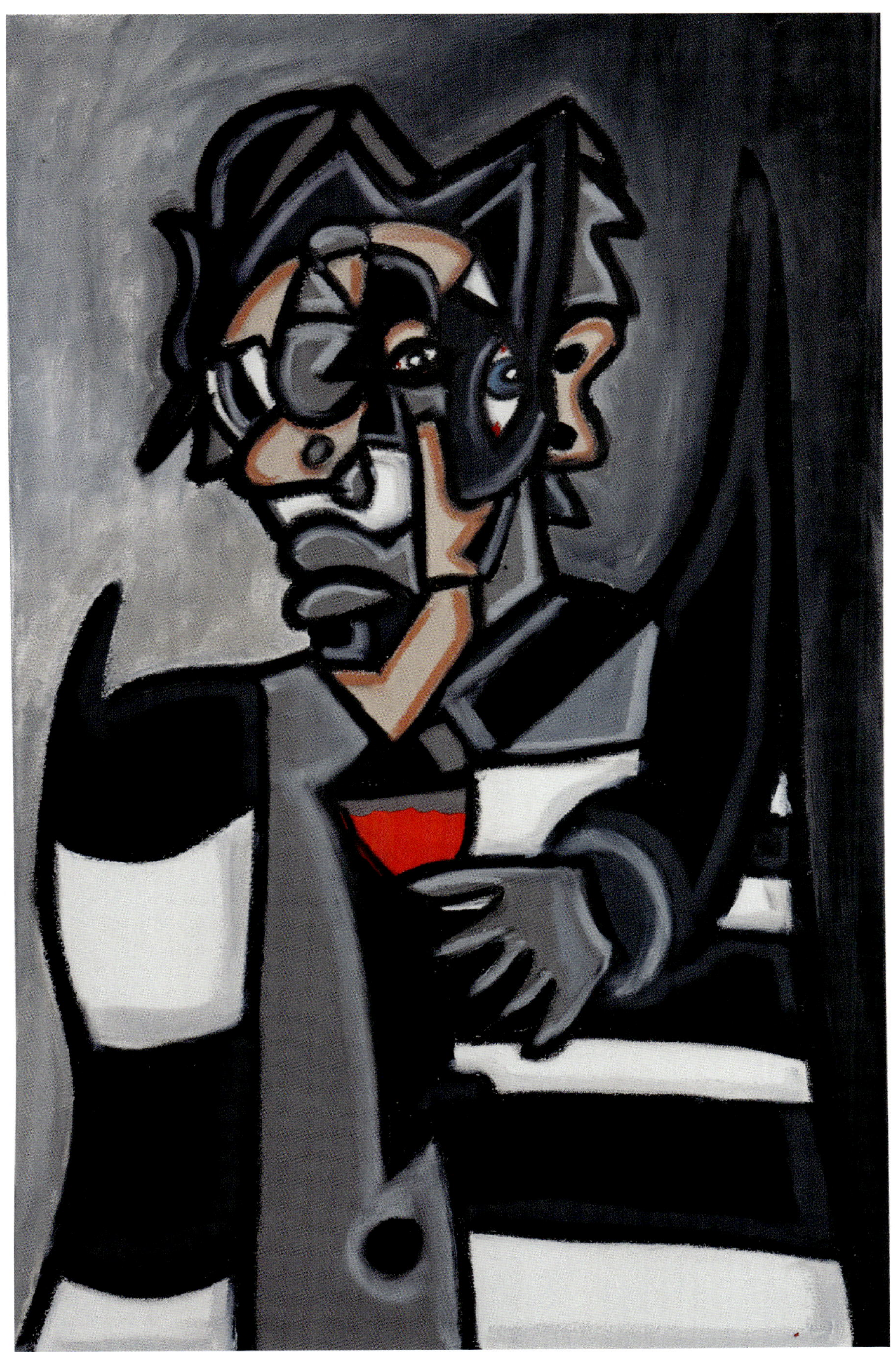

Surreal Man, 2023 | acrylic and oil pastel on canvas, 32 × 20 in

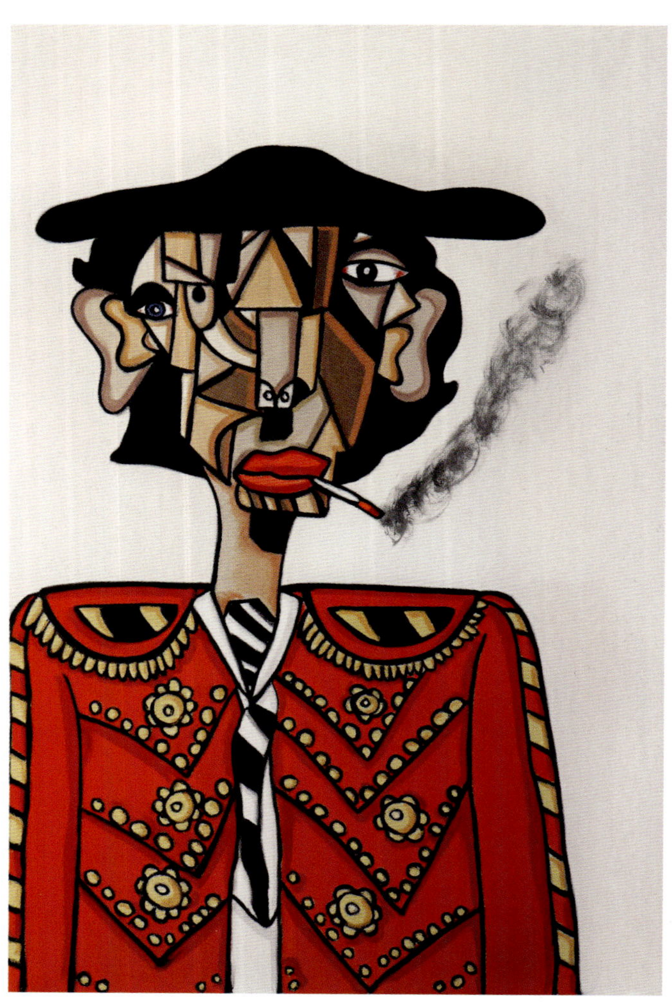

Magnifico Torero, 2023 | acrylic and oil pastel on canvas, 60 × 40 in

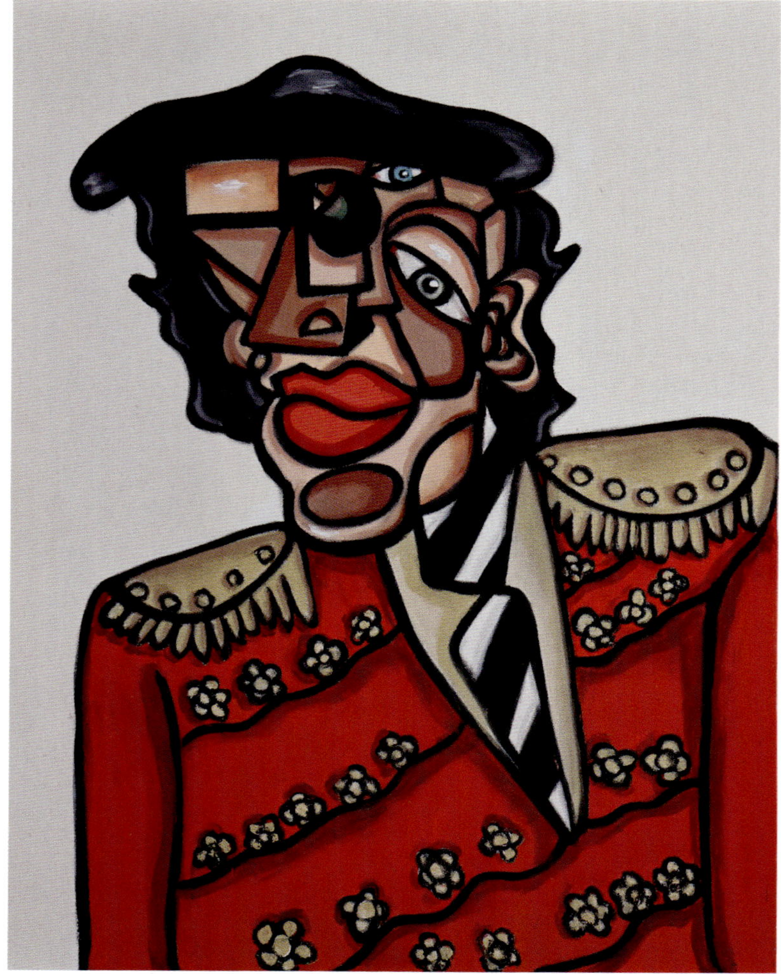

Traje De Luces, 2023 | acrylic and oil pastel on canvas, 36 × 28 in

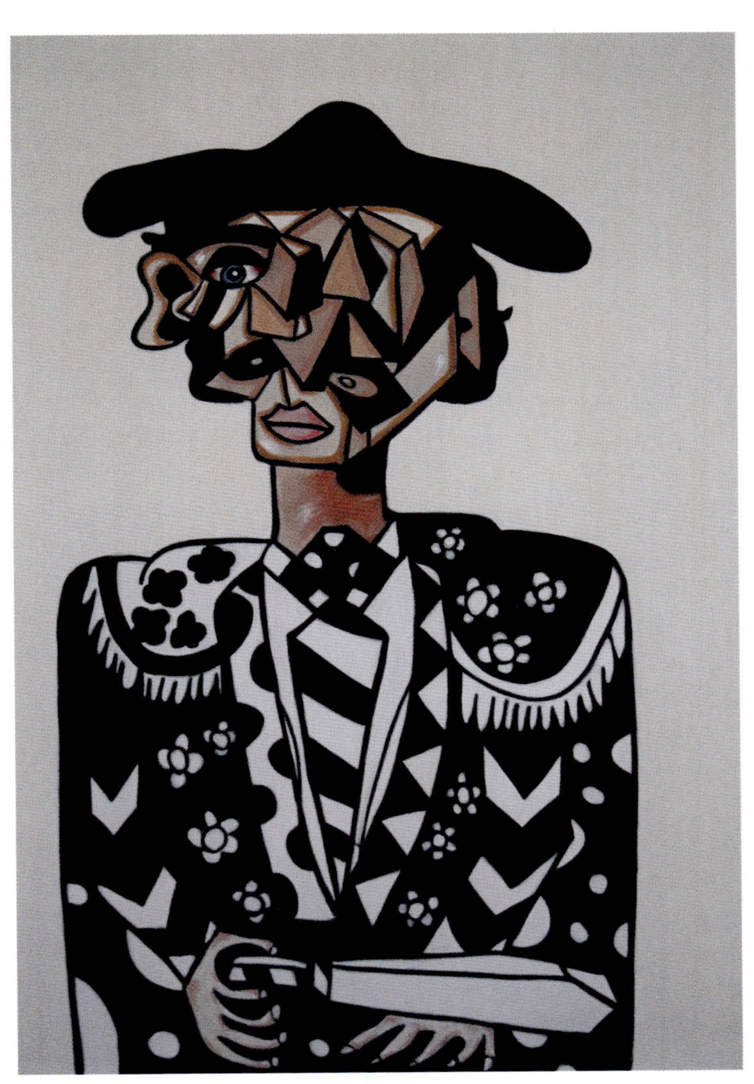

El Matador, 2023 | acrylic and oil pastel on canvas, 60 × 40 in

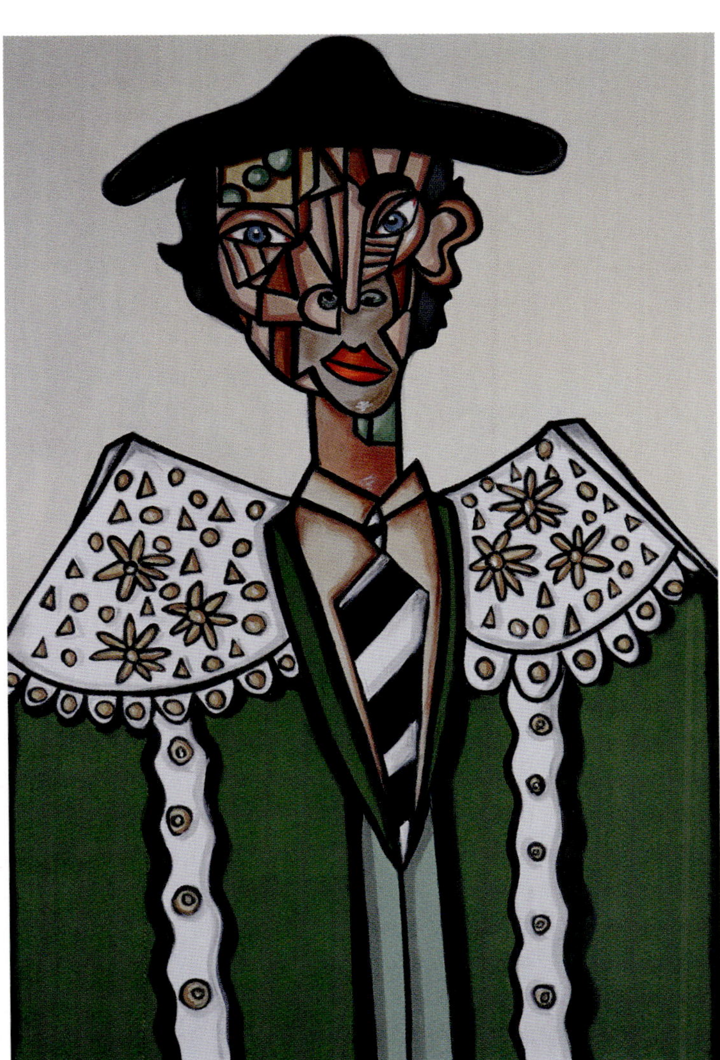

Torerito, 2023 | acrylic and oil pastel on canvas, 60 × 40 in

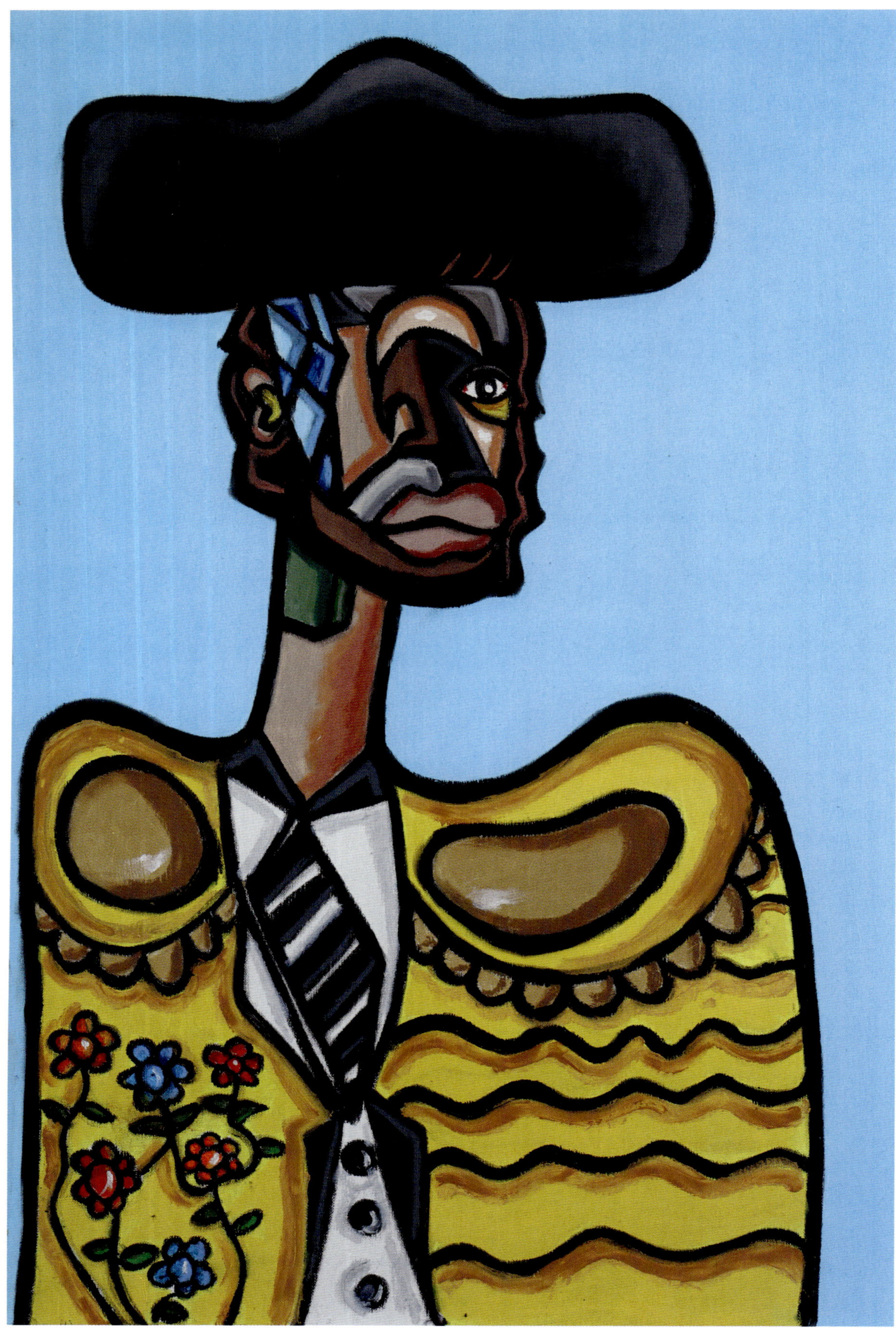

Sebastian, 2023 | acrylic and oil pastel on canvas, 36 × 24 in

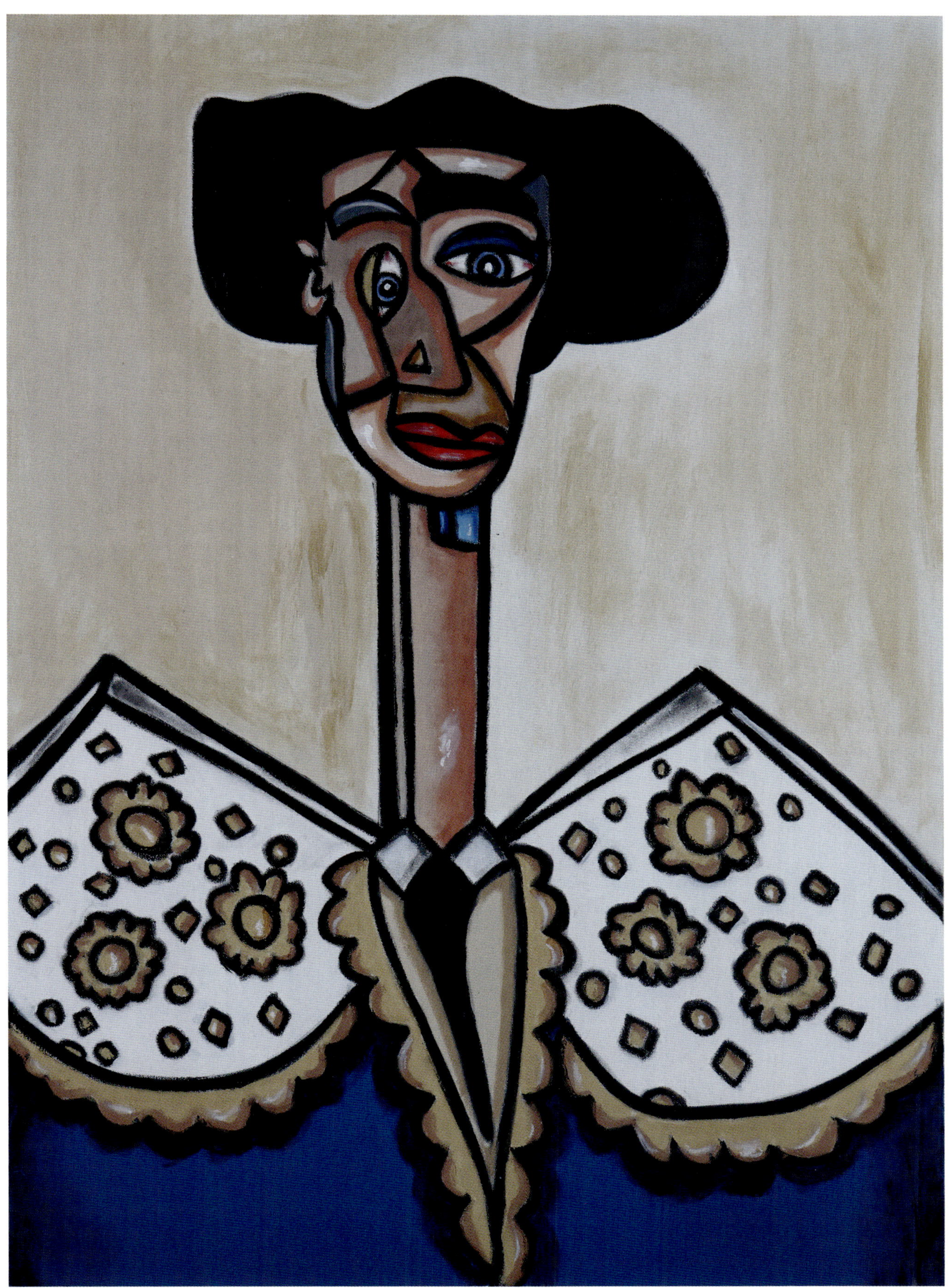

Gran Torero, 2023 │ acrylic and oil on canvas, 42 × 30 in

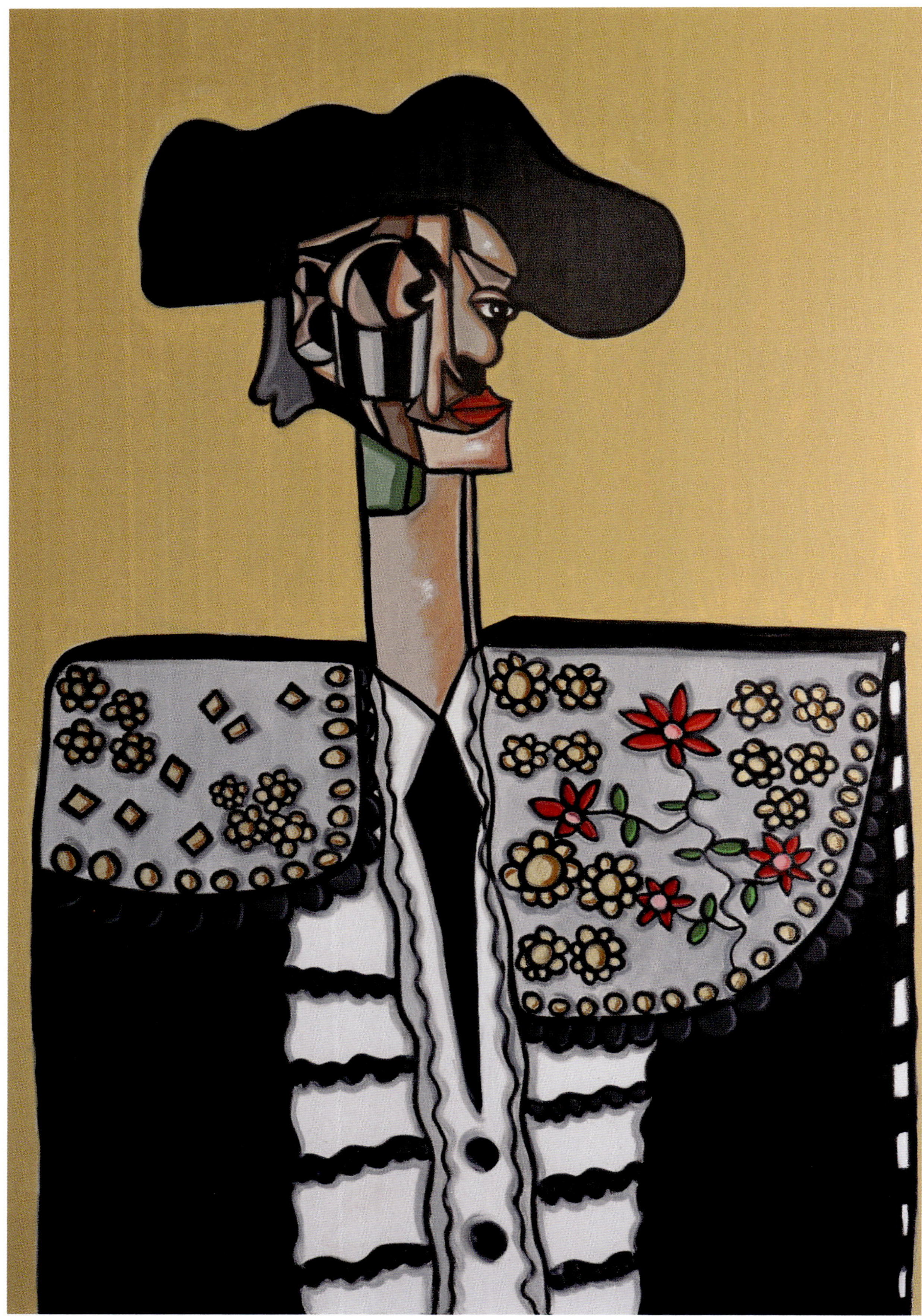

Romero, 2023 | acrylic and oil pastel on canvas, 72 × 48 in

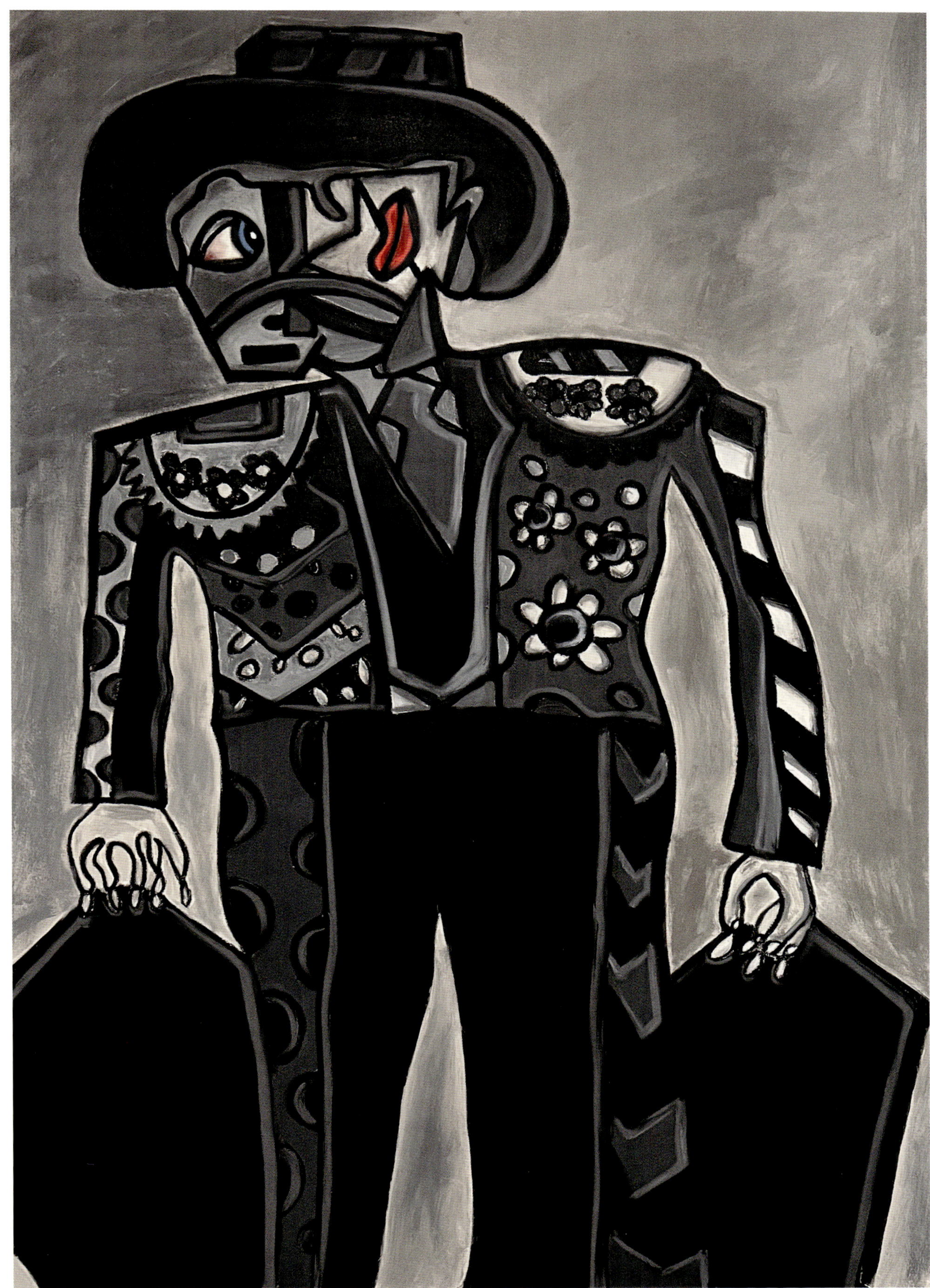

Torero, 2023 | acrylic and oil pastel on canvas, 60 × 40 in

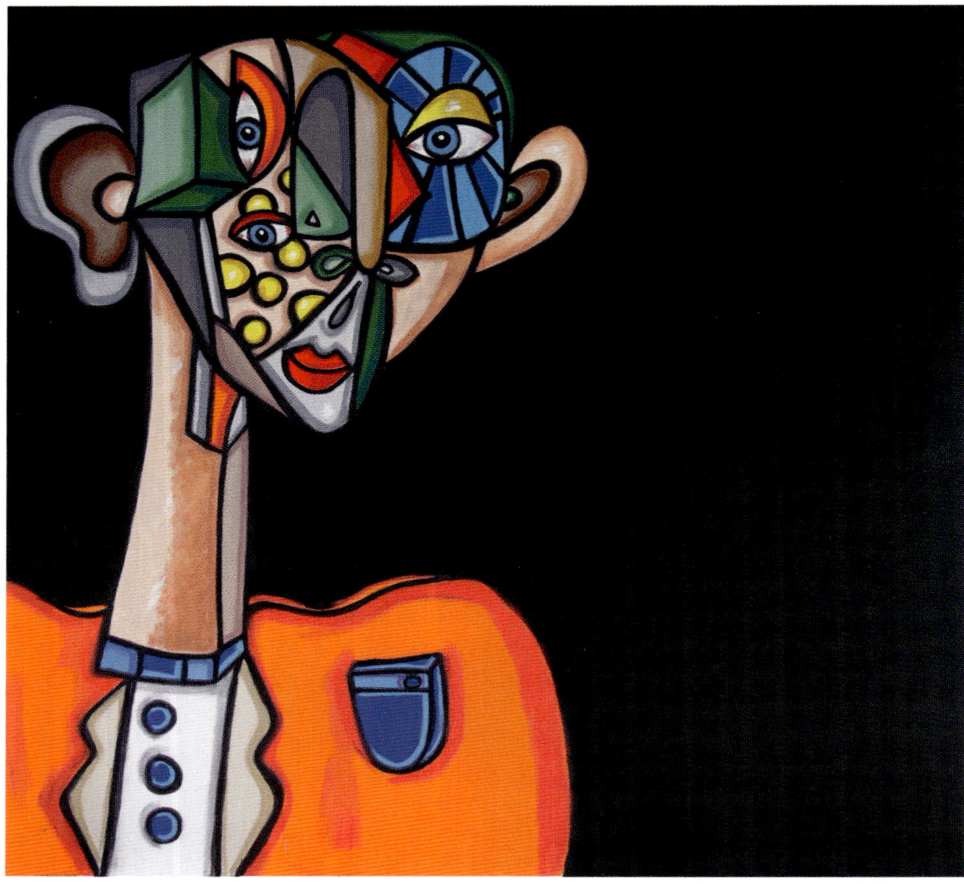

Minds in Motion, 2023
acrylic and oil pastel on canvas, 60 × 60 in

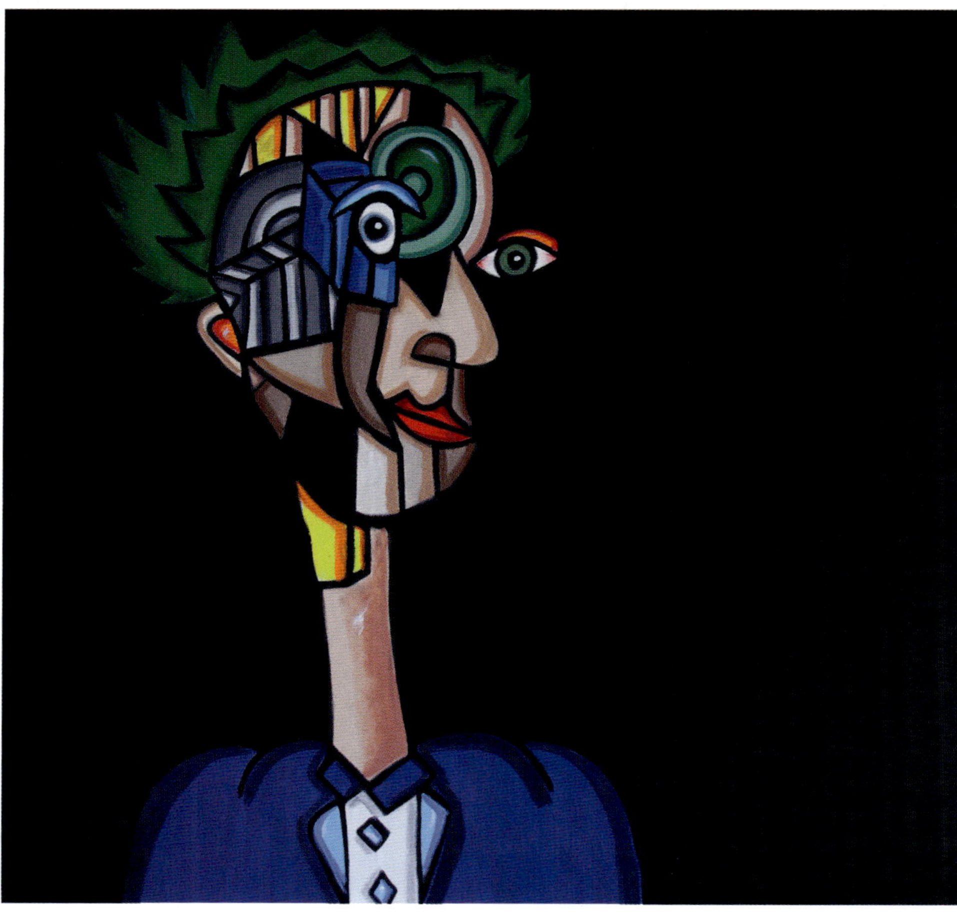

Sharp Man, 2023
acrylic and oil pastel on canvas, 60 × 60 in

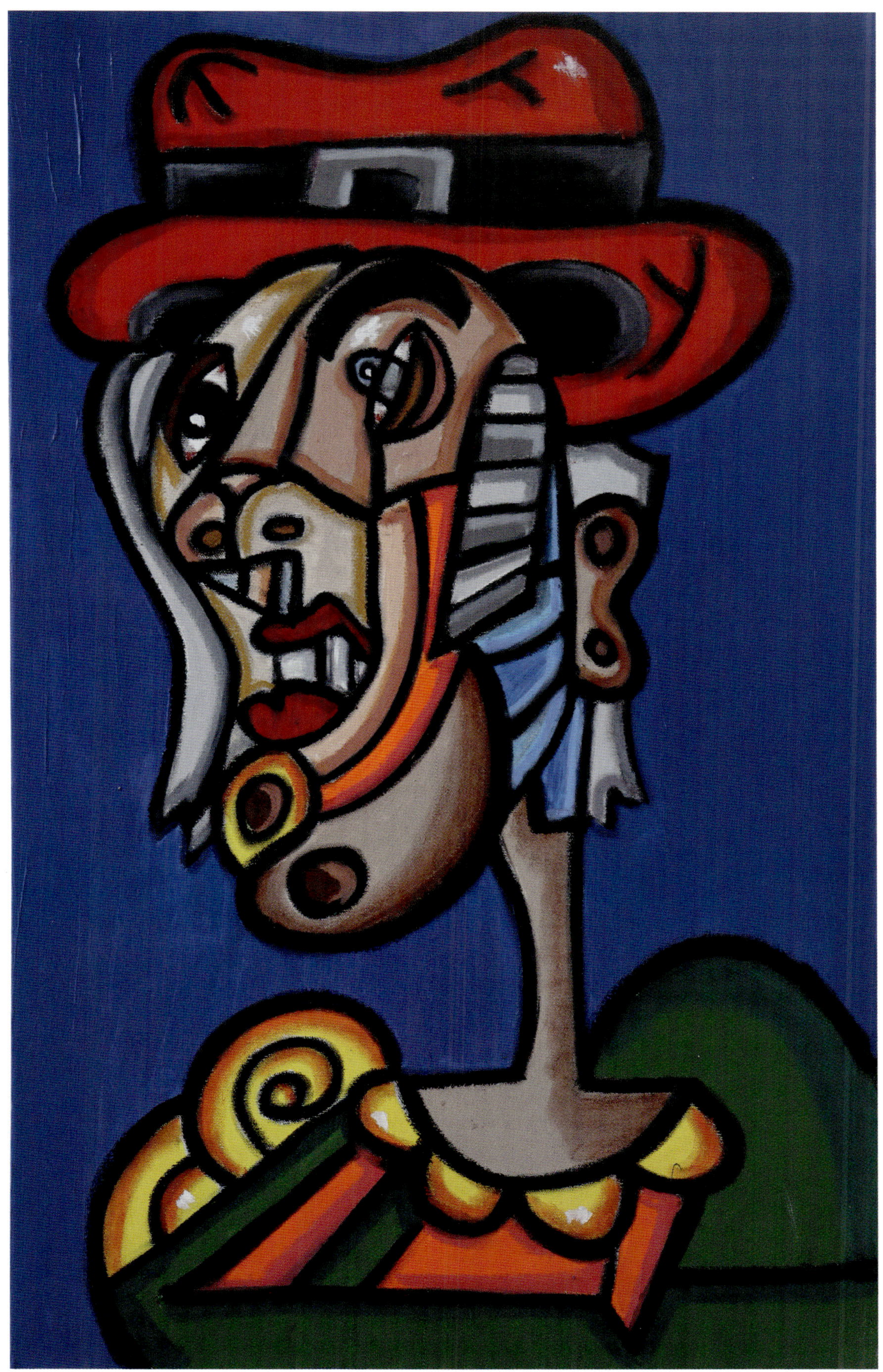

Rock Star, 2024 | acrylic and oil pastel on canvas, 29 × 18 in

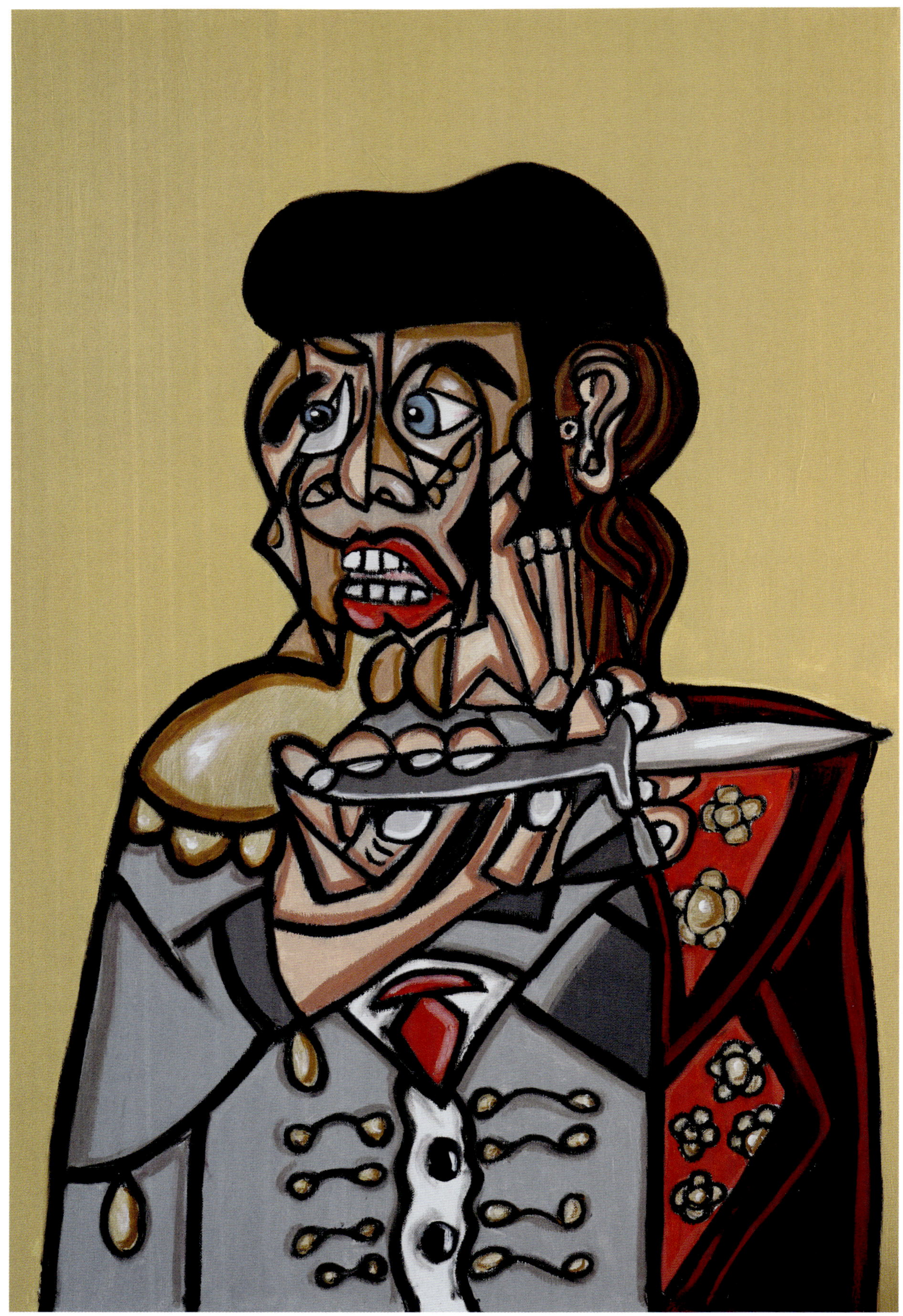

Benito, 2024 | acrylic and oil pastel on canvas, 36 × 24 in

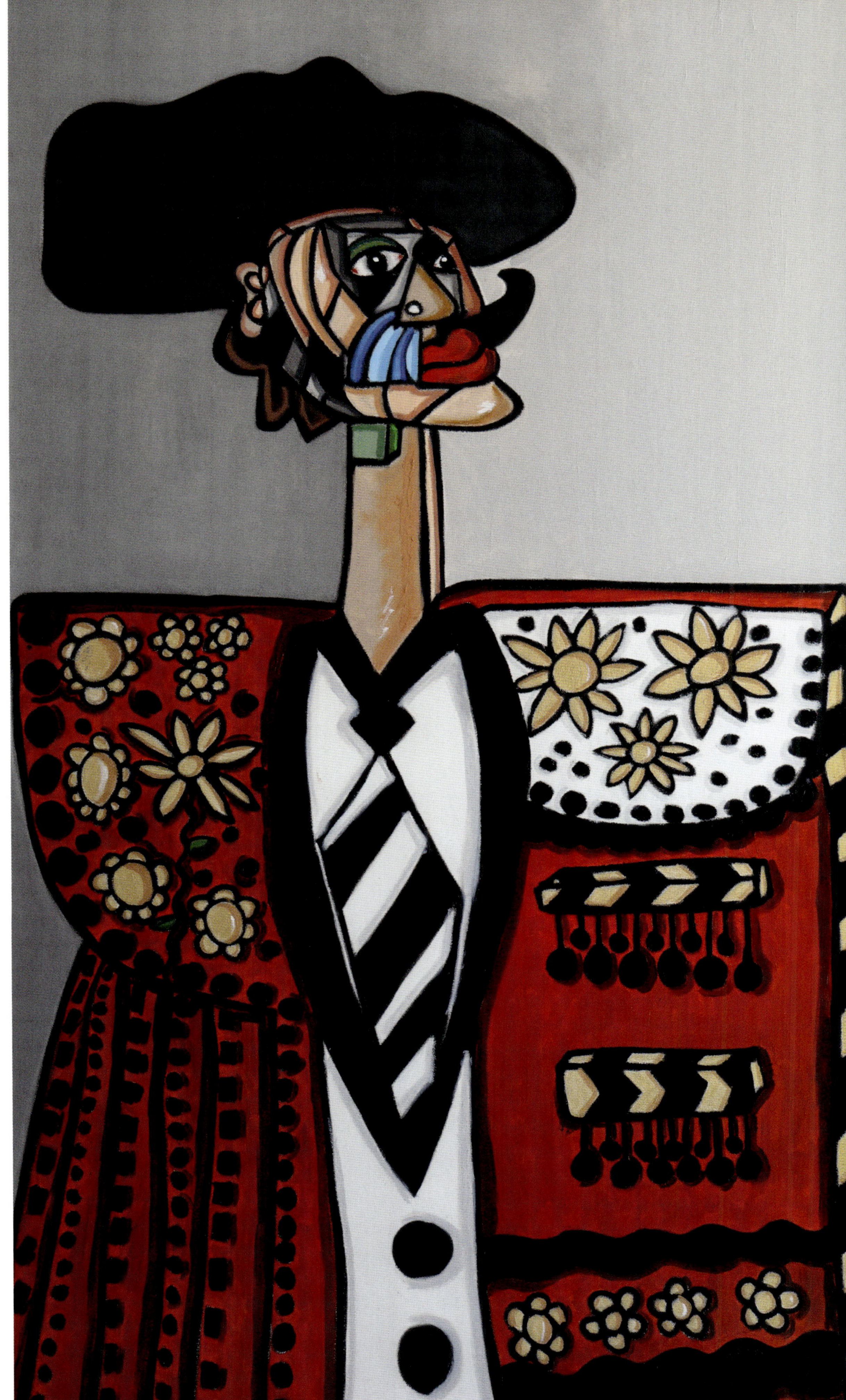

Francisco, 2024
acrylic and oil pastel
on canvas, 72 × 48 in

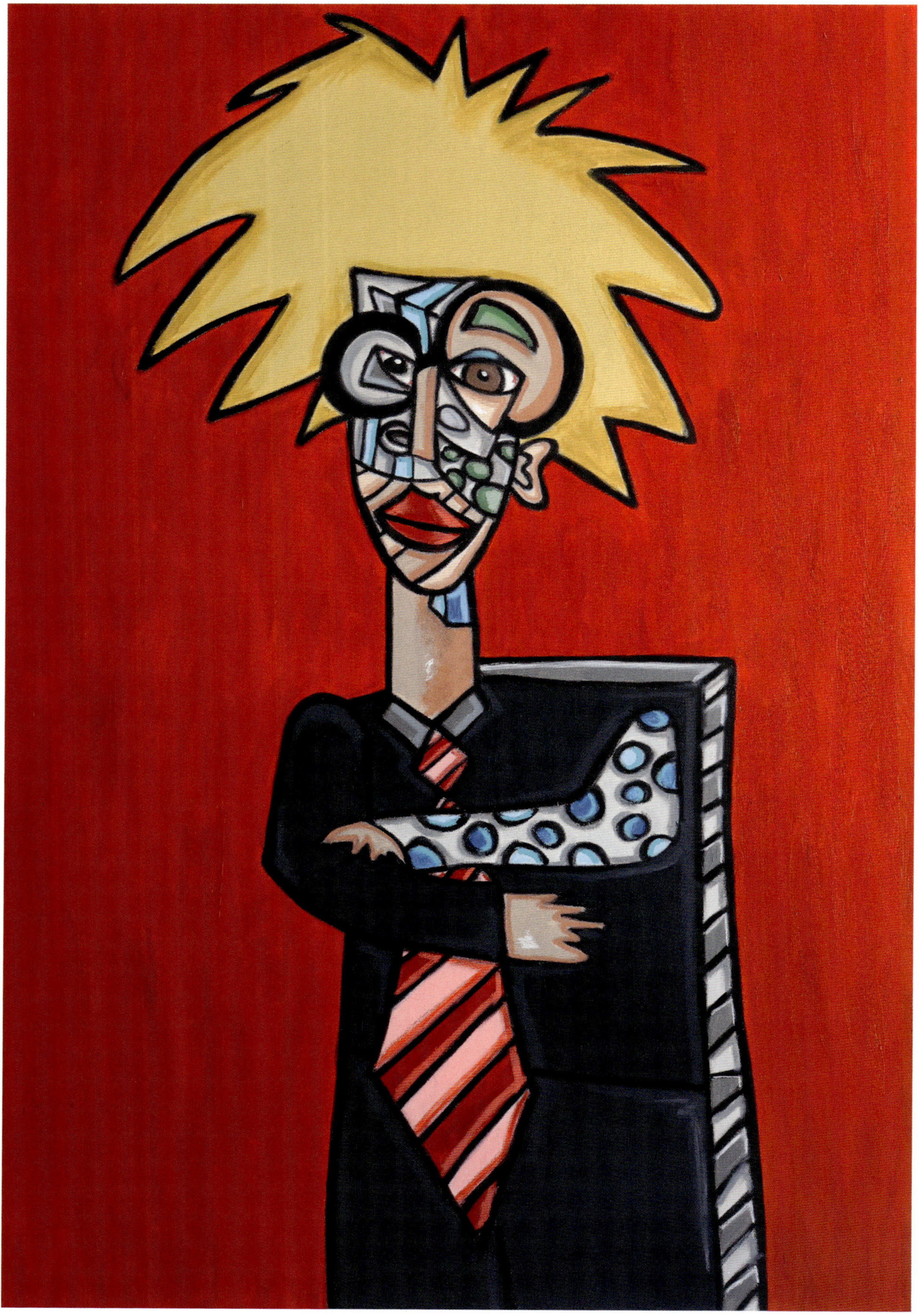

Andy Warhol, 2024 | acrylic and oil pastel on canvas, 60 × 40 in

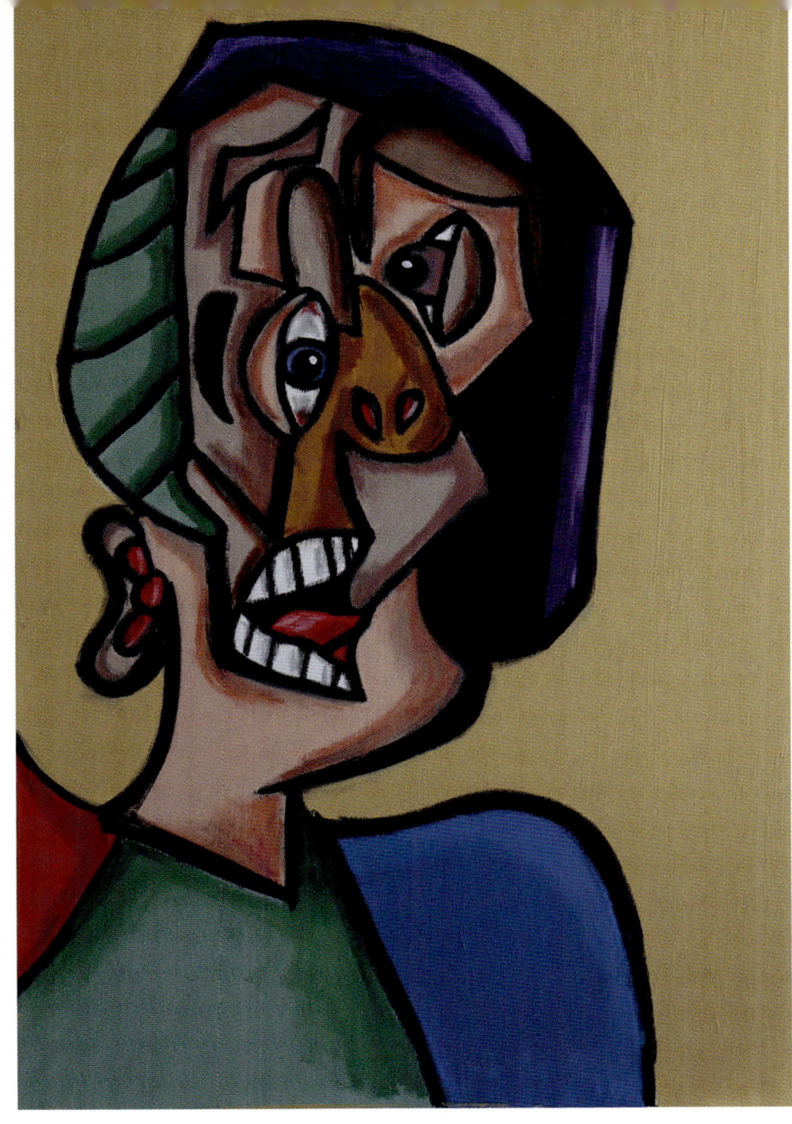

Roberto, 2024
acrylic and oil pastel on canvas, 36 × 24 in

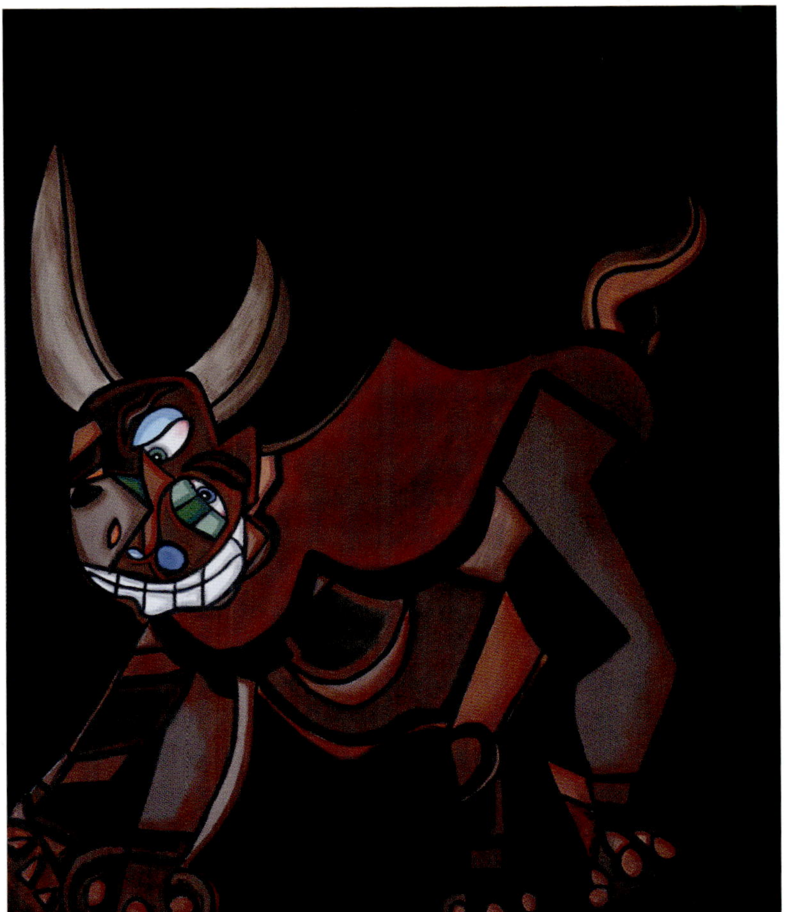

Sagrado Toro, 2024
acrylic and oil pastel on canvas, 72 × 60 in

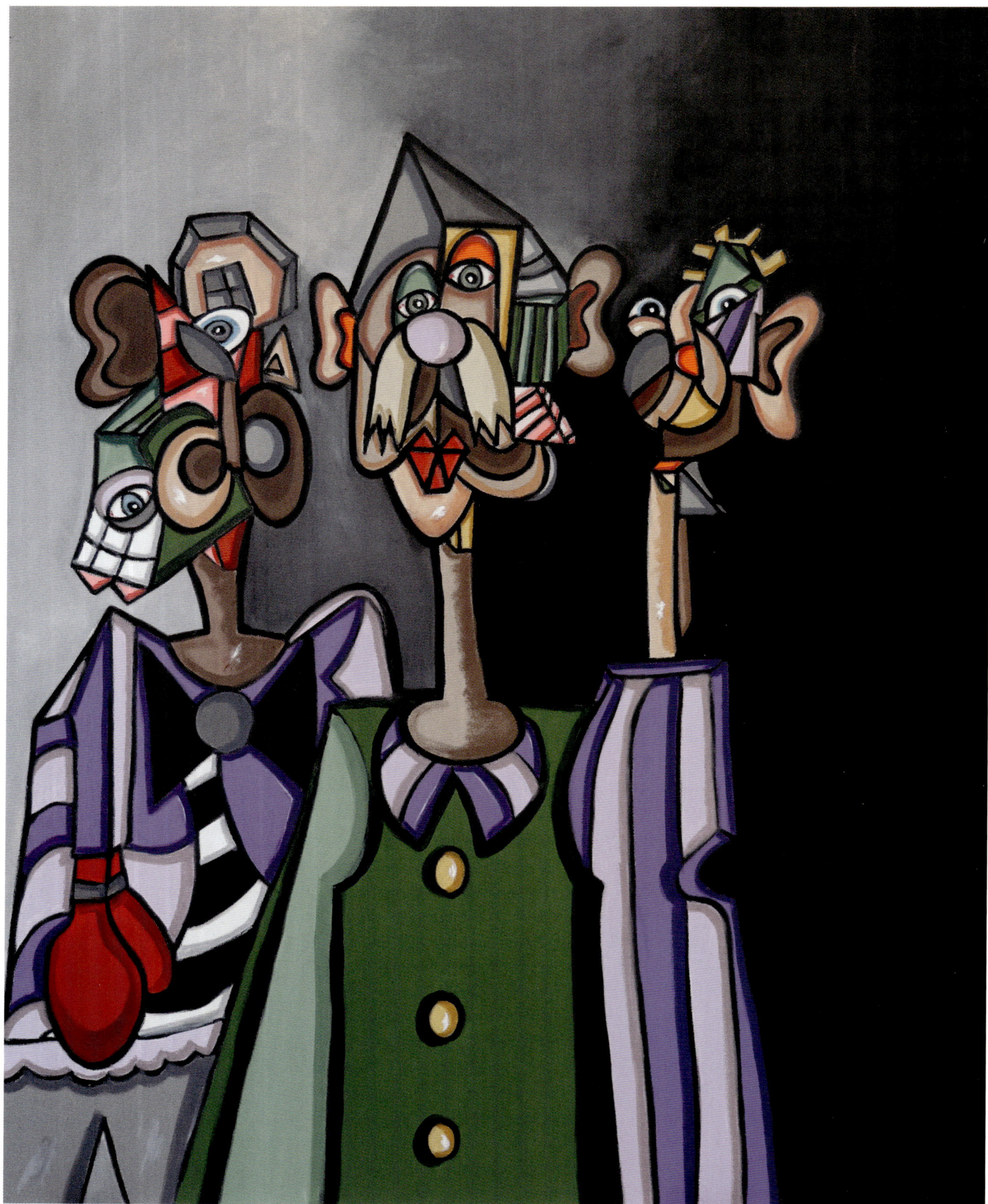

The Untouchables, 2024 | acrylic and oil pastel on canvas, 72 x 60 in

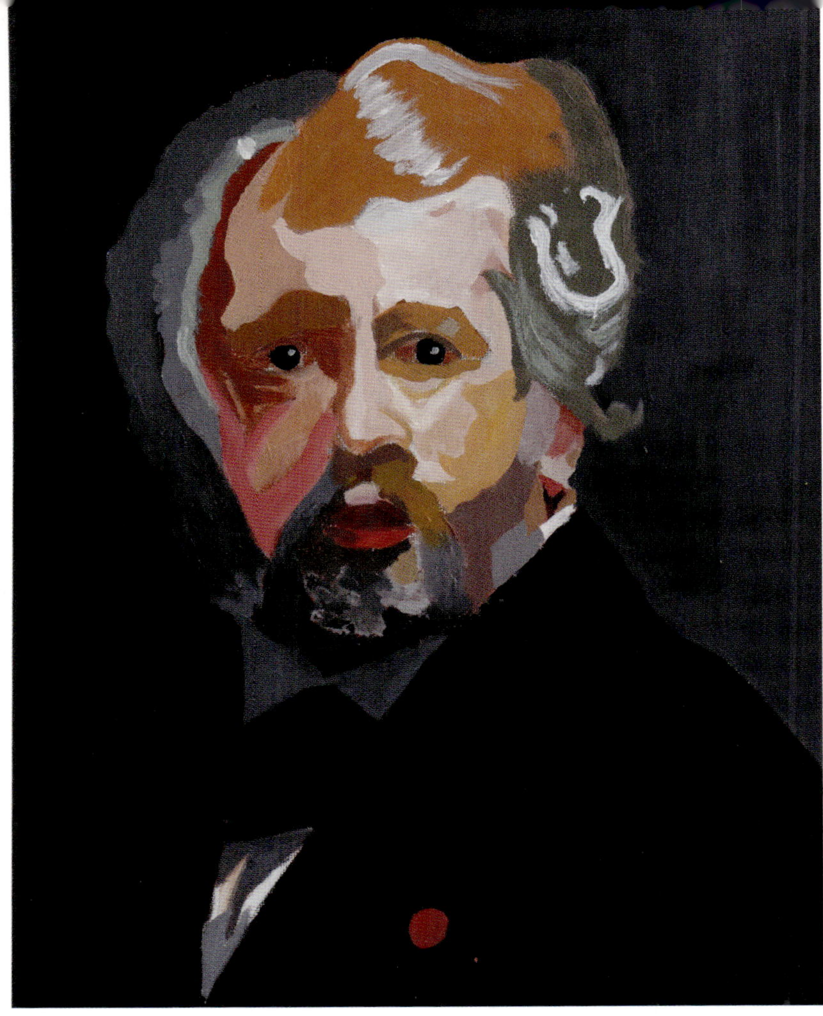

William Adolphe Bouguereau, 2024
acrylic and oil pastel on canvas, 14 × 11 in

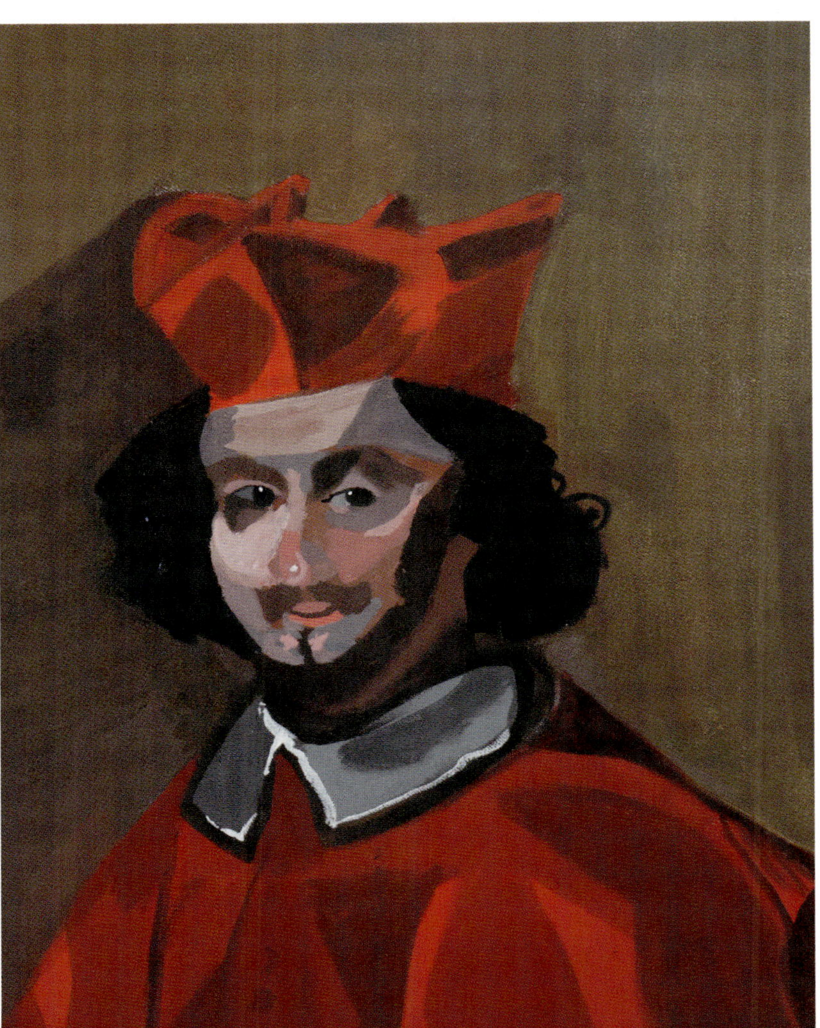

Cardinal Camillo Astali Pamphili, 2024
acrylic and oil pastel on canvas, 20 × 16 in

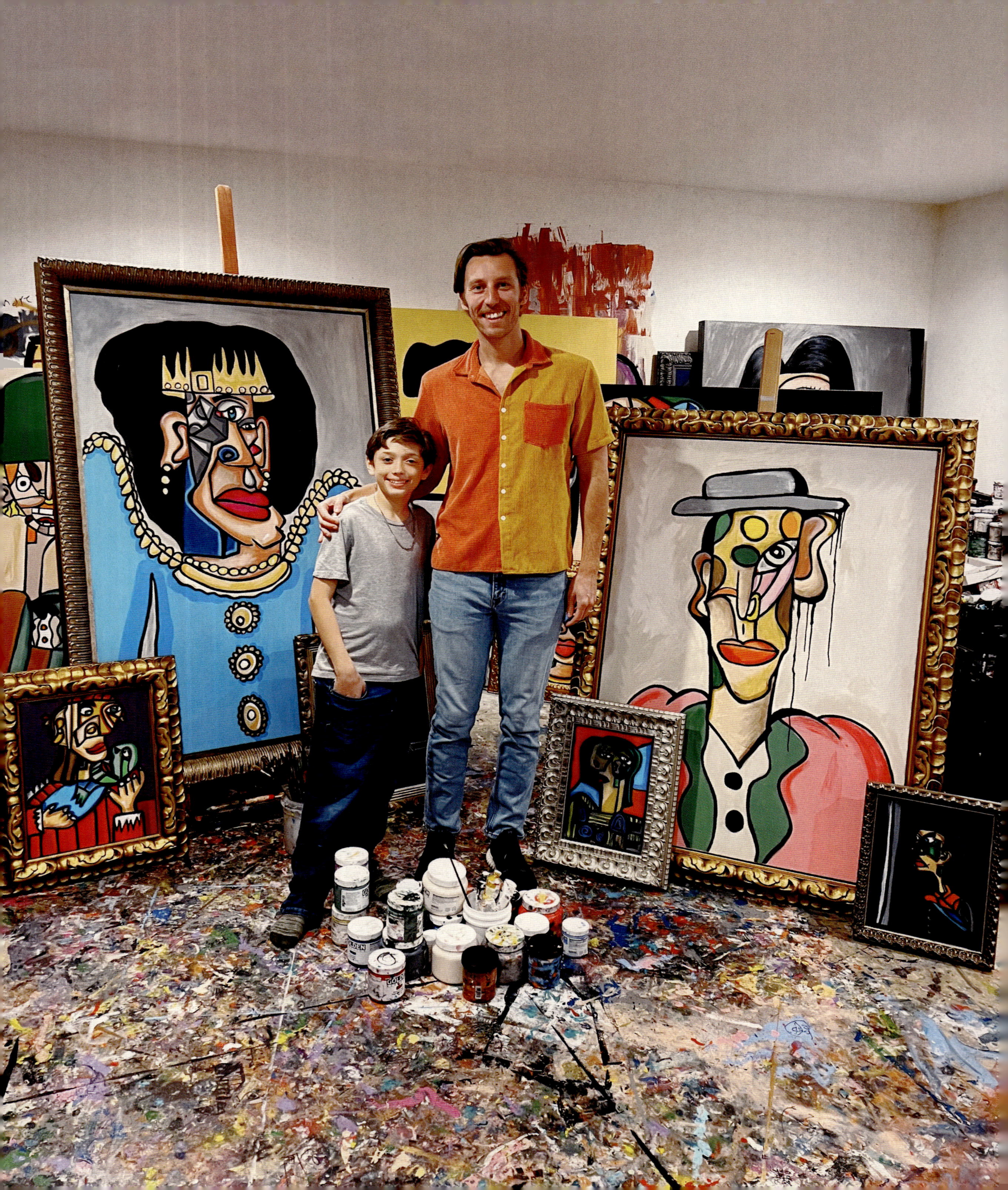

Acknowledgments

ANDRES:

I would like to thank my parents for helping me with my art career my whole life, and my sister Atiana for her support. Thank you to Bernie Chase for giving me the opportunity to showcase my art with the world. I would also like to thank my dog Nieva for appearing in some of my videos.

ALEXANDER:

When I first learned of Andres Valencia in the *New York Times* article about him in September 2022, I was immediately impressed with his artwork and creative energy. Fast-forward to two years later, and I am so grateful for the opportunity I've had to work with Andres and his family on this book about his artistic process. I want to give a huge thank you to Lupe and Elsa Valencia for helping to make this project a reality. Throughout our time putting this book together, you were both such a joy to work with. Thank you for all of the conversations and interviews, for providing me with photographs, for connecting me with others, and for welcoming me into your home. I will never forget the time we spent discussing Andres and his art surrounded by his incredible paintings. Thank you to Bernie Chase and Nick Korniloff for sharing your stories about Andres and how you helped bring his artwork to the public's attention. I would also like to thank my team at DK, who helped bring this book together: to Joanna Price, thank you for designing such a beautiful book, and for always being such an upbeat, optimistic colleague, you make working on books together so much fun; to Mike Sanders and Ann Barton, thank you for believing in me and for allowing me to not only acquire this book, but to write it as well. Thank you to my partner, Bobby, for always supporting me and for sharing in my excitement about this project. And finally, thank you to Andres, for trusting me with your story, for sharing your paintings with me, and for our conversations about art and creativity. I am so inspired by your love of art and the way in which you create from a place of joy, uninhibitedly. You have already accomplished so much at a young age, and I can't wait to see what you do next. I know you are going to have an amazing lifelong career as a celebrated artist. Thank you for making this book with me.

Opposite: Andres and Alexander in the artist's studio, March 2024.

Index

About the Authors

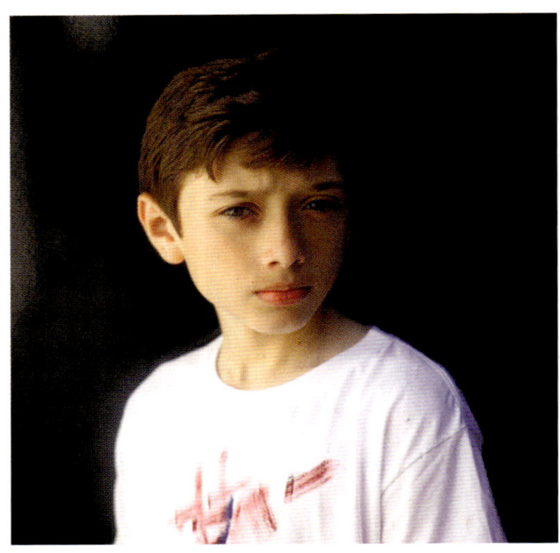

Andres Valencia (b. 2011) is a California-based contemporary artist known for large, dramatic, colorful figurative paintings that are deeply influenced by cubism. Valencia has been painting since he was five years old. He creates large-scale works with a mix of oil pastel and acrylic paint, seeking to pair bold colors with wildly imaginative fragmented facial compositions. Surrounded by art at home, Valencia is inspired by Pablo Picasso, George Condo, and Amedeo Modigliani. At the age of ten, he became the youngest artist in history to have his own booth at Art Miami, where his works on display quickly sold out. He has donated over $1 million in proceeds from his artwork to charities around the world.

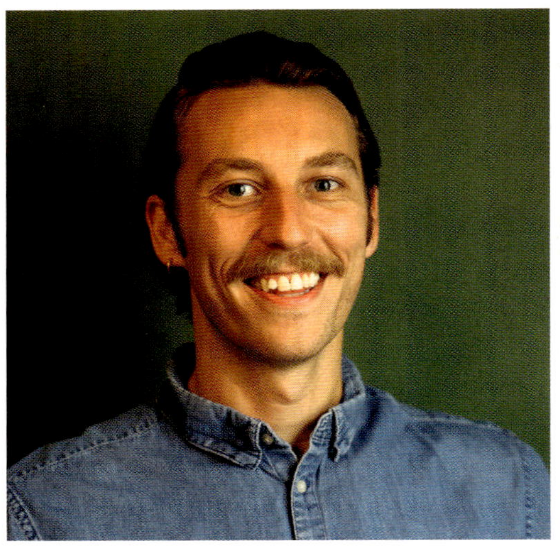

Alexander M. Rigby is a *New York Times* best-selling editor at Penguin Random House. He holds an MFA from Stonecoast at the University of Southern Maine. A lifelong lover of art and avid outdoorsman, Alexander enjoys working with other creatives and hiking in the wilderness. He lives in Pittsburgh, Pennsylvania.

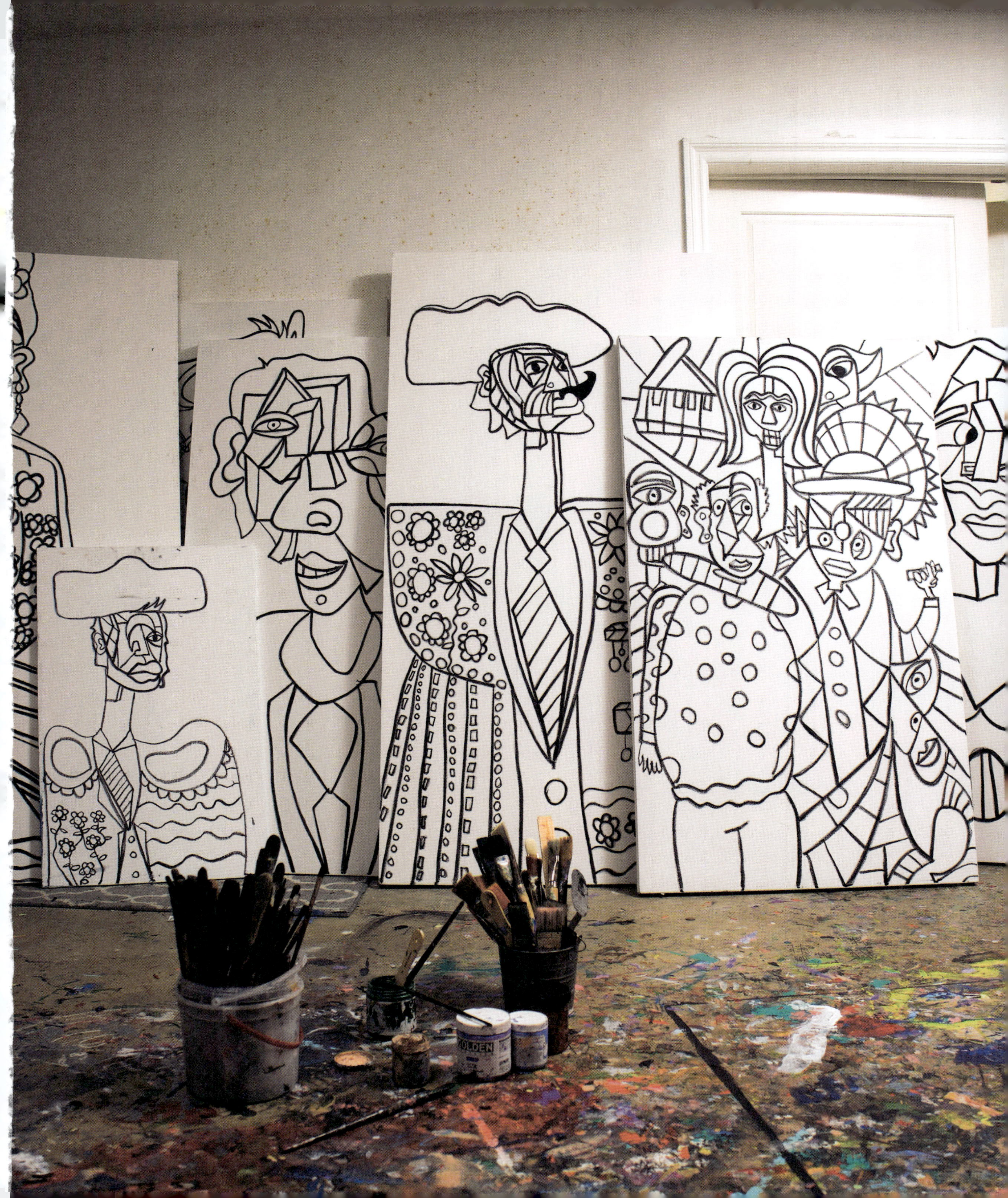

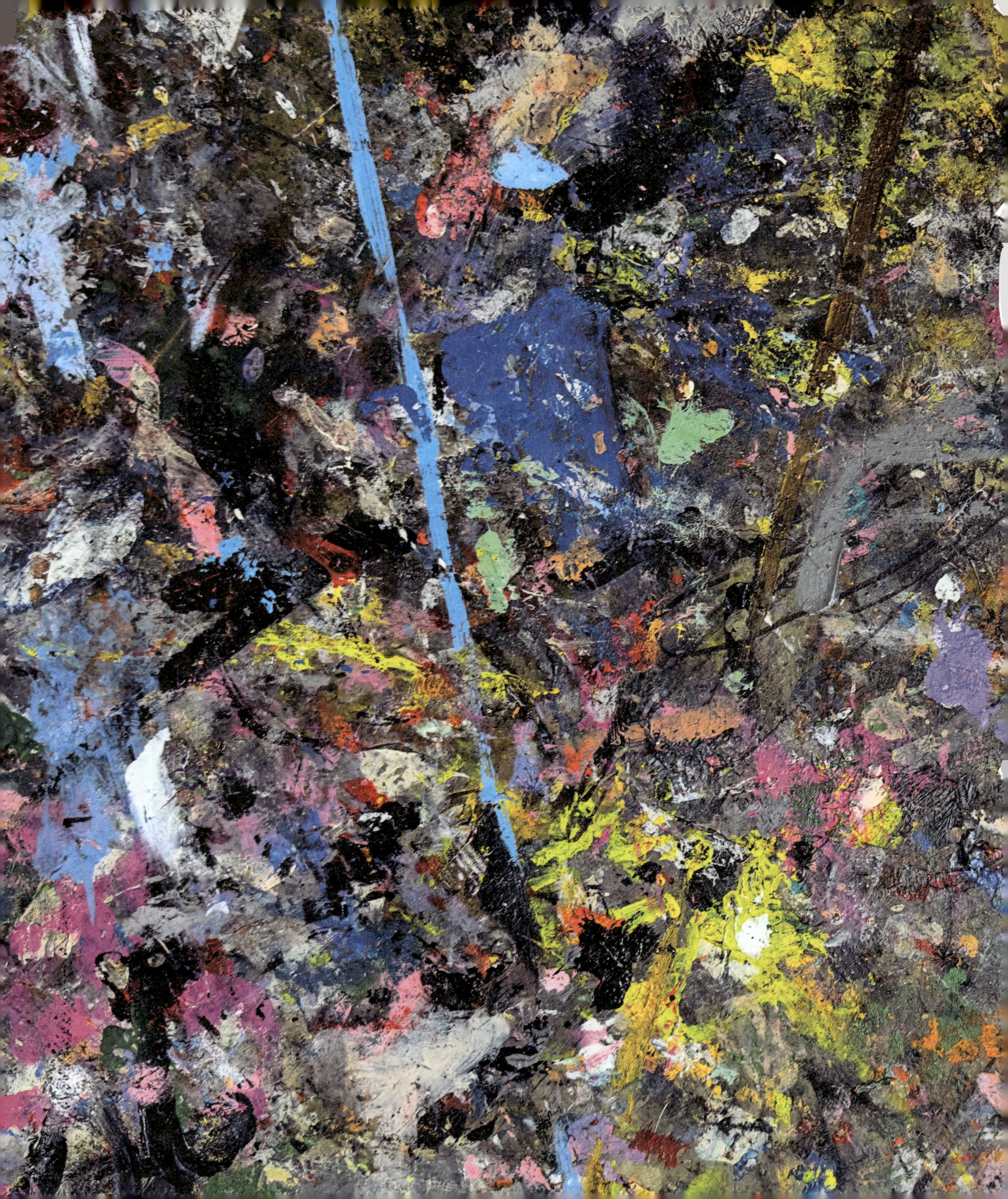